THE GENERAL INQUIRER

THE GENERAL INQUIRER:

A Computer Approach to Content Analysis

Philip J. Stone
Dexter C. Dunphy
Marshall S. Smith
Daniel M. Ogilvie
with associates

The M.I.T. Press
Massachusetts Institute of Technology
Cambridge, Massachusetts, and London, England

To
Robert F. Bales

Foreword

A remarkable fact about our civilization is the spread of scientific modes of thought and observation to the study of man's subjectivity and to all his devices of communication. Although earlier civilizations cultivated a scientific approach to the natural order, they did little more than speculate about human thought and action. Hence no record can be found of systematic attempts to test speculations about personality and culture by taking note of the frequency with which subjective and behavioral events confirm or disconfirm to an explanatory model. It is thus accurate to refer to the universalization of science and technology as a principal characteristic of our epoch. The phrase is accurate on two counts. The first is territorial. A civilization originally consolidated in Western Europe is moving to comprehend the globe. The second is internal. The scientific frame of reference is directed at internal no less than external events — at events internal both to a social process and to the individual participant in the process. Our records are increasingly full of data obtained by introspection or by extrospection of what we take to be the behaviors of ourselves and others. Many procedures have been invented to relate the observer to his field of observation and to produce a record that can be related to the terms of an explanatory model.

It is evident therefore why the procedures that pass under the label "content analysis" are among the distinctive achievements of modern civilization. The scientific quest is a search for procedures that allow rational choices to be made between competing explanatory concepts. Explanations take the form "events of category x are precipitated by events of category y." Sometimes the problem is deliberately limited to physical events. For instance, the volume of sound uttered by a group may rise or fall as the temperature of the room varies. A more intensive research may attempt to account for deviations from this pattern by showing that the temperature factor is of trivial importance if the statements made by the participants are conflicting. "Conflict" may be measured by counting the number of sentences in which the sentence maker uses words that communicators competent in the language understand to indicate disagreement. Words like "disagree," "deny," and "refute" are examples.

The person who classifies an uttered word as "disagree" is making a record that goes beyond registering a mass-energy dimension, such as the sounds involved. The sounds also refer; they allude to a pattern of subjective events called "comprehending the sounds." The classifiers *register* sound; they *characterize* referents.

It is unnecessary to belabor the point that any attempt to introduce orderly procedures for describing the flow of "reference-making" utterances will stir up a cloud of uncertainty, confusion, and controversy. Sometimes the dissent is generated by the "meanings" that different scientists or sciences find salient to their problems. This leads one to ask: "Is it possible to devise a procedure that will produce an inventory of meanings that will satisfy all possible objectives of social researchers?" For shorthand purposes, we may call this the quest for a universal dictionary. Dissent is also generated by the *procedures* used in analyzing the verbal data. (In the present context, the task is restricted to verbal rather than other modes of communication.) Should the basic texts be rewritten in conformity with some standardized format, or is the natural language and style to be retained? Should the text be analyzed on a word-by-word basis, or should there be options to use larger syntactic units?

The emergence of the computer has made it feasible for social and behavioral scientists to make a fresh start on content analysis. The vast potentialities of content analysis, though foreseen for some years, have been poorly realized, owing chiefly to the onerous task of scanning texts and processing data. The latter operation — data processing — has been successfully improved, and there is promise of automatic scanners that, when appropriately joined with panels of human judges, will accelerate the turning of raw records into data.

The supreme virtue of the General Inquirer method devised by Dr. Stone and his associates is that it keeps conceptual issues in the foreground and refuses to give undeserved prominence to the computer. Dr. Stone is thoroughly justified in insisting that the problem of inference should receive top billing in any appraisal of results or evaluation of future alternatives. The General Inquirer gives promise of providing a means by which a particular investigation can be conducted in the light of accumulated knowledge about content analysis without losing the possibility of adding detail as required to revise, respecify, or generalize the dictionaries and programs at hand.

The essential problem of content analysis is to provide a procedure that preserves and codes as economically as possible the meanings relevant to social theories. The scientist who works with samples of data with which he is concerned can now hope eventually to identify the universe of referents pertinent to his theory. His instruments will then faithfully present the distribution of relevant meanings intended or perceived by the participants in the social process. In the universalizing civilization of tomorrow, taking samples of communication at strategic spots will, when properly harnessed in an inclusive man-machine network, keep signs and meanings in very close harmony with one another. Or if not, the discrepancies will reflect the vagaries of policy rather than the dimness of incapacity.

HAROLD LASSWELL

Preface

Since 1961, we have been investigating computer-aided content analysis as a research technique. The use of computers has allowed us to circumvent some of the tedium and limitations of manual coding and to explore research procedures that had previously been neglected. This book reports our efforts.

We hope that the work described here will be useful to students of human behavior, whether trained as scientists or humanists. An attempt is made to supply sufficient information for the reader to judge the general utility of our approach and its value for specific research projects. Our concern is with basic issues of content analysis rather than technical details of current computer implementation. Throughout the book, we insist that the computer only aids and does not replace human endeavor.

Although some familiarity with general problems of research is assumed, the presentation has been designed for both lay and professional readers. No previous experience with computers is assumed. While some experience with statistics is relevant, the purposes of using statistics in content analysis are carefully discussed.

The name "General Inquirer" was chosen to complement the "General Problem Solver" of Herbert Simon and Allan Newell at Carnegie Institute of Technology, and thus the name acknowledges the place of the system in a tradition of list processing. The early seminars held at RAND were attended by Robert F. Bales and George Miller from Harvard, who passed on the idea of list processing to us.

While technical discussions are omitted from this book, the reader is assured that the procedures have been carefully documented and are available. For those interested in using the computer procedures, a supplementary operations manual may be obtained.[1] Copies of programs and actual data used in most past studies are available from the archives of the Inter-University Consortium for Political Research, University of Michigan.

OVERVIEW

This book is intended both to introduce a method and serve as a reference work on content analysis. The book is divided into two parts. Part I presents the system in the context of past content analysis research. At several points, information is presented in detail for purpose of reference, and the reader who is interested in grasping the general character of the system may prefer to skim these sections in his initial reading. Part II presents applications of method within a variety of social science areas, and one criterion for their selection was that they illustrate different research procedures. Chapter 7 (Part I), with its detailed tables, and the editorial comments prefacing each application section (Part II) are designed to guide the reader to those studies most relevant to his interests.

Our intention has not been to produce final answers but to develop content analysis procedures to a level of effectiveness and sophistication useful in future research. Many of our conclusions in Part I are at best tentative: for each issue studied, a number of additional issues tend to be raised. Similarly, because the method is new, the examples in Part II should be viewed as illustrations of ways the method can be used to develop and test theory. They are not final confirmations of theory. Often they report early steps in continuing research endeavors.

Chapter 1 introduces content analysis, defines it, and discusses our definition in detail, together with a model of the content analysis process. Chapter 2 contrasts several past approaches to content analysis research. Applications in various fields are compared. Techniques often used with, or as alternatives to, content analysis are discussed. The requirements of content analysis are considered in relation to other computer "text-processing" applications. Against this background, Chapter 3 presents the rationale and procedures of the General Inquirer system.

---

[1] This *Users Manual,* prepared by Cambridge Computer Associates, Cambridge, Massachusetts, is published by the M.I.T. Press.

Since category construction plays a crucial role in the system, we devote Chapters 4 and 5 to a discussion of this task. Chapter 4 reviews issues that need to be considered in constructing a category system. Chapter 5 describes three category systems in detail.

Chapter 6 considers the General Inquirer as a measuring instrument. A number of approaches to problems of reliability and validity are considered in a perspective relevant to content analysis.

Chapter 7 presents and discusses a classification system for the applications in Part II. While the goals and procedures of content analysis strategies are introduced in nontechnical terms, each section ends with a few paragraphs of comments for those familiar with statistics. The chapter ends with a nontechnical discussion of strategies for the efficient use of the Inquirer.

Part I represents a joint effort of all four authors and includes many ideas from others who have used the system. However, clear differences of style and approach are evident in the seven chapters and therefore the main author(s) responsible for the final draft are identified at the beginning of each chapter.

Part II, edited by Daniel Ogilvie, includes contributions by a number of researchers who have used the method, often working quite closely with the authors in exploration of issues discussed in Part I. Brief introductions to each of the seven areas of application point up some of these issues. We hope the reader will find applications of interest in fields outside his own.

The editing of other people's contributions is always difficult. We are grateful to the many contributors who revised and shortened their chapters at our request. Several contributions that might otherwise have been included have been omitted because of lack of space.

ACKNOWLEDGMENTS

Many of the ideas expressed in these pages have developed from discussions with our colleagues using the General Inquirer. Past and present members of our project include J. Zvi Namenwirth, William McPherson, Mrs. Louise Woodhead, Miss Janica Towne, Barry McLaughlin, Mrs. Evelyn Glenn, and John Williamson. These colleagues contributed substantially to our thinking and to the production of this book.

We also express our thanks to a number of associates, both at Harvard and elsewhere, who have used the General Inquirer in their research and have provided us with many insights concerning its application. Several of these associates have written chapters in Part II describing their work. Others who have used the General Inquirer include Victoria Bricker, Harvard University; Tara Dinkle, University of Chicago; John Ford, Systems Development Corporation; Bruce Frisbie, University of Chicago; Sally Frisbie, University of Chicago; John Hartman, University of Michigan; Earl Hunt, U.C.L.A.; Rosemary Jchnson, University of Edinburgh; Pierre Maranda, Harvard University; John Masters, Stanford University; Dorothy Meier, Washington University; James Peacock, Harvard University; Michael Ross, Harvard University; Erwin Scheuch, University of Cologne; Arthur Stickgold, Washington University; and Richard Suzman, Harvard University, plus a number of students who have used the Inquirer for their projects in our graduate seminar on content analysis.

The importance of assistance at the very early stages remains vivid in the memory of the senior author. He would like to extend personally his grateful appreciation to Carol Bosche of Bell Telephone Laboratories, Ann Congleton of Wellesley College, and John Bennett of IBM, San Jose, all at that time members of the M.I.T. COMIT project, directed by Victor Yngve, for their many hours of on-call assistance in implementing the system. He thanks the many people who have offered advice and encouragement in travels outside Harvard, including Harold Borko, System Development Corporation; Karl Deutsch, Yale University; Harold Guetzkow, Northwestern University; Francis Levy, Maison des Sciences de l'Homme; Thomas Milburn, Project Michaelson; and Fred Strodtbeck, University of Chicago. We would like to acknowledge a special debt of gratitude to Daniel Lerner at M.I.T. and Harold Lasswell at Yale, who read the final draft of the manuscript.

The contributions of many of the people who have worked on later revisions of the Inquirer programs are acknowledged in several points in Chapter 3. Many important contributions to the system have stemmed from the ideas of Aram Grayson, Robert McCarthy, Horace Enea, Donald Davis, Philip Miller, Erik Steiner, and most recently, Victor Oppenheimer, Anthony Marotto, and Cary Wyman. The implementation and testing of programs over the years were facilitated by the active interest and cooperation of the Harvard Computer Center operating staff, including such veteran experts as Joseph

Lewko, Richard Delery, and Arthur Dolan. We also thank the staffs at Project MAC, the M.I.T. Computation Center, and Western Data Processing Center for their assistance with our work, and Ralph Bisco and the Consortium for providing data archive facilities.

This book would not have been completed without the editorial assistance of Miss Susan Wright. Her efforts to coordinate and integrate Part I and to assist with the editorial tasks of Part II are deeply appreciated. We also extend our thanks to Miss Susan Easton, our secretary, who not only typed and retyped considerable portions of the manuscript but did so with good humor despite the vagaries of the editors. In preparing Chapters 1 and 2, we have benefited greatly from sharing the literature summaries prepared by Joanne Loomba for Ole Holsti's chapter on content analysis for the *Handbook of Social Psychology*. We acknowledge with appreciation the authors and publishers who gave permission for use of the quotations appearing in this book.

The bulk of the General Inquirer research has been supported by grants from the National Institute of Mental Health and the National Science Foundation (NIMH USPH M-4169, NSF GS-178) and administered by the Laboratory of Social Relations under the conscientious direction of Mrs. Bette Burnham. In particular, we would like to thank Dr. Robert Hall, former director of the NSF Program in Social Psychology, for his interest and suggestions. His years spent away from the campus to administer this program were greatly appreciated by many members of the behavioral science community.

This system evolved from Robert F. Bales' insistence that an approach such as this is both necessary and possible. We are grateful for his initial contribution, encouragement, and continued enthusiasm. It is in fond respect that we dedicate this book to him.

Department of Social Relations   PHILIP J. STONE
Harvard University   DEXTER C. DUNPHY
Cambridge, Massachusetts   MARSHALL S. SMITH
August 1966   DANIEL M. OGILVIE

Contents

PART I

CONTENT ANALYSIS

CHAPTER ONE

A Perspective on Content Analysis[1]

When we conceive the same things differently, we can hardly avoid different naming of them. For though the nature of that which we conceive be the same, yet the diversity of our reception of it, in respect of different constitutions of body, and prejudices of opinion, gives every thing a tincture of our different passions. And therefore in reasoning a man must take heed of words; which besides the signification of what we imagine their nature, have signification also of the nature, disposition, and interest of the speaker.

Thomas Hobbes, *Leviathan,* 1651 (1928 ed., 17–18)

A symbol may be a myth, a root metaphor, or a clinical symptom. "Meaning," likewise, is neither signification or denotation. It is anything from a stimulus-response relation to the wish behind the dream . . . There is little the poor epistemologist can do about such encroachments of the jungle on his garden.

Suzanne K. Langer, *Philosophical Sketches,* 1962, 55

Words and sentences are important human artifacts. As products of social experience, they serve as the everyday media for much thought and communication; what people say and write is a basic source of evidence about individual and social processes. A psychologist, for example, hands a subject an inkblot and asks him to describe what he sees. A public opinion interviewer asks for an

---

[1] The main author of this chapter is Philip J. Stone.

answer to his questions. A sociologist studies conference-group processes and makes transcripts of his tape recordings. A political scientist collects diplomatic notes. In each case, the data are the same: words and sentences such as you are now reading.

For the behavioral scientist, this is raw data, collected from appropriate sources and consisting of words and punctuation marks recorded on paper. Through the analysis of these data, he can often learn much about the personality and preoccupations of the writers and the sociocultural processes in which they are involved. Verbal data, however, are extraordinarily rich and varied, reflecting ideas, attitudes, and styles partly unique to the individual and partly derived from the particular cultural milieu. How can the infinite variety of words, phrases, sentences, and styles be the source of stable, scientific conclusions?

A model for such abstraction can be found in our many day-to-day conclusions drawn on the basis of what people say and write. Upon reading a personal letter or a newspaper editorial, we might remark that the author is "taking a softer line on . . ." or "certainly emphasizes the fact that. . . ." Sometimes such informal judgments reflect an extended inference process, and we decide, "He must have been influenced by . . ." or "If he were given the chance, I bet he would. . . ." The use of some intuitive standard or norm derived from past experience is usually evident and consciously employed in such statements as, "I would never have expected him to say . . ." or "It was the same old story."

While impressionistic conclusions may satisfy the needs of day-to-day living, they do not usually form the reliable resource needed for testing research questions. The impressionistic conclusion may depend upon the individual's idiosyncratic frame of reference and may be influenced by the way he feels at a particular moment.

To overcome these problems, social scientists have developed various procedures, generally known as "content analysis," to explicate such judgmental processes more clearly and to make them more objective. If, for instance, we wish to rate a series of editorials on whether they are for, against, or neutral toward a particular policy, we can be more certain of the reliability of our results if the judges follow explicit scoring rules, for we can check the extent to which they agree in their rating of the same editorials. Rating a large number of editorials by such procedures, however, can be a tedious process.

This book describes a system of content analysis that places heavy emphasis on procedures for transforming intuitive judgments into explicit rules. It uses computers to aid this process of explication, to extend the scope of content analysis, and to ensure reliability and speed of coding while reducing its tedium. The system, however, is not independent of past efforts to develop content analysis as a method. Before presenting the system, we shall outline a definition of content analysis, and in Chapter 2 discuss the system in relation to the past development of the field.

A DEFINITION OF CONTENT ANALYSIS

The following definition summarizes our view of what content analysis is and what it does for the social scientist. We shall examine this definition in some detail, specifying its implications on a few key issues.

Content analysis is any research technique for making inferences by systematically and objectively identifying specified characteristics within text.[2]

Let us separately consider each component of this definition.

"For Making Inferences"

This phrase is by far the most important and perhaps the most controversial element of our definition. Inference is presented in our definition as the *raison d'être* of content analysis. The fundamental assumption appears in the quotation from Hobbes, that words not only reflect "the signification of what we imagine their nature" but "have a signification also of the nature, disposition and interests of the speaker." The "disposition and interest" of the speaker partly reflect the pressures of the current social situation, which may determine the topic being discussed and engender a need to make a particular effect on others. The "nature of the speaker" includes personality characteristics and styles of expression, derived in part

---

[2] This definition was developed jointly with Dr. Ole Holsti at Stanford University in conjunction with his chapter on content analysis in the revised *Handbook of Social Psychology* (in press).

from the individual's past experience in family, neighborhood, school, and work situations.

The verbal record, then, is a piece of evidence that may be used to make inferences about any and all of these factors. The inference may be fairly direct, or, as indicated in our opening quotation from Langer, it may involve a web of overt and latent levels. For example, one standard procedure in psychological testing is to ask a person to construct a story about a picture shown to him, a story telling who is in the picture, what has happened, what the people are thinking, and what will happen next. This procedure, the thematic apperception test (TAT), yields stories that are thought to reflect the subject's social history, his values, needs, and defenses, his current concerns in life, and the impression he wishes to make on the psychologist. In meeting the demands of this task, a subject draws on a set of beliefs, wishes, and expectations both to interpret the picture and to plan the story. The projective content of the stories may be used to infer characteristics of the subject, some of which may be unknown to the subject himself. By comparing stories told by subjects from different social classes, family constellations, and so on, an investigator may extend these inferences to more general cultural characteristics.

The social scientist may also go directly to cultural rather than to personal language products. The content of folktales or the scripts of traditional plays and songs may reflect the characteristics of an entire culture. Such materials, as suggested by their repetition over many generations, may depict persisting focal concerns and problems within the social life of a culture.

A text thus represents the author and the social situation in which it was produced; if it is also a significant social document, it may also set a framework for further perceptions and actions. For example, the symbols developed in a political acceptance speech may set the stage for an election campaign. The importance of such effects of communication was well recognized by G. H. Mead:

> The social process, as involving communication, is in a sense responsible for the appearance of new objects in the field of experience of the individual organisms implicated in that process.
> Symbolization constitutes objects not constituted before, objects which would not exist except for the context of social relationships wherein symbolization occurs. Language does not simply symbolize a situation or

object which is already there in advance; it makes possible the existence or appearance of that situation or object, for it is part of the mechanism whereby that situation or object is created.

(G. H. Mead, 1934, 77–78)

From this point of view, content not only reflects but directs. The document itself becomes a pivot for further discourse and action; inferences and predictions may be made about its effects.

Thus there are many kinds of inferences that might be made from the written or verbal record. Taken together, we think these inferences constitute a significant element in understanding man's behavior.

"Identifying Specified Characteristics"

The content analysis procedure involves the interaction of two processes: the specification of the content characteristics to be measured and the application of rules for identifying and recording the characteristics when they occur in the data. The categories into which content is coded vary widely from one investigation to another and are dependent on the investigator's theory and the nature of his data.

Categories used in content analysis may be relatively simple, consisting, for instance, of various names for a particular person or place. To use such simple categories alone often results in simple frequency counts that reaffirm the obvious. To go beyond this requires the recognition that language offers many alternative ways in which concepts may be expressed.

Suppose we want to identify the extent to which "conservatism" is expressed in writing or speech. Investigators would undoubtedly differ in their intuitive interpretations of the meaning of this concept. Their lack of agreement would be evident if they were asked, without any prior discussion, to make over-all ratings of the presence of conservatism in particular speeches. However, by thinking about and discussing the different aspects of the concept, they might well agree on characteristics they would consider signs of conservatism, and if given an explicit set of scoring directions, they would identify them as such. In examining the concept in detail, they may find it necessary to distinguish between two or more forms of conservatism. They will also need to be specific in distinguishing it from related concepts.

At the simplest level, the characteristics that are considered signs of conservatism might consist of lists of words and idioms.[3] For example, one list might be a category of signs indicating RESTRAINT: careful, caution, cautious, restrained, with care, and so on. Similarly, another list might consist of alternative ways of expressing OBLIGA-TION: conscience, duties, obliged, ought, proper, and so on. The specification for scoring might then require a co-occurrence of entries from the lists, and in some cases a noun-modifier relationship, as in the larger concept OBLIGATION OF RESTRAINT: "obligation to carefully," "duty to be cautious about," "conscience to be restrained in," "use proper caution in."

Conservatism can, of course, be expressed in many different ways other than a simple concern for OBLIGATION OF RESTRAINT. We might, for example, reason that a conservative person tends to express concern for matters getting out of hand, especially economic matters, and thus we might want to identify references to EXCESSIVE ECONOMIC COSTS. This category might signify a co-occurrence between ECONOMIC COSTS, such as budget, cost, deficit, expense, price, tax, and so on, and words indicating EXCESSIVE QUANTITY, such as beyond . . . means, costly, excessive, exorbitant, expensive, and so on, to produce such combinations as "deficit is too costly," "budget becomes excessive," "exorbitant tax on," "at a price beyond our means," "costs too much."

A complete procedure for measuring conservatism would require a number of additional specifications. It might be questioned whether some of the measures really reflect conservatism; indeed, if categories and procedures are explicit, such questions are more easily debated.

How does the investigator know when he has specified all the alternative ways in which a characteristic can be expressed? He usually does not. On making further applications of his categories, he will often find new and unanticipated alternatives. He may fail to remember that certain words and phrases are signs of a social or psychological variable. He may also forget about the usages of a word or phrase under certain circumstances, which differ from those he has in mind. Most of these errors can be avoided if the investigator collects a number of instances of actual word usage in context. Chapter 4 discusses some empirical procedures we have assembled

---

[3] The term *idiom* will be used in this book to refer to all word clusters that have a single meaning quite apart from their components. Most of them are the common units of everyday speech, such as with care, or care for, break through, break out, break up.

to aid the process of developing comprehensive lists of signs within categories. Yet inasmuch as the investigator is making statistical judgments, he can sometimes afford to tolerate a certain amount of error in his measurement procedures. The errors found in the course of present research can be used to make better specifications for the future.

In specifying alternative forms of expression, the investigator may choose to limit his coverage to a particular kind of language, such as the conversational language used by particular occupational groups or the editorial language of certain newspapers. Such focused coverage will often show a higher degree of accuracy, capitalizing on idioms and idiosyncracies of language usage within a particular linguistic community. In reporting categories of signs, the investigator should make clear the population of language users and situations for which the specifications are intended. Occasionally, categories will be found to have a wider range of successful application than originally intended. Such new applications for old categories, however, need to be made with care.

The problem of category construction is widely regarded as the most crucial aspect of content analysis. It is the step in which the data are tied to theory, and it serves as a basis for drawing inferences. As Berelson has indicated,

> Content analysis stands or falls by its categories. Particular studies have been productive to the extent that the categories were clearly formulated and well adapted to the problem and to the content. Content analysis studies done on a hit or miss basis, without clearly formulated problems for investigation and with vaguely drawn or poorly articulated categories are almost certain to be of indifferent or low quality as research productions. Although competent performance in other parts of the analytic process is also necessary, the formulation and the definition of appropriate categories takes a central importance. Since the categories contain the substance of the investigation, a content analysis can be no better than its system of categories.
>
> (Berelson, 1952, 147)

Unfortunately, although our social scientific theories may lead us to the concepts we wish to study, we lack an adequate theory of language to direct us in finding the alternative signs that express a particular concept. In a situation where something is to be said, there is no theory to tell us what words will be used to say it. Lasswell, Lerner, and Pool have summarized this dilemma in this way:

> There is as yet no good theory of symbolic communication by which to predict how given values, attitudes or ideologies will be expressed in manifest symbols. The extant theories tend to deal with values, attitudes, and ideologies as the ultimate units, not with the symbolic atoms of which they are composed. There is almost no theory of language which predicts the specific words one will emit in the course of expressing the contents of his thoughts. Theories in philosophy or in the sociology of knowledge sometimes are used to predict ideas that will be expressed by persons with certain other ideas or social characteristics. But little thought has been given to predicting the specific words in which these ideas will be cloaked. The content analyst, therefore, does not know what to expect.
>
> (Lasswell, Lerner, and Pool, 1952, 49)

To be useful, such a theory will have to combine specific knowledge of the individual speaker and the perceived social situation, together with a general knowledge of language. The learning of the language takes place within a social context but is a highly individualistic experience. Each word comes to be the name of a particular set of experienced events, objects, or other referents. From various associations with these experiences, including personal reactions, the reactions of other people, other events, and so on, the name also comes to be associated with a certain set of properties. Carnap (1947) and other semanticists have distinguished between a word's "extension" to a class of referent objects and its "intension" to a list of properties. Many of the intensions and extensions of a word can be inferred from a sample of how it is used. Usually there will be remnants of prior extensions and intensions that are no longer obviously apparent in the individual's word usage but still influence his thoughts and attitudes. Given the desire to put an idea into words, we assume that the individual selects those words most relevant to his own associations as well as acceptable and relevant to his listeners'. As Carroll (1953) has emphasized, the problem is also complicated by the fact that the selection of words to express an idea is not a series of independent decisions but must interdependently combine to fit into a hierarchical structure. Once the words most central to the expression of the idea are chosen, the other words tend to become highly determined by the context of the developing thought structure.

OVERVIEW: A MODEL OF CONTENT ANALYSIS

Our definition presents content analysis as a research tool to be used by the social scientist in making inferences; what is measured in content analysis depends on the theory being investigated. This context is needed not only to gain a proper perspective on content analysis but to differentiate it from other activities that may appear to be similar but are for other purposes. In this section, we shall present a content analysis model, and we shall then use this model to specify what content analysis is not.

Past discussions of content analysis have often given little consideration to its larger context. While Berelson's definition specifies that content analysis is "a research technique," little further emphasis is made of its research purpose. In fact, Berelson argues that many valid content analysis studies are undertaken solely or primarily to describe characteristics of content:

> In a great many studies there is no real problem of inference at all. This is true for all those content analyses in which the description of content itself is the primary objective. Such studies can be said to contain implicit inferences about the causes or the consequences of the content — and some contain them explicitly — but such inferences are in the nature of addenda to or reformulations of the basic data. Thus a trend study of newspaper content can be considered material for inferences about the changing character of press controls and/or about the changing character of public attention. But such "inferences" are usually nothing reformulations in other terms of the content analysis itself.
>
> (Berelson, 1954, 516–517)

...el that the researcher has an obligation both to himself and ...public to explicate clearly the inferences he is making. As we ... in Chapter 2, many content analysts, often preoccupied with ...ment, have felt that they should stay at the level of fact and ...reader draw the conclusions. Actually content analysts in-...use at least a rudimentary theoretical framework in the very ...f categories and rules for their application. Its rationale, ...and implications when applied to the data should be made

...ntent analysis model is represented in Figure 1.1. Primary ... is given to the theory being investigated. The theory ...the texts to be compared (that is, the research design), the

Lacking an adequate theory of the relationship between social scientific variables and how they are expressed in language, the social scientist falls back on his intuitive understanding, which is naturally subject to error. As the material in this book will reveal, much of our current success in content analysis derives from the lessons of past research. These lessons lead to further refinements and practical means of compensating for the inadequacies of the theory. Chapters 4 and 5 consider these lessons in further detail.

"Systematic and Objective"

These are the aspects of content analysis most stressed by previous writers. Berelson, in probably the most widely referenced definition of content analysis, defines it as "a research technique for the objective, systematic and quantitative description of the manifest content of communication." (Berelson, 1954, 489). Berelson uses the term "objective" to indicate that the procedure should be explicit, one that can be replicated exactly by other analysts. "Systematic" for Berelson means that "*all* the relevant content is to be analysed in terms of *all* the relevant categories" (Berelson, 1954, 489) in order to secure unbiased information for the hypotheses being tested. Similarly, Cartwright proposes to "use the terms 'content analysis' and 'coding' interchangeably to refer to the objective, systematic, and quantitative description of any symbolic behavior" (Cartwright, 1953, 424). Objectivity and systemization are requirements not specific to content analysis, but they are necessary for any procedure to be appropriate for scientific inquiry.

Contrary to its apparent implication, to be "systematic" does not always require that all the sampled text be inspected. Often the question is whether or not a characteristic appears in a text, not how often it appears. In such cases, the text need be inspected only until an occurrence is found.

Similarly, a scientific inquiry need not have the additional characteristic of being quantitative in the sense of counting frequencies. The qualitative-quantitative dimension, which will be discussed in Chapter 2, has been a source of considerable confusion and argument. The procedure of content analysis refers only to the systematic and objective identification of specified characteristics. Whether these occurrences are counted after they are identified depends on the hypotheses being investigated.

The implementation of procedures on a computer insures that they are both systematic and objective. The nature of a computer program requires that both the categories and the rules for identifying and recording characteristics occurring in the data be explicitly stated. The computer then systematically applies the categories and rules to the data in a completely objective manner. Whether the measurement procedure was reasonable or best suited to the inferences being made may be debated, but the procedures themselves are explicit and clear. The fluctuations resulting from the biases and fatigue of the coder do not enter into the analysis process itself when a computer is used, nor is there any problem of securing intercoder reliability.

"Within Text"

Our definition is not concerned with problems of record*ing* information but of analyzing the patterns of information as contained in a record*ed* text. Within this book, all texts analyzed are in English. There is no reason why the text need be limited to English; indeed, General Inquirer procedures are currently used to study text in Tzotil, the language of the Zinacanten Indians in the Chiapas Highlands of Mexico. Another project is currently under way that will require the analysis of text in German. The General Inquirer procedures described in this book might also be used to study a phonetic transcription or the notation text of an observer's recording of playground interaction.

Working with text materials often provides information not otherwise available. Many important changes of society and of the people who live in it are richly documented by text information. Text often becomes the most important resource for testing hypotheses about changes over the years. The investigator need not be present with his measuring instruments either before or after or during the event. Text is also often naturally produced and available in situations in which the investigator could not or cannot intrude.

Past definitions of content analysis have not limited it to text material but have included all aspects of communication or symbolic behavior. In verbal behavior, the text may be only part of the communication. Indeed, as Bernstein (1964*a*) has pointed out, the language used in many social situations is a "restricted code in which the text content is actually of secondary importance in the communication process." A number of writers, including Allport and Vernon

(1933), Ruesch and Kees (1956), and contributors to the Sebec Hayes, and Bateson volume (1964), have stressed the importance various paralinguistic cues. In limiting our definition to text, we not denigrating the importance of these phenomena. Rather w stressing they will be adequately handled by content analysi when they can be notated in textual form.

"Research Technique"

The final component of our definition emphasizes tha analysis is carried out in the context of a research design findings are always relative, based on the characteristics as compared with another. The texts to be compared de hypotheses being tested. For example, if we compare one speeches with another man's family dinner conversa probably learn more about the differences between publ family dinner conversations than we will learn abou between the two men. Some studies will attempt to h constant while studying different respondents. O purposely vary the situation to study its effect.

If the hypotheses concern differences in the tr the first task is to select documents relevant to that a study of newspaper editorial changes in attitude market (Chapter 11) first must select editor topic. Procedures for choosing text to be incl be explicit.

For some research problems, the investig amount of data and "wash out" unrepresen effects as much as possible. For example, self-analytic groups (Chapter 8), it is diffic member absences or particular variatic sampling an adequate amount of materia the sample comes to represent the ove and topic concerns of the group.

Research design, then, is an import content analysis takes place. We hav it in Chapters 6 and 7.

We fe
to his
describ
measur
let the
variably
design
purpose,
explicit.
Our co
importanc
determines

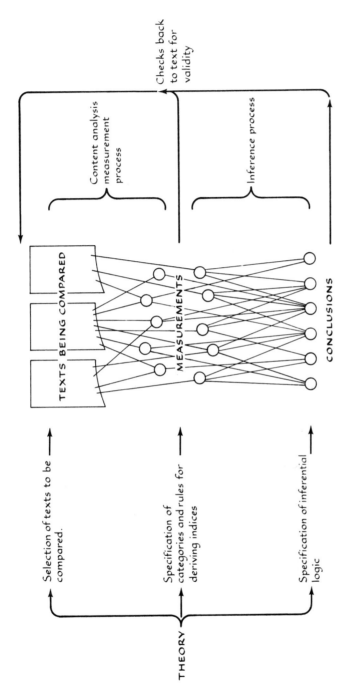

FIGURE 1.1. Representation of content analysis model.

categories and rules for application that must be constructed, and the kinds of inferences that might be drawn from the results of measurement. The content analysis process is but one part of the model. Upon selection of texts and specification of procedures, the content analysis process makes systematic and objective measurements on the texts by identifying occurrences of specified characteristics. These measurements then serve as a reference for drawing inferences. While the content analysis process is objective and direct, the inferences drawn from the results may be quite subtle and indirect. Whether the measurements and conclusions follow reasonably from the text may be ascertained by checking back to the text.

Often an important part of the inference process (not represented in Figure 1.1) is information external to the texts themselves, with comparisons made to the text measures. Such external information is used to support inferences made from the content analyses of the texts.

This over-all content analysis model represents the pattern of measurement and inference common to scientific research of all kinds. Measurement is used to operationally define, single out instances, and describe variations of those aspects of the environment in which the investigator is interested. It is these measurements, made in the context of a research design, that are used to test hypotheses and draw conclusions.

In clinical analysis, as well as in much of literary analysis, emphasis is often placed on understanding as thoroughly as possible a particular instance or event. Inferences are made from the careful inspection of the text itself rather than from the intermediary steps of formal measurement. Each inference is made from the full context of a particular instance or event, rather than from the measures abstracted by the content analysis process.

We have taken the position that these two approaches are complementary, and thus we have designed the procedures described in this book to facilitate the interaction of one with the other.[4] Prior to making a formal content analysis, the investigator can and should carefully inspect a sample of his data, drawing on his intuitive powers

---

[4] Essentially this distinction and our strategy in regard to it parallel the discussion by P. E. Meehl in *Clinical Versus Statistical Prediction* (1954). For another presentation of this distinction applied to content analysis, see Marsden (1965).

to identify the unforeseen circumstances that might be affecting the data. This inspection is used in developing categories and application rules. Formal content analysis is then applied to describe the data as a whole.

Past definitions, such as Berelson's, have emphasized the "manifest" aspects of content analysis, often putting aside the utility of content analysis in drawing conclusions about "latent" implications. The content analysis process itself, being systematic and objective, must be based on manifest characteristics of the text. Berelson points out that "the results of content analysis, however, frequently serve as the basis for these 'interpretations' of latent content" (Berelson, 1954, 489). In our model, such interpretations are represented by the stage of inference. The interpretation of "latent" as well as "manifest" meanings is a valid exercise within the model.

Often different inferences will be drawn from the same content analysis measure. Thus in one study, a category, MALE-ROLE, consisting of terms he, king, man, prince, and so on, might be inferred to indicate simply that overt, manifest attention is being given to persons in male roles, while in another study, the same category may be used to infer an unintentionally expressed concern about masculinity. As a general rule, the more latent the phenomenon inferred, the more internal consistency among categories and external evidence the investigator will want for its support.

By our definition, making inferences from communication content is considered the primary function of content analysis, not addenda or reformulation. This is not a trivial change from past definitions, for it imposes upon the researcher the burden of integrating theory with method, of being dissatisfied with mere description of phenomena. This does not restrict the researcher to strictly hypothesis-testing studies, but it does require him to construct categories that he believes are relevant, either singly or in combination, to his conceptual framework.

This context, represented by a research model (Figure 1.1), distinguishes content analysis from several related activities. Considered apart from the emphasis on research design and inference, the content analysis process is basically the task of applying descriptors; that is, of making a particular many-to-few mapping of the text. Viewed this way, it does not differ from any cataloging or concordancing activity, such as produced the index to this book. A book index or catalog may reflect a theoretical orientation. But by our over-all definition, they are not content analyses.

Our definition thus differs from a number of past definitions in distinguishing between the relatively small amount of content analysis research and the large amounts of cataloging done every day. Unfortunately, as broad, operations-centered terms such as "information processing" or "information retrieval" come into vogue, investigators sometimes tend to lose sight of their research purposes, and important distinctions can become blurred. The general flexibility of the computer has on occasion led the investigator to forget what he is doing, but this need not be the case.

Our definition also distinguishes content analysis from similar operations in related areas involving the study of language. The term "semiotic," originally used in medicine to refer to the study of "signs" or symptoms, was first put forward by John Locke in the latter part of the seventeenth century to refer to the general study of the nature of signs and the use to which the mind puts them in understanding things. The term was subsequently used by philosopher Charles Pierce and gained wide currency from the writings of Charles Morris (1946). Morris divided semiotics into semantics, syntactics, and pragmatics:

> *pragmatics* is that portion of semiotic which deals with the origin, uses, and effects of signs within the behavior in which they occur; *semantics* deals with the signification of signs in all modes of signifying; *syntactics* deals with combinations of signs without regard for their specific significations or their relation to the behavior in which they occur.
>
> (Morris, 1946, 219)

Within semiotics, content analysis becomes one aspect of pragmatics. As a set of operations, however, it closely resembles uses of descriptors in the area of semantics. One cannot read the "Structure of a Semantic Theory" in *The Structure of Language* by Katz and Fodor (1964) without sensing a remarkable operational parallel with the content analysis procedures described in this book. However, content analysis differs in purpose from semantics. For the behavioral scientist, the purpose of content analysis is to infer the "origin, uses, and effects of signs within the behavior in which they occur."

While it is important to distinguish content analysis from what it is not, we would emphasize that advances in related activities may have important implications for content analysis. Thus, reference to semiotics, information retrieval, and information processing may serve a useful purpose in keeping these ties explicit.

In summary, content analysis does not study behavior itself; rather it focuses on artifacts produced by behavior; that is, recorded speech and writing. Much as the archaeologist infers the life of a culture from the pattern of remnants, so the content analyst infers the orientation and concerns of a speaker, subculture, or culture from the record of what is said.

Studying artifacts rather than studying behavior itself has its drawbacks, but also its advantages. The artifact is static, not a fleeting event as is behavior. Text can be copied and shared with other investigators. It can be analyzed and reanalyzed until the investigator is satisfied with his work; and it can be reused later to test other hypotheses. Text is usually readily available, often being produced naturally as part of an event. Because it extends through history, text is an excellent vehicle for studying long-term changes of attitudes, concerns, and styles.

However, like the archaeologist's diggings, the available text fragments may be trivial and insignificant data about the situations they represent. The really significant documents may never become available or, for that matter, may not have been produced. Despite this, as Langer makes clear in the quote at the head of this chapter, the scope of symbolic meaning is wide. The diversity of possible interpretations, the proximity of verbal expression to the pressures of the situation, the multiple levels in which personality is reflected through speech and writing, usually all make the content of what is said an interesting subject of study, suitable for testing a number of hypotheses. Sensitively chosen text, like a well-chosen archaeological site, can yield very worthwhile rewards.

CHAPTER TWO

Trends and Issues in Content Analysis Research[1]

> . . . our power of interpreting the psychological records embodied in words is increasing and capable of immense increase in the future. Among the means to this end a combination or co-operation of psychology and literary analysis, or criticism, seems the most hopeful. Neither alone can do much, both together may go far. There is a possibility that something parallel to recent advances in physics might be achieved if we could combine them.
>
> I. A. Richards, *Practical Criticism,* 1929, 208

> . . . the study of language and communication phenomena . . . is beginning to emerge as one of the most fundamental disciplines in the psychological and social sciences — quite as important, for example, as the study of molecular physics in the natural and biological sciences.
>
> J. B. Carroll, *Study of Language,* 1953, 6

The General Inquirer is a recent contribution to a continuing tradition of theoretical debate and empirical research. In this chapter we shall review the major trends and issues of this tradition in order to convey an understanding of the purposes content analysis serves, the concepts we here draw upon, and the problems the system was designed to handle.

[1] The main authors of this chapter are Philip J. Stone and Dexter C. Dunphy.

THE HISTORICAL DEVELOPMENT
OF BASIC ISSUES IN CONTENT ANALYSIS

Historically, the label "content analysis" has been primarily associated with research in the field of journalism. This research considerably influenced early empirical political science, which borrowed the term and strengthened the method. Most of the debates and criticisms reviewed on the following pages have been directed toward this main stream of studies.

In addition, however, content analysis has been undertaken in a variety of other disciplines. Formal content analysis research has appeared within anthropology, education, history, literature, philology, psychiatry, psychology, and sociology. The range of material varies from fan mail to folklore, from public speeches to private diaries. Often this research is not explicitly called content analysis. In psychology, for example, topic labels, such as "study of mental content" or "study of personal documents," are frequently used rather than the procedural label of content analysis.

As the following pages make evident, our thought has been largely influenced by American research. However, a small number of European investigations, including Busemann's work in Germany on the "action quotient," Bernstein's analysis of interaction processes in England, Propp's analysis of plot in Russian folktales, and Lévi-Strauss's work from France in the study of mythology, have certainly played a role in our thinking.

This chapter contrasts approaches to content analysis research. A thorough review of past research would be a book in itself and is beyond our immediate purposes.[2] We shall first draw on past content analysis trends within journalism and political science to identify important strategies and to provide a context for the discussion of unresolved issues. Next we shall illustrate content analysis strategies and applications in other fields. Techniques often used with, or as alternatives to, content analysis will be discussed with the field in which they are most frequently used. Finally, a brief review is presented of recent concepts and procedures used in linguistics, and comparisons are made with other computer "text processing" applica-

[2] General reviews are available in Berelson (1952, 1954), Barcus (1959), and more recently in Holsti (in press). Occasional reviews within a particular field are available; for example, recent reviews of content analysis in the study of therapy processes appear in Marsden (1965) and Jaffee (in press).

tions, including indexing, concordances, and mechanical translation. With this background, we turn in the next chapter to a description of the General Inquirer itself.

Early Beginnings

There are probably a number of instances in history where systematic content analysis has been undertaken as part of a debate, especially for the purpose of censorship. Dovring (1954), for example, cites an interesting case of sophisticated content analysis in Sweden in the 1640's. At that time, the publication of a collection of ninety hymns, entitled *Songs of Zion* created a considerable controversy concerning their effects on the people and their threat to the organized Lutheran religion. Both sides of the controversy engaged in measurement, including counts of how often various religious themes and values were mentioned, the way they were treated in the hymns (positive-negative-neutral), the complexity of the style, and the context in which such presentations were made. Counts were made by using the official church hymnal for reference. It was argued that "symbols describing Jesus as a bleeding and loving savior occurred more frequently in the songs than those dealing with other Christian values cherished by orthodox Lutheranism" (Dovring, 1954, 392). The pietists countered that the songs were repeating the scope of traditional values in simpler words. Inasmuch as inferences were made about the values and intentions of these hymnals and the probable effects on those who used them, such research clearly fits our definition.

The tradition of research eventually labeled content analysis had its beginning in the field of American journalism about the turn of the twentieth century; by the 1920's it was centered in the School of Journalism of Columbia. Perhaps one of the first quantitative studies of communications media in the United States was by Speed (1893), a comparison of changes in the Sunday editions of New York newspapers between 1881 and 1893. During this period, *The New York Times* attempted to increase circulation by lowering its price from three cents to two cents and greatly enlarging its size, forcing the other papers to follow suit. By measuring number of column inches devoted to different topics, Speed found that the number of inches and the proportion of the newspaper devoted to gossip and scandal had greatly increased at the expense of literature, religion, politics, and other categories. While Speed's case against the New York newspapers rested heavily on the measurement of column inches, he also emphasized the level of sensationalism of reporting within categories. He lamented that in order not to offend their readers, even Chicago newspapers found it necessary to tone down the extreme stories of scandal taken from New York newspapers.

Several additional studies of the mass media were undertaken early in the twentieth century by Matthews (1910), Tenney (1912), Garth (1916), and others, but the hallmark study was sociologist Willey's *The Country Newspaper* (1926), a model of carefully planned content analysis. Willey was concerned with the role of the country weekly in face of the circulation of the large city dailies. Prior to 1784, the United States had no daily newspapers; the entire struggle for independence, for example, had been reported by a number of small weekly papers. By the early twentieth century, the weekly had acquired a distinctly different role. Willey made an intensive study of the development of the Connecticut weeklies.

Typically, the early investigators measured the attention devoted to straight topic categories, such as fashion, sports, and so on. The actual measures were usually in terms of the amount of space (such as column inches) devoted to the topics, the allocation of space in terms of page and location on the page, and the size of headlines. During the 1930's, this form of content analysis expanded into the analysis of other mass communications media, particularly radio (Albig, 1938), and later, movies and television. Content analysis of this kind continues today. It has come to include nearly all forms of communications, among which are textbooks, children's readers, speeches, novels, poetry, advertising, and comic strips.

The rate of content analysis growth in communications research has been phenomenal. Barcus' review (1959) of content analysis in communications research from 1900 to 1958 cites over 1,700 references, including some 500 Master's theses. Three fourths of these references are dated after 1940. This rapid growth has not occurred without arousing criticism. The term, content analysis, has acquired some pejorative associations, and with good reason.

A Period of Preoccupation with Measurement

A large proportion of studies bearing the label of content analysis have been mechanical, superficial tabulations of who says how much of what to whom. The procedure has often become its own *raison d'être*. Lazarsfeld at Columbia (1951) has criticized what he calls the tendency toward "administrative communications research," and Cartwright comments in a review,

> One of the most serious criticisms that can be made of much of the research employing content analysis is that the "findings" have no clear significance for either theory or practice. In reviewing the work in this field, one is struck by the number of studies which have apparently been guided by a sheer fascination with counting.

(Cartwright, 1953, 447)

When content analysts did seek to link their work to a systematic theory of human action, they often drew on stimulus-response behaviorism. The stimulus-response framework fits the communication situation very well. The communication message can be regarded as an event. On the stimulus side, the investigator catalogs the occasions on which such events occur. On the response side, he catalogs the apparent effects on the audience. Behavioristic theories had the unfortunate effect of allowing the investigator to be satisfied with a low level of inference. Yet, behaviorism did offer a needed framework for abstracting patterns in verbal content from myriad details.

More recently, the stimulus-response framework has tended to be recast in terms of information theory. The message is an event within a system. Stimulus and response tend to be replaced by references to the input and output of the system. Such factors as communication noise, encoding, and decoding become important within this framework. Our own view is that the depth of inference remains quite shallow.[3]

World War II and Political Symbol Analysis

The work of Lasswell, Leites, and associates in the 1940's put both content analysis theory and method in a much more refreshing and meaningful perspective. Based on an extensive background in the study of propaganda (Lasswell, 1927), their work at the University of Chicago and at the Experimental Division for the Study of Wartime Communications at the Library of Congress offered a major

---

[3] For more details, Osgood and Sebeok (1954) provide an excellent comparison of learning theory and information theory as they relate to psycholinguistics in general.

opportunity to make advances both in conceptualization and technique, summarized in their *Language of Politics* (1949).[4]

Lasswell, Leites, and associates make their theoretical focus the political myth, quoting Dicey:

> The whole body of beliefs existing in any given age may generally be traced to certain fundamental assumptions which, at the time, whether they be actually true or false, are believed by the mass of the world to be true with such confidence that they hardly appear to bear the character of assumptions.
>
> (Dicey, 1924, 20, quoted by Lasswell, 1949, 9)

Lasswell further states that "a key symbol is a basic term of the political myth" (Lasswell, 1949, 13). For example,

> In the United States, key words are "rights," "freedom," "democracy," "equality." Such terms figure in the recondite treatises of the professors, in the opinions of the courts, and in the arguments heard in the halls of Congress or the street corners of the nation.
>
> (Lasswell, 1949, 13)

With this focus, the task of content analysis becomes fairly explicit:

> One of the principal problems of political science is the study of factors making for the restriction or diffusion of political doctrines and formulas. This calls, of course, for the study of historical and contemporary trends in the distribution of political myths, and the analysis of facilitating or retarding factors.
>
> (Lasswell, 1949, 14)

Considered in this light, much of the research reported in this book studies the facilitating and retarding factors associated with the appearance of symbols and myths, not just in the political realm but extended to both the spectrum of cultural institutions and to the private world of the individual. Human beings apparently need symbols and myths, in Lasswell's sense, to explain the world about them. While there is a cynicism (witness modern reactions to the myth writers of Plato's *Republic*) toward using myths in society, their importance for societal, as well as for individual, solidarity and stability cannot be disregarded by the social sciences. Within this book,

---

[4] *Language of Politics* has been reprinted in 1965 by the M.I.T. Press as part of the same *Symbols* series in which this book appears.

we shall discuss the attributes associated with symbols as problems of *image* and the combination of symbols into Lasswell's myths as problems of *theme* and *plot*.

The technical advances of the Lasswell group focused on systematic sampling. On the one hand, the care of Sherlock Holmes was needed to identify clues and to make inferences from available data. On the other, Lasswell was critical of the sampling procedures used in previous propaganda analysis, including his own past research. In past work,

> "excerpts were chosen to illustrate what was circulated to different publics and what themes were used. The authors left unspecified their criteria of choice . . . no explicit justification was given of most of the excerpts chosen to illustrate a specific theme, to characterize the content of any particular channel, or to describe propaganda directed toward or reaching any given audience"
>
> (Lasswell, 1949, 42–43)

Within *Language of Politics,* a number of chapters are devoted to problems and studies of method. Detailed consideration is given to problems of validity in content analysis and the reliability of content analysis categories. Irving Janis argues that the validity of the procedure is inferred from its productivity and proposes the following principle of validation:

> The larger the number of relationships established by the use of a content analysis technique, the higher the probability that the procedures estimate signification responses correctly, and hence the higher the degree of validity.
>
> (Janis, in Lasswell, 1949, 72)

In this way, a strong emphasis is placed on ties to other measures. Until a procedure is fully validated, negative results "will fail to increase substantially the probability that a hypothesis is false." One cannot know whether there is a true lack of relationship or an inappropriate measurement procedure.

Several applications are reported in *Language of Politics*. Each combines systematic rigor with a careful political analysis of the data. For example, in the analysis of Soviet May Day slogans from 1918 to 1943, a procedure is defined, graphs of symbol frequencies are presented with comments as to over-all trends, and then a year-by-year analysis is presented, noting the political situation of each year and its relation to shifts in the frequency of particular symbols. Correlations between successive time periods are used to identify major occasions of over-all shift.

Several agencies during World War II had responsibilities for monitoring large amounts of propaganda. A. L. George (1959*a*) has reviewed the successes and failures of inferences made during the war by The Foreign Broadcast Intelligence Service of the American Federal Communications Commission. While procedures used in these agencies attempted to be systematic, the day-to-day demand for interpretations and predictions made systematic procedures not always feasible.

After World War II, the study of political symbols continued for a number of years at the Hoover Institute, Stanford University, with Lasswell's supervision and the direction of Daniel Lerner and Ithiel de Sola Pool. The study of symbols in elite press editorials and major policy speeches from 1890 to 1950 in Great Britain, Russia, United States, France, and Germany was paralleled with studies on the composition of elite powers. The content analysis was immense. Using careful sampling procedures, some 105,004 symbols were identified in 19,553 editorials. Yet, since 416 different symbols were counted, the sample was often not large enough. The symbol "balance of power" occurred only 31 times; "freedom of assembly" occurred 17 times. "Such frequencies, scattered over five papers and sixty years, are not likely to be useful" (Lasswell, Lerner, and Pool, 1952, 60).

In *The Comparative Study of Symbols,* Lasswell, Lerner, and Pool discuss the lessons learned from their content analysis studies: when content analysis is useful, what insights it can offer, its costs, and what comprises a desirable content analysis procedure. Concerning when to use content analysis, they stated,[5]

> Content analysis will not tell us whether a given work is good literature; it *will* tell us whether the style is varied. It will not tell us whether a paper is subversive; it *will* tell us if the contents change with party line. It will not tell us how to convince the Russians; it *will* tell us what are the most frequent themes of Soviet propaganda.
>
> (Lasswell, Lerner, and Pool, 1952, 45)

The real issues behind what is often referred to as the "qualitative-quantitative" argument were faced directly; however, in the context

---

[5] The Hoover *Symbol Studies* will also be republished as part of this M.I.T. Press *Symbols* series.

of today's computer power and flexibility, the distinction can be less absolute than it appeared to the authors at that time:

> It should be frankly recognized that content analysis is a procedure of deliberate simplification, Such deliberate simplification is painful. Coders are pained at losing some of the richness of the meaning in the text. Invariably, a reader will bring to his supervisor some passage full of innuendo, metaphor, or double entendre, and protest that the scheme being used distorts its real meaning. Toward such difficulties the analyst may well be ruthless. When the questionable passage has become but one of fifty-seven checks in category *xyz*, the analyst will have neither time nor cause to consider its individuality. Content analysis is a statistical procedure, and, like any statistical procedure, it disregards the individuality of the particular case for the sake of discovering the uniformities in the mass.
>
> (Lasswell, Lerner, and Pool, 1952, 52)

Other content analysis problems explicitly discussed include validity, category consistency, category domination by a few frequent words, language translation, combining categories, coder reliability, selection of units, and differences between handling nouns and verbs. Often what is suspected to be a difficult problem is not very severe, while problems that might not be anticipated prove very difficult. For example, the problem of translation from different languages becomes much simpler because of content analysis categories. The reader need not be concerned with capturing the entire meaning of a word, but only considering those aspects relative to the categories being scored. Thus "VATERLAND and PATRIE may be somewhat different; so, too, may REICH and STATE. But, by the time all of these and other symbols have been lumped into national self-references, the particular mode of expression assumes little statistical importance" (Lasswell, Lerner, and Pool, 1952, 59). On the other hand, a task of combining category counts caused difficult technical problems, which now can be handled by the computer facilities described in this book.

In recommending an over-all procedure, Lasswell, Lerner, and Pool strongly advocated combining a clinical and statistical understanding, with clinical understanding taking precedence:

> Content analysis should begin where traditional modes of research end. The man who wishes to use content analysis for a study of the propaganda of some political party, for example, should steep himself in that propaganda. Before he begins to count, he should read it to detect charac-

teristic mechanisms and devices. He should study the vocabulary and format. He should know the party organization and personnel. From this knowledge he should organize his hypotheses and predictions. At this point, in a conventional study, he would start writing. At this point, in a content analysis, he is, instead, ready to set up his categories, to pretest them, and then to start counting.

(Lasswell, Lerner, and Pool, 1952, 65)

In hand content analysis, the clinical analysis comes first, followed by the development of a fixed content analysis schedule. In the procedures to be described in this book, the clinical stage need not cease when the content analysis begins. With the computer to do the leg work, the data can be rapidly reanalyzed as new insights are acquired.

Finally, Lasswell, Lerner, and Pool spoke eloquently for the importance of pretesting, a stage that cannot be slighted even with computers.

The purpose of pretesting is to determine objectively how well one's "impressionistic" reading of the media has served in working out a research plan which gets the most of what one needs (and the least of what one does not need) to test the hypotheses of the study. To pretest the research scheme, one simply applies it to limited portions of the material to be analyzed. Thereby, one tests whether the periodization chosen gives useful results; whether the symbol lists include the specific words actually used by the medium being studied (and excludes words not used); whether the recording procedures adequately reflect the grammatical-syntactical-semantic habits of the medium; whether these procedures are adequately understood and uniformly applied by the coders.

(Lasswell, Lerner, and Pool, 1952, 73)

The results of the Stanford *Symbol Studies* took a variety of forms. With Yule's K statistic, analyses were made of symbol variety to identify those papers and time periods in which there is a concentration of fewer symbols. Reports analyzing frequency patterns of internationalism, democracy, freedom, and doctrine were separately issued. Attitudes toward symbols were scored as being favorable, unfavorable, or neutral. Results were often rather complicated. For example, while references to symbols of democracy markedly increased over time, this increase was only proportional to the space given subject matters related to democracy in editorials; beyond this, an increase in references to the symbol itself scarcely occurred.

Although the Stanford studies yielded a number of important insights and greatly improved the standards of content analysis research,
large-scale studies by this group were not continued. Lerner and
Pool both went to M.I.T. and became immersed in other research.
The labors of large-scale hand content analysis discouraged its further
use. Already Lasswell, Lerner, and Pool were aware that the future
feasibility of the method might very well depend on the computer:

> Perhaps the evolution of modern computing machinery may prove to
> be the key to the tremendously complex problems involved in the sta-
> tistical analysis of language. . . . The advantage of a sufficiently flexible
> mechanical system would have been that we could have gone back to
> the original data at will. With the system actually used, tabulation was
> so laborious that, once the summary tables by periods were made up, it
> was almost never possible to go back for another look at them.
>
> (Lasswell, Lerner, and Pool, 1952, 63)

The 1940's and 1950's also witnessed a rapid increase in the
sophistication of content analysis apart from the groups associated
with Lasswell. Investigators in general were less willing to count for
the sake of counting. While Barcus' review of content analysis literature from 1900 to 1958 places 70 percent of the studies after 1940,
some 88 percent of the 240 primarily concerned with content analysis
theory and methodology appeared after 1940.

A Review of the 1950's

In the early 1950's, the Social Science Research Council's Committee on Linguistics and Psychology held two summer conferences
on psycholinguistics. Considerable interest was expressed in problems
relating to content analysis, and a third conference was called in the
winter of 1955, resulting in *Trends in Content Analysis,* edited by
Pool (1959). Participants represented a number of different disciplines.

At the time of the conference, it was assumed by many that content
analysis was on the decline. The conference participants were surprised
to find that others were still working in the field and had the same
concerns about methodological sophistication. Pool described the
situation as follows:

> If one listed the persons who were publishing in the field of content
> analysis in the decade of the 1940's (Lasswell, Leites, Berelson, Lerner,
> Janis, Pool, etc.) one would have difficulty in finding one of them still

engaged in that kind of research. One could easily find among them persons who had quite consciously rejected the field as an unprofitable enterprise, while others, though retaining their faith in the ultimate value of the method, had turned for the present to greener pastures.

It was, therefore, somewhat of a discovery for a group of scholars assembled in the mid-1950's, when content analysis seemed to be on the decline, to find that each one was not alone in the research which he was doing, and that other scholars also had seen unexplored potentials in content analysis if certain new tacks were taken to meet the unsolved problems of the previous decade. The conferees, each starting from different directions and unaware of each other's work, did not of course see eye to eye on all issues. The discussions were vigorous. Some of the participants were explicitly critical of what they thought content analysis had been, others hopeful, others, having approached the field from novel direction, somewhat unaware of their predecessors. Issues remained at the end of the conference as well as the beginning. But the striking fact was the degree of convergence.

(Pool, 1959, 2)

According to Pool, the conference found the convergence to center on two points:

1. a sophisticated concern with the problems of inference from verbal material to its antecedent conditions, and
2. a focus on counting internal contingencies between symbols instead of the simple frequencies of symbols.

(Pool, 1959, 2)

The first point raised the question of what can be inferred from a frequency count. If one author uses a symbol twice as often as another author, then what can we say about the authors? The second point reflected an increased awareness that contingencies between symbols may take a variety of different forms. The results of a study may be very much influenced by the rules selected for determining what is and what is not a contingency. Within a research project, such rules for determining more complex units of analysis are part of what we call a "content analysis program."

Since much of the failure of content analysis was seen to hinge on these issues, we should consider the alternatives that were possible.

Frequency Counts as a Source of Inference

A few proponents of content analysis frequencies have been quite clear in stating their inferences. Baldwin's success in using frequency counts in studying *Letters from Jenny* (Allport, 1942) led him to conclude that "the frequency with which an item appears in the case material may be used as a measure of its importance in the personality" (Baldwin, 1942, 168).

Actually, Baldwin's claim that frequency indicates "importance in personality" is a stronger inference than most investigators have been willing to make. More commonly, the statement has been made that frequency counts measure the "intensity of an attitude" or "amount of concern" or "attention" devoted to a topic.

In reviewing previous research, Pool concludes that such inferences are, in fact, often reasonable:

> The assumption that the frequency of statements provides a good index of intensity of attitude is probably reasonable for a large class of cases. By "attitude" here, of course, we mean the attitude expressed in the body of the text, not the covert feelings of the author. Even with this limitation, the assumption baldly spelled out sounds absurd, because it is perfectly clear that frequency is only one of a variety of devices by which feeling is expressed. But the experience of more than one analyst who has tried refinements in measuring intensity has been that nothing much is added by other measures than the frequency one.
>
> (Pool, 1959, 194)

Attempts to refine simple frequency counts have usually been made at considerable expense in manual labor and have therefore been largely avoided. With the General Inquirer, many of these refinements can be obtained at little cost. We agree with Pool that the power of simple frequency counts is not to be underrated, but further refinements have often proved worthwhile. Let us review here some of the possibilities.

First, the words within a category may be weighted to indicate the extent to which the category is present. For example, if a category were developed to measure a SENSE OF ACTIVENESS, such words as madhouse, speed of sound, frenetic, racing, and zooming might be weighted heavily, while such other phrases as "bit hasty," "kept going," "moved along" would indicate a less intense salience. A category score would be the number of mentions, each mention multiplied by its appropriate weight. As we describe later in this chapter, Osgood, Saporta, and Nunnally (1954, 1959) have made a three-point scale weighting an important part of their "evaluative assertion analysis" procedure. In research using the General Inquirer, Holsti at Stanford (see Chapter 9) has used a similar weighting scale for each of his category dimensions.

A second modification of simple frequency concerns the assumption of an equal-interval scale. Is it as much of a jump to go from the second mention to the third as it is to go from the seventh to the eighth? In fact, the investigator may want to make a scale transformation for two reasons. First, he may adjust the distribution of scores so that they will be more suitable for the assumptions of particular statistical tests; for example, Namenwirth's study (Chapter 11) used an arc sine square root transformation before subjecting his data to an analysis of variance model. A second type of transformation involves identifying major thresholds of intensity change. The first threshold, of course, is to go from no mention at all to a single mention. The single mention indicates that the reference is in the author's repertoire and is elicited by the situation being studied. When a category has appeared once, the probability of a second reference becomes relatively high. However, after a particular category has been used a number of times, a second threshold will develop against its further occurrence, representing the need to put more variety in the document by shifting to other topics and/or styles of expression. Beyond this second threshold, a higher frequency may indicate a preoccupation with a topic or way of speaking. Even higher rates, beyond further thresholds, may represent forms of perseveration characterizing delusional speech.

Occasionally, past studies have measured only passage of the first threshold; that is, whether or not a category is present in a document. For example, in studying a large number of editorials, a count would be made of how many editorials mentioned a category rather than how many times it was mentioned within each editorial. In a similar fashion, studies of delusional speech might well focus on identifying category frequencies beyond normal thresholds.

A third modification of simple frequency considers the question of distribution. A document may have a very high frequency for a particular category, but it may result from occurrences clustered in one section. If the sampling procedure had not happened to include that section of the document, the frequency count would have been quite low. Thus, an ideal index should actually be a measure of permeation; that is, it should consider both frequency and distribution information. One simple procedure for handling this is to divide each document being studied into several sections, making separate measurements on each section, and checking to see that frequency rates hold up across sections. Those categories that permeate the document will have high frequencies in each section. A category that clusters in one or two sections will show very uneven frequencies across sections.

Taken together, these three additional considerations can greatly increase the sophistication of simple frequency measures. Only rarely might one have occasion to take the time and effort to utilize all three at once. Individually, they appear in various applications described in this book and often make a critical contribution.

Critics of simple frequency counts have often ignored the different forms that frequency measurement procedures can take. Persons measuring presence versus absence have often claimed to be "qualitative," ignoring the fact that this is also a form of measurement yielding what is formally called a "nominal" scale. As Barcus (1959), Holsti (in press), and others have pointed out, the quantitative-qualitative distinction "has merit when used to describe a general orientation of social scientists toward their data, but the dichotomy is so oversimplified as to have little theoretical significance" (Barcus, 1959, 21).

Levels of Symbol Complexity

Since all more complex contingency measures are based on the identification of elementary symbols, the first question is, "What are the 'atoms' in content analysis?" Pool reports that the 1955 conference found it necessary to "leave the matter of 'basic units' vague."

> It is a problem the conferees discussed but not one they could resolve. It is one of the problems of content analysis to which psycholinguistics may help produce an answer. But as of now, it is not clear how one identifies a basic unit of meaning.
>
> (Pool, 1959, 204)

In fact, content analysis studies have used a variety of different elementary units. These range from just part of a word, such as the "ly" or "ed" suffix, to a multiword string, such as "United States of America." These elementary units have been described by a variety of terms, such as morpheme, semanteme, word, idiom, sign, and unit symbol. However, for specific studies it is fairly easy to determine the basic meaning units to be considered. Some content analysis studies simply measure the number of references made to a particular elementary unit. One study may look at the number of "hmms" made by a psychiatrist. Another study may look for mention of a particular geographical place.

Categories usually take the form of classes of elementary units, and category selection depends on the hypotheses being tested. As we have indicated, if a variety of words and phrases are combined within a certain category, this does not mean they are all considered identical in meaning, but that they share a common aspect which is being measured in order to test a hypothesis. For example, if dog and cat are classed together in the category ANIMAL, it does not mean there are no differences between them, but that they are of interest as examples of animals.

However, before making an inference from category frequencies, it is often important to check back to see which of the elementary units comprising the category were actually used. If the frequency of political mentions is to be used to indicate *level of political salience,* the investigator may well be advised to see what kinds of political forms are cited. It may be that all the mentions refer to FASCISM, the documents in fact showing little interest in other political phenomena.

In developing contingency measures, various categories may be developed not as indexes in themselves but for use in conjunction with other categories. Examples of contingency measures ("obligation of restraint," "excessive economic costs") were given in Chapter 1. As discussed, a number of different contingency measures may be combined to produce an over-all index.

Contingency procedures may vary in complexity. Examples of three different levels of complexity are represented by *image and theme, analysis of plot,* and *patterns of beliefs and arguments.*

Image and theme. Berelson defines a theme as "an assertion about a subject matter." We would roughly divide such assertions into two varieties. One employs an active verb and a noun to describe events, the noun being either a subject or an object of the verb. Examples include "maltreat minorities," "soldiers revolt," "dictator attacks," "underpay workers," as well as complete transitive statements, such as "shopowners underpay workers." A second form is a static assertion described by a word and its modifiers, such as "nasty neighbor" or "healthful exercise."

Repetitions of the first kind of assertion often result in generalizations described by the second. For example, the specific statements

"Communist China constructs foundry equipment."
"Communist China makes tractors."
"Communist China assembles automobiles."

might first be generalized into the statement

"Communist China manufactures industrial goods."

and then further generalized to a more static image, as

"Communist China is industrialized."

or finally,

"Industrialized Communist China today announced. . . ."

Within this book, we use the *theme* primarily to refer to an assertion involving events described by active verbs. The more static assertions, implicit in many noun-modifier relationships, are called *images*.

Images and themes are often studied in political science. In looking at themes in a set of documents, the political scientist is likely, for example, to ask, Who sees which groups as being aggressive toward which other groups? His task is then to locate descriptions of aggression and to identify the roles associated with the aggression. A second kind of question concerns attitudes held toward certain political symbols, treaties, political programs, or countries. Are they regarded positively or negatively? Are they seen as important or inconsequential?

A number of image studies have focused on the treatment of particular people or groups of people. Daykin (1937) has traced the representation of Negro types in American fiction; Foff (1958) has studied the stereotype of the American teacher in American novels. Deegan (1951) has studied the "single woman" image. Images of the United States and Great Britain as portrayed by the Communist press have been studied by Davison (1947), Dallin (1947), and Bassow (1948). In this book, Dunphy (Chapter 8) studies differences in the ways members of self-analytic groups describe other group members in their essays; Paige (Chapter 12) describes differences in the ways one individual portrays significant figures in her life.

One of the better-known content analysis procedures that measures psychological assertions is McClelland's (1953) "Need-Achievement." By looking primarily at different kinds of thematic contingencies, an over-all score is made as to whether achievement imagery is present in a story. The procedure is explicitly worked out and has been carefully reported. In Chapter 5, Ogilvie and Woodhead describe the translation of the hand scoring into General Inquirer categories and scoring directions for the computer.

Analysis of plot. Plot analysis has been particularly important in studying literature, drama, and film. A number of plots are compared to draw conclusions about major psychological themes, audience expectations, or theories of drama that characterize an era, culture, or media. Most analyses, such as Wolfenstein and Leites's study of movies (1950), employ an informal analysis procedure, often quite anecdotal. A few, such as Propp's classic study of Russian folktales, are quite formal.

TABLE 2.1. Major Action Categories in Propp's Analysis of Folktales

Preparatory section
  (includes description of an absence, an interdiction, a punishment, a hero or villain obtaining information, the use of a magical agent, preliminary misfortune caused by a deceitful agreement, and so on)
Villainy
Elements lacking, missing
The connective item
  (call, dispatch, release, announcement of misfortune, and so on)
Consent to counteraction
Dispatch of the hero from home
The first function of the donor
Reaction of the hero
Control of a magical agent
Transference to a designated place
Struggle with the villain
Victory of the villain
Branding or marking the hero with a sign
The liquidation of a loss or harm
Return of the hero
Pursuit of the hero
Rescue, salvation of the hero
Unrecognized arrival
Claims of a false, bogus hero
Difficult task
Solution of task (within given period of time)
Recognition of the hero
Exposure of the false hero
Transfiguration
  (new physical appearance, new palace, new garments, and so on)
Punishment of the false hero or of the villain
Wedding and accession to the throne

Propp's study, published originally in Russian in 1928 and translated into English in 1958, is an extensive comparison of a hundred Russian folktales, focusing on the sequence of plot and the functions of the dramatis personae. Propp finds that Russian folktales have a shared pattern of sequences. The sequence formula branches partly into two main paths. A number of alternative events are generally listed as possibly fulfilling the function of a particular stage in the sequence. Table 2.1 presents the main action categories used by Propp. Within each category, a number of subcategories may be specified. VILLAINY, for example, contains 19 subcategories; the FIRST FUNCTION OF THE DONOR contains ten alternatives.

Propp's over-all characterization of the Russian folktales is in terms of a particular problem-solving sequence. Unfortunately, the conclusions stated in the report are not supported with statistical tables.

More recently, extensive work has been done on mythology structure by Lévi-Strauss and his students. One form of analysis is to group myths according to the kinds of transformations represented. For example in Lévi-Strauss's recent *Le Cru et Le Cuit* (1964), over 170 South American myths are compared, focusing on the transformation from nature (the "raw") to culture (the "cooked"), especially as symbolized by the development and control of fire.

Both B. N. Colby and Pierre Maranda have been exploring the possibility of utilizing the General Inquirer in the study of plot, with folktales as texts. As described in Chapter 21, Colby (1966) has divided each folktale into ninths and looked for recurrent shifts in his various frequency counts across sections. Maranda has developed a more structural analysis of sequence development for the study of "Ge" folktales. Analysis of plot with the General Inquirer is in a very early stage of development.

Patterns of beliefs and arguments. Content analysis studies of rhetoric and propaganda techniques form a special area of interest dating back to the 1930's. Much of this development can be traced to the appointment by the Social Science Research Council in 1931 of a Committee on Pressure Groups and Propaganda. Basically, this involved discovering various propaganda tricks of the trade within the content of a document. Such tricks identified by the Institute of Propaganda analysis in the 1930's included "selecting the issue," "card stacking," "name calling," "glittering generality," "testimonial," "plain folks," "bandwagon," and "hot potato." While most of these tricks can be identified directly from the content of the text, occasionally it is necessary to have specific knowledge about the actual situation that is being described.

Another approach to patterns of argument has been developed by Shneidman (1961) in what he calls "psycho-logic." Taking the point of view that "everyone thinks with some kind of logic," Shneidman identifies a collection of logical procedures, rhetorical devices, and psychological mechanisms as they serve to reflect personality patterns in speech and writing. Shneidman uses the strategy of contralogic to test the adequacy of his explanations.

Shneidman's approach when applied to such documents as the Nixon-Khrushchev "kitchen debates" shows a very complex level of scoring that requires considerable training, sensitivity, and intelligence on the part of human scorers. It would be a formidable task to describe such complex procedures well enough for a computer to use them.

With the computer more in mind, Abelson (1963) has undertaken a major effort to develop a model of "hot cognition," identifying defense mechanisms and other strategies employed by individuals to resolve discrepancies between incoming information and their belief systems. Similarly, K. Colby (1963) has focused on models to identify the neurotic logic expressed by a patient over the course of therapy. Neither approach attempts to handle arguments as they occur in natural text; instead they both first reduce the text to a sequence of simplified sentences.

The Analysis Program

In addition to the development of units, categories, and contingency measures, a content analysis must also include a program: a set of rules for organizing the data, applying categories, determining contingencies, and arranging the results for inspection and further statistical tests. The program is essentially a set of consecutive procedures for processing data.[6]

As an example of a fairly simple program, we may cite that given for value analysis by White in his study of *Black Boy* (1947).

1. Put in the margin a symbol corresponding to each goal and each value-judgment that is explicitly stated in the material or clearly implied by it.

---

[6] The program is roughly equivalent to what Cartwright (1953) describes as the "analysis outline."

2. Tabulate these symbols.
3. Interpret each numerical result in the light of the picture as a whole, with special attention to the person's possible reasons for conscious concealment or unconscious self-deception.

(White, 1947, 445)

Although White provides a list of value categories, symbols and symbol combinations, such a program obviously leaves many detailed aspects to the coder's interpretation.

In general, content analysts have varied considerably in the extent to which they have made their program steps explicit. Programs also vary greatly in complexity, depending upon whether they are concerned with simple word frequencies or a set of thematic contingencies.

Probably the most sophisticated and explicit manual content analysis program is Osgood's "evaluation assertion analysis" (1959). This procedure identifies both themes and images within the text which contain references to a particular person, idea, or object, and then combines these in a multistep procedure to obtain an over-all assessment of how each object is evaluated.

The purpose of evaluative assertion analysis is to extract from messages the evaluations being made of significant concepts, with a minimum dependence on the effects of messages on coders or on their existing attitudes. It begins with a sample of "raw" messages received from some source and ends up with an evaluative scaling of the attitude objects referred to by the source.

(Osgood, 1959, 42)

The steps to the procedure are briefly as follows:

Evaluative assertion analysis involves several stages which can be done serially by a single coder, or, preferably, serially by a set of different coders. In Stage I, the attitude objects (AO) in the message are identified, isolated linguistically, and then masked [by the substitution of non-sense-letter pairs.] In Stage II, this masked message is translated into an exhaustive series of evaluative assertions which are standard in structure, but semantically equivalent to the original message. In Stage III, the assertions and common-meaning evaluations are assigned directions and weights. Finally, in Stage IV, assertions relating to each attitude object are collected and averaged in terms of common meaning evaluation, thereby allocating each attitude object to a common evaluative scale.

(Osgood, 1959, 43)

It is evident that much of the labor of evaluative assertion analysis is in masking the text into nonsense-letter pairs. If the documents are at all famous, such masking may not be very successful. Turning to a computer greatly simplifies evaluative assertion analysis, for the computer is without historical bias and disguising is unnecessary.

Space does not permit a detailed presentation of evaluative assertion analysis. The original references are highly recommended. Evaluative assertion analysis has been used extensively by Holsti and his group at Stanford and has influenced much of their computer content analysis reasearch reported here.

Part of the content analysis program includes the specification of certain boundary conditions, particularly the *recording unit* and the *context unit*. Past empirical research, such as that of Grey, Kaplan, and Lasswell (1949), has shown that the size of these units can significantly affect the findings of a study.

The *recording unit* is the smallest section of text in which the appearance of a reference is counted. It may be a word, sentence, paragraph, or entire document, depending on the appropriateness to the hypothesis being tested. The level at which this unit is specified determines how the analysis will be carried out. For example, if the unit is the word, the maximum number of occurrences would be the number of words in the document. If the unit is the sentence, the maximum scoring is once per sentence. If it is the document, the question becomes whether or not a reference occurs in a document.

A *context unit* enters into contingency scorings. Before the co-occurrence of two categories can be scored, it is necessary to determine the maximum allowable distance between mentions of the categories. Often this unit boundary is simply stated as a number of words distant, such as, "Score co-occurrence if X is within five words of Z." Sometimes direction is also included, such as, "Score co-occurrence if X is within three words *before* Z." Often the context direction pays heed to the natural unit of the sentence, such as, "Score co-occurrence if X is in the same sentence as Z." Sometimes the boundary is syntactic in nature, such as, "Score co-occurrence if X is a modifier of Z."

There has been considerable argument about whether context units should consider the structure of language or simply the mechanical distance such as would be specified by "within so many words away." The mechanical distance procedure has been justified on the grounds (1) that it is simpler to access and (2) that the investigator is really interested in *associations* within language irrespective of language structure. Curiously, justifications for this have been attributed to both stimulus-response theory and psychoanalytic models. Both emphasize that the mention of one word sets up a probability of mention of another, which carries across sentence boundaries.

In the General Inquirer system, one of the fundamental decisions has been to recognize the sentence as a meaningful unit. Provision is made for measurement of within-sentence patterns and between-sentence sequences. By taking the sentence as a major unit of context, a basis is laid for the future study of image, theme, and plot.

The Issue of Standardized Categories and Procedures

While the emphasis of the 1955 conference was on the careful design of measurement units, categories, contingency indexes, and analysis programs to fit the hypotheses being tested, the question was also considered of whether it is necessary for each content analysis study to be designed completely from scratch. Might there not be a store of categories and procedures developed in the past that could provide components for testing new hypotheses?

Previous reviewers had been quite pessimistic about standardized categories, partly because they had served as an excuse for preoccupation with method apart from any immediate hypotheses. The 1955 conference was more willing to recognize, with caution, that past misuses of the standardization banner need not negate its importance for the future. Pool summarized the consensus of the conference in this way:

> . . . standardized content analysis categories . . . could be used by different researchers in different studies to the end that studies would be more comparable and additive. Clearly this is a laudable aspiration and one that has been with content analysts from the beginning. . . . In other fields of social science general tools of a similar kind have proved of great use. The intelligence quotient is such a standardized measure. In studies of the relation of intelligence to some other variable, it is most convenient that there is a standardized measure for at least one of the variables. Garraty noted how useful it would be for historians if relevant precut content analysis categories existed.
>
> It is questionable, however, how ready we are to establish standard measure of that sort in content analysis. Such a measure is convenient when a considerable number of researchers are working on the same

variable, and when someone succeeds in working out good categories for that variable. It is doubtful that either of those criteria can be met in most areas of content analysis.

(Pool, 1959, 212–13)

With the availability of the computer as a content analysis aid, the issue of standardization takes on a new perspective. In past manual content analyses, the development of a scoring procedure usually was a minor task compared to the sheer labor of applying it to the data. Usually the amount of labor involved meant that the data could only be analyzed once. With a computer to carry out the analysis, the investigator can easily try out several different approaches on the same data. More important, the specification of units, categories, contingency indexes, and analysis programs for the computer encourages careful identification of these components. Rather than borrow an entire procedure, the investigator may combine certain components from several past studies to test the hypotheses under consideration.

A content analysis category may be general in two ways. First, it may be constructed to include a variety of words and idioms representing the category as it is used in different kinds of formal writing and informal speech. Such a category may be relevant to only one specific theory, but it is general in picking up manifestations in a variety of different kinds of text. Second, a category may be general inasmuch as it serves as an important component in a number of theoretical viewpoints. In Chapter 4, considerable attention is given to general categories that have been found to serve as common components in testing a variety of different kinds of hypotheses.

Similarly, a content analysis *program* may function as a component in a number of different measurement procedures. For example, the "product-image-analysis" framework, described in Chapter 22, presents an over-all strategy that may be adopted to the vocabulary and categories of different product analysis situations.

The computer setting thus encourages borrowing both complete scoring systems and their component parts in constructing new systems. The implications of a previous content analysis procedure on new data can be quickly checked. Cumulative research, in fact, becomes more likely.

The alternatives faced by the 1955 conference take on a new importance with the flexibility of computer implementation. With a considerable history of content analysis behind them, the participants of the conference were well aware that many of the potentialities of content analysis were yet to be demonstrated.

The General Inquirer approach has expanded over the past five years to applications in a number of different fields. Considerable borrowing across fields has occurred in the past and will undoubtedly continue in the future. It is to the content analysis research outside the traditional mainstream that we now turn.

RESOURCES AND STRATEGIES
IN DIFFERENT AREAS OF APPLICATION

Each field brings to content analysis a specialized set of problems and experiences, representing different sensitivities to various aspects of message content and the context in which it appears. Inasmuch as content analysis is part of an inference-making process, the text measurements are usually only a piece in the chain of evidence needed to support the inference. When several inferences are possible, further research on language meaning often can be used to select the correct one.

Despite the continued separation of content analysis research by field, we believe that the element of striking convergence of interests experienced in the 1955 conference still holds true today. We shall briefly illustrate some of the different analysis uses and problems in fields other than journalism and political science. We shall note techniques developed in the study of language meaning and use which supplement content analysis research.

Psychiatry

Psychiatry offers perhaps the most intensive analysis of language use, often combining semantic, syntactic, and paralinguistic information in one analysis. Pittenger, Hockett, and Danehy (1960) devote an entire book to an extensive "microscopic" anlysis of the first five minutes of a therapy interview, using both a text transcription and a phonetic transcription, as well as information on pausing, movement, and other events. Similarly Gottschalk (1961) brings together a number of analysis approaches to gain a variety of perspectives in describing two therapy sessions.

Content analysis of therapy has often been hampered by a lack of clear criteria in making inferences. The basic issue is whether (and in what way) the patient improves. Valid external criteria are hard to come by. Furthermore, the complexity and unique nature of each case often make generalizations difficult. Yet a number of studies have been carried out and have been reviewed by Auld and Murray (1955), Marsden (1965), and Jaffee (in press).

While generalizations across cases may be difficult, content analysis inference within a case is occasionally at its best in psychiatry. Laffals study (1960) of the Schreber case is an example of this. Schreber's autobiography (1903) was a considerable source of debate in psychoanalytic circles. Much of the argument concentrated on the symbolism of the sun as it appeared in Schreber's accounts. Freud (1911) took the view that for Schreber the sun was a father symbol. Macalpine and Hunter (1955) translated the case into English and took a contrary position that "all the evidence goes to show that the sun, far from representing only the father, mirrored Schreber's own ambisexuality, being both male and female" (1955, 378).

Laffal did a content analysis of the autobiography using a rather comprehensive set of some 60 content analysis categories. A count was made of the number of times each category was used in conjunction with mention of the sun, of female persons, and of male persons; the context unit was defined as the co-occurrence within the same, preceding, or following sentence. On the basis of similarities of these co-occurrence profiles, the problem was then approached: Was the sun treated in the text more like a male or a female figure?

Laffal developed his 60 content analysis categories (later expanded to over 100 categories) from the patterns in word-association test norms and from his own experience on how language is used in the clinical situation. His categories represent a major attempt toward standardization, and their usefulness is demonstrated in a number of different studies in addition to the Schreiber case. While Laffal does not relate his research to the field of traditional content analysis, both his category system and its applications represent a major contribution.

In general, the medical field offers a number of unique resources for the further understanding of language functions. The clinical evidence provided by delusional speech patterns, effects of brain damage on speech, verbal behavior under drugs, aphasic speech, and the effects of brain stimulation provide important insights into the function of speech in thought and behavior. In many cases, the ability of people to function cognitively without certain language resources provides a constant reminder that language is only one medium of symbolic representation. In short, medical evidence also plays an important role for a much needed theory of language. As such medical evidence is further explored and assimilated, insights concerning possible inferences from the content of what is said should become evident.

Psychology

With its extensive testing and assessment, psychology has the day-to-day task of making standardized assessments and evaluations from the content of what is said or written in a test situation. Many psychological tests elicit verbal responses, ranging from sentence completion to construction of TAT stories. Additional verbal data are gathered in autobiographies and interviews.

Much of psychological content analysis is on an intuitive level; the analyst makes assessments based on his impression of a protocol compared with others in his experience. A number of efforts have been made, usually quite apart from traditional content analysis, to formalize such assessments. Following from the framework of "needs" and "presses" developed by Murray (1938), McClelland first developed a well-specified content analysis procedure for measuring "need-achievement" imagery (1953) and demonstrated its relationship to risk taking and a number of other performance measures in characterizing both the individual and the society (1961). Need-achievement today is a standard variable used in a wide range of research studies. Similar measures have been developed by Atkinson and others (1958) for the measurement of need-power and need-affiliation.

Although formal procedures are essential for the research setting, the large volume of content analysis by psychologists in schools, hospitals, counseling offices, and clinics usually makes the time and expense of formal procedures prohibitive. Usually the psychologist prefers to assess many different aspects of a protocol by inspection rather than formally measure a few variables.[7]

Psychology has also emphasized the use of personal documents in the study of personality. Attention was drawn to the fruitfulness of this area by Allport's *The Use of Personal Documents in Psychologi-*

[7] One formal content analysis procedure that appears to have considerable clinical utility is Arnold's story sequence analysis (1962) based on the TAT. This procedure evaluates "imports" of the stories and thus is somewhat different from the detail of most content analysis tasks.

cal Science (1942), a strong argument for the contribution that can be made by nomothetic and idiographic studies of personal documents.

Two empirical studies in the 1940's suggested that Allport's emphasis on the idiographic approach was sound. Baldwin's application of "Personal Structure Analysis" (1942) indicated the usefulness of formalizing intuitive procedures for the exploration of personality structure. Baldwin used contingencies among content categories in the letters of a woman to reveal major configurations in her personality. Similarly, White's study of *Black Boy* (1947) outlined a procedure for arriving at a set of categories for the study of an individual's goals and values and used the study to give a concrete picture of the personality.

The early work by Baldwin in studying *Letters from Jenny* has been carried on by Paige (Chapter 12) in this volume. Hopefully, the simplicity of the computer techniques described by Paige will encourage more such idiographic studies. Garraty, in the 1955 conference, considered Baldwin's approach useful to the study of personal documents in history.

On the nomothetic side, personal documents have been employed to draw generalizations about patterns in the ways groups of people approach a situation or set of circumstances. Allport, Bruner, and Jandorf (1953) studied 90 essays submitted to a prize competition on "My Life in Germany before and after January 30, 1933" as a source of insight into personality function under the catastrophe of the Nazi revolution. The study focuses on how attitudes were developed toward different sources of frustrations and how defense mechanisms entered to delay making an escape. After the war, Allport and Gillespie (1955) conducted a study in which youth from different parts of the world were asked to write an essay, "From Now to the Year 2000 A.D." While most of the formal analyses stem from a questionnaire that accompanied the essay assignment, the essays were important in assessing ways in which national character influenced the structuring of goals, values, and expectations for the future. Some of these original essays were studied by Dahlberg and Stone (Chapter 20), using formal content analysis techniques.

The use of personal documents has been combined with depth interviews to assess determinants of attitudes on particular topics. In *Opinions and Personality* by Smith, Bruner, and White (1956), an autobiography written by the subjects was supplemented by extensive interviews on childhood memories, family backgrounds, personal education, occupational and participational history, health and sex history, how a particular day was spent, assessment of abilities, and temperamental traits. This information, plus a number of intelligence and other tests, was used in analyzing an additional series of interviews and tests concerning attitudes toward Russia. Categorizing and relating the wealth of verbal information collected posed a major problem. Much of the analysis was informal and the conclusions tentative. The sample consisted of only ten men.

More recently, a related emphasis on depth interviewing has been presented by Robert Lane in his *Political Ideology* (1962). Lane focuses on those opinions, attitudes, and values that the individual uses in perceiving the operations of, and his relations to, the different levels of government. Using a sample of 14 working-class men in an eastern town, he especially probes those factors that provide the subjects with a sense of equality, freedom, and security.

Occasionally, a large number of people are interviewed at length to obtain information about attitudes and practices. Sears, Maccoby, and Levin (1957) interviewed 379 mothers on patterns of child rearing. They "obtained the information by long interviews that allowed the mothers to talk fully and freely about the joys and problems they had had, their feelings before and after their child was born, and the methods they had used for training and for making him — or her — happy" (foreword, 1).

Psychology has also contributed to an understanding of the various ways people use language. For example, Osgood, Suci, and Tannenbaum in the *Measurement of Meaning* (1959) offer a major tool, the semantic differential, as a method for mapping certain aspects of an individual's semantic speech.

In this procedure the subject relates a number of adjective dimensions to a specified object. This is accomplished by a checking procedure; the concept being evaluated is given at the top, and a check is made for each adjective's dimension; for example,

LADY

rough———:———:———:———:———:———:———smooth
fair———:———:———:———:———:———:———unfair
active———:———:———:———:———:———:———passive, etc.

Both the objects described and the adjective dimension may be either words supplied by the investigator or words taken from the vocabulary of the subject. The analysis techniques allow the "distance" between objects to be represented in a multidimensional factor space.

In applying this instrument format to a number of research situations, Osgood found that factor analysis techniques would repeatedly produce roughly the same three factors. These factor dimensions, in order of their importance in accounting for variance, were labeled positive evaluation versus negative evaluation, strong versus weak, and active versus passive.

Despite the criticism by Carroll (1959) and others that situations could be constructed where these factors would not show up, Osgood and his associates were encouraged to apply this technique on a variety of different languages to test the extent to which they had discovered a universal phenomenon. A list of objects common to most environments was prepared and translated into a number of different languages. Persons in various cultures were then asked to provide adjective dimensions for each of these objects. The adjective dimensions were sorted, grouped, and formed into semantic differential scales by a computer. The resulting semantic differential forms were used to provide adjective dimensions for each of the objects, and these forms were then sent back to the culture in question for scoring by subjects. Osgood found that the first two factors held up quite well as language universals (1963*a*).

Given the empirical importance of these three dimensions, they suggest a framework of content analysis categories of possible relevance to a number of different hypotheses. These categories have been used by Holsti and associates at Stanford and are discussed in Chapter 5.

Psychology has also developed techniques for identifying those particular language constructs that are important to the individual in characterizing his social universe. Kelly, in *Psychology of Personal Constructs* (1955), presents a *"Rep"* test in which a person is asked to identify a number of significant persons in his social universe, including members of his family, liked and disliked teachers, neighbors, and work associates. The subject is then presented with three of these names at a time and is asked, "In what ways are two of these people alike?" After a choice is made, the subject is then asked, In what ways is the third person different? By exploring a number of possible triads, significant personal constructs relative to the individual's social perceptions become evident.

Psychological, psychiatric, and psychoanalytic theories are often utilized by the content analyst in making inferences from verbal and written data. As general theories of behavior, they offer a common referent in explaining aspects of social, political, and economic attitudes, as well as in general styles of expression.

Research on face-to-face groups (which, for convenience, we place as a subcategory of psychology) has been an important area of content analysis studies. Usually what is said is analyzed from the point of view of its implications for group process. For example, in Bales's *Interaction Process Analysis* (1950), a statement like, "I think we should . . ." would be scored within the scheme as an "act of suggestion," but the actual content of the suggestion is not part of the scoring. Observer categories often use information other than verbal messages. For example, within the Bales's scheme, a subject may "show tension" by nervously lighting a cigarette, fidgeting with a pencil, or a number of other nonverbal cues.

We have found it useful to distinguish between scoring schemes of *process* from schemes concerned with the discussion *content*. The difference can be identified by the information that must be considered by the scorer. A good scorer of Interaction Process Analysis can sit in a corner of a group meeting or behind a one-way mirror and code the events as they occur; yet after the meeting is over, he may be hard pressed to tell you much about what was discussed. In making classifications into such process categories as "gives opinion," "gives suggestion," "asks for information," "agrees," and "shows solidarity," the scorer does not need to consider the content of what was actually said, indeed the busywork of his scoring tends to divert his attention from it.

In contrast, a content-oriented procedure is concerned with the topic that is discussed and how it is treated. Since the group usually has considerable latitude in how it selects topics and works on them, a large number of categories usually need to be used, making observer scoring somewhat difficult.

The transcripts of small-group discussions often prove quite difficult to analyze. The discussion often contains many sentence fragments and vague references to what has been said before. A sentence beginning, "Well, they might take what he implied to suggest that . . ." may be very clear to the members present, but considerable ambiguity may be found on later inspection by a content analyst. As groups develop over a series of meetings, they often form their own set of metaphors, making understanding difficult for the newcomer or outsider.

Several systems of scoring group interaction have been developed for making special kinds of contrasts. A system design by Mann (1966) has focused on the implications of statements as they relate to the group leader. The Sign Process Analysis system of Mills (1964) is designed to note parallels in the treatment of objects both internal and external to the group. In Mills' system, a statement is scored as either characterizing a principal object ("He looks sad") or as stating a relationship between a principal object and a secondary object ("He agrees with me"). Objects are scored according to whether they are groups, things, or people, and if people, their sex, and whether they are superior or subordinate. Each statement is scored in terms of whether it is positive, negative, or neutral.

Much of the analysis of small-group data has been concerned with the sequence of group development, both within the phases of a single meeting or in terms of changes in the group over the course of many meetings. Thus, in a sense these studies are concerned with deciphering recurring sequences in the "plot" of group transformation and change. Several theories concerning such change have been put forward by Bion (1961), Bennis and Shephard (1956), and others.

In this volume, Dunphy (Chapter 8) focuses on perceived changes within a self-analytic group. The data are not what was said but rather analyses by each member about the meetings.

History

The field of history offers a number of important purposes for content analysis, only a few of which have yet been explored. Often the historian is concerned with changes in concerns and attitudes recorded in archives of written data. Archives may be large, and there may be many relevant content patterns that could be profitably explored. The kinds of problems for possible investigation are best illustrated by some examples.

Merton (1957) has examined the appearance of socioeconomic implications in the reports of eminent seventeenth-century English scientists. In examining the minutes of the Royal Society for the years 1661–1662 and 1686–1687, Merton classifies items as (1) directly related to current socioeconomic demands, (2) having clear-cut implications that were not explicitly mentioned by the author, or (3) treated as pure science, without any particular socioeconomic application. Merton finds that less than half of the contributions to the Royal Society could be described as pure science. Problems of marine transport attracted the most attention, but the influence of military exigencies was almost as strong. Mining also was found to have an appreciable influence.

Valuable archives of verbal text often take some unexpected forms. Cochran's book, *Railroad Leaders 1845–1890* (1953), is based on the some 100,000 letters written by managing executives of a number of American railroads. In those years before the telephone, letter communication was particularly important to maintain the widely dispersed railroad management operations. The letters were assembled from company and family archives, and in some cases, from collections already placed in a university or in special libraries. The sample is somewhat biased, since only some of the better operated railroads of the period have archives available. Yet the letters form an important base for the analysis of ideas and attitudes toward such issues as expansions and innovations, relations with competitors, labor relations, relations with the government, and the role of railroads as an agency of regional growth.

Barton Hacker (1965) has taken a more quantitative approach to the analysis of changes of attitudes toward the natural environment as revealed in a comparison of the 13th and 16th century encyclopedias. The treatment of different animals is compared, ranging from the domestic (cat) to local wild (fox) to exotic (elephant) to the mythical (dragon). Questions are asked concerning changes in the treatment of these topics that might reflect the renaissance and the beginnings of the scientific revolution.

An extensive collection of grievance documents (*cahiers de doléances*) produced at the beginning of the French Revolution has been assembled and is being content analyzed by Shapiro (1965). Some 23,000 of the original 40,000 documents are available, representing the views of different regions and estates. This study considers a number of methodological problems and will provide examples of several content analysis approaches in the field of history.

Content analysis can be of considerable utility in many situations in which there are a number of documents that repeatedly reflect attitudes and ideologies of a time and situation. Regularly occurring events, whether they be ministers' sermons (Hamilton, 1942) or convocation addresses, often serve an important norm-setting or reaffirmation role at the time they are produced; and they thus constitute an important resource of historical evidence.

Anthropology

Anthropology has a traditional concern with studying patterns in myth and folklore and relating these patterns to other characteristics of a culture.

Two of the articles in the second part of this volume are concerned with comparisons of folktales from different cultures. Such comparisons across cultures illustrate several problems. The folktales have been translated into English, but the translations in the sample vary from King James English to modern English to a literal translation that attempts to maintain the lack of sentence structure which characterizes the language of the culture in question. Sometimes missionaries translated the folktales into Latin, occasionally deleting passages offensive to Western morals.

The comparison of folktales raises the question of whether categories can be created that are valid for different cultural frames of reference. An example of the problems that arise is illustrated by Maranda:

> If "tapir," for instance, is tagged as "wild animal," it does not mean that it should always belong there. It occurs most frequently as wild game in the data. It is a heavy kill that requires strength to be carried to the village. In the Kayapo texts, the Tapir plays an important role of "monstrous lover," while the Apinaye just allude to it as a "monster."
> (Maranda, 1965, 4)

In some cases, universal connotations may be impossible.

The validity of cross-cultural comparisons often needs to be supported by results from other sources of evidence. For example, Colby (Chapter 21) has compared the patterns found in Navaho and Zinacantan folktales with the patterns obtained in TAT's and dreams of current members of the culture. Inasmuch as salient concerns and themes are represented by the folktales, they should also find representation in other forms of projective and symbolic materials.

Anthropological work has been responsible for some of the earliest experimentation in computer content analysis. Sebeok and Zeps (1958) programmed a computer to search for patterns in Cheremis folktales, a transliteration being necessary to match the characters of the Cheremis alphabet to the available characters of the computer. One General Inquirer study is currently under way to test hypotheses concerning patterns of humor in Tzotzil. The entire test and the scoring categories are in the Tzotzil language, as transliterated for the computer. A further consideration of some computer content analysis applications in anthropology has recently appeared in *The Use of Computers in Anthropology* (Hymes, 1965).

Anthropology provides important lessons on how to understand the uses of language in cultures far different from our own. The simplest method has been that of the bilingual informant. More recently, anthropologists have given considerable emphasis to the development of more formal techniques for identifying the referents of particular words. For example, procedures of "componential analysis" are designed to determine which cues are important in assigning one plant name versus another, or labeling a condition with one disease name rather than another, or identifying the collection of persons included by a particular kinship term. Essentially, componential analysis is a systematic procedure of obtaining information about language usage from an informant. By making a number of comparisons, the cues actually used in categorizing instances of a semantic concept can be identified empirically.

Education

The field of education includes both standard content analysis problems and some issues unique to its own area. Some special problems that we shall discuss here concern the content of children's readers and measures of readability.

Children's readers have always been a target for close content inspection by educational theorists, teachers, parents, and school board members. Over a number of years, several formal studies have been carried out. In 1936, for example, Martin examined a number of children's readers for amounts of nationalism. A second kind of study has examined children's readers as reflections of the values held by the nation's youth. McClelland (1961) has cross-culturally related the imagery of the readers to later shifts in national economic growth.

Different formulas for the assessment of the readability of materials have been developed by investigators both in journalism and education. Usually research is first carried out on a set of documents that have already been ranked by experts for degree of reading difficulty. Measurements are made on such variables as average number of syllables per word, average sentence length, and number of words prespecified as being difficult. These measurements are then correlated with the ranking of the documents. In this manner, formulas represent a weighted selection of the measurements based on the regression coefficients that maximally correlate with the experts' rankings. Danielson and Bryon (1963) have demonstrated that most of these types of measurements, once developed, can easily be carried out by a computer.

Some exploratory research currently being conducted by Page (1965) attempts to define a set of parameters that can be measured by computer and will predict English grades given to essays written in a standardized situation. Page's object is twofold: to gain insight into the human grading process and to explore the potential of the computer in the analysis of prose writing.

As the body of data collected within education becomes better organized, much of it is becoming available in files for testing hypotheses concerning patterns and effects of education. The Project Talent file at Pittsburgh, Pennsylvania, contains data from 500,000 students in a sample of high schools across the United States. Occasionally, such files contain autobiographical material, assigned essays, and other written information. Content analysis could play an important role in the study of such data.

Research is yet to be done to determine the order in which language concepts are acquired by young children. Concepts learned at an early age will presumably be more diffuse in their semantic value. A knowledge of which word groups are learned at a particular age might offer important insights into patterns of language use at a later age. While some study of language acquisition has been conducted in conjunction with norms for verbal intelligence tests, the understanding of acquisition patterns has only begun. Piaget's *Language and Thought of the Child* (1926) as well as Vygotsky's comments in *Thought and Language* (1962) present an important set of initial strategies.

Sociology

Sociology could potentially utilize content analysis in research ranging from opinions and attitudes expressed in large-scale surveys down to the details of the "dramaturgical script" of an individual role performance. Since many of the more important connotations within language usage are often shared within the boundaries of a subculture, the sociologists' contributions to the study of language itself could be immense. Perhaps one of the most common language subcultures is that of the family, where years of shared experience provide a language context of nuances and innuendos that are not picked up by the casual outsider. Other subcultural boundaries include social class, occupational, and regional factors. Sociology can make a contribution by identifying such subcultures and studying them through their use of language.

Unfortunately, sociologists have not given language the attention that might be expected, both in its use in content analysis and in its further elucidation through the tools of sociology. Bernstein has commented,

> What is a little odd is the negligible contribution of sociology to the study of language. The textbooks celebrate the fact of man's symbolic possibilities in chapters on culture and socialization and then the consequences are systematically ignored. One might go as far as saying that the only time one is made aware that humans speak in the writings of contemporary sociologists is incidentally through the statistical relations induced from social survey inquiries. And here all that is required is that the subjects can read; speech confounds the later arithmetic.
>
> (Bernstein, 1965)

Recently, both linguists and sociologists have begun to give more attention to the relationships between sociological variables and the use of language. "Sociolinguistics" is on the verge of becoming a field in its own right.

Within sociology, survey research constitutes an important area of content analysis applications. Several research organizations in the United States and in other countries staff nationwide networks of interviewers, trained in the administration of lengthy, complex questionnaires that are frequently concerned with sensitive topics. Often the interviewer will not place the respondent's views into one of the alternative categories provided by the questionnaire but will be instructed to write down the respondent's views as he gives them. Such responses are called open ended. For example, a nationwide survey conducted by the Michigan Survey Research Center during each of the recent presidential election campaigns began each interview with open-ended questions of what was liked and disliked of each of the parties and candidates. As described in the *American Voter* by Campbell *et al.* (1960), the free responses are analyzed for candidate image, salience of issues, sophistication (or "level") of attitude, conflicted attitudes, and ideology. Open-ended responses are related to the responses to closed-end choices appearing later in the questionnaire, including social class, party identification, and voter turnout.

A discussion of content analysis, qualitative analysis, or simply of coding (these terms, plus several others, seem to be used interchangeably in survey research) can be found in articles by Lazarsfeld and Barton (1951), Cartwright (1953), or in the staff manuals maintained by several of the research organizations. Experiments in the application of the General Inquirer to the analysis of national samples of open-ended material is currently in process at Harvard, using the 1964 presidential election survey from the Michigan Survey Research Center.

Survey research today provides a meeting point for psychology, sociology, and political science. For example, as illustrated by *Candidates, Issues, and Strategies* by Pool, Abelson, and Popkin (1964), behavior often can be predicted by sociological variables such as education, political party affiliation, religion, regional location, or social class identification, provided that such variables are consistent in the pressures they bring to bear on the individual. When an individual finds himself under cross pressure as to which way he should behave, predictions may become much more complex. At this point, a number of possible psychological mechanisms can come into play in resolving the pressures; the balance of forces and interplay of mechanisms must be considered in combination. As demonstrated by Campbell *et al.* (1960), open-ended questions then become important in assessing the salience of conflicting factors in a cross-pressure situation and in identifying some of the mechanisms by which they are resolved.

Philology and Literary Analysis

Philology and literary analysis have contributed to filling a gap left by sociologists. Such books as H. L. Mencken's *American Language* supplemented by such journals as *American Speech* provide a sociologically sensitive perspective on American language usage as it has developed and exists today within different occupational, regional, and social class groupings. Studies of literature stemming from particular subcultures often provide considerable insight into the subcultures themselves.

Many studies of literature and poetry are thorough in identifying the occurrences of specified characteristics. Leites (1953), for example, has carefully traced appearances of affectlessness in Camus' *The Stranger* and has used this information to draw inferences about the intelligibility of the hero. A number of studies focusing on the occurrence of a particular kind of symbolism in literature appear in the psychoanalytic journal, *American Imago*. An extensive content analysis of English poetry has been made by Josephine Miles (1951, 1957, 1960), in which she has compared word usages of poets over several centuries; the data have been assembled in a number of ways for testing a variety of inferences.

I. A. Richards' *Practical Criticism* (1929) studies a number of student essays about a series of poems, whose authors were unidentified to the students. Richards draws inferences concerning both the readers and the poems themselves.

Often the General Inquirer is used to find indexes that will discriminate between two text sources. While making such discriminations is indeed a problem in identifying authorship, it usually differs from the classical authorship problems (Federalist papers, Shakespeare-Marlowe, books of Homer, and so on) in several respects. First, each source is usually not a single author but rather a group of people. Second, the would-be goal is not simply to make an efficient discrimination but also to gain further understanding of the psychological forces and perceived demands of the situation in which the document was produced. If our goal was to identify authorship, usually we could find our best clue in idiographic stylistic differences (noun-declension preferences, "while" versus "whilst") rather than in content themes.

At present, we have just begun to explore possible General Inquirer applications in literary analysis. The kinds of explorations that might be made are briefly illustrated in this book by Ellis and Favat's report of their analysis of Huck Finn (Chapter 23).

Content Analysis and Linguistics

While the purposes of the behavioral scientist as an analyst of text content may be quite different from those of the linguist, there appears to be an overlap in procedures, which has important bearings for content analysis work. For example, Z. Harris, when presenting "distributional structure analysis" in 1954, made explicit a procedure for identifying elements that share similar linguistic environments. Specifically,

> The distribution of an element will be understood as the sum of all its environments. An environment of an element *A* is an existing array of its co-occurrences, i.e., the other elements, each in a particular position, with which *A* occurs to yield an utternace. *A*'s co-occurrents in a particular position are called its selection for that position.
>
> (Harris, in Fodor and Katz, 1964, 33)

Using a now famous example, Harris discusses how probabilities of elements sharing the same selections are described.

> If we consider *oculist* and *eye doctor,* we find that, as our corpus of actually occurring utterances grows, these two occur in almost the same environments, except for such sentences as *An oculist is just an eye doctor under a fancier name,* or *I told him Burns was an oculist, but since he didn't know the professional titles, he didn't realize he could go to him to have his eyes examined.* If we ask informants for any words that may occupy the same place as *oculist* in sentences like the above (i.e., have these same environments), we will not in general obtain *eye doctor,* but in almost any other sentence we would. In contrast, there are many sentence environments in which oculist occurs but lawyer does not; e.g., *I've had my eyes examined by the same oculist for twenty years,* or *Oculists often have their prescription blanks printed for them by opticians.* It is not a question of whether the above sentence with *lawyer* substituted is true or not; it might be true in some situation. It is rather a question of the relative frequency of such environments with *oculist* and with *lawyer* or of whether we will obtain *lawyer* here if we ask an informant to substitute any word he wishes for *oculist* (not asking what words have the same meaning). These and similar tests all measure the probability of a particular environment occurring with particular elements, i.e., they measure the selections of each element.
>
> (Harris, in Fodor and Katz, 1964, 43)

It should be apparent that the distributional structure analysis procedure might be useful to identify words and idioms belonging together in the same content analysis category. If the content analyst could specify a few examples of his intended category, the rest of this list might be filled out by this empirical procedure.

Saporta and Sebeok (1959), however, are careful to point out that distributional structure may be quite different from the groupings of words used in content analysis. For example, "sit" and "chair" are hardly substitutable, having membership in different grammatical classes and being quite different in their environment. Yet for the content analyst, they may share considerable meaning, more than, for example, "sit" and "slam" or "chair" and "door." "In short," conclude Saporta and Sebeok, "how do we know that sit and chair are more similar in meaning than sit and door?" (Saporta and Sebeok, 1959, 136)

While there are similarities between activities of linguists and content analysts, they may be more apparent than real. The content analyst, for example, is very much concerned with meaning and will use whatever he has at his disposal to identify conscious and unconscious intentions. Harris is explicit and in this sense represents an ideal of most linguists: that their conclusions are to be strictly based on the information contained in language structure.

> Since there is no independently known structure of meanings which exactly parallel linguistic structure, we cannot mix distributional investigations with occasional assists from meaning whenever the going is hard.
> (Harris, in Fodor and Katz, 1964, 39)

Although the content analyst does not necessarily impose the same restrictions on himself as the linguist, a number of current activities in linguistics have implications for future content analysis work. Several of these, concerning syntactic structures and semantic projection rules, are discussed in Chapter 4.

SUMMARY OF SUPPLEMENTARY RESOURCES

Suppose that the investigator has well in mind the hypotheses he wants to test, but suppose also that he is taking the text from an occupational, social, or regional subculture, so that it is difficult to determine precisely which words and phrases should be included in his categories. He may find it necessary to obtain further information about possible shades of meaning of certain words and phrases within that subculture. Several possible techniques for doing this have been discussed in this chapter and are brought together here for comparison.

Interviewing Informants

In the tradition of the anthropologist, the investigator can simply make contact with a member of the subculture and ask him to describe the meaning of certain words in certain contexts. Further probing can aid in determining what contextual cues are important in using a word for a particular occurrence. The informant can be asked to read samples of the text under study and relate what the text means to him. Or he can be asked to make up sentences using particular words and idioms.

Semantic Differential Test Profiles

The investigator may want to assess certain connotations of particular words and phrases by collecting semantic differential information from members of a subculture. The word or phrase becomes the object rated, and the connotations are specified in the scale dimensions. By examining the ratings, the investigator can assess whether or not a connotation is generally present and the amount of agreement there is on this within the subculture.

"Rep" Test Profiles

Often the investigator may want further information about how certain objects are perceived. Rather than supply dimensions as in the semantic differential, he may ask members of a subculture to compose their own categories to describe how various pairings of objects are similar or opposed.

Componential Analysis

Often the investigator will want to know why one term rather than another is used to refer to certain objects or processes of the environment. By conducting a systematic inquiry as to what objects are considered to have a particular label, the investigator can determine which of the characteristics or attributes of the object itself are responsible for the assignment of that label.

Word Associations

Finally, at a more indirect level, the investigator may want to explore relationships between terms by use of free association. Word relationships may appear that are unique to a subculture and therefore quite helpful in understanding word usage in the text material being studied.

Distributional Analysis of Text

Often when an investigator is uncertain of the meaning of a word or phrase, he can look in other available texts for more familiar words or phrases used in the same context. The technique described by Harris becomes useful in taking an unknown and relating it to references that are more familiar. This becomes an especially important strategy when the investigator is studying documents produced many years ago, or where suitable informants are alive but, perhaps because of political considerations, are not available for comment.

Whether or not the investigator finds it necessary to use such resources beyond the text being analyzed depends, in the last analysis, on his intuitive assessment of his success in understanding the text relative to the hypotheses being tested. If the analysis has been straightforward and if he has not felt any difficulties in making the categorizations necessary to test his hypotheses, no further resources are necessary. Occasionally, the investigator may sense minor difficulties but may not feel that these will affect his results strongly enough to merit further investigation. After the formal content analysis has been made, it is important to again return to an intuitive inspection asking whether the categorization really represents the text relative to the hypotheses being tested.

THE COMPUTER AND CONTENT ANALYSIS

Even with explicit sets of categories and an analysis program, it has generally been difficult, expensive, and time consuming to employ human coders to follow complex content analysis directions in analyzing large amounts of verbal material. "Content analysis usually requires skilled and sensitive coders, the very type of persons who soon become bored and frustrated by the tedious and repetitive nature of the task" (Holsti, in press). Individual differences in actual coding practices often occur and the same coder may show considerable fluctuation over time. Hence, articles on methods of content analysis have devoted considerable attention to problems of interscorer reliability. As indicated by Lasswell, Lerner, and Pool's remarks on the future of content analysis, quoted on page 30 of this chapter, the advantages of the general purpose computer in taking over the tedious aspects of handling text material and providing increased content analysis flexibility was already envisioned in 1952.

Some of the first actual text-processing studies, however, were concerned with indexing and constructing word concordances. A project for constructing concordances of the *Dead Sea Scrolls* and St. Thomas Aquinas' *Summa Theologica* was reported by Tasman (1957) and Busa (1957) as part of a joint international pioneering project.

The first application of computer content analysis that we know of was Sebeok's study (1958) on an IBM 650 computer of 4,000 Cheremis folktales. A number of co-occurrence patterns were counted in testing a variety of hypotheses about these tales. In 1960, David Hays of the Rand Corporation explored possibilities in a paper entitled, "Automatic Content Analysis." In early 1961, Stone and Bales, who were then studying content themes in the interaction of long-term, face-to-face groups and were unaware of Sebeok's or Hays' work, designed and programmed the initial version of the General Inquirer system described in this book. A set of categories was designed during that summer, and initial processing of transcript material began in September 1961, on an IBM 709 computer at M.I.T.

Starting in the late 1950's, a number of investigators began working on general problems of automatic syntax analysis and synthesis, mechanical translation from one language to another, storage and retrieval of large amounts of text information, indexing, and the design of question and answer systems. Basic computer routines and "programming languages" became available to assist in giving text-processing commands to machines that were designed more for processing numbers. One of these languages, called COMIT, was developed by the Mechanical Translation Group at M.I.T. under Victor Yngve. Stone accidentally became acquainted with Yngve and learned about COMIT just as it was about to become operational. Without the extensive programming simplifications offered by the COMIT language, the task of designing and coding the General Inquirer would not have been undertaken at that time. The COMIT system provided a crucial initial flexibility in which a number of strategies could be tried and adjusted. In turn, the General Inquirer was an important initial application for testing the text-processing power of COMIT and for locating "bugs" in the COMIT programs.

An early project in information retrieval was the question-and-answering system developed by Wolf, Chomsky, and Green (1963) called "Baseball," designed to interpret natural language questions and to find the correct answer from tables. For example, suppose the user typed, "How many times did the Red Sox beat the Yankees in 1958?" The computer would then untangle the syntax of the question and supply the correct answer.

More recently, the growth of work in almost all aspects of text processing has accelerated rapidly. Extensive work in indexing and concordance constructing has been done by the Euratom group in Ispra, Italy, and by the Cornell Project at Ithaca, New York. A number of large information retrieval systems have appeared, including the SMART system at Harvard and the SYNTOL system of the C.R.N.S. group in Paris. In addition to reports in both computing and documentation journals, a special English journal, *Information Storage and Retrieval,* has recently appeared. Applications in the humanities were reviewed at a conference held in the fall of 1964 at the IBM center in Yorktown, New York published in the *Proceedings, 1964.* Library applications have been reviewed at Woods Hole, Massachusetts, during the summer of 1965, resulting in a book entitled *INTREX* (Overhage and Harman, 1965). A more futuristic perspective of computerized libraries has been presented by Licklider (1965). Question-and-answer systems have been recently reviewed by Simmons (1965).

A number of computer programs have recently been developed for performing word-count measurements on text material. Starkweather and Decker (1964) report a program for producing frequency counts and type-token ratios of the different words occurring in the text. Categories of words may also be specified, and the category counts may be used in further statistical procedures. Similar word-counting procedures have been developed by Couch and his associates (1966) within the context of an extensive library of statistical analysis techniques. Harway and Iker (1964) have produced a program for tabulating word frequencies for each specified interval of text, producing correlations between specified sets of words and deriving a factor structure from these correlations. Carstensen and Stolz (1964) have developed a number of computer procedures in conjunction with research on the "cloze" technique.[8]

As computer techniques reduce the amount of tedious effort in content analysis, it should be interesting to observe how this affects the issue of measurement for measurement's sake. The availability of a powerful computer makes it even more tempting to forget about theory and hypotheses and simply let the method tell the story. Data can be mechanically described with indexing and correlation procedures; the results can be mechanically summarized by factor analysis procedures. Given such resources, the human being and his categories can begin to look like a prejudiced voice of bias in a mechanical realm of hard facts.

Social scientists, with their very complex data and their continual shorthandedness of usable theory, have tended to be prime targets for these rationalizations. Indeed the management of computer operations at a number of installations have insightfully used two epithets, the "wheelbarrow" and "G.I.G.O." to refer to this approach. The "wheelbarrow" refers to the quantities of data the new-fashioned empiricist tends to haul in and out of the computing center. "G.I.G.O." stands for "garbage in, garbage out," emphasizing that the quality of the results from the computer can be no better than the quality of what goes in.

In brief, the presence of the computer serves to dramatize a choice. As a powerful machine, it can extend purely mechanical methods into a high-volume production, or as a reliable aid to the scientist, it can serve as a flexible adjunct to human thinking, extending the awarenesses of human intuition, and handling the mechanics of formal analyses.

There is little doubt that the mechanical approach in content analysis will occasionally make some interesting and perhaps important discoveries. The earlier hand labors of methods-oriented analysts were not without occasional value. Yet the telling cost of a preoccupation with automated methods is not the amount of computer time nor the acres of forests that are converted into computer paper but rather the psychological effects of returning to an administrative research mentality.

[8] The most elaborate existing integrated word-count and retrieval systems that we are acquainted with are unfortunately proprietary to IBM Federal Systems Division Bethesda, Maryland, for certain government agencies with textual information processing problems and cannot be discussed here.

The computer procedures described in this volume have been set up with the second approach in mind. The system is not just a set of steps that can be set loose on data; it requires that the investigator present his ideas in terms of a set of content analysis categories and scoring procedures. The data analysis is not designed to be a one-step processing operation but instead to encourage repeated, cumulative interaction between the processing of the machine and the thinking of the investigator.

Yet, there is nothing built into these computer programs that guarantees this second approach. The categories and procedures can be unthinkingly borrowed from a previous investigator. At best, we can design the repertory of computer operations to encourage the second approach, emphasizing that the researcher repeatedly ask himself, "But what is my purpose?"

CHAPTER THREE

The General Inquirer[1]

In this chapter, we outline the entire General Inquirer system. The first section is a brief introduction to the computer as a content analysis tool. A delineation of the General Inquirer preparation and processing procedures follows. The chapter is not intended as an operations manual to instruct the reader in the details of how to push computer buttons or prepare control cards. An operations manual updated to the most recent machine configurations is available as a supplement to this chapter.[2] Instead, we consider here the possible flows of information through the system and illustrate our discussion with brief examples. The chapter ends with a summary diagram showing the interrelationships between the different parts of the system.[3]

THE COMPUTER AS A CONTENT ANALYSIS TOOL

Computers and Text

Computers are machines that compare and rearrange information and not just devices that do arithmetic. The term computer, with its emphasis on calculation, presents too narrow an image of the machine's capabilities. It often comes as a surprise that computers can

---

[1] The main author of this chapter is Philip J. Stone.

[2] As noted in the preface, this supplement is published by the M.I.T. Press.

[3] The reader may wish to consult this diagram (Figure 3.25) to trace his course through the description of the system.

also "read" text and manipulate this text within their processing and memory units.

Although the provision for handling alphabetic data has been standard since the earliest days of computer technology, few computers offer more than minimal consideration to the requirements of text processing. Most computers do not provide for the differentiation between small and capital letters, for a full set of punctuation marks, or for the extra characters necessary for foreign alphabets. Methods of giving the computer its instructions (programming) for processing text often involve awkward steps to arrange information in a memory basically designed for numbers.

The General Inquirer is a set of computer programs to (a) identify systematically, within text, instances of words and phrases that belong to categories specified by the investigator; (b) count occurrences and specified co-occurrences of these categories; (c) print and graph tabulations; (d) perform statistical tests; and (e) sort and regroup sentences according to whether they contain instances of a particular category or combination of categories. Contrary to occasional impressions, the General Inquirer is not a particular category system. As described in Chapter 4, a number of different category systems have been used by the Inquirer, each representing a different point of view.

It is useful to liken the Inquirer to an energetic, compulsive, but stupid clerk who has been trained in content analysis mechanics. This clerk has no ideas of his own but waits for the specification of categories and scoring procedures supplied by the investigator. Once these instructions are received and not found to be self-contradictory, the clerk is able to apply them systematically to endless amounts of data.

General Inquirer programs free the investigator from the details of machine operations. Just as people can drive cars without being auto mechanics, so investigators can use the Inquirer system without concern for programming details or the insides of computers. Just as people are able to use one car to get to a variety of different places, so the investigator can employ the General Inquirer in a wide variety of ways, using many kinds of categories, research designs, and data manipulation strategies.

The General Inquirer programs represent five years of evolution. The experience accumulated from different applications has led to numerous changes in strategy and format. Unneeded procedures have been trimmed; other procedures have been added. Where it has been possible to rewrite programs for smaller, more accessible computers, such steps have been taken. The General Inquirer programs have been completely rewritten three times and partly modified on a number of other occasions. Yet, text data and category specifications prepared for the system five years ago can be processed with current programs.[4]

Through these five years of evolution, the following goals have been continually before us.

Explication and Operationalization of Theory

In content analysis research prior to the computer, it was often difficult to determine exactly how the investigator translated hypotheses stemming from his theory into measurement procedures. Judgments were often intuitive, making replication almost impossible. However, when measurement categories have to be made explicit enough to be used by a computer, there remains little question of what is measured.

In the past, it has often been simpler for the investigator to construct his own categories rather than to try to figure out those of his colleagues. Because categories now must be clearly defined for computer use, an investigator can inspect categories from a previous study to determine their relevance to his own concerns. When a category is relevant, it can be borrowed directly or modified to suit the particular needs of the investigator and then added to his computer content analysis. The effort involved in adding such borrowings is minimal. Consequently, it is more likely that further research will build upon the theory and categories developed by others.

Comparability of Procedures

By setting certain conventions, investigators can use the computer to try out their categories and scoring systems on data collected by others or to compare the effectiveness of several different category systems in analyzing one set of data. Statistics produced from one study can be directly compared with those of another. Studies using a specific set of categories can be combined to produce norms for future studies.

---

[4] When formats have changed, computer programs have been written to update automatically before processing. In no case has it been necessary to reprepare data or categories.

Often minor idiosyncracies in method have prevented content analysis studies from being comparable. The Inquirer attempts to maintain comparability at a number of crucial points while allowing for wide flexibility in procedures. An analogy might be made to the development of a standard track width in railroading. Once the width was specified, a variety of types of railway cars could be built to run on the track. Similarly, before the radio could be used for its wide variety of communication purposes, basic signal characteristics had to be specified for transmitters and receivers. Certain decisions had to be made in the design of the Inquirer. We have tried to be as flexible and foresighted as possible.

Closeness to Data

The word "computer" often conjures the image of a remote method of processing data. Yet one of the purposes of the General Inquirer is to enable the investigator to be closer to his data. The investigator can devote his energies to the careful study of a relatively small sample of the data, using the computer to check out his hunches from that small sample on the whole data. Since the computer can quickly go through the data again and again, the investigator can reformulate and retest his ideas until he understands them thoroughly; sheer labor no longer leads him to stop after the first rough analysis.

Furthermore, the computer provides a variety of different procedures with which the investigator can look at his data. The computer routinely lists the text, showing exactly how the categories have been applied. The investigator can ask for sentences containing specified characteristics to be regrouped together and printed separately from the rest of the text for his inspection.

In such ways, the investigator gains acute awareness of his data through his application of different categories and analysis strategies. The General Inquirer programs feed into each other in a variety of ways so that a series of strategies may be used. Unanticipated differences can be quickly checked to their source in the data.

Ease of Use

Computer procedures often appear very elegant but in fact are difficult to follow. After five years of experience with a number of content analysis applications, we have learned how to remove sources of disruption. The system can be used in natural, easily remembered steps. Housekeeping details are kept at a minimum. The user does not have to remember complicated code words or format requirements. Mistakes in coding will generally not stop computer processing; instead, they are automatically noted and corrected if possible.

Given the ease with which General Inquirer programs can be used, many investigators with little knowledge of computers have found it convenient and useful to direct the computer processing themselves. Those research results that are more extensive or complicated than expected can be immediately explored further; analysis designs that the researcher finds irrelevant to the data can be quickly dropped from further applications.

It would be a mistake to assume that our four over-all goals are now completely achieved, that the Inquirer is fixed, and that further changes will not be made. As new computers are developed, programs will be rewritten to fit their specifications. New ideas will continue to be incorporated into the system, and old procedures will continue to be simplified.

Description of Computers

Computers, like Detroit automobiles, come in a variety of sizes and models, usually with a number of optional features that for certain users may not be so optional. They can be regarded in a number of ways: from the viewpoint of the user who wants a machine for a particular task, the enthusiast who is interested in the elegance of the machine's capabilities, or the mechanic who must consider fixing it. Our own concern is in having computers effectively serve content analysis tasks.

As of 1966, the General Inquirer programs operate on three different types of machines: large-memory computers, small-memory computers, and special time-shared computers. Considering present technology, it is both economically sensible and convenient for the user to take advantage of the different capabilities of these machines. Hopefully, soon there will be computing systems in which all three kinds of facilities are integrated and the user can draw on just those features of the system that he needs for a particular phase of his work, with the data automatically stored and available as needed. This re-integration of facilities of different sizes and purposes into single machine systems will bring added convenience, but it will probably not significantly change the sequence of computer content analysis procedures from what is described here.

Let us consider the features of these three types of machines.

Large-Memory Computers

These machines allow many category lists to be stored inside the computer memory. As the text material is processed through the computer, the applicability of various content analysis categories can rapidly be checked.

Large-memory computers are expensive and should not be kept waiting. Devices with high speeds of information transfer, such as magnetic tape drives, are used to feed information in and out of large computers at speeds up to many thousands of characters per second. The magnetic tapes are then brought to smaller computers where the information they contain is printed on paper or punched on cards. Similarly, small computers are used to transfer information punched on cards onto magnetic tape for use by a large-memory computer.

At present, the assignment of categories to text is programmed to operate on large IBM 7090–7094 computers.[5] Over 6,000 words and phrases (together with the computer program) can be simultaneously stored in the computer memory. As text is processed, thousands of lookups and checks are made per second (the basic memory reference time being under two microseconds). Depending on the complexity of the content analysis scheme, text is processed through this phase at between 7,000 and 12,000 words per minute. The computer, together with enough tape drives needed for General Inquirer operations, is shown in Figure 3.1.

A large random-access memory can also be provided for small computers by means of a rapidly revolving mechanical disk.[6] The

---

[5] Originally the entire General Inquirer system was programmed for the 709–7090–7094 series in the COMIT language by Philip Stone. Later, just the category assignment phase was kept on the 7090–7094 series, this time in COMIT II. In 1964–1965, a much faster version of the assignment phase was written in the BALGOL language by Horace Enea at Stanford University. The BALGOL language program has since been transliterated into the MAD language by Erik Steiner at Yale.

[6] A random-access storage device can have any of its information rapidly consulted. Thus a phonograph record is random access inasmuch as the user can play any part of the record by putting the needle on the chosen section. This differs from tape recordings, where the user must spin through to the section he wants to hear. If the section is far down on the tape, this takes a while.

different category lists are stored on the surface of the disks. Whenever one of these categories is to be checked, the computer must wait until the information next passes under a reading head. Storage capacity is very large; even a small disk can easily handle 20,000 words

FIGURE 3.1. The IBM 7090 computer.

and phrases. Yet, the processing speed at best is only a few hundred words of text per minute.

Using this second strategy, the assignment-of-categories phase is also programmed to operate on the much smaller IBM 1401–1460

FIGURE 3.2. The IBM 1311 disk storage unit.

series machine *together with the IBM 1311 disk attachment.*[7] Procedures are logically parallel to, albeit much slower than, those who have operated on the larger machine. A picture of the disk device, which stands the size of a small desk, is shown in Figure 3.2.

[7] The programs using the disk were designed and written by Phillip Miller at Washington University in St. Louis.

Small-Memory Computers

After categories have been assigned, further General Inquirer processing can be successfully handled without large computer memories. These additional steps involve printing various reports and retrieving sentences in the text which have specified characteristics in common. As the initial results suggest further ideas to be checked, the investigator may want to work closely and repeatedly with the machine.

These further operations are designed for the smaller IBM 1401 or 1460 series machine with at least two magnetic tape drives and an 8,000-character core memory.[8] The machine, as illustrated in Figure 3.3, also includes a printing device that prints at up to 600 lines per

FIGURE 3.3. The IBM 1401 computer.

minute, plus a card reader (800 cards per minute) and a 250 cards-per-minute punch. Processing again is in the order of microseconds.

When appropriately used, the IBM 1401–1460 series machine is an extremely powerful and flexible instrument; yet its low costs come as a surprise. Many university and nonprofit installations, using special rental discounts, are able to break even at an hourly charge of $20, a considerable portion of this being used to pay for large amounts of paper. Commercial rates begin at about twice that figure. The hourly rate is thus comparable to that charged by many professionals, such as lawyers, psychiatrists, and business consultants. A comparable amount of discretion is warranted in the use of the computer. Usually,

---

[8] An alternative minimum 1401–1460 specification for the General Inquirer programs is a 4,000-character core and four magnetic tape drives. The 1401–1460 programs have been written by Aram Grayson, Robert McCarthy, and Donald Davis.

a very large volume of work can be done in an hour, with several minutes to spare for making on-the-spot checks and decisions.

An important additional reason for our choice of the IBM 1401–1460 series machine is that there are so many of them distributed across the United States and other countries. As of 1965, over 12,000 machines in this series have been manufactured. Usually arrangements can be made with a government agency or a local business to use their 1401 or 1460 during off hours. Data may be sent away to a large computer for the category assignment phase. The magnetic tape that is returned can then be used on a nearby, smaller machine.[9]

Time-Shared Computers

Recent technical advances have made it possible for a user to share a computer with a number of others. Each user has a typewriter console connected to the computer via a teletype or phone line. The computer processes requests from users as they arrive, interacting with each user on a one-at-a-time basis. While information is being typed (or a user is busy thinking), the main computer processor shifts to other users; each user thus experiences delays of only a few seconds in having any reasonable request processed. A time-shared computer may not be extremely large; however, it invariably requires a large, random-access information storage device for fetching information associated with each user's problem as the user requests it. The user is generally charged only for the processing time. Usually, this totals less than two minutes for each hour spent at the typewriter console.

Early in 1964, we began to design and program General Inquirer content analysis procedures for the "Project MAC" time-shared system at the Massachusetts Institute of Technology.[10] Several applications employing these additional time-shared facilities are reported in this book. Since the data are stored on a disk, the investigator, sitting at a typewriter console, can repeatedly regroup sentences according to different characteristics and identify patterns in the text relevant to

[9] While the large 7090–7094 machines have been available at Cambridge, New York, New Haven, Stanford, Bonn, Paris, London, Chicago, Princeton, Los Angeles, and so on, only the IBM 1401 or 1460 has been available for content analysis work at such places as Santa Fe, New Mexico, Edinburgh, Scotland, and Cologne, Germany. With the gracious cooperation of government and industry, we have been able to process General Inquirer programs at civil engineering, bank, and factory offices.

[10] The General Inquirer time-shared programs were written by Stephen Sacks at Harvard University.

the hypotheses being tested. He can thus rapidly rework his data until he is satisfied with his analysis.

While the time-shared system offers flexibility, ease of use, and closeness to data, two factors in the present M.I.T. system greatly limit its utility. First, the user is held to the printing speed of a typewriter, which can be tediously slow when compared to a 600-lines-a-minute printer. A device is needed that at least matches the reading speed of most users. Second, storage costs have not as yet reached the point where it is feasible to keep large amounts of data on the disks. At present, the information to be analyzed must be transferred to the disk from magnetic tape at some time before the analysis is to begin. Usually, storage allocation logistics require that this information be deleted or returned to magnetic tape before other information can be put on the disk. We expect that all these present difficulties will be resolved in the near future. Indeed, in the future reintegrated system, the user should be able to use the time-shared aspect of the system to monitor all phases of his content analysis processing.

In the meantime, the 1401–1460 machines have proved to be the preferred device for regrouping operations. Large files can be kept on tape and passed through the smaller computer for regrouping, any resulting new files being either printed or written on another tape. Complicated analysis procedures may involve handling a number of different tapes. Yet one can duplicate all the regrouping operations possible on the time-shared system.

PREPARING DATA AND CONTENT ANALYSIS DICTIONARIES

After the data have been gathered and the investigator has decided on his categories, all this material must be transferred into a form that the computer can process. In the future, optical readers that can convert any printed text directly into computer code may become common. At present, optical readers are useful for only a very limited number of printing fonts and formats. If the investigator is analyzing printed material and can obtain copies of the punched tapes that were used to direct the typeset machine, facilities are available for converting and editing these typeset codes into computer format (Kehl, 1965). For the vast bulk of procedures, however, it is necessary manually to transfer handwritten notes, sound recordings, or whatever other forms the data take, directly onto IBM cards.

Information is keypunched on IBM cards using a keyboard similar to that of an electric typewriter. An IBM card contains 80 columns; each column may represent an alphabetic, numeric, or punctuation character, or it may be left blank. As the operator transcribes the text, the characters are printed at the top of successive columns, and holes, representing the characters, are punched at different places in each column. Thus, one IBM card is made for each line of text. A double-spaced typewritten page is represented by 20 to 30 successive cards. (The cards are inexpensive, about ten for a penny.) The computer is sensitive to the placement of the holes and "reads" the text through them.

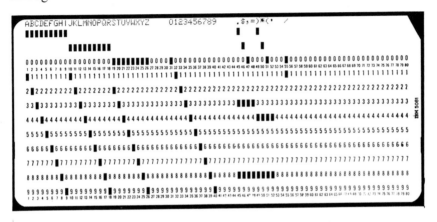

FIGURE 3.4. IBM card with punches illustrating alphabetic, numeric, and punctuation code conventions.

Figure 3.4 illustrates column placement of the code for different characters. With the alphabet and numbers presented in sequence, the pattern of code placement in each column becomes evident. Figure 3.5 shows a section of transcript from a family discussion as keypunched on two successive IBM cards. While the pattern of holes may appear more chaotic, the code in each column can easily be identified from the pattern given in Figure 3.4.

After the cards are keypunched, they can be listed on any one of a series of IBM printing machines, one line per card. Some samples

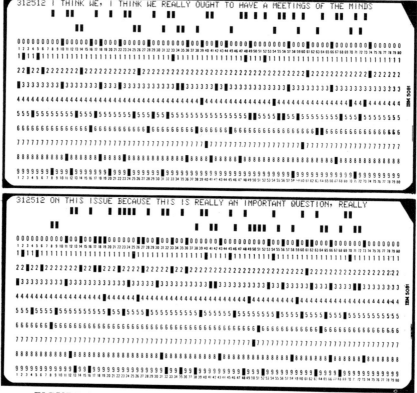

FIGURE 3.5. Two IBM cards with text from small-group discussion.

of different text used in General Inquirer content analysis studies are shown in Figure 3.6.

Once the text is on IBM cards, it can be reprocessed from a variety of points of view. Usually, the computer procedures discussed in this book have been used for moderate amounts of data, where a number of different measurements are to be made. However, if the data are without much further interest, and if only a simple content analysis is desired, a quick manual content analysis may be more practical than undertaking the effort of keypunching.

Text Preparation Conventions

The limited number of punctuation characters available on the keypunch machine keyboard has necessitated developing a set of general conventions. For example, two commas (,,) serve as quotation marks; a dollar sign ($) represents a question mark, and so on, as indicated in Table 3.1.

TABLE 3.1. Keypunching Conventions

.	= period
$	= question mark
+	= edited break point
-s	= possessive (at end of word)
-	= hyphen (hyphenated word treated as one word)
(	= open parentheses
)	= closed parentheses
,,	= quotation marks
,	= comma

A hyphen at the end of the last word on a card means word is continued on next card.

The General Inquirer considers the first word of each card an identification code. This word may consist of numbers, letters, or a mixture of both. A sentence is assigned the identification code appearing on the card on which the sentence ends. If a code begins with a hyphen, the last preceding identification code not beginning with a hyphen is assigned instead. The code associated with the first sentence is used by some operations to identify the document as a whole. An identification code must begin in the first card column and may extend across as much as the first 70 columns of the card. A blank column indicates the end of the identification code and the beginning of the text.

Several other general conventions merit comment. A word at the end of a card may be hyphenated and continued as the first word on the next card. Hyphenated words appearing elsewhere, however, are treated as one word with a hyphen. A card with a dollar sign ($) in the first column is considered a title card; its message is used on page headings of reports prepared by the computer. A new title card may be inserted at any point in the data. Finally, a card with a star (*) in the first column is used to mark the end of a document and the beginning of a new one. The importance of this star marker will become apparent later in the chapter.

Optional Text Editing

In most General Inquirer studies, indeed better than 90 percent, the researcher has chosen to use straight keypunched text such as illustrated in Figure 3.6. Certain content analysis strategies may require additional text descriptors that at present must be supplied with

```
122  I WENT TO THE CIRCUS AND LOAFED AROUND THE BACK SIDE TILL THE
122  WATCHMAN WENT BY AND THEN DIVED IN UNDER THE TENT.  I HAD MY
122  TWENTY DOLLAR GOLD PIECE AND SOME OTHER MONEY BUT I RECKONED
122  I BETTER SAVE IT BECAUSE THERE IS NOT NO TELLING HOW SOON YOU ARE GOING TO
122  NEED IT AWAY FROM HOME AND AMONGST STRANGERS THAT WAY.  YOU CAN NOT
122  BE TOO CAREFUL.  I AM NOT OPPOSED TO SPENDING MONEY ON
122  CIRCUSES WHEN THERE IS NOT NO OTHER WAY BUT THERE IS NOT NO USE
122  IN WASTING IT ON THEM.  IT WAS A REAL BULLY CIRCUS.  IT WAS THE
122  SPLENDIDEST SIGHT THAT EVER WAS WHEN THEY ALL COME
122  RIDING IN TWO AND TWO AND GENTLEMAN AND LADY SIDE BY SIDE THE
122  MEN JUST IN  THEIR DRAWERS AND UNDERSHIRTS AND NO SHOES NOR STIRRUPS
122  AND RESTING THEIR HANDS ON THEIR THIGHS EASY AND
122  COMFORTABLE THERE MUST HAVE BEEN TWENTY OF THEM AND EVERY LADY WITH A
122  LOVELY COMPLEXION AND PERFECTLY
122  BEAUTIFUL AND LOOKING JUST LIKE A GANG OF REAL SURE ENOUGH
122  QUEENS AND DRESSED IN CLOTHES THAT COST MILLIONS OF
122  DOLLARS AND JUST LITTERED WITH DIAMONDS.  IT WAS A POWERFUL
122  FINE SIGHT I NEVER SEE ANYTHING SO LOVELY.  AND THEN

                        HUCKLEBERRY FINN


3006111  LAGOS WOKE UP TO A DISGRACEFUL INCIDENT ON THURSDAY BECAUSE THE OCCUPANT
3006111  OF THE SLUM AREAS OF THE CAPITAL CITY REFUSED TO BE REASONABLE.  THE
3006111  SPECTACLE WAS SADDENING, AND IT WAS BOUND TO AROUSE THE ANGER OF EVERY
3006111  LOVER OF NIGERIA AND THOSE WHO RIGHTLY FEEL THAT LAGOS SHOULD, AND CAN,
3006111  BE A WORTHIER CAPITAL.  IT SHOULD HAVE OCCURRED TO THE OCCUPANTS, AND THE
3006111  LEADERS IN PARTICULAR, THAT BY INDULGING IN THIS FOOLHARDINESS, THEY HAD
3006111  ONLY THEMSELVES TO BLAME IF THE POLICE WITH NIGERIA BEHIND THEM GOT

                      NIGERIAN EDITORIAL


-00683      DEMOCRATIC PARTY BELIEVES ALL PEOPLE SHOULD HAVE EQUAL RIGHTS.
-00683      DEMOCRATIC PARTY LETS THE WORKING MAN HAVE MORE WORK TO DO.
-00683      YOU GET A BETTER WAGE UNDER THE DEMOCRATS.
-00693      I DO NOT PAY MUCH ATTENTION TO ALL OF THAT.

-00163      YOU UNDERSTAND, I WAS JUST BORN A DEMOCRAT + AND I WILL DIE ONE.
-00163      YES, IT IS THE PARTY MY PEOPLE HAVE ALWAYS SUPPORTED + AND I AM FOR
-00163      IT TOO.
-00163      THAT IS THE BEST THING ABOUT IT.

-00053      + BUT I DO NOT BELIEVE IN HANDING THEM THINGS ON A SILVER PLATTER.
-00053      THE DEMOCRATS ARE MORE ON THE LIBERAL SIDE.
-00053      THEY HAVE GONE TOO FAR WITH THIS LIBERTY.
-00053      I BELIEVE IN PEOPLE GETTING HELP IF THEY CANNOT HELP THEMSELVES,

                      SURVEY RESEARCH RESPONSES
```

FIGURE 3.6. Examples of text from The General Inquirer as listed from IBM cards.

the text. The General Inquirer computer programs carry the necessary machinery and formats to handle these extra optional conventions.

Proper Name and Pronoun Identification

At present the General Inquirer procedures cannot directly associate pronouns with their correct preceding proper names. One way to make this association explicit is by adding parenthetical remarks to the text.

```
25243111211137 THIS PICTURE SHOWS A WEALTHY MAN WHO HAD THE FORTUNE OF HAVING
25243111211137 BEING LEFT A HERITAGE BY HIS FATHER. THE FATHER OWNED A LOT OF
25243111211137 CATTLE AND WHEN HE DIED LEFT THEM FOR HIS SON, BUT THE SON WENT
25243111211137 AND SOLD THEM, WHEN HE GREW UP TO BE A MAN. HE FIRST PAID FOR HIS
25243111211137 LOBOLA AND MARRIED THE WOMAN HE WANTED.
25243111211137 IN THE PICTURE HE IS SEATED COUNTING HIS MONEY AND THE WIFE IS
25243111211137 LOOKING ON ADMIRING HIS RICHES. THOUGH THEY ARE DISCUSSING AND
25243111211137 THE WIFE INTENDS HIDING THE MONEY WHILST THE MAN WANTS TO TAKE
25243111211137 IT TO THE POST OFFICE.
25243111211137 THEY COME TO AN AGREEMENT TO DIG A HOLE IN THE HOUSE AND HIDE THE
25243111211137 MONEY ESPECIALLY THAT THE CHILDREN ARE STILL PLAYING OUTSIDE AND
25243111211137 WILL NOT DISTURB AND SEE WHERE THE MONEY IS HIDDEN.
```

SOUTH AFRICAN TAT


```
221432 YOU DID NOT LIKE GRAMMAR SCHOOL$

221423 NO.

221432 GRAMMAR, PUBLIC GRAMMAR SCHOOLS ARE SO HORRIBLE, THEY ARE A SIN-

221423 BUT HIGH SCHOOL, I LIKED, THE SUBJECTS I LIKED, I DID WELL IN.
221423 THE SUBJECTS I DID NOT LIKE, I DID NOT DO TOO WELL IN- LIKE YOU.
221423 LIKE YOU. BUT, IN COLLEGE, I REALLY ENJOYED COLLEGE. THE, THE
221423 WHOLE ATMOSPHERE, THE, THE CAMPUS, THE AHH, I DO NOT KNOW. I FELT
221423 GROWN UP. AND I WORKED HARDER.

221432 THE FACT THAT YOUR FATHER OBLIGED YOU TO BE IN SORORITY$

221423 EVEN THAT. YOU KNOW, I DID NOT LIKE THAT PART OF IT, BUT I
221423 ADJUSTED TO IT. AND I, I ENJOYED THAT. I ADJUSTED TO IT AND I
221423 ENJOYED IT. I DID NOT WANT TO JOIN A SORORITY. (LAUGH)

221430 SO. I WILL GO ALONG WITH MOMMY. (LAUGHTER)

221423 (LAUGH)
221430 DADDY HATES TO ADMIT DEFEAT.
```

FAMILY INTERACTION


```
3034 JESUS THEN GOT INTO THE BOAT, AND HIS DISCIPLES FOLLOWED.  ALL AT ONCE A
3035 GREAT STORM AROSE ON THE LAKE, TILL THE WAVES WERE BREAKING RIGHT OVER THE
3036 BOAT,. BUT HE WENT ON SLEEPING.  SO THEY CAME AND WOKE HIM UP, CRYING.
3037 ,SAVE US, LORD,. WE ARE SINKING/.,  ,WHY ARE YOU SUCH COWARDS  , HE SAID,.
3038 ,HOW LITTLE FAITH YOU HAVE/.,  THEN HE STOOD UP AND REBUKED THE WIND AND
3039 THE SEA, AND THERE WAS A DEAD CALM.  THE MEN WERE ASTONISHED AT WHAT HAD
3040 HAPPENED, AND EXCLAIMED, ,WHAT SORT OF MAN IS THIS, THAT EVEN THE WIND AND
3041 THE SEA OBEY HIM  ,  WHEN HE REACHED THE OTHER SIDE, IN THE COUNTRY OF THE
3042 GADARENES, HE WAS MET BY TWO MEN WHO CAME OUT FROM THE TOMBS,. THEY WERE
```

NEW TESTAMENT

FIGURE 3.6. continued.

For example, the text,

WHERE IS JOHN? HE WENT TO FLORIDA.

might be more useful for the content analysis edited as

WHERE IS JOHN (COMPANY TREASURER)?

HE (COMPANY TREASURER) WENT TO FLORIDA (WARM VACATION PLACE).

Care should be taken to see that the definition of the proper name represents its true meaning within the text. In the example just given, John might have been referred to in his role as Community Fund Chairman; his trip to Florida might have been for business purposes.

An alternative procedure, especially used by Holsti at Stanford (Chapters 5 and 9), is to put proper names and places in category lists and then parenthetically add the name references after all relevant pronouns. Thus, in our example, "John" and "Florida" would both be assigned to appropriate categories to indicate that John is company treasurer and Florida is a warm vacation place. The only editing then needed would be after the pronoun, "he":

WHERE IS JOHN? HE(JOHN) WENT TO FLORIDA.

Another alternative is to use *alphabetic subscripting* facilities. Special single-letter codes appearing as subscripts after a word can cause that word to be assigned to a specified category. For example, we might use the letter "T" as a code designating United States towns. The keypunched sentence would read,

THE FARMER WENT TO BUFFALO/T.

The computer would identify Buffalo as a town rather than as an animal.

More than one alphabetic subscript may be added to a word.

BUFFALO/TBX

could mean that not only is Buffalo a United States town but that it has a population of over 500,000 (B) and is located on a river (X).

To indicate that the categories originally assigned to the text word should not be removed, we use two slashes in the subscript.

BUFFALO//T

would refer to the animal "buffalo" as well as to the category "T."

Regardless of which procedure is used, we have found it important that such proper names and place referents be assigned to special categories. By doing this, the main set of categories remains constant, while special adjustments for topics, names, and places are handled separately. The effect is that frequency counts for studies using a particular content analysis system remain comparable. If the main categories were even slightly altered for each study, comparability would be difficult.

As discussed in Chapter 4, a major project currently under way includes the development of procedures for automatic identification of pronoun referents. "He" or "she" pronoun references to preceding names should be relatively simple for a computer to handle. Many of the uses of the pronoun "it" are very difficult even for the human editor to assess, as for example, "It then led me to conclude. . . ." Partial human editing will probably prove helpful for some time to come.

Syntactic Relationships

When the General Inquirer was first constructed in 1961, there was considerable debate about the feasibility of reliable syntactic identification by a computer. Rather than become involved in such a large problem, we decided to maintain our primary concern with the development of content analysis categories and wait to see the results of on-going research on computer syntax analysis.

Content analysis can use syntactic information in several ways, none of which is as demanding as the syntactic requirements for computer translation from one language into another. First, in assigning content categories a number of words, such as judge, mind, patient, or court, change meaning depending on their syntactic position. To identify whether a word occurs as a noun, verb, or modifier requires only a rudimentary syntax. Similarly, a relatively low level of syntactic information can be used to associate a modifier with its correct referent; for example, if the investigator wants "huge man" in the same category with "giant," syntactic information can correctly associate "huge" with "man," even when "huge" occurs in a later modifying phrase.

A second somewhat more complicated use of syntactic information in content analysis is the problem of keeping track of "who is saying what to whom." This is especially important in analyzing diplomatic notes, plot structure, and so on. Identification of the subject and object relationships within the sentence is required.

It is now well demonstrated that available procedures for computer syntax analysis procedures can adequately handle all these needs. Further discussion of our plans to implement automatic routines will appear in Chapter 4.

While waiting for the outcome of the research on computer syntax analysis, it was important to provide facilities for handling syntax in current studies, especially in those cases where "who is doing what to whom" was necessary information. The early versions of the General Inquirer were designed so that syntax position could be identified by optional numerical subscripts added to the text. The earlier General Inquirer systems at Harvard (Stone *et al.,* 1962) handled nine different syntactic codes. The first system installed at Stanford (North *et al.,* 1963; Holsti, 1964*a*) used a two-digit numerical subscript system to obtain an even more elaborate syntactic identification. Since then, both the Harvard and Stanford subscripting procedures have been considerably simplified.

An elaborate syntactic system, combined with even a moderate-sized set of semantic categories, often cuts the data too finely to be of much use in frequency studies. Sometimes investigators have carefully edited their data for syntax, only to find that they actually made very little use of this information; the semantic categorizations alone gave them all the information they could comfortably handle. With the computer making basic semantic analyses, any further syntactic sorts could usually have been quickly made by hand.

Thus, most of the existing studies using the General Inquirer have not been edited for syntax or have proved not to need syntax information. We describe syntax editing here to illustrate how it has been used by the authors of several studies reported in this volume. As discussed in Chapter 4, at least a rudimentary automatic editing of syntax will shortly be added to the Inquirer itself.

We describe here the General Inquirer as it is set to handle four-category syntax editing (subject, verb, object, and unclassified). Within this scheme, function words, such as prepositions and auxiliary verbs, are left in the unclassified position. The numerical assignments are selected to be compatible with previous, more elaborate editing procedures.

/1 subject position
/3 verb position
/5 object position
/8 attributive subject
/9 attributive verb
/0 attributive object

When one of these numerical subscripts follows a word, a syntax marker is associated with each of the content analysis categories that the computer lookup assigns to that word and its alphabetic subscripts. A numerical subscript can be mixed in with alphabetic subscripts in any order.

To reduce syntax marking to such a rudimentary level, the editor must first divide complex sentence structures into as many independent clauses as possible. This is done by the insertion of plus signs (+), which are treated by the computer as end-of-the-sentence marks. Occasionally, this means inserting a verb or a noun that was originally shared between two clauses. Since syntax editing can be done at several levels of complexity and thoroughness, the investigator who decides to edit must in addition carefully formulate his needs.

All phrases indicating the source behind a statement, such as "I think," "John says," or "he believes that," are called attributives. By use of the numerical code categories 8, 9, and 0, the computer is able to automatically separate the attributive phrases from the rest of the sentence. The separation is represented by a plus sign. For example, a sentence edited as

JOHN/8 SAID/9 TO MARY/0 THAT BOSTON/1 NEEDS/3 RAIN/5

would automatically be separated into the attributive phrase plus the main sentence:

JOHN SAID TO MARY THAT + BOSTON NEEDS RAIN.

Figure 3.7 presents two "Letters from Jenny" (Chapter 12) as they have been edited for both names and syntax. Complex sentences are broken down into simpler units by the use of plus signs. Implied words and unusual names are parenthetically identified. The subscript "R," which appears in the first letter, is used to identify references to her son, Ross. Attributive phrases, such as "nature intended" or "I believe," also appear in the first letter.

The example of *Letters from Jenny* represents only one type of thoroughness and elaboration in editing. Other syntax editing has varied from the simple insertion of occasional plus signs to the development of elaborate codings.

Representation of Content Analysis Categories

In discussing content analysis, we have spoken first of categories and then of the words and idioms belonging to those categories. The

```
EXAMPLE OF SYNTAX EDITED TEXT.    LETTERS FROM JENNY.    LETTERS 146 AND 147.
                                  JOURNAL OF ABNORMAL AND SOCIAL PSYCHOLOGY.

14620 MY DEAREST GIRL.
14621 I/1 HAVE DECIDED/3 NOT TO SLEEP/3 ALL OF THIS WINTER, + AS I/1 DID
14621 LAST, BETTER DIE/3 AT ONCE. SO I/1 HAVE STARTED MY STUDY/3 OF GRECIAN/5
14621 HISTORY/5 ALL OVER AGAIN. I/1 HAVE ALWAYS BEEN A STRONG/1 ADMIRER/1
14621 OF THE GREEKS/5, THEIR WARS/5, DRAMAS/5, LITERATURE/5 AND ART/5. THIS
14621 HISTORY/5 I/1 AM ON NOW (READ/3) STARTS OFF ON THE HELLENES/5, BUT
14621 THAT IS FAR ENOUGH BACK FOR ME. ROSS/1R GLORIED/3 IN GREEK/5 (LIKE/3)
14621 (ART/5) SCULPTURE/5, + MANY A DAY WHEN IN CHICAGO/C I/1 HAVE CARRIED/3
14621 HIM/5R THROUGH THE ART/7 GALLERIES/7 ON MY/1 BACK/1 + HIS/1R DRAWINGS/1
14621 WERE LATER HUNG/3 AT THE STUDENTS/5 EXHIBITION/5, + HE/1R ATTENDED/3
14621 THE SCHOOL/5 THERE. THE ART/1 INSTITUTE/1 IN CHICAGO/1 IS, IN MY
14621 OPINION, MUCH MORE/1 BEAUTIFUL/1 THAN THE METROPOLITAN (MUSEUM/1) HERE.
14622 I/1 INTEND/3 TO GO/3 TO THE METROPOLITAN/5 (MUSEUM/5) OFTEN THIS
14622 WINTER + THEY (MUSEUM/1) HAVE/3 LECTURES/5, AND ,,GALLERY/5 TALKS/5,,
14622 ALMOST EVERY DAY. MY/1 REASON FOR NOT GOING/3 MORE LAST WINTER IS
14622 BECAUSE + THEY ARE (LECTURE/3) MOSTLY DELIVERED BY WOMEN/1, + AND
14622 I/8 DO NOT BELIEVE/9 NATURE EVER INTENDED WOMEN/3 FOR THAT (SHOULD/3
14622 LECTURE/3) PURPOSE. THEY/1 (WOMEN/1) GRIN/1 AND LAUGH/1 TOO MUCH +
14622 I/1 (DISLIKE/3) CANNOT BEAR ,,SMILERS/5,, + WE HAVE DOZENS OF THEM HERE
14622 IN THIS PRISON, WHAT THEY FIND TO GO ABOUT GRINNING AT IS A MYSTERY
14622 TO ME.  LADY M.

14720 MY DEAREST GIRL.
14721 WHAT A PERFECTLY/1 LOVELY/1 SHIRTWAIST/1 (CLOTHING/1), IT CAME YESTERDAY
14721 YOU MIGHT HAVE HEARD MY ,,OH,, OF SURPRISE, THERE. IT IS MY TASTE
14721 EXACTLY, AND THE STRANGE PART IS (CLOTHING/1) THAT IT IS A PERFECT/1
14721 FIT/1. BECAUSE OF MY/1 GORILLA/1 LIKE LONG/1 ARMS/1 I/1 HAVE ALWAYS
14721 HAD TO BUY/3 MY/5 SHIRTWAISTS (CLOTHES/5) TOO LARGE/5, + OTHERWISE
14721 THE SLEEVE/1 WOULD BE UP/3 TO MY/5 ELBOW/5, + BUT THIS (CLOTHES/1) ONE
14721 IS JUST RIGHT/1.
14722 I/1 WENT/3 OUT EARLY ON CHRISTMAS (HOLIDAY/1) MORNING + SOON AS THE
14722 PRISON/1 DOORS/1 WERE UNLOCKED/3,  AND + (I/1) STAYED/3 OUT/3 ALL
14722 DAY. THE CHRISTMAS (HOLIDAY/1) SHOW/1 AT RADIO/1 CITY/1 WAS JUST ABOUT
14722 PERFECT/1, ALL EXCEPT THE ADMISSION PRICE, + IT ALWAYS MAKES ME/1 SORE
14722 (ANGRY/1) TO SEE/3 THE PRICES/5 RAISED/5 ON THE VERY DAY + WHEN MEN/1
14722 WANT/3 TO TAKE/3 THEIR/5 CHILDREN/5, FAMILY/5 AND FRIENDS/5 TO THE
14722 GREATEST THING/7 IN THE SHOW/7 LINE THAT CAN BE PRODUCED. IF THOSE
14722 GRAFTERS WERE (CRIMINALS/1) REALLY CHRIST/1 LIKE/1 THEY WOULD LOWER/3
14722 THE PRICES/5 + SO THE WHOLE/1 FAMILY/1 COULD/3 ENJOY/3 IT (SHOW/5).
14722 IT MUST BE TERRIBLE/1 FOR A FATHER/1 TO HAVE TO LEAVE/3 OUT/3
14722 (BOY/5 GIRL/5) LITTLE/5 JOHNNY/5 OR MAY/5 BECAUSE HE HAD COME TO THE
14722 END OF HIS DOLLARS. NO WONDER MEN/1 STEAL/3.
14723 I/1 WAS ALONE/1 ALL DAY, + (I/1) NEVER OPENED/3 MY/5 LIPS/5 TO A SOUL/7.
14723 WHAT SHALL I/1 WISH/3 YOU/5B IN THE NEW YEAR$ DOUBTLESS YOU/1B WILL
14723 GET/3 ALL/5 THAT IS COMING TO YOU IN ONE WAY OR ANOTHER, + AND THAT
14723 MY/1 WISHES/1 WILL NOT HAVE A (NOTHING/1) THING TO DO WITH IT. I/8 CAN/9
14723 ONLY SAY AGAIN WITH THE IMMORTAL WILLIAM (POET/1) ,,SEE WHAT IS BEST,
14723 THAT BEST/5 I/1 WISH/3 IN THEE/5B,,. LADY M.
```

FIGURE 3.7. Example of syntax- and pronoun-edited text: Letters from Jenny.

actual content analysis procedures work in reverse. The computer program begins with the words in the text and uses them to assign appropriate categories. This is accomplished by looking up each word of the text in a "dictionary" stored inside the computer. Rather than giving alternative definitions, this dictionary is ultimately concerned with assigning categories. If a word of the text is in the dictionary, it can also assign the word to one of the investigator's categories and specify whether further checks should be made to see if the word is part of a specified idiom.

A dictionary, then, represents a collection of content analysis categories that the investigator wants to process together. We have used as few as a dozen categories and as many as over 200 at once. Since most content analysis dictionaries to date have involved less than 100 categories, we shall consider a version of the General Inquirer in which each category can be identified by a two-digit number.[11] While the user must use category numbers in giving directions to the computer, the computer will respond with category names or, if preferred, with both the category names and numbers.[12]

Each entry for a dictionary is punched on a separate IBM card. The entry word is punched beginning in column one and is immediately followed by an equal sign. Each category to which this word belongs, as illustrated in Figure 3.8, appears as a two-digit number to the right

```
JUDGE=21,64      JOB   LEGAL
KEEPER=21        JOB
LAWYER=21,64     JOB   LEGAL
MAGICIAN=21,71,34      JOB   MYSTIC   PERFORMER
MANAGER=21,62    JOB   ECONOMIC
```

FIGURE 3.8. Illustration of dictionary format.

of the equal sign. The categories assigned are called *tags*. Following a blank column, the investigator may add comments, usually the names of the tags assigned.

An idiom is tested by directions that are part of the dictionary entry for the last word of the idiom. Two kinds of directions are used. In the first of these, the computer is instructed to look for a specific pre-

---

[11] During the first few years of using the Inquirer, we found that many users would first build dictionaries having many categories, and then on succeeding revisions they tended to combine those categories that had very low frequency counts. Considering the shift toward dictionaries of fewer than 100 categories, we decided to increase the efficiency of storage by using two-digit numbers. More recently, some plans have been proposed that would greatly increase the number of categories. Several of these are discussed in Chapter 4. At present, the General Inquirer is programmed to allow the user to go up to 300 categories by borrowing part of the machinery normally reserved for syntax procedures. If many dictionaries return to more than 100 categories, we can easily switch to a three-digit system.

[12] Earlier versions of the Inquirer allowed the user to use names that were then automatically translated into numbers. Constant difficulties occurred with misspellings to the point that the strategy was abandoned. For example, a category name might be RECREATION, but on occasion recreational or recreations might be written instead and missed in proofing. Direct use of numbers has proved more satisfactory.

ceding word or words. This is indicated by the code "w." For example,

BELFRY = (w,3,BAT,41)

If the computer comes across the word "belfry" in the text, it looks for the test word "bat" within the three preceding words and if found, assigns the tag 41. By allowing for three words, the phrase may be "bats in his belfry," "bats in the belfry," and so on.

An idiom test may also involve a string of words. For example,

TREATY = 53,(w,3,NORTH ATLANTIC ALLIANCE,35)

will normally assign tag 53 to "treaty" unless it is the "North Atlantic Alliance Treaty," whereupon tag 35 is assigned. The sequence of test words "North Atlantic Alliance" must be adjacent in the text; again the computer searches through the number of words specified after the "w."

For a single entry, a list of idioms may be specified:

OFF = 48,(w,1,KNOCK,52),(w,2,PULL,42,27),(w,2,KNOCK IT,83), (w,3,PAID,64)

The computer will test the idiom routines from left to right. If none are satisfied, any initial first tags are applied (in this case, the tag 48). The list of idioms may extend to several cards.[13]

From experiences with earlier versions of our test routines, we found it very important to be able to specify the allowable number of previous words. Thus in our last illustration, the first test requires that "knock" be immediately followed by "off" ("They will knock off after lunch"). The idiom "knock it off," which is tested later, or idioms having other words between "knock" and "off" will not satisfy this first test. On the other hand, the test of "paid off" specifies a search of three words, thus allowing "paid off," "paid them off," "paid them all off." If the idiom is found, tags already assigned to the previous test words are removed.

In the second test procedure, indicated by a "T," the computer is instructed to look for a specific tag previously assigned. Again the investigator specifies how many previous test words should be considered. For example,

PLAY = 68(T,7,49,34)

[13] Continuations are made from column 80 in one card to column 1 in the next. The first blank column indicates the end of directions associated with that entry.

tells the computer that normally tag 68 is assigned to the word "play." However, if tag 49 has been assigned to one of the seven previous words in the sentence, then tag 34 is applied instead. As we shall see, this is but one initial test for tag co-occurrence patterns.

The over-all size of the dictionary is considerably reduced by the following strategy. The computer first attempts to look up a word in the dictionary exactly as it appears in the text. Thus, the words walked, walks, or walking may each be assigned different categories. However, if the exact word is not found in the dictionary, the computer attempts to remove regular prefixes and suffixes. An often-used removal procedure for English text, involving only suffixes, is illustrated in Figure 3.9. If a suffix is found, the word without the suffix is looked up in

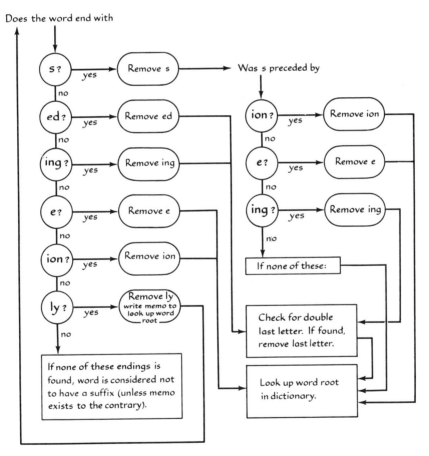

FIGURE 3.9. A suffix-editing procedure for English.

the dictionary list. For example, if a separate entry was not found for walked, walks, or walking, each of these would be reduced to the root "walk," which would then be looked up as a second try.

The suffix routine shown in Figure 3.9 makes some fairly elaborate tests. If the word "swimming" was not in the dictionary, the computer would first remove the "ing" and then the second "m" before finding the root "swim" on the second try. Suffix removal routines can easily reduce the number of dictionary entries needed by a factor of two or three.[14]

All words used within idiom test directions must also appear as dictionary entries. Rather than check back to the actual text words, the computer looks in a list to see if these dictionary entries have been matched. This strategy allows the idiom test to take advantage of previous prefix or suffix removals. For example, if a dictionary has an entry for "knock" but not "knocked," then occurrences of "knocked" in the text will be found by entry "knock" on the second lookup. Since successful lookup was made on this entry, an idiom test direction (w,1,KNOCK,52) will match the previous word "knocked." By thus coordinating idiom tests and entries, it is possible to avoid separate idiom directions for each suffix ending of each test word. If on the other hand the investigator does not want "knocked" matched by the idiom test of "knock," he need only enter "knocked" as a separate dictionary entry.

The computer keeps track of all cases where it cannot find a word or word root in the dictionary. These are printed out as a *leftover list* for the investigator's inspection. An "N" following the equal sign of a dictionary entry indicates that a word is not to be tagged and is not to appear on the leftover list. This device is primarily used in two cases: when a word is part of an idiom test but is not tagged when it stands outside the idiom, and when the investigator wants to keep highly frequent but untagged words (a, the, and so on) off the leftover list.

The investigator may add new entries to a dictionary immediately prior to a run, either as temporary or permanent additions. Temporary categories are often added to identify proper names and places in particular documents under study.

Special computer programs are available to assist the investigator in preparing a dictionary. The investigator may choose, for example,

---

[14] Procedures for changing those removal routines for both prefixes and suffixes are described in the supplementary operations booklet.

to make a separate pile of entry cards for each category. A title card with the category name and number is placed on the top of each pile. One program will then merge the information from the different category piles, producing an alphabetical dictionary. Another program will take an existing alphabetical dictionary and convert it to a listing of entries and idioms by category. Such listings by category are called *cross-sorts.*

While the computer programs do not require alphabetizing of the dictionary entries, the investigator will often have use for an alphabetized listing. The alphabetized dictionary, together with the cross-sorts by category, provides two contrasting ways of checking for dictionary inconsistencies. The utility of these two kinds of listings is illustrated in Chapter 4.

Although several categories may be associated with any one entry word, such *multiple tagging* can cause complications. Problems of multiple tagging and strategies for handling them are discussed in Chapter 4.

Optional Sentence and Document Summaries

After the computer has assigned tags to a sentence, it can be directed to examine the list of tags for certain co-occurrence patterns. If such patterns are found, additional tags are added to the end of the list.

For example, in the Need-Achievement Dictionary (Chapter 5) the sentence "He has always wanted to become a doctor" would be assigned the tags NEED, TO-BE, and ROLE-POSITIVE. When the computer finds this pattern, it is instructed to add the tag ACHIEVEMENT-INDICATE to the end of the list.

This scoring of co-occurrence can be extended across sentence intervals. For example, in the need-achievement procedure, if FAILURE is indicated in one sentence and ANXIETY is indicated in the next, an ACHIEVEMENT-INDICATE tag is added to the second sentence. Another kind of cross-sentence check takes place at the end of each TAT story. When a sentence summary tag is assigned, a marker "flag" is set inside the computer. The pattern of flags is examined at the end of each story, and an appropriate need-achievement evaluation is written as a comment following the last sentence. The flag settings are, of course, removed before the next story is processed.

The within-sentence co-occurrence tests are represented by Boolean statements that are prepared by the investigator. While complete directions are given in the operations supplement, a few examples should give an idea of their format. For example, the statement

IF OCCUR(77) AND (OCCUR(63) OR OCCUR(84)) $ PUT(90)$

says, "If tag combination 77 and 63 occurs or if tag combination 77 and 84 occurs, then add tag 90 to the list." Other functions test not only whether a tag co-occurrence exists but whether the co-occurrence is in a particular sequence, and if also desired, whether the sequence is on adjacent words. Negation and various truth-table relationships can also be tested. To cite but one more example:

IF ORDER (12, 13) AND NOT OCCUR(15) $(PUT (86) $PJ = 1)$

would check if tags 12 and 13 occurred in that order and if tag 15 did not appear anywhere, in which case tag 86 would be added and flag "PJ" set to 1.

The testing of flags across sentences follows a similar format. These procedures are described in the forthcoming operations supplement. Flag setting is the basic mechanism for handling plot analysis problems discussed in Chapter 2.

Summary

The text to be analyzed, the content analysis dictionaries, and the co-occurrence summary rules must all be keypunched on IBM cards before any computer content analysis begins. In accordance with the investigator's hypotheses, the data may be edited for identifying proper names, pronoun referents, and syntactic relationships. The dictionary entries include procedures for identifying idioms. Co-occurrence rules include procedures for both within-sentence patterns and between-sentence patterns. The between-sentence patterns may be used to make a summary evaluation of the entire document.

COMPUTER PROCESSING PROCEDURES

The General Inquirer represents a number of programs that interleaf through several different machines. As a basic reference machine, all operations can take place on an IBM 1401 or 1460 [15] with an IBM 1311 disk attached if larger computers are not available. When large

[15] For our purposes, the IBM 1401 and the IBM 1460 are identical machines. Their main actual difference is in operating speed.

computer memories or time-shared facilities are appropriate, they have also been used. The General Inquirer thus offers a number of different paths of information processing. By keeping the different parts of the system compatible, so that information may flow from one program into another and from one machine to another, the user has a variety of possible content analysis strategies available. In this section, we examine the General Inquirer programs and the flow of information between one program and another. Different analysis strategies are illustrated with examples.

"Tagging": The Assignment of Content Analysis Categories

This is the first step of content analysis processing. A computer scans the text from beginning to end. Each successive text word is looked up in the content analysis dictionary provided by the investigator. The tags assigned by each successfully matched entry word or idiom test routine are stored in sequence on a list. If the word is syntax edited, a syntax code indicating subject, verb, or object is stored with each tag; otherwise, the tag is marked with a "U" as unclassified. If a word is not found in the dictionary upon first lookup, the computer attempts to remove a regular suffix and try making a lookup again. If no suffix is found, or if a second lookup also fails, the computer writes a copy of the word on a leftover list:

The General Inquirer is oriented to the sentence as a basic unit. When a period, a dollar sign (serving as a question mark), or a plus sign is reached in the text, the following information is written on a tape:

a. the sentence number and number of words in the sentence,
b. the last preceding identification code that did not start with a hyphen,
c. a copy of the text of the sentence,
d. an equal sign (=) as a marker followed by a list of the tags in the order in which they were assigned, each tag being a two-digit number followed by an S, V, O, or U to indicate syntax position.

In addition to assigning categories, the tagging program also keeps separate counts of how often each dictionary entry was matched in the course of processing text. These counts may be printed at any point in the course of processing or they may be saved on magnetic tape or on a disk and cumulated over several runs. The counts can be printed in several formats. Most commonly, they are printed in cross-sort format, that is by tag category, showing the counts for each entry word in the category. Within each category, the entries may be ordered alphabetically or by descending frequency. This listing is important in that it shows which entries are most responsible for the tag frequencies. If desired, those entries having zero frequencies may be omitted from the listing. Another format is to have entries and their frequency counts for the entire dictionary listed alphabetically. Still another is to have the entries of the entire dictionary listed in order of descending frequency.

This last format is technically important. Tagging proceeds faster if the most frequently used entries appear earlier in the dictionary. The entry counts from past runs can be used to reorder the dictionary by frequency. The machine is then able to process text faster in the future on the basis of its past experience.

The tagging procedure for the IBM 7090–7094 series machines is outlined in Figure 3.10. The dictionary is identified by a card marked

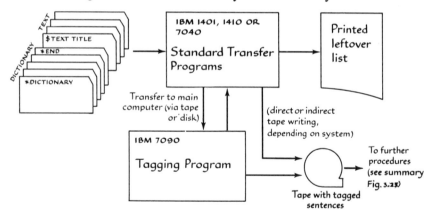

FIGURE 3.10. Tagging procedure using the IBM 7090–7094.

*DICTIONARY and followed by a card marked *END. The text cards immediately follow on the same deck.[16] The information in this deck is usually transferred by standard procedures to magnetic tape, or at some

---

[16] In addition, any sentence and document summary rules are inserted directly into the General Inquirer program. This permits preparing highly complex contingency tests with complete computer language flexibility. The cost is that the program subroutine must be compiled each time these rules are changed. The procedures are completely described in the operations supplement.

installations, to a disk storage unit, before it is processed through the computer. The computer program first reads and stores the dictionary. Then, as the computer scans the text and assigns tags, the sentences with their tags are written on magnetic tape, either directly by the IBM 7090–7094 itself or indirectly via a disk intermediary. In addition, a list of leftovers is prepared by the 7090–7094 on magnetic tape or an intermediary disk and afterwards is printed by a smaller machine.

Dictionary storage within the IBM 7090-7094 computer memory is very compact. Idiom tests are especially compact; directions involving a single test word require one third the space needed for a dictionary entry. Thus, it is possible to process 5,000 entries, 3,000 idioms, and several hundred sentence and document summaries all at once. Since a dictionary with 3,000 to 4,000 words will often identify over 90 percent of the text, leftover lists can be quite short.

The tagging sequence for the IBM 1401–1460 series with IBM 1311 disk attachment is shown in Figure 3.11. First, a special program

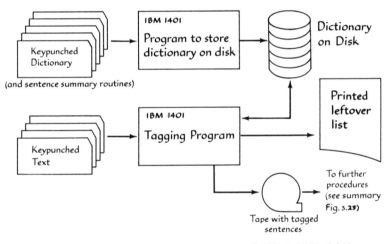

FIGURE 3.11. *Tagging procedure using the IBM 1401–1460.*

is used to read the dictionary and store it on the 1311 disk. This takes several minutes; however, the disks are removable and can be stored between runs to avoid the reloading problem. With this arrangement, disk storage capacity is even larger than that of the 7090–7094. A second program reads the keypunched text and assigns categories from the disk. A printed leftover list and a magnetic tape with the tagged sentences are prepared as the text is processed.

The main results of tagging, then, are the leftover list and a tape containing a series of tagged sentences. This tape serves as input to the next operation: the text and tag listing.

Text and Tag Listing

This is an IBM 1401–1460 program, using the magnetic tape of tagged data generated by the tagging program. The text and tag listing program unpacks the information stored on the magnetic tape and prints it in the bilingual book format illustrated in Figure 3.12. The text is listed on the left by sentence, with each sentence serially numbered and printed with its identification code. The tags are listed in rows on the right in the order in which they were assigned to the sentence. The first example (suicide notes) shows highly edited text with syntax position (S, V, O, U) indicated after each tag. Note that attributive clauses are marked with parentheses and printed separately with their tags. The second example (Presidential Acceptance Speeches) shows unedited text; syntax identifications are omitted. Each sentence is thus paralleled by its "tag translation." Any sentence summary tags appear at the end of the list.

The text and tag listing program prints tags as names rather than numbers, making the changes to names as it goes along. The program requires a keypunched set of tag names before it begins processing data. Since some 90 milliseconds are available for computing each 100 milliseconds it takes to print a line, the program also uses some of this time to take care of housekeeping matters and to write a new tape of tagged sentences. It is this new tape format that is used for all further operations. Again, full details are in the operations supplement.

The investigator is encouraged to inspect the text and tag list to make sure that words and idioms are tagged as expected. If inappropriate tagging occurs, he can note it and make changes in the next dictionary revision. Inspection of the text and tag listing will often point up important co-occurrence patterns that might not otherwise be noticed.

The text and tag listing becomes a basic reference document in all further data analysis with that dictionary. The further steps are all concerned with handling the information in this listing.

Tag Tally Procedures

The IBM 1401–1460 tag tally procedures provide statistics on how many times each tag was assigned to a document. First, the tags assigned to each sentence are counted at about the rate of 300 sentences per minute. At the end of each document, that is, whenever a card marked with a star (*) is encountered, the totals are printed as tables, punched on cards, or written on tape.[17] Both raw tag frequencies and tag indexes scaled proportional to document length are provided. The index score is a percentage, indicating roughly the number of occurrences divided by the number of possible occurrences.

Where document lengths differ, both raw counts and index scores are often needed in making comparisons between documents. For example, let us suppose a comparison is to be made between documents A and B. Document A is twice as long as document B. Although both documents give equally exhaustive treatment to topic X, document A goes on to consider several additional topics, using different tags. The raw tag counts for tags relative to topic X may be the same for both documents. However, if frequencies are adjusted proportional to total document length, document A will have lower indexes for these tags. A description of this situation requires two statements: the frequency of mention was the same, but the extent of saturation was less in document A because of document A's inclusion of additional topics.

The tag tally program offers two alternative basic counting procedures. The *word count* is used if the analyst is primarily interested in specific references and images. The number of actual times the tag was assigned to each sentence is tallied. An index score proportional to document length is provided by dividing the word count by the total number of words in the document, the results rounded to the nearest tenth of a percent. However, to the extent some tag assignments are based on multiword idioms, division by total number of words only approximates the figure needed for a true percentage.

If an analyst is studying themes within a document, the *sentence-count* procedure is more relevant. The number of sentences in which a tag was assigned is tallied. This tally is divided by the total number of sentences in the document to create an index score. Thus, the sentence-count index score represents the number of sentences to which a tag was assigned as a percentage of the total number of sentences to which it could have been assigned. The sentence-count tallies directly correspond to the statistics produced by the 1401 retrieval program and the time-shared "tree-building" program described later in this chapter.

---

[17] These options are controlled by switches on the computer, as explained in the operations supplement.

```
                SENTENCE   1    TOTAL WORDS=   2    IDENTIFICATION 192
DEAR MARY.
                                     AFFECTION    U  SIGN-ACCEPT  U  FAMILY       U

                SENTENCE   2    TOTAL WORDS=   4    IDENTIFICATION 192
(YOU ARE CONVINCED THAT )
                                     OTHER        S  COMMUNICATE  V  SIGN-AUTH    V

                SENTENCE   2    TOTAL WORDS=   6    IDENTIFICATION 192
SINCE YOU ARE CONVINCED THAT YOU ARE AN INVALID
(SICK) +
                                     TIME-REF     U  OTHER        U  BAD          S  DISTRESS  S  SIGN-WEAK   S

                SENTENCE   3    TOTAL WORDS=   6    IDENTIFICATION 192
AND NO ONE CAN HELP YOU.
                                     NOT          U  QUAN-REF     U  GUIDE        S  SIGN-STRONG V  SIGN-ACCEPT V
                                     OTHER        O

                SENTENCE   4    TOTAL WORDS=   2    IDENTIFICATION 192
(I HOPE )
                                     SELF         S  SIGN-ASCEND  V  URGE         V

                SENTENCE   4    TOTAL WORDS=   9    IDENTIFICATION 192
I HOPE MY THREE THOUSAND DOLLARS OF INSURANCE WILL
HELP YOU +
                                     SELF         S  QUAN-REF     S  OVERSTATE    S  MESSAGE-FORM S  ECONOMIC   S
                                     MESSAGE-FORM S  SIGN-STRONG  S  ECONOMIC     V  GUIDE        V  SIGN-STRONG V
                                     SIGN-ACCEPT  V  OTHER        O

                SENTENCE   5    TOTAL WORDS=   7    IDENTIFICATION 192
TO (YOU) SEE THE TRUTH ABOUT YOURSELF +
                                     OTHER        O  SENSE        V  IDEAL-VALUE  O  ACADEMIC     O  OTHER      U

                SENTENCE   6    TOTAL WORDS=   8    IDENTIFICATION 192
AND (YOU) GET RID OF YOUR MENTAL SICKNESS.
                                     OTHER        O  GET          S  SIGN-REJECT  V  EXPEL        V  OTHER      O
                                     THINK        O  ACADEMIC     O  DEVIATION    O  MEDICAL      O
```

FIGURE 3.12a. Samples of text and tag listings. Example 1: Suicide notes.

```
SENTENCE  25     TOTAL WORDS=  22     IDENTIFICATION 364

THE NEEDS WE SEEK TO FILL, THE HOPES WE SEEK TO
REALIZE, ARE NOT OURS ALONE, THEY ARE THOSE OF OUR
PEOPLE.

   URGE          SELVES          ATTEMPT      SIGN-ACCEPT   SIGN-ASCEND
   URGE          SELVES          ATTEMPT      SIGN-ACCEPT   SENSE
   NOT           SELVES          QUAN-REF     OTHER         QUAN-REF
   SELVES        LARGE-GROUP     COMMUNITY


SENTENCE  26     TOTAL WORDS=   8     IDENTIFICATION 364

MOST AMERICANS WANT MEDICAL CARE FOR OLDER
CITIZENS.

   QUAN-REF      OVERSTATE       NEUTER-ROLE  POLITICAL     URGE
   MEDICAL       GUIDE           TIME-REF     HIGHER-STAT   NEUTER-ROLE
   POLITICAL     PEER-STATUS


SENTENCE  27     TOTAL WORDS=   4     IDENTIFICATION 364

AND SO DO I.

   SELF


SENTENCE  28     TOTAL WORDS=   9     IDENTIFICATION 364

MOST AMERICANS WANT FAIR AND STABLE PRICES FOR
FARMERS.

   QUAN-REF      OVERSTATE       NEUTER-ROLE   POLITICAL     URGE
   GOOD          UNDERSTATE      IDEAL-VALUE   SIGN-STRONG   QUAN-REF
   ECONOMIC      JOB-ROLE        TECHNOLOGICL


SENTENCE  29     TOTAL WORDS=   4     IDENTIFICATION 364

AND SO DO I.

   SELF


SENTENCE  30     TOTAL WORDS=  12     IDENTIFICATION 364

MOST AMERICANS WANT A DECENT HOME IN A DECENT
NEIGHBORHOOD FOR ALL.

   QUAN-REF      OVERSTATE       NEUTER-ROLE   POLITICAL     URGE
   SOCIAL-PLACE  FEMALE-THEME    FAMILY        SOCIAL-PLACE  COMMUNITY
   QUAN-REF      OVERSTATE


SENTENCE  31     TOTAL WORDS=   4     IDENTIFICATION 364

AND SO DO I.

   SELF
```

FIGURE 3.12b. Samples of text and tag listing. Example 2: Presidential Acceptance Speech.

GENERAL INQUIRER WORD TAG TALLY

DOCUMENT   1   FIRST ID 00130

LETTERS FROM JENNY.   SECTION ONE.

4541 WORDS   502 SENTENCES

Category	RAW SUB	RAW VRB	RAW OBJ	RAW UCL	RAW TOTAL	INDEX SUB	INDEX VRB	INDEX OBJ	INDEX UCL	INDEX TOTAL
SELF	219	1	42	123	385	4.8	.0	.9	2.7	8.5
SELVES	13		3		16	.3	.0	.1		.4
OTHER	36		19	30	86	.8	.0	.4	.7	1.9
MALE-ROLE	79		18	26	123	1.7	.0	.4	.6	2.7
FEMALE-ROLE	45		23	29	97	1.0	.0	.5	.6	2.1
NEUTER-ROLE	15		6	14	35	.3	.0	.1	.3	.8
JOB-ROLE	2		2	3	7	.0	.0	.0	.1	.2
GROUPS										
SMALL-GROUP	2			2	4	.0	.0		.0	.0
LARGE-GROUP	6		1	9	16	.1	.0	.0	.2	.4
PHYSICAL OBJECTS										
BODY-PART	11		5	4	20	.2	.0	.1	.1	.4
FOOD	1		1	1	3	.0	.0	.0		.1
CLOTHING	1		8	6	15	.0	.0	.2		.3
TOOL	11	2	5	10	28	.2	.0	.1	.2	.6
NATURAL-OBJ	24		9	8	41	.5	.0	.2	.2	.9
NON-SPC-OBJ	6	3	8	81	98	.1	.1	.2	1.8	2.2
PHYSICAL QUALIFIERS										
SENSORY-REF	8		1	4	13	.2	.0	.0	.1	.3
TIME-REF	15	5	7	174	201	.3	.1	.2	3.8	4.4
SPACE-REF	8	14	18	194	234	.2	.3	.4	4.3	5.2
QUAN-REF	20	3	21	146	190	.4	.1	.5	3.2	4.2

Category	RAW SUB	RAW VRB	RAW OBJ	RAW UCL	RAW TOTAL	INDEX SUB	INDEX VRB	INDEX OBJ	INDEX UCL	INDEX TOTAL
AROUSAL	3	2		5	10	.1	.0	.0	.1	.2
URGE	2	16	3	10	31	.0	.4	.1	.2	.7
AFFECTION	4	5	3	10	22	.1	.1	.1	.2	.5
PLEASURE	8	2	2	3	15	.2	.0	.0	.1	.3
DISTRESS	18	17	1	4	40	.4	.4	.0	.1	.9
ANGER	2	3			5	.0	.1	.0	.0	.1
THOUGHT										
SENSE		15		11	26	.0	.3	.0	.2	.6
THINK	5	21	4	33	63	.1	.5	.1	.7	1.4
IF	3	1	1	44	49	.1	.0	.0	1.0	1.1
EQUAL	2	7	1	7	17	.0	.2	.0	.2	.4
NOT	5	4	3	82	94	.1	.1	.1	1.8	2.1
CAUSE										
DEF-MECH				7	7	.0	.0	.0	.2	.2
EVALUATION										
GOOD	21	1	7	14	43	.5	.0	.2	.3	.9
BAD	11			3	14	.2	.0	.0	.1	.3
OUGHT	5	1		49	55	.0	.1		1.1	1.2
SOCIAL-EMOTIONAL ACTIONS										
COMMUNICATE	2	22	6	34	64	.0	.5	.1	.7	1.4
APPROACH		34		7	41	.0	.7	.0	.2	.9

FIGURE 3.13. Sample of word tag tally: Harvard III Dictionary.

The tally is printed as a rotated table. It has two parallel panels, each giving four sample counts, a total count (N), and the corresponding percentage (rate) columns.

Panel 1

Category	S1	S2	S3	S4	N	%1	%2	%3	%4	%
ENVIRONMENTS										
SOCIAL-PLACE	8	7	26	43	84	.1	.2	.6	.9	1.8
NATUR-WORLD	6	12	2	11	31	.1	.3	.0	.2	.7
CULTURE										
IDEAL-VALUE	11	3	7	7	28	.2	.1	.2	.2	.6
DEVIATION	3	8		2	13	.1	.2	.0	.0	.3
ACTION-NORM	5	3	11	17	36	.1	.1	.2	.4	.8
MESSAGE-FRM	21	4	64	23	112	.5	.1	1.4	.5	2.5
THOUGHT-FRM		2		7	9	.0	.0	.0	.2	.2
INSTITUTIONS										
ACADEMIC	5	6	5	19	35	.1	.1	.2	.4	.8
ARTISTIC	4	2	7	3	16	.0	.0	.2	.1	.4
COMMUNITY	1	3	3	3	10	.0	.1	.1	.1	.2
ECONOMIC	22	19	37	31	109	.5	.4	.8	.7	2.4
FAMILY	8	5	12	16	41	.2	.1	.3	.4	.9
LEGAL	2	8	1	4	15	.0	.2	.0	.1	.3
MEDICAL	6			7	13	.1	.0	.1	.2	.3
MILITARY	1				1	.0	.0	.0	.0	.0
POLITICAL	6	3	3	7	19	.0	.1	.1	.2	.4
RECREATIONAL	8	2	2	8	20	.2	.0	.0	.2	.4
RELIGIOUS	2	2	1	4	9	.0	.0	.0	.1	.2
TECHNOLOGICL	12	16	7	16	51	.3	.4	.2	.4	1.1
STATUS CONNOTATIONS										
HIGHER-STAT	6	5	7		18	.1	.0	.1	.2	.4
PEER-STATUS	13	2	2		17	.3	.0	.0	.1	.4
LOWER-STATUS	7	1	7	4	19	.2	.0	.2	.1	.4

Panel 2

Category	S1	S2	S3	S4	N	%1	%2	%3	%4	%
GUIDE	1	22	4	12	39	.0	.5	.1	.3	.9
CONTROL		5		3	8	.0	.1	.0	.1	.2
FOLLOW		4		1	5	.0	.1	.0	.0	.1
ATTACK	1	3		4	8	.0	.1	.0	.1	.2
AVOID	1	21	4	10	36	.0	.5	.1	.2	.8
IMPERSONAL-ACTIONS										
ATTEMPT	1	5	3		9	.0	.1	.1	.0	.2
GET		28	1	5	34	.0	.6	.0	.1	.7
POSSESS	1	48	1	38	88	.0	1.1	.0	.8	1.9
EXPEL	1	9	1	1	12	.0	.2	.0	.0	.3
WORK	1	30	17		48	.0	.7	.4	.0	1.1
MOVE	8	22	9		39	.2	.5	.2	.0	.9
PSYCHOLOGICAL THEMES										
OVERSTATE	22	6	15	117	160	.5	.1	.3	2.6	3.5
UNDERSTATE	10	2	8	70	90	.2	.0	.2	1.5	2.0
SIGN-STRONG	13	56	3	12	84	.3	1.2	.1	.3	1.8
SIGN-WEAK	20	24	3	10	57	.4	.5	.1	.2	1.3
SIGN-ACCEPT	11	54	7	18	90	.2	1.2	.2	.4	2.0
SIGN-REJECT	12	43	4	30	89	.3	.9	.1	.7	2.0
MALE-THEME	6	1	2	4	13	.1	.0	.0	.1	.3
FEMALE-THEME	29	8	22	29	88	.6	.2	.5	.6	1.9
SEX-THEME	13	10	15	17	55	.3	.2	.3	.4	1.2
SIGN-ASCEND	19	23	6	60	108	.4	.5	.1	1.3	2.4
SIGN-AUTH	8	2	2	16	28	.2	.0	.0	.4	.6
DANGER-THEME	2	1	3	7	13	.0	.0	.1	.2	.3
DEATH-THEME	12	24	5	18	59	.3	.5	.1	.4	1.3

FIGURE 3.13. Sample of word tag tally: Harvard III Dictionary.

Since the probability of a tag appearing in a sentence is correlated with sentence length, the sentence-count procedure may present problems. If sentence-count index scores tend to be higher for a particular document, it may be because the document tends to have longer sentences. This possibility can be quickly checked. Average sentence length information is automatically provided by the tag tally program at the end of each run.

Tag tally results are printed on a one- or two-page table, depending on the number of tags used and the table format desired. Format is controlled by a keypunched deck of instructions as outlined in the operations supplement. Figures 3.13 and 3.14 compare a word-count tally and a sentence-count tally of the same document.[18]

Each tag tally may be printed with a title card heading supplied at the time the tally is made. The identification code associated with the first sentence of the document is also printed at the top of each table.

Since our current content analysis dictionaries often have noun, verb, and other syntactic usages mixed in the same category, the tag tally is designed to provide separate syntax counts within each category. The format is set to correspond to the four-position syntax-editing procedure discussed earlier in this chapter. For example, in Figure 3.13 we are told that the tag DISTRESS appeared five times as a subject and four times as a verb. The writer obviously is talking about DISTRESS words as subject as well as using DISTRESS words as verbs. Interestingly, in this text the category does not occur as the object of a sentence. By using the retrieval procedures, which will be described, we could print the sentences in which DISTRESS occurs for further inspection.

Note that in the sentence count (Figure 3.14), a tag may occur for several parts of speech in the same sentence but is only counted once in the total column. The sum of the different tallies for each part of speech may thus exceed the figure in the total column.

As discussed in Chapter 4, more recent dictionaries have tended to have separate content analysis categories for different syntax usage. The advantages are such that we may expect even more use of syntax-specific categories in the future. For example, distress words as nouns

---

[18] The dictionary used in Figures 3.13 and 3.14 is the Harvard III Psycho-sociological Dictionary described in Chapter 5. The section of the dictionary illustrated in Figure 3.15 is the Product Image Dictionary discussed in Chapter 22.

GENERAL INQUIRER SENTENCE TAG TALLY

LETTERS FROM JENNY.   SECTION ONE.

DOCUMENT 1   FIRST ID 00130

4541 WORDS   502 SENTENCES

	RAW SCORES					INDEX SCORES AS PERCENT				
	SUB	VRB	OBJ	UCL	TOTAL	SUB	VRB	OBJ	UCL	TOTAL
SELF	216	1	39	105	309	43.0	.2	7.8	20.9	61.6
SELVES	13			3	16	2.6	.0	.0	.6	3.2
OTHER	35	1	17	29	76	7.0	.2	3.4	5.8	15.1
MALE-ROLE	77		14	23	106	15.3	.0	2.8	4.6	21.1
FEMALE-ROLE	43		20	22	75	8.6	.0	4.0	4.4	14.9
NEUTER-ROLE	15		6	14	34	3.0	.0	1.2	2.8	6.8
JOB-ROLE	2		2	3	7	.4	.0	.4	.6	1.4
GROUPS										
SMALL-GROUP	2		2		4	.4	.0	.4	.0	.8
LARGE-GROUP	6	1		8	14	1.2	.2	.0	1.6	2.8
PHYSICAL OBJECTS										
BODY-PART	11		5	4	20	2.2	.0	1.0	.8	4.0
FOOD	1		1	1	3	.2	.0	.2	.2	.6
CLOTHING	1		7	6	13	.2	.0	1.4	1.2	2.6
TOOL	9	2	5	8	22	1.8	.4	1.0	1.6	4.4
NATURAL-OBJ	24		8	8	38	4.8	.0	1.6	1.6	7.6
NON-SPC-OBJ	6	3	8	71	86	1.2	.6	1.6	14.1	17.1
PHYSICAL QUALIFIERS										
SENSORY-REF	7		1	4	12	1.4	.0	.2	.8	2.4
TIME-REF	14	5	7	138	154	2.8	1.0	1.4	27.5	30.7

	RAW SCORES					INDEX SCORES AS PERCENT				
	SUB	VRB	OBJ	UCL	TOTAL	SUB	VRB	OBJ	UCL	TOTAL
AROUSAL	3	2		5	10	.6	.4	.2	1.0	2.0
URGE	2	16	3	10	30	.4	3.2	.6	2.0	6.0
AFFECTION	4	5	3	10	22	.8	1.0	.6	2.0	4.4
PLEASURE	8	2	2	3	15	1.6	.4	.4	.6	3.0
DISTRESS	17	17	1	4	37	3.4	3.4	.2	.8	7.4
ANGER	2	3			5	.4	.6	.0	.0	1.0
THOUGHT										
SENSE		15		10	25	.0	3.0	.0	2.0	5.0
THINK	5	19	4	33	59	1.0	3.8	.8	6.6	11.8
IF	3	1	1	43	48	.6	.2	.2	8.6	9.6
EQUAL	2	7	1	7	16	.4	1.4	.2	1.4	3.2
NOT	4	4	3	73	84	.8	.8	.6	14.5	16.7
CAUSE										
DEF-MECH				7	7	.0	.0	.0	1.4	1.4
EVALUATION										
GOOD	20	1	7	14	41	4.0	.2	1.4	2.8	8.2
BAD	10		5	3	13	2.0	.0	1.0	.6	2.6
OUGHT		5	1	48	54	.0	1.0	.2	9.6	10.8
SOCIAL-EMOTIONAL ACTIONS										

FIGURE 3.14. Sample of sentence tag tally: Harvard III Dictionary.

might then be a separate category from distress words as verbs, with distress words as modifiers possibly put into a third category.

If such changes are made, the present automatic division of each category into separate syntax counts will probably be dropped. Instead, more categories will be used. Even at present, a number of cells in the tag tally table tend to appear as one part of speech and not as another. For example, the role tags in our example (SELF, SELVES, OTHER, MALE-ROLE, FEMALE-ROLE, NEUTER-ROLE, and JOB-ROLE) never occur as verbs unless there is a mistake in editing. While future dictionaries may have more categories, the array of numbers appearing on future tag tally tables will probably be reduced.

At present, if syntax editing is not used, all counts occur in an unclassified column. Part of a tally for unedited text is shown in Figure 3.15.

Several cards may be punched for each tag tally. The first card contains the identification code that is printed at the top of the page. The remaining cards contain the word- or sentence-index scores (depending on which count is being made) that appear in the total column. The divisor number used to produce the index score (that is, the total number of words or the total number of sentences) is also punched on the last card.

The punched cards are designed so that they can be directly used as data for analysis of variance, factor analysis, and other statistical computer programs. Again, complete descriptions and directions are in the operations supplement.

Finally, a tape may be written that contains all the information appearing on a tag tally table, both raw and index scores for all syntax positions, plus the total columns. The user may decide to make this tape and not to take the time to also print tables. The output tape information serves as data for several supplementary IBM programs.

Transpose Program

The tag tally program adds to the output tape each time a tag tally is printed; thus the output tape is organized by document. To do further graphing or statistical work, it is necessary to have information organized across documents by tag. The IBM 1401-1460 transpose program does this reordering. The investigator supplies a control card specifying the kind of score (raw, index, particular part of speech, and so on) plus what columns of the identification code are to be

GENERAL INQUIRER SENTENCE TAG TALLY

DOCUMENT   1   FIRST IC 11811

5572 WORDS

263 SENTENCES

Left panel

	RAW SCORES SUB	VRB	OBJ	UCL	TOTAL	INDEX SCORES AS PERCENT SUB	VRB	OBJ	UCL	TOTAL
PRODUCT PROPERTIES										
STRENGTH				35	35	.0	.0	.0	13.3	13.3
VERSATILI				65	65	.0	.0	.0	24.7	24.7
ECONOMY				25	25	.0	.0	.0	9.5	9.5
RELIABILI				7	7	.0	.0	.0	2.7	2.7
BEAUTY				79	79	.0	.0	.0	30.0	30.0
GOOD				78	78	.0	.0	.0	29.7	29.7
TOTAL ASSET				172	172	.0	.0	.0	65.4	65.4
WEAKNESS				16	16	.0	.0	.0	6.1	6.1
EXPENSE				20	20	.0	.0	.0	7.6	7.6
BAD				22	22	.0	.0	.3	8.4	8.4
T. LIABILIT				52	52	.0	.0	.0	19.8	19.8
QUANTITY										
MANY-LARG				61	61	.0	.0	.0	23.2	23.2
FEW-SMALL				24	24	.0	.3	.0	9.1	9.1
METRICS				103	103	.0	.0	.0	39.2	39.2
RELATICNA				52	52	.0	.0	.0	19.8	19.8
TOTAL-QUANT				152	152	.0	.0	.0	57.8	57.8
HIGH-RATE				31	31	.0	.0	.0	11.8	11.8
LOW-RATE				11	11	.0	.0	.0	4.2	4.2

Right panel

	RAW SCORES SUB	VRB	OBJ	UCL	TOTAL	INDEX SCORES AS PERCENT SUB	VRB	OBJ	UCL	TOTAL
INSTITUTIONAL REFERENCE										
RCLES				34	34	.0	.0	.0	12.9	12.9
ORGANIZAT				31	31	.0	.0	.0	11.8	11.8
MANAGEMEN				26	26	.0	.0	.0	9.9	9.9
FINANCE				14	14	.0	.0	.0	5.3	5.3
MARKETING				11	11	.0	.0	.0	4.2	4.2
CONSUMPTI				8	8	.0	.0	.0	3.0	3.0
SCIENTIFI				81	81	.0	.0	.0	30.8	30.8
TECHNOLOGI				65	65	.0	.0	.0	24.7	24.7
STYLE										
EMPHASIS				88	88	.0	.0	.0	33.5	33.5
UNDEREMPHA				37	37	.0	.0	.0	14.1	14.1
EMOTICNAL				6	6	.0	.0	.0	2.3	2.3
CHANGE										
INCREASE				51	51	.0	.0	.0	19.4	19.4
DECREASE				14	14	.0	.0	.0	5.3	5.3
STASIS				8	8	.0	.0	.0	3.0	3.0
TRANSFORM				73	73	.0	.0	.0	27.8	27.8
TOTAL-CHANG				122	122	.0	.0	.0	46.4	46.4
SUM-DECLINE				6	6	.0	.0	.0	2.3	2.3
SUM-IMPROVE				30	30	.0	.0	.0	11.4	11.4

FIGURE 3.15. Example of tag tally using unedited text: Product Image Dictionary.

taken from the output tape. Only one kind of score can be transposed at a time. A new tape is written with the transposed data.

Graphing Program

The IBM 1401 graphing program prepares pictorial bar graphs comparing tag scores for different documents. A title of the study and name of the tag being graphed appears at the top of each page. Those columns of the identification code selected by the investigator are listed for each document on the left. To the right of each code, a horizontal bar graph is printed with a two-digit number at the end of each bar indicating the score for the document. The length of the bar, of course, is proportional to the magnitude of the score.

The bar graph is printed up to a hundred positions long. If this is not adequate, the investigator can specify a "scale factor" to be used in computing the graph. For example, a "scale factor" of four will divide all scores by four (and round them) before graphing them. If certain bars still exceed the hundred units available, the hundred's position is printed as a digit to the left of the graph.[19]

```
GENERAL INQUIRER TAG TALLY GRAPH.  TAG  5   FEMALE-ROLE

          LETTERS FROM JENNY.    INDEX CHANGES OVER TIME.  SCALE FACTOR  1       PAGE  1

DOCUMENT IDENTIFICATION *          *           *          *          *          *          *   -N-

     001   *-------------------21                                                         *   4541
     007   *-----------------17                                                           *   3494
     016   *---------------------23                                                       *   4041
     025   *------------------20                                                          *   1966
     034   *-----------------------------31                                              *   4996
     045   *-----------------------------31                                              *   2437
     053   *-------------------------------34                                            *   1518
     058   *----------------------------------37                                         *   2432
     068   *----------------------------------37                                         *   2229
     079   *----------------------22 24                                                   *   2573
     092   *----------------------------29                                               *   2677
     107   *----------------------------29                                               *   2934
     116   *------------------------26                                                    *   2684
     129   *-------------14                                                               *   2111
```

FIGURE 3.16. Illustration of tag tally bar graph: Time trend changes on FEMALE-ROLE *in* Letters from Jenny.

Figure 3.16 illustrates the graph format. Time-trend changes are shown here for reference to FEMALE-ROLE in *Letters from Jenny.* Graph examples can also be found in later chapters; for example,

---

[19] Horizontal format is also directed by control cards. The computer can be directed to skip a line every time the character in a specified column of the identification field changes. The bar graphs are thus blocked into groups according to document number.

Chapter 10 presents several graphs showing tag changes in U.S. Presidential nomination acceptance speeches over the last 36 years.

Other 1401 Statistics Programs

Often, an investigator will want to graph information in several different ways. For example, if comparing scores of political acceptance speeches, the investigator may want graphs both by year and by political party. A special document-sort program is used to rearrange the document order within each tag before regraphing.

A second special 1401 program is designed for those cases where many documents may be available, and the investigator wants information on arithmetic means, standard deviation, and range. Control cards are used to group a specified number of successive documents and give them a title.

Summary

The tag tally output tape thus feeds into a number of supplementary procedures. These procedures are outlined in relation to the basic tag tally program in Figure 3.17. Together they constitute a useful resource for many of the counting tasks in the General Inquirer System.

Retrieval and Co-occurrence Tests

The IBM 1401–1460 retrieval program forms the basis for image and thematic co-occurrence analyses not directly included as part of the tagging phase. It is the basis for much of the General Inquirer's clinical exploratory power.

The retrieval program reads one or more questions keypunched by the investigator and then searches the tagged text on magnetic tape for sentences that match the question specifications. When a sentence successfully matches all the specifications within a question, a tally is made in a counter associated with that question. In addition, a retrieval of that sentence may also be made. The form of the retrieval is directed by one or more keypunched codes that follow each question. These codes are explained in Table 3.2.

Upon reaching the end of a document (that is, a card keypunched with a star), the different frequency counts are listed on the printer. Each question is printed together with its raw frequency and its index score. The index score, like the sentence tag tally, is obtained by divid-

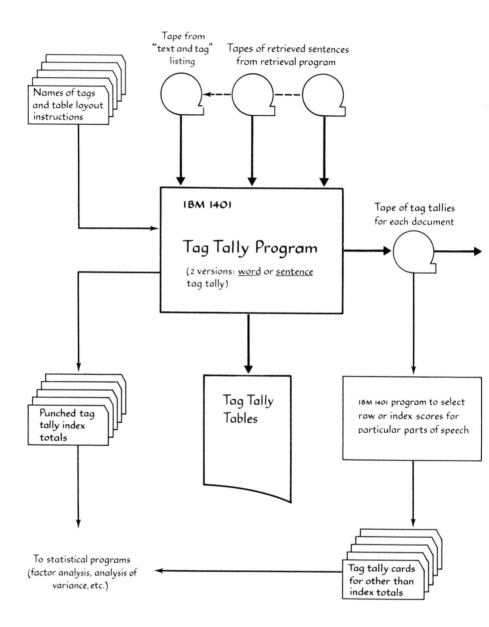

Tape from "text and tag" listing

Tapes of retrieved sentences from retrieval program

Names of tags and table layout instructions

IBM 1401

Tag Tally Program

(2 versions: word or sentence tag tally)

Tape of tag tallies for each document

Punched tag tally index totals

Tag Tally Tables

IBM 1401 program to select raw or index scores for particular parts of speech

To statistical programs (factor analysis, analysis of variance, etc.)

Tag tally cards for other than index totals

FIGURE 3.17. *Summary diagram:*

Note: dash line denotes tapes of identical format.

An IBM 1460 may be substituted at each step for an IBM 1401.

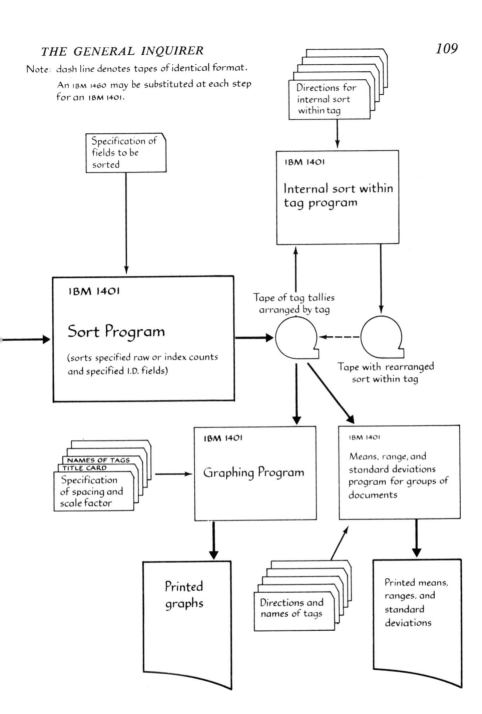

Tag tally procedures.

TABLE 3.2. Codes for Retrieval Options

P: The matched sentence is printed, together with its identification code and sentence number. All questions having code "P" that the sentence matched are printed afterwards. For example:

SENTENCE 86   TOTAL WORDS = 6   IDENTIFICATION 211
THEN I TOLD YOU MY TROUBLES
QUESTION + 01s + 43v = P (SELF AS SUBJECT, COMMUNICATE AS VERB)
          + 01s + 03∅ = P (SELF AS SUBJECT, OTHER AS OBJECT)

C: For each question matched, the identification code and the sentence number are punched on a card, together with the number of the question.

2, 3, 4, ... 9: A complete copy of the sentence, together with its identification code and assigned tags, is written on the tape unit designated by this code number. The retrieval written on tape is identical in format to what was read in. Thus the information retrieved on tape can be used in making further retrievals or in making tag tallies. (Imput is no tape 1.)

X: The question is included only for counts; no retrievals are to be made.

---

ing the frequency count by the total number of sentences in the document. In addition, separate raw-frequency and index-score totals are then printed to indicate the number of retrievals sent to each of the places listed in Table 3.2. Thus the investigator knows exactly how many sentences were printed, punched, and written on the different magnetic tapes.

After the processing of the last document is complete, the grand totals are automatically printed. These include total counts and index scores for each of the questions, plus total counts of sentences sent to each of the retrieval units.

Much of the power of the retrieval program comes from the flexibility of the question-writing procedure. Each question consists of a list of one or more specifications. Each specification is preceded by a plus or a minus sign, indicating whether successful match should be based on presence or absence. Specifications can refer to tags, the sentence text, or the identification codes.

Tags

A tag is referred to by its two-digit number. Thus $+32$ would specify that the tag 32 must be assigned to a sentence in order for a match to be successful. Conversely, -32 specifies that tag category 32 must not have been assigned to the sentence.

The tag number may be followed by a letter specifying further syntax restrictions. The syntax letters permitted in the present procedures are

s = subject
v = verb
o = object
u = unclassified

Thus, +32s would specify category 32 in the syntax position of subject.

Text Words and Phrases

The retrieval program can search the text of the sentence for particular words, phrases, or parts of words. Specifications referring to the text are identified by parenthesis marks on each side. The computer searches the text of the sentence for the string of characters contained within these marks. The string of characters within the parenthesis marks may include blanks and extend for a total length of several words. The computer would then check for this entire sequence. The string may also just contain part of a word; thus, the computer can search for letter combinations like "tion."

Each of the parentheses serves an important function of being what we call a *boundary marker*. A "correct" parenthesis (that is, a parenthesis facing the string of characters) indicates a *closed boundary*. It causes the computer to test if the position next to the end of the string in the text marks the end of a word. The position just before the beginning of a word in a sentence, of course, might be a space, an open parenthesis, or our comma quotation marks. The position following the end of a word in a sentence might be a space, a period, a comma, a closed parenthesis, or our dollar-sign question mark. Thus, if a string of characters is written with closed boundary markers at both ends, the exact word or words must appear in the text. For example, the specification

+(PARENT)

would identify only the word "parent," while

+(NORTH ATLANTIC ALLIANCE TREATY)

would cause the computer to search for that exact phrase.

An *open boundary marker* is represented by a parenthesis that looks incorrect inasmuch as it faces away from the string of characters. When this is used, the computer does not check to see what follows the end of the string. That end of the string may be embedded in part of a larger word. The investigator can make either one or both of the boundaries open. Thus,

+(PARENT(would not only match the word "parent" but also "parents," and so on.

+)PARENT)   would not permit any letters following, but would permit prefixes resulting in such words as grandparent.

+)PARENT(would allow for a string of characters embedded in a larger word with additions at either end.

Boundary markers can be used to identify any letter sequences and to specify whether they may occur at the beginning, end, or anywhere in the word. Thus the number of occurrences of "re" could be tested by the specification

+(RE(

which would match those occurrences of this letter combination at the beginning of words. On the other hand, the specification

+)RE(

would look for that letter combination either at the beginning, middle, or end of words, including remit, are, secret, and so on.

Identification Code

The investigator may also direct one or more of the specifications to check on information contained in the identification code associated with each sentence. These specifications are identified by the use of a slash mark (/). A two-digit number preceding the slash specifies a column of the identification code. The computer begins its check in that column. It looks for the sequence of characters indicated after the slash. Thus,

03/EJ4   causes the computer to look for "EJ4" beginning in column three of the identification code.

03/E   causes the computer to look just for an "E" in column three of the code.

Question Structure

Questions are written as a sequence of specifications without intervening spaces. The sentence must meet all the specifications in order to be matched. The last specification is followed by an equal sign (=) and a list of either one or more retrieval unit codes (Table 3.2) or the code X.

As might be expected, it takes the computer much longer to search the text of the sentence than it takes to check for the presence of a particular tag or check the identification code. Since the specifications within a question are tested from left to right, it is always a good idea to put the text specifications last. These will be actually tested only when all the specifications to the left have been successfully matched. For example,

$$+ 32 - 46 - 05/\text{z} - (\text{PEACE}) = \text{P4}$$

would only search the text for the absence of the word peace when tag 32 is found to occur, when tag 46 is not present, and when column 5 of the identification code does not contain a z. If the sentence also does not contain the word "peace," it is counted, printed, and written on tape unit #4.

Let us now examine some contingency strategies using these retrieval procedures. Optional comments may follow after a space.

1401 Contingency Strategies[20]

Combined Text and Tag References

Often an investigator will want to know how a particular reference is treated in the text he is studying. For example, a survey researcher, in assessing respondents' statements toward Medicare might want to make the following retrievals:

+ 41 + (MEDICARE) = P	BAD
+ 76 + (MEDICARE) = P	SIGN-REJECT

and then retrieve

+ 40 + (MEDICARE) = P	GOOD
+ 75 + (MEDICARE) = P	SIGN-ACCEPT

[20] Our examples in this section use the Harvard III Dictionary described in Chapter 4.

In the first case, the computer would search for sentences containing co-occurrences of the word Medicare with occurrences of tag categories BAD or SIGN-REJECT (tags 41 and 76), sending matching sentences to the printer. In the second case, sentences containing co-occurrences of Medicare with tags GOOD or SIGN-ACCEPT are sent to the printer. Upon completing each task, the computer prints the number of sentences retrieved.

Unless pronouns have been edited carefully, the researcher may be quite dissatisfied with the quality of his retrievals. For example, the sentence, "It will only cause trouble" would not be retrieved unless the pronoun "it" is edited as referring to Medicare.

Retrievals are often used to modify tag categories after the data have been tagged. For example, Dahlberg and Stone in Chapter 20 use the tag GUIDE to connote possible interpersonal structuring in the "future" autobiographies of Egyptian female students. However, since these students were studying to become teachers, the many references to teaching, teach, and educate were usually in direct connection with their intended vocation, and for Dahlberg's purposes were best separated from the other words and idioms in the GUIDE category. By making the retrieval specification

$$+ 45 - (\text{TEACH}(- (\text{EDUCAT}(= \text{P}$$

only those sentences to which the tag GUIDE (tag 45) was assigned, and those not containing words beginning with "teach" or "educat" were retrieved. While this modification somewhat reduced the differences in the GUIDE category scores between Egyptian girls and their Radcliffe comparison group, enough difference still remained to justify keeping the GUIDE tag as an important discriminator.

Retrievals to Tape Combined with Tag Tallies

Often an investigator will note that the counts for a certain tag are quite high and will want to explore further possible co-occurrences with this tag. For example, in the comparison of Egyptian and Radcliffe future autobiographies, references to MALE-ROLE were quite frequent in both groups, appearing in 14.8 percent of the Egyptian sentences and 12.1 percent of the Radcliffe sentences. Because the perception of the male figures is important to the syndrome being studied, the investigator looked further for tag co-occurrences. Sentences containing reference to MALE-ROLE but not FEMALE-ROLE were first separated onto another computer tape with the following retrieval question:

$$+ 04 - 05 = 2$$

(where tag 04 is MALE-ROLE and tag 05 is FEMALE-ROLE). A tag tally was then taken of the retrieved sentences. It was found that in the Egyptian girls' sentences containing MALE-ROLE there were more references to JOB-ROLE, SIGN-STRONG, SIGN-ACCEPT, HIGHER-STATUS, and RELIGION and less to SIGN-WEAK, PEER-STATUS, and WORK than in the sentences of their Radcliffe counterparts.

An evaluation of co-occurrence differences, however, requires that we go back to the original tag tallies to see if the co-occurrence scores are really different from what we would expect. In the subset of sentences containing MALE-ROLE, for example, the tag SIGN-WEAK occurs in 7.4 percent of the Radcliffe sentences, and only 2.4 percent of the Egyptian sentences. While this difference is dramatic, perhaps the tag SIGN-WEAK functions this way in the data as a whole. Looking at the subset of sentences containing MALE-ROLE has not added anything.

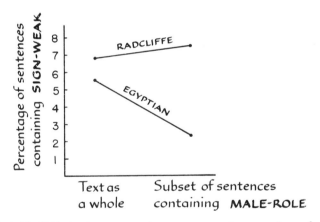

FIGURE 3.18. *Shift in frequency of* SIGN-WEAK *references for subset of sentences containing* MALE-ROLE.

In fact, SIGN-WEAK occurs in 6.9 percent of the total Radcliffe sentences and 5.6 percent of the total Egyptian sentences. By singling out co-occurrences, a shift has occurred as represented in Figure 3.18. We see that SIGN-WEAK does somewhat differentiate the two kinds of documents, but this difference is greatly heightened by considering the co-occurrence with MALE-ROLE. The main shift is a drop in the Egyptian count.

The combination of retrieval and tag tally operations in this way forms an important strategy for General Inquirer operations. As we shall see, it constitutes a means for carrying out the tree-building procedures to be described.

Printed Retrievals of Tag Combinations

In making tag tallies of the MALE-ROLE subset just described, it was noted that the tag WORK showed a considerable increase in discrimination. (In the total data, WORK (tag 51) is applied to 14.4 percent of the Egyptian sentences and 18.8 percent of the Radcliffe sentences, while in the MALE-ROLE subset, this shifts to 8.2 percent of the Egyptian sentences and 25.0 percent of the Radcliffe sentences.) What then is the context of this concern for MALE-ROLE and WORK? For the Radcliffe group, a retrieval on

$$+04 + 51 = \text{P} \quad (\text{MALE-ROLE and WORK})$$

shows considerable concern for working together with the husband,

> I will help my husband in his work.
>
> I will aid my husband in making reports.
>
> The task of my husband and I . . .

and for the husband's eventual success,

> My husband continued to sell his works
>
> My husband earned enough so . . .
>
> Suddenly my husband discovered a revolutionary new method of building suspension bridges.

The Egyptian students, in contrast, show more concern for the work of their brothers and future sons, emphasizing contributions to the country rather than personal or family gains:

> My son came back to devote his life for the service of his country, I hope that he will be a doctor in the army.
>
> . . . so that my work in medicine in the future world would have supplemented my brother's work.
>
> After my sons graduate, they will become men who are useful to their country through great service and profitable projects.

Often the investigator may want to specify syntax relationships in making retrievals of tag co-occurrences. For example, at one point, Paige, in the study of *Letters from Jenny* is concerned with the writer's perception of hostility in herself. By making the retrieval questions

$$+ 01s + 32v = P \text{ (SELF AS SUBJECT, ANGER AS VERB)}$$
$$+ 01s + 48v = P \text{ (SELF AS SUBJECT, ATTACK AS VERB)}$$

sentences are retrieved such as

However, I am not grumbling, not kicking, not wholly discouraged yet.

I despise him.

I fought and screamed and . . .

I kicked the stopper out with my left foot.

I rather resent my country woman's joyous appearance.

I have always resented Tennyson's, "Ring out the wild bells to the wild sky."

I should destroy the books.

I will try not to bother you too terribly with my little woes.

But I never deliberately planned to injure anyone.

I hated myself for doing it.

Similarly, sentences describing ATTACK as a verb and not SELF-REFERENCE as subject can be separately retrieved with the questions:

$$- 01s + 32v = P \text{ (SELF NOT AS SUBJECT, ANGER AS VERB)}$$
$$- 01s + 48v = P \text{ (SELF NOT AS SUBJECT, ATTACK AS VERB)}$$

yielding such sentences as

Why she thought to trap me into living with her.

If there is no other course open to you, then take the child to the sea and shove him in.

She dislikes me, has from the first moment.

Their little faces will haunt me as long as I live.

Then they got whacked (hit) to stop crying.

I reminded her that she had ruined the children.

It is not in his power to disappoint or hurt me, ever again.

But Ross would be angry and resent it terribly.

He will murder the chip or +

She will murder him.

The old uncle came along and protested.

She killed him morally and physically.

Who can fight fate?

For Jenny, anger and aggression are perceived in a number of different ways, the more violent forms of interpersonal attack being attributed more to other people. A recurring theme during a later part of Jenny's life was that her son's mistress killed her son (although he had died from natural causes). Statements of anger and aggression are indeed a characteristic of Jenny, especially attributed to women; yet beyond this, the statements take so many different forms that further generalizations are difficult to make.

As more specifications are added to a retrieval question, fewer sentences are retrieved. We often find that users at first tend to write extremely specific questions, only to find that the text contains very few instances of the exact kind of statement they have in mind. A better strategy is to write a set of questions that will pick up a number of different alternative forms in which a theme or idea might be expressed. The final check and selection can quickly be made by hand after the bulk of the sorting has been done by machine.

Printed retrievals often suggest further retrieval questions. Having looked at the results of one retrieval, the investigator may want to sharpen up his retrieval questions in order to avoid certain kinds of statements, or to broaden his questions (often by adding more questions) in order to pick up statements that he has perhaps missed. The danger remains, however, that such procedures are always *post hoc,* and the investigator may be shaping his procedures to fit the peculiarities of his sample.

Co-occurrences Using Identification Field Information

Often an investigator will want to pick out sentences that have a certain character in their identification field. For example, in research not reported in this book, S. Frisbie focused on transcripts of family interaction. Usually the document unit was the family discussion. For parts of her analysis, Frisbie needed to sort out and analyze separately the contributions of the father, mother, and child. Since the fourth character in the identification field indicated who was speaking, the questions,

$$+ 04/1 = 2 \qquad \text{(father)}$$
$$+ 04/2 = 3 \qquad \text{(mother)}$$
$$+ 04/3 = 4 \qquad \text{(child)}$$

sorted out the sentence onto separate tapes according to speaker. Further retrievals from these tapes would then represent a co-occurrence of speaker identification and the retrieval specification.

Occasionally, the investigator may be concerned with a co-occurrence within the identification field itself. Let us say Column 7 of Frisbie's identification field indicated the person *spoken to,* and the investigator was interested in separating all sentences of the father speaking to the mother. The retrieval

$$+ 04/1 + 07/2 = 2$$

would transfer all these sentences to tape 2.

Summary

We have considered a number of basic contingency procedures for exploring and testing data characteristics with the IBM 1401–1460 series machines. After describing the time-shared procedures, we will consider further contingency strategies that can be implemented on either the time-shared system or on the 1401–1460 series machines.

Before considering the additional time-shared procedures, the reader may want to review the summary flow chart (Figure 3.25) presented at the end of this chapter. At this point, we have already described all the basic operations of the General Inquirer. These are the tagging, text and tag listing, tag tally, and retrieval procedures. Together they form a self-contained system.

The Time-Shared Programs

The General Inquirer time-shared programs are designed to facilitate the comparison of two texts. The assumption is made that the investigator wants to develop an efficient set of rules that will enable him to effectively describe, in terms of tag assignments, the differences between two texts. Confronted with any sentence, the investigator, using these rules, should be able to identify the text to which the sentence belongs.

As discussed in Chapter 6, several standard statistical procedures based on separate tag distribution frequencies might be used for making such discriminations. Using stepwise multiple regression, a formula could be developed by the computer that would identify each sentence by the probability of certain tags occurring within it. The formula, however, usually considers the probability of each tag separately, and not information of co-occurrence.[21]

The potential importance of co-occurrence relationships within the sentence can be illustrated by a simple example. Say that the co-occurrences with the same sentence of LOWER-STATUS and GIVE or HIGHER-STATUS and RECEIVE both indicate that the message is from text A, but that the co-occurrences of LOWER-STATUS and RECEIVE or HIGHER-STATUS and GIVE indicate text B. Thus, knowing the over-all frequency counts for each text on the tags HIGHER-STATUS, LOWER-STATUS, GIVE, and RECEIVE is little help in identifying a particular sentence. The question is, What are the patterns of co-occurrence?

The time-shared procedures focus on co-occurrence patterns within sentences, using the tree-building procedure, described next, to regroup sentences according to whether or not certain tags are present. The data are transferred from magnetic tape to the time-shared computer disk at some time prior to the session at the typewriter. The investigator interacts with the computer and his data via the typewriter console and transmission line. In order to save disk space, only the tag descriptions, not the original text itself, are stored. Rather than print retrieved sentences, the computer types the document and sentence numbers, and the investigator can quickly look up sentences in the "text and tag listing." Because of the relatively slow typewriter speed, the programs do not print out tables of frequency counts but rather just print those tags and tag combinations that show a specified frequency relationship between the two texts.

The investigator begins by calling the content analysis program and specifying the names of the texts he wants to compare. Further commands will be presented in conjunction with the description of tree-building strategy. As in using the 1401 retrieval program, tags are referred to by number rather than by name; the number may be followed by a letter indicating syntax restriction.

[21] Co-occurrence information can be added as additional variables to multiple regression procedures; the problem, of course, is that a variable has to be added for each co-occurrence possibility that the investigator wants to consider. The number of variables soon becomes unwieldy.

Further Contingency Applications: Tree-Building Strategies[22]

As an example, let us compare the Radcliffe and Egyptian future autobiographies, using half the data to check our findings on the other half. We begin with ten future autobiographies from each source, totaling 1,221 Radcliffe sentences and 818 Egyptian sentences (the tendency of the Egyptians to write somewhat less is a rather efficient discriminator in itself).

From our previous sentence tag tally on the IBM 1401, we know that FEMALE-ROLE appears in many more Egyptian sentences than Radcliffe sentences, even though there are fewer Egyptian sentences in all. We might begin by asking that the data be divided according to whether FEMALE-ROLE is present. This division of the sentences is represented by the branch in Figure 3.19. The sentences on the left

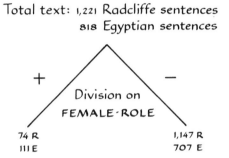

Total text: 1,221 Radcliffe sentences
818 Egyptian sentences

+   Division on   −
FEMALE-ROLE

74 R   1,147 R
111 E   707 E

FIGURE 3.19. Tree format of representation: Separating sentences containing reference to FEMALE-ROLE.

contain FEMALE-ROLE; those to the right do not. Seventy-four Radcliffe and 111 Egyptian sentences had been assigned FEMALE-ROLE; 1,147 Radcliffe and 707 Egyptian sentences had not. The time-shared computer will now ask whether we want to further divide those sentences containing FEMALE-ROLE. If not, we type QUIT, at which the computer turns its attention to those sentences *not* containing FEMALE-ROLE. Since we have been interested in the treatment of MALE-ROLE, let us divide the sentences on the basis of this frequently assigned tag, even though the MALE-ROLE tag counts in themselves are not dis-

[22] The tree-building techniques discussed in this section stem from work on inductive concept learning with E. B. Hunt at the University of California. Examples of the tree-building strategy applied to other kinds of problems as well as text discrimination is discussed in *Experiments in Induction* by Hunt, Marin, and Stone (1966).

criminating. This brings us to a second stage of the tree, shown in Figure 3.20.

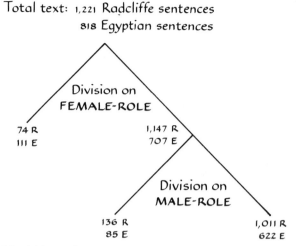

FIGURE 3.20. *Additional separation of sentences* not *containing* FEMALE-ROLE *according to presence of* MALE-ROLE.

Next, we might, from our previous 1401 example (page 115) divide the sentences containing MALE-ROLE (but not FEMALE-ROLE) according to whether they contain JOB-ROLE or SIGN-WEAK, thus yielding two more highly discriminating divisions: this is shown in Figure 3.21.

The investigator can continue to divide any branch of the tree until the numbers become so small that further division is unprofitable. Should he be dissatisfied with his work, he can condense back his most recent divisions or by a simple command start the tree over at the top. At this point, the divisions in our tree to the left of JOB-ROLE and SIGN-WEAK are probably best left as end points. The other branches remain to be further explored.

The commands and procedures for making these divisions are quite simple. If the investigator types "USE 34s" (tag 34, syntax as subject), then the division is directly made according to that specification. If the investigator instead types "TRY 34s," then the computer provides counts of how many sentences in each source contain tag 34 as subject without actually sorting the sentences. The computer program assumes that the investigator will build a tree from left to right. That is, after a branch is made, the computer shifts its attention to the sentences on the left until either there are no more sentences in our source or the investigator sends a QUIT message. The computer then moves its attention to the nearest branch to the right and starts dividing it, again working to the left. Tree building stops when the program runs out of sentences on the far right side.

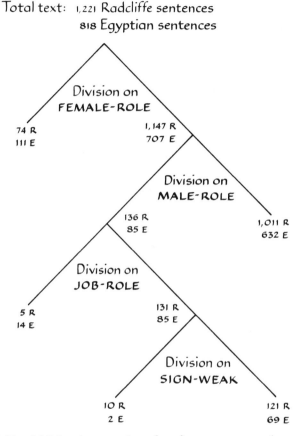

Total text: 1,221 Radcliffe sentences
818 Egyptian sentences

Division on
FEMALE-ROLE

74 R
111 E

1,147 R
707 E

Division on
MALE-ROLE

136 R
85 E

1,011 R
632 E

Division on
JOB-ROLE

5 R
14 E

131 R
85 E

Division on
SIGN-WEAK

10 R
2 E

121 R
69 E

FIGURE 3.21. Additional separations based on presence of JOB-ROLE *and* SIGN-WEAK.

Usually, of course, the investigator at the time-shared console will not be guided by the findings of previous 1401 retrieval and tag tally analyses of the data, but will want the time-shared computer to provide whatever information is needed to select an appropriate tag at each node. Some of the most important considerations in selecting tags are the following:

a. At this point in the tree, which tags are most relevant to the theoretical interests of the investigator? Thus, for example, in our example, MALE-ROLE was selected as a tag for dividing the data because of its high frequency and relevance to the syndrome being studied and not because it discriminated in itself.

b. Do we want to continue to build further branches to the left or do we want a tag that will terminate the left branch at this point? If further building is anticipated, then tags must be selected with high enough frequencies in both sources to make further divisions possible. If termination is preferred, then a highly discriminating tag may be chosen that will reduce the number of sentences in one source to near zero; JOB-ROLE and SIGN-WEAK are examples of this in our earlier tree.

c. What is the ratio between the two sources of sentences that do not contain the tag? With the sentences divided on the tag FEMALE-ROLE, what is the ratio to the right?

A number of options to meet these issues are provided by the time-shared system. If, for example, the investigator is interested in further branching to the left, he may want a listing of those tags that offer adequate frequencies. The typewriter command ORDERS plus a number will list all tags for which the sum of the counts from the two sources at this point in the tree is greater than a specified minimum. From such lists, the investigator can select a tag relevant to his theoretical interests.

Often the investigator will want a list of tags that offer further discrimination between the two sources than already exists at that point in the tree. Let us further consider the cluster of sentences containing FEMALE-ROLE. There are 74 Radcliffe and 111 Egyptian sentences at this point in the tree, making a ratio of 1:1.5, and enough sentences in each source to make further divisions feasible. Are there any additional tags that might be used for further branching to improve this discrimination ratio?

An immediate set of terminating tags at this point are those occurring in one source but not the other. All the some-none tags, as we call them, with at least five occurrences in the "some" source at this point are shown in Table 3.3. Each of these some-none tags could be used as a short terminal branch in a tree structure such as Figure 3.22. However, only a small amount of data is accounted for by each branch,

TABLE 3.3. "Some-None" Tags with Counts over Four in Sentences Containing Female-Role

Tag	Number of Radcliffe Sentences	Number of Egyptian Sentences
GUIDE as verb	0	9
ARTISTIC	0	6
FOLLOW as verb	0	6
SIGN-AUTHORITY as verb	0	6
LEGAL as subject	0	5

perhaps not enough to make inclusion worth while. Note, however, that most of the some-none tags in this case probably relate to a syndrome of interpersonal structuring.

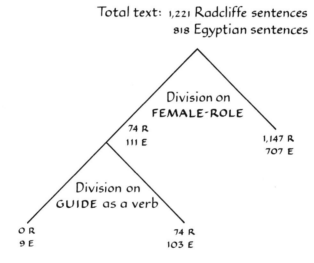

Total text: 1,221 Radcliffe sentences
818 Egyptian sentences

Division on
FEMALE-ROLE

74 R
111 E

1,147 R
707 E

Division on
GUIDE as a verb

0 R
9 E

74 R
103 E

FIGURE 3.22. Tree representation of "Some-None" terminal nodes.

Looking next at those tags that occur in both sources, we list in Table 3.4 all tags showing a ratio between sources greater than the initial difference of 1:1.5.

It is immediately evident that many of the more impressive ratios are based on small numbers, and thus are not very useful for tree branching. However, such tags as GUIDE, LOWER-STATUS as subject, LOWER-STATUS, SIGN-AUTHORITY, and MALE-ROLE each represent healthy discriminations with more than 20 sentences on the larger

TABLE 3.4. Tag Counts of Sentences Containing Female-Role which Show Ratios Greater than 1.50

Tag	Number of Radcliffe Sentences	Number of Egyptian Sentences	Ratio (larger over smaller)
LEGAL	1	9	9.00
GUIDE	3	22	7.33
SIGN-ACCEPT as verb	2	13	6.50
POLITICAL	3	17	5.66
ACTION-NORM	3	16	5.33
LOWER-STATUS as subject	8	40	5.00
OUGHT	4	19	4.75
MALE-ROLE as subject	3	14	4.67
NATURAL-WORLD	3	14	4.67
GOOD	4	18	4.50
APPROACH as verb	2	9	4.50
SIGN-AUTHORITY as subject	2	9	4.50
LOWER-STATUS	19	76	4.00
DISTRESS	4	1	4.00
FAMILY	7	2	3.50
SEX-THEME as verb	3	10	3.33
SIGN-AUTHORITY	9	28	3.11
MALE-ROLE	12	36	3.00
WORK as verb	11	4	2.75
URGE as verb	3	8	2.67
LARGE-GROUP	5	13	2.60
URGE	8	20	2.50
ACADEMIC as object	4	10	2.50
EQUAL	2	5	2.50
RECREATION	7	3	2.33
MESSAGE-FORM	4	9	2.25
SIGN-ACCEPT	12	25	2.08
GET	6	12	2.00
APPROACH	6	12	2.00
THINK	10	5	2.00
COMMUNICATE as verb	6	3	2.00
WORK	26	14	1.86
SIGN-ASCEND	19	35	1.84
OTHER	10	18	1.80
ACADEMIC as subject	4	7	1.80
ACADEMIC	15	27	1.75
SEX-THEME	9	15	1.66
IF	8	13	1.62

side; and considering their probable reference to interpersonal structuring, they are certainly suitable candidates for further branching.

Since there are more Egyptian sentences to begin with, most of the tags listed in Table 3.4 show larger numbers in the Egyptian column.

These tags, however, offer increased discriminating power at the expense of reducing the ratio between sources of sentences *not* containing that tag closer to one. For example, the tag LOWER-STATUS as subject branches the sentences as shown in Figure 3.23. The ratio of

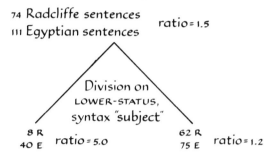

Total sentences containing **FEMALE-ROLE:**

74 Radcliffe sentences
111 Egyptian sentences   ratio = 1.5

Division on
LOWER-STATUS,
syntax "subject"

8 R   ratio = 5.0   62 R   ratio = 1.2
40 E   75 E

FIGURE 3.23. Division on LOWER-STATUS *as sentence subject.*

sentences having LOWER-STATUS increases from 1.5 to 5.0, but at the expense of lowering the ratio of sentences not containing LOWER-STATUS from 1.5 to 1.2. Occasionally, the investigator may want a branch point to function in this way, picking off extra Egyptian sentences obtained by the previous division on FEMALE-ROLE, leaving the remaining sentences with a ratio closer to 1 for further division work.

If, on the other hand, the investigator picks a tag with more Radcliffe sentences, the ratio on both sides is increased. The first example in Table 3.4 of a tag showing Radcliffe to have a worthwhile numerical advantage is WORK, which, being well down on the list, divides as follows in Figure 3.24.

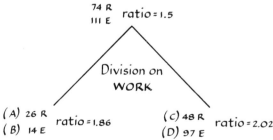

Total sentences containing **FEMALE-ROLE**

74 R   ratio = 1.5
111 E

Division on
WORK

(A) 26 R   ratio = 1.86   (c) 48 R   ratio = 2.02
(B) 14 E   (D) 97 E

FIGURE 3.24. Division on WORK.

In addition to the ratio used to order the tags in Figure 3.24, the time-sharing program is provided with an index that also considers the resulting ratio of sentences *not* containing the tag in question. If we assign the labels *A, B, C,* and *D,* as indicated in Figure 3.24, to the results of the branching operation, we can describe the new index as consisting of

$$J = \frac{A \times D}{B \times C}$$

The applications of this function to content analysis have been explored by J. Levine (1964, 1965)[23]. This index balances any gains made in the ratio of sentences containing a tag against any reduction in the ratio of sentences not containing a tag. A tag increasing the ratio on both sides (as in Figure 3.24) will receive additional weight, while a tag decreasing one of the ratios (as in Figure 3.23) is somewhat discounted. For example, the tag WORK, with more Radcliffe sentences, has an index of 3.75, while SIGN-ASCEND (the next tag in Table 3.4) with a similar difference magnitude but more Egyptian sentences has an index score of only 1.33.

If two tags in Table 3.4 have the same ratio in the same direction, the "J" index will pick the one having the larger numbers. This weighting away from ratios based on smaller numbers is a useful feature. To take another example from Table 3.4, the division on LOWER-STATUS as subject yields an index of 4.42, while POLITICAL, with a considerably higher ratio in the same direction but with fewer sentences, yields only 4.28. Still another index, namely the ratio multiplied by the absolute difference, has also been included in the time-shared program to offer even more weighting against small number differences.

Thus, the investigator at the time-shared typewriter has several commands available that will cause the tag counts at the tree node being considered to be ordered and printed according to a particular criterion based on size of frequencies, ratio of difference, or a combination of both. With each command, he must also give a cutoff value at which the listing should stop. After the tags are listed, he can divide the tree further by selecting a tag with adequate discrimination efficiency, adequate frequencies, and appropriate relevance to his theoretical interests and purposes at this point in the tree.

As still another strategy, the investigator can abandon the right to

---

[23] This function is the odds ratio and has a 1:1 correspondence to Yule's Q.

choose tags from a list and permit the computer to do the selection. The investigator first tells the computer that he wishes to make a LIST. He then types in the names of a series of tests and minimum parameters. The computer will then apply these tests in the order specified until it finds a tag that meets the associated minimum parameter. It then uses this for dividing a branch, announces the division on the typewriter, and automatically continues to the next branch and repeats the process. The investigator may stop the operation or make changes in the list of directions at any time.

Generally, we find that the automatic mode of operation can be counted on to make some interesting suggestions but will often select tags that are not of particular theoretical interest for that part of the tree. The automatic division process needs to be watched carefully so that it can be stopped when it goes off on a wrong track. A list of relevant tags could be put in at each stage of operation, with relative weights assigned, but this would be more work than letting the machine order tags and then manually pick one. The automatic mode of selection, at least in the immediate future, will continue to be an experimental feature rather than a basic procedure in content analysis.

While the time-shared system offers the convenience of computing indexes, all the basic reordering and counting necessary for growing trees can also be achieved by the IBM 1401–1460 retrieval and tag tally procedures. Any branch of a tree can be represented by a retrieval question. Thus, to go back to Figure 3.21, the question

$$-05 + 04 - 10 - 76 = \text{P2} \quad (\text{MINUS FEMALE-ROLE, PLUS MALE-ROLE, MINUS JOB-ROLE, PLUS SIGN-WEAK})$$

would send 121 Radcliffe and 69 Egyptian sentences to the printer and tape 2. A tag tally of the retrieved sentences on tape 2 would suggest possible tags for further division at this point in the tree.

No matter what procedures are used, when the work is completed the question remains whether an efficient tree has been produced. Could the same level of discrimination have been produced with fewer nodes and branches?

Several factors can greatly affect the efficiency of a tree. Some tags deferred to later in the tree might have functioned much more effectively if they had been used higher up in the tree. Tags that did not appear to have any discriminatory power in themselves, and

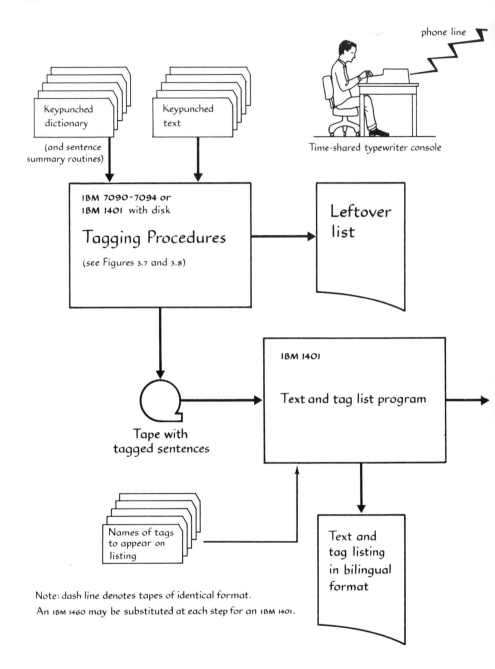

FIGURE 3.25. Summary representation

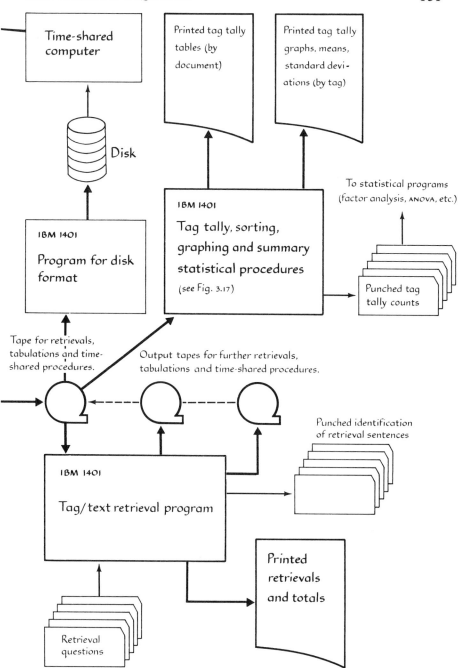

of General Inquirer System.

were thus not used, might have "unlocked" a number of powerful, discriminating co-occurrences. For example, MALE-ROLE in the Radcliffe-Egyptian data does not in itself discriminate; yet it is a high frequency tag and its use led to discriminating co-occurrences. Unfortunately, there is no simple rule for unraveling the most efficient tree. For the computer to try out all likely trees would take an immense amount of time.

Often, it is possible to come up with two equally efficient but completely different trees for describing the same data. Each tree may represent a different theoretical orientation, the branches of the tree representing difference co-occurrence themes. The principle of efficient discrimination often cannot in itself decide which tree best describes the data.

Tree building, like making retrievals, is usually a *post hoc* operation. Branches can be added to branches until the data run out. As unsuccessful strategies are discarded and new ones are tried, sooner or later a significant discrimination is bound to emerge. Investigators tend to forget about the discarded ventures and keep only the more profitable analyses. Incredible ingenuity can often be marshaled to weave a theory that explains the obtained tree. On the other hand, to be overly rigorous — to deny oneself the opportunity to be Sherlock Holmes, rapidly following up clues, uncovering new and exciting information as one proceeds, and changing analysis strategy as one comes to know the data better — would result in the loss of important insights.

We feel that the problem of *ex post facto* analysis is best met by putting a random half of the data aside and then using it to test if the findings still hold up. If a tree, for example, represents basic differences rather than idiosyncrasies in the sample, it should effectively discriminate the second data sample. Tree branches that make theoretical sense tend to hold up better on new data than tree branches that are hard to interpret. Tree branches based on relatively large numbers of sentences have generally proved to be more reliable in handling the new data sample than short "twigs" based on relatively small numbers.

We have here attempted to describe some of the basic issues and strategies of a tree-building approach. A presentation and discussion of several complete trees for one set of data would lengthen this discussion out of proportion. Examples of complete tree discriminations, based on several kinds of text, can be found in Hunt, Marin, and Stone (1966).

The tree-growing strategies, however, are intended to serve a broader set of needs than just mapping complete trees. A single complete tree tacks a particular sentence at the end of only one branch. The other tags in that sentence (and there may be many of them) are no longer considered in building further branches to the right of the tree. Instead of completing the entire tree, the investigator may want to allow sentences to play a part in a number of regroupings. He may want to focus primarily on branching to the left and start again at the top with new tags rather than extensively branch downward to the right. This restarting is easily done with either the time-shared or the 1401–1460 procedures.

Summary

We have presented the possible flows of General Inquirer analyses through a number of programs and computers. The over-all schematic representation shown in Figure 3.25 summarizes the relation of these steps. Unless otherwise indicated, information is stored on magnetic tape when the analysis process moves from one program to another. The ever-present investigator is able to work directly with his data at all stages and levels of analysis and is able to use the results at one stage in the scheme for planning his actions in another. All stages of the scheme attempt to represent the goals of explication, comparability, closeness to data, and ease of use outlined at the beginning of this chapter. There is no limit to the number of times the investigator can come back to his data, beginning, if he wishes, with a new dictionary at the upper-left corner of the scheme.

With this introduction to the system itself, we now turn to a closer examination of the crucial upper corner of Figure 3.25, the design and preparation of a dictionary.

CHAPTER FOUR

The Construction of Categories for Content Analysis Dictionaries[1]

INTRODUCTION

Over the last five years, a number of research groups and individual researchers using the General Inquirer have evolved dictionaries for use with the system. Some dictionaries have been constructed for a specific project and were employed only on data for that particular project. Others have been used again and again for a variety of projects and on a range of textual data. Consequently, a considerable amount of experience has accumulated about optimum methods of category and dictionary construction. In this chapter, we explore problems involved in constructing useful categories and assembling them within the framework of a dictionary. As emphasized in Chapter 1, no matter how sophisticated the method employed, content analysis stands or falls by the quality of its categories.

A content analysis category consists of a number of *language signs* (words, idioms, phrases, and so on) that together represent a variable in the investigator's theory. For example an investigator concerned with self-image may well be interested in identifying the number of self-references within documents written by different individuals, and so construct a category, SELF, composed of the following

---

[1] The main author of this chapter is Dexter C. Dunphy.

signs: I, me, mine, my, myself. The basic procedure in content analysis is to identify these signs when and if they occur in text as instances of a particular semantic category, scoring them as such.

However, the investigator seldom carries out a content analysis with a single semantic category. Instead, he is usually interested in examining relationships of a number of semantic categories as they appear within specific documents. Most content analysis studies therefore use a cluster of categories, referred to as a *content analysis dictionary*.

THE NATURE OF CONTENT ANALYSIS DICTIONARIES

A content analysis dictionary is similar to any dictionary in that it gives descriptions or meanings of words. However, it differs from a standard English language dictionary, such as Webster's, in that the meanings of words are given by a semantic classification indicating the relevance of the particular words to a social science theory being used by the investigator. Thus, a content analysis dictionary is a concrete representation of the investigator's theory as it relates to verbal data. It consists of an entry list of those words he wishes recognized, with the appropriate categorizations for each word. The first phase of a content analysis procedure is the application of a dictionary to verbal text, with the result that many characteristics within the text are translated into a new (social science) language of considerably smaller vocabulary. In this way, the large number of words occurring within the text are reduced to a few basic variables by a many-to-few mapping procedure.

The semantic classification aspect of a content analysis dictionary is its most distinctive attribute and one that makes its structure more analogous to a thesaurus, such as Roget's, than to a standard English language dictionary. A content analysis dictionary and a thesaurus both arrange words of similar meaning under conceptual headings so that the meaning of any word can be summarized by listing the headings under which it occurs.

Like *Roget's Thesaurus,* a content analysis dictionary can be listed in two forms, each of which has its uses. The main bulk of *Roget's Thesaurus* is composed of category lists; all words in a particular category are listed under it, as shown in Table 4.1 for the categories SELF and SELVES.

TABLE 4.1. Entries for Tags Self and Selves

SELF	SELVES
I	we
me	us
my	our
mine	ours
myself	ourselves

The other form is the alphabetical list of all entry words in the dictionary, with the categories to which they have been assigned. In Table 4.2, we give an example of a small section taken from an

TABLE 4.2. Comparison of Content Analysis Dictionary with Thesaurus and Standard Dictionary

Standard Dictionary (Webster)	Thesaurus (Roget)	Content Analysis Dictionary (Harvard III)
ache = 1. To have or give dull, steady pain 2. (colloq.), to yearn or long 3. n. a dull, continuous pain	ache = pain	ache = DISTRESS
achieve = 1. to do; do successfully; accomplish 2. to get or reach by exertion; attain, gain	achieve = end produce achieve accomplish	achieve = GET
achievement = 1. an achieving 2. a thing achieved, especially by skill, work, or courage; feat; exploit	achievement = sign feat	achievement = GET
acquaintance = 1. knowledge got from personal experience 2. knowledge (of a person) got by casual personal contact; less intimate than friendship 3. a person or persons whom one knows only slightly	acquaintance = knowledge information friend	acquaintance = COMMUNITY PEER-STATUS NEUTER-ROLE

alphabetical list. The example is arranged to compare the treatment of the same four words in Webster's, Roget's, and a content analysis dictionary (Harvard III).

As illustrated in Table 4.2, the definition of a specific entry word in a content analysis dictionary and a thesaurus is given in terms of one or more of a limited number of concept names. In contrast, an entry word in a standard dictionary is defined by synonyms or sentence explanations.

It is apparent that both the standard dictionary and the thesaurus definitions make clearer distinctions between syntactically variant meanings and between homographs than the content analysis dictionary. This limitation of existing content analysis dictionaries has been partially overcome in dictionaries more recent than the Harvard III, and we hope it will be fully overcome in the next year or so.

The two ways of listing dictionary entries, categorically and alphabetically, have different advantages. Listing by tag category makes it possible to receive an immediate impression of the meaning of a tag, which is specified by the entries appearing under it. On the other hand, if the investigator is interested in the meanings associated with a particular entry, it is easier to find it in an alphabetical list.

Specifying the concrete form of a dictionary is simpler than formulating the principles that the social scientist uses to construct content analysis dictionaries comprising a range of related and interdependent categories. Because it takes a form similar to a thesaurus, a content analysis dictionary shares with it the problem of arriving at the most useful set of conceptual headings (tags). Words, like other objects, can be classified in many different ways. If we have some lemons, some bananas, and some apples, we can classify the lemons and bananas together on the ground that they are yellow and the apples red; we can put the lemons and apples together on the ground that they are round and the bananas long; or we can put the apples and bananas together because they are sweet and the lemons sour. The number of possible classifications of words in a language on a semantic basis is infinite. If we wish to limit the number of classifications, it is important to consider the reasons for classification. In everyday life we make the kinds of classification that are most useful at the moment. In the example just given, we classify differently according to whether we wish to make an artistic arrangement of the fruit or select a dessert.

In devising categories for a dictionary, the social scientist works in the same way. He makes the kinds of classifications he believes will be most useful to him: those relevant to his theory and the hypotheses he wishes to test and those of practical use in analyzing the kinds of documents in which he is interested. In the classification of lemons, bananas, and apples, it is unlikely that a social science investigator would be interested in either an aesthetic or dietary classification; but he might consider these objects as instances of a more general class, *food,* which might be one indicator of, say, ORAL CONCERN. It is the choice of tag categories on the basis of their relevance to the theories and hypotheses of the investigator that most distinguishes a content analysis dictionary from either a regular thesaurus or dictionary.[2]

In fact, however, some of the categories may look very similar to those in a thesaurus, for a content analysis dictionary may use everyday denotative categories as semantic units. For our purposes, we may refer to such denotative categories as *natural language units* since they are everyday distinctions recognized across a language community. The category *male,* for example, is a natural one within the language, and there would be little disagreement among language users or linguists as to which of the following words belonged in it: ant, John, potato, moon, he, automobile, man, run, father. Natural language categories of this kind become social science variables when they are incorporated, singly or in combination, into a proposition concerning human behavior. Such a proposition states that a particular relationship exists between at least one such variable and at least one other behavioral variable which may or may not itself be another language category. Such propositions are parts of a more general theory, composed therefore of a set of interrelated propositions.

For example, the following statement is a social science proposition involving two natural language categories:

> In groups meeting for an academic year on Task A, *member identification with the group,* as indicated by the ratio of words tagged SELVES (we, us, ours, our, ourselves) to the words tagged SELF (I, me, my, mine, myself) increases significantly over group sessions.

In this proposition the social scientific variable is *member identification with the group.* This theoretical construct is operationally defined in terms of the ratio of two natural language categories, SELVES and SELF, and a relationship is postulated between this variable and stage in group evolution. This proposition could then be linked to others specifying, for example, a relationship between certain personality characteristics of members and differential rates of change in member identification with the group. This set of interrelated propo-

---

[2] From this point on, the word dictionary will refer to the content analysis dictionary unless otherwise specified.

sitions would then represent a theory concerning member identification with the group. Agreement among language users as to which words should be entered into a category is an adequate measure of denotative meaning. Another approach (discussed in Chapter 2) that may in the end yield similar results would be to analyze a sample of text, identifying grammatical classes and then examining words within those classes that appear in similar environments.

However, a content analyst may have good theoretical reasons for grouping together a number of signs that do not share similar environments, belong to the same grammatical class, or even belong to what language users would recognize as the same class. The ways of arriving at denotative meaning may be poor ways of arriving at connotative meaning. For example, all the following words are part of a more inferential category used in the Harvard III Dictionary called SIGN-AUTHORITY: responsibility, obedience, obey, regulation, law, duty, regulate, officer. To take a more extreme example, a psychoanalyst might establish a class of signs representing unconscious symbols of masculinity. In the case of emotions, values, cognition, or norms, the distinction between denotation and connotation is important. On the one hand, we may be interested in whether the writer is expressly aware of emotions in himself and others. On the other, we may be interested in signs, both direct and indirect, that connote emotional states of the writer. Similarly, we may need to distinguish between categories that denote how much reference is made to thinking and categories assessing how much thinking went into the making of the document.

Although connotative categories are more difficult to validate than denotative categories, they can legitimately be included in a content analysis dictionary provided they have theoretical relevance.

PROBLEMS OF DICTIONARY CONSTRUCTION

A content analysis dictionary is a collection of content analysis categories. It is not, however, simply a collection of *any* content analysis categories. Ideally, a dictionary is constructed with a view to testing one or more theories. The language relevant variables in these theories are clearly specified in terms of content categories, and (again ideally) the hypothesized relations between variables are also specified.

To our knowledge, 17 dictionaries have been developed for use with the General Inquirer. These dictionaries are not entirely independent since some of them have a number of categories in common.

TABLE 4.3. General Inquirer Dictionaries: Fall 1965

Harvard III Psychosociological Dictionary. A second revision of the Psychosociological Dictionary. The number of tags has been reduced from 164 to 83 in describing some 3,500 entries. The dictionary has been used with considerable success in a wide variety of studies.

Yale additions to Harvard III Dictionary. An additional 16 tags developed by Z. Namenwirth at Yale for the analysis of "prestige paper" editorials about the common market.

National Opinion Research Council Survey Research Dictionary. A dictionary roughly following the category scheme of the Harvard III Dictionary, making considerable adjustment for survey response language used by middle and lower class subjects. Contains over 500 idioms. Developed by Bruce Frisbie at the University of Chicago.

Psychoactive Drug Study Dictionary. Developed by T. Dinkel at the University of Chicago to delineate different modes of reaction of psilocybin, the dictionary builds upon the Harvard III Dictionary base.

Stanford Political Dictionary. Developed by Ole Holsti, this dictionary focuses on Osgood's three semantic differential dimensions: positive-negative, strong-weak, active-passive. Each dimension has tags for six levels of intensity, three for each pole. Additional tags are provided for classifying names and places in political documents.

Santa Fe Third Anthropological Dictionary. Developed by B. N. Colby at the Museum of New Mexico, this dictionary is for cross-cultural comparison of folktales and projective test materials. Originally centered on the Kluckhohn value categories and a number of specific concepts, the third version takes a more general framework.

Davis Alcohol Dictionary. Built by William Davis at Harvard for testing hypotheses concerning relations of themes in a world-wide sample of folktales to cultural uses of alcohol, the dictionary currently contains 99 tags, 3,600 entry words, some 90 idioms, and several "sentence summary" scoring routines.

McPherson Lobbying Dictionary. Developed by William McPherson for the study of lobbying communications, the design of the dictionary draws heavily on Parsonian theory. 38 tags are used in classifying some 2,400 words. This dictionary has also been used in the analysis of political acceptance speeches.

Lasswell Value Dictionary. A dictionary centered around the eight value categories outlined in Lasswell's and Kaplan's *Power and Society.* Developed by Z. Namenwirth and H. Lasswell at Yale University.

Who-Am-I Dictionary. Developed by B. McLaughlin at Harvard for analyzing multiple open-ended responses to the question, Who am I? The dictionary uses 30 tags in describing 3,000 entries, including about 50 idioms.

Simulmatics Dictionary. Developed by Stone and Dunphy in conjunction with the Simulmatics Corporation for the analysis of product and corporation images, the dictionary base contains some 70 tags for about 2,500 entries, including a number of idioms and sentence summary routines.

TABLE 4.3. (*continued*)

Need-Achievement Dictionary. Developed by D. Ogilvie and Mrs. L. Woodhead, the dictionary closely follows the hand-scoring directions outlined by D. C. McClelland for the scoring of "need-achievement" imagery in projective test materials. The dictionary has 25 tags, 1,200 entries, about 30 idioms, and a number of sentence-summary routines. A special set of scoring procedures is programmed to analyze the pattern across sentences and provide a net "need-achievement" score for each story. The computer scoring correlates well with hand-scoring methods.

Need-Affiliation Dictionary. Developed by J. Williamson at Harvard for scoring "need-affiliation" imagery in projective materials, the dictionary uses similar strategies to those employed in the Ogilvie and Woodhead procedure. The construction of this dictionary has pointed up the need for further theoretical clarifications concerning this topic. Further refinements can then follow.

Icarian Dictionary. Developed by D. Ogilvie and D. Dunphy at Harvard for measuring symbolism associated with the Icarian myth. Used in a number of personality and cross-cultural studies in relation to early father absence.

Tzotzil Humor Dictionary. A 2,500 word dictionary developed by V. R. Bricker to be used in analyzing Tzotzil humor texts. Tzotzil is a Maya Indian language spoken by the Zinacanteco's of Chiapas Highland, Mexico. The tags reflect themes important in Zinacanteco culture.

Gê Mythology Dictionary. Anthropological dictionary developed by Pierre Maranda at Harvard for the analysis of plot within Gê mythology. 2,000 words defined by 99 categories, based on Lévi-Strauss theory of the structure of myths.

Edinburgh Dictionary. Developed by T. Burns and Miss R. Johnson of the Department of Sociology at the University of Edinburgh for the analysis of case discussions by panels representing various professions. Contains numerous idioms.

But of the 17 listed in Table 4.3, each has at least ten distinctive categories of its own.[3]

Because category construction efforts for the General Inquirer have taken one or the other of two broad approaches, two kinds of dictionary are represented in Table 4.3. Some investigators have used the method for very specific research projects centering around the testing of hypotheses related to a restricted range of data. Such studies generally begin with a rather clear theory and very specific hypotheses derived from it. As a consequence, the resulting dictionary usually contains a limited number of tag categories which operationalize the

---

[3] Table 4.3 does not include earlier versions of current dictionaries, even though they are often quite different and in several cases have continued to be used for the sake of comparability with earlier findings. Also omitted are often rather extensive name-and-place dictionaries developed for different political studies by the Stanford group (Chapters 5 and 9). Most of the minor variants not listed have been based on a version of the Harvard Psychosociological Dictionary. In some studies, these categories are added by the use of alphabetic subscripts in editing the data.

variables in the theory, Co-occurrences between lower-order variables may well be prespecified for scoring particular images and themes that are anticipated. Since the number of variables is usually limited, the number of entry words in the dictionary also may be limited. Words irrelevant to the specific variables being measured will therefore be discarded in the tagging process. Because a dictionary of this kind is usually designed with specific text materials in mind and at least a sample available, the meanings that words will have can be fairly easily determined with key-word-in-context procedures, to be described later.

We have referred to dictionaries emerging from projects of this kind as *specific dictionaries*. The Need-Achievement Scoring System, described briefly at a later point in this chapter (and more fully in Chapter 5) is the most developed example of a dictionary of this kind. In this dictionary, 25 basic tag categories are supplemented with approximately 50 rules for scoring co-occurrences between tags in arriving at a summary evaluation as to whether a TAT story contains need-achievement imagery. Since only entry words relevant to achievement are listed in the dictionary, the evaluation is made without reference to many of the text words appearing in a particular document.

Social scientists who are more interested in operationalizing, developing, and testing a general theory have evolved a second line of approach. The approach has resulted in *general dictionaries*. Because the theory tends to be more inclusive, dictionaries of this kind usually incorporate a relatively large number of categories and are designed to anticipate a wide range of possible hypotheses to be derived by particular investigators. The larger number of variables generally makes the entry lists of such dictionaries more comprehensive. As a result, a higher proportion of text is covered in the tagging process. Because specific hypotheses cannot be anticipated, co-occurrence scoring for higher order units, such as images and themes, is usually not specified in the dictionary. Another difficulty in attempting general dictionaries arises from the variant meanings attributed to words in different subcultures. For certain types of studies, this results in a high proportion of errors from inappropriate tagging.

Two dictionaries in particular represent the second approach: the Harvard III Dictionary developed by Stone, Bales, Namenwirth, Ogilvie, Dunphy, McPherson, and others at Harvard (see Chapter 5) and the Santa Fe Anthropological Dictionary developed by Colby at the Museum of New Mexico in Santa Fe (see Chapter 20).

While these two approaches to dictionary construction are clearly discernible in the studies in Part II of this book, theoretically, at least, a number of dimensions are involved that need not necessarily be associated in this dichotomous way. A dictionary may use a small number of categories but attempt a wide text coverage. The Stanford Political Dictionary, for example, classifies a large entry list into only six evaluative categories derived from Osgood. Similarly, future general dictionaries may well incorporate thematic as well as tag scoring by prespecifying particular co-occurrences, in a manner similar to the current Need-Achievement Dictionary.

Considerable variation exists in the extent to which the 17 dictionaries represent a clear theory stated in propositional terms. Generally speaking, specific dictionaries are much more likely to do so, since large-scale social theories tend to be rather ill-defined. The state of social theory is such that it is often difficult to know exactly which variables are likely to have the most explanatory power in a given situation, and even more difficult to hypothesize beyond mere guessing the relationships that might hold between them. In such cases, the only reasonable approach is to conduct an exploratory study. As far as content analysis is concerned, this implies that the roster of social science variables specified as tags will be tentative, and relationships will be examined *ex post facto* rather than hypothesized in advance. One would hope, of course, that studies of this kind would lead to the formulation of specific propositions, the clarification of theory, and further testing on new data. In fact, one of the important functions of general dictionaries is to facilitate the process of operationalizing, testing, and refining broad social theories as they relate to verbal data. When a researcher is beginning to work on an area in which he wishes to originate rather than test hypotheses, he may find the measurements offered by a generalized dictionary very helpful. His results may in turn provide important information about the usefulness of categories in the dictionary, especially by indicating the extent to which individual tags represent homogeneous variables and by indicating empirical interrelationships of tags. Applications of the exploratory, hypothesis-generating type often lead to dictionary refinements.

Thus, the general character of the dictionary required by a research project is determined by the scope and definitional clarity of the theory employed by the investigator. These factors will have a direct effect on the number of tags, their level of abstraction, and the extent to which relationships between tags are specified in advance of data analysis for hypothesis testing or examined *ex post facto* for hypothesis generating. In this regard, it is instructive to compare how different dictionaries categorize a given content area. For example, one area relatively easy to discuss is pronouns and role designations. Let us compare four dictionaries:

In the Harvard III Dictionary, there are three categories that consist only of personal pronouns:

SELF: I, me, mine, my, myself
SELVES: we, us, our, ours, ourselves
OTHER: you, your, yours, yourself, yourselves

Masculine and feminine pronouns (he, she, and so on) are not given separate categories but are entered into MALE-ROLE and FEMALE-ROLE along with such sex-specific nouns as man, woman, husband, lover. Other role designations are put into either JOB-ROLE (lawyer, magician, mayor, merchant) or into NEUTER-ROLE, a category composed mainly of ascribed, non-sex-specific roles (adolescent, acquaintance, neighbor, foreigner, taxpayer, and so on). In addition, finer distinctions are obtained by a cross-cutting set of institutional and status references. For instance, "doctor" is MEDICAL, HIGHER-STATUS, and JOB-ROLE. There are twelve institutional categories: ACADEMIC, ARTISTIC, COMMUNITY, ECONOMIC, FAMILY, LEGAL, MEDICAL, MILITARY, POLITICAL, RECREATIONAL, RELIGIOUS, and TECHNOLOGICAL. Status is divided into HIGHER, PEER, and LOWER.

Colby's Santa Fe Anthropological Dictionary makes a parallel division of pronouns and nouns into SELF, SELVES, OTHER, SEX-FEMALE, and SEX-MALE. Since the dictionary is concerned with material from primitive, and hence less occupationally differentiated societies, there is no JOB-ROLE category. On the other hand, three categories are created for kinship concepts: KIN-AFFINAL (terms for husband, wife, in-laws), KIN-CONSANGUINEAL (lineal, collaterate, and nonnuclear family terms), and CHILDREN. The dictionary thus reflects the concern for kinship within anthropological theories.

The Stanford Political Dictionary is very much oriented to identifying the role positions and country of political figures, and is supplemented by separate dictionaries, specific to each study, for identifying proper names. For example, "Lyndon Johnson" might be tagged, HEAD, USA, DEMOCRAT. Subscripts or parenthetical comments are assigned to pronouns at the time of editing to assist in identifying referents intended, the pronoun itself not being of interest. Role names appearing in the text (president, clerk, dictator) are tagged according to their relative position on Osgood's three dimensions. For example, "dictator" might be tagged as $+++$NEGATIVE, $+++$STRONG, $++$ACTIVE.

The Need-Achievement Dictionary places no theoretical importance on pronouns and therefore does not consider them; role references are classified according to their status relative to achievement. POSITIVE ROLES include doctor, lawyer, banker, and so on.

It should be pointed out that even where there is correspondence between dictionaries in the names given to a category the entry words and idioms included in that category may differ. Thus, MALE-ROLE in the Harvard dictionary resembles, but is not identical to SEX-MALE in the Santa Fe dictionary. Comparisons made between such categories must recognize the different variables.

We have deliberately chosen a relatively simple area to use in comparing four different dictionaries. The words we have discussed relate to social roles, an area for which the social sciences have fairly well-developed categorization schemes. In addition, these words belonged to the grammatical classes — personal pronouns and nouns — which are linguistically less complex than are other classes — verbs, for instance. Categorization schemes in other areas become far more varied than this particular example indicates. The example does show that the number of social science concepts and their level of abstraction are derivative of the investigator's theory. This is particularly the case when the investigator is working at the hypothesis-testing stage with a well-defined theory, for it is here that the appropriate number of social science concepts and level of abstraction should be self-evident. In the case of Need-Achievement theory, for example, variables such as URGE and BLOCK are clearly specified in the theoretical model.

When the investigator is working in an hypothesis-generating mode, the necessity for including some variables is fairly obvious; but there may be a range of others that are conceptually vague and of dubious relevance. Theoretically, there is no limit on the number of tags that can be used, but we have found from our own and others' experience that it is confusing to work with more than 100 tags because the resulting frequency-count tables are overwhelming. Of course, this holds only where the tags are used as individual entities and are not incorporated in higher-order co-occurrence units such as themes and images. In the case of such procedures, one is concerned with the higher-order units rather than the individual tags of which they are composed.

One practical way to decide on the number of categories needed is to establish general levels of abstraction for clusters of variables. As stated before, the authors of a dictionary reduce a large number of words and idioms to a smaller number of categories. If too much reduction is made, a category may be too broad to be of much use. On the other hand, too little reduction will leave the categories too specific for an investigator's purposes. Consider, for example, the following categories in Figure 4.1, which represent one possible break-

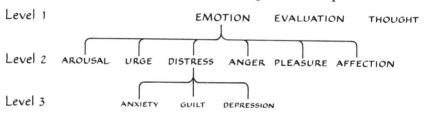

FIGURE 4.1. Levels of category abstraction.

down into different levels of abstraction in the area of words relating to emotion. It would be possible simply to have categories representing the level of EMOTION, EVALUATION, and THOUGHT, and let the matter go at that. However, the author of a general dictionary has the option of making finer distinctions such as those represented in Figure 4.1 at Level 2, or even the specificity represented by Level 3. Some spheres of a dictionary are often theoretically important enough to merit such detailed specification. For example, categories concerned with values, norms, action words, cognitions, and emotions may be especially important aspects of the investigator's theory. Those category areas that are usually of less interest to the behavioral scientist can be left more global. The decision as to what category level to use is important; nevertheless, a dictionary can be designed to allow the investigator some freedom to move up and down between category levels. Ramallo (Chapter 17), for example, contrasts a "thinking" versus "involvement" attitude expressed in reports from field volun-

teers. This is actually a higher level of abstraction than directly represented in the Harvard III Dictionary, which he uses; and it requires
merging of categories (see Figure 17.1). Conversely, occupations indicated by POSITIVE ACHIEVEMENT ROLES in the Need-Achievement
Dictionary roughly correspond to a more specific category represented
by intersection of JOB-ROLE and HIGHER-STATUS in the Harvard III
Dictionary.

The strategy of deliberately creating a category or categories with
subsections is relatively new, currently existing only in the Santa Fe
Anthropological Dictionary. It seems useful and will probably be used
heavily in future general dictionary construction. With this approach,
only one tag category level is tallied and appears in the tag tally tables.
However, if a certain tag looks sufficiently "frequency rich" to merit
further study, the investigator can ask for counts on its different subsections. Using this approach, we might decide, for example, to maintain only regular tag counts for a category called CONSUMABLE SUP-
PLIES. Whenever this count appears high enough, and if it is relevant
to the inferences being tested, we might look further into it, perhaps
obtaining counts for the subsection FOOD, perhaps within that obtaining counts for the subsections MEATS, VEGETABLES, FRUITS, and so
forth. By having the computer tally concurrently on many tag levels,
while keeping most of the lower levels out of sight, the investigator is
not bothered with unnecessary details but has access to more detailed
information when he wants it.

A major factor influencing the choice of a category level for a
general dictionary is the frequency with which the resulting category
would be applied in an average text from the target population of the
study. If an instance of a category is only assigned on the average of
once every 1,000 words of text, then it is best to move up to a higher
level. Most content analysis studies are done on rather small samples
of content. If a category is unlikely to appear, then its inclusion in
the study is useless and creates statistical problems by the inclusion
of zero cells in the tag tally matrixes. Thus the language characteristics
of the target population of the study affect the dictionary by establishing which theoretical distinctions will be meaningful in practice and
by affecting the assignment of entry words to particular tags on the
basis of their usage. We increasingly use samples of the text to be
analyzed in creating lists of entry words, determining the most appropriate definitions (on the basis of the usage exhibited in these

samples from documents of this particular language community), and checking whether the levels of abstraction of our tag categories are feasible. A dictionary is the product that emerges from the dual demands of theory on the one hand and concrete data on the other.

PROBLEMS OF CATEGORY CONSTRUCTION

Most of the dictionary revisions tend to be changes in category levels. An example appears in Figure 4.2, which considers changes

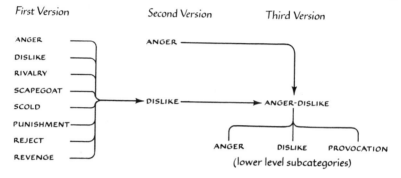

FIGURE 4.2. Successive category revision: Section of Santa Fe Anthropological Dictionary.

made by Colby in successive revisions of one section of his dictionary. The area of negative emotions was originally represented by a highly differentiated set of eight tags. Low counts on seven of these led to their merging in a single tag, DISLIKE, in the second dictionary, so that the whole negative-emotion area was represented by two tags rather than by eight. This yielded higher counts for the categories. But in the third dictionary, another solution was found by merging these two tags into a single tag with three subsections. Counts for each subsection could be examined if the total count was sufficiently high on the single higher-order tag.

Some categories with only a few signs have a very high average frequency and merit a place in a dictionary. For example, the SELF category, discussed on page 136 of this chapter, has only five entries but usually has a very high frequency of occurrence. The FOOD category in the Harvard III Dictionary contains a number of different entries, yet we find that food is so rarely mentioned in most kinds of text we study that the category is rarely of use. In addition, few social science theories are concerned with food; none of the specialized dictionaries, for example, include a category of this kind. On the other hand, food assumes an important place in primitive societies, so the Santa Fe Anthropological Dictionary categorizes a large range of terms for food.

Highly frequent words tend to be a source of considerable difficulty in constructing a general dictionary. Often their frequency counts will dominate an entire category; the counts on that category essentially become counts of one or two words. To make matters worse, such high-frequency words tend to be highly varied in their meanings. Lorge (1951) concludes from his compilation of the *American College Dictionary* that *"Most* of the words that occur with great frequency are words used in many different senses" (italics ours). Writers of a specialized dictionary can often anticipate the way these words will be used in the kind of language they are studying. The authors of a general dictionary have a more complicated problem. For example, words like "left" or "play" change their meanings depending upon their contexts.

One strategy used by Colby in constructing his dictionary is to ignore ambiguous, high-frequency words in favor of less frequent but more reliable indicators. There is considerable merit in this approach. We have learned from experience that certain high-frequency words like "get" or "go" should never be taken at face value and if defined should be given variant meanings based on context. High-frequency words of this kind can usually be correctly identified with idiom routines.

Occasionally, the author of a dictionary will want to provide special routines for a word, not because it is ambiguous but because it is often used in a special way. Two examples of this are the words "think" and "feel" in such expressions as "He thinks that . . ." or "I feel that. . . ." These attributive usages usually outweigh other uses of these two words as the main verbs in a sentence (for example, "I feel energetic"). The attributive uses occur so often that they will dominate the frequency of most categories in which they appear. It helps to provide routines that will identify attributive uses and handle them separately.

Another problem derives not from the fact that the same word form may have a number of meanings but from the nature of classificatory systems. The simplest classification system would be one that defined each entry word in terms of one tag and one tag only. It is questionable, however, whether this gives the best characterization of semantic meaning. The word "king," for example, carries the meanings male, social-role, high-status, political, and so on. The word usually means all these things, and all of them could be of theoretical importance from a social science point of view. It might be asked, why select one rather than all of these meanings? If all meanings are relevant to theoretical categories, why not classify "king" into all of them?

There are major advantages to be gained by avoiding multiple tagging of words or idioms. Applying a single tag avoids overlapping categories. The intercorrelations between categories do not then simply result from the fact that they share entry words and idioms. Contingency measures can be made, knowing that within-sentence co-occurrences will be represented by two different words, rather than by a shared word.

Even if categories do not have any entry words or idioms in common, this is not to say that the categories can be considered independent. As discussed in Chapters 6 and 7, the nature of language itself denies the possibility of complete independence. Research does not assume independence, but rather compares the extent of contingencies between different texts.

In the early versions of several dictionaries, multiple tagging often caused very high correlations between certain categories because of a few high-frequency words in common. Some correlations would remain greater than +.80 in study after study. There was little practical utility in maintaining such overlapping measures.

Our own current handling of the multiple-entry problem in the Harvard III Dictionary is designed to keep the user maximally aware of interrelationships due to overlapping categories. We make a distinction between what we call *first-order* and *second-order* tags. First-order tags represent our estimate of the most usual and explicit denotative meanings. Words and idioms are assigned to one and only one first-order tag category. Thus these categories are mutually exclusive in the sense that there is no overlap between them. In addition, as many second-order tags are assigned as are needed to complete the description. These categories are explicitly recognized to have considerable overlap, and the investigator must take this into account. In the Harvard III Dictionary, there are 57 first-order and 26 second-order tag categories.

Another approach to the solution of this problem of multiple tagging is adopted by the authors of the Stanford Political Dictionary. That dictionary uses, in the main, three dimensions, each with a positive and negative end and differing levels of intensity. Judges assign words to an intensity level on one or more of these dimensions.

The problem of reconciling the respective demands stemming from the nature of language and the requirements of analysis procedures is not really solved by such strategies. As yet, however, we have no clear alternative answer to offer.

A final issue that we shall consider in the construction of categories is the question of using dimensions. A number of dimensions such as good-bad, male-female, or abstract-concrete can prove to be highly useful categories. The question is how this technique can be extended. We find that the tendency to use dimensions has its dangers. Often one end of the dimension proves to be well defined, whereas the other end becomes more heterogeneous. Identifying words in terms of their contrast with other words can result in strange groupings. For example, higher-status is a fairly well defined sociological concept, referring to a rather useful set of ascribed and achieved roles. Its opposite, lower-status, is defined more in terms of lacking status qualities, rather than having qualities in common. In the Harvard III Dictionary, it includes all nonadults: babies, children, and adolescents. It also includes working members of the society, such as worker, clerk, servant. Finally it includes a number of deviant roles that are held in low esteem, including murderer, prostitute, witch, and spy. It is obvious that lower-status is a less unified category than higher-status.

In the following chapter, three dictionaries constructed from different perspectives for different purposes will be examined in detail. Before moving on to this, however, we shall discuss our latest methods for constructing categories and dictionaries. The reader may find this section useful in evaluating the dictionaries presented in the next chapter.

AN EMPIRICAL BASE FOR
DICTIONARY CONSTRUCTION [4]

The construction of a dictionary can be represented as involving two stages. In the first stage, the investigator must decide what kinds of categories are to be used, depending on the theoretical frame of reference under consideration. In the second stage, he must specify which words and idioms belong to particular categories. If similar categories exist in other dictionaries, the investigator can look to them to see what has been done before. However, if the category represents a relatively new concept, appropriate entries must be decided on.

Two questions must be asked in the second stage. First, how can one obtain a list of possible word and idiom entries for the category? Second, how is one to decide which entries to select? As discussed in Chapter 1, acquiring a list of entries is an empirical problem, requiring that words and idioms be culled out as they appear in the kinds of language usage to be studied. Once such a list is available, there are several possible aids to selection, as indicated in Chapter 2. If the categories are fairly denotative and the investigator has little difficulty in understanding how language is being used, he may be able to make the assignments himself. However, the categories may be quite connotative, and the question frequently may arise of whether a word or idiom really has a certain implication in a particular language subculture. In this case, the investigator may want a sample of people from that subculture to make semantic differential ratings, word associations, or other evaluations that test for the actual implications.

Most of our early dictionaries for the General Inquirer were intuitive products of a committee. Words from the Thorndike-Lorge count appearing with minimum frequency in the English language were put on cards for possible categorization. The committee members assigned those words to the categories that seemed most appropriate. Often there was some debate among members as to whether a particular word was appropriate for inclusion in a category. Occasionally *Webster's Dictionary,* the *American College Dictionary,* or *Roget's Thesaurus* was consulted. Unfortunately for our purposes, the standard dictionary lists only the alternative meanings of words; it

[4] The procedures described in this section are being developed by Louise Woodhead, together with Philip J. Stone, Dexter C. Dunphy, and Marshall S. Smith, under an NSF grant due completed by June 1967.

does not tell how much more predominant in which situations one meaning is over another. Further, a dictionary tends to be filled with specialized word usages; sorting out the really common meanings from the less common ones is tedious. We found that we could usually think of the common meanings ourselves, even if it was difficult to evaluate their relative frequency. Neither the standard dictionary nor the thesaurus was of much help.

In these initial efforts, the Thorndike-Lorge count itself proved somewhat inadequate even as an indication of frequency of usage. Heavily weighted toward such language sources as popular magazines and the Bible, it reports relatively high counts for words not particularly frequent in the kinds of text we were studying. Conversely, the Thorndike-Lorge list assigns deceptively low frequencies to words associated more with speech and informal writing. The counts on alternative word meanings used in constructing the *American College Dictionary* (1951) could have been an additional useful source of information for making category assignments, but it too suffers from the same sampling problems.

We thus used the Thorndike-Lorge list to help solve the problem of finding suitable entry words for category construction. We felt that at least the 3,000 most frequent words from this list should be included, but found it necessary to supplement these words with about 500 others that occurred with high frequency in the data we were analyzing.

As we pointed out earlier, the high-frequency words in the language are often homographs; that is, the same form carries alternative meanings in differing contexts. The early General Inquirer dictionaries handled alternative meaning problems in several different ways. Because the first Harvard Psychosociological Dictionary used highly connotative categories derived from psychoanalytic theory, it was decided to consider all relatively high-frequency meanings of a word, assigning a number of different tags for each occurrence. Our reasoning was that even though a word may have only one meaning in a particular context, it carries connotations of its other meanings, and these might be of assistance in identifying "deeper" interpretations. Since the reader is quick to focus on the intended meaning, having the computer label some of the "unintended" meanings might be of considerable use in making interpretations. As might seem obvious (things always seem obvious in retrospect), this strategy caused more confusion than insight. In subsequent revisions of the dictionary, while idiom procedures were yet to be written, we decided not to define a word with all its alternative meanings. Rather, when a word had multiple meanings, a judgment was made as to the most common usage, and this was attached as the only meaning recognized by the system. This single meaning was expressed in terms of one or a few tag names.

It should thus be emphasized that the assignment of tags to entry words for the dictionaries described here was done by an individual or a group of judges. In most cases, the judges did not work from an empirical base, showing how words are actually used, because data of this kind were not available. Instead they drew upon their collective experience as language users in deciding which meaning should be regarded as most common and which tags should be chosen to make the best representation of that meaning. If a word was felt to be particularly ambiguous, it was omitted.

At this point, therefore, we had two problems. We were knowingly working with an inadequate model of language which ignored the problem of multiple meaning; and in filling in the content of that model, we had to work intuitively instead of from empirical evidence about usage. We needed, first of all, ways of handling alternative meanings for words, and then appropriate language data organized so as to identify clearly the appearance and frequency of alternative word meanings.

Some dictionaries took advantage of syntax editing by assigning semantic meaning on the basis of grammatical usage. Thus the word "judge" marked as a verb would be tagged differently from "judge" as a noun. Similar distinctions were made for such words as force, project, court, dump, spring, watch, and associate. The drawback to this, of course, was that most data were not marked for syntax. Thus syntax-edited data were being tagged differently from data not syntax edited, making it difficult to compare tag frequencies across studies.

Another attempt to allow for more flexibility in assigning meanings took the form of *idiom routines*. Through these routines, it became possible to attach alternative meanings to a dictionary entry. A definition was selected on the basis of prespecified clues found in the immediate context of the word. As the name suggests, these routines were most useful for handling standard idioms, and their usefulness extended to certain classes of homographs. To find an entry list of idioms, we first consulted several of the existing published dictionaries of idioms. Although these lists were useful, once again we found that such dictionaries are too concerned with literary usage for our purposes. They do not list many of the idioms that are so much a part of common speech as to be unremarkable. Nevertheless the more frequently used idioms from these idiom dictionaries were incorporated into content analysis dictionaries. Using idiom dictionaries, we identified many more "literary" idioms but failed to include the more unremarkable ones important to a successful content analysis.

The basic problem remained that we had no catalog of what ways and how often words and idioms were being used in the kinds of languages we were studying. B. Frisbie (personal communication) of the National Opinion Research Center suggested that the problem might be handled for special dictionaries by running a sample of the keypunched data through key-word-in-context computer procedures. These programs print each occurrence of a word, together with the context of a few words that preceded and followed it. Words occurring in the document are listed alphabetically, in each case showing the different ways in which they were used. This strategy was first employed in constructing a specialized dictionary for analyzing product images (Chapter 22). A sample of the kinds of promotion material to be analyzed was keypunched and put through this program. Specialized word usages and idioms were quickly identified, and tagging errors made by the resulting dictionary were greatly reduced.

The success in using key-word-in-context procedures in the construction of a specialized dictionary suggested the possible advantages to be gained from preparing a similar listing of a sample of all keypunched text used in General Inquirer studies. Several lines of thinking converged to convince us of the usefulness of such a listing. First, it would provide a list of entry words with frequencies derived from the kinds of data we actually process (a replacement for the Thorndike-Lorge list). Second, it would similarly identify common idioms and their frequencies of occurrence. Third, it would provide an important data reference for constructing syntax procedures.

Our dictionary construction procedures have tended more and more to consider syntactic distinctions in making divisions between categories. The first Harvard Psychosociological Dictionary often grouped words of different syntax into the same tag category, but we found that such mixed categories often led to confusion, especially because we could not avoid many unwanted retrievals. In making the third revision, we tended to separate categories by syntax, especially nouns from verbs. Thus the category THINK (decide, interpret, resolve) is separated from THOUGHT-FORM (idea, scheme), COMMUNICATE is separated from MESSAGE-FORM, and so on. This process was taken even further with the Need-Achievement Dictionary. Such distinctions, however, do not resolve syntactic ambiguities. A rising interest in images and thematic analyses led us to consider working toward inclusion of the automatic syntax-scoring procedures which would facilitate this. In undertaking this major step, we have been encouraged by the conclusions of other users of the system, one of whom concluded a recent paper on the system with the following remarks:

> The hope then, in summation, is that greater efforts will be made to move away from the preformed categories made by researchers to the more basic research which still remains to be done concerning the actual usage of words, their frequencies of usage, the particular content of other words, situations and settings in which these usages occur, the peculiar idiomatic constructions which give different meanings to words and the serious adaptation by the content analyst of the subjective perspective of the actor so that the categories will be constructed in terms which reflect the actual usages and meanings made by speakers of the language. This latter point is one which requires more careful attention by the content analyst to his own assumptions of the everyday common sense meanings of words. He "cannot afford to rely on his own commonsense understanding" [Cicourel, p. 155] because he would then be unable to differentiate between what he can understand because of his own theoretical framework and what can be understood by "members of society; the users and the audience of the particular communication."
>
> (Psathas, 1965)

By late 1964, some six million words of text had been keypunched for various General Inquirer studies. A sample of about half a million words (510,976 to be exact) was drawn from 56 of the different available sources. The sources were divided into nine category areas, the amount of material included in each approximately representing the importance of that area in our past research. These areas include conversational material, personal documents, dreams, responses to survey research questions and TAT's, literary sources, editorials, speeches, and folktales. An example of the resulting key-word-in-con-

```
CUT HIM UP FOR US. AND THE EAGLE      BIT  A HOLE IN THE SKIN ON THE RUMP. THE       8L1 OMAHA
THIS SUMMER. I HAVE LEARNED QUITE A    BIT  ABOUT ETHIOPIA AND ITS PEOPLE BUT I        2K1 RAMALLO
MY HUSBAND. I HAVE WORRIED QUITE A     BIT  ABOUT HIS ILLNESS. I JUST HOPE THIS        4B2 FRISBIE DETROIT SAMPLE
MORE TO DRINK. I CAN TELL A LITTLE     BIT  ABOUT IT. THIS HERE GIRL, SHE WAS UP       5A2 HARTMAN DETROIT GANGS
IN THE SHOP WINDOWS NOT FEELING A      BIT  ALONE IN THIS STRANGE TOWN WHEN A          0B1 CHILDREN S DREAMS
VERY SOON AT THE TOP I FOUND A LEVEL   BIT  AND THEN A LAST RIDGE OVERLOOKING          6A3 T E LAWRENCE
THEY FINISH DANCING THEY ATE A LITTLE  BIT  AND WENT HOME. WELL THE MAN IS KIND        5G1 NAVAHO TATS
GROUP GOES. IN DOING THIS, HE SEEMS A  BIT  ANTAGONISTIC. AND, WHETHER HE HAS          2H3 SHAPIRO SMALL GROUP
OBJECT WHICH IS FILLING THE NEK AS     BIT  AS A MOUNTAIN THAT IS KHOLUMOLUMO.         8B1 BASUTO TALES
LIVE WITH IT., THE OLDER MAN SMILES A  BIT  AS HE REMEMBERS HIS OWN YOUTH, BUT         5D1 WILLIAMSON UNDERGRAD
REDICULOUS SPEAKING ABOUT IT A LITTLE  BIT  ASHAMED I GUESS BUT I DONT KNOW AND        1F1 JAFFE CASE
BUT I/8P FIGURE/9 IT MIGHT BE LITTLE   BIT  BETTER IF HE/1C GOT/3 OUT AND MET/3        1G4 MILLS
I KNOW ARE THE ONES INFLUENCED QUITE A BIT  BY WHAT I SAY. -UH -HUH. AND I             1A1 FAM INTERACTION FRISBIE
A RESPONSIBLE PERSON + A LITTLE 2O191  BIT  COCKY + LOYAL TO MY FRIENDS + A PLAY       9C2 WHO AM I
TO THEM. THE OTHER THREE MEN ARE A     BIT  CONCERNED WITH WHAT IS BEING TOLD          5F2 N ACH TAT
ADDITIONS TO THE GROUP. I AM A         BIT  DISAPPOINTED THAT THERE IS NOT MORE        2K4 RAMALLO
SURREALISTIC HE SEEMED HE LOOKED A     BIT  DISTORTED POSSIBLY WITH HIS EYES IN        2E3 PSILOCYBIN
THE FOOD YOU ARE GIVING ME. I FEEL A   BIT  DOWN WITH A COUGH I SAID. YOU SEE AH       0A3 ZINACANTAN DREAMS
OF ANY READER WHO MAY HAVE FELT A      BIT  FRAYED AROUND THE EDGES AT ONE TIME        7F1 CITIZEN S COUNCIL
SLIPPING THROUGH THE UNIVERSE WAS A    BIT  FRIGHTENING OR RATHER TENSION              2E3 PSILOCYBIN
THE GRATING SOUNDS OF OX CARTS, ALL A  BIT  FRIGHTENING TO ONE WHO HAD JUST LEFT       2D3 PEACE CORPS
COOKING AND CLEANING FOR US. I FEEL A  BIT  FUNNY ABOUT THIS AS I HAVE NEVER           2K4 RAMALLO
THINGS BROUGHT OUT THIS WEEK WENT A    BIT  FURTHER IN FORMULATING THE OPINION         2F1 CLEVELAND DIALOGUES
OF COURSE IT/1 (SPECULATION) IS A      BIT  FUTILE/1, BUT PERHAPS INTERESTING/1.       2C5 RADCLIFFE EGYPT
GOOD. SOME OF THE AFRICAN FOOD IS A    BIT  HARD TO GET USED TO BUT THE MORE I         2K4 RAMALLO
I AM UNHAPPY IT SEEMS. I LIKE IT A     BIT  HE SAID. WHY HE WAS ASKED. AH             0A2 ZINACANTAN DREAMS
PLAYING WITH HIS DOG WHEN THE ANIMAL   BIT  HIM ON THE WRIST. THE CUT BLED             0B2 CHILDREN S DREAMS
VERY CLOSE TO THE LITTLE BOY THE BOY   BIT  HIS (SAINT MICHAEL S) THUMB AND            0B1 CHILDREN S DREAMS
,KIND SIR,. BOYS WHO WERE PERHAPS A    BIT  INTIMIDATED BY THE MERE PRESENCE OF        2D3 PEACE CORPS
RIGHTNESS OF THIS. I BEGAN TO SEE A    BIT  INTO THE FUTURE. I UNDERSTOOD THAT I       2E2 PSILOCYBIN
MY HEALTH HAS BEEN WORRYING ME QUITE A BIT  LATELY. I HAVE BEEN WANTING                4B3 FRISBIE DETROIT SAMPLE
STATES A BIT MORE DOMESTIC HELP, AH WAIT A BIT LESS OF OTHER CONVENIENCES, BUT NOT     2D5 PEACE CORPS
TOO MUCH ALREADY HE SAID. AH WAIT A    BIT  LET ME FINISH SPLITTING MY WOOD HE         8A1 ZINACANTAN FOLK
NOT LOVE ME + A GOOF OFF AT TIMES + A  BIT  LOST + I AM. THE LAST TIME I SAW           9C4 WHO AM I
WITH LIFE IN THE UNITED STATES A       BIT  MORE DOMESTIC HELP, A BIT LESS OF          2D5 PEACE CORPS
ENOUGH SHE SAID I MUST ADD A LITTLE    BIT  MORE SO THAT THE BAG CAN BE FASTENED       8J1 KIKUYU
NEW/1 YORKERS/1, + HOWEVER, (CHANGE) A BIT  MORE/1 BUSTLE/1 ONCE/4 IN/4 A              4D4 MASTERS NEW CASTLE
SPRING WAS BEAUTIFUL IT WAS NOT A      BIT  MUDDY. ALL THE FECES CAME OFF MY           0A1 ZINACANTAN DREAMS
HOURS. I MUST SAY I FIND DOING THESE A BIT  OF A NUISANCE SINCE I WRITE THE SAME       2K4 RAMALLO
DO IF WE HAD BETTER FINANCES. IT IS A  BIT  OF A SMALL PROBLEM WITH THE CHILDREN       4B3 FRISBIE DETROIT SAMPLE
I HAD THE TIME AT SCHOOL) ACTRESS + A  BIT  OF A SNOB + A LOVER OF SHAKESPEARE,        9D2 ALYMER SENT COMP
HAVING READ THE PAPERS HAVE A LITTLE   BIT  OF ACQUAINTANCE WITH WHAT IS GOING         1A1 FAM INTERACTION FRISBIE
I DID OR THOUGHT MADE THE SLIGHTEST    BIT  OF DIFFERENCE. I WOULD HAVE GIVEN          2E2 PSILOCYBIN
WE NEED THE CAR AND IT NEEDS QUITE A   BIT  OF FIXING. SICKNESS. I AM AFRAID I         4B1 FRISBIE DETROIT SAMPLE
FOR THE MOST PART. WE DID HAVE A       BIT  OF FRUSTRATION WHEN WE HAD TO SIT          2K1 RAMALLO
```

FIGURE 4.3. Sample of Key Word in Context: Bit.

text appears in Figures 4.3 and 4.4. Figure 4.3 shows listings for the word "bit," Figure 4.4 for the word "play."

At the end of the listing for each word (not shown in the illustration), a number of summary statistics are provided. These include the number of listings and the number of the nine different areas which are represented. The word "coyote," for example, occurs 127 times in the listing but is drawn exclusively from the area of folktales.

On an intuitive basis, a word such as "bit" can take a variety of meanings. Our early dictionaries assumed the predominant meaning was "a piece of," but a number of other meanings were certainly possible:

> Try a *bit* harder. Please give me a *bit* of that. There is no *bit* in the carpenter's shop. In communication theory, the unit of information is the *bit*. He *bit* a piece out of the apple. The horse dug into his *bit*. He gave the boy *two bits*.

The key-word-in-context listing shows that the meaning of "somewhat" (as in "bit of a nuisance") is actually much more frequent than the meaning of "piece" (as in a "bit of gold"). References to the act of biting occur occasionally ("Buzzard bit off a piece of fat," "He bit the lids") but appear to be easily identified as a verb use. The senses of the word "bit" as it is used in carpentry, information theory, or in the sense of a horse's bit do not occur at all and thus could well be ignored in a general dictionary without much risk of error. Some examples reflect a particular dialect, such as, "We are quite a bit on family outings," "He started thinking about the crime bit again," or "Throwing a bit of a liquor party." Information on dialect differences in meaning (for example, how much is "a bit of") might require obtaining further interviews from members of the subculture.

The availability of the key-word-in-context listing for this sample completely changes the situation for the person attempting to write a dictionary. Rather than guess how the word "bit" is to be used, he has information on how many times per half million words the word is used in a particular way for this kind of data. He can avoid word meanings occurring too rarely to be of importance and can locate and evaluate idiom, syntax, and other signs to aid in identifying the correct meaning.

Much has been written on the importance of considering context in

Left Context		Right Context	Code
A VIOLINIST OF THE HIGHEST CALIBRE	PLAY	A CONCERTO. JIMMY HAS BEEN TAKING	5C1 WILLIAMSON UNDERGRAD
IN HIS ROOM, HE WOULD HALF-HEARTEDLY	PLAY	A FEW SCALES, AND THEN WOULD PUT	5D1 WILLIAMSON UNDERGRAD
LEADERSHIP, THAT SCOTT WILL PROBABLY	PLAY	A LARGER ROLE IN THIS AREA, AND	2H4 SHAPIRO SMALL GROUP
BEST BUDDY. ..HOW ABOUT COMING OVER TO	PLAY	A LITTLE BALL... HIS FRIEND	5D1 WILLIAMSON UNDERGRAD
WHILE HE IS YOUNG HE SHOULD LEARN TO	PLAY	A MUSICAL INSTRUMENT, THE VIOLIN.	5D1 WILLIAMSON UNDERGRAD
A GREAT DEAL TO US) COULD CONCEIVABLY	PLAY	A SIGNIFICANT PART. IT SURPRISES ME	2H5 SHAPIRO SMALL GROUP
AN AIR OF DISDAIN. HOW CAN HE POSSIBLY	PLAY	A SOLO IN THE CONCERT TOMORROW	5C1 WILLIAMSON UNDERGRAD
COME TO PLAY A TUNE I HAVE COME TO	PLAY	A SONG. WILL YOU GIVE ME YOUR	OA3 ZINACANTAN DREAMS
MIGUELITO HOW ARE YOU. I HAVE COME TO	PLAY	A TUNE I HAVE COME TO PLAY A SONG.	OA3 ZINACANTAN DREAMS
A VIOLIN, HE WANTED TO LEARN HOW TO	PLAY	A VIOLIN. GO TO THE NEXT ONE$ HE	5A1 HARTMAN DETROIT GANGS
SEEM, YOU KNOW, ENCOURAGED ENOUGH TO	PLAY	AN INSTRUMENT AND I DO NOT THINK HE	5A1 HARTMAN DETROIT GANGS
PARENTS HAVE DECIDED THAT HE SHOULD	PLAY	AN INSTRUMENT, AND HAVE BOUGHT HIM	5D1 WILLIAMSON UNDERGRAD
WELL GROWN THEY USED TO GO OUTSIDE TO	PLAY	AND HAVE FRESH AIR. THEY WENT ON IN	8J1 KIKUYU
THINGS, THE CHILDREN WOULD ASK HER TO	PLAY	AND THAT IF SHE SEES THAT IT IS	1A1 FAM INTERACTION FRISBIE
BOY. WHEN I WAS DOWN SOUTH, I USED TO	PLAY	AND THEN I WOULD GET MAD AND GO IN	5A2 HARTMAN DETROIT GANGS
WE WANTED SOMETHING, AND SO WE WOULD	PLAY	AND THROW BOXES ALL OVER THE ROOM,	5A2 HARTMAN DETROIT GANGS
I-VE DECIDED TO TAKE YOUR OFFER AND	PLAY	AT THE ,,POPS,, TONIGHT. HOW MUCH	5D1 WILLIAMSON UNDERGRAD
YOU SEE I WILL BE BACK I AM GOING TO	PLAY	AT THE HOUSE OF OUR FRIEND MANVEL	OA3 ZINACANTAN DREAMS
AND SCOLD HIM AND TELL HIM HE CANNOT	PLAY	BALL AT ALL TODAY SINCE HE DID NOT	5C1 WILLIAMSON UNDERGRAD
IS A NICE SPRING DAY AND HE WANTED TO	PLAY	BALL, INSTEAD. HE IS NOW TRYING TO	5D1 WILLIAMSON UNDERGRAD
CONSOLE HIMSELF BY GOING OUT TO	PLAY	BALL, AND RESIGNEDLY RETURN TO	5F1 N ACH TAT
HE IS IN THE ATTIC, WATCHING SOME BOYS	PLAY	BASEBALL ON THE OPPOSITE HILL. HE	5D1 WILLIAMSON UNDERGRAD
I GO AROUND THERE WITH MY FRIENDS AND	PLAY	BASKETBALL ALL THE TIME. THAT IS	5A2 HARTMAN DETROIT GANGS
AFRICANS IN BASKETBALL, AND I OFTEN	PLAY	BASKETBALL WITH THE LEBANESE.	2C2 PEACE CORPS
WORK AND SO THEN I GOES DOWN THERE AND	PLAY	BASKETBALL, BECAUSE THAT HELP FIND	5A2 HARTMAN DETROIT GANGS
BIT COCKY + LOYAL TO MY FRIENDS + A	PLAY	BOY + LENIENT TOWARD SOCIAL 20191	9C2 WHO AM I
HE GREW A LITTLE BIGGER HE LEARNED TO	PLAY	BY HIMSELF AND WHEN HE GOT BIGGER	5G2 NAVAHO TATS
HAD TO SIT THERE AND LET THE PIANO	PLAY	BY ITSELF. HE WAS IN SCHOOL AND THE	OB2 CHILDREN S DREAMS
IN THE EVENINGS WE TALK, WRITE,	PLAY	CARDS OR SCRABBLE. WE HAVE A NEW	2K1 RAMALLO
(THAT HE/5C HAS ROBBED/5 HIS FATHER).	PLAY	EENY MEENY MINEY MO$ WE/1 HAVE/3	1G1 MILLS
BE THAT IN SIX OR SEVEN YEARS HE WILL	PLAY	FAIRLY WELL AND BE EXTREMELY	5D1 WILLIAMSON UNDERGRAD
OURS THOU WHO ARE IN MAPANAL. DO NOT	PLAY	FALSE BUT TURN THOU SOON ASIDE.	8E1 IFUGAO
JUNIOR YEAR + ON THE HOUSE COMMITTEE +	PLAY	FOOTBALL + PLAY TENNIS + ENJOY	9C4 WHO AM I
I SELDOM PLAY I DONT KNOW AND I PLAY I	PLAY	FOR MY OWN NO I CANT NOW I LEARNED	1F1 JAFFE CASE
I WAS ON THE PITCHING MOUND. I	PLAY	FOR THE DETROIT TIGERS. WELL, I	5A1 HARTMAN DETROIT GANGS
TWO TO TWELVE. WE COMB THEIR HAIR,	PLAY	GAMES WITH THEM, SEW CLOTHES FOR	2C5 PEACE CORPS
TO TALK WITH THEM, SHOW AND	PLAY	GAMES, SING AND WATCH THEIR FACES	2K2 RAMALLO
OBSERVE THE RITUAL PROHIBITIONS. THEY	PLAY	GONGS AND DANCE. ON THE EIGHTH DAY	8E1 IFUGAO
WE WILL GET SUGAR CANE TODAY. THEY	PLAY	GONGS FOR THE SUGAR CANE. THEY CUT	8E1 IFUGAO
WENT STRAIGHT TO MWENENDEGAS HOUSE TO	PLAY	HAVOC. A LONG BLAST FROM A HORN WAS	8J1 KIKUYU
MIGUEL HE SAID. NOW BASTARD LET US	PLAY	HE SAID. TAKE OFF YOUR CLOTHES WE	OA1 ZINACANTAN DREAMS
TO HIS WOMANS HOUSE HE WOULD COME TO	PLAY	HIS GUITAR. WELL NO THE OLD MAN	8A1 ZINACANTAN FOLK
EVEN LEARN THE PIANO AND I I SELDOM	PLAY	I DONT KNOW AND I PLAY I PLAY FOR	1F1 JAFFE CASE
I I SELDOM PLAY I DONT KNOW AND I	PLAY	I PLAY FOR MY OWN NO I CANT NOW I	1F1 JAFFE CASE
AND SADDLES. THAT WAS OUR GREATEST	PLAY	IN OUR VILLAGE IN BASUTOLAND. THE	5B1 SUZMAN SOUTH AFRICAN

FIGURE 4.4. Sample of Key Word in Context: Play.

order to achieve correct word identification. Writers have generally assumed that the context unit needed is rather large. People about to use the General Inquirer often have reservations about working with the sentence as a major context unit. Yet in our use of the key-word-in-context procedure, we have found that the amount of context needed to make correct category assignments is surprisingly small, usually much less than the line provided by the context program.

A major exception to the general requirement of "small context" is pronouns. Such words as "it" or "they" tend to be used ambiguously. This ambiguity is often ignored in casual communication, but a closer examination of the text shows that one must guess what the pronoun really refers to from among several alternatives. A valuable addition to the dictionary would be a routine to assign, where possible, the correct referent to each pronoun occurrence. The context for other words, then, would consist not only of the pronoun but of its referent, even if it appeared in a previous sentence.

Apart from pronouns, then, even such an unusually ambiguous word as "play" can be identified with only a few words of context. Of the 176 occurrences of the word in our sample (Figure 4.4), only a few such as the following still remain ambiguous with the context provided.

> . . . BE THAT IN SIX OR SEVEN YEARS, HE WILL *play* FAIRLY WELL AND BE EXTREMELY . . .
>
> . . . I SELDOM PLAY I DONT KNOW AND I *play* I *play* FOR MY OWN NO I CANT NO I LEARNED . . .
>
> . . . MIGUEL HE SAID, NOW BASTARD LET US *play* HE SAID. TAKE OFF YOUR CLOTHES WE . . .
>
> . . . AND SADDLES. THAT WAS OUR GREATEST *play* IN OUR VILLAGE IN BASUTO LAND. THE
>
> . . . TO TALK AT THAT HOUSE WHERE HE WENT TO *play*. SENOR SAN MIGUELITO HOW ARE YOU . . .

While such cases of ambiguity may be of interest to the linguist, the important fact for the content analyst is that some 95 percent of the occurrences of even such an extreme example as "play" can be correctly identified with only a few words of context. For most words, all occurrences can be identified accurately.

Future Procedures

From the key-word-in-context listings, it becomes quite apparent that the correct assignment of words to categories will frequently draw on the following routines:

Idiom Procedures

As used in reference to the General Inquirer, an idiom is any clue to word meaning based on the presence of another word or tag category within a specified number of words in the text. For example, the idiom "break down" or "break up" can be used as a verb and be quite different from the use of "break" as in "If we break a bowl. . . ." The idiom in this sense remains the workhorse of context identification, providing essential, yet quick and simple, distinctions in word meaning where needed.

Syntax Rules

When the General Inquirer was first constructed, a number of persons maintained that a reliable, comprehensive syntax analysis by computer was too complex to be considered. Rather than venture upon these uncharted waters ourselves, we decided to use hand syntax coding where needed and wait to see the outcome of ongoing research on computer procedures. Since then, Kuno (1965), Salton (1965), Robinson (1965), Stolz, Tannenbaum, and Carstensen (1964), and others have shown that such a system is feasible. Kuno's syntactic analysis system for the IBM 7094 is the most comprehensive we know of to date.[4]

Many early attempts at automatic syntactic analysis were limited in their success partly because they tried to get by with small dictionaries. For words not in the dictionary, suffix endings such as "ly," "ment," and so on as well as contextual position were used to make syntactic assignments. If, however, a large dictionary had been available, the less frequent and syntactically more stable words could have been identified and used to provide contexts for identifying less stable and usually more frequent words. Stolz, Tannenbaum, and Carstensen (1964), for example, in their use of a moderate-sized dictionary, achieved considerable success at syntactic identification with relatively simple pro-

---

[4] Philip Stone has continued to keep in touch with the development of these procedures.

cedures. In analyzing erroneous classifications made by the machine, they found that the largest single source of improvement would be simply having a larger dictionary.

We are now experimenting with a set of syntactic procedures to be used in conjunction with future dictionaries. Tentative syntactic assignments can be made part of the dictionary lookup, a final selection of syntax being based on the pattern of sentences. Table 4.4 demon-

TABLE 4.4. Sample Syntax Assignments

a. Possible syntax categories assigned by dictionary				
the	dress	pattern	was	ugly
article	noun or verb	noun or verb	verb	adjective
b. Probable syntax structure selected by computer rules				
THE	DRESS	PATTERN	WAS	UGLY
ARTICLE	NOUN	NOUN	VERB	ADJECTIVE

strates the syntax assignments that the dictionary might make for the sentence, "The dress pattern was ugly." These assignments would then determine the most probable structure, which in turn would be used in making a final selection of tags:

THE (ARTICLE) DRESS (NOUN/CLOTHING) PATTERN (NOUN/ FORM) WAS (VERB/EQUAL PAST) UGLY (ADJ/BAD ARTISTIC SIGN- REJECT).

Thus, we could readily identify this sentence as an evaluation, phrased in the past tense, concerned with a clothing form and offering a negative aesthetic evaluation.

The syntactic analysis programs for assigning correct word meanings usually need only consider relatively simple distinctions, such as the noun "mind" distinguished from the verb "mind," or the adjective "patient" distinguished from the noun "patient." This level of simplicity is quite different from the syntax requirements in theme analysis for determining who is doing what to whom. In addition to specifying which words are nouns, the computer must also specify which nouns are in the subject position, which are in the object position, and so on. We hope to have available eventually a syntax-analysis procedure that can handle both functions.

Semantic Rules

Similarly, we may wish to have the computer assign alternative tags to the text and wait to determine the over-all topic of the sentence before making a final decision. In assigning tags to the word "play," the computer might, for example, be unable to use a simple clue to decide whether the word refers to playing an instrument or playing a recreational game. The computer could consult the semantic context of preceding sentences or assign tags appropriate to both usages and make a final decision after the tagging of the sentence has been completed. A final sentence summary routine or procedure using flags (as discussed in Chapter 3) could be used to choose between alternatives based on the over-all topic of the text.

Special Topic and Name Identifications

A number of special word usages appearing in the key-word-in-context emphasize the need to provide a list of special word usages depending on the particular topic being considered. If, for example, the document is concerned with carpentry, appropriate additions to the dictionary can be inserted just before the data are processed to anticipate special uses of such words as "bit." Similarly, proper names and places should be identified for the computer before processing begins. "Rocky Green," for example, should be identified as a male person and not a hard color. "New Castle" should be identified as a Midwestern town and not a renovated high-status building. In future procedures, the investigator will normally provide a list of topics, dramatis personae, names of places, and directions on how to process them.

With all these new procedures, there will still be situations where the computer is unable to choose between alternative meanings, or when in assigning tags it may indicate that something is peculiar in the data. Considering the extended development and uses of computer time sharing, we anticipate that it will soon be possible to combine regular processing with occasional time-shared pauses in which the investigator is asked for advice as needed.

The Source Dictionary

The key-word-in-context procedure, complemented by appropriate computer context procedures, provides a long-needed resource for construction of both general and specific dictionaries. It also provides a guide to the most frequently used words as well as to the number of words one can profitably include in the dictionary. For example, if we remove the 20,302 occurrences of proper names from our 510,976 words, we find that the 5,000 most frequent words account for 95.6 percent of the text. Table 4.5 shows the rank frequency order of

TABLE 4.5. Statistics from 500,000-Word Sample of Texts

Word Rank	Frequency	Cumulative Text Percentage Covered
10	6,797	25.4
50	1,528	47.1
100	663	57.5
500	103	76.5
1,000	43	83.5
3,000	11	92.5
5,000	5	95.6
7,500	3	97.5
10,000	2	98.6
15,000	1	99.6
16,000	1	99.9

words and the cumulative percentage of text accounted for by that number of words.

In Table 4.5, 16,596 different words, aside from proper names, account for the entire text sample of 500,000 words. Having listed our

TABLE 4.6. Statistics with Noun Plurals and Regular Verb Paradigms Combined with Root Forms

Word Rank	Frequency	Cumulative Text Percentage Covered
10	6,883	25.4
50	1,591	47.5
100	722	58.7
500	109	80.0
1,000	45	87.1
3,000	9	95.4
5,000	4	97.7
7,500	1	98.9
10,000	1	99.4
11,500	1	99.9

frequency distribution in this manner, we decided to combine regular verb paradigms (ed, ing, s) and noun plurals,[5] and this reduced the 16,596 word figure to approximately 11,500. Table 4.6 shows this distribution.

These figures indicate that a relatively small number of words (3,000 to 5,000) account for the greatest bulk of the text. An increase in dictionary entries, for example, from 5,000 to 7,500 (a 50 percent increase) would cover only an additional 1.2 percent of the text. For most general dictionaries, there comes a point where the effort of making further additions is not worth the gain in textual coverage. Proper names and words specific to a particular topic in the text being studied can be added as extra categories for each study.

Therefore, in the construction of the source dictionary, we use the 5,000 most frequent words from the KWIC sample. The source dictionary will consist of a set of direction sheets, each summarizing a major word or word root. These sheets will describe the different meanings for each word, including the idiomatic, syntactic, semantic, and special topic considerations to be used in their identification. Also included is frequency information on each kind of use, as well as information on unusual usage in certain types of data. These summary sheets, when collected, are called a source dictionary. Table 4.7 presents two examples of a summary sheet.

It should be noted that the information provided by the key-word-in-context would also be quite useful for Harris' "distributional structure analysis," discussed in Chapter 2. The main difference in approach, we believe, is that the content analyst does not impose on himself the rule that he cannot use further information on meaning. In making the source dictionary for the key-word-in-context listing, a highly judgmental process is involved in picking out the patterns of word usage with similar meaning. If the investigator finds himself in doubt, he can ask people to make word associations or semantic differential ratings, using their replies to assist him in making assignments. The key-word-in-context listing thus provides the candidates to be described. The reduction to a source dictionary comprises the first round of judgments as to what meanings words take on in different usages. Distributional similarities may provide an important piece of evidence, but the final decision must be based on human judgment.

[5] In other words, we considered hat–hats and walk–walks–walked as single words.

TABLE 4.7. Source Dictionary Summary Sheet Examples

Example Word: KIND   Total Occurrences   257
   "Kind" is a case where the ambiguity is syntactic and the problem is solved
by identifying the part of speech.

Part of Speech
Noun	1. like class or group of same type	159
Adjective	2. benevolent	48
Adverb	3. rather	47

Idioms
4. in kind (retaliation)	1

Imperative-Adjective Use
  be kind to
  be kind with
  be so kind as

Rules for Differentiating Senses

  Sense 1
    1. *DET + KIND + OF + NOUN
      Kind is preceded by a determiner, followed by *of* plus a noun.
      Example = the kind of leather
    2. NOUN + OF + DET + KIND
      Kind is the object of a prepositional phrase headed by a noun.
      Example = a horse of that kind
    3. DET + KIND + (a period that ends the sentence)
      Example = He is of another kind.
    4. DET + KIND + REL. CASE
      Example = He is the kind who would come.

  Sense 2
    5. ∅ DET + KIND + ∅ OF
      Kind is *not* preceded by a determiner or followed by *of*.
      Example = He is kind.
    6. DET + KIND + NOUN
      If kind is preceded by a determiner within 2 words and followed by
      a noun.
      Example = He is a kind person.

  Sense 3
               adjective or past participle
    7. KIND + OF + have and phrase
               like
      "Kind of" followed by one of the above generally means "rather" or
      "sort of."
      Examples = She got kind of dizzy.
               I kind of have that impression.
               It was kind of like being reborn.

TABLE 4.7. (continued)

Example Word: DEGREE   Total Occurrences   51
   Degree, with three noun meanings, is therefore semantically ambiguous
   three ways. This presents a much more difficult problem since the part-of-
   speech grammatical cues for distinguishing meanings cannot be relied on.

Part of Speech
  Noun 1. A stage in a scale of intensity or amount   34
         2. An academic title   16
         3. Unit in measurement of temperature   1

Rules for Differentiating Senses

 Sense 1
   1. TO + DET AND/OR QUANTIFIER* + DEGREE
     Examples: *Quantifiers* = some, considerable, growing, slight
                            small, greater, lesser, large
   2. TO + DET + DEGREE + THAT + Sentence Clause   4

 Sense 2
   3. ART + NOUN* + DEGREE
   4. ART + DEGREE + OF + NOUN*
                AT
                FROM
    *Nouns: college, Ph.D., university, B.A., bachelor's, doctor, honors,
    history, art, etc.

   5. POSSESSIVE + DEGREE   Example = His degree
   6. VERB* + ART/POSS + DEGREE
    *Verbs: earn, have, get, take, receive, and so on

---

* Determiner refers to the following words: a, the, this, that, these, those, one, two . . . ,
first, second . . . , any, either, many, much, all, both, half, enough, more, most, such, some,
and so on.

SUMMARY

   As this chapter makes evident, the construction of category systems has been one of the major activities in General Inquirer research.
In terms of time and effort, it occupies a much more extensive investment than the programming of computers. We feel that it is one of the
most important and interesting aspects of content analysis, having important implications for developing theories in the behavioral sciences.
The source dictionary that is now occupying our attention involves a
considerable investment of time and resources. However, it will reduce
the work involved in constructing content analysis dictionaries and will

increase the accuracy of analysis based upon their use. It will also extend the range of types of content analysis that can be attempted by providing a solid structural basis for image, theme, and plot analysis. We hope to use the source dictionary ourselves both in developing specialized dictionaries for specific projects and in making a thorough revision of the Harvard III Dictionary. If others use it also, it may well provide a common link between a number of theoretical positions.

CHAPTER FIVE

Presentation of Three Content Analysis Dictionaries[1]

It is instructive to examine a small number of dictionaries in some detail, keeping in mind the kinds of decisions that go into making a dictionary. We have selected three dictionaries for detailed comparison: the Harvard III Psychosociological Dictionary, the Stanford Political Dictionary, and the Need-Achievement Dictionary. These dictionaries have been constructed by different people working in varied settings with differing theoretical viewpoints and many kinds of text materials. They therefore present interesting contrasts, but together they demonstrate the main idea we have tried to convey: that any set of categories is a compromise between theoretical concepts, the nature of the data, and the stage of the research; and that, because of these factors, it is legitimate to expect considerable variation in the character of content analysis categories.

In selecting these three dictionaries, we have attempted to cover a range from general to specific. The dictionaries in this chapter are samples of three general types: those having many entries for many categories, many entries for few categories, and relatively few entries for few categories. The Need-Achievement Dictionary is

---

[1] The descriptions of the various dictionaries are, with only slight editorial modifications, those of the authors of the respective dictionaries. The description of the Harvard III Dictionary was written by Dexter C. Dunphy, that of the Stanford Dictionary by Ole Holsti and his associates, and that of the Need-Achievement Dictionary by Daniel M. Ogilvie and Louise Woodhead.

included as our best example of more complex contingency scorings.

Several additional dictionaries are described in Part II of this book. Namenwirth's additions and changes to the Harvard III Dictionary are briefly described in Chapter 11. Categories used by McPherson in his political dictionary are listed in Table 10.2, Chapter 10. Colby's anthropological dictionary procedures are discussed in Chapter 21. The "alcohol" dictionary is briefly described by Kalin *et al.* in Chapter 19. A "product image" dictionary is outlined in general terms in Chapter 22.

To describe and compare a large number of different dictionaries at this point in our exposition would be extremely tedious reading. Although we originally planned to have appendixes presenting complete descriptions of each dictionary, it was decided to drop this idea since it would greatly increase the size of this already large book. Instead we describe here only three dictionaries that represent the approaches we have discussed.

We recommend that the reader skim this chapter lightly on first reading in order to obtain an idea of the variety of categories represented and the decisions made in their selection. The reader may well come back to the details of the chapter in considering his own areas of interest.

THE HARVARD THIRD
PSYCHOSOCIOLOGICAL DICTIONARY

Number of Language Signs Classified: 3,564
Number of Tags: 83

The Harvard III Dictionary is the work of a number of faculty members and graduate students at Harvard who took part in the General Inquirer project. The following persons were actively involved in the construction of the dictionary at various stages of its development: P. J. Stone, R. F. Bales, D. C. Dunphy, and D. M. Ogilvie at Harvard; Z. Namenwirth, now at the Department of Sociology, Yale; and W. McPherson, now at the Department of Sociology, American University.

Throughout the course of the General Inquirer project, the research team at Harvard has been evolving a general purpose dictionary for use in conjunction with research of a psychological and sociological character. This dictionary has now gone through three major revisions, the current revision first appearing in March 1963. All who have helped to construct this dictionary have had a common background in the interdisciplinary Department of Social Relations at Harvard. In one sense, therefore, the dictionary represents a further step in the long-term interest of many in the department in evolving a general theory of action. In fact, the dictionary has been developed under the general guidance and with the active participation of R. F. Bales who has been a major contributor to this theoretical tradition. The dictionary is an attempt to apply an operational form of a general theory of action to the analysis of documents. Table 5.1 lists the tags in the Harvard III Dictionary, and Table 5.2 gives brief definitions of them and sample entry words. Following the samples, a number indicates the total number of entry words in the category.

We have termed this particular dictionary a "psychosociological" dictionary because it was designed primarily for those investigators with psychological and sociological objectives and theories. Hence, those in other disciplines, such as anthropologists and political scientists, have usually preferred to construct dictionaries that represent more closely the theories and categories of their own concerns. Yet, psychologists and sociologists who have used the system have generally felt satisfied with limited revisions or additions, if any, to the categories, although to a large extent these investigators have been working in terms of general action theory (to use that term loosely).

The first psychosociological dictionary was the work of Stone and Bales and combined psychoanalytic associations with action theory. In subsequent revisions of the dictionary, the association principle was abandoned in favor of categories based on a combination of grammatical classes (noun, verb, modifier) and more formal classifications derived from sociological and psychological theory. Another major difference between the first and third revisions of the dictionary was the introduction into the latter of the distinction between first-order and second-order tags.

In constructing categories for the Harvard III Dictionary, it seemed to us that, on the whole, sociology furnished a set of categories better suited to classifying roles, objects, and cultural artifacts than did psychology. On the other hand, psychology presented more clearly defined categories for dynamic processes. We proceeded, therefore, to give most nouns (object names) a sociological definition and most

TABLE 5.1. Harvard Third Psychosociological Dictionary: List of Tags

---

FIRST-ORDER TAGS

OBJECTS

   Social Realm

Persons
SELF
SELVES
OTHER (suggested additions:
     males, females)

Roles
MALE-ROLE
FEMALE-ROLE
NEUTER-ROLE
JOB-ROLE

Collectivities
SMALL-GROUP
LARGE-GROUP

   Cultural Realm

Cultural Objects
FOOD
CLOTHING
TOOLS

Cultural Settings
SOCIAL PLACE

Cultural Patterns
IDEAL-VALUE
DEVIATION-VALUES
ACTION-NORM (norms)
MESSAGE-FORM
THOUGHT-FORM (concepts)
NONSPECIFIC-OBJECT

   Natural Realm
BODY PART
NATURAL OBJECT
NATURAL WORLD

PROCESSES

   Psychological Processes

Emotions
AROUSAL
URGE
AFFECTION
ANGER
PLEASURE
DISTRESS

Thought
SENSE
THINK
IF
EQUAL
NOT
CAUSE

Evaluation
GOOD
BAD
OUGHT

   Behavioral Processes

Social-Emotional Actions
APPROACH
GUIDE
CONTROL
ATTACK
AVOID
FOLLOW
COMMUNICATE

Instrumental Actions
ATTEMPT
WORK
MOVE
GET
POSSESS
EXPEL

QUALIFIERS

TIME REFERENCE
SPACE REFERENCE

QUANTITY REFERENCE
QUALITY (SENSORY) REFERENCE

TABLE 5.1. (continued)

SECOND-ORDER TAGS	
INSTITUTIONAL CONTEXTS	*PSYCHOLOGICAL THEMES*
ACADEMIC	*a.* OVERSTATE
ARTISTIC	UNDERSTATE
COMMUNITY	*b.* SIGN-STRONG
ECONOMIC	SIGN-WEAK
FAMILY	*c.* SIGN-ACCEPT
LEGAL	SIGN-REJECT
MEDICAL	*d.* MALE-THEME
MILITARY	FEMALE-THEME
POLITICAL	SEX-THEME
RECREATIONAL	*e.* ASCEND-THEME
RELIGIOUS	*f.* AUTHORITY-THEME
TECHNOLOGICAL	*g.* DANGER-THEME
	DEATH-THEME
STATUS CONNOTATIONS *	
HIGHER-STATUS	
PEER-STATUS	
LOWER-STATUS	

* Assigned to roles only

verbs a psychological definition at the denotative level. In the listing of tags, the first-order distinction refers to the primary explicit, denotative meanings of words. We will begin with an explanation of first-order tags and then proceed to the second-order tags.

As the tags are listed, the left-hand column of first-order tags represents our categorization scheme for nouns. The right-hand column of first-order tags represents our categorization scheme for verbs, with the exception of the tags IF, EQUAL, NOT, CAUSE, GOOD, BAD, and OUGHT. The tags IF, EQUAL, NOT, and CAUSE are primarily expressive rather than denotative of thought processes; and the tags GOOD, BAD, and OUGHT are denotative of evaluative and moral processes, but in most cases are not verbs. In addition, at the bottom is a set of categories under the heading *qualifiers.* These represent categories of modifiers that are applied to nouns or verbs.

Objects

Upon more detailed examination of the first-order classification, it is apparent that we have divided the world of objects up into three major areas: the social, cultural, and natural realms. By the social world, we mean references to *persons,* to *social roles,* and to *collec-*

TABLE 5.2. Harvard Third Psychosociological Dictionary (brief definitions)

FIRST-ORDER TAGS
Social Realm
Persons

SELF — all pronoun references to the personal self (I, me, mine, myself) 5

SELVES — all pronoun references to the inclusive self (we, us, ours) 4

OTHER — all non-sex-specific pronouns for other (you, yours, they, theirs) 7

Roles

MALE-ROLE — all roles with specific male references (actor, boy, brother, Christ) 35

FEMALE-ROLE — all roles with specific female references (actress, aunt, bride, daughter, fairy) 28

NEUTER-ROLE — all role names not connoting sex or occupations (baby, American, anybody, child) 83

JOB-ROLE — all roles with clear occupational reference, theoretically open to both sexes (agent, artist, author, captain) 72

Collectivities

SMALL-GROUP — groups in which members are usually able to have face-to-face interaction (agency, band, board, club) 21

LARGE-GROUP — collectivities usually too large for face-to-face interaction (administration, army, church) 44

Cultural Realm
Cultural Objects

FOOD — articles or types of food (bean, beer, candy, cherry) 37

CLOTHING — articles or types of clothing (button, dress, fur, garment) 30

TOOLS — instrumental objects or artifacts of any kind [broader category than hand tools] (bag, automobile, ambulance) 114

Cultural Settings

SOCIAL PLACE — buildings and building parts; political, social, and economic locations (abroad, America, bedroom, cabin) 118

Cultural Patterns

IDEAL-VALUE — culturally defined virtues, goals, valued conditions and activities (ability, able, beauty, bold) 179

DEVIATION — culturally devalued goals, conditions and types of activity (abnormal, blind, crazy, drunken) 70

ACTION-NORM — normative patterns of social behavior (agreement, business, commission, credit) 93

MESSAGE-FORM — names of communication media, in a broad sense including art objects and money (art, book, cash) 102

THOUGHT-FORM — units and styles of reasoning (abstraction, basic, contrast, estimate) 59

NONSPECIFIC-OBJECTS — abstract references to objects [connoting intellectualization] (affair, aspect, capital, detail) 48

Natural Realm

BODYPART — parts of the body (arm, body, brain, cheek) 55

NATURAL-OBJECT — objects not made by man (plants, animals, minerals, fish) 70

NATURAL-WORLD — geographical places, weather reference and cosmic objects (air, beach, gulf, meadow) 71

TABLE 5.2. (continued)

Qualifiers

SENSORY-REF — smells, colors, tastes, etc. (aloud, black, fresh) 67

TIME-REF — references to measurement of time (after, again, began, daily) 154

QUANTITY-REF — references to units and measures of quantity (add, any, big, exact) 122

SPACE-REF — references to spatial dimensions (about, ahead, back, bent) 116

Psychological Processes

Emotions

AROUSAL — states of emotional excitement (attitude, awaken, felt, habit) 40

URGE — drive states (dream, eager, incentive, intend) 21

AFFECTION — indicants of close positive, interpersonal relationships (admire, affection, charm, dear, flirt) 43

PLEASURE — states of gratification (cheer, delight, funny) 43

DISTRESS — states of despair, fear, guilt, shame, grief, failure or indecision (afraid, alarm, break, conflict) 120

ANGER — forms of aggressive expression (angry, boil, burn, detest) 31

Thought

SENSE — perceptions and awareness (appear, attend, aware, read) 50

THINK — cognitive processes (assume, choice, doubt, mind) 70

IF — conditional words (almost, chance, else, if) 28

EQUAL — words denoting similarity (alike, same, consist) 11

NOT — words denoting negation (cannot, not, differ, none) 19

CAUSE — words denoting a cause-effect relationship (affect, cause) 19

Evaluation

GOOD — synonyms for good (admirable, clean, fair, suitable) 44

BAD — synonyms for bad (awful, bitter, cheap, crude) 39

OUGHT — words indicating a moral imperative (duty, ought, proper) 13

Behavioral Processes

Social-Emotional Actions

COMMUNICATE — processes of transmitting meaning (address, admit, answer, boast) 101

APPROACH — movement toward (arrive, attach, bring, brought) 48

GUIDE — assistance and positive direction (aid, allow, benefit) 66

CONTROL — limiting action (appoint, arrest, bind, bound) 44

ATTACK — destructive, hostile, action (annoy, attack, beat, betray) 110

AVOID — movement away from (abandon, absent, conceal) 53

FOLLOW — submissive action (agree, apology, consent) 40

Impersonal Actions

ATTEMPT — goal-directed activity, implying effort (aim, apply, bid, effort) 35

WORK — task activity (adjust, construct, cook, create) 82

GET — obtaining, achieving action (afford, attain, beg) 41

POSSESS — owning, consuming (belong, occupy, lock) 37

EXPEL — ejecting (blew, cast, defecate, drop) 41

SECOND-ORDER TAGS

Institutional Contexts — specification of the social context of rules and actions

ACADEMIC (assignment, correct, teach, editor) 135

ARTISTIC (performance, charm, display, actress) 60

COMMUNITY (accustom, custom, tradition, visit) 70

TABLE 5.2. (continued)

ECONOMIC (business, cost, debt, finance) 134
FAMILY (engagement, marital, marriage, dear, marry) 77
LEGAL (agreement, trial, condemn, confirm) 68
MEDICAL (therapy, treatment, injury, sickness) 40
MILITARY (war, attack, fight, raid, uniform) 49
POLITICAL (appointment, partisan, taxation, campaign) 113
RECREATIONAL (sport, swam, band, trail, holiday) 79
RELIGIOUS (magic, ritual, devotion, pray) 80
TECHNOLOGICAL (job, ability, engineer, hunter, print) 106
Status Connotations — male, female, neuter, and job-role status implications
HIGHER-STATUS (aunt, analyst, doctor, devil, opera) 70
PEER-STATUS (mate, bride, wife, fellow, lover) 24
LOWER-STATUS (baby, child, boy, mistress) 49
Psychological Themes
OVERSTATE — emphatic or exaggerated words, generally adjectives or adverbs [connotes a defensive style] (gratefully, terrible, badly, hopelessly) 208
UNDERSTATE — words, generally adjectives or adverbs, connoting doubt or uncertainty [connotes a defensive style] (tend, hesitate, fair, partially) 80
SIGN-STRONG — words connoting strength or capacity for action (magic, encouragement, professional) 222
SIGN-WEAK — words connoting weakness or incapacity for action (sorry, postpone, sank, shy, admit) 207
SIGN-ACCEPT — words implying interpersonal acceptance (encouragement, admire, appreciate) 168
SIGN-REJECT — words implying interpersonal rejection (anger, betray, jealousy, sulk) 272
MALE-THEME — psychoanalytic symbols of masculinity (limb, beast, cock, staff) 66
FEMALE-THEME — psychoanalytic symbols of femininity (blood, button, velvet, weep) 81
SEX-THEME — direct or indirect references to the sex act (engagement, attractive, embrace, kiss) 127
ASCEND-THEME — words associated with rising, falling, fire and water, indicating concerns relating to the Icarus complex (burn, arousal, awaken, assert) 271
AUTHORITY-THEME — words connoting the existence or exercise of authority (custom, establish, admit, forbid) 36
DANGER-THEME — words connoting alarm or concern with danger (blast, deviant, warn, stretch) 99
DEATH-THEME — words connoting dying, end (crush, degrade, burnt) 106

tivities, and, in fact, these represent three subgroups within this area, as discussed in Chapter 4. References to SELF are to the individual self or first person singular. References to SELVES are to the inclusive self or first person plural. References to OTHER are to the words "you" and "they" and their derivatives. Thus, these three tags represent a classification of personal pronouns. However, "he" and "she" and their derivatives were classified for the purposes of this dictionary under MALE-ROLE and FEMALE-ROLE, respectively, along with nouns such as husband and wife. On the basis of our experience with this, we have concluded that in the next revision of the dictionary, it would be advisable to make this classification more logically complete by separating the pronouns he and she and their derivatives from the roles. At the moment we find that because of a large count on pronoun references, the MALE-ROLE and FEMALE-ROLE tags are not sensitive to references to nonpronoun roles.

The tags relating to roles are given an assignment on the basis of whether they are sex specific or relate to the occupational structure of the society. NEUTER-ROLE, therefore, is essentially a list of ascribed roles which are not sex specific and do not relate to the occupational system. Sex attribution plays such an important part in our system primarily because the dictionary was originally constructed as a tool to analyze small-group interaction in groups where displacement phenomena play an important part. Therefore it was of particular importance to identify the sexual relevance, if any, of roles mentioned by those in the groups. Similarly JOB-ROLES, particularly high-status JOB-ROLES, were likely to be the object of displaced feelings about the group trainer, and so this also seemed an important category for our purposes. This raises a basic question of the usefulness of these categories to researchers engaged in other problems. Our experience has been that the divisions are useful to other researchers and have a significance beyond that of the displacement phenomenon. On the other hand, anthropologists concerned with kinship, for example, find the lack of separate kinship categories confusing for their purposes.

As far as *collectivities* are concerned, we have divided them into two general categories of SMALL-GROUP and LARGE-GROUP on the basis of the distinction between small face-to-face groups and the larger, more impersonal collectivities. Thus, SMALL-GROUP includes such words as clique, club, gang, team, while LARGE-GROUP includes army, church, college, population, society. This distinction was useful to us in small-group research, since it allowed us to differentiate between references to the group itself (along with other analogous groups) and the major institutional collectivities. However, other kinds of categorization are conceivable and might be more useful for some purposes. For instance, it would be possible to make a distinction between organized and unorganized groups, or to make a separate category referring to classes of people rather than to collectivities, which in the strict sense of that term would include only general words: race, humanity, mankind, public, population.

We have defined the *cultural realm* as consisting of all the material and nonmaterial objects created by man. Within this area we make three major subdivisions: *cultural objects,* which are physical man-made objects; *cultural settings,* which are man-made milieux consisting essentially of complexes of physical artifacts; and *cultural patterns,* which are essentially the values, norms, and concepts of the society. This tripartite division is along the lines of the usual gross distinctions made by anthropologists in studying particular cultures.

We have further divided *cultural objects* into three main categories: FOOD, CLOTHING, and TOOLS. FOOD and CLOTHING are fairly straightforward lists, but the category TOOLS consists of all other concrete man-made objects and, therefore, the term TOOL has to be interpreted in a much wider sense than in ordinary usage. Apart from such regular tools as file, hammer, and knife, there are other artifacts such as ambulance (medical tool), weapon (military tool), and pen (academic tool). The practicality of this particular list is questionable unless the list is used in conjunction with second-order tags. FOOD and CLOTHING also present problems since they are relatively short lists and usually accumulate low or zero counts. Two factors contribute to this. The first is that the lists are extremely impoverished. Considering the wealth of words in the language referring to food and clothing, which can be culled from the advertising sections of any newspaper, these lists are incredibly short. There is a second reason, however. In most of the text we have analyzed, little attention is devoted to these basic essentials of life. It seems also that this must be a characteristic of those sources from which Thorndike-Lorge drew their word counts since we have included their high-frequency words as the basic vocabulary for our dictionary. Thus, to add enough words in these categories to make a real difference to counts would take a large amount of storage space in the computer with little return per word. As we go into larger dictionaries, however, these categories need to be built up. Certainly, for any anthropological work with materials from primitive societies, many additional entries would seem appropriate at this point, for concern with food and clothing usually bulks larger in material from these sources. In addition each culture has its own distinctive cultural items.

There is just one tag under *cultural settings* in this dictionary; and as one user of the General Inquirer remarked, "This category includes everything from 'bath' to 'kingdom.'" Originally there were two: BUILDING PART listed items of furniture such as bed, chair, bath, and SOCIAL SETTINGS listed words for other socially defined situations such as prison, village. However, like TOOL, the entries on this list are more useful in conjunction with second-order institutional tags. The list includes, for instance, the words heaven and hell, defined as RELIGIOUS SOCIAL PLACES. "Temple" is tagged a RELIGIOUS SOCIAL PLACE, but "kingdom," for example, is tagged a POLITICAL SOCIAL PLACE. The entries on these two lists were merged into one list because of the low counts on both categories.

In the area of cultural patterns, we accept the division proposed by Parsons and Shils (1954) between values, norms, and concepts. We recognize the existence of deviance in relation to values as well as positive values themselves. On the IDEAL-VALUE or positive-value list, we have such words as beauty, confidence, companionship, experience, and faith, while on the DEVIATION list we have words such as deviant, foolish, and wicked.

ACTION-NORM, as the name suggests, refers to norms guiding and controlling action. Ideally if we were to be consistent with the value categories, there should be an ANOMIE list to act as the opposite for the ACTION-NORM category. However, there seemed to be few high-frequency words to compose such a list.

Concepts are divided into three groups: MESSAGE FORM consists of nouns referring to types of objects involved in communication (for instance, speech, song, novel, message, money), while THOUGHT FORM entry words consist of a list of abstract nouns referring to thought processes (for instance, abstraction, analogy, belief, concept, topic, theory).

The tag NONSPECIFIC-OBJECT includes all nouns with vague referents, such as thing, piece, anything, stuff, phenomena. We have found empirically that a high rate of use of words in this category implies vagueness and when associated, as it often is, with OVERSTATE and UNDERSTATE, seems to indicate prose with a defensive quality.

Processes

The right-hand column of first-order tags refers to processes that are subdivided into the two major areas of *psychological* and *behavioral* processes. The psychological processes are divided into the familiar categories of *emotions* (affect), *thought* (cognition), and *evaluation* (conation). The area of behavioral processes is subdivided into *social-emotional* and *instrumental* actions.

Within the general class of *emotions,* we distinguish six kinds of emotions. AROUSAL consists of a list of words referring to a generalized state of emotional arousal (for instance, arousal, concern, curiosity, excitement, interest, passion). URGE refers to drive states where an object is implied: for instance, desire, intend, motivation, urge, want, wish. The other categories consist of two sets of opposites: AFFECTION-ANGER and PLEASURE-DISTRESS. AFFECTION and ANGER refer to the two opposite poles of affectional relationships: love and hate. AFFECTION includes such words as admiration, devotion, embrace, love, thank. ANGER includes such words as detest, dislike, hate, hostile. PLEASURE needs little explanation, for it is a very straightforward list of such words as cheerful, fulfill, pleasure, rapture. The DISTRESS category includes all references to unpleasure or pain, many of the words being related to anxiety, depression, and guilt.

Thought processes are represented chiefly by two important tags, SENSE and THINK. Words under the heading of SENSE refer to the process of perception, aware, conscious, gaze, perceive, recognize, smell, watch. Words under the heading THINK refer to processes of rational thought such as analyze, classify, conclude, consider, prove, reflect. The remainder of the tags under *thought* are expressive rather than indicative of thought processes; that is, they are words that imply cognitive processes rather than directly refer to them. Words listed under IF (for example, if, either, might, probably) imply consideration of alternatives involved in choice behavior. Words under EQUAL imply the process of determining similarity (alike, equal, identical, similar). The category NOT consists of words implying negation (no, none, not, nor), and CAUSE is a list of words connected with the issue of causality (cause, consequency, because, result). Together with IF, EQUAL, and NOT, it is a category that indicates a set of rational processes is in operation ordering alternatives (if), classifying ideas as similar (equal), or dissimilar (not), determining causal sequences, and probably effects (cause).

Evaluation

The psychological process of *evaluation* is represented by three tags: GOOD, BAD, OUGHT; the lists for GOOD and BAD are comprised of synonyms for these words. There is a close connection here between the IDEAL-VALUE and DEVIATION categories, but we decided to separate the categories, for one set seemed more cultural, the other more personal. The individual uses culturally provided values to make decisions, but the decision as to whether X is good or bad is his own. OUGHT words (conscious, duty, must, obligation, should) also imply evaluative processes and so OUGHT is included under this heading.

The area of behavioral processes is subdivided into social-emotional and instrumental actions. This follows the scheme advanced in action theory and embodied in one of the most widely used scoring systems for small-group behavior, Bales' Interaction Process Analysis (1950). The categories themselves, however, do not follow the IPA model in detail because words rather than whole acts are being scored. IPA categories tend to be more complex in nature and could not be replicated by a simple tag count.

Social-Emotional Actions

In devising categories for the description of behavioral processes, we made use of a simplified version of Leary's scoring scheme (1957), which has been found useful in small-group studies and has received considerable support from factor analytic studies in the same area. The "Leary wheel" consists of a set of related and counterposed categories arranged in their relationship to the two main factors of domination-submission and affection-antagonism. Figure 5.1 shows the way in which we have attempted to construct categories to follow this model. It should be pointed out that the lower segment of the diagram has

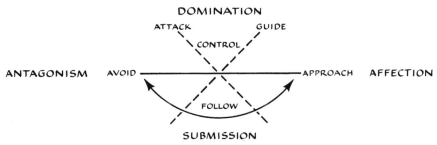

FIGURE 5.1. Categories of socioemotional actions (*derived from the Leary scheme*).

only one category (FOLLOW) instead of the three the scheme logically requires. Our failure to find sufficient words to make three categories of the kind needed would suggest that there is a relative absence of such terms in the language. In addition, the tag COMMUNICATE is a generalized category of words referring to the communication process but not specific in terms of the Leary scheme.

Instrumental Actions

The categories of *instrumental action* were designed to represent consecutive stages in the work process. Thus, the cycle begins with ATTEMPT, continues with WORK and MOVE, proceeds to GET, culminates in POSSESS, and is concluded with EXPEL. The following lists show sample entry words under these categories:

ATTEMPT	WORK	MOVE	GET	POSSESS	EXPEL
attempt	build	chase	accomplish	eat	bury
bid	construct	fly	achieve	hold	discharge
compete	count	hurry	acquire	have	dispose
pursue	cultivate	move	attain	keep	expel
search	invent	raise	reach	occupy	hurl
venture	study	slide	seize	save	throw

When the categories were constructed, it was hoped that a systematic shift through them might appear over the course of work-group process in a manner analogous to the systematic shift in Interaction Process Analysis categories. We have found no evidence to support such a movement although no systematic study has been undertaken to confirm or disprove the hypothesis.

These categories seemed to be fairly straightforward lists of words when we constructed them. However, many of these words have multiple meanings, and a number of high-frequency words (for example, make, use, get) are also components of important and recurrent idioms. Consequently, counts on the categories can be misleading. As a result of this and similar problems with some other entry words in the dictionary, we have added idioms which we hope will solve the problem of multiple meaning for some of these words.

The final set of categories in the dictionary consists of lists of words used primarily to modify or amplify the meanings of nouns and verbs. We have classified entry words of this type into the familiar TIME, SPACE, QUANTITY, and QUALITY categories.

The first-order tags represent a set of mutually independent categories for classifying words according to their denotative meanings. Each entry word is included under one and only one first-order tag,

Second-order tags are designed to identify pervasive qualities of the text and thus to indicate significant generalized concerns with the external or internal worlds. Categories refer both to denotative and connotative levels of meaning. They are not independent entities since the meaning of any entry word can be filled out with the addition of more than one second-order tag. The distinction between nouns, verbs, and qualifiers is not maintained at the second-order level.

Second-Order Tags

The left-hand column of second-order tags is subdivided into two general areas: *institutional contexts* and *status connotations. Institutional contexts* suggests the institutional character of objects and actions, while *status connotations* indicates important levels of hierarchical concern. The right-hand column lists a number of psychological themes indicating significant inner concerns.

Second-order tags fill out the limited meaning given by the assignment of a single first-order tag. When a word has been assigned a first-order tag (for instance, sword = TOOL), its meaning can then be enlarged with one second-order tag from within as many of each of nine subsets as seem relevant. The nine subsets are indicated in the table. Thus "sword" can have one institutional context tag added if appropriate; in this case the proper tag would be MILITARY. If it describes a role, the entry word might be assigned a status connotation, for instance "queen" would be HIGHER-STATUS. Status connotations are not used for objects. Their psychological symbolic meanings can be given by adding not more than one tag from as many of subsets *b* through *g* as seem appropriate. In this case, we decided that sword = DANGER-THEME, MALE-THEME, SIGN-STRONG, MILITARY, TOOL.

Thus second-order tags are designed to transcend the object-action basis for classification used in the first-order section of the dictionary and to "fill out" additional levels of meaning.

Institutional Contexts

In typical sociological fashion, we have divided the external world into a number of institutional spheres that indicate the social contexts to which the speaker or writer is orienting himself. Our choice of these twelve contexts has been influenced by schemes found useful in other areas. The German philosopher Spranger, for instance, advanced a sixfold classification of values which was later incorporated into the "Allport-Vernon Study of Values" (Allport, 1961, 454). His six value areas were the theoretical, economic, esthetic, social, political, and religious. These correspond, respectively, to our ACADEMIC, ECONOMIC, ARTISTIC, COMMUNITY, POLITICAL, and RELIGIOUS tags. We have found it useful to distinguish an additional six contexts: FAMILIAL, LEGAL, MEDICAL, MILITARY, RECREATIONAL, and TECHNOLOGICAL.

These 12 institutional context categories can be used in two main ways. They may be used as simple indicators of relative concern; for example, we may find that of two writers we are comparing, the writing of one is primarily POLITICAL in emphasis, while the other's is primarily RELIGIOUS. Alternatively, these tags may be used in conjunction with first-order tags in the way suggested earlier. This results in contingency counts, which can reveal useful distinctions within first-order categories. We may find, for example, that our two writers are both high in referring to JOB-ROLES, but that one is primarily interested in COMMUNITY JOB-ROLES, while the other is primarily interested in RELIGIOUS JOB-ROLES; or again, that one is primarily interested in RELIGIOUS JOB-ROLES, while the other is primarily interested in FAMILY FEMALE-ROLES.

Status References

The assignment of status tags (higher, peer, and lower-status) poses a number of problems. Originally these tags were applied to any entry words where their use seemed appropriate. However, this resulted in their application to few words other than those referring to roles or collectivities, so that we decided to include only words referring to roles.

Psychological Themes

When the third dictionary was constructed, an attempt was made to set up tag lists which would measure important psychological themes. From the discussion of the thematic analysis in Chapter 2, it should be apparent that this was a rather naive and simplistic attempt. If a theme is essentially a conjunctive relationship between tags, as we have proposed, it cannot be measured by a simple tag count. In fact, we have found the usefulness of some of these tags to be limited and have moved in the direction of writing specialized dictionaries such as those for Need-Achievement and Icarianism. Therefore, we foresee the eventual abandonment of at least some of these categories and their replacement with sets of categories and special programs for scoring conjunctive relationships within these sets. Another problem with this aspect of the dictionary is that it does not represent a comprehensive coverage of the area of psychological needs or complexes in the way that the institutional and status tags provide a basic coverage of an area of sociological concern.

The OVERSTATE list consists of words which tend to enlarge and exaggerate the content of the communication, while the UNDERSTATE words tend to modify, restrict or "tone down" the content. Empirically, we have found these categories highly correlated with NON-SPECIFIC-OBJECT, which is a list of vague references to objects and another indication of unclear communication.

SIGN-STRONG and SIGN-WEAK and SIGN-ACCEPT and SIGN-REJECT were devised to operationalize two of the Osgood evaluative dimensions.

The first Harvard dictionary included ORAL, ANAL, and GENITAL categories which comprised words denoting the standard psychoanalytic symbols of sexuality relating to these modes. These categories were abandoned as impractical in subsequent revisions. They were replaced with the present tags, MALE, FEMALE, and SEX-THEME. Both direct and symbolic references are included in these tag lists. Our experience suggests that the direct entries are useful for indicating an overt interest in sexuality, but that the attempt to pick up latent imagery has not been successful. It may well be that there is no extensive common language of sexual symbolism so that the attempt to score imagery in this way is not possible; alternatively, it may be that the lists need to be far more extensive than they are at present.

ASCEND-THEME was designed to identify the concerns referred to by Murray (1955) as the Icarus Complex. It was included as a category here because Couch (1960) had found Icarianism to be a significant factor in his factor analysis of the psychological determinants of interpersonal behavior in small groups. The list of entry words is extremely long and includes words connoting fire, water, flying, falling, excitement, height, ambition. The degree to which these words, in fact, are related in a theme is an empirical question and, therefore, we have gone over to a specialized dictionary that examines the contingency relations among tags of this order.

AUTHORITY-THEME. This tag list is an attempt to measure authoritarianism through use of the normal verbal productions of individuals rather than by standard questionnaires. The list is made up of words with authoritative overtones, the theory behind the category being that a person concerned with authority would tend to use a high proportion of such words.

DANGER-THEME. The tag includes words that betray an underlying worry or anxiety. No attempt was made at the time to relate this category to other anxiety measures used in content analysis. To do this could be a profitable undertaking.

DEATH-THEME. The tag name DEATH-THEME is probably too dramatic. While this category includes references to death, the entries predominantly refer to ending or completion of activities. This was formed primarily because it was thought to be useful for the analysis of small-group processes. As the end of a group approaches, groups become very concerned with handling the disbandment of the group, and this tag was designed to pick up this concern.

Summary

This presentation has outlined in some detail the existing classification system for entry words included in the Harvard III Dictionary. As far as possible, we have attempted to explain the rationale behind the present tag categories and, at the same time, given some insight into the dilemmas and complexities of dictionary construction. To review a dictionary such as this is to realize that the construction of a generalized dictionary is a continuous process guided by feedback from retrievals carried out on data to which the dictionary has been applied. It is only through modifications that a dictionary of this kind begins to assume a satisfying level of accuracy in categorizing text.

THE STANFORD POLITICAL DICTIONARY

Number of Language Signs Classified: 3,500+
Number of Tags: 9+

This dictionary is the work of North and Holsti of the Political Science Department, Stanford University.

Since inception in the late 1950's, the team concerned with the Stanford Studies in International Conflict and Integration has undertaken a variety of studies. Many have been of an exploratory nature, with the purpose of isolating and, where possible, quantifying the fundamental patterns of conflict and integrative behavior at the international level. From the many approaches available to the investigator, a decision was made to undertake the analysis primarily at the perceptual level of the key decision makers. The primary source of data would be those documents authored by the decision makers themselves, and therefore a search was made for various techniques of content analysis meeting the requirements of methodological rigor and quantifiability.

An early pilot study using data from the crisis in the summer of 1914 indicated that the systematic content analysis of diplomatic documents offered a fertile field for the study of international conflict (Zinnes, North, Koch, 1961). It also became evident that analytic units must be measured for intensity as well as frequency.

At that time, the Stanford Studies undertook the investigation of Communist Chinese and Soviet Russian relations during three recent periods: January 1960, May 1960, and April 1961 (Holsti, 1964*b*). That study demonstrated that through content analysis of documents, it is possible to measure various subjective dimensions of international tensions on a global scale. The study also revealed, however, that so long as the time-consuming methods of manual content analysis were employed, the feasibility of such investigation would remain in doubt. The task of generalizing and analyzing adequate data for the comparative, cumulative, and replicable studies necessary to theory building might prove to be unmanageable within the limits of the normal social science research budget.

In April 1962, the Stanford Studies undertook a methodological review of existing techniques and new approaches to content analysis which make more extensive use of electronic computers. Contact was soon made with the General Inquirer Project at Harvard and further exploratory work revealed the feasibility of the General Inquirer for use in connection with the Stanford Studies.

About the same time, an arrangement was made with the Center for Advanced Studies in the Behavioral Sciences at Stanford to bring together a small work group of behavioral scientists. As the outgrowth of these conferences during the summer of 1962, Charles E. Osgood and Robert C. North undertook the task of establishing a rough foundation for the development of a theory appropriate to the systematic study of international politics. Hypotheses deriving from this theory have been tested, and many have received at least initial confirmation in studies of high-tension and low-tension situations.

The chief theoretical basis for the Stanford Political Dictionary is the semantic differential developed by Osgood and others (Osgood, Suci, and Tannenbaum, 1957) and Osgood (1959, 1963a). The dictionary makes use of three dimensions corresponding to the evaluative, potency, and activity factors found by Osgood and others to be primary in human cognition irrespective of culture. The Stanford dictionary thus reflects the premise that when decision makers (or any human beings) perceive themselves, other decision makers, nations, events, or any stimulus, the most relevant discriminations are made in a space defined by these three factors. This does not assume, however, that two people will agree on whether the stimulus is good or bad, strong or weak, active or passive; it assumes only that these factors account for a large proportion of discrimination variance. The three dimensions yield six tags which form the core of the dictionary:

POSITIVE AFFECT . . . . NEGATIVE AFFECT
STRENGTH . . . . WEAKNESS
ACTIVITY . . . . PASSIVITY

In constructing these tags, entry words were gathered from four main sources. The basic entry list consisted of the 3,000 most frequently used words in the English language drawn from Thorndike-Lorge (1944). In order to make the entry list more appropriate for the analysis of political documents, the sources were also examined for additional words:

1. Documents relating to the outbreak of World War I in 1914.
   a. British documents
   b. French documents
   c. Russian documents
   d. German documents
   e. Austro-Hungarian documents
2. Chinese Communist and Soviet Russian documents relating to
   a. The signing of the Japanese-American security treaty (January 1960)

b. The U-2 incident (May 1960)

c. The Bay of Pigs Invasion (April 1961)

3. American, Soviet, and Chinese documents relating to the Cuban Crisis of October 1962

It is felt that these sources provide a good cross section of the vocabulary of politics. Experience in studies completed to date indicates that the current dictionary is capable of analyzing over 98 percent of the text.

Assignment of entry words to the three dimensions was undertaken in the following way. Three or more judges were asked to indicate which dimensions were relevant to each word. Because it was assumed that the paired dimensions are independent, any word might be tagged for one, two, or three dimensions; that is, a word might be rated positive–strong–active, but not positive-negative or strong-weak. This resulted in six lists corresponding to the six ends of the two dimensions. A series of judges then rated the words on each list in terms of three intensity levels, and the results of these judgments were averaged. The word list for each of the six tags was then forced into a 30 percent–40 percent–30 percent distribution: words whose average ratings were in the top 30 percent were given the intensity rating of 3, the next 40 percent were rated 2, and the lowest 30 percent were assigned the intensity rating of 1.

The core of the dictionary is therefore 3,500 words tagged for the dimensions of affect, strength, and activity, with each of the dimensions scaled for six levels of intensity. Some words of course are tagged for only one or two dimensions. Table 5.3 lists the tags, and gives examples of entry words.

TABLE 5.3. Stanford Political Dictionary: List of Tags

Tag	Number of Words	Examples of Words
POSITIVE AFFECT	977	mutual, natural, normal, pure
NEGATIVE AFFECT	1,513	scandal, profane, refuse, repugnant
STRENGTH	1,391	steel, stone, sword, tough
WEAKNESS	579	thin, unaware, under
ACTIVITY	1,218	react, reign, touch, travel
PASSIVITY	722	unchanged, utter, wait
OVERSTATE	128	absolutely, accurately, always
UNDERSTATE	50	although, apparently, approximately
NOT	6	unlike, neither

A second set of categories completes the main dictionary. These minor categories relate to the perceiver's style of expression. The tags OVERSTATE and UNDERSTATE derived from the Harvard dictionary indicate emphatic and hesitant styles. Words of negation (NOT) are also treated as a separate category. It is quite evident that the first dictionary is completely connotative in character.

A third set of categories is incorporated in a separate dictionary which is used in a second-pass on the computer. The second dictionary is denotative, consisting entirely of geographical and biographical proper name entries. Names of persons and places serve as the entry words, which are tagged with relevant information necessary for identification. Examples of entries used in the analysis of the Cuban Crisis of 1962 include

> GROMYKO = SOVIET — UNION + FOREIGN — MINISTER +
> EXECUTIVE + COMMUNIST
> WASHINGTON = UNITED — STATES + CAPITAL
> MAO TSE-TUNG = CHINA + CHAIRMAN + COMMUNIST —
> PARTY

The geographical-biographical dictionary serves three major purposes. First, it relieves the coder from the necessity of memorizing and adding all desired identification information each time such a term appears in the text. The dictionary also serves to cross-reference proper names in order to permit more economical retrieval. For example, references to the Soviet Union are commonly made through a number of terms referring to the nation (Soviets, Russia, U.S.S.R.), to decision makers (Khrushchev), or institutions (the Kremlin). In the dictionary, each of these terms is identified as a synonym for "Soviet Union." Thus the analyst may use a single question set to retrieve all information concerning the Soviet Union regardless of the terms used in the document.

The geographical and biographical dictionary is a useful tool in problems that depend on discriminating among subunits of a larger class. The analyst may, for example, wish to compare the perceptions of Democrats with those of Republicans, or the perceptions of members of the legislature with those of the executive. Such information may not be explicit in the text but can be inserted automatically through dictionary entries such as

KENNEDY = UNITED — STATES + PRESIDENT + EXECUTIVE +
    DEMOCRAT
FULBRIGHT = UNITED — STATES + SENATE + LEGISLATURE +
    DEMOCRAT
  KEATING = UNITED —STATES + SENATE + LEGISLATURE +
    REPUBLICAN

Thus the dictionary may be used to aggregate subunits of proper name references, such as Republicans and Democrats, for efficient retrieval.

The amount and type of information in the second-pass dictionary will vary according to the particular research problem. The nature of politics makes it likely that a thorough revision of the second-pass dictionary will be necessary for each new research problem. The entries for American decision makers in a study of the U-2 incident (Eisenhower, Herter, Dulles, Lodge, and so on) would clearly be inadequate for an analysis of the Cuban missile crisis. A research application using this dictionary is presented in Chapter 10.

THE HARVARD NEED-ACHIEVEMENT DICTIONARY

Number of Language Signs Classified (omitting *N* words): 855
Number of Tags: 14

The Need-Achievement Dictionary was developed primarily by two members of the Harvard research team, Daniel Ogilvie and Louise Woodhead. The dictionary was developed to duplicate an existing hand-scoring system of content analysis for TAT responses developed by David McClelland of the Department of Social Relations at Harvard.

Unlike the Harvard and Stanford dictionaries, the Need-Achievement Dictionary does not attempt a near-complete word coverage of a document. It is only concerned with detecting the existence of an expressed need for achievement, and all words irrelevant to such a need are discarded. The size of the entry list is therefore considerably smaller than for these other dictionaries.

Purpose

To this date, the users of the General Inquirer have concerned themselves primarily with the frequency of various tag applications to particular texts. This procedure aids the investigator in itemizing *differences* between documents. Once tag differences were determined, investigators have attempted to discern the meaning of these differences and to reconstruct the diversity of ideas and thoughts conveyed through written materials. The development of retrievals based on the co-occurrence of tags and the use of factor analytic methods of data organization have aided the investigator in attaching meanings to various tag profiles. This "attachment of meaning" has often taken the form of labeling particular tag clusters or combinations. Labels are usually selected that summarize the arrangement of variables in some understandable way. For example, a certain constellation of tags might be interpreted as a *theme,* a *trait,* or a *value orientation,* and so forth. The choice of terminology depends largely on the nature of the materials and the interests of the investigator. But the important point here is that the choice has always been made *by the investigator.* We have never relied on the computer to make such interpretive decisions.

We are now in the position of at least attempting to construct rules enabling the computer to make these kinds of decisions. Thus we no longer will be solely concerned with the frequencies of various concepts, but instead more directly involved in the problems of dealing with sequences of words and phrases. In doing so, we feel that we are attacking an important issue inherent in the heavy reliance on frequencies of words or tag occurrences in most General Inquirer studies. For example, a writer of a suicide note might have to say, "I am going to kill myself, kill myself, kill myself, kill myself" before the General Inquirer would (through tag counts) convey this central theme of self-destruction. Just one statement to that effect could well get lost in a maze of other more "significant" discriminators.

In conceptualizing a computer model for making decisions about the nature of a document we confront the issue of the kinds of decisions we wish it to make. One possibility can, at this point, be dismissed. That is the possibility of constructing a system that is capable of reconstructing a theme, no matter what that theme may be. This would entail the prestoring of information and rules relevant to every theme that exists or could exist. We have not been that ambitious.

Another more promising possibility is to concentrate on one theme, thus drastically simplifying the problem. By so limiting our interest, we could attempt to construct a system that would answer the question,

Does this sentence, paragraph, document, and so forth, contain X theme or does it not? This, of course, is not an artificial problem. In fact, a number of hand-scoring systems have been developed to answer this type of question. With this in mind, we decided to approach the task just set forth by attempting to duplicate a hand-scoring system on the computer. Therefore, our goal was to construct rules enabling the computer to make decisions that are reliably similar to the decisions of a skilled judge. In making such an attempt, we have had in mind the following question: At our present level of technology, what are the possibilities of computers making interpretive judgments? As we come nearer to an answer to this question we also hope to illuminate more sharply some of the difficulties inherent in translating rules governing human strategies of decision into rules governing automatic strategies of decision.

The Search for a System

A primary consideration in selecting a hand-scoring method to "mechanize" was that it be reasonably objective, yet complex enough to provide an adequate answer to our question. David McClelland's system for scoring Need-Achievement fulfilled both criteria. First, it is objective enough to enable general agreement between scorers. Second, its complexity requires a good simulation which considers contingencies of words rather than relying solely on the appearance of a few key words.

Another reason for selecting the "N-Ach" scoring system was that we were encouraged by George Litwin's previous attempt to duplicate the system (1962). Although Litwin's early work with simulating McClelland's system was not programmed, he successfully demonstrated that the possibility of automation existed by outlining a system that distinguished between 30 TAT stories in much the same manner as McClelland's system. Litwin's goal, however, differed from our present goal in that he was interested in empirically revising the existing hand-scoring method by making use of correlational and factor analytic studies of words and phrases. Our goal is more modest insofar as we are just trying to duplicate the system as it currently exists. We have no theoretical investment in its revision. Revision is important to us only if we discover inconsistencies in the system as we attempt to simulate it.

A final reason for focusing our efforts on the N-Ach scoring system is that it is widely used. Not only has it been used extensively by McClelland and his associates in scoring TAT themes and stories written for children, but other investigators have used it in a variety of studies. By way of agreement that it can be successfully used as a measure for achievement, it has become a model for other scoring systems designed to score for "Need-Affiliation," "Need-Power," and "Need-Competence."

Overview of the Need-Achievement Scoring System

Following Murray, McClelland takes the position that responses to ambiguous stimuli (for example, TAT's) can reveal the underlying motivational or need structure of the individual. That is, if an individual has a high need for achievement, then his apperceptions should reveal this fact. It would take us too far away from the purpose of this paper to review in detail what is meant by "need for achievement," but a partial understanding would be helpful. Suffice it to say that it is a label attached to the motivation behind a fairly well defined syndrome of behavior. This syndrome includes postponement of gratification, moderate risk taking, sublimation of aggressive energies into entrepreneurial activities, independence, and so forth.

McClelland's task was to devise a scoring system that would reveal whether or not an individual's response to a TAT contained images and themes that could reliably be characterized as achievement related. The system that emerged from this effort first places each story in one of three categories: (1) definitely containing achievement imagery (AI); (2) having doubtful achievement imagery (TI); or (3) containing no achievement imagery (UI or unrelated imagery). The criteria for scoring AI will be considered in detail when we discuss the construction of tag categories.

If the story cannot be scored AI but contains some references to achievement, it is scored for doubtful achievement imagery (TI). McClelland explains his choice of T as a symbol for this category as follows

> (T) indicates that most frequently the stories to be classified as doubtful are ones in which one of the characters is engaged in a commonplace *task* or solving a routine problem. Whenever there is doubt about whether or not one of the three criteria for Achievement Imagery has been met, and the story is not totally unrelated to achievement, it is classified as TI.
> (McClelland, Atkinson, Clark, and Lowell, 1953, 114–115)

If the story cannot be placed in either of the categories, it is classified UI.

Finally each story that is scored AI is further checked for the appearance of one or more "subcategories." Although strategies for scoring subcategories have been partially worked out, most of our efforts have centered around accurate initial placement of a story in the AI, TI, or UI categories. Before discussing this, it is important to point out that this is an operating system and with the limited amount of test runs that have been performed, it is operating successfully. In all, 240 TAT compositions have been categorized by the computer (in batches of 60 stories) and the percent of agreement between the automatic method and trained scorers has varied from 82 to 86 percent. We view this degree of success as encouraging for eventual simulation of the entire N-Ach scoring system (including the subcategories).

Tag Categories and the Rationale for Them

The most crucial and probably the most difficult stage in developing a system using General Inquirer principles is the formulation of tag categories. Careful selection of tag headings tends to reduce the problem of filling out the categories with words that are likely to appear in texts. Our search for relevant tags was greatly facilitated by McClelland's proposed "behavioral sequence" related to the achievement activity. In brief, this sequence

> originates when an individual experiences a state of *need*. He may . . . be anticipating *successful attainment* of his goal or anticipating frustration and *failure*. He may engage in *activity instrumental* to the attainment of his goal . . . Sometimes his goal-directed activity will be *blocked*. He may experience strong *positive* and *negative affective* states while engaged in solving his problem . . . He is likely to experience a state of positive affect in goal attainment, or a state of negative affect when his goal-directed activity is thwarted or he fails.
>
> (McClelland, Atkinson, Clark, and Lowell, 1953, 108)

Before discussing the definition of what constitutes an achievement goal, we shall itemize the tag headings extracted from the preceding quotation. First, the individual experiences a state of need. It seemed reasonable to tag as "need" words such as wants, desires, hopes, and yearns. Similarly, since anticipation of success or failure is considered an important aspect of the behavioral sequence, they, too, were taken as tag headings. Fame, success, glory, honor, and praise are a few of the words entered under SUCCESS; error, incorrect, mistake, ruin, and blunder are tagged as FAILURE.

A very important category for the achievement dictionary was developed from the aspect of the behavioral sequence termed instrumental-activity. This category has been given the name VERB-POSITIVE and is used to tag over 100 activity words specific to the concept of achievement (that is, doing, making, inventing, working, and so on).

In addition to the four tags already discussed, three others were selected from McClelland's behavioral sequence. These were BLOCK, AFFECT-POSITIVE and AFFECT-NEGATIVE. BLOCK contains words indicating difficulties or obstacles standing in the way of goal attainment. At present, most of the words in this category connote environmentally induced blocks; for example, the words test, broken, damage, examination, crisis. McClelland calls such blocks "environmental obstacles." The other subdivision of the category BLOCK in McClelland's scheme is "personal obstacle." This refers to a personal lack of confidence, ineptitude, awkwardness, and so on. We have found that for over-all scoring of achievement imagery this subdivision is not important. However, our work with subcategories has indicated that the addition of a *personal obstacles* category would be to our advantage.

Finally AFFECT-POSITIVE and AFFECT-NEGATIVE were two of our most straightforward categories. The former includes such words as joy, happy, cheerful, delighted; and the latter includes sad, disappointed, sorry, angry, worried, unhappy, and so on.

We have now introduced seven of the fourteen tags currently used in the achievement dictionary. As will be made clear later, none of these tags are important in and of themselves. That is, it can easily be seen that an individual can express negative affect in a variety of different circumstances. He can be "sad" about a death in the family, he can be "unhappy" about a scar created by an automobile accident, or he can be "disappointed" by a rainy day. Likewise, a person might express a "need" to go on a vacation, he may "want" to destroy a relative, or he may "desire" to win an essay contest. A mere total of the number of times these seven categories define various words in a document can tell us little about the document itself. It is only when two or more concepts co-occur that we can begin to reconstruct the meaning of a sentence as it relates to a particular theme. Since the theme in this case is achievement, we must specify the nature of an achievement goal more precisely. In the process of defining achievement goals, we shall itemize seven more categories. This will complete our list of 14 definitions.

McClelland defines achievement goal as "success in competition with some standard of excellence" (1953, 110). The important criteria here is *concern* over competition with a standard of excellence and not whether the individual successfully attains his goal. Following from this general definition, McClelland lists a series of three criterion used in scoring for achievement imagery. For a story to be scored AI, it must clearly fall within the boundaries of one or more of these criteria.

   I. *Competition with a standard of excellence.*
     A. One of the characters in the story is engaged in some *competitive activity* (other than pure cases of aggression) where winning or doing as well as or better than others is actually stated as the primary concern.
     B. If one of the characters in the story is engaged in some competitive activity (other than pure cases of aggression), but the desire to win or do as well as or better than others is not explicitly stated, then 1) affective concern over goal attainment, and 2) certain types of instrumental activity are considered as indicating that the desire to compete successfully with a standard of excellence is implicit in the story.
     C. Often the standard of excellence involved no competition with others but meeting self-imposed requirements of good performance. In this case, in order to score for AI what is needed are words to the effect that a *good, thorough, workmanlike job,* and so forth is desired, or statements showing the affective concern or instrumental activity that will allow such an inference. . . .
        (McClelland, Atkinson, Clark, and Lowell, 1953, 111–112)

Two tags were derived from this criterion. A list of words suggesting that an effort is being made to excel at a competitive activity were placed under the general heading COMPETE. Win, gain, overtake, and surpass are examples of words included in this list. The other tag category was constructed from criterion IC. This tag, ADVERB-POSITIVE, was chosen to assist in picking up parts of sentences suggesting that a "good, thorough, workmanlike job" is desired. Since this concern is often expressed in verb-adverb combinations (for instance, work carefully, study thoroughly, and probe cautiously) and since we already have the tag VERB-POSITIVE, the addition of ADVERB-POSITIVE allows us to focus on such relevant combinations.

> II. *Unique Accomplishment*
> One of the characters is involved in accomplishing other than a run-of-the-mill daily task which will mark him as a personal success. Inventions, artistic creations, and other *extraordinary accomplishments* fulfill this criteria. . . .
> (McClelland, Atkinson, Clark, and Lowell, 1953, 113)

We have divided "extraordinary accomplishments" into two tags. The first is called VALUE-POSITIVE. Words classified under this category are most often nouns relevant to culturally valued goals — but only those goals that are related to achieving activity (for instance, discovery, creation, curiosity, intelligence, skill). The second list of words are modifiers that are related to the "extraordinary" aspects of the accomplishments. These words (such as great, powerful, promising, splendid) are placed under the general heading ADJECTIVE-POSITIVE.

> III. *Long-term Involvement*
> One of the characters is involved in attainment of a *long-term achievement* goal. Being a success in life, *becoming* a *machinist, doctor, lawyer,* successful *businessman,* and so forth, are all examples of career involvement which permit the inference of competition with a standard of excellence unless it is made explicit that another goal is primary, e.g. food for the kids, personal security.
> (McClelland, Atkinson, Clark, and Lowell, 1953, 113)

The final three tags were taken from this criterion of "long-term involvement." From our experience, the least useful category (one that may eventually be dropped) is TIME. Words like lifetime, life, years that on the surface appear to be very important in achievement scoring have been more misleading than useful. However, this is not true for the next two tags: TO-BE and ROLE-POSITIVE. The tag TO-BE defines three "idioms" and two words: to be, to become, of becoming, become, becomes, and becoming. By themselves, these words and phrases do not give us much information about a document; but when used in conjunction with other key words, they provide crucial links in scoring achievement imagery. Detailed examples of these contingency relationships will be presented shortly.

One remaining tag not yet discussed is ROLE-POSITIVE. This almost self-explanatory category includes titles of various roles that are valued by our "achieving" society. Some examples are doctor, surgeon, lawyer, thinker, professor, and executive.

This concludes the presentation of the tag categories for the Achievement Scoring System. A list of these tags plus a sample of words defined by them appears in Table 5.4.

TABLE 5.4. Tag Names and Sample Words

Tags	Examples	Number
NEED	wants, desires, hopes, yearns	57
TO-BE	become, becoming, to become	6
COMPETE	win, gain, overtake, surpass	28
VERB-POSITIVE	doing, making, inventing, working	136
ADVERB-POSITIVE	carefully, properly, cautiously, thoroughly	50
ADJECTIVE-POSITIVE	great, powerful, promising, splendid	166
VALUE-POSITIVE	discovery, creation, curiosity, intelligence	142
ROLE-POSITIVE	surgeon, lawyer, executive, professor	38
BLOCK	test, broken, damage, crisis	53
SUCCESS	fame, success, glory, honor	23
FAILURE	error, incorrect, mistake, blunder	43
AFFECT-POSITIVE	joy, happy, cheerful, delighted	27
AFFECT-NEGATIVE	sad, anxious, sorry, worried	82
TIME	lifetime, life, years, weeks	4

Up to this point, we have presented our tag categories piecemeal, without stressing how they function as a system. Some of the tags, such as VERB-POSITIVE, ADVERB-POSITIVE, are based on a "part-of-speech" division. Dividing our categories grammatically seemed a requirement for the effective analysis of themes. Since a theme is essentially a set of relationships, either among words or other structural units (phrases, sentences), the identification of these sequences of patterns is crucial for thematic analysis. Because language is a system and meaning is conveyed through an organized combination of component parts, we have tried to base our categories on those parts.

The thematic relationships that this system has enabled us to score as Need-Achievement imagery will be outlined in the following presentation of rules.

Rules and Reasons

It was noted that words defined by our tag categories could be used in a variety of contexts that are in no way related to achievement imagery. To circumvent these difficulties and additional problems of relying on the appearance of one word or one tag for scoring a document, we formulated a number of rules prescribing sets of tag sequences that are likely to occur only in documents containing achievement imagery.

Since our rules have been constructed directly from McClelland's criteria for manual scoring of achievement, we shall go back to his statements and extract the sections that have proved helpful. Although we have quoted McClelland extensively, the repetition of some of that material is unavoidable.

Recall that Part A of the first criterion, "Competition with a Standard of Excellence," states, "One of the characters in the story is engaged in some competitive activity where winning or doing as well as or better than others is actually stated as the primary concern" (McClelland, Atkinson, Clark, and Lowell, 1953, 113). Statements like "he is *determined* to *win*," "he *wants* to *excel*," "he *dreams* of *succeeding*" all fulfill this criteria. The first underlined word in each phrase is defined NEED by our dictionary and the second series of words has been included in our COMPETE category. Therefore, every time a sentence contains words defined by NEED and COMPETE (in that sequence) it is scored for achievement. It is important to note that that sequence alone is sufficient for scoring the entire document AI.

Part B of the first criterion includes the following statement:

> If one of the characters in the story is engaged in some competitive activity . . . but the desire to win . . . is not explicitly stated, then affective concern over goal attainment . . . [indicates] that the desire to compete successfully with a standard of excellence is implicit in the story.
> (McClelland, Atkinson, Clark, and Lowell, 1953, 111)

Two related rules have been drawn from this criterion. The first is SUCCESS followed by AFFECT-POSITIVE. This rule is meant to cover statements indicating that a goal has been successfully attained and that the hero is happy about his triumph: "He received lots of recognition (SUCCESS) for his efforts and was pleased (AFFECT-POSITIVE). A special feature of this rule and the next rule to be discussed is that affective concern need not be expressed in the same sentence that conveys SUCCESS. Our example could just as well have been expressed in two sentences: "He received lots of recognition for his efforts. This pleased him very much." The computer routine we use to identify these "cross-sentence" sequences works in the following manner. When a word in the text is defined AFFECT-POSITIVE, the *preceding* sentence is checked for the occurrence of SUCCESS. If SUCCESS is found, the document is scored AI. Empirically we have found that most instances of successful activity combined with affective involvement are conveyed either in one sentence or in two sequential sentences. Therefore the computer routine terminates its search for SUCCESS after the sentence preceding the instance of AFFECT-POSITIVE has been scanned.

The other rule developed from criterion IB is FAILURE plus AFFECT-NEGATIVE. As McClelland notes, an indication of failure is not enough to warrant the inference that success was desired. On the other hand, failure followed by negative affect (angry, upset, distressed) suggests more than peripheral involvement in goal-directed activity. Examples are "He *lost* the game and was *disgusted* with himself," "The problem remained *unsolved* and his *anxiety* remained high." The cross-sentence routine would score sentences like the following: "George *failed* the exam for the second time. This made him *furious*."

The sequence of tags developed from Part C of the first criterion was discussed during the presentation of tag categories. This criterion was formulated by McClelland to include statements that indicate that a "good, thorough, workmanlike job" is desired. Phrases like "train regularly," "raise carefully," or "study diligently" indicate that the individual is competing against self-imposed standards. With evidence to this effect, direct competition with others is not necessary for AI scoring. As just mentioned, the rule intended to locate these co-occurrences is any combination of a VERB-POSITIVE and an ADVERB-POSITIVE in one sentence.

The second criterion in McClelland's system is "Unique Accomplishment." To fulfill this criterion, "there need be no explicit statement of concern over the outcome or direct statement that a good job is wanted when someone is working on a new invention or is in the process of doing something unique which will be generally accepted as a personal accomplishment." Concern with inventions, artistic creations, and other extraordinary, non-run-of-the-mill activities satisfies this criterion. As we have mentioned, words like discovery, creation, and invention have been defined VALUE-POSITIVE. When a VALUE-POSITIVE is found in conjunction with a word defined as instrumental activity (VERB-POSITIVE), AI is scored. *"Working* on a *masterpiece,"* *"building a fortune,"* and *"conducting research"* are a few examples.

A less satisfactory but still generally useful rule is the combination of ADJECTIVE-POSITIVE with VALUE-POSITIVE. The examples *illustrious refinement, magnificent progress,* and *great industry* give some idea of the nature of the adjective-noun combinations scored as achievement related by this rule.

Two of our most reliable rules have been developed from McClelland's third criterion for scoring AI. This criterion concerns longterm involvement with an achievement goal. "Being a success in life, becoming a machinist, doctor, lawyer . . . are all examples of career involvement which permit the inference of competition with a standard of excellence . . ." Statements like "He wants to become a doctor," "He dreams of becoming an inventor," and "He wonders if he will ever become famous" all fulfill this criterion. The words wants, dreams, and wonders have been classified as NEED; and the words to

TABLE 5.5. Summary of Rules

Rule 1: NEED + COMPETE
"He *wants* to present a clearcut synthesis of these two conflicting philosophies, to satisfy his own ego and *gain* academic recognition from his professor.
Rule 2: SUCCESS + AFFECT-POSITIVE (within- and cross-sentence routine)
"The worker wanted *fame* and got it. He died a *happy* man."
Rule 3: FAILURE + AFFECT-NEGATIVE (within- and cross-sentence routine)
"The invention will be a *failure. Discouraged* and financially bankrupt, the man will drown himself with liquor."
Rule 4: VERB-POSITIVE + ADVERB-POSITIVE
"The operator is hoping that everything will *pan out properly.*"
Rule 5: VERB-POSITIVE + VALUE-POSITIVE
"The first man wants to get it *fixed* and do a *good job.*"
Rule 6: ADJECTIVE-POSITIVE + VALUE-POSITIVE
"He will wander from this *steadfast purpose* but eventually achieve it."
Rule 7: NEED + TO-BE + ROLE-POSITIVE
"For a long time he has *wanted to become* a *mechanic.*"
Rule 8: NEED + TO-BE + ADJECTIVE-POSITIVE
"All he *wanted* was *to become great* at something."
Rule 9: TO-BE + SUCCESS (last sentence routine)
"Mutual compromise and the machine *will be* a *success.*"

---

become, of becoming, and become are defined TO-BE. "Doctor" and "inventor" are ROLE-POSITIVE, and "famous" is an ADJECTIVE-POSITIVE. Thus the two rules NEED + TO-BE + ROLE-POSITIVE and NEED + TO-BE + ADJECTIVE-POSITIVE have been formulated to detect sentences suggesting long-term involvement in an achievement goal.

Our final rule is not as directly related to McClelland's criteria as are the ones just presented. After processing numerous stories, we discovered that a few of the documents, which should have been scored AI but were not, contained a last sentence stating that the hero was (or would be) successful ("He will become a success," "The experiment will be successful"). Since none of our existing rules covered such a sequence, we added the rule TO-BE + SUCCESS. This rule only operates on the last sentence of a document and thus far appears to be a helpful addition.

Since our presentation has been a gradual and somewhat tedious summary of the rules, an example of sentences identified by each of these rules should be helpful. This summary appears in Table 5.5.

We end this discussion of the construction of rules with a description of our strategy for scoring documents for Doubtful Achievement Imagery (TI). It has already been noted that stories that do not fulfill any of the three criteria for AI scoring but contain some references to

TABLE 5.6. Example of Story Scored AI

Sentence 1: The student is *dreaming* about *becoming* a *great inventor*.	NEED TO-BE ADJECTIVE-POSITIVE ROLE-POSITIVE SENTENCE SUM = AI
Sentence 2: After *years* of *labor* the crucial moment arrives.	TIME VERB-POSITIVE SENTENCE SUM = UI
Sentence 3: He *hopes* everything will *turn out well*.	NEED VERB-POSITIVE ADVERB-POSITIVE SENTENCE SUM = AI
Sentence 4: But the *experiment* will *fail*.	VALUE-POSITIVE FAILURE SENTENCE SUM = UI
Sentence 5: *Displeased* but still *confident* he will modify his procedures and try again.	AFFECT-NEGATIVE VALUE-POSITIVE SENTENCE SUM = AI

****SUMMARY****THIS DOCUMENT CONTAINS ACHIEVEMENT IMAGERY.

achievement are scored TI. More specifically, these are stories in which one of the characters is engaged in a *commonplace task* or in *solving a routine problem.*

Empirically, we have found that stories that have not been scored AI but which contain a word tagged BLOCK are (almost without ex-

TABLE 5.7. Example of Story Scored TI

Sentence 1:
The persons are *studying*.   VERB-POSITIVE SENTENCE SUM = UI

Sentence 2:
The central object is *daydreaming*,   NEED VERB-POSITIVE SENTENCE SUM = UI
not *concentrating*.

Sentence 3:
He is probably in a world of   SENTENCE SUM = UI
fantasy, or reliving some past ex-
perience.

Sentence 4:
The boy attended classes and got   BLOCK
assignments to do.   SENTENCE SUM = TI

Sentence 5:
He has balanced his time so he has   SENTENCE SUM = UI
a little extra.

Sentence 6:
He should be *studying* but he is not.   VERB-POSITIVE SENTENCE SUM = UI

Sentence 7:
Some problem is bothering him,   SENTENCE SUM = UI
probably lack of concentration.

Sentence 8:
The boy *wants* to remember some-   NEED SENTENCE SUM = UI
thing pleasant.

Sentence 9:
Perhaps he is not, perhaps reliving   SENTENCE SUM = UI
his past summer and the fun he had.

Sentence 10:
The outcome *will be* he will snap   TO-BE VERB-POSITIVE SENTENCE SUM = UI
out of it and get back to *work.*

Sentence 11:
The *daydreaming* will surely *become*   NEED TO-BE TO-BE TIME SENTENCE SUM = UI
part of his subconscious *to be*
relived again at some *future* time.

*******SUMMARY***THIS DOCUMENT CONTAINS DOUBTFUL ACHIEVEMENT IMAGERY.

---

ception) placed in the TI category by the hand-scoring method. This is reasonable when we consider the fact that BLOCK words include test, grade, exam, hardship, stuck, and so forth — all of which definitely connote concern with a *task*. In this case, we do not rely on a contingency of words; one such word has been sufficient for TI scoring.

The other rule for TI scoring is the presence of two verbs that have been identified as VERB-POSITIVE. We have found that VERB-POSITIVE occurs frequently in UI (Unrelated Imagery) stories but two or more such words usually means that task activity is being conveyed. In summary, then, one BLOCK or two words defined by VERB-POSITIVE are our only rules for scoring TI.

This concludes our discussion of rules for scoring Need-Achieve-

TABLE 5.8. Example of Story Scored UI

Sentence 1: A father and son are having a very *serious* discussion.	ADJ-POSITIVE SENTENCE SUM = UI
Sentence 2: The son has gotten into *serious* trouble with the police.	ADJ-POSITIVE SENTENCE SUM = UI
Sentence 3: He has gambling debts and has taken some of the family jewels to pay the debt, without telling the father.	SENTENCE SUM = UI
Sentence 4: The father suspects the son but does not accuse him directly.	SENTENCE SUM = UI
Sentence 5: He *wants* the son to confess himself.	NEED SENTENCE SUM = UI
Sentence 6: The son is very *troubled* and *afraid* to tell the truth.	AFFECT-NEG = AFFECT-NEG SENTENCE SUM = UI
Sentence 7: The son will finally break down and confess in tears.	SENTENCE SUM = UI
Sentence 8: The father will give him money to get the jewels back and reprimand although compassionately.	SENTENCE SUM = UI

*****SUMMARY***THIS DOCUMENT CONTAINS UNRELATED IMAGERY.

ment. To summarize and clarify our procedures, we list three stories (Table 5.6, AI; Table 5.7, TI, and Table 5.8, UI) showing the format of the printout from this computer scoring system.

In Table 5.6, text words are listed on the left, and the tags applied to each sentence appear on the right. Text words that have been tagged have been italicized for the reader's convenience. Referring back to Table 5.5, we can see that Sentence 1 fulfilled both Rules 7 and 8. Sentence 3 fulfilled Rule 4 and Sentence 5 contained AFFECT-NEGA-TIVE preceded by FAILURE in Sentence 4, thus fulfilling Rule 3.

The story in Table 5.7 fulfills both criteria for scoring **TI**. The BLOCK in Sentence 4 would have been sufficient. In addition to this BLOCK, 4 words have been tagged VERB-POSITIVE.

Although six words in the text shown in Table 5.8 were identified by tags, none of them appeared in relevant sequence for an AI score nor were the TI rules matched.

CHAPTER SIX

The Development of a Content Analysis Measuring Instrument[1]

INTRODUCTION

The preceding chapters have described a system of interrelated computer programs designed to aid researchers in quantitative content analysis research. To a large extent, the application of the system is independent of the particular content being analyzed and the particular classifying scheme (dictionary) employed. Thus the procedures and the nature of the output produced by various analyses generally take a common form.

We now consider the system as a general procedure for the measurement of certain content characteristics. Many problems common to all forms of measurement are discussed, including reliability, validity, and some aspects of inference. Basic assumptions about the procedure itself are explicated.

The following pages often will be long on suggestions and short on results. This can be traced to two factors: the rapid and widespread use of the instrument before it was comprehensively measured for reliability and validity and the fact that the research was aimed toward developing content analysis procedures as well as using them. The latter is reflected in a continually changing system.

---

[1] The main author of this chapter is Marshall S. Smith.

THE GENERAL INQUIRER
AS A MEASURING INSTRUMENT

> In its broadest sense, measurement is the assignment of numerals to objects or events according to rules.
>
> (Stevens, 1951, 1)

In the context of the General Inquirer system, it is convenient to consider the role of measurement at each of two stages.

The Stage of Dictionary Construction

Dictionary construction consists of two complementary processes: the classification of language signs (words, word roots, and phrases) into a set of theoretically relevant categories and the definition of these categories by the language signs specified for them.[2] Thus in the Psychosociological Dictionary, the language sign "physician" is classified as MALE-ROLE, HIGHER-STATUS, and MEDICAL. The tag category SELF is defined by the language signs I, me, my, mine, and myself. The two processes proceed concurrently as a dictionary is being constructed, and it is often difficult to objectively separate them. However, as the researcher assigns language signs to a category, the definition of that category may subtly be altered from his original intent. The careful researcher, therefore, must be aware of the possible interactive effect of these processes.

Two common implications of classificatory measurement are particularly important: First, the terms of any one category must be equivalent in the property being scaled. Thus all signs in a given tag are generally considered equal and interchangeable.[3] Second, to help ensure this condition of equivalency of terms in a category, a dictionary should be constructed for application to data originating from a specified language community and in response to stimuli from a specified class. As more progress is made in refining general dictionaries, this

---

[2] In terms of Stevens' definition of measurement, the general procedure of dictionary construction can be characterized as the assignment of tag category names (numerals) to language signs (the objects) according to some strategy (rules).

[3] In most dictionaries discussed here, we assume that any given entry in a tag category is as strong an indicator of that category as any other. However, we could differentially *weight* the various terms (entries) of a category, a procedure used in the Stanford Political Dictionary (see Chapter 5).

requirement may become less binding. At the present time, however, error through misclassification does sometimes result from applying a dictionary to inappropriate data.

The Stage of Text Analysis[4]

Three sets of operations can be distinguished at this stage.

Tagging

In this operation, prespecified labels (tags) are assigned to the meaning units contained in the text. This operation is conceptually different from the construction of a dictionary. The objects of measurement in the dictionary construction stage are the various signs of the language community as defined by the investigator. The objects of measurement in the tagging operation are the meaning units contained in the text being analyzed. As explained in Chapter 3, tags are not assigned to the meaning units themselves but rather to the sentence in which the meaning units appear. Although the meaning unit is the object of measurement, the tagging operation carries out labeling on the sentences. Thus for retrieval operations, the sentence is the unit of analysis.

Tag Tally

This operation consists of counting the number of times the text's meaning units are classified into each of the tag categories. A primary assumption of this operation is that each occurrence of a tag is equivalent in emphasis for the property being scaled.[5] The tag tally operation results in the assignment of two types of numbers to each document analyzed: one set represents the absolute frequency of occurrence (raw scores); the second represents the relative frequency of occurrence (index scores). In the tag tally operation, the object of measurement is the document. The computation of index scores allows comparison between documents of varying lengths. This comparison requires the assumption that the length of a document and the relative frequency of occurrence of a tag are independent.

---

[4] In this stage, the dictionary and programs comprise the rules by which numerals (tag names) are assigned to the objects (documents or segments of verbal data) of measurement.

[5] This assumption is derived from the initial procedure of dictionary construction.

Retrieval

As described earlier, this operation may take a number of forms. In every case, however, retrieval operations have two measurement characteristics in common. The objects of retrieval are sentences, and the numbers resulting from a retrieval operation characterize the total document. This set of numbers differs from those resulting from the tag tally procedure. The particular numbers obtained by the retrieval operation are those *requested by the researcher, and they only represent a sample of all possible retrievals that could be made.* In general, then, retrieval operations are far less comprehensive than tag tally operations. The most frequent use of retrieval procedures is *not* the assignment of numbers to documents but the effective exploration of data in order to determine the specific meaning units that contribute to tag tally counts, to investigate possible mistagging of meaning units, and to collect examples and ideas about the data in the context of sentences.[6]

The measurement stages just listed will serve as a primary reference in the following discussion. A second reference is the discussion of dictionary construction that appears in Chapter 4. We shall continually trace content analysis measurement problems back to the stage of dictionary construction. The procedures and strategies employed in dictionary construction influence the resulting reliability and validity of the instrument.

A third reference point might be considered the objective of a psychometric type of analysis. In the following discussion of procedures and assumptions, our primary aim is to develop a framework for the efficient and accurate exposure and assessment of information contained in verbal protocols. The objective of obtaining such information is to make inferences about the source and the antecedents or effects of the language production. The approach advocated here is largely deductive: that is, we superimpose on the data a theoretical framework in the form of a set of content categories and rules for measuring these categories. To justify such a deductive approach, considerable attention must be paid to the empirical nature of the categories as well as to their theoretical relevance. Ideally, in a science with carefully constructed and demonstrated theories, the task of evaluating a measuring

[6] A number of possible uses of the retrieval procedures are discussed in detail in Chapter 3.

instrument is simply one of comparing empirical outcomes to theoretically expected products. Behavioral science theories, however, cannot be claimed to be demonstrated, and thus the construction of an instrument may, in fact, involve the construction of a theory. The interplay between the construction and evolution of a theory in conjunction with the construction and evaluation of a measuring device may be serious. We may be able to distinguish analytically the questions of developing a theoretical system of categories and the actual construction of these categories, but in practice we are not usually able to separate the two operations. The discussion of dictionary construction in Chapter 4 and the present discussion concerning assessment of the functional properties of content categories can be considered a step in the separation of the two operations. Our objective here, however, is not to force this distinction but to show the interactive nature of the two operations while focusing on the empirical nature of the categories.

RELIABILITY

A reliable measuring instrument and procedure produces stable, dependable, and accurate measurements. One of the primary ways of assessing a measure is to determine the amount of error of measurement when the measure is applied. Error of measurement is generally considered to be unsystematic random error. In the measurement of documents it is considered to be the result of chance fluctuations in conditions affecting the source when the document was produced or in conditions affecting the application of the measure. A measurement is unreliable to the extent that it reflects these temporary and shifting influences.

If we can demonstrate that our measures and procedures are reliable, we have a basis for later demonstrating that they are valid. In the assessment of reliability, we ask, for example, if our instrument dependably measures a stable characteristic of certain documents and, more specifically, if the language signs comprising the tag categories have stable meanings over a variety of situations.

Generally, the techniques and approaches used to assess reliability have been developed with the short-answer test in mind. Although the content analyst often can adopt the general goals and framework of the psychometrician, in most cases he must modify or alter the actual procedures. In this discussion, we shall consider four approaches to the assessment of the reliability of content analysis category systems.

Coder Reliability

Traditionally, content analysts have been concerned with the reliability of applying the rules of coding to the data (Berelson, 1954; Holsti, in press). This particular form of reliability is estimated empirically by the degree of correlation between results obtained by independent coders scoring the same data and using a common set of categories. Many studies employing a number of coders have paid considerable attention to this problem and frequently report high levels of coder reliability (Berelson, 1954; Barcus, 1959). To attain high coder reliability, decisions about the major issues of content analysis, units, categories, and coding rules must be specified.

In the General Inquirer system, the tagging procedure corresponds to the operations that would normally determine coder reliability, but because the machine and program replace the human coder, decisions are entirely uniform and perfect coder reliability is obtained.[7] By largely eliminating this problem, the researcher is able to consider more closely the other forms of reliability.

Category Consistency

Category consistency refers to the internal consistency of the list of entries comprising a category.[8] Do the entries in our tag category all appear to measure the same thing? Are they equivalent and interchangeable in the property being scaled?

Two levels of this requirement are apparent: first, the internal consistency of the category when it is developed, and second, the textual equivalence of meaning units to the elements of a category. An

---

[7] To some users of the system, problems of coder reliability are still important. The hand coding of syntactic position of key words in sentences and the coding of proper names and pronoun usage create two such problems, although considerable progress is being made toward an automatic solution of both.

[8] This form of reliability is analogous to the reliability of aptitude or personality scales as measured by the analysis-of-variance method and the split-half method. An example of a procedure of this sort is to divide a scale into two parts, administer the test to a group of people, compute the scores on each half separately, and then correlate the two scores. The correlation coefficient is then considered as the reliability measure.

example should clarify this distinction. Suppose that a researcher desires to assess the attention given by a source to the topic ECONOMIC and develops a category that includes the term "bank." At the level of category construction, the term "bank" might be considered to be consistent with other terms, such as "finance" or "money," in the measurement of the attribute ECONOMIC. In a text, however, the symbol "bank" might be used in the context of "river bank" or "one can bank on it." Thus, at the level where the category is applied to the text, the category cannot be considered to be internally consistent. Although this is a trivial example and an error such as this would probably not be made, the lack of correspondence between the apparent meanings of terms within a category and the use of the terms in a text presents a major problem to content analysts. The many homographs in the English language and the frequent use of idiomatic language contribute to this problem.

In an initial approach to the problem, we may separate the two levels. At the level of classification of language signs into a category, one procedure for obtaining reliability would have a number of qualified persons independently build a content category by selecting language signs from a large pool of possible entries. A reliable category would be signaled by lists with many entries in common. The measure of reliability would have to take into account two variables: (1) the number of agreed-upon entries and (2) the number of singular entries.

The obvious approach to the assessment of category consistency at the level of application of the category to data is to take a set of documents, count the number of times the individual entry terms appear in each document, intercorrelate these counts, and perhaps intercorrelate the counts with the total category scores. A grosser measure would be to split the entry list randomly in half, separately compute scores for each half, and then intercorrelate the scores. The solution is complicated, however, in the content analysis of natural language productions because the source(s) generating the documents may not use, or even know, all the entry words in the tag list. Thus correlations between the individual entries in a category cannot generally be relied upon. Indeed, to the extent that category entries are substitutable forms of expression, they cannot be expected to correlate positively with one another. The split-half approach may be less sensitive to this objection, but the results would still be influenced by it. Furthermore, the objection absolutely rules out one by-product of assessing reliability: the selection or rejection of particular entry words in a category based on their correlations with the total tag score.

Generally, the solution to this problem is pragmatic. The principal purpose of assessing the internal consistency of a category is to aid the researcher in category construction and interpretation of his results. If we can initially assess the level of internal consistency at the time of category construction and apply the category to a sample of data to see how well our category operates in a practical situation, then we have the beginning of a limited feedback loop. This loop would begin with category construction, proceed to application of the category to some data and assessment of the category's behavior, and then feed back to category construction. Careful category construction in content analysis, as in other research situations, often requires the researcher to proceed from the theoretical to the practical and then back to the theoretical; it requires the researcher to integrate the deductive with an inductive approach.[9]

Category Stability[10]

After it has been established that a category is internally consistent, the assessment of reliability turns to the question, "Is the measure dependable?" Scores obtained from reliable measurement of a stable characteristic should not vary over short periods of time or with small changes in the stimulus situation.[11]

[9] Other approaches to the assessment of category consistency may exist. Insofar as entries within a category list are substitutable, the entries should be able to correlate negatively with one another, while having similar patterns of positive correlation with other categories.

[10] The measurement of a similar form of reliability, test-retest reliability, is common practice in the construction of objective measurement devices. Often, this measurement can take the form of an item-by-item correlation. However, in content analysis the responses cannot be fully defined, and the correlation must be made on total scale scores.

[11] In a discussion of the Achievement Motive, Roger Brown (1965, 433) remarks. "If testing situations are kept the same, perhaps just neutral, the absolute scores as well as relative order ought to remain the same if it is true that scores are chiefly determined by the controlled orientation and a stable personality characteristic. There are, however, other possible determinants. Individual scores might be chiefly determined by recent random events. Plays seen on television the night before, a novel just put down, a conversation before class could all affect the stories people tell on a given occasion. Insofar as these events are the effective determinants, scores would not remain constant or preserve their order."

Two factors complicate the measurement of this form of reliability, here called *category stability:*

1. Often content categories are constructed to be sensitive to subtle changes in the stimulus situation and to changes over time. Other categories are constructed to be stable over time and in different situations. The researcher must be careful to differentiate between the two types of categories before blindly applying his measurement procedures.

2. In the assessment of a content analysis category, it must be recognized that the domain of responses in the natural language protocol cannot be completely controlled. Thus, even though a category is internally consistent, the document may contain meaning units that should be but are not included as entry terms for that category.

A sensitive researcher should be able to deal with the first factor. The second poses a more difficult problem, although a number of studies reported on here have attempted to approximate a solution. Category construction is the crucial factor. If a category could contain the entire population of entry terms relevant to it, the problem is solved; but the limits on dictionary size and the immense number of possible terms in any language community militate against this solution. To overcome this problem, researchers have made extensive use of lists of frequently used words and large comprehensive key-word-in-context samples. In pilot studies, examination of leftover lists and careful analysis of other pre-existing dictionaries are often valuable. In most cases, however, the tags will still contain only a sample of the population of possible entry terms. Researchers applying an existing dictionary to the analysis of data should be aware of this problem. Their data may contain important signs that were not anticipated by the dictionary architects, and the researcher may be required to expand or reconstruct some of the dictionary categories.[12]

Two other more practical alternatives exist. The first is the more conventional measurement of this form of reliability. Two samples of data are drawn and processed; the researcher matches the sources in the two samples into pairs and then correlates the tag category

---

[12] Alteration of existing dictionaries by different researchers makes cross-study comparisons of results difficult, but the alteration procedure is often necessary.

scores across the sampled pairs. A variation on this approach is to split half a set of documents, match the documents into pairs, and then correlate the tags across pairs. The same problems exist for both approaches. It is often very difficult to match pairs, and frequently the matching must be made on some gross level (such as on documents originating from the same newspaper or folk culture). Further, the matching is not always consistent across pairs.[13]

The second alternative also involves two samples or a sample split in half and then matched. In this situation, the matching is by groups. The objects of comparison are the tag mean and standard deviation scores for the matched groups rather than correlations. It may be argued that large discrepancies between the group means on a tag signal an unreliable category. Those categories showing discrepancies may either be discarded or reconstructed.

A note of caution should be sounded about exercises such as these. The best vehicle for the examination of reliability is an experimental situation in which the researcher is in control of the circumstances under which the data are collected. Furthermore, the data should be collected for the purpose of reliability analysis and preferably should not also be used for testing experimental hypotheses.

Another appropriate situation is a pilot study on available data. In both cases, the object of the research is an evaluation of the dictionary categories. Problems arise when the same data used to investigate and search for hypotheses are also used to evaluate dictionaries, for even the most careful and honest researcher will often find it difficult not to stack the deck subtly in his favor by convenient changes in the dictionary.

Interpretive Reliability

When a large number of variables are measured, a broad range of interpretations, perhaps conflicting, is always possible. Interpretive reliability is the degree to which independent researchers, familiar with the method of content analysis and the particular study being made, arrive at similar interpretations of the results. When specific hypotheses are being tested and when the investigators share a common

---

[13] An example of an approach such as this is found in Chapter 19. Kalin, Davis, and McClelland gathered two samples of folktales from 46 cultures, matched pairs by culture, and then correlated across pairs.

theoretical framework, the problem of interpretive reliability is minimized.

VALIDITY

To the researcher, validity information indicates the degree to which a measuring instrument is capable of achieving the aims for which it was constructed, for measuring what he thinks he is measuring. Suppose, for example, the researcher defines a content category and labels it SELF-REFERENCE. The category is defined by its entry terms: I, me, mine, myself, and my. Suppose also that through appropriate techniques he determines that the category is internally consistent and stable. Moreover, he has an idea about what this measure should be tapping. In constructing the category, he tried to operationally define a theoretical construct. The category should appear to measure a manifestation of this construct in the source of the document to which it is applied.[14] He further has an idea about the way in which the usage of the terms of the category will vary under different stimulus situations. He might expect the category to predict some criterion measure or to discriminate between certain defined groups. At a more advanced level, he might expect the category to fit into a theoretical network, to correlate positively with certain variables, to operate independently of others, and to vary in a negative relationship with others.

Validation is the process by which the researcher examines a measure to see if it fits these expectations. It may be argued that in every content analysis there is an inference made from the characteristics of the document being measured to the source of the document. Three basic premises underlie this inference: that some manifestation of the theoretical construct for which our category was designed to assess actually exists in the source of the document; that the terms of the category indicate this manifestation; and that the meaning of the terms as they are used in the document is equivalent to the meaning of the terms at the stage of category construction. In quantitative content analysis, a fourth premise is often added: the frequency of occurrence

---

[14] In this chapter and in Chapter 7, the term "source" will be used to signify the person or persons who were responsible for generating the data (documents, text). The reader could substitute "author(s)" or "speaker" or "writer(s)" for the term if he wishes. Also, as discussed in Chapter 4, the categories being validated may be single tags or combinations or co-occurrences of tags.

of the terms in the document should correspond to the intensity of the manifestation. This set of premises is similar to those underlying most measurement in the behavioral sciences. To assess these premises, a generally accepted set of procedures has been developed. These procedures delineate four types of validation techniques that should be considered in the development of a measuring instrument: content validity, concurrent validity, predictive validity, and construct validity.

Content Validity

Generally two broad questions are evaluated in the process of assessing content validity:

1. Does the measure look as though it is measuring what the researcher wants it to measure? In the context of the content analysis systems described here, the question becomes, "Do the entry terms in a tag appear to measure the concept that the tag is constructed to measure?"

This question can be divided into two parts. Do the entry terms look as though they are indicants of the source manifestation of the theoretical construct? Generally, the researcher makes only a qualitative estimate of this question merely by looking at the various entry terms when he constructs the category. Perhaps if the construct that he wishes to operationalize were completely defined by a number of independent judges, and if he were then to ask these judges to rate the category as to its content validity, he could get some form of empirical test for this part of the question.

The second part of the first question relates to the correspondence between the meaning of the terms intended by the analyst in construction of the category and the meaning of the terms as they are used in the document. This problem was considered in the discussion of category consistency.

2. Is the amount of text sampled adequate to produce stable assessments of the concept? And a related question for content analysts: Have we included all or most of the relevant entries in the construction of our category?

Both parts of this question point to important differences between the measurement problems of content analysis and those of standard psychometric tests. In relation to standard psychometric tests, the problem generally can be translated into one question: Have enough items been included in the scale to make stable assessments of the concept to be measured? To have relevance to content analysis, the question must be stated in two parts, one corresponding to the size of the text being measured and the second corresponding to the completeness of the entry list.

The second part of this question has already been considered in the discussion of reliability, where it was argued that one of the crucial elements in developing category stability is the completeness of the entry list.

However, we have not considered the problem of ascertaining whether an adequate amount of text has been sampled. This problem often arises when researchers initially consider the use of content analysis, and it generally takes the form, How large must a document be in order to obtain a good estimate of the mean rate of usage? Unfortunately there is no quick and easy answer. The solution varies from one research application to another. We can, however, outline some general rules for the decision process.

One rule of thumb has been that there should be roughly 1,000 words for each tag tally when a researcher is using the Psychosociological Dictionary or some modification of it.[15] A review of the basic statistics of this dictionary gives some insight into this rule. Of these 1,000 words, roughly 925 will be looked up and found in the dictionary, and about 600 of these will be tagged. Thus about 75 of the words will be assigned to the leftover list and 325 will be looked up but not tagged. If it is assumed that on the average two tags are assigned to each word — one first-order and one second-order tag — the average index and raw scores for the tags can be estimated. For the 53 first-order tags, the average is about 11 occurrences per 1,000 words of text, and for second-order tags the average is roughly 19 occurrences per 1,000. Of course, tags vary greatly in their average tag scores. But in our experience, documents of 1,000 words have a minimum of zero scores for tags. A thousand-word document will thus give a rough guideline.

Two other guidelines should be considered. The first is the degree to which the document being analyzed was generated in a structured

---

[15] We shift terminology here from "meaning unit" to "word" for two reasons. The Psychosociological Dictionary looks up words and their roots; our experience is based largely on this dictionary. Words also represent an unequivocal measure of the length of the document.

situation. Generally, as the situation in which documents are generated becomes more unstructured, the necessary sample size and the number of relevant tags both increase. This is a common sense result; if the researcher knows that the situation is well structured, we can expect to tap the source's few alternatives with fewer words and fewer tags than if the source had many alternatives. Luckily, the average size of documents produced seems to correlate positively with the structured-unstructured dimension.

The second factor to be considered is the possibility of grouping documents to increase the stability of the tag scores, often an effective technique. The crucial factor is whether the grouped documents were generated by the same sources and under roughly the same stimulus conditions. Dunphy (Chapter 8), in his analysis of reports about self-analytic group meetings, grouped together three and four reports from the same group member to aid in stabilizing his scores. By grouping documents in an uncontrolled situation, however, the researcher often runs the risk of missing important information in one particular document by averaging the score over many documents.

After the researcher is satisfied by intuitive or empirical analysis that the categories are reliable and content valid, the next step is to relate the measurements to the manifestation of the construct in the source.

The use of the term *source manifestation* deserves some clarification. It is intended to mean simply the manner and degree to which the source possesses an indication of the theoretical construct operationally defined by the content category. Thus the research may have categories to measure the frequency of occurrence of references to certain values, and one inference might be that the more a value is mentioned, the more important its manifestation in the person who generated the document. Allport takes a similar position in a discussion of traits and calls the position "heuristic realism."

> Heuristic realism, as applied to our problem, holds that the person who confronts us possesses inside his skin generalized action tendencies (or traits) and that it is our job to discover what they are. Any form of realism assumes the existence of an external structure (out there) regardless of our shortcomings in comprehending it. Since traits, like all internal variables, are never directly observed, but only inferred, we must expect difficulties and errors in the process of discovering their nature.
>
> (Allport, 1966, 3)

The term source manifestation does not need to take on the purely psychological sense of needs, motives, drives, or traits. It may merely relate to the degree and amount of attention directed toward a topic.

Relating the content characteristics to the source manifestation involves (1) a demonstration that the theoretical construct is appropriate to the source(s) being studied and (2) a demonstration that the document produced by the source contains a manifestation of the construct and that the category taps this manifestation. If the investigator has taken sufficient care in the definition of the language community appropriate to his dictionary, and if he has attained a reasonable level of reliability and content validity, he has to some extent demonstrated the first step: that the theoretical construct, as it is operationally defined by the entry list, may be appropriate for study.[16]

Generally, if the purpose of a study is to assess validity, the researcher chooses documents from sources that are expected to produce relevant indicators. Though this is most easily carried out in experimental situations, the opportunity often arises with available data. If the relevant indicators are found, a contribution is made toward establishing content validity. If the indicators are not found, the measures or the sources selected may be inappropriate, or there may be other suppressing factors that have not been considered.

The actual process of demonstrating that we are assessing the manifestation of a particular trait is indirect. The researcher must find apart from the document a characteristic of the source that reflects the manifestation. Generally this is done by obtaining external measures, such as membership in various groups, personality scores on standardized tests, sex, IQ, income, child-rearing practice, or any of the multitude of variables measured by behavioral scientists.

Predictive and Concurrent Validity

Both predictive and concurrent validity can be characterized by prediction of an outside criterion.[17] Predictive validation is the assess-

---

[16] We have not shown that the organizing theory is correct but we have demonstrated that given the theory, the language indication of the construct to be assessed is, or should be, in the repertoire of the source.

[17] Three important points about concurrent and predictive validity should be noted: (1) The demonstration of concurrent validity does not guarantee predictive validity or vice versa. Although this may appear obvious, the point becomes important if the two types of validity are not adequately delineated. (2) Probably the most crucial aspect of carrying out these types of validation is the definition of the criterion measures. (3) The tag categories that are being analyzed for predictive

ment of the instrument's power to predict a future outcome. Thus we might measure some personality variables when students enter college and from these measurements predict future grade point averages. We use a rather loose definition of predictive validity because we require only that future outcome follows the production of the document, and we do not require it to follow the analysis of the data. Thus *ex post facto* research on available data may be admitted to the class of prediction studies.

Concurrent validation is the assessment of the instrument's power to predict an external variable that can be measured at the same time or before the document is produced. Studies that determine whether a test discriminates between presently identifiable groups are concerned with concurrent validity.

This volume contains no reports of analyses designed solely to assess predictive or concurrent validity. To carry out such a study, the researcher would have to limit his research and theoretical interests. However, a considerable amount of indirect evidence can be gleaned by studying the research reported later.

Ramallo's analysis of reports by Crossroads Africa volunteer workers (Chapter 17) is an example of research bearing on the question of predictive validity. He developed criteria based on contingencies between tags, which represent concepts of thought and action, for the prediction of successful field volunteers. He then postulated that successful and unsuccessful field workers could be distinguished on the basis of their use of these categories in written reports. The criteria for his predictions were supervisor ratings. The assessment of the volunteers by the supervisors followed the production of the reports.

Further examples of studies relating to the question of concurrent validity are Namenwirth's analysis of prestige newspapers (Chapter 11) and Ogilvie, Stone and Shneidman's study of simulated and real suicide notes (Chapter 13). In each case, the criterion measure is

---

and concurrent validity may be considered in isolation or in the context of many of the other variables.

There are two implications of the third point. The first is that we might use multivariate statistical procedures to predict or discriminate our criterion variable. The choice of the procedures would depend on the theory and research question being considered by the investigator. The second is that we might attempt to validate a particular tag category while holding constant other tag categories. An example of this would be to try to validate an achievement-oriented category in the context of an educational situation while holding constant a tag designed to measure academic orientation.

unambiguous, and the object of the research is discrimination based on that criterion. These studies are typical of many of the analyses reported on here. Both were conducted on available data, discriminated between defined sources, and were carried out with the object of making behavioral science judgments based on the analyses. The contribution of these studies to our assessment of the validity of our instrument can be considered an important by-product of the research.

This, then, is the mode of attack necessary for the assessment of these types of validity. The evidence is large but irregular and often secondary to the object of the reported research.

Construct Validation

Construct validity is evaluated by investigating what psychological qualities a test measures, i.e. by demonstrating that certain explanatory constructs account to some degree for performance on the test. To examine construct validity requires both logical and empirical attack. Essentially in studies of construct validity we are validating the theory underlying the test. The validation procedure involves two steps. First, the investigator inquires: From this theory, what prediction would we make regarding the variation of scores from person to person or occasion to occasion? Second, he gathers data to confirm these predictions.

(APA Technical Recommendations, 1954, 14)

Through content validation procedures, we can demonstrate that the tag category appears to measure the theoretical construct and that we seem to have an adequate sample of language signs. Through predictive and concurrent validation procedures, we can demonstrate that relevant outside behaviorial criteria are related to our measures. The final step is to test for the validity of the theory, a procedure requiring an awareness of two large sources of error: error in theory and error in the operational definition of the theory.

If the researcher requires that his tag categories have demonstrated reliability and content validity, he has to some extent controlled for the source of error contained in the operational definition of his theory. The task is then to concentrate on the validation of the theory.

It is convenient to consider two types of construct validation procedures: those using only variables internal to the content analysis and those using both external and internal variables. We make this distinction because most of the work presented here that is relevant to construct validation has used internal measures. By internal measures, we mean tag categories; all other measures are external. If we accept a working definition of theory to be a coherent group of general propositions used as principles of explanation for a class of phenomena, a crucial idea tested in construct validation is the idea of coherence. One way of testing coherence is through the use of factor analysis techniques. The application of factor analysis to a correlation matrix results in the reduction of the matrix into a set of dimensions, less than the original number of variables, which account for a large percentage of the variance of the measures. Thus factor analysis can be considered as a refined technique for looking at the way a variable correlates with a large number of other variables. Since the researcher concerned with construct validity is attempting to discover the relationship of the variable he is validating with other variables, factor analysis can be quite useful. Examples of this approach are found in Dunphy's analysis of self-analytic groups (Chapter 8), and in Namenwirth's analysis of prestige newspaper editorials (Chapter 11). Both researchers factor analyzed a tag-by-tag correlation matrix to discover important dimensions of their data and to gain insight into the interrelationships among the dictionary variables.

In a sense, every study that uses a particular dictionary adds some information to the assessment of the construct validity of that dictionary. As various researchers interrelate variables and use the tags to discriminate and predict differing external variables, they add to a common fund of information relating to the theory embodied in the dictionary. Even though the research is not carried out as a validation examination, the ideas are cumulative. An interesting example of this occurred in the application of the Harvard Third Dictionary. In one of the first studies using this dictionary, Dunphy (Chapter 8) factor analyzed his small-group data and discovered a dimension characterized by a particular stylistic way of expressing ideas. The tags relevant to the dimension include OVERSTATE, UNDERSTATE, SELF, THINK, and SIGN-REJECT. Some individuals appear to have a particular expressive style in threatening situations; they tend to protect themselves by exaggeration, underplaying, qualification (by use of such terms as "I think"), or rejection. Later, in their analysis of Presidential Nomination Acceptance Speeches (Chapter 10), Smith *et al.* factor analyzed their data and uncovered a very similar clustering of tags: those candidates who scored high on the tags in that cluster appeared to be exhibiting much the same style of expression as those in Dunphy's analysis.

The deductive approach presented here is predicated on the plausibility of demonstrating construct validity. By developing a number of tag categories based on some relevant theoretical notion, we are in a sense beginning at the end. We are operationalizing a theory before demonstrating its validity. To some extent, this impasse is overcome by developing only those categories based on theoretical notions that have previously been demonstrated to be valid by other research. In doing so, however, we somewhat preclude the development of theory.

A second way of overcoming the problem of simultaneously developing and assessing a theory and a measurement instrument is to tailor a dictionary for a specific type of data and for a specific set of theoretical concepts. This is roughly the approach taken in the development of specific as contrasted to general dictionaries. As discussed in Chapter 4, a progression from general to specific dictionaries may be a desirable research goal. This development may indeed be equivalent to the progression from descriptive, hypothesis-generating studies to hypothesis-testing studies, from the development of theory to the construct validation of that theory.

An Overview

Two components, reliability and validity, have been defined on the previous pages as essential to the development of an accurate and sensitive measurement instrument. In practice, the measurement of these two components can proceed concurrently. Conceptually, however, the two components should be distinguished in that high reliability is a necessary condition for the demonstration of validity.

For the researcher interested in developing and applying a content analysis measuring instrument, one procedure for conceptualizing and possibly constructing his instrument might be as follows:

1. Define the target for his eventual measurements, the set of documents that he wishes to analyze.
2. Define the language community for which his instrument will be applicable.
3. Operationally define his theoretical framework in terms of categories containing symbols of the defined language community,

and develop a set of rules for applying these categories to verbal data.

4. Ascertain by appropriate procedures a measure of the category consistency and content validity. If these measurements do not reach a satisfactory level, the researcher would loop back to Step 3 and re-evaluate the instrument. The procedure of evaluating category consistency involves looking at the internal consistency of the tags. The procedure of content validation is a way of qualitatively assessing the relationship between the researcher's theoretical scheme and the operational definition of his constructs.

5. Assess the degree of category stability by applying the instrument to different sets of documents obtained from the same sources in various situations and over a time interval. This reliability assessment is designed to help ensure that the categories do not contain large amounts of random error from slight changes in stimuli and situation. This often involves looking at large amounts of data and correcting misclassifications and oversights in the category construction procedure.

6. Once the researcher has demonstrated that his measurements are sufficiently stable, the problem becomes one of demonstrating the correspondence of the objects of measurement to properties of the source and to his theoretical constructs. An initial approach to this is to gather two or more sets of documents that differ on some known, operationally defined and measured characteristics. A test is applied to see if the measured characteristics differentiate between the sets of documents. The procedure then leads to the assessment of concurrent and predictive validity.

7. The final stage is to carry out construct validation. At this level, the researcher is checking the coherence of the theory and the validity of the various implications of the theory. Construct validation represents the most advanced stage of verification of the inference processes.

THE NATURE OF DATA
FROM THE TAG TALLY PHASE

Earlier we noted that two general sets of numbers can be conveniently assigned to content documents processed by the General Inquirer system. In the tag tally phase of the operation, raw and adjusted (index) scores are automatically assigned to the document for every tag concept in the dictionary. In the retrieval phase, scores often represent selected combinations of occurrences of tag concepts, with one another or with specified outside variables.

Our concern is with the first set of assigned numbers, since these numbers are automatically generated in every analysis and are the most frequently used in later statistical manipulations. For each tag concept, four numbers in this set generally can be computed: (1) the raw frequency of occurrence of the tag concept in the document as measured by the sum of the occurrences of all of the entry words of the tag concept in the document; (2) the raw frequency of sentences in the document which contain at least one of the entry terms of the tag concept; (3) the raw frequency of (1) divided by the number of words in the document (word index score)[18]; (4) the raw frequency of (3) divided by the number of sentences in the document (sentence tag tally). The most frequently used of these four numbers is the word index score. The others, though easily available, are not as convenient for between-document comparison: the raw word and raw sentence scores are difficult to use if the documents vary in length. The sentence index score is not useful if the length of sentences varies considerably between documents.

As mentioned earlier, the use of the word index score usually means that the researcher has made the assumption that relative frequency of mention is a stable index of intensity over documents of varying lengths. Thus, the use of the word index scores equates two documents on the tag SELF if the first document, which has only one hundred words, contains one reference, and the second, which has one thousand words, contains ten references.[19]

In most of the content analyses represented here, it is also assumed that any one entry in a tag category is as strong an indicator of that category in the document as any other entry. The only dictionary

---

[18] Since the use of entry terms that are composed of more than one word (for instance, idioms) is becoming more common, some adjustment in the division of the word index scores should be made. The number of words is obviously only an estimate of the "true" number of individual units.

[19] Statistical methods can be exercised to test for and control for deviations from this assumption. Ramallo (Chapter 17), for example, using counts derived from retrievals, controls for the length of sentences by statistical methods. In true experimental work, the effect of different lengths can be controlled by the researcher by specifying a required constant length.

that employs weighted entry terms is the Stanford Political Dictionary (see Chapter 4).

Relationship of Index Scores to Source Characteristics

Since the index scores on a particular tag count are considered as indicants of some property of the source of the measured document, the properties measured in the document should somehow reflect the corresponding properties of the source, but it is important to realize that the metric of the measured behavior may not be isomorphic to the "natural" metric of the source property. The weakest statement we can make about two or more sources with different tag scores in their respective documents is that the sources may differ on some characteristic because the documents differ on the corresponding property.

A slightly stronger statement is that we can *order* sources on the basis of tag scores in their respective documents. This statement partially restricts the assignment of numerals in the conventional measurement situation because by specification of an *ordinal* property we must meet the criterion of transitivity; thus if we measure A and B and find that $A > B$, and measure B and C and find that $B > C$, then the ordinal property requires that the comparison of A and C must be compatible with the previous measurements and assignments of numerals such that $A > C$. The critical relationship missing in an ordinal specification can be expressed as a question — "How much different is A and B or A and C?" — for if we only insist on specification of greater than, equal to, or less than, we cannot specify how much different A and B or A and C are. Since we do not know how much different A and B are, then we do not know how much to increment B for it to be equal to A. Thus ordinal measurement allows us to assign only a rank-order position to the sources on the property being measured. Ordinal scales do not possess the characteristic of equal intervals, and without at least this property arithmetic operations on the raw data are not legitimate. For this and other reasons a class of statistics called nonparametric (the computation of parameters usually involves arithmetic operation) has been developed. Their use has been strongly advocated by Stevens (1951) and Seigal (1956) on the grounds that only ordinal measurement is achieved by most social scientific endeavors. It is not until we have restricted our assignment of numbers (with the requirement that there is at least equality of interval at all levels of the scale) that we can appropriately employ parametric statistical tests which require the use of arithmetic manipulation. However as Stevens notes,

> In the strictest propriety the ordinary statistics involving means and standard deviations ought not to be used with these scales, for those statistics imply a knowledge of something more than the relative rank order of the data. On the other hand, for this "illegal" statisticising there can be involved a kind of pragmatic sanction; in numerous instances it leads to fruitful "results."
>
> (Stevens, 1951, 26)

How does this discussion relate to tag tally count scores? The manifest behavior that we measure (the count or percentage of times certain words occur) can certainly be considered as exhibiting interval measurement properties. We can compare documents *A* and *B* and spell out the difference between them on some tag scores in terms of behavior (the number or percentage of words). Arithmetic manipulations are meaningful; the mean number of words in documents from source A has unambiguous meaning. The problem arises when we relate the behavior back to the property of the source that it is designed to indicate. Can we equate an increment of one in the tag score with an increment of one in the source concept? Often not! In some cases, it is further likely that even an ordinal ranking of the sources based on an ordinal ranking of the documents on the property indicated may be incorrect. Consider a possible tag designed to measure the intensity of preoccupation with sexual activity in a set of documents. The measure used is a count of the number of, or percentage of, words that denote manifest SEX references. We score the documents and then rank them in accordance with the magnitude of their various scores, even though it is possible that a high level of preoccupation with sexual activity might be manifested either by many references to manifest sex or, if repressed, by few references, thus making our monotonic relationship between frequency of reference to words in the SEX category and level of preoccupation with sexual activity inaccurate. The problem is complicated when we consider that every tag indicator in a dictionary may have a unique (different from all other tags) relationship with the concept that it was designed to indicate. To a large extent, the researchers using the General Inquirer have as-

sumed at least ordinal (monotonic) and usually interval (linear) correspondence between the indicator and the manifestation in the
source.[20]

In practice the choice between ordinal and internal correspondence
is important in two ways: (1) As we noted earlier, the appropriateness of certain statistical techniques is somewhat dependent on the
type of relationship that is assumed between measured behavior and
the source property. One of the assumptions underlying many of the
parametric statistical techniques is interval measurement and correspondence, while in most cases the nonparametric tests require only
nominal or ordinal assumptions. (2) If we do not assume interval
measurement and interval correspondence between measured behavior
and source characteristic, it is only natural to formulate other hypotheses about the nature of the relationship between the measured
indicators and the source. That is, if we feel that we can assume only
ordinal measurement and correspondence, what hypotheses about the
data can we make to explain our weaker assumption? Note that we
are not concerned here with the observed distribution of scores but
with the nature of the relationship between the observed behavioral
indicators and the properties of the source. One hypothesis in particular
has been suggested (Stone, 63): the saturation hypothesis. Stone
postulates that the occurrence of a word in a document that is tagged
with a certain concept is not necessarily independent of the occurrence of other words in the document tagged with the same concept.

At any point in a document, the probability of making a reference to a
category very much depends on the number of previous references made.
If no references have been made, the probability of a first reference is
quite low. Perhaps that kind of reference is not part of the speaker's
active vocabulary. Perhaps there are situational forces inhibiting its
mention. Once a single reference has been made, the probability of a
second reference is usually quite high. The pressures inhibiting first
reference have been broken. Further clarification and expansion on the
topic is likely. However, as still more references to a category are made,
forces of saturation develop. Lauguage by nature involves the interplay
of a number of different semantic and syntactic categories, not the dominance by a single kind of referent. Even more limiting, the speaker often
purposely will diversify his references to hold the interest of his audience.

[20] The researcher can, of course, assume that nonlinear or nonmonotonic relationships occur between the behavior and the characteristic, but assumption of the
linear or monotonic relationship is generally preferred.

It would be most useful to have empirical studies on the forces of continuation and saturation. As McKeon's analysis of delusional speech in schizophrenics indicates such continuation and saturation forces are quite different in delusional patients than in normal people. One major characteristic of delusional speech is not to diversity, but instead to perseverate with a particular semantic and/or syntactic reference.

(Stone, 1963)

The true relationship between measured behavior and source characteristic does not conform to the interval measurement model in every case or to proposed models such as the one just given, which may be more appealing than a bland acceptance of the interval model. Stone's model, however, is difficult to verify; and indeed if it is verified, it might be difficult to deal adequately with it because "the forces of saturation and continuation fluctuate" (Stone) at various frequency levels, over different situations, and certainly for different people. Even though the particular model may be difficult to verify, the hypothesis that the General Inquirer tag scores are not examples of measurement on an interval scale has considerable support among various users. This has led to some use of the nonparametric statistical techniques. Their utility, however, is limited for two reasons: (1) Nonparametric techniques have only been developed for straightforward, univariate problems. Thus for almost any multivariate procedure, the availability of known statistical methods and computer programs tends to help convince the investigator to use parametric methods. (2) If only nonparametric techniques are used in an analysis, cross-study comparison becomes very difficult.

Often when an investigator has made a decision to use parametric methods, the question arises as to how the tag tally scores are distributed. They are concerned because many of the standard parametric methods contain the assumption that the data be normally distributed. The problem is simply that if the distribution is unknown or recognized to be not normal, the results of the computation of significance levels based on statistical tests requiring normality may be in error. The problem becomes more complicated when multivariate tests are applied, since often the assumption of multivariate normal distribution is required. The question is often asked in hopes that a simple transformation applied to the data will assure that the assumption is met.

Unfortunately, no such simple transformation is known to us. If it were, we would have built it into the system long ago. One particular transformation, however, has been argued for and applied. Perhaps the most critical assumption in the use of analysis of variance is that of homogeneity of variance. This means simply that the variances in the cells of the ANOVA table are roughly equal. Inspection of the results of a number of studies, however, reveal that homogeneity of variance of tag tally scores across groups is surely not the rule. In fact, the size of the variance seems to depend roughly on the size of the mean scores, and often they are roughly equal. This suggests the Poisson distribution and an appropriate transformation to stabilize and to roughly make the variances homogeneous. The transformation under these circumstances is the square-root transformation.[21]

Namenwirth (Chapter 11) has applied the square-root transformation in the analysis of results from the tag tally phase of the General Inquirer. Aside from Namenwirth, however, only passing attention has been given to the problems in this area. Part of the reason may be that much of the work reported on here is nonexperimental in nature, and researchers have used parametric methods because they are well known and have considerable heuristic power rather than for their usefulness in computation of confidence limits and significance levels. Considerable work should be put into this area. We do not expect the results to be simple, but rather that scores for different tags may be distributed in different ways.

[21] The reader should note that some authors of studies later in this book multiply index scores by 1,000, while other investigators use the index scores in the form of percentages. These forms can be considered as alternative. No difference in computation of statistical significance should result, except, perhaps, through rounding error.

CHAPTER SEVEN

The Application of the General Inquirer to Research Problems[1]

INTRODUCTION

In the preceding chapter, we emphasized problems involved in the development of a content analysis measuring instrument. We shall now turn our attention to techniques of applying the instrument in research situations.

Our initial step is to propose a general scheme for classifying types of quantitative content analysis research. This scheme is concerned with the various types of research design, the nature of the research questions that can be asked, the extent to which inferences can be drawn, and the appropriate statistical procedures. A number of research strategies are reviewed, and a general strategy for efficient use of the General Inquirer system is proposed. The emphasis of the strategy is upon a continual interaction between the researcher and the original data. The proposal is for a three-stage procedure integrating the use of statistical and retrieval processes.

Using the studies contained in Part II of this book, this discussion evaluates procedures that have been employed, suggests some that should or might be used, outlines problems that have been solved, and isolates particular problem areas that require further research. We offer no final answers but we hope that the spirit of this discussion does justice to a quote from John W. Tukey:

[1] The main author of this chapter is Marshall S. Smith.

233

Data which is heterogeneous in precision, or in character of variation, and data that is very incomplete, offer challenges that we have just begun to meet. Beyond this we need to stress flexibility of attack, willingness to iterate, and willingness to study things as they are, rather than as they hopefully should be.   (1962, 4)

A CLASSIFICATION OF CONTENT ANALYSIS RESEARCH

Researchers choose their measuring instrument according to its effectiveness in organizing the particular type of data involved and in answering the particular type of research questions to be asked. There seem to be three criteria for data and research questions appropriate to the General Inquirer:

1. Data generated in a relatively constant stimulus situation. This does not mean that we cannot compare documents generated in different stimulus situations, rather the requirement is that a particular document or speech be produced in a stable stimulus situation. Examples of this type of data are TAT protocols, newspaper editorials, post-meeting reaction reports, and acceptance speeches. One type of data that does not meet this requirement is verbal interaction data. Unless the interaction is very structured, as by an interview schedule, the cues to the source are constantly changing, and the ideas, emphasis, and themes exposed may have been elicited by extraneous and accidental stimuli, making it very difficult for the researcher to design his research with appropriate controls.

2. Questions that can be answered about data by the analysis of simple elements, measured by their frequency of occurrence within the document. One way of approaching this type of question is through analysis of results from the tag tally phase of the measurement operation combined with appropriate supporting retrievals. This criterion is becoming less crucial as greater strides are made toward the analysis of themes in documents through the analysis of conjunctions of tags within and across sentences. The work of the political scientists at Stanford (Chapter 9) represents a departure from this general rule, as does Colby's analysis of themes in folktales and myths (Chapter 20). The problem of thematic analysis, however, is not yet solved, and the

researcher should not expect all of the answers. This also applies to researchers interested in the analysis of logical arguments, a particularly difficult area to subject to automated scoring.

3. Since the system described here is based primarily on the semantic analysis of content, little research requiring structural analysis of language has been or can be carried out. Possibilities exist for automating structural analysis (Chapter 4), but the only research reported on here that attempts this is the system for scoring Need-Achievement (Chapter 5). The same restriction applies to the field of literary analysis. Insofar as particular semantic usages are required, the system is adequate, but it is not designed for the analysis of stylistic qualities such as alliteration or rhyme. (See Ellis and Favat, Chapter 23).

Even with these restrictions, the variety of sources of data and possible research questions is large. One of the ways to facilitate discussion of this variety is to introduce a scheme for classifying types of research. In imposing such a scheme, we make no claims about its ultimate efficiency or value; it is used as a convenient heuristic.

Three dimensions are suggested for the classification of research. The first dimension generally corresponds to the amount of control that the investigator has over the set of data as it is generated. In the experimental design literature, this dimension is generally thought of in terms of a nonexperimental versus an experimental dichotomy, although recently the labels quasi-, pseudo-, and *ex post facto* experimental have been applied to research appearing in a form similar to true experimental research but differing in the degree of control exercised by the experimenter. In discussing this dimension, we will speak of a trichotomy, and we will use the labels historical, concurrent, and experimental.

Historical, Concurrent, and Experimental

Under the historical label, we can conveniently class a number of studies reported on in this volume; Smith's study of Presidential Nomination Acceptance Speeches (Chapter 10), Namenwirth's study of elite newspaper editorials (Chapter 11), Paige's analysis of *Letters from Jenny* (Chapter 12), and others. The primary criterion here is that the data existed even before the research. The researcher exerts no control over this form of data; his knowledge of its conception is truly historical. In a large sense, the facility to conduct quantitative and systematic studies on historical data represents the most powerful use of content analysis, since the most systematically recorded behavior of the past is often the written document.

The second label, concurrent, can be understood as a compromise between historical and experimental. In this category, Dunphy's study of self-analytic groups is a good example (Chapter 8). Dunphy was aware of, and actively engaged in, analysis of the set of data as it was being generated. The study differs from a true experimental study in that a minimum of control was exercised over the persons generating the data. The subjects were self-selected, and the controls exercised by the researcher were often not preplanned or systematic.

The third label, experimental, describes only one study in this book. In this classification scheme, an experimental study is one in which the researcher has the power to assign persons to the various groups involved in the study and to manipulate the independent variables in the study. The need for such studies (particularly for the assessment of reliability and validity) is great.

Descriptive and Hypothesis Generating versus Hypothesis Testing

The second dimension suggested here is described by the dichotomy *hypothesis generating* versus *hypothesis testing*. In a sense, this dimension is not independent of the first dimension. The studies that can be classified generally as descriptive or hypothesis generating here usually fall into the historical and concurrent categories, and studies labeled as hypothesis testing may often be those described as experimental. However, the distinction is useful. The dimension we wish to discuss here could be called the preinvestigation set of the researcher. It is intimately related to the state of the researcher's theory, and is one of the same dimensions that is used to classify dictionaries in Chapter 4. In a strictly hypothesis-testing study, the researcher enters the research with an explicit set of hypotheses worked out and operationally defined in terms of the variables that he is measuring. Ordinarily, a specific dictionary is used in this situation. It must be stressed that this type of research can be conducted in a situation that is not truly experimental. In our terms, it can be conducted in an historical or a concurrent research situation. The type and degree of inference that validly can be made will depend on the situation or type of data.

As discussed in Chapters 1 and 2, our definitions of the labels hypothesis generating and descriptive are not interchangeable, although generally the behaviors the labels describe will occur together. Together they represent the stage of research at which the investigator's particular theory and hypotheses are not fully worked out. In this stage, the research questions are not completely specified and the relevant variables may not be entirely operationally defined. In this type of analysis, a descriptive phase usually precedes the hypothesis-generating phase: the researcher begins a project with an area that he wishes to investigate, describes his data, and then sets down a series of possible hypotheses to be tested in future research. The interplay with theory at this stage of research is very important; the investigator is in the process of inventing a set of theoretical constructs that fit in some manner and can later be put to empirical test.

No study reported on in this book could be considered to be solely hypothesis testing. In general, the research represented here falls into both the hypothesis-testing and the hypothesis-generating categories. To some extent, this can be best understood by examining two aspects of our content analysis research. As discussed in Chapter 4, the dictionary used by a researcher represents a systematic explication of some elementary variables that alone or in some combination are considered to operationally define some social science concepts. Thus, to some extent, the actual use of a dictionary entails the operation of hypothesis testing. On the other hand, much of the theory involved in our research is still in the exploratory phases, and much of the data being analyzed are rich but hitherto untilled, a situation that leads to descriptive, hypothesis-generating procedures.

Directions of Inference

The third classification dimension might be called the purpose, the object, the orientation, or perhaps the direction of inference in the study. In the previous discussion, we couch our approach to inference in the general context of validating the measuring instrument. In this discussion, we look at the inference problem from the viewpoint of the researcher.

Three directions of inference are commonly considered in content analysis literature. These directions are depicted in Figure 7.1.

The direction of inference can be noted by the direction of the arrows. The arrow labeled (1) leading from document to source refers to a direction of inference that has been previously discussed: the inference that the characteristic measured in the document has some relationship to characteristics of the source. To substantiate this involves the research problems of relating known characteristics of the sources to the documents, describing time trends in context, and comparing content with norms. In the study of Presidential Nomination Acceptance Speeches (Chapter 10), the initial analyses relating the characteristics of the speeches with political party and with year of delivery would be considered inferential to source alone.

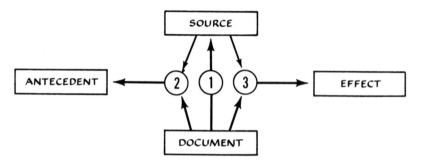

FIGURE 7.1. Directions of inference.

Continuing this example, the investigator might then ask, *Why* do these particular tags (and their characteristics) vary linearly with time? This leads us to arrow (2) in the figure: the making of inferences as to the antecedent of the communication. Thus in the acceptance-speech analysis, the researchers note that the tag ECONOMIC decreases over time from 1928 to 1964, and from this they make two general inferences: (1) that the concern of the nominees with economic matters decreases over time, and (2) that possible reasons may be the depression of the thirties which raised the concern, the war of the forties which lowered it somewhat, and the over-all affluence of the fifties and sixties which contributed to making economic issues less of a campaign concern.

Many of the studies in this book contain inferences of this second sort. One of the few that does not is Ogilvie, Stone, and Shneidman's study of suicide notes (Chapter 16). In this study, the primary emphasis was to find characteristics of the texts that separated genuine from simulated notes. Inferences to the sources were made. The words used and tag counts of the simulated notes were found to indicate a greater tendency for these note writers to intellectualize compared to the genuine note writers; but inferences to antecedents, to child-rearing practices, to marital or financial problems were not made.

One other important point about the relationship between inferences to sources and inference to antecedents should be noted. The inference from a document to antecedent condition(s) is almost always made with the characteristics, both known and inferred, of the source in mind. Thus there is an interaction between the inferences to the source and to the antecedents: we often cannot make an inference to antecedents without initially making an inference to the source.

The third direction of inference in the figure refers simply to the question, What are the effects of communication? No analysis of this sort is included in this book. Such an analysis again raises the issue mentioned in the discussion of inference to antecedents: the interaction between the source of the document and the document itself.[2]

We must emphasize that the general problems of inference in content analysis are no different than in any other research area. Inference to antecedents, to effects, or to characteristics of a source is a very tricky exercise at best. In the framework of our other classifying dimensions, an experimental, hypothesis-testing study is probably the most appropriate vehicle for legitimately making inferences. Appropriate controls, samples, statistical measures, and a careful, sensitive researcher are important elements. The fact of the matter is that often some or many of these elements are missing and that theorizing and inference making goes on. Combine a sensitive and spirited researcher with a powerful measuring tool, interesting data in a promising area, and the result may be both exciting and suspect. The reader is offered the choice in many of the studies in this book, as in much of the literature, of accepting or rejecting the findings offered. However, he must remember that rejection implies that an alternative theory or inference can be generated which will better account for the research evidence.

Table 7.1 classifies the research in Part II by the three-dimensional

---

[2] By inference to "effects," we mean the effects of the document. This is obviously partly dependent on the identity of the source of the document. For example, the effect on the public of a columnist pundit saying "We may go to war in six months" would be measurably different from the effect on the public if the President made the same statement.

TABLE 7.1. A Classification of Content Analysis Research*

	HISTORICAL		CONCURRENT		EXPERIMENTAL	
Direction of Inference	Descriptive and Hypothesis Generating	Hypothesis Testing	Descriptive and Hypothesis Generating	Hypothesis Testing	Descriptive and Hypothesis Generating	Hypothesis Testing
To Source Alone	Psychotic Language (14) Product Image (22) Study of Literature (23) Suicide Notes (16)	Psychotic Language (14)	Case of Windle (13) Field Work Reports (17)	Field Work Reports (17)	Analog Therapy Interviews (15)	
To Source and to Antecedents	Acceptance Speeches (10) Elite Editorials (11) Letters from Jenny (12) Folktale Themes and Use of Alcohol (19) Anthropological Dictionary Applications (21)	Sino-Soviet Communications (9) Elite Editorials (11) Folktale Themes and Use of Alcohol (19)	Self-Analytic Groups (8) Who-Am-I? (18) Future Auto-biographies (20)	Self-Analytic Groups (8) Who-Am-I? (18) Future Auto-biographies (20)		
To Source and to Effects						

* Numbers in parenthesis refer to chapter numbers in Part II.

scheme just described. Many of the studies are listed more than once because they contain elements that are descriptive and hypothesis generating and/or hypothesis testing.

STRATEGIES OF CONTENT ANALYSIS RESEARCH

The preceding discussion and classification of research should underline the fact that many content analysis studies do not fall into the areas generally discussed in textbooks on research design. Only one of the studies presented here is categorized as experimental, and only a few are classified as hypothesis testing. In a sense, many of the research strategy problems that content analysts face are similar to those faced by field observers. Little or no control can be exercised, or is desired, over the behavior being studied, and only very general ideas and measurements can be utilized to assess the importance of the many external influencing variables. Thus many of the studies are justifiably open to the criticism that they cannot examine causal relationships, that without statistical or physical control over many important independent variables, there is no sure way of knowing that the crucial variables are even those being investigated. On the other hand, content analysts can amass the many arguments of the naturalistic observer to justify the utility of their research. Furthermore, they can argue that verbal behavior can be analyzed and gathered in a systematic, efficient, and comprehensive fashion that is often impossible for other forms of natural behavior, and that the analyst is often unusually confident that his own particular biases do not affect the initial collection and early analysis of data.

The two most powerful reasons for the utility of content analysis research have been the objects of much discussion in the preceding chapters. Both reasons are predicated on the assumption that words and symbols used in verbal communication are indicative of many latent and manifest attributes of the source of the communication.

First, given this assumption, the researcher is able to gather measurements on a large number of dependent variables from one piece of behavior. The behavior (document) can be recorded and subjected to extensive analysis and reanalysis. It will often reveal characteristics of the source that were unanticipated by the researcher and unknown to the source; in fact, the research use for which the document is collected is usually unknown to the source before and during generation of data.[3]

Second, many research questions can be approached efficiently only through the use of available verbal data. Often the only type of systematically retained data containing clues relating to the attitudes and personalities of historical figures is public and private verbal communications. One of the few ways to study the dominant concerns of a primitive culture in an efficient manner is through its myths and folktales. One major source of insight into the personalities of mental patients is their own written records as in personal letters and autobiographies. One of the few ways of assessing the general attitudes, opinions, and beliefs of a society without conducting extensive surveys is through a content analysis of the output of its mass media.

It should be recognized that the analysis of available data often makes it impossible for the researcher to claim that his data are a

[3] This points to an important difference between the clinical use of content analysis procedures and standardized tests. In the administration of standardized tests, the source is usually aware of the potential use of the tests, a situation that may, in fact, affect his response.

sample representative of some population of data. In fact, it is often more convenient to analyze data of the entire population. Even in those cases in which samples of data are drawn from some defined population, there are often numerous problems in ascertaining that the sample is representative. Thus the methods employed in the content analysis studies of this book are often similar to those of case studies. Statistical inference to populations based on the analysis of a sample of data is rare. At the same time, an exciting aspect of this approach is apparent. A primary thrust of theoretical inquiry among users of this system is in the study of the processes of change. An emphasis has been directed toward the analysis of the change over time in content characteristics and their inferred source characteristics.

In the following pages we consider some of the comparisons made in content analysis research. We begin with a discussion of the case study approach in content analysis.

Content Analysis Case Studies

The use of the label case study to characterize research often implies a clinical as opposed to statistical approach. We do not intend to imply this distinction. Our general position is that all content analysis research should combine the clinical and the statistical approaches. Researchers using a quantitative content analysis system must be prepared to remain in close contact with their original data as they apply and interpret summary statistical measures. In earlier chapters, we emphasized the investigation of leftover lists, the use of retrievals, and the examination of the text and tag listings to facilitate the interpretation of statistical results.

An example of research classified here as case study is Dunphy's analysis of self-analytic groups (Chapter 8). In this study, comparisons are made between the written reports of members in two self-selected groups of college students. Dunphy's focus was on differences between the groups, trends over time common to both groups, and types of role differentiation occurring in the groups. If the membership of the groups could have been considered as representative of some population of college students the study may not have been classified as a case study. The group members, however, self-selected the groups and therefore certain characteristics of the group members are known to differ even from the characteristics of a college population. Thus Dunphy considered it inappropriate to make statistical inferences to a larger population of possible groups. Further, because the type of group studied differed in a number of ways from other self-analytic groups studied it becomes difficult to make statistical inferences to a larger population of groups. His study can thus be considered as a case study. This study, however, did test hypotheses that were based on other research and generated a number of hypotheses that might be considered to be important enough to be tested by other researchers with slightly different types of groups. The problem in this research as in other research classified here as a case study is a problem familiar to most field study researchers. To retain the natural characteristics of the object being studied often requires a sacrifice of the opportunity to make statistical inferences.[4]

One further important point should be noted in this discussion of case studies. Although no statistical inferences are made in these studies, the use of statistics from which statistical inferences are generally made is a common practice. The reasons for this practice are clear but should be carefully outlined. The statistics are used as a heuristic device for the analysis of content comparisons (group differences, trends over time, and so on) in order to sort out and possibly order the generation of hypotheses for future research. This reason is thus closely related to the making of statistical inference. Instead of using the findings to generalize to a larger population, these researchers use the findings to suggest hypotheses for future research. The approach to the problem of suggesting hypotheses is thus similar to the approach taken in making statistical inferences.

Suppose a researcher is interested in generating hypotheses from a comparison of two groups of documents. His approach may take the form of a two-pronged attack. The first prong is theory, not the testing of particular hypotheses suggested by a particular theory but a tendency to prefer and trust differences of potential theoretical pertinence. By chance in the selection of documents, or through an error in tagging, a partcular variable may appear to be a fine discriminator. If, however, the meaning of this tag category (the concept implied by it) has little or no theoretical relevance either to existing theories or a potential theory of the researcher, the difference should be questioned, and the researcher should not blindly accept it. Similarly, a tag that

---

[4] We make a distinction between logical inference and statistical inference. In our other use of the term inference (to sources, to antecedents, and to effects) the inferences are logical. When we discuss inferences made from a sample of data to a larger population of data, we are referring to statistical inference.

shows only slight discriminating power but fits nicely into an existing theory might be closely considered.

The second prong of the approach generally takes a form such as this; if everything else is equal, the researcher is more likely to prefer those differences between two sets of documents that are large. This is a question to be considered in the context of the research, but the meaning is at least intuitively obvious. The researcher also would prefer the large differences to be relatively stable; that is, that most of the documents from one of the groups have less mention of a concept than most of the documents in the other group. The researcher thus wants a measure, a heuristic device, which, together with his theoretical understanding of the problem, will help him select those variables (tags and/or their combinations) that best distinguish between the two sets of documents.

He also wants a measure that will be understood by other behavioral scientists. These conditions for the choice of a heuristic device suggest measures very similar to common statistical measures. Comparison between the groups weighted by some measure of the internal variation is a characteristic of both parametric and nonparametric statistical tests. The use of significance levels, confidence limits, and measures of degree of association in the experimental literature suggest possible cutoff values for the choice of potentially important stable differences. Furthermore, the form and calculation of most of the mentioned statistics are familiar to researchers and are programmed for electronic computers.

Thus, in the research reported upon in this book, one use of statistics is primarily for interpretation, description, and hypothesis generation rather than for significance testing. Statistics are used in conjunction with the theoretical orientation of the researcher to help explain his data rather than to make statistical inferences.

The following four sections of this chapter correspond to the last four headings of Table 7.2. Each of these headings can be considered a classification of a type of data comparison. These particular headings do not include all research comparisons made by content analysts, or even by the content analysts sampled in this volume. It is evident from the table that most research studies involve one or more comparisons. It is also evident that the comparisons suggest particular forms of statistical tests that might be employed to examine the data. In the following discussion of the types of comparisons, it is useful

TABLE 7.2. Comparisons of Content Analysis Research

	1. Case Study	2. Analysis of Group Differences	3. Relating of Content Characteristics to Quantified Variables Outside of Text Analysis	4. Analysis of Change over Time	5. Within Document Analysis
Small Group					
Self-Analytic Groups (8)	×	×		×	
Political Science					
Sino-Soviet Communications (9)	×	×		×	
Acceptance Speeches (10)	×	×		×	
Elite Editorials (11)		×		×	
Personality					
Letters from Jenny (12)	×			×	
Case of Windle (13)	×		×		
Clinical Psychology					
Psychotic Language (14)		×	×		
Analog Therapy Interview (15)	×	×			
Social Psychology					
Suicide Notes (16)	×	×			
Field Work Reports (17)		×	×	×	
Who-Am-I? (18)		×	×	×	
Cross Cultural					
Folktale Themes and Use of Alcohol (19)		×	×		
Future Autobiographies (20)	×	×			
Anthropological Dictionary Applications (21)		×			×
Other Applications					
Product Image (22)	×	×			
Study of Literature (23)	×				×

to bear in mind that we might be suggesting statistical tests either for
heuristic purposes (to give us a trowel to better dig at these data for
description, generation of hypotheses, and hypotheses testing) or for
significance testing. We shall consider each of the four headings separately, looking at the tests each suggests: both univariate and multivariate, parametric and nonparametric.[5] The use of factor analytic
techniques for the reduction of the number of content variables will
then be considered in relation to the four types of comparisons.

Analysis of Group Differences

The object of this type of analysis is the comparison and delineation
of the differences in the content of documents generated by members
of different groups. To explain the differences, inferences are usually
made to the characteristics of the groups. Tests for differences may
arise from specific hypotheses about the groups and their documents or
from a descriptive search for characteristics that discriminate between
the groups. The groups may be formed by experimental manipulation
or may have existed prior to the study. Different statistical inferences
may be made about the results of the study dependent on the manner
in which the groups are formed, but often the ways of looking for
or testing for differences are the same.

The most common parametric tests for group differences are based
on variations of a comparison between the *internal* variation within
the groups and the *external* variation between or among the groups.
In the simple case of two groups and one dependent variable, the
most commonly used statistical test involves the computation of a
measure of the difference between the means of the two groups divided
by an estimated standard deviation of the difference between the
means. The means of the two groups of documents may be considered
as estimates of the means of two populations of documents for
which the groups are samples.

The computed measure is considered, given the acceptance of some
assumptions, to be distributed according to a particular distribution
that is partially determined by the size of the two groups of documents.
If the computed measure exceeds some prespecified value, the in-

---

[5] In the discussion of statistical methods presented here, the variables being
analyzed may be individual tag, raw, or index scores; counts of combinations of
tags within text; or any of the variables resulting from the content analysis procedures. The type of variable and the assumptions made about it may help to determine the particular test that is made.

vestigator has some confidence that the means of the two populations differ. This statistical test, the Student's t-test, is considered in detail in most elementary statistical texts. The extension of this test to situations in which there are many groups and one dependent variable is the well-known Snedecor F-test. The use of the F-test in designs, usually called analysis of variance, is widespread in the literature of behavioral sciences. In the application of the t-test, we are often concerned with testing whether the means of two populations, represented by the two sample means, are different. The F-test is a technique to measure the significance of the differences between two or more means.

The t-test and the F-test are used to compare the means of different groups in a number of studies in Part II. These tests consider the dependent variable to be an interval- or ratio-scaled variable. Thus we can perform such arithmetic operations as adding, dividing, and multiplying for the purpose of arriving at parameters. The independent variable is usually a nominal variable.[6] If we have more than one independent variable, F-tests may also be employed. The case of one independent variable is usually called one-way analysis of variance, for two independent variables, two-way analysis of variance, and so on. In the two-way design, three statistical tests can be made, one for the effect of each of the variables independently and one for the result of the interaction between the two effects. For example, suppose that samples of editorials were drawn from eight newspapers in four major American cities and that one newspaper from each city could be considered to be an elite newspaper and one newspaper from each city a tabloid. Instead of looking for differences between the eight newspapers, we might be more interested in looking at differences between the newspapers of the four cities (one independent variable) and the difference between elite and tabloid newspapers (the second independent variable). We would thus have a four-by-two analysis of variance design, four cities and two types of newspapers. Each of the eight cells of this design contain a sample of editorials from a newspaper. The within-cell samples serve as a measure of variation within each newspaper; when pooled, these measures are used to

[6] The independent variable might also be an ordered variable. Thus we might be considering a set of newspapers and ordering them on the basis of the size of circulation. Supposing that we did this, techniques are available for the study of trends (for instance, the gradual decrease in reference to the concept ECONOMIC as the size of the newspaper circulation increases). More complicated ordered relationships can also be analyzed.

assess the significance of mean differences between cities and types of newspaper. We can then obtain a measure of the differences on the dependent variables for each of the two "main" effects. A third effect, the interaction effect, might also interest us. It may be that the combination of one particular city and one particular type of newspaper yields a higher occurrence of reference to economic matters than would be expected. To take a trivial example, those cities with major stock markets may have elite newspapers that are relatively more concerned with economic matters than other elite newspapers, while the tabloid newspapers of that city are no more concerned with economic matters than would be expected of tabloid papers in cities without stock markets. In this case, the interaction of particular cities and elite newspapers is an important effect to measure. It should be evident that many-dimensional analyses of variance are possible. In the multiway designs, a number of more complex interaction effects are possible, as well as a number of main effects equal to the way of the design.[7]

Up to this point, we have considered the case of differences between groups for only one dependent variable. Generalizations of analysis-of-variance techniques exist for the cases with more than one dependent variable. These generalizations are also based on comparisons of the *within*-group and *between*-groups variance. In the most general case, Wilk's lambda is an appropriate statistic for testing group differences. If possible, it is preferable to use multivariate techniques. Often, however, we run into situations in which the computation of multivarious techniques is arduous if computer programs are not available. Even when programs exist, interpretation of results is often a major problem. The argument for the use of multivariate methods is simple: the analysis of a set of variables allows us to consider the interrelationships among them in much more detail. It should be noted that multivariate analysis of this sort can also be utilized as an intermediate measure. If a multivariate test meets an appropriate criterion of significance, we will usually have more confidence in the significance of the results derived from univariate procedures on these same data.

Two problems should be considered by the content analyst when

---

[7] For more complete discussion of analysis-of-variance techniques, see a statistical text: McNemar (1959) or Edwards (1963); and for the more advanced, Winer (1962) or Scheffe (1959).

using analysis-of-variance designs. One of the primary assumptions made in using the F-statistic is that the variances are homogeneous; that is, they are equal across groups. As we mentioned in Chapter 6, the square-root transformation might be appropriately applied to index scores to help stabilize the variance and thus to help meet this assumption.

The second problem is that tests of significance with parametric methods generally require the assumption that the dependent variable is distributed in the population according to the normal distribution. Although we have little reason to expect that this is the case with most of the variables obtained from analyses using the General Inquirer, the F-statistic is known to be sufficiently robust to give good estimates even under rather drastic deviations from the assumption.[8]

When we are unwilling to make the assumption that our dependent variables are interval- or ratio-scaled measurements, or when we feel that other assumptions about the techniques are too rigid, we can use statistical tests that do not require such rigorous assumptions. As we have stressed earlier, the important relationship is the degree of isomorphism between the object being measured and the object to which we wish to infer. Often, as in the case of index scores, we are confident that the measurement of word counts conforms to interval measurement, but not so confident that the assessment of the intensity of the concept supposed to be indicated by the words is also an interval measurement. When there are two groups and one dependent variable, a number of nonparametric tests are available. Probably the most widely used is the Mann-Whitney U-test. This test requires the assumption that our dependent variables are only instances of ordinal measurement. For the case of a number of groups in a one-way design, the Kruskal-Wallis One-Way Analysis-of-Variance procedure is appropriate. For the one-dependent-variable, two-way ANOVA case with matched pairs and without a measure of interaction, the Friedman's Two-Way Analysis of Variance is appropriate. Each of these

---

[8] Another parametric multivariate technique for the analysis of differences between groups should be mentioned: that of discriminant analysis, used to find the maximum (subject to certain assumptions) weighting of dependent variables to discriminate between groups. A short discussion of discriminant analysis is contained in Cooley and Lohnes (1962). This book also contains discussions of computer programs for parametric statistical analyses. See also Rulon and Brooks (1961) for a discussion of techniques for generalized analysis of variance.

tests assumes only that the dependent variable is ordinally distributed. However, they represent about as complicated a form of design as can be handled by nonparametric statistical techniques.[9]

Two other points should be mentioned because they are important to content analysts interested in ascertaining group differences. The first, already referred to briefly, is sample size. It is a major problem in any type of analysis and is accentuated by the availability and appropriateness of multivariate techniques. When a researcher is dealing with available data, the number of variables he is measuring (for instance, tag categories and relevant combinations) often comes close to, or even exceeds, the number of cases being analyzed. Small samples make accurate and dependable estimation of parameters very difficult. In the multivariate case, the situation becomes critical when the number of cases is less than the number of variables. The procedure generally chosen to help overcome this problem is a reduction of the number of tag variables. In the studies reported on in Part II, this tactic has generally been carried out in two ways. The number of tag categories can be reduced by discarding all variables that appear to be theoretically unimportant, or appear to have too much within-group variance, or are regarded as unreliable or invalid. Unless very specific criteria are followed for reduction of the variables, this procedure raises the possibility of researcher bias and opens the door to the possibility of discarding important variables along with the unimportant. The other procedure for reducing variables will be given greater attention later in this chapter; it involves employing factor analytic procedures to discover a few important dimensions in the data. After the dimensions have been isolated, the documents in the study are scored on the variables defined by the dimensions. These new variables are then subjected to univariate analyses.

In the general discrimination of groups, techniques outside of the range of common statistical approaches can be considered. Among these is the tree-building procedure described in Chapter 3. It should be noted that in this procedure, we are discriminating between sentences from the documents of the two groups. The procedure entails finding combinations of tags appearing in one set of sentences from one group and not appearing in the sentences from the documents

[9] For more information about nonparametric methods, see Siegel (1956). See Wilson (1956) for a proposed solution to the nonparametric analysis-of-variance problem. Note McNemar's (1957) criticism of this solution.

in the other group. An example of an analysis employing this technique is Ogilvie's study of Windle (Chapter 13).

Analysis of Relationship Between Content Characteristics and Quantified Variables Outside of Text Analysis

This type of analysis attempts to measure the relationship between content variables and outside measures on the sources (other than those measures defining groups). Some of the problems that can arise are considered in the discussion of predictive validity. Analyses of this sort are contained in only 5 of the 16 studies in the book. (The lack of studies using this approach may be attributed to the use of nonexperimental data. Often, for the source being studied, there are no important systematically available measurements outside of the content.) Probably the best examples of this type of research in this book are the study of the use of alcohol in various societies (Chapter 18) and the study of the identity of college students (Chapter 19). In each, rather complete information has been collected about the sources of the content being analyzed.

The general statistical techniques used for the assessment of these relationships are parametric univariate- and multiple-correlation procedures and nonparametric correlation procedures. In the univariate case, both the parametric and nonparametric procedures result in a figure which lies between -1 and $+1$. A negative figure signifies a negative relationship; a zero figure signifies no relationship; and a positive figure signifies a positive relationship. For example, the researcher may have an independent measurement of the concept *avoidance* and may wish to see how this measure relates to the tag AVOID. He would compute a correlation coefficient for those two variables, expecting the relationship to be positive. His choice of a parametric or nonparametric measure would depend on his judgment of whether or not the two variables meet the necessary assumptions. As in the analysis of variance situation, procedures exist for computing correlations on interval-scaled data and on ordinal-scaled data.[10]

[10] The Pearson product-moment correlation coefficient is the usual parametric measure. See McNemar (1959). Generally the nonparametric measure used is Kendall's tau. See Kendall (1955).

Some care should be taken in the interpretation of correlations between tag category index scores. A certain amount of spurious association is introduced into the calculations by variables that have been divided by a common denominator (in this case, document length). Although this problem is apparently not serious for most of the studies reported here, the effect of this source of association should be

Confidence limits and levels can also be computed for these measures. Again the computation and use of these levels will depend on the research demands. If inferences to populations are made from sampled data, the confidence setting can be used in the standard manner. If no statistical inferences are being made, the setting may be used for heuristic purposes.

Before we mention the multivariate case, the use of multiple correlation and regression, two important interrelated points about the use of measures of correlation should be mentioned. In our discussion of analysis-of-variance and discrimination procedures, there was little ambiguity in distinguishing between independent and dependent sets of variables. In the case of correlation, the distinction is not so clear. In the discussion of analysis of variance, we avoided the issue of *causation,* but we cannot ignore it here. Strictly speaking, we hold to the point of view that causation can never be proved. However, there are times when we can state with some confidence that a causal effect is operating, and there are other times when we have little or no confidence that a causal chain exists between two or more variables. Often in the type of research reported on here causal effects can only be tenuously stated. The problem lies in the type of research that is predominant in content analysis. As we stated earlier, many analyses are conducted on historical or concurrent data; data generated in situations over which the researcher had little or no control. The researcher cannot control for important, unknown effects by randomly assigning various subjects to groups, and often he cannot even include statistical controls in his study for variables known to be important. The researcher has no assurance that important relationships between outside variables and the variables generated in the content analysis procedures are not the result of some unexplored outside variables.

In the search for techniques to assess group differences (discussed in the preceding section), the implication that membership in the groups may cause the differences was prominent. The question was by-passed in our discussion because the definition left no doubt which variable, the group-membership variable or the tag variable, preceded the other, and thus there could be no ambiguity about the potential causal variable. In the analysis of relationships of content variables

---

more closely investigated. One technique of controlling for this effect is to use document length as a variable and to partial out its effect on the other correlations before investigating variable-by-variable associations.

to other outside variables, there may be some doubt about which variable precedes the other. It may be hard to imagine that just the occurrence of a particular concept in a document will ever act with causal effect on some other behavior of the source, but the possibility cannot be ignored.[11] However, an attitude or motive, as it is reflected by the mention of a particular concept in a document, may act with a causal effect.

It should be noted that the methods we have mentioned for assessing the relationship between two variables are testing for a linear or a monotonically increasing relationship. There are measures for assessing curvilinear relationships. In attempting to assess other than the obvious linear relationship between two variables, the problem becomes one of choice. There are so many other relationships that may be tested. If an investigator has a hypothesis of a particular relationship other than linear, it may be easily tested; but if he is simply looking for other fits, the procedure is usually most easily implemented by plotting and visually inspecting his data.

In the multivariate case, a number of situations can be considered. The first is the case of more than one independent variable and of one dependent variable. This is generally called multiple correlation when we are simply looking for the relationship between the best linear combination of the independent variables and the dependent variable. It is a widely used method in the behavioral sciences. Suppose we are concerned with the relationship between certain personality variables and the level of academic achievement of a number of college students. To obtain measures of the personality variables, we might require each entering freshman to write an essay on his conception of himself. We would then construct tags to assess the personality variables we are interested in and process the essays. After the students had completed their first year of college, we might then run a multiple correlation, using the set of tag variables as independent variables and the students' grade point average as the dependent variable. We might, of course, control either statistically or physically for certain other variables, such as sex, aptitude scores, and types of courses taken.

The use of multiple correlation, of course, does not restrict us to

---

[11] It is possible, however, that the mention of a particular word can have a reinforcing effect on the attitude of a person, and thus the mention itself may be considered as causal in some sense.

using the tag variables as independent or preceding variables; we may wish to measure the association between a set of variables that precedes the production of a document and a particular tag variable in it.

In conjunction with the use of multiple-correlation procedures, we may also ask, How well are we *predicting* the dependent variable of each case by the independent variables? This technique is called multiple regression; and it involves computing "optimal" weights for the dependent variable(s) to find how well those weights, in combination with the original scores, predict the scores on the independent variable.[12]

In conjunction with correlation and regression, one further topic should be mentioned. Recently, there has been considerable interest in the analysis of residuals and, in particular, of "outlying" residuals. Residuals are normally defined as the deviations of the actual scores from the scores predicted by the model being used. In regression analysis, the residual score of a person (case or document) is defined as the actual score minus the predicted score. We note that this is a deviation from a linear model and can have either a positive or negative value. Since the regression model is linear and additive, researchers are interested in the study of residuals to see, for example, if interactions between some of the independent variables might not add substantially to the predictions already made through the linear additive technique. A second area of interest is in isolating those cases that deviate greatly from the expected or predicted score. In analyses conducted primarily for exploratory, descriptive, and hypothesis-generating purposes, the study of deviating cases may be of extreme value.

Analysis of Change Over Time — Analysis of the Process of Change

As we discussed earlier, the major orientation of much of the research in this book is directed toward the study of change. It is a wry

---

[12] The use of correlational and regression techniques requires that certain distributional assumptions be met if they are employed for the ascertainment of confidence limits and intervals. Discussion of these assumptions can be found in most intermediate statistical textbooks. We might note, too, that there are generalized cases of multiple-correlation and regression analysis. In the first generalization, a set of independent variables is maximally weighted to predict a set of unweighted dependent variables. In the second case, both the independent and dependent variables are weighted. This technique is commonly called canonical analysis. Both a discussion of the various assumptions and the generalizations mentioned are beyond the scope of this book.

coincidence that it is also here that we run into our greatest problems in measurement and assessment. It may be argued that many of the tactics used in the research represented here are inappropriate, but they are often the only techniques available to, and understood by, the researchers. In the discussion of change, we are concerned with the change in some variable(s) measured on the same source over a number of time periods. The question is not of a trend analysis of the type that we discussed earlier; we are not concerned with systematic differences of dependent variables for various sources differing on some independent variable.

Since the measurements are made on the same source but at different times, the measurements cannot be considered to be uncorrelated. That is, if a certain person tends to mention economic matters frequently in documents and this tendency changes over a certain time period so that a second measure of the amount of attention given to economic reference is made, then the absolute value of the second measure will depend to some extent on two factors: the source's initial frequency of mention and the degree to which he was affected by his experiences during the interval between the measurements. Both factors are crucial in the measurement of change.

In measuring change over time, we must emphasize the dangers of attributing causal influence to certain variables in uncontrolled conditions. In addition, we must point out that visual procedures rank among the most important for assessing and evaluating change. By visual procedures we mean straightforward plotting of the variables with time as one dimension. As with most other problems of analysis, it is only as the researcher becomes closely involved with the data that he becomes sensitive to and aware of the subtle, the unexpected, and the exciting. We stress the point in the context of discussing problems of change only because the more mechanical techniques are not as well known here as in the other comparisons. However, the method could have been appropriately suggested in any part of the preceding discussion, particularly in the discussion of residual analysis.[13]

---

[13] It should be noted that plotting and visual inspection of data can be a sophisticated process. In residual analysis, for instance, the plots may consist of comparisons of the residuals with the original raw scores, with the expected scores, or with some third variable. The plotting may be made on normal graph paper, on log paper, on log-log paper, or on any of a number of different kinds of paper that immediately effect certain transformations on the data. For some discussion of this, see Anscombe and Tukey (1963).

Because of the complexity of measuring change, we shall limit our discussion to the examination of two commonly occurring cases.[14]

One Dependent Variable, One Person,
Many Measurements over Equal Periods of Time

This situation often occurs in analyses of the content of therapy sessions. In the studies reported here, no research exactly fits this case. Three studies, however, come close to meeting the description and, in fact, could employ techniques similar to those suggested here. Paige's study (Chapter 12) of the *Letters of Jenny,* an analysis of the personality of an elderly woman as reflected in her published letters, varies because the letters do not occur at equally spaced intervals. The study of Presidential Nomination Acceptance Speeches (Chapter 10) differs from the description in that two documents are analyzed for each of ten equally spaced time periods. Ogilvie's study of the personality and behavior of small-group members over a number of meetings (Chapter 13) also deviates from the description in the matter of equally spaced time intervals.

In looking at change of this sort, the procedure again depends to some extent on the orientation of the research: if the investigator is interested in testing a particular hypothesis or a set of particular alternative hypotheses on the nature of the change, he may consider the use of a different strategy than if he were simply interested in exploring or generating hypotheses. In the second instance, we would suggest that the researcher begin by plotting and visually inspecting his data. From this inspection, he can form certain *post hoc* hypotheses to test out in subsequent research.

The second part of the analysis consists of defining a model or models and testing the fit of the data to these models. This procedure, although preferable to a blind orientation to available models, is difficult in most types of analyses. The most common model is the one described by a linear relationship between time on one dimension and the dependent variable on the other. In the case that we are presently describing, a convenient measure of the fit to this model is the Pearson correlation coefficient. For the case of a monotonic and not necessarily linear model, a nonparametric rank-order correlation coefficient such

[14] A recent collection of articles discussing methods of measuring change is contained in *Problems in Measuring Change,* edited by Chester Harris (1962). See also Campbell and Stanley in Gage (1963) for an important discussion of *ex post facto* and quasi-experimental designs.

as Kendall's tau is appropriate (Kendall, 1955), a measurement requiring only a monotonic assumption for unequal time intervals.

The model fitted in the case of linear relationship is of the form $y = ax + b$, where y is the dependent variable, x is the independent variable (in this case taking on values from 1 to n where n equals the last of the repeated measurements), and a and b are appropriate constants. By visual inspection or through theoretical considerations, other simple models could be suggested and tested. The use of the nonparametric test removes the restriction of linearity and allows perfect fit to a variety of curves that are all monotonic in direction.

In analyses of this sort, the computation of significance levels is difficult to rationalize. However, a procedure for comparison of models is suggested by the ease with which alternative hypotheses can be tested. Within the limits of possible theoretical relevance, it is advisable to look at the fits to the curve of as many alternative models as seem appropriate. Comparisons between the fits of the various models then allows the researcher some grist for his choice of the best model.

One Dependent Variable, a Group of Cases, a Number of Observations

This is probably the most recurrent situation in studies assessing change. The situation can usually be handled in the same general manner as the comparison of group means was handled, through analysis-of-variance procedures. In the terms of analysis of variance, the problem is generally labeled "repeated measurements." In the case of one dependent variable and two observations, an appropriate statistic, the t-test for correlated groups, is available. In cases of more than two measurements, the initial analysis procedure closely follows that of the standard analysis-of-variance procedures, with the exception that the correlations between the various repeated measurements on the same individual are taken into account. This procedure usually affects the results by reducing the within-group variance (the error term) and thus often intensifies the significance of the results. The tests for change over time then take the form of looking at the group means and testing to see whether they fit a linear relationship. When enough repeated measurements are available, tests for cubic and quadratic fits can be applied.[15]

[15] See Winer (1962) for a good discussion of repeated-measurements designs.

In situations with repeated measurements, the analysis becomes difficult to conduct when certain measurements are missing. In the experimental situation, it is occasionally justifiable to throw out those cases with incomplete data. In analyses of available data over which the researcher has had no control, the cases with missing data are generally self-selected and as such are very important to the researcher interested in a faithful analysis of his data. An example from the studies reported on later will serve to strengthen this point. In his study of change in self-analytic groups, Dunphy attempted to collect six sets of reports from each member of two groups. There was a considerable number of missing observations because people dropped out of the groups during the study and reporting was voluntary. Dunphy was concerned with changes within the groups, a process which was intimately affected by those members who dropped out over the year and by those who saw fit not to write some of the reports. He could not afford to remove from his analysis those persons with missing observations. His solution to the problem was the heuristic sort so often seen in the analysis of actual data. He ignored the fact that the design was a repeated measurements design and treated the observations in the six time periods as though they were independent of one another.

The cases of multivariate assessment of the process of change have not been considered. Although they are generally similar to univariate methods, the manipulation of many variables adds to the complexity of analysis and interpretation. Appropriate statistical controls should always be considered for use. Some discretion should be employed in using controls, however, for important relationships can be canceled out if they are misused. Aside from the approach of controlling, however, the multivariate problem is only approximated in the studies here, although procedures analogous to those suggested earlier for ANOVA with more than one dependent variable can be used. The approximations here take the form of reducing the variables through factor analysis and then dealing with the factors as separate, independent variables in univariate analyses.

Internal Document Comparison

We shall briefly consider this topic since it is peculiar to only two studies. The object of this analysis is the study of patterns of the frequency of occurrence of a particular tag in various parts of a document. One example of this would be the study of whether a certain concept is more frequently mentioned in the beginning, middle, or end of a certain story. Colby makes an analysis of this sort in his study of the myths of various cultures (Chapter 20). He divided his data into a number of sections and then ran tests for the best fit of his data to a number of models. Two approaches can be taken. A chi-square type of analysis can be run with expected values specified by the researcher. These expected values would define a certain model that the data were expected to fit. In one case, where all of the expected values could be the mean value, the test might be called a "flatness" test. In another case, the expected values might define an increasing amount of occurrence. A simpler approach is to test the alternative hypotheses by setting up some dummy variables that define certain models and then run rank-order correlations between the dummy variables and the variables (tag categories) that interest the researcher.

The Use of Factor Analysis Techniques for the Reduction of Data

In the studies reported here, factor analytic techniques are used a number of times to fulfill a need for reducing the many tag variables ordinarily measured by General Inquirer content analyses. Factor analysis is that branch of multivariate analysis that deals with the internal structure of correlation matrices. The correlation matrices factored in the studies here are the tag-by-tag correlation matrices. Generally, no variables other than tags are factored, and usually all of the tag categories are included in the matrix. Frequently, that form of factor analysis called principal components analysis is chosen.

This approach has certain distinct advantages:

1. If we do not wish to make tests of significance on the outcome of the analysis, components analysis requires no hypotheses about the data other than that the observations are independent.
2. Components analysis is a technique to isolate the major orthogonal (uncorrelated) dimensions. It reduces the number of variables to interpret and the opportunities for chance association with our external variables of interest. A solution can be found for the situation of fewer observations than variables, where the reduction of variables is particularly convenient.
3. Scores for the observations on the isolated components can be computed easily.

Once the dimensions are interpreted and the observations scored on each of the retained dimensions, they may be considered as variables and subjected to some of the univariate analyses of the sort described earlier. Frequently, only the first two or three factors are retained (if they are apparently related to the areas of interest of the investigator), and thus the problems of analysis are reduced.

Since this use of factor analytic procedures is somewhat unconventional, a description of a strategy for the interpretation of the factors might be appropriate. This strategy involves two steps. The first is an interpretation of the multidimensional space defined by the retained factors. Previous to this stage, some cutoff point for the number of retained factors has been decided. The interpretation of the two dimensional spaces requires us to go beyond merely labeling the primary dimensions. It follows an approach advocated by Kassebaum, Couch, and Slater (1959). In this approach, the researcher analyzes and names not only the primary reference dimensions but also those axes at 45-degree angles to the primary dimensions. Kassebaum, Couch, and Slater cite two particular advantages for the identification of these new axes called "fusion factors" (228).

1. Conceptual clarity: "a better understanding of the fixed position factors is produced when they are examined in relation to other dimensions in the factor space."
2. Increased probability of continuity of studies: ". . . the arbitrary placing of axes according to the simple structure criterion maximizes apparent diversity of findings if fusion factors are not interpreted."

The interpretation of the multidimensional space must, of course, be theoretically consistent.[16] Once we have completed our interpretation of the space defined by the factors, the factor scores for the documents on the composite measure defined by the factor loadings can be plotted and interpreted in a factor score space.

The strategy of plotting the factor scores of observations in the factor score space and then interpreting the positions has been used to great advantage in three studies of change over time. In two of the studies Dunphy (Chapter 8) and Namenwirth (Chapter 11), the analysis consisted of looking at the change in groups as represented

---

[16] There are, of course, other fusion factors to be analyzed; for instance, those defined by the combination of three dimensions, four dimensions, and so on.

by the movement through the factor space of the means of the groups for a number of repeated measurements. In the other study, Smith (Chapter 10), the actual observations were plotted because the number of cases was so small. The advantage of such a strategy is that we can look at the processes of change in a well-defined multidimensional space.

Two particular problems in the use of factor analytic techniques should be stressed. In the use of the technique to look for dimensions important in the analysis of change, the researchers in this book often violate the assumption that each of the observations is independent. In the usual case, the analysis is conducted on an original data matrix of N observations and p variables. If we are studying how certain sources have changed over periods of time, the observations may not all be independent; that is, we may have two or more observations at different time periods for each of the particular sources. Ledyard Tucker (1962) has suggested an appropriate way of handling this situation; a technique called Multi-Mode factor analysis.

The second problem has already been discussed in some detail in Chapter 4. The use of factor analysis of matrices, including both first- and second-order tags, leads us to the problem that some correlations between tags are large because the tags have entry words in common; for instance, the meaning unit "teacher" is tagged NEUTER-ROLE, ACADEMIC, and HIGHER-STATUS in the Harvard III Dictionary. The statistical interdependence of the first- and second-order tags should be recognized both by users contemplating intercorrelating them and by analysts in their interpretation of results; often just one or two entry words in common may be causing high intercorrelations. Again, we argue for the use of the approach, even given the violation of some assumptions on the basis of the utility of the results.

The use of factor analysis and other multivariate techniques is one approach to the analysis of tag contingencies in the data. As stressed in earlier chapters (2 and 4) and in the 1959 report on content analysis (Pool, 1959), contingency analysis is the wave of the future in content analysis. The concerns of investigators are shifting from the analysis of single variables to analysis of the relationships between variables in the context of the data being analyzed.

> Contingency analysis asks not how often a given symbolic form appears in each of several bodies of text, but how often it appears in conjunction with other symbolic units. (Pool, 1959, 196)

Factor analytic techniques represent an approach to contingency analysis that is based on the linear association of frequencies of tag occurrences in the several bodies of text. The contingencies found in factor analysis are between pairs or sets of tags within a total document. The documents receiving high positive factor scores are those which have generally high relative frequencies of occurrence on those tags defining the positive end of the factor and low relative frequency of occurrence on those tags defining the negative end of the factor. This approach can possibly be considered as an efficient way of suggesting contingencies between tag categories within sentences. The initial analysis of the suggested sentence contingencies can be easily conducted using the retrieval procedures; later more sophisticated techniques can be built into the tagging program if they appear important.

A STRATEGY FOR THE EFFICIENT USE OF THE GENERAL INQUIRER CONTENT ANALYSIS SYSTEM

Throughout this book, we have stressed the importance of working closely with the data. In the discussion of reliability and validity, we noted the importance of the researcher watching for possible mistagging and for crucial terms on his leftover lists. In the discussion of inference and of statistical techniques, we noted the necessity of checking and rechecking hypotheses that are suggested by analyses of the summary numbers derived from the General Inquirer procedures.

The system of content analysis described in this book was developed with these needs directly in mind. With many variables being computed automatically for a number of documents, it was anticipated that content analysts would have difficulty remaining in close contact with their data. The bilingual listing resulting from the text and tag list program and the retrieval procedures of the system were developed to help the researcher stay close to his data while applying the appropriate statistical procedures.

To facilitate this communication between the researcher and his data, a strategy for the coordination of statistical and retrieval procedures has been developed, based on a three-level conception of potential analysis procedures. Any particular study could use the techniques of analysis of only one or of two or of all three of the levels and satisfy requirements for a sensitive, solid piece of research. Although the levels have an apparent relationship with the degree of complexity of the analysis procedures, complexity itself should not necessarily be equated with the value of research.

Table 7.3 outlines the three levels of analysis. This framework is obviously not appropriate for all quantitative content analyses. As a rough guideline, however, it does provide a flexible framework for the ordering, application, and communication of simple and complex measures while it also suggests techniques enabling the researcher to remain constantly in close touch with his original data. The approach suggested by Table 7.3 is obviously tailored for a descriptive, hy-

TABLE 7.3. A Scheme of Research Procedures in Content Analysis

Level	Statistical Procedure	Retrieval Procedure	Object of Analysis
I	Graphing tag index scores	Hand retrievals using the text and tag "bilingual" listing.	To appraise validity of tagging procedure. To suggest hypotheses for research at levels II and III below.
II	Univariate analysis procedures	Single tag retrieval procedures to study context in which tags occur and to study the words contributing to tag counts.	To assess the power of individual variables in the relevant comparisons.
III	Multivariate analysis procedures	Co-occurrence analysis and retrievals.	To describe and interpret the data through sensitive interplay with the statistical measures and retrievals.

pothesis-generating type of study. A strictly hypothesis-testing researcher would immediately apply the appropriate measure to assess the relationship that interests him. The three levels imply a hierarchy of procedures that can often be efficiently employed.

The first level suggests combining the visual inspection of the tag tally graphs with a qualitative hand retrieval analysis using the text and tag listing output. This is a very crucial stage in any analysis. It is at this point that the researcher receives his initial feedback on the reliability and validity of his tagging procedure, and the verification of his initial hypotheses about the data. It is also at this stage that certain seeds of possible future hypotheses are suggested. Many researchers return many times in their subsequent, more complex analyses to examine both the graphs and the text and tag listing output.

The second level of analysis outlined can be described as a mechanical, univariate approach. At this point, we are investigating the nature of tags individually. The analysis might be directed toward seeing how well individual variables discriminate between groups, how well they predict some outside variable, or perhaps how they vary internally within the document. The particular comparisons made at this level may have been suggested by the earlier analysis at the first level; they may be the result of *ad hoc* hypotheses; or they may result simply from the choice of an over-all shotgun approach. The retrieval procedures at this level would generally take the form of single tag retrievals for the purpose of studying the context in which tags occur and the particular words contributing to the tag counts. An understanding of the interaction between the statistical results and the meaning units contributing to the tag counts is crucial here, not only for the theoretical interpretation of the results at this stage but for the eventual interpretation of results at the third level of analysis.

The third level of analysis is represented by multivariate techniques on the statistical side and complex retrieval and second-order analysis on the retrieval side. This is the stage at which we are investigating the interrelationships among the tags and the multiple relationships of the tags to outside variables. An adequate understanding of the individual variables is crucial to understanding combinations of variables. The multivariate techniques might be as complex as multivariate analysis of variance or discriminant analysis, or as simple as a three-variable multiple-correlation analysis. However, the relationship that is suggested by the analysis should be verifiable by appropriate retrievals. As discussed in Chapter 3, retrieval procedures can be used to obtain information not only of co-occurrences within documents but of co-occurrences within sentences as units of information. Such additional information allows us to go beyond the over-all characterization of tag usage to the identification of themes.

Researchers should not, however, restrict their analyses of co-occurrences to those suggested by statistical multivariate procedures based on the frequencies of tags within documents. Often equal frequencies of occurrence within two sets of documents mask certain important within-sentence interactions.

CONCLUDING REMARKS

The following pages of this book contain descriptions of studies that have been carried out by a number of different researchers using the General Inquirer system. The number of approaches used by these various researchers in the analysis of data is equal to the number of researchers. Any suggestion implied in this chapter that there is a "right" way to analyze content data should be rejected by the reader. We hope rather to have prepared the reader to some extent for the variety of procedures used in the following research and to have impressed upon him the idea that although content analysis, like other forms of measurement, is not completely simplified because a computer method is available, it is not too complex to be successfully used by sensitive, careful researchers.

BIBLIOGRAPHY

Abelson, R.
   1963   "Computer Simulation of 'Hot' Cognition." In S. Tomkins and S. Messick (eds.), *Computer Simulation of Personality*. New York: John Wiley & Sons.

Albig, William
   1938   "The Content of Radio Programs, 1925–1935." *Social Forces,* Vol. 16, 338–349.

Allport, Gordon W.
   1942   *The Use of Personal Documents in Psychological Science.* New York: Social Science Research Council.
   1946   "Anonymous Letters from Jenny." *Journal of Abnormal and Social Psychology,* Vol. 41, 315–350.
   1961   *Pattern and Growth in Personality.* New York: Holt, Rinehart and Winston.
   1965   *Letters from Jenny.* (ed.) New York: Harcourt, Brace & World (Harbinger Book).
   1966   "Traits Revisited." *American Psychologist.* Vol. 21, No. 1, 1–10.

Allport, G. W., and J. S. Bruner, and E. M. Jandorf
   1953   "Personality and Social Catastrophe: Ninety Life Histories of the Nazi Revolution." In C. Kluckhohn, H. Murray, and D. Schneider (eds.), *Personality in Nature, Culture, and Society*. New York: Knopf. Revised Edition.

Allport, G. W., and J. M. Gillespie
   1955   *Youth's Outlook on the Future: A Cross-National Study.* Garden City, N.Y.: Doubleday.

Allport, G. W., and Philip E. Vernon
   1933   *Studies in Expressive Movement.* New York: Macmillan.

Anscombe, F. J., and J. W. Tukey
  1963 "The Examination and Analysis of Residuals." *Technometrics,* Vol. 5, No. 2, 141–160.
Arnold, Magda B.
  1962 *Story Sequence Analysis: A New Method of Measuring Motivation and Predicting Achievement.* New York: Columbia University Press.
Atkinson, John W. (ed.)
  1958 *Motives in Fantasy, Action, and Society: A Method of Assessment and Study.* Princeton, N.J.: Van Nostrand.
Auld, Frank W., and Edward J. Murray
  1955 "Content Analysis Studies of Psychotherapy." *Psychological Bulletin,* Vol. 52, 377–395.
Baldwin, A. L.
  1942 "Personal Structure Analysis: A Statistical Method for Investigating the Single Personality." *Journal of Abnormal and Social Psychology,* Vol. 37, 163–183.
Bales, Robert F.
  1950 *Interaction Process Analysis: A Method for the Study of Small Groups.* Reading, Mass.: Addison-Wesley.
Barcus, Francis E.
  1959 "Communications Content: Analysis of the Research, 1900–1958 (A Content Analysis of Content Analysis)." Ph.D. dissertation, University of Illinois. Ann Arbor, Mich.: University Microfilms, Inc.
Bassow, Whitman
  1948 "*Izvestia* Looks inside U.S.A." *Public Opinion Quarterly,* Vol. 12, No. 3, 430–439.
Bennis, Warren G., and Herbert A. Shepard
  1956 "A Theory of Group Development." *Human Relations,* Vol. 9, 415–437.
Berelson, Bernard R.
  1952 *Content Analysis in Communication Research.* Glencoe, Ill.: The Free Press.
  1954 "Content Analysis." In Gardner Lindzey (ed.), *Handbook of Social Psychology.* Vol. 1. Reading, Mass.: Addison-Wesley.
Bernstein, B.
  1961 "Social Class and Linguistic Development: A Theory of Social Learning." In A. Halsey, J. Floud, and C. Anderson (eds.), *Education, Economy, and Society.* Glencoe, Ill.: The Free Press.
  1964a "Aspects of Language and Learning in the Genesis of Social Process." In D. Hymes (ed.), *Language in Culture and Society: A Reader in Linguistics and Anthropology.* New York: Harper & Row.
  1964b "A Socio-Linguistic Approach to Social Learning." Unpublished paper.
Bion, Wilfred
  1961 *Experiences in Groups and Other Papers.* New York: Basic Books.
Brown, Roger W.
  1965 *Social Psychology.* New York: The Free Press of Glencoe.

Busa, R.
   1957   *I Principali Problemi dell' Automazione del Linguaggio Scritto,*
          Rome.
Campbell, Angus *et al.*
   1960   *The American Voter.* New York: John Wiley & Sons. (Abridged
          Edition, 1964.)
Carnap, Rudolf
   1947   *Formalization of Logic.* Cambridge, Mass.: Harvard University
          Press.
   1956   *Meaning and Necessity: A Study in Semantics and Modal Logic.*
          2nd Edition. Chicago: University of Chicago Press.
Carroll, John B.
   1953   *The Study of Language: A Survey of Linguistics and Related Disci-
          plines in America.* Cambridge, Mass.: Harvard University Press.
   1959   "Some Cautionary Notes on the Semantic Differential." Presented
          at a Symposium, American Psychological Association, Cincinnati,
          September 1959.
   1964   *Language and Thought.* Englewood Cliffs, N.J.: Prentice-Hall.
Carroll, John B., and Joseph H. Casagrande
   1958   "The Function of Language Classifications in Behavior." In E. Mac-
          coby, T. Newcomb, and E. Hartley (eds.), *Readings in Social
          Psychology.* 3rd Edition. New York: Henry Holt.
Carstensen, F., and W. Stolz
   1964   "Cloze Procedure Analysis Programs." *Computer Newsletter,* Vol.
          3, 5–6.
Cartwright, D.
   1953   "Analysis of Qualitative Material." In L. Festinger and D. Katz
          (eds.), *Research Methods in the Behavioral Sciences.* New York:
          Holt, Rinehart and Winston.
Cochran, Thomas C.
   1953   *Railroad Leaders, 1845–1890: The Business Mind in Action.* Cam-
          bridge, Mass.: Harvard University Press.
Colby, Benjamin N.
   1966   "Cultural Patterns in Narrative." *Science,* Vol. 151, No. 3712,
          793–798.
Colby, B. N., G. Collier, and S. Postal
   1963   "Comparison of Themes in Folktales by the General Inquirer Sys-
          tem." *Journal of American Folklore,* Vol. 76, No. 302.
Colby, Kenneth
   1963   "Computer Simulation of a Neurotic Process." In S. Tomkins and
          S. Messick (eds.), *Computer Simulation of Personality: Frontier
          of Psychological Theory.* New York: John Wiley & Sons.
Cooley, William W., and P. R. Lohnes
   1962   *Multivariate Procedures for the Behavioral Sciences.* New York:
          John Wiley & Sons.
Couch, Arthur
   1966   "Psychological Determinants of Interpersonal Behavior." Unpub-
          lished Ph.D. dissertation, Department of Social Relations, Harvard
          University.

Couch, Arthur, David Peizer, and Mary Hyde
    1965   "The Data Text System: Program Description and Operating In-
            structions. Preliminary Manual." Department of Social Relations,
            Harvard University.
Dallin, Alexander
    1947   "America through Soviet Eyes." *Public Opinion Quarterly,* Vol. 11,
            No. 1, 26–39.
Danielson, W., and S. Bryan
    1963   "Computer Automation of Two Readability Formulas." *Journalism
            Quarterly,* Vol. 40, 201–206.
Davison, W. P.
    1947   "An Analysis of the Soviet-Controlled Berlin Press." *Public Opinion
            Quarterly,* Vol. 11, 40–57.
Davitz, Joel R., *et al.*
    1964   *The Communication of Emotional Meaning.* New York: McGraw-
            Hill.
Daykin, Walter L.
    1937   "Negro Types in American White Fiction." *Journal of Sociology
            and Social Research,* Vol. 22, 45–52.
Deegan, Dorothy Yost
    1951   *The Stereotype of the Single Woman in American Novels: A Social
            Study with Implications for the Education of Women.* New York:
            King's Crown Press.
Dicey, Albert Venn
    1924   *Lectures on the Relation Between Law and Public Opinion in Eng-
            land during the Nineteenth Century.* London: Macmillan and Com-
            pany, Ltd.
Dovring, Karin
    1954   "Quantitative Semantics in 18th Century Sweden." *Public Opinion
            Quarterly,* Vol. 18, No. 4, 389–394.
Edwards, Allen L.
    1950   *Experimental Design in Psychological Research.* New York: Holt,
            Rinehart and Winston.
    1963   *Statistical Methods for the Behavioral Sciences.* New York: Holt,
            Rinehart and Winston.
Foder, J. A., and J. L. Katz
    1964   *The Structure of Language: Readings in the Philosophy of Lan-
            guage.* Englewood Cliffs, N.J.: Prentice-Hall.
Foff, A.
    1958   "Scholars and Scapegoats." *English Journal,* Vol. 47, 118–126.
Foster, H. S.
    1935   "How America Became Belligerent: A Quantitative Study of War
            News." *American Journal of Sociology,* Vol. 40, 464–475.
Freeman, M., and J. Tukey
    1950   "Transformation Related to the Angular and the Square Root."
            Annals of Mathematical Statistics, Vol. 21, 607–611.
Freud, Sigmund
    1911   "Psychoanalytic Notes upon an Autobiographical Account of a
            Case of Paranoia (Dementia Paranoides)." In *Collected Papers of
            Sigmund Freud.* Vol. XIII. Alix and James Strachey (trans.).
            London: Hogarth Press.

Frisbie, Bruce
    1964   Personal Communications.
Gage, N. L. (ed.)
    1963   *Handbook of Research on Teaching*. Chicago: Rand McNally.
Garraty, John A.
    1959   "The Application of Content Analysis to Biography and History."
            In Ithiel de Sola Pool (ed.), *Trends in Content Analysis*. Urbana,
            Ill.: University of Illinois Press, 1959.
Garth, T. R.
    1916   "A Statistical Study of the Content of Newspapers." *School and
            Society*, Vol. 3, 140–144.
George, Alexander L.
    1959a   *Propaganda Analysis: A Study of Inferences Made from Nazi
            Propaganda in World War II*. New York: Harper & Row.
    1959b   "Quantitative and Qualitative Approaches to Content Analysis."
            In I. de Sola Pool (ed.), *Trends in Content Analysis*. Urbana, Ill.:
            University of Illinois Press.
Gottschalk, Louis A. (ed.)
    1961   *Comparative Psycholinguistic Analysis of Two Psychotherapeutic
            Interviews*. New York: International University Press.
Green, Bert F.
    1963   *Digital Computers in Research: An Introduction for Behavioral and
            Social Scientists*. New York: McGraw-Hill.
Grey, Alan, David Kaplan, and Harold D. Lasswell
    1965   "Recording and Context Units — Four Ways of Coding Editorial
            Content." In Harold D. Lasswell, Nathan Leites, and associates,
            Language of Politics: Studies in Quantitative Semantics. Revised
            Edition. Cambridge, Mass.: The M.I.T. Press.
Guiliano, Victor
    1964   "The Interpretation of Word Associations." Proceedings of a Sym-
            posium on Statistical Association Methods for Mechanized Docu-
            mentation. Washington, D.C.: National Bureau of Standards and
            American Documentation Institute.
Hacker, B.
    1965   "Content Analysis by Computer of Bartholomew's *De Proprietati-
            bus Rerum* and Topsell's *Historie of Foure-Footed Beasts*." Paper
            presented at the Midwest Junto of the History of Science Society,
            Stillwater, Oklahoma.
Hamilton, Thomas
    1942   "Social Optimism and Pessimism in American Protestantism." *Pub-
            lic Opinion Quarterly*," Vol. 6, 280–283.
Harris, Chester (ed.)
    1962   *Problems in Measuring Change*. Madison, Wis.: The University of
            Wisconsin Press.
Harris, Z.
    1964a   "Co-occurrence and Transformation in Linguistic Structure." In
            J. Foder and J. Katz (eds.), *The Structure of Language*. Engle-
            wood Cliffs, N.J.: Prentice-Hall. Reprinted.
    1964b   "Distributional Structure." In J. Fodor and J. Katz (eds.), *The
            Structure of Language*. Englewood Cliffs, N.J.: Prentice-Hall. Re-
            printed.

Harway, N., and H. Iker
   1964   "Computer Analysis of Content in Psychotherapy." *Psychological Reports,* Vol. 14, 720–722.
Hays, David
   1960   *Automatic Content Analysis.* Santa Monica, Calif.: RAND Corporation Publication.
   1962   "Automatic Language and Data Processing." In H. Borko (ed.), *Computer Applications in the Behavioral Sciences.* Englewood Cliffs, N.J.: Prentice-Hall.
Hobbes, Thomas
           Leviathan. Edition used, London: J. M. Dent & Sons, Ltd. Everyman's Library, 1928.
Holsti, Ole
   1964*a*   "An Adaptation of the General Inquirer for the Systematic Analysis of Political Documents." *Behavioral Science,* Vol. 9, 382–388.
   1964*b*   "The General Inquirer System Applied to Sino-Soviet Relations." Paper read at The American Psychological Association Convention, September 5, 1964.
   1964*c*   "Perceptions of Time, Perceptions of Alternatives, and Patterns of Communication as Factors in Crisis Decision-Making." Stanford, Calif.: Stanford University Studies in International Conflict and Integration.
   in press   "Content Analysis." A prepublication draft of a chapter to appear in G. Lindzey and E. Aronson (eds.), *The Handbook of Social Psychology.* 2nd Edition. Reading, Mass.: Addison-Wesley.
Holsti, Ole, R. Brody, and R. North
   1964   "Measuring Affect and Action in International Reaction Models: Empirical Materials from the 1962 Cuban Crisis." Paper read at International Peace Research Society Conference at Ghent, Belgium, July 18–19, 1964.
Holzinger, Karl J., and Harry H. Harman
   1941   *Factor Analysis: A Synthesis of Factorial Methods.* Chicago, Ill.: University of Chicago Press.
Hunt, Earl B., J. Marin, and P. J. Stone
   1966   *Experiments in Induction.* New York: Academic Press.
Hymes, Dell (ed.)
   1965   *The Use of Computers in Anthropology.* London: Mouton.
Jaffee, J.
   in press   "Computer Analysis of Verbal Behavior in Psychiatric Interviews." To appear as a chapter in S. Arieti (ed.), *American Handbook of Psychiatry.* Vol. 3, New York: Basic Books.
Janis, Irving L.
   1965   "The Problem of Validating Content Analysis." In Harold D. Lasswell and Nathan Leites and associates, *Language of Politics: Studies in Quantitative Semantics.* Revised Edition. Cambridge, Mass.: The M.I.T. Press.
Kassebaum, G. G., A. S. Couch, and P. E. Slater
   1959   "The Factorial Dimensions of the M.M.P.I." *Journal of Consulting Psychology,* Vol. 23, 226–236.

Katz, J., and J. Fodor
    1964   "Structure of a Semantic Theory." In J. Fodor and J. Katz (eds.),
            The Structure of Language: Readings in the Philosophy of Language. Englewood Cliffs, N.J.: Prentice-Hall.
Kehl, W. (ed.)
    1965   Fall Joint Computer Conference Proceedings (1965). Baltimore, Md.: Spartan Books.
Kelly, George
    1955   *The Psychology of Personal Constructs*. 2 vols. New York: Norton.
Kendall, Maurice G.
    1955   *Rank Correlation Methods*. 2nd Revised Edition. New York: Hafner.
Kuno, S.
    1965   "The Predictive Analyzer and a Path Elimination Technique."
            Communications of the Association of Computer Machinery, Vol. 8, No. 7, 453–462.
Kuno, S., and A. Oettinger
    1962   "Multiple-Path Syntactic Analyzer." *Proceedings of IFIP* (International Federation of Information Processing). Munich, Germany.
Laffal, Julius
    1960   "The Contextural Associates of Sun and God in Schreber's Autobiography." *Journal of Abnormal and Social Psychology*, Vol. 61, No. 3, 474–479.
    1964   "Freud's Theory of Language." *Psychoanalytic Quarterly*, Vol. 33, 157–175.
    1964   "Psycholinguistics and the Psychology of Language: Comments."
            American Psychology, Vol. 19, 813–815.
    1965   *Pathological and Normal Language*. New York: Atherton Press.
Lane, Robert E.
    1962   *Political Ideology*. Glencoe, Ill.: The Free Press.
Langer, Susanne K.
    1962   *Philosophical Sketches*. Baltimore, Md.: The Johns Hopkins Press. Mentor Book, 1964.
Lasswell, Harold D.
    1927   *Propaganda Technique in the World War*. New York: Knopf.
Lasswell, Harold D., Daniel Lerner, and Ithiel de Sola Pool
    1952   *The Comparative Study of Symbols*. Hoover Institute Studies, Series C: No. 1., Stanford, Calif.: Stanford University Press.
Lasswell, Harold D., and Nathan Leites and associates
    1965   *Language of Politics: Studies in Quantitative Semantics*. Revised Edition. Cambridge, Mass.: The M.I.T. Press.
Lazarsfeld, Paul F.
    1941   "Remarks on Administrative and Critical Communications Research." *Studies in Philosophy and Social Science*, Vol. 9, No. 1, 2–16.
Lazarsfeld, Paul F., and Allen H. Barton
    1951   "Qualitative Measurement in the Social Sciences: Classification, Typologies, and Indices." In D. Lerner and H. D. Lasswell (eds.), *The Policy Sciences: Recent Developments in Scope and Method*. Stanford, Calif.: Stanford University Press.

Lazarsfeld, Paul F., Bernard Berelson, and Hazel Gaudet
    1948   *The People's Choice: How the Voter Makes Up His Mind in a Presidential Campaign.* New York: Columbia University Press.
Leary, Timothy F.
    1957   *Interpersonal Diagnosis of Personality: A Functional Theory and Methodology for Personality Evaluation.* New York: Ronald Press.
Leites, Nathan C.
    1964   "Trends in Affectlessness." In C. Kluckholn, H. Murray, and D. Schneider (eds.), *Personality in Nature, Society, and Culture.* Revised Edition. New York: Knopf.
Lévi-Strauss, Claude
    1964   *Le Cru et Le Cuit.* Paris: Plon.
Levine, Joel
    1964   "Measurement of Association." Unpublished manuscript, Laboratory of Social Relations, Harvard University. Revised, 1965.
Licklider, J. C. R.
    1965   *Libraries of the Future.* Cambridge, Mass.: The M.I.T. Press.
Litwin, George Henry
    1965   "The Language of Achievement: An Analysis of Achievement-Related Themes in Fantasy Using Mechanical Methods." Unpublished Ph.D. dissertation, Harvard University.
Lorge, Irving
    1944   "Predicting Readability." *Teacher's College Record,* Vol. 45, 404–419.
    1951   "Selection of Entries and Definitions." In C. Barnhart, *American College Dictionary.* New York: Harper & Bros.
Macalpine, Ida, and R. A. Hunter
    1955   "Discussion of the Schreber Case." In Daniel Paul Schreber, *Memoirs of My Nervous Illness.* Ida Macalpine and R. A. Hunter (trans.), Cambridge, Mass.: Robert Bentley.
McClelland, David C.
    1951   *Personality.* New York: Holt, Rinehart and Winston.
    1961   *The Achieving Society.* Princeton, N.J.: Van Nostrand.
McClelland, David, *et al.*
    1953   *The Achievement Motive.* New York: Appleton, Century, Crofts.
McNemar, Quinn
    1957   "On Wilson's Distribution-Free Test of Analysis of Variance Hypothesis." *Psychological Bulletin,* Vol. 54, No. 4, 361–362.
    1959   *Psychological Statistics.* New York: John Wiley & Sons.
Mann, R. D.
    1966   "The Development of the Member-Trainer Relationship in Self-Analytic Groups." *Human Relations.* Vol. 19, No. 1.
Maranda, P.
    1965   Personal communication.
Marsden, Gerald
    1965   "Content Analysis Studies of Therapeutic Interviews, 1954–1964." *Psychological Bulletin,* Vol. 63, No. 5, 298–321.
Martin, Helen
    1936   "Nationalism and Children's Literature." *Library Quarterly,* Vol. 6.

Matthews, Byron C.
1910 "A Study of a New York Daily." *Independent,* Vol. 68, 82–86.
Mead, George H.
1934 *Mind, Self, and Society from the Standpoint of a Social Behaviorist.* Chicago, Ill.: University of Chicago Press. Ed. by Charles W. Morris.
Meehl, Paul E.
1954 *Clinical Versus Statistical Prediction: A Theoretical Analysis and a Review of the Evidence.* Minneapolis, Minn.: University of Minnesota Press.
Mencken, H. L.
1936 *The American Language.* 3 vols. New York: Knopf.
Merton, Robert K.
1957 "Science and Economy of 17th Century England." In R. Merton (ed.), *Social Theory and Social Structure.* Glencoe, Ill.: The Free Press. Revised Edition.
Miles, Josephine
1951 *The Continuity of Poetic Language.* Berkeley, Calif.: University of California Press.
1957 *Eras and Modes in English Poetry.* Berkeley, Calif.: University of California Press.
1960 *Renaissance 18th Century and Modern Language in English Poetry.* Berkeley, Calif.: University of California Press.
Mills, Theodore M.
1964 *Group Transformation.* Englewood Cliffs, N. J.: Prentice-Hall.
Morris, Charles
1946 *Signs, Language and Behavior.* New York: Prentice-Hall. (George Braziller, 1955.)
1964 *Signification and Significance: A Study of the Relations of Signs and Values.* Cambridge, Mass.: The M.I.T. Press.
Murray, Henry A.
1938 *Exploration in Personality.* New York: Oxford University Press.
Murray, Henry A.
1955 "The American Icarus." In Burton and Harris (eds.), *Clinical Studies of Personality.* Vol. II. New York: Harper & Bros.
North, R., with Ithiel de Sola Pool
1952 *Kuomintang and Chinese Communist Elites.* Hoover Institute Studies, Series B: Elite Studies No. 8, Stanford, Calif.: Stanford University Press.
North, Robert C., *et al.*
1963 *Content Analysis.* Evanston, Ill.: Northwestern University Press.
Osgood, Charles E.
1959 "The Representational Model and Relevant Research Methods." In Ithiel de Sola Pool (ed.), *Trends in Content Analysis.* Urbana, Ill.: University of Illinois Press.
1963a "Language Universals and Psycholinguistics." In J. Greenberg (ed.), *Universals of Language.* Cambridge, Mass.: The M.I.T. Press. 2nd Revised Edition.
1963b "On Understanding and Creating Sentences." *American Psychologist.* Vol. 18, 735–751.

Osgood, C. E., S. Saporta, and J. C. Nunnally
   1954   "Evaluative Assertion Analysis: A Method for Studying the Semantic Content of Messages." Unpublished manuscript, University of Illinois. Institute of Communications Research.
   1956   "Evaluative Assertion Analysis." *Litera.* Vol. 3, 47–102. Summa-
   1959   rized in Ithiel de Sola Pool (ed.), *Trends in Content Analysis.* Urbana, Ill.: University of Illinois Press.

Osgood, C. E., and T. A. Sebeok (eds.)
   1954   "Psycholinguistics: A Survey of Theory and Research Problems." *Journal of Abnormal and Social Psychology* (Supplement), Vol. 49, No. 4, Part II.
   1965   *Psycholinguistics: A Survey of Theory and Research Problems,* with A. Richard Diebold's *Survey of Psycholinguistic Research 1954–1964.* Bloomington, Ind.: Indiana University Press.

Osgood, C. E., G. J. Suci, and P. H. Tannenbaum
   1957   *The Measurement of Meaning.* Urbana, Ill.: University of Illinois Press.

Osgood, C. E., and Evelyn Walker
   1959   "Motivation and Language Behavior: A Content Analysis of Suicide Notes." *Journal of Abnormal and Social Psychology,* Vol. 59, 58–67.

Overhage, C. F. J., and R. Harman
   1965   *INTREX: Report of a Planning Conference on Information Transfer Experiments.* Cambridge, Mass.: The M.I.T. Press.

Page, E.
   1965   "Measurement Frontiers Symposium, Essay Grading by Computer." American Psychological Association, Chicago, Illinois, September 7, 1965.

Parsons, Talcott, and Edward Shils (eds.)
   1951   *Toward a General Theory of Action.* Cambridge, Mass.: Harvard University Press.

Piaget, Jean
   1926   *Language and Thought of the Child.* New York: Harcourt Brace & World.

Pittenger, R. E., C. F. Hockett, and J. J. Danehy
   1960   *The First Five Minutes: A Sample of Microscopic Interviews Analysis.* Ithaca, N.Y.: Paul Martineau.

Pool, Ithiel de Sola
   1959   "Trends in Content Analysis, A Summary." In Ithiel de Sola Pool (ed.), *Trends in Content Analysis.* Urbana, Ill.: University of Illinois Press.

Pool, Ithiel de Sola, Robert P. Abelson, and Samuel L. Popkin
   1964   *Candidates, Issues, and Strategies.* Cambridge, Mass.: The M.I.T. Press.

Pool, Ithiel de Sola, Harold D. Lasswell, and Daniel Lerner
   1951   *Symbols of Internationalism.* Hoover Institute Studies. Series C, Symbols: No. 3. Stanford, Calif.: Stanford University Press.
   1952a   *The Prestige Papers: A Survey of their Editorials.* Hoover Institute Studies. Series C, Symbols: No. 2. Stanford, Calif.: Stanford University Press.

1952*b*   *Symbols of Democracy.* Hoover Institute Studies. Series C, Symbols: No. 4. Stanford, Calif.: Stanford University Press.

"Proceedings of the IBM Literary Data Processing Conference," (Bessinger, Parrish, Arader).
1964   Yorktown Heights, New York: IBM Corporation.

Propp, Vladimir I.
1958   *Morphology of the Folktale.* Laurence Scott (trans.), Bloomington, Ind.: Indiana University Research Center in Anthropology, Folklore, and Linguistics, Publication 10.

Psathas, George
1965   Paper read at Mid-West Sociological Meeting, Chicago.

Révész, Géza (ed.)
1954   *Thinking and Speaking: A Symposium.* Amsterdam: North Holland Company.

Richards, I. A.
1929   *Practical Criticism: A Study of Literary Judgment.* New York: Harcourt, Brace & World. Harvest Books.

Robinson, J.
1965   *Parse: A System for Automatic Syntactic Analysis of English Text.* RM-4654-RR, Santa Monica, Calif.: *RAND* Corporation.

Ruesch, Jurgen, and Weldon Kees
1956   *Non-Verbal Communication: Notes on the Visual Perception of Human Relations.* Berkeley, Calif.: University of California Press.

Rulon, P., and W. Brooks
1961   *On Statistical Tests of Group Differences.* Cambridge, Mass.: Educational Research Corporation.

Salton, George
1965   "Information Storage and Retrieval." Scientific Report No. 1SR-9. Cambridge, Mass.: Computation Laboratory of Harvard University.

Saporta, Sol, and Thomas A. Sebeok
1959   "Linguistics and Content Analysis." In Ithiel de Sola Pool (ed.), *Trends in Content Analysis.* Urbana, Ill.: University of Illinois Press.

Scheffe, H.
1959   *The Analysis of Variance.* New York: John Wiley & Sons.

Schreber, Daniel Paul
1903   Denkwürdigkeiten eines Nervenkranken. Leipzig: Oswald Mutze. Translated by Ida Macalpine and R. A. Hunter, *Memoirs of My Nervous Illness.* Cambridge, Mass.: Robert Bentley, 1955.

Sears, R., E. E. Maccoby, and H. Levin
1957   *Patterns of Child Rearing.* Evanston, Ill.: Row, Peterson

Sebeok, Thomas A.
1953   "The Structure and Content of Cheremis Charms." *Anthropos: International Review of Ethnology and Linguistics.* Vol. 48, 369–388. Summarized in *Style and Language.* Cambridge, Mass.: The M.I.T. Press. 1966.

Sebeok, Thomas A., and Valdis J. Zeps
1958   "An Analysis of Structured Content, with Application of Electronic Computer Research in Psycholinguistics." *Language and Speech,* Vol. 1, 181–193.

Sebeok, Thomas A., Alfred S. Hayes, and Mary C. Bateson (eds.)
    1964   *Approaches to Semiotics.* The Hague: Mouton.
Shapiro, G.
    1965   "Public Opinion in the Revolutionary Process: A Quantitative Study of the *Cahiers de Doléances* of 1789." Paper delivered at the 1965 Conference, American Association for Public Opinion Research. May 15.
Shneidman, E. S.
    1961   "Psycho-Logic: A Personality Approach to Patterns of Thinking." In J. Kagan and G. Lesser (eds.), *Contemporary Issues in Thematic Apperception Methods.* Springfield, Ill.: Thomas.
Siegal, Sidney
    1956   *Nonparametric Statistics for the Behavioral Sciences.* New York: McGraw-Hill.
Simmons, R.
    1965   "Answering English Questions by Computer. A Survey." *Communication of the Association for Computing Machinery,* Vol. 8, 53–70.
Smith, M. B., J. S. Bruner, and R. W. White
    1956   *Opinions and Personality.* New York: John Wiley & Sons.
Speed, J. G.
    1893   "Do Newspapers Now Give the News?" *The Forum,* Vol. 15, 705–711.
Starkweather, J., and J. Decker
    1964   "Computer Analysis of Interview Content." *Psychological Reports,* Vol. 15, 875–882.
Stevens, S.
    1951   "Mathematics, Measurements and Psychophysics." In S. Stevens (ed.), *Handbook of Experimental Psychology.* New York: John Wiley & Sons.
Stoltz, W., P. Tannenbaum, and F. Carstensen
    1964   "A Stochastic Approach to the Grammatical Coding of English." Unpublished paper, Center for Cognitive Studies, Harvard University.
Stone, Philip J.
    1963   Dittoed paper. Laboratory of Social Relations, Harvard University.
Stone, Philip J., Robert Bales, V. Zvi Namenwirth, and Daniel Ogilvie
    1962   "The General Inquirer: A Computer System for Content Analysis and Retrieval Based on the Sentence as a Unit of Information." *Behavioral Science,* Vol. 7, No. 4, 484–498.
Tannenbaum, P., and M. Lynch
    1960   "Sensationalism: The Concept and its Measurement." *Journalism Quarterly,* Vol. 37, 381–392.
Tasman, P.
    1957   "Literary Data Processing." *IBM Journal of Research and Development,* Vol. 1, No. 3, 249–250.
"Technical Recommendations for Psychological Tests and Diagnostic Techniques."
    1954   *Psychological Bulletin* (Supplement), Vol. 51, No. 2, Part 2.
Tenney, Alvin A.
    1912   "The Scientific Analysis of the Press." *Independent,* Vol. 73, 895–898.

Thorndike, E. L., and Irving Lorge
   1944   *The Teacher's Word Book of 30,000 Words.* New York: Bureau of Publications, Teachers College, Columbia University.

Tukey, J.
   1962   "The Future of Data Analysis." *Annals of Mathematical Statistics.* Vol. 33.

Tucker, L.
   1963   "Implications of Factor Analysis of Three-Way Matrices for the Measurement of Change." In C. Harris (ed.), *Problems in Measuring Change.* Madison, Wis.: University of Wisconsin Press.

Vygotsky, Lev S.
   1962   *Thought and Language.* Eugenia Hanfmann and Gertrude Vakar (trans.), Cambridge, Mass.: The M.I.T. Press.

White, Ralph K.
   1947   *"Black Boy:* A Value Analysis." *Journal of Abnormal and Social Psychology,* Vol. 42, 440–461.

Willey, Malcolm K.
   1926   *The Country Newspaper.* Chapel Hill, N.C.: University of North Carolina Press.

Wilson, K. V.
   1956   "A Distribution-Free Test of Analysis of Variance Hypotheses." *Psychological Bulletin,* Vol. 53, No. 1, 96–101.

Winer, B. J.
   1962   *Statistical Principles in Experimental Design.* New York: McGraw-Hill.

Wolf, A. K., C. Chomsky, and B. Green, Jr.
   1963   "The Baseball Program: An Automatic Question-Answerer." Cambridge, Mass.: Lincoln Laboratory, Technical Report 306. April 1963.

Wolfenstein, Martha, and Nathan Leites
   1950   *Movies: A Psychological Study.* Glencoe, Ill.: The Free Press.

Yngve, V. H. (ed.)
   1963   *COMIT Programmers' Reference Manual.* Cambridge, Mass.: The M.I.T. Press.
   1962   *Introduction to COMIT Programming.* Cambridge, Mass.: The M.I.T. Press.

Zinnes, Dina A., R. C. North, and H. E. Koch, Jr.
   1961   "Capability, Threat and the Outbreak of War." In J. N. Rosenau (ed.), *International Politics and Foreign Policy.* New York: The Free Press of Glencoe.

Zwicky, A., J. Friedman, B. Hall, and O. Walker
   in press   "The MITRE Syntactic Analysis Procedure for Transformational Grammars." The MITRE Corporation. Abridged in the Proceedings of the Fall Joint Computer Conference of 1965.

PART II

STUDIES

Preface to Part II[1]

The system of content analysis described in this book grew out of a need to analyze verbal interaction in small groups. For several years, socioemotional and task interaction between group members had been scored and summarized with Bales's Interaction Process Analysis (IPA). Although all of the 12 IPA categories rely to some degree on the content of spoken or written materials (for example, Gives Suggestion, Asks for Opinion), the nature of the suggestion or the theme of the question is essentially ignored. If it were possible to measure group interaction in terms of what was being said, this system could be used in conjunction with IPA, and more adequate descriptions of group interaction could be made. This was an ambitious undertaking. So ambitious that, as yet, no one has completed this sort of joint analysis.

This is not to say that the area of small groups has been totally ignored. In fact, the largest and most detailed report in Part II (Dunphy, Chapter 8) deals directly with small-group materials. Instead of using verbal behavior as it occurred in the groups' setting, Dunphy relied for his analysis on reports written by group members. Despite this deviation from our original goals in kind of materials used, Dunphy was able to study some central issues (phase movements and role differentiation) that we had hoped could be investigated when the General Inquirer was first conceived.

Another study, Chapter 13, is related to our original goals insofar as IPA scores for one member of a group were compared with the

[1] The main editor and author of editorial notes for Part II is Daniel M. Ogilvie.

scores of the group as a whole and, in turn, scores that distinguished this member from the others were related to the content of his written reports. However, the bulk of this study lies outside the more traditional problems of small-group analysis and veers in the direction of a clinical study, with emphasis placed on the interpretation of tag scores.

The rest of the studies in Part II are representative of the kinds of work that have been or are in the process of being conducted. Together these studies reflect the manner in which the General Inquirer has been used, modified, and adjusted to assist in the investigation of problems outside of the realm of small-group research. Some of the studies were selected because they are clear examples of the General Inquirer method of analysis or because they help clarify particular issues mentioned in earlier chapters. Others illustrate how the dictionaries discussed in Chapter 5 have been put to use, and some demonstrate various stages of development of the General Inquirer and have been instrumental in advancing the method.

One criterion that applied to all articles selected was that they either add or show promise of adding to our knowledge of a particular area. As we have emphasized, we do not count words for the sake of counting words. In most of the studies reported here, important questions are being asked. What are some of the relationships between personality, culture, and themes expressed in folktales? (Kalin). Is it possible to identify characteristics of psychotic language pathology? (Maher). What are some of the features of Presidential Nomination Acceptance Speeches that distinguish between candidates and between political parties? (Smith). In other studies, Heider's balance theory is applied to international relations (Holsti); Allport's persistent request for methods that aid in the study of a single individual is partially answered (Paige); and an attempt is made to provide a method to analyze interaction in psychotherapeutic interviews (Psathas).

We have also strived for diversity, selecting topics over a wide range of social science areas. The coverage goes from a paper on self-perceived identity (McLaughlin) to an analysis of elite newspapers (Namenwirth), from a study of successful and unsuccessful volunteers for a program called Operations Crossroads Africa (Ramallo) to an analysis of Huck Finn (Ellis). The interests and background of the reader will dictate which articles attract his attention.

We have divided Part II into the following sections: Sociology,

Political Science, Personality, Clinical Psychology, Social Psychology, Cross-Cultural Studies, and Other Applications. Some articles were easier to classify under these headings than others, and some of the sections contain a more homogeneous array of studies than others. For example, the papers written by Smith, Holsti, and Namenwirth clearly belong under Political Science, whereas the articles appearing under Social Psychology are more heterogeneous, so much so that the heading may be somewhat misleading. However, this state of affairs is not terribly distressing to us since the headings are merely intended to be rough guides to content areas.

As a further guide to the reader, we have provided an introduction to each section that briefly summarizes the section's contents and highlights some of the distinctive features of the papers included in it. In addition, a few of the papers have been edited and summarized, and notes to that effect are included in an introduction to these studies. Such editing is one of the unfortunate but inescapable tasks in arranging a section of readings. When editing was necessary, we went through the articles with a reluctant pen, crossing out passages that were often interesting in themselves but represented excess baggage as far as our immediate needs were concerned. For example, if we selected a paper because it contained a good discussion of the application of a particular dictionary in a certain content area, we tended to focus on that point and summarize other details not directly related to it. Undoubtedly, some of our editorial decisions will return to haunt us.

With these points in mind, we turn to our sample of General Inquirer applications.

SMALL GROUPS

INTRODUCTION

Dunphy's article has already been introduced in the preface to Part II. We add here that many of the current statistical techniques and factor analytic strategies of data reduction were first tried on Dunphy's small-group materials. We feel that the results of this analysis, the scope of the study, and the theoretical and empirical implications of the research represent a fitting tribute to Robert F. Bales, who has continually encouraged this sort of integration of intuitive understanding and empirical demonstration.

CHAPTER EIGHT

Social Change in Self-Analytic Groups

Dexter C. Dunphy
Harvard University

INTRODUCTION

This chapter reports a study of change in small groups. The empirical investigation is concerned specifically with two sections of *Social Relations 120: Analysis of Interpersonal Behavior* (a Harvard undergraduate course) which met for an academic year. These groups are referred to as "self-analytic groups," since a major part of the group task is the study of behavior within the group itself.

The study arose out of an extensive review of previous theories and empirical research relating to process and change in small groups. Three general problems have been of continuing importance: to establish the existence and nature of generalized phase movements that are hypothesized to characterize the development of groups of many different kinds; to identify and describe characteristic role types that emerge in groups; and finally to determine the relationship of these role types to phase movements and the major functions they perform in the personality systems of group members and in the emerging social system of the group.

The following conclusions may be drawn from studies of process and change in small groups:

a. *Phase process over sessions:* The generalization of results of empirical studies of experimental groups is hindered by the fact that the groups studied operated for very limited time periods, lacked strong ego involvement, presented little opportunity for extensive and stable forms of structural differentiation or for a strong group culture. There is some evidence (mostly intuitive observational reporting) from long-term, self-analytic groups with high ego involvement. Two empirical studies of Mills (1964) and of Mann (1966) are particularly noteworthy, and there are some suggestive similarities between the results of these studies.

b. *Role differentiation over sessions:* A task-socioemotional dichotomy is suggested by the work of Bales (1953) and others, but short-term groups provide little indication of the direction of further differentiation. Again self-analytic groups provide some suggestive ideas in this regard (Arsenian *et al.,* 1962; Bennis and Shepard, 1956; Bion, 1959) but leave open the question of the relationship of role differentiation to phase movements.

It seems fairly obvious that further empirical studies of long-term, self-analytic groups should provide real insight into the question of whether or not there are predictable phase movements and patterns of role differentiation and of the conditions that induce and modify these patterns. The research discussed here is an empirical study of developmental processes in two such groups and focuses on the two issues of phase sequence and role differentiation.

The study also assumes a particular theory of the relationship between personality and the emerging structure and culture of groups undergoing change. The integrative core of the personality is found to consist of images of persons and groups which, in the course of the individual's socialization, have been significant in satisfying and frustrating drives. Group integration is a possibility because individuals in group situations are able to relate these images to new social objects through projective identification. Within groups of all kinds, role specialists emerge who facilitate projective identification by playing roles representing important elements in the internal phantasies of group members. Through the actions of these role specialists, the internal phantasies of group members are externalized and dramatized; and their acting out in the group results in the development of a generalized group phantasy or "mythology." Thus nonrational role specialists play a central part in the integration of the phantasies of individual members.

Because the mythology incorporates generalized images from the individual phantasies of members, it acts as an overarching symbol system, coordinating the drives of individual members to common purposes and unifying group action. In self-analytic groups, the central aspect of a mythology is an idealized representation of the authority figure (therapist, trainer, or instructor). However, the projected images of authority are thought to undergo a series of changes in response to the changing emotional states of group members. These changes are reflected in the distinctive phase movements through which the groups pass, the relative significance of the various nonrational roles in these phases, and the character of the central myth on which the group operates.

The primary focus of this investigation is change in the content of weekly reports, written by individual members of the two self-analytic groups. The reports describe and comment upon group interaction. Using the group members' written reports rather than their verbal interaction reduced the amount of verbal data to be processed, ensured contributions from all members, and focused the study on those aspects of the group interaction that members themselves regarded as important. The instructors for the two groups were respectively the author and Professor R. F. Bales, Director of the Harvard Laboratory of Social Relations. The specific hypotheses tested were as follows:

I. *Hypotheses relating to phase movements*
  1. That the content of the written reports from the two self-analytic groups will show similar quantitative and qualitative changes over time, that is, common phase movements.
  2. That these phase movements will explain more variance in the data than will differences between the two groups.
  3. That the characteristics of consecutive phase movements will reflect an emerging group unity and an increasing emotional involvement on the part of group members.
II. *Hypotheses relating to role differentiation and group mythology*
  4. That analysis of the *role images* of the most psychologically salient members will reflect a process of role differentiation in the group, that is, a movement from functionally diffuse to functionally specialized roles with a consistent rather than random order in the division of major functions.

5. That the process of role differentiation bears a clear relationship to the identifiable common phase movement, with the role specialists functioning as important symbols of alternative responses to the focal conflicts of each major stage of development.
6. That both the common phase movement and the accompanying process of role differentiation are paralleled by identifiable changes in a group mythology centering about idealized images of the formal authority figure (the instructor) and the group.

Basic Research Design

The weekly reports submitted to the group instructors by the two *Social Relations 120* groups were processed in sets of four consecutive notes; that is, the reports submitted by each member over a four-week period were combined into a single document referred to as a basic data unit. Each four-week period was referred to as a *phase,* so that the basic unit of data is this combined report by an individual on a four-week phase period. There were six phase periods for the entire year, each four weeks long, except the last, which was three weeks. This gave a basic design as shown in Table 8.1.

TABLE 8.1. Basic Research Design

Phases		Semester 1			Semester 2		
		1	*2*	*3*	*4*	*5*	*6**
Bales group	A	23	21	21	19	17	17
	B	22	19	16	17	15	12
	C	78	68	48	49	42	30
Dunphy group	A	26	26	25	24	24	24
	B	26	26	22	19	17	13
	C	88	80	64	70	49	28

A. Number of people in section.
B. Number of people writing at least one note.
C. Number of notes received.
Note: The figures in Row B represent the number of basic data units.
* Three weeks only.

Each cell in this matrix then contained the basic units of data from each group member, and the number of these is shown in Table 8.1. After processing, these text units were replaced with the person's score on each of the 83 variables (tags) in the Harvard III Dictionary. Statistical tests were then applied to assess the significance of the major changes in content revealed by these scores and to estimate the implications of these results for theories of group development.

PHASES IN GROUP DEVELOPMENT

In order to test for the existence, extent, and nature of common phase movements (Hypotheses 1 through 3), use was made of the entire text of the written reports produced by the members of the two groups (approximately 300,000 words). Three major statistical techniques were used to identify changes in content: analyses of variance, means trend tests, and a factor analysis.

We will take up each of these methods in turn, explaining their relevance to the theories being tested and the implications of the findings.

Group Trends: The Analysis of Variance

An analysis of variance was performed for each of the 83 tags, using a 6×2 matrix (6 phases, 2 groups). Through this method it was possible to estimate the relative contribution to the total variance made by factors peculiar to

1. particular phases ("phases")
2. one group or the other ("group")
3. the interaction of these two effects ("interaction")

In terms of the analysis-of-variance design employed here, trends common to both groups are represented by tags for which *phases* make a significant contribution to the total variance, while particular group characteristics are represented by tags for which *group* makes a significant contribution. On the other hand, a significant contribution by *interaction* indicates a complex effect through a combination of the *phases* and *group* effects. Tags for which none of these effects is significant are ignored. For such tags, individual (error) variance is so great that the effects that are our primary concern here do not make a significant contribution to the total variance. Therefore, these tags presumably are being influenced by factors largely external to the evolving group culture, either individual traits of group members or factors in a more inclusive culture.

However, 51 of the 83 tags (or 78 [1] of 249 tests of significance,

[1] Twelve tests would be expected to be significant by chance at the .05 level.

three tests on each tag) do yield significant results for one or more
of the effects. Table 8.2 presents a grouping of the 51 tags according

TABLE 8.2. Results of Analyses of Variance
(Significance levels of the f-tests)

Only Phases Significant		*Only Group Differences Significant*	
NEUTER-ROLE	.01	JOB-ROLE	.01
SPACE-REFERENCE	.01	GUIDE	.01
QUANTITY-REFERENCE	.01	PEER-STATUS	.01
ACTION-NORM	.01	OTHER	.05
THOUGHT-FORM	.01	IDEAL-VALUE	.05
AROUSAL	.01	FAMILY	.05
GET	.01	SIGN-ACCEPT	.05
COMMUNITY	.01	FEMALE-THEME	.05
OVERSTATE	.01		
UNDERSTATE	.01		
SELF	.05		
SMALL-GROUP	.05	*Only Interaction Significant*	
LARGE-GROUP	.05	DISTRESS	.01
OUGH	.05	POSSESS	.01
APPROACH	.05	AUTHORITY-THEME	.01
ATTACK	.05	SIGN-REJECT	.05
POLITICAL	.05		

Both Phase and Group Difference Significant

	Phase	Group
EQUAL	.01	.01
ACADEMIC	.01	.01
DANGER-THEME	.01	.01
DEATH-THEME	.01	.05
TIME-REFERENCE	.05	.05
LEGAL	.05	.05

Both Group and Interaction Significant

	Group	Inter-action
DEVIATION	.01	.05
HIGHER-STATUS	.01	.05
URGE	.05	.05

Both Phase and Interaction Significant

	Phase	Inter-action
MALE-ROLE	.01	.01
AVOID	.01	.01
SIGN-WEAK	.01	.01
SOCIAL-PLACE	.01	.01
AFFECTION	.01	.01
RELIGIOUS	.01	.05
FEMALE-ROLE	.05	.01

All Three Significant

	Phase	Group	Inter-action
SEX-THEME	.01	.01	.01
MESSAGE-FORM	.01	.01	.05
NATURAL-WORLD	.01	.05	.01
SENSORY-REFERENCE	.05	.01	.05
ASCEND-THEME	.01	.05	.05
NATURAL-OBJECT	.05	.05	.05

to the source of the contribution. If the tags are assumed to be equivalent variables, the *phase* effect accounts for a significant amount of
variance for the largest number of these tags (36), whereas *group* and
interaction effects account for significant variance on only 22 and 20

TABLE 8.3. Tags for Which "Phases" Make a Significant Contribution to Tag Variance (Ranked by phase averages: only 1st and 2nd ranks given)

"Supertag" Category	Phase					
	1	2	3	4	5	6
Persons	SELF NEUTER-ROLE	SELF MALE-ROLE*	NEUTER-ROLE MALE-ROLE*	FEMALE-ROLE*	FEMALE-ROLE*	
Groups	LARGE-GROUP				SMALL-GROUP	SMALL-GROUP
Physical objects				NATURAL-OBJECT*	NATURAL-OBJECT*	
Physical qualifiers	SPACE-REF. QUAN-REF.	SPACE-REF.	SENSORY-REF.*	TIME-REF. QUAN-REF.	SENSORY-REF.*	TIME-REF.
Environments	SOCIAL-PLACE*				NATURAL-WORLD*	SOCIAL-PLACE* NATURAL-WORLD*
Culture	ACTION-NORM	MESSAGE-FORM*	THOUGHT-FORM† MESSAGE-FORM*	THOUGHT-FORM	THOUGHT-FORM	ACTION-NORM
Emotions				AROUSAL	AROUSAL AFFECTION*	AFFECTION*
Thought						
Evaluation	OUGHT	OUGHT		EQUAL	EQUAL	EQUAL
Socioemotional actions		APPROACH ATTACK		ATTACK	AVOID*	APPROACH AVOID*
Impersonal actions					GET	GET
Institutional-contexts	POLITICAL-COMMUNITY	POLITICAL	ACADEMIC	RELIGIOUS* ACADEMIC LEGAL	LEGAL	COMMUNITY RELIGIOUS*
Status						
Psychological themes		SEX-THEME*	SEX-THEME*	OVERSTATE UNDERSTATE SIGN-WEAK*	UNDERSTATE SIGN-WEAK* ASCEND-THEME* DANGER-THEME DEATH-THEME	OVERSTATE ASCEND-THEME* DANGER-THEME DEATH-THEME

* Tags for which the interaction effect is also significant.
† THOUGHT-FORM appears three times because phases 3 and 5 tied for second place; phase 4 represents the peak for this tag.

tags, respectively.[2] The contribution of *phases* appears even more powerful if one considers the significance levels of these tests: 24 out of 36 tags (66 percent) to which *phases* makes a significant contribution are significant at the .01 level, whereas for *group* only 11 of 22 tags (50 percent), and for *interaction* only 11 of 20 tags (55 percent) are significant at the .01 level. This indicates that common time trends are affecting the use of more tags and affecting their use to a greater extent than are the other effects: that is, individual group differences are of less importance than are common phase trends in explaining variance in the use of tags. For some tags, however, unique group differences are the most important source of variance. There is convincing evidence for common group trends in the two groups, but the analysis also indicates that each group exhibits some unique characteristics.

Table 8.3 shows the two phases of the six in which each of the tags was most used. It therefore illustrates the changing thematic pattern — the content trends common to both groups — occurring throughout the year. Table 8.4 lists the tags for which the *group* effect made a significant contribution to the total variance and is therefore illustrative of the characteristic and persistent differences between the two groups. Similarly, Table 8.5 lists the tags for which *interaction* made a significant contribution to the total variance, showing the effect of group differences interacting with common phase patterns.

An attempt will now be made to show the relationship between the variance on the tags and the evolving pattern of group events and reactions to these events by group members. It should be realized that the General Inquirer provides a highly abstract synthesis of the content of the members' notes, pointing up the main changes in terms of a number of theoretical variables. Having distinguished the salient characteristics of the data and essayed an interpretation in theoretical terms, one must once more work from the abstract to the more specific to check the validity of the interpretation. In order to do this, detailed retrievals were made on these tags in order to identify the words that led to the changes and the contexts in which the words were used. Because this is a brief summary of the original work, these lengthy retrievals and the close analysis made of them will not be presented here.

---

[2] There is a problem in interpreting significant main effects when the interaction effect is also significant. In most cases, however, the retrievals point to the plausibility of the main effects being significant.

TABLE 8.4. Group Differences: Tags for Which "Group" Makes a Significant Contribution to Tag Variances

"Supertag" Category	Bales's Group Higher	Dunphy's Group Higher
Persons	JOB-ROLE	OTHER
Groups		
Physical objects	NATURAL-OBJECT	
Physical qualifiers	SENSORY-REFERENCE*	
Environments		NATURAL-WORLD
Culture	MESSAGE-FORM	IDEAL-VALUE, DEVIATION
Emotions		URGE
Thought		EQUAL*
Evaluation		
Actions	GUIDE	
Institutions	ACADEMIC, LEGAL	FAMILY
Status	HIGHER-STATUS	PEER-STATUS
Psychological themes	SIGN-ACCEPT	SEX-THEME
	FEMALE-THEME	ASCEND-THEME
	DANGER-THEME	
	DEATH-THEME*	

* The results of these tags were biased by the fact that two members of Bales's group and one member of Dunphy's group had names that corresponded with entry words; that is, Rocky (SENSORY-REFERENCE) Don/e (DEATH-THEME) and Sam/e (EQUAL). Because of this, these tags are not discussed in the text.

Only the conclusions are summarized to indicate what the changes revealed about the attitudes, emotional involvement, and learning of those undergoing the training experience.

TABLE 8.5. Interaction Effects: Tags for Which "Interaction" Made a Significant Contribution to the Total Variance

"Supertag" Category	Tags
Persons	MALE-ROLE, FEMALE-ROLE
Groups	
Physical objects	NATURAL-OBJECT
Physical qualifiers	SENSORY-REFERENCE
Environments	SOCIAL-PLACE, NATURAL-WORLD
Culture	DEVIATION, MESSAGE-FORM
Emotions	URGE, AFFECTION, DISTRESS
Thought	
Evaluation	
Actions	AVOID, POSSESS
Institutional contexts	RELIGIOUS
Status connotations	HIGHER-STATUS
Psychological themes	SIGN-REJECT, SIGN-WEAK, AUTHORITY-THEME, SEX-THEME, ASCEND-THEME

Phase Characteristics: Common Trends

Inspection of Table 8.3 reveals some major changes that describe a common pattern in the evolution of the two groups. Using the classification according to the general areas in the Harvard III Dictionary, we can follow changes in the dominant themes expressed in the weekly reports over the course of the year. Perusal of the table reveals a strong tendency for the two peaks for each tag to occur in adjacent phases, thus indicating a persisting concern with the area to which the tag refers. This tendency is significant at the .001 level. There is also another distinguishable pattern in the distribution of tags in Table 8.3. A small number of tags (SOCIAL-PLACE, ACTION-NORM, and COMMUNITY) are high in the first and last phases, indicating that some concerns are common to both the beginning and the ending of the course.

Persons. In the category of persons, the highest ranks in the first semester are for SELF, NEUTER-ROLE, and MALE-ROLE, while in the second semester, FEMALE-ROLE is high. The high counts on SELF at the earliest stages of the groups' development reflect an initial individualism that subsequently declines. The high counts for NEUTER-ROLE in Phases 1 and 3 arise from use of words such as member, role, person, individual, and leader, and they reflect an emotionally distant manner of discussing others. As far as MALE and FEMALE-ROLES are concerned, the high counts arise largely from pronoun references (he, she, and so on) linked with the names of group members. The relatively high count for MALE-ROLE in the latter part of the first semester, and the high count for FEMALE-ROLE in the early part of the second semester reflect the differential participation of males and females at these different times.

Thus as far as PERSONS are concerned, there is a change in emphasis between semesters. Concern with self, males, and other members regarded impersonally is relatively high in the first semester, while in the second semester females receive relatively more attention than earlier.

Groups. References to *groups* show an initial concern with LARGE-GROUP (Phase 1 [3]) and an ultimate concern with SMALL-GROUP. This reflects a changed concern with the group's own culture rather than the external culture and for the group as an entity rather than as a collection of individuals. The references to LARGE-GROUP occur in the context of attempts by group members to structure the situation in

[3] Ties for second rank account for this tag appearing once only.

terms of the usual set of external norms. The failure of the instructor to fulfill normative expectations makes this impossible, so that the group has to work through the problem of anomie to an indigenous set of norms.

Actions and emotions. It is appropriate at this point to move from a discussion of the main categories of nouns and pronouns used to the categories of verbs with which they were associated. The general area contains tags from the higher-order tag categories labeled *emotions, thought, evaluation, socioemotional actions,* and *impersonal actions.* In addition, SEX-THEME is included since, unlike other second-order tags, it consists mainly of direct references to sexuality. Thus the words in these categories relate to actions rather than to objects, persons, or situations.

The analysis of tags in this area reveals a marked change in group atmosphere from the first to the second semester, with the main transition taking place in Phase 4. Of particular interest in the first semester is the relative lack of reference to emotions. At this stage the members appear to be writing predominantly about overt behavior (APPROACH, ATTACK, SEX-THEME) rather than about inner feelings. The high counts on OUGHT are the only exception to this, and seem to indicate a reaction to the disintegration of established norms and an attempt to impose superego demands on the situation.

This early period in the development of both groups is characterized by an extensive concern with overt aggression and sexuality (AT-TACK, SEX-THEME). Attack shows particularly high counts, the words most frequently used being attack, against, criticize, and assert, although a large number of other words (threaten, trap, fight, oppose) also make contributions. The sentences tagged ATTACK convey a clear picture of the prevailing tone of antagonism and rivalry in the groups. SEX-THEME will be discussed in more detail later since it reveals interesting group differences as well as common trends. For both groups, however, direct references to sexuality are higher at this time than at others. Thus we have here some empirical evidence that two basic responses to a state of anomie are direct expressions of aggression and sexuality.

Retrievals on approach show that words tagged in this category can be divided into two clear subcategories: (1) *contribute* (initiate, propose, contribute) and (2) *physical approach* (come, contact, encounter). The tagged words divide fairly evenly between these two subdivisions. The high counts on the physical approach section of the category suggest that at this time the first serious attempts are being made to initiate closer personal relationships. It is interesting that sentences with words indicating contribution also show this same theme, for what is being contributed is largely personal information. The response to these early attempts at interpersonal intimacy and sharing is indicated by the high counts on ATTACK, and not until Phase 4 is the second peak for this tag reached.

There seems to be a successive change in the expression of libidinal drives throughout the year; the shift is reflected in the movement from SEX-THEME (Phases 2 and 3) to AROUSAL (Phases 4 and 5) to AFFECTION (Phases 5 and 6). Expressing this in more familiar terms, the change is from words directly expressive of sexuality, to words indicating a generalized emotional involvement in the group situation, and finally to words specifically referring to affection. AROUSAL (felt, feel, feeling, concern, interest, emotion, react, reaction) acts as an index of emergent emotional involvement. But as the end of the course becomes imminent, members pass from expressing increased emotional involvement to direct concern with the problem of affection and love between group members.

Just as the expression of libidinal drives changes over the course of the year, the expression of negativity changes also. The expression of negativity in the first semester takes the form of open and direct aggression toward other group members, but in the final two phases negativity takes the form of avoidance (AVOID). Concern over handling this problem is high at this time. Avoidance words relate both to physical avoidance (absence from the group) and psychological avoidance (ignore, deny). Members are concerned with the threat to group progress and unity posed by avoidance in the final phase of the year.

Tags in the more impersonal areas (*thought and impersonal-actions*) also reveal changes in attitude in the second semester. The tag EQUAL shows two general areas of concern. Most frequent is use of the words same or similar to denote generally the recurrence of phenomena that have previously been obscured in the group.

> "This is the *same* as earlier phantasies, *like,* say that of going behind the glass."

This is closely related to TIME-REFERENCE, which is also high at this time, and together these tags indicate the perception of growing areas of stability and recurring patterns of behavior in the course of the groups' evolution.

But EQUAL words are also used in metaphors where concrete imagery is employed to convey insight into group phenomena. For example,

"Cliff has been behaving *like* a raven, a ferocious phallic marauder."

This is another aspect of the phenomenon to be noted in the discussion of NATURAL-OBJECT and NATURAL-WORLD, that is, the development at this stage of a multiplicity of concrete images to describe aspects of the group process.

The high counts for GET for the last two phases indicate a concern with contributions to the group's task and with reaching a desirable level of achievement before the end of the course.

Culture. ACTION-NORM shows a high level of concern with means of control both at the beginning and at the end of the year. Retrievals reveal that initially the concern is with maintaining an external set of normative standards, while finally it is concerned with the new normative standards that have developed within the group itself.

The change in emphasis from MESSAGE-FORM (Phases 2 and 3) to THOUGHT-FORM (Phases 3, 4, and 5) indicates a shift from external and outward modes of communication (the assigned cases, statements, explanations, stories) to internal, cognitive concerns (problem, relationship, interpretation, fact). This parallels the rise in emotional involvement and indicates that involvement is accompanied by an increased attempt to work toward an intellectual understanding of group processes.

The changes within the cultural area can therefore be seen as proceeding from external to internal aspects of the culture. Attention moves from

1. A set of social norms deriving from the environment external to the group, to
2. concern with objective forms of communication within the group, to
3. concern with forming an internal intellectual understanding of these external processes and, finally, to
4. a concern with the indigenous normative system.

Physical world. In the category of *physical qualifiers,* a change is manifested from an early emphasis on SPATIAL-REFERENCE and QUANTITY-REFERENCE to SENSORY-REFERENCE and TIME-REFERENCE.

This reflects a general shift from a view of the group as a collection of external and discrete objects (SPATIAL-REFERENCE and QUANTITY-REFERENCE) to a more inward and sensitive view (SENSORY-REFERENCE) of the group as an evolving entity (TIME-REFERENCE).

The drop in percentage scores between the first and second semesters for SPATIAL-REFERENCE is dramatic. Considering the high frequency of the commonplace words in this category, such a change was unexpected and demanded explanation. Consideration of the retrievals suggests that in a number of related ways members are attempting in the first semester to stand apart from the group, to remain emotionally uninvolved, and to determine analytically the structure of the rather confusing situation with which they are faced. Since the other group members, the group itself, and other major elements in the situation (ideas, topics) are regarded as external to the self, they are discussed as external objects interacting in physical space. This is literally true at the physical level where students are *looked upon* from *behind* mirrors, sit *in* the *corners* of the room, and so on.

However, the interaction in the group is also treated metaphorically as space, in a way similar to the use of the term psychological field in psychology. Here the field seems to be composed of the focus of attention for the group members so that a member stays "in" the field of action, moves "out" of the spotlight, is pushed "out" of the group. Interaction between actors is also described in a way that gives spatial concreteness to psychological relationships: for example, well-aimed darts are directed "at" persecutors and incidents awaken dormant conflicts "between" members. This leads to the creation of a cognitive map of the emerging social structure, again expressed in physical terms. There are, for instance, gradually coalescing subgroups "within" the class, hierarchies are set "up," leaders fortify their "positions" or are pushed "into" them, members feel they are "under" authority.

Finally, it is not only the social structure of the situation that is treated as analogous to physical reality but also the emerging culture of the group. The individual appears to use the same method to orient himself to the realm of expressed opinions and ideas where he cannot put his finger "on" an issue, perceives conflicts where "opposing" lines and issues are unclear, sees the discussion spread "out" to other topics, puts a discussion off "at" a distance and views it more objectively.

Thus, while the individual remains emotionally distant from other members and their ideas, they are discussed as objects in a space external to the self. When ego boundaries become relatively fluid, there is a significant drop in the use of spatial terms.

In Phase 5 the word "silence" accounts for 60 percent of the words tagged SENSORY-REFERENCE in Bales's group and 38 percent in Dunphy's group. It was in this period, for both groups, that protracted silences occurred during sessions. Protracted silence represents an immobilization of the group resulting from ambivalence about the loosening of personality defenses as the process of internalization begins to take place.

TIME-REFERENCE reaches two peaks in the first and last phases of the second semester, is generally higher throughout the second semester than the first (except for Phase 1), and shows a dramatic rise in the final phase. This indicates a growing awareness of the group as an evolving entity with a definite beginning and end.

Retrievals on NATURAL-OBJECT and NATURAL-WORLD show a number of references to animals, other inanimate objects, and aspects of the natural world. The choice of concrete symbolism seems to emphasize an open system: the objects on the whole lack definite boundaries (sea, world, waves, universe, land, ocean, river). Thus, over-all references on these two tags indicate a richer use of symbols and images at this stage of development, the nature of these symbols being energy and life. But they also reveal a sense of lack of control over these forces in that they refer to relatively unconfined objects. It will be recollected also that high counts on the word "like" under the tag EQUAL reflected an increasing use of simile at this time. Of course, some of these images are used once or twice and fail to recur, while others are taken up and elaborated into a system of meaningful symbols.

Institutional contexts. Within the area of institutional contexts, the emphasis changes from POLITICAL to ACADEMIC to LEGAL and RELIGIOUS. In addition, COMMUNITY is high in the initial and final phases. These tags characterize very clearly the way in which the frame of reference through which the group is viewed changes over the course of the year.

In the early stage of the groups' development, action is described primarily in political terms, the emphasis being on power maneuvers and positions of power. This manipulative mode reveals a lack of positive emotional relationships between the group members and thus supports the other signs of impersonality noted for this period. A large number of references to political role types (leader, authority, president) suggests that members are at this point highly concerned with identifying authority figures in the group. High counts on ACADEMIC in the midyear phases emphasize a shift from interest in interpersonal power play to the academic content of the course. As MESSAGE-FORM and THOUGHT-FORM are also high at this time, Phases 3 and 4 appear to represent a more work-oriented and intellectual stage in the groups' development. At this time, there seems to be the greatest interest in reading, discussing, and analyzing the cases and relating them to problems in the group.

The shift to a higher proportion of LEGAL references in Phases 4 and 5 immediately precedes the high counts for ACTION-NORM in Phase 6. Retrievals also show that within the category itself there is an increasing emphasis on obligatory norms and a marked drop in references to negative sanctions over the year. It seems that this tag also reveals the progressive development of an internalized set of normative standards.

The increased references to religion (RELIGIOUS) in the second semester are undoubtedly stimulated by readings on religion assigned for this period. However, one cannot help being struck both by the readiness with which members applied these readings to the group process and by the religious references that do not stem directly from the readings. The groups seem to be involved in creating an elementary form of mythology in which the actions of the instructors and others who play distinctive roles are given a religious dimension, and actions of symbolic significance for the group are seen as religious rituals. As emotional involvement in the group increases and as the end of the course approaches, a search develops for religious symbols to convey a sense of the emotional significance of the group experience.

The recurrence of high counts on COMMUNITY (Phases 1 and 6) is associated with use of more impersonal social references and its reoccurrence at the conclusion of the course suggests the use of a "distancing mechanism" to handle the end of the group.

Psychological themes. We have found from the analysis of other kinds of data that high counts on UNDERSTATE and OVERSTATE indicate defensiveness, and excessive use of these words modifies otherwise simple, direct statements. Retrieval of sentences making use of these tags indicates in many cases an underlying note of repressed or suppressed hostility either toward the instructor or other group members. Since OVERSTATE and UNDERSTATE both reach a peak when there is maximum strain in the group culture, they appear to be indices of strain experienced by individual group members. The individual in these groups, in writing to the instructor, is in a difficult position in that the direct expression of hostility to the instructor is threatening, and the expression of hostility to group members seems incongruous with the ideal set up for the course: the understanding and appreciation of the motives and actions of oneself and others. The high counts on these categories at this time suggest that, at this point, hostility is felt most strongly, but that there are conflicting impulses to express hostility while at the same time disguising its expression.

In the latter part of the group's development, anxiety and depression (SIGN-WEAK) are increasingly expressed. The expression of this general feeling at this time finds other concrete manifestations in the high rate of absenteeism and long periods of silence in group sessions.

Increased counts on SIGN-ASCEND appear to indicate an endeavor to escape the patterns of behavior that characterized earlier phases of the group's activity. These group patterns are seen to inhibit free and honest communication of emotional reactions. The wish is expressed to rise above defensiveness and anxiety and to enter a new phase of understanding based upon respect for, and appreciation of, the positive contributions others can make.

High counts on DANGER-THEME and DEATH-THEME toward the end of the year suggest emotional threat and mourning. At this point, an internal emotional involvement corresponds sharply with the mood of notes written earlier in the year.

Summary of Trend Analysis

We are now in a position to summarize in more general terms the major shifts in theme in the analyses from both groups. The analyses of variance have shown that in his initial view of the group, the individual member differentiates himself (self), the instructor, and other individuals who are able to gain the attention of the group (leaders), and an undifferentiated collection of others (people). At this time, little coordination of group activity is perceived, and members appear to be striving at cross-purposes. The group is viewed primarily in terms of categories of structure and power, and, after a short period of trying to maintain a traditional normative pattern, action takes on a strongly manipulative character. Behavior is seen as increasingly directed toward the satisfaction of aggressive and sexual drives, with men particularly active and women largely withdrawn. The viewpoint taken by members in the analyses is that of the detached observer. Descriptions deal primarily with external objects and concrete behavior. Early attempts to achieve interpersonal closeness are strongly resisted; emotional involvement in the group is avoided; and, with the aid of the superego, ego boundaries are maintained with increasing rigidity. It is as if the disintegration of the external normative system is reacted to as a threat to the internalized normative system so that a barrier is thrown up around the ego for its protection and stability.

In the first part of the second semester (Phase 4) a major change in this pattern becomes evident. Rigid ego boundaries are undermined as involvement in the group increases markedly. As some sense of individual identity is lost in the "oceanic" experience of merging with the group, there is a consequent feeling of personal weakness and of threat. There seems to be an increased sensitivity to the qualities of external objects complemented by a new concern with internal objects, emotions, and cognitive processes. Depression and anxiety increase markedly. Libidinal drives are sublimated in the interest of stronger affective ties within the group, and increased efforts are devoted to the realization of group goals. The primary concerns in interpersonal relationships are with personal involvement with others and affection. Women play a relatively more active role at this time, a role with considerable significance in working through problems of acceptance and the expression of affection. Toward the end of the course, a view develops of the group as an evolving communal entity with coordinated emotional states and persistent patterns of behavior. In referring to the group, members attribute human qualities to it as if by "giving themselves" to the group it had acquired some of their own human qualities. Thus in some way, the loss of individual identity contributes to a sense of group identity, and the common extension of personality boundaries leads to greater coordination of the emotions and actions of the individual members of the group. An elementary set of symbols, derived from readings and from phantasy, develops toward the end of the year, and these symbols are employed to give a deeper level of meaning to the group experience. This process is accompanied by the development of an indigenous set of group norms. The interiorization of the group is responded to, however, by a deeper set of defenses. The earlier defense of noninvolvement, which found its active expression in aggression, gives way to the deeper defenses of resistance and denial, actively expressed in avoidance. Considerable concern about the reactions is exhibited in the group reports, for they are seen as detracting from an idealized form of group life toward which many group members are now consciously striving. As the group ends, concern is expressed for the loss of the group and for its relative state of unity and achievement.

Group Differences

Those tags for which the group effect was significant are shown in Table 8.4. As one group or the other scored consistently higher on these tags, the two lists in Table 8.4 represent the distinctively different qualities of the reports from the two groups.

The Bales group is consistently higher on tags indicating a more structured social situation (JOB-ROLE, MESSAGE-FORM, GUIDE, ACADEMIC, LEGAL, HIGHER-STATUS), while the Dunphy group is higher on tags indicating the lack of an ordered social structure (NATURAL-WORLD, IDEAL-VALUE, DEVIATION, URGE, PEER-STATUS, SEX-THEME, ASCEND-THEME). Similarly, the Bales group shows more awareness of the vertical dimension (HIGHER-STATUS), while the Dunphy group shows more awareness of the horizontal status dimension (PEER-STATUS). These differences seem to stem primarily from the age and status differences of the instructors. Professor Bales has an established reputation as a behavioral scientist and is Director of the Laboratory of Social Relations, a professor in the Department of Social Relations, with responsibility for the *Social Relations 120* course as a whole. The author, on the other hand, was at the time a graduate student, 28 years old, with no former experience in teaching the course. This difference was reinforced in the minds of members by the way in which the two groups were formed. Because there were too many students, Professor Bales divided the course into a second section at the beginning of the second week by choosing each alternate person in the room.

This initial experience had a marked effect on the two groups. In both groups, those who were chosen to go with Bales were referred to as "the chosen people," the frequencies for SELVES show clearly the initially high "we feeling" created in the Bales group by this event and the relatively low "we feeling" created in the Dunphy group by the same event. The result was a sense of relative security in the Bales group and reinforcement of the significance of the presence of an experienced, high-status authority figure. The sense of stability in the Bales group is reflected in the number of tags that refer to structure and authority. In the Dunphy group, however, the separation brought a feeling of abandonment with an unknown "peer" as a replacement of Bales. Hence, the feeling of anomie heightened.

Related to these group differences are the higher counts for the Bales group on ACADEMIC, LEGAL, MESSAGE-FORM, and GUIDE. Members of Bales's group used more academic and legal (formal) language in their reports. That the greater formality in language might accurately be attributed to a sense of Bales's greater authority is suggested also by higher counts for his group on GUIDE and MESSAGE-FORM. Retrieval of sentences referring to the "instructor guiding" or "members guiding" shows that not only is Bales's group generally higher on references to guidance but that members are also more concerned with the instructor guiding and less concerned with members guiding. This is particularly characteristic of Phase 2: in Dunphy's group only 9 percent of sentences tagged GUIDE refer to the instructor guiding, while in Bales's group 16 percent refer to the instructor guiding. Interestingly enough, both groups show a marked decline over time in instructor GUIDE sentences, presumably reflecting a general decline in dependency on the instructor. Nevertheless Bales's group is consistently higher in instructor GUIDE sentences than the other group throughout the year.

Bales's group also shows both quantitative and qualitative differences on MESSAGE-FORM. In particular, the words question and opinion, implying hesitancy, are very high in comparison with Dunphy's group. On the other hand, Dunphy's group, though generally lower on most words, is higher on story, statement, and suggestion, implying more certainty in contributing to the group.

While the members of Bales's group show more overt awareness of the superior status of the instructor and more formality and deference in the style of writing they adopt to communicate with him, they show more sympathy when discussing one another. Retrieval on SIGN-ACCEPT shows higher counts on the following words, for instance, for Bales's group: support, affection, commitment, kindly, trust, offer, sympathy, cooperation. In Dunphy's group, less acceptance of others is shown by higher counts on OTHER. Members of Dunphy's group tend to identify less with each other, perceive each other to be more external to the self than do members of the Bales group. However, as SIGN-REJECT is not characteristic of Dunphy's group, it seems that this is more a case of a lack of mutual identification than of a rejection of others. As the counts for SELVES show, it was not until the final phase of the year that a level of mutual identification, similar to that in Bales's group, was achieved.

These basic differences between the groups have other, less immediately obvious, concomitants. Bales's group, for instance, shows more underlying anxiety than does Dunphy's group. Upon closer examination of retrievals, the tags DANGER-THEME, FEMALE-THEME, and NATURAL-OBJECT reveal the anxiety as having two major causes: Bales was a more appropriate source of superego anxiety than Dunphy, and this anxiety was reinforced by the presence of unseen observers, behind a one-way screen, under whose gaze Bales's group met. Words tagged DANGER-THEME and used with greater frequency in Bales's group included crisis, silence, trouble, destruction, dangerous, murder, destroy. The impression created by these words is enhanced by NATURAL-OBJECT references to such phrases as the beast, playing cat and mouse, throwing sticks and stones, clutching at straws, retreating into one's shell.

FEMALE-THEME references were higher mainly because of higher use of the word *into,* frequently used in conjunction with phases referring to being drawn *into* self-disclosure, being assimilated *into* the group, being seduced *into* making personal revelations. Thus, Bales's group is seen as threateningly seductive in that members feel increasing pressure to abandon impersonality for personal revelations in a situation where they are exposed to the judgment of a superego figure backed by unseen observers.

If the Bales group shows more anxiety, the Dunphy group shows more striving (URGE, SEX-THEME, ASCEND-THEME), which is apparently connected with handling the problem of openness (NATURAL-WORLD, IDEAL-VALUE, DEVIATION). On URGE, the Dunphy group uses such words as need, want, and hope more frequently, and these are probably related psychologically to the higher references to life and water words (wave, ocean, sea, river) tagged NATURAL-WORLD. Within the IDEAL-VALUE category, words concerned with friendship and group solidarity receive more attention; and, since there is more attention also to deviation, this undoubtedly reflects an attempt to

handle the problem of anomie. The larger use of sexual words probably reflects this as well as the less-inhibited style of writing by members of Dunphy's group.

Thus most of the consistent differences between the two groups can
be related in fairly obvious ways to the initial method of forming the
groups, the different status characteristics of the instructors, and to
a lesser extent, to the different settings in which the groups met.

Interaction Effects

Table 8.4 shows those tags for which "interaction" makes a significant contribution to the total variance. The analysis of variance
indicates that a significant amount of variance is not attributable to
individual, group, or phase properties alone. This portion of the variance must be attributed instead to the interaction of the particular
characteristics of the group with the common characteristics of a particular phase. For any given phase, therefore, the groups are significantly different, but it is not possible to predict from a knowledge of
the group and/or phase what the group means for the next phase will
be.

No attempt will be made here to identify the underlying causes for
interaction effects. They are usually complex, and a more detailed
analysis appears in Dunphy (1964).

Conclusion

On the basis of the analysis of variance, the phase effect was shown
to be most significant. The main trends showed a shift from an impersonal concern with authority structure and power maneuvers (first
semester) to a greater emotional involvement, an increased sense of
personal weakness, and a new view of the group as an evolving entity
with projected human qualities. The result of this change was a
clearer sense of group identity and more coordination of the actions
and emotions of the groups' individual members. Each group also
developed a distinctive set of images deriving from its unique history,
setting, and authority relationships.

Means Trend Tests

A second method employed to measure significant change over time
was a means trend test (Crow *et al.,* 1960, 63–64), which tests consistency of trend in either an upward or downward direction and also

alternating up and down fluctuations. Each group was considered separately, and for each tag the test was applied to the six successive phase means. The purpose of using this test was to identify consistent *directional* patterns of change in either or both groups. It was apparent from the results that

1. Relatively few tags showed consistently maintained directionality of change. This can be interpreted to mean that groups of this kind do not work more and more or less and less on a particular problem or topic but rather take it up, drop it, and then return to it again.
2. No tag appeared in lists for the two groups so that there were no linear trends common to both groups. It is clear that the strong similarities in pattern shown to exist for the two groups are not of this simple linear sort.
3. There was evidence of a good deal more consistent directionality of change in Dunphy's group than in Bales's group. In this regard, comparison of graphs for the tags showing directionality revealed the importance of the early disequilibrium in Dunphy's group. For a number of these tags, there was a linear relationship for Dunphy's group, but a curvilinear relationship for Bales's group. The clearest example of this was for the tag SELVES. Bales's group started comparatively high, indicating the solidarity created by the splitting of the group and the presence of Bales, while Dunphy's group started comparatively low, indicating the lack of solidarity created by the loss of Bales. Both groups, however, ended at approximately the same level. The means trend tests revealed that change in the groups was not linear in character but was of a more complex crisis type. The nature of these changes was then explored more fully through factor analysis to establish a basic factor structure for the reports and to trace changes on this factor structure over time.

Factor Analysis

The factor analysis and the analysis of variance use the same basic units. Factor analysis, however, tests the degree of association between the 83 tags within a basic data unit; that is, a person's reports from a particular phase. The first factor analysis discussed was performed on all the reports for the year. This means that each person contributes six sets of scores to the factor analysis. When the analysis has been performed for the whole year, tags loading high together on a factor are those tags that correlate with each other throughout the year.

The advantage of this kind of analysis is that it yields a measure of co-occurrence of tags, unlike the analysis of variance, which examines each tag separately. Hence we can determine how tags cluster and how the clusters change over the year.

The type of factor analysis used was a principal components analysis; that is, the factors were chosen to maximize the amount of variance accounted for. Only the first three factors are used in this analysis. The rapidly decreasing amount of variance accounted for by the rest of the factors and the encouraging nature of the plausible interpretation of the first three factors led us to analyze the space defined by these three factors rather than attempt an analytic rotation or use of more than three factors. The first three factors derived from the data accounted for the following percentages of the total variance:

Factor I: 6.83 percent
Factor II: 5.21 percent
Factor III: 4.21 percent
TOTAL   16.25 percent

This appears a small proportion of the variance, but it should be recognized that in constructing this dictionary an attempt was made to devise categories as independent of each other as possible. Use was

TABLE 8.6. Factor I—Expressed Negativity versus Denied Negativity

EXPRESSED NEGATIVITY		DENIED NEGATIVITY	
Tag	*Percent of Total Variance*	*Tag*	*Percent of Total Variance*
SIGN-REJECT	.5884	NONSPECIFIC-OBJECT	−.6423
ATTACK	.5662	QUANTITY-REFERENCE	−.6306
MILITARY	.4507	UNDERSTATE	−.6179
MALE-ROLE	.4065	OVERSTATE	−.5590
SIGN-WEAK	.3593	IF	−.5082
DISTRESS	.3484	NOT	−.4411
SIGN-STRONG	.3212	SELF	−.3979
SEX-THEME	.2749	OUGHT	−.3654
ANGER	.2629	SENSE	−.3692
DEVIATION	.2418	THINK	−.2962
COMMUNICATE	.2719	LARGE-GROUP	−.2694
GUIDE	.2613	COMMUNITY	−.2937
DANGER-THEME	.2585		
FAMILY	.3225		
ARTISTIC	.2835		

made of factor analysis to adjust categories to reduce intercorrelation so that it was expected that the factors would account for a relatively small proportion of the variance.

As shown in Table 8.6, the positive end of Factor I is concerned with aggression (SIGN-REJECT, ATTACK, MILITARY, ANGER, SIGN-STRONG), the anxiety underlying aggressive acts, and the effects of aggression (SIGN-WEAK, DISTRESS, DEVIATION, DANGER-THEME). With this interpretation, it is particularly interesting that MALE-ROLE is also highly loaded on this factor. In the discussion of analysis of variance, it has already been noted that males tended to dominate the first phases of the group when ATTACK was a prominent theme. The negative end of Factor I shows high loadings for a number of tags which in other studies have been found to indicate defensiveness. This is particularly true of OVERSTATE and UNDERSTATE and generally true of NONSPECIFIC OBJECT, the high use of which indicates vagueness. IF, NOT, SENSE, and THINK also convey a lack of certainty. The tag IF, for example, contains words suggesting indecision, such as maybe, possible, perhaps. Similarly, NOT indicates a euphemistic way of avoiding direct statements. THINK and SENSE appear because the attributive phrases "I think" and "I feel" are used similarly to indicate uncertainty. Since this is the negative end of a factor with aggression as the positive end, it appears that members using words in these categories avoid discussion of the problem of aggression.

TABLE 8.7. Factor II: Normative Structure versus Anomie

NORMATIVE STRUCTURE		ANOMIE	
Tags	*Percent of Total Variance*	*Tags*	*Percent of Total Variance*
MESSAGE-FORM	0.5751	FEMALE-ROLE	−0.4267
ACADEMIC	0.5651	MALE-THEME	−0.4091
SIGN-ACCEPT	0.4748	DEVIATION	−0.3766
POLITICAL	0.4115	DISTRESS	−0.3846
NEUTER-ROLE	0.3846	EQUAL	−0.3678
AUTHORITY-THEME	0.3825	SIGN-WEAK	−0.3466
GUIDE	0.3470	LOWER-STATUS	−0.3170
JOB-ROLE	0.2796	AVOID	−0.3198
FOLLOW	0.2725	SEX-THEME	−0.3116
SMALL-GROUP	0.2690	NATURAL-OBJECT	−0.3084
		DEATH-THEME	−0.2696
		SIGN-REJECT	−0.2557

It is significant that SELF is associated with the negative end of Factor I, indicating that when members talk about themselves they are most likely to be defensive. Considering that these notes are written to the trainer, this seems a very reasonable finding.

Table 8.7 shows that the tags clustered about the positive end of Factor II are closely related to the institutional structure of the course. ACADEMIC MESSAGE-FORM, for instance, is the tag definition for "case," that is, references to the assigned cases for group discussion. Similarly, professor and instructor are both defined ACADEMIC and JOB-ROLE. SMALL-GROUP consists mainly of references to the group itself with some references to the family. On this factor, actions are represented by GUIDE and FOLLOW with the associated institutional context being POLITICAL. Inspection of intersection lists in the dictionary gives some idea of the type of actions being spoken about here. For instance, words defined POLITICAL GUIDE in the dictionary are assemble, elect, influence, reform. Similarly, words defined POLITICAL FOLLOW are vote and follow. The words most used on the SIGN-ACCEPT–FOLLOW intersection are accept, agree, follow, conform, participate, respect. The words most used on the SIGN-ACCEPT–GUIDE intersection are approve, assist, encourage, guide, help, support. Clearly this end of the factor derives from sentences dealing with the formal institutionalized structure of the course and the patterned behavior deriving from this structure.

Clustered about the negative end of the factor is a mixed group of tags with the unifying theme of an awareness of lack of controls and structure. DEVIATION, DISTRESS, SIGN-WEAK, AVOID, SIGN-REJECT, LOWER-STATUS, and DEATH-THEME are all fairly clearly aspects of this pattern. Interesting also is the presence of SEX-THEME and MALE-THEME along with FEMALE-ROLE. In the notes, discussions of distress, deviance, and sexuality are clearly divided from discussion of the normative structure of the situation. The high counts on EQUAL (the words like, similar, and so forth) show that the language used in referring to anomie tends to be metaphorical rather than direct.

Tags appearing in Factor III are shown in Table 8.8. The positive end of this factor is most highly loaded on SIGN-STRONG, and the notion of strength seems to characterize most of the other tags on this end of the factor, particularly when first- and second-order tags are considered in conjunction. Words defined SIGN-STRONG–IDEAL-VALUE are, for example, authority, independence, and freedom. Similarly,

TABLE 8.8. Factor III: Strength versus Weakness

STRENGTH		WEAKNESS	
Tags	Percent of Total Variance	Tags	Percent of Total Variance
SIGN-STRONG	0.4027	TIME-REFERENCE	−0.4786
MALE-ROLE	0.3775	SIGN-ACCEPT	−0.4507
SPATIAL-REFERENCE	0.3286	DANGER-THEME	−0.4331
ACTION-NORM	0.2851	COMMUNICATE	−0.4120
IDEAL-VALUE	0.2810	SENSORY-REFERENCE	−0.4066
POLITICAL	0.2683	SIGN-WEAK	−0.3899
FEMALE-ROLE	0.2542	ACADEMIC	−0.3469
FAMILY	0.2503	DEATH-THEME	−0.3314
		AVOID	−0.3086
		THOUGHT-FORM	−0.2568

leadership is tagged POLITICAL, ACTION-NORM. The references to father and mother figures account for the loading on FAMILY. MALE-ROLE is particularly high, as it is for Factor I also, and thus males appear to be associated with both strength and negativity.

The negative end of Factor III is characterized by tags indicating indecision and weakness. SIGN-WEAK is rather highly loaded on the end of the factor. Particular words which are frequently used and defined with tags loaded highly on this end of the factor are silence (DANGER-THEME, SIGN-WEAK, SENSORY-REFERENCE), discuss, discussion (ACADEMIC, SIGN-ACCEPT, COMMUNICATE), end (TIME-REFERENCE, DEATH-THEME), suicide, leave, left (DEATH-THEME, AVOID).

Figure 8.1 schematically outlines the factorial structure just identified. In addition, vectors lying midway between the primary reference axes have been added. This follows the approach advocated by Kuder (1954), Leary (1957), and Kassebaum, Couch, and Slater (1959).

Fusion Factors

Those tags that are most highly loaded on the fusion factors are listed in Table 8.9. Only a general discussion of the fusion factors will be given here in order to show how they are related to the primary factors and to indicate how the interpretive names for the fusion factors were derived. The fusion factor *INFLUENCE,* for example, lies between *EXPRESSED NEGATIVITY* and *NORMATIVE STRUCTURE.* It has high loadings on both MESSAGE-FORM and COMMUNI-

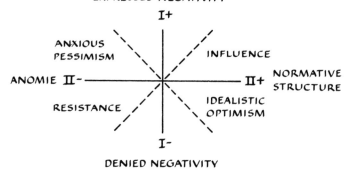

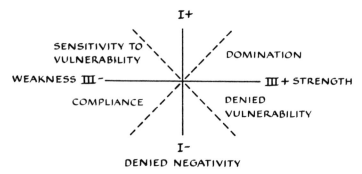

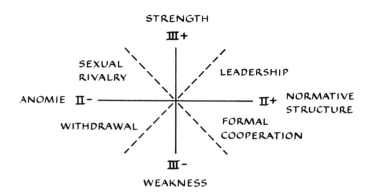

FIGURE 8.1. Factors and fusion factors.

TABLE 8.9. Tags Highly Loaded on Fusion Factors

Projection: Factor I on Factor II

influence
POLITICAL, GUIDE, MESSAGE-FORM, MALE-ROLE, COMMU-NICATE, SIGN-STRONG, HIGHER-STATUS

versus

resistance—
NONSPECIFIC-OBJECT, QUANTITY-REFERENCE, UNDERSTATE, OVERSTATE, IF, NOT, SELF

anxious pessimism
SIGN-REJECT, ATTACK, SIGN-WEAK, DISTRESS, MILITARY DEVIATION

versus

idealistic optimism
ACADEMIC, OUGHT, COMMUNITY, ACTION-NORM, IDEAL-VALUE

Projection: Factor II on Factor III

leadership
POLITICAL, SIGN-STRONG, MALE-ROLE, ACTION-NORM, AUTHORITY-THEME, IDEAL-VALUE, HIGHER-STATUS

versus

withdrawal
SIGN-WEAK, DANGER-THEME, DEATH-THEME, SENSORY-REFERENCE, AVOID

sexual rivalry
FEMALE-ROLE, LOWER-STATUS, OTHER, PLEASURE, FAMILY, SEX-THEME, NOT, IF, ATTACK

versus

formal cooperation
SIGN-ACCEPT, ACADEMIC, COMMUNICATE, TIME-REFERENCE, MESSAGE-FORM, SMALL-GROUP, FOLLOW

Projection: Factor I on Factor III

domination
ATTACK, MALE-ROLE, SIGN-REJECT, MILITARY, SIGN-STRONG, FAMILY, POLITICAL, ANGER, SEX-THEME

versus

compliance
UNDERSTATE, NONSPECIFIC-OBJECT, QUANTITY-REFERENCE, OVERSTATE, SELF, GOOD, DEFENSE-MECHANISM, TIME-REFERENCE, ACADEMIC

sensitivity to vulnerability
SIGN-WEAK, COMMUNICATE, HIGHER-STATUS, DANGER-THEME, DEATH-THEME, SENSORY-REFERENCE, AVOID, NATURAL-OBJECT, DISTRESS

versus

denial of vulnerability
IF, NOT, SENSE, OUGHT, THINK, COMMUNITY, LARGE-GROUP, AROUSAL, ACTION-NORM

CATE, it is manipulative in character (POLITICAL, GUIDE, SIGN-STRONG), and it is closely associated with high-status males (HIGH-STATUS, MALE-ROLE). One can contrast *INFLUENCE* with *LEADERSHIP,* which lies between *STRENGTH* and *NORMATIVE STRUCTURE. LEADERSHIP* is also high on POLITICAL, SIGN-

STRONG, MALE-ROLE, and HIGH-STATUS but shows high loads on AC-
TION-NORM and IDEAL-VALUE as against MESSAGE-FORM and COM-
MUNICATE. Therefore, this fusion factor seems appropriately named
LEADERSHIP since leadership is defined as POLITICAL, ACTION-
NORM in the Harvard III Dictionary. Similarly *INFLUENCE* seems
an appropriate name for the other, since influence implies communica-
tion and is defined by the two tags which have the highest loadings on
the factor, POLITICAL, GUIDE. Both of these fusion factors can be contrasted again with *DOMINATION,* which lies between *EXPRESSED
NEGATIVITY* and *STRENGTH.* On this factor, POLITICAL, SIGN-
STRONG, and MALE-ROLE are high, but the distinctive quality is the
number of tags implying negativity: ATTACK, SIGN-REJECT, MILITARY,
ANGER. Thus, if we compare the fusion factors that lie between the
positive ends of the three primary factors, we find a common theme
for that area of the factor space. Text highly loaded in this area shows
concern with men engaged in strong power maneuvers. These maneuvers range from influence attempts, through leadership, to domination.
Interestingly enough, MALE-ROLE loads higher on each fusion factor
in that order. In other words, the more the text is concerned with
strong, negative, manipulative behavior, the higher the probability
that men will be mentioned.

A similar comparison of the upper-left-hand quadrants of Figure
8.1 shows that area of the factor space to be concerned primarily
with anxiety, depression, and sexuality. FEMALE-ROLE and SEX-
THEME are both closely related on all projections of the factor space
and load highly on both *ANXIOUS PESSIMISM* and *SEXUAL
RIVALRY. SEXUAL RIVALRY* is the opposite of *FORMAL
COOPERATION,* particularly case discussion. Generally speaking,
therefore, the factor analysis shows women to be closely associated
with *ANOMIE, ANXIOUS PESSIMISM,* and *SEXUAL RIVALRY,*
while men are associated with *NEGATIVITY, STRENGTH,* and
DOMINATION.

The four factor fusions that are associated with the negative end of
Factor I are all strongly influenced by the tags that load highly on it.
The defensive character of the tags NONSPECIFIC-OBJECT, OVERSTATE,
UNDERSTATE, QUANTITY-REFERENCE, IF, NOT, THINK, SENSE, and
OUGHT has already been discussed. All four fusion factors *RESIST-
ANCE, IDEALISTIC OPTIMISM, COMPLIANCE,* and *DENIAL
OF VULNERABILITY* are highly loaded on these tags and therefore

have a strongly defensive character. They seem to represent a defense against clear specification of the problem openly dealt with in text loaded highly on the other end of these fusion factors. The two remaining fusion factors represent a combination of *WEAKNESS* with Factor II *NORMATIVE STRUCTURE* versus *ANOMIE*. They point to two clear behavior patterns in these groups, withdrawal (notably absenteeism) and formal cooperation (particularly case discussion). Both of these are seen as weak solutions to the normative problems of the groups as contrasted with *LEADERSHIP* and *SEXUAL RIVALRY,* which are seen as *strong* reactions to the same problems.

The factor analysis is an abstract representation of the major dimensions present in the weekly analyses presented to the group instructors. With two qualifications, it seems reasonable to regard the factor space as a model of the shared frame of reference in terms of which members perceive the group situation. The first qualification is the degree to which the frame of reference can be represented by the categories of the dictionary, and the second is the degree to which the frame of reference is openly communicated to the instructor. It is not possible to estimate the adequacy of Havard III tag categories, but it is clear from the factor analysis that in writing the group reports many members are essentially camouflaging aspects of their frame of reference.

Changes on the Factor Structure

The factor analysis was employed to reduce the large number of individual variables to a smaller number of composite variables and to use these to define a perceptual domain common to the reports of the group members. Each person's reports for a single phase can be located at a particular point within this domain, the point being determined by the three factor scores for the phase. The changing emphasis in a person's reports from the first to the last phase can then be traced by following his six successive positions within the factor space. Thus a particular individual may move from a high concern with *NORMATIVE STRUCTURE, STRENGTH,* and *NEGATIVITY* in the first two phases, swing to the discussion of *LEADERSHIP, DOMINATION,* and *WEAKNESS* in the third, and finally be predominantly concerned with *WITHDRAWAL, COMPLIANCE,* and *RESISTANCE* throughout the second semester. We are particularly interested here, however, in determining general trends of this kind for the majority of individuals' scores. We now take up the problem of measuring the extent to which the general emphasis on different areas of the domain changed over time and whether these differences resulted primarily from phase or group effects.

In order to study change of this kind on the factor structure, the three factors are treated as three variables. Each person has a score on each of these variables for those phases where he submitted group reports, and these factor scores are now used as the basic data units. A univariate analysis of variance, applied separately to each of the three factors, tests for change in exactly the same way as was done for each individual tag in the first part of this chapter. This makes it possible to determine whether a significant amount of variance on the factor over time can be attributed to phase, group, or interaction effects.

The results of the univariate analysis of variance show that for Factor I no effects were significant. The implication is, therefore, that *NEGATIVITY* is an element of continuing importance in the way members view the group, but that there are no significant shifts in the emphasis over time, nor are there important differences between the groups in the extent to which it is emphasized. However, we know from the discussion of the analyses of variance performed for individual tags that a qualitative change takes place within this factor; for instance, while *DENIAL OF NEGATIVITY* remains an important element in the reports, in the first semester it takes the form of high counts on QUANTITY-REFERENCE and SPATIAL-REFERENCE, while in the second semester it takes the form of high counts on OVERSTATE and UNDERSTATE.

For Factor II, all three effects are significant (phase and group effects at the .001 level), but interaction is barely significant at the .05 level. Consistent with previous findings, the reports from Bales's group maintain greater concern with *NORMATIVE STRUCTURE* throughout the year. However, equally evident is the phase movement: in both groups *NORMATIVE STRUCTURE* is emphasized in the first semester while attention turns toward *ANOMIE* in the second semester.

For Factor III the interaction effect is not significant, and both phase and group effects are significant at the .001 level. Dunphy's group is consistently higher in the emphasis given to *STRENGTH*, but both groups show an increasing emphasis on *WEAKNESS* over time.

Bales's final phase is the only major exception to this pattern, showing a reversal of trend but still remaining on the *WEAKNESS* end of the factor. This general pattern also seems consistent with the conclusion that concern with *WEAKNESS* was characteristic of the second semester and seemed to represent consciousness of the loss of rigid ego boundaries.

Since the three factors define a common perceptual domain, it is possible to use a multivariate analysis-of-variance technique to test simultaneous change on all three factors; that is, what is being tested are the effects of group, phase, and interaction on each individual's profile on all three factors. The results of this test indicate that both group and phase exercise a significant effect (.001) but that the interaction effect is not significant. We know that we may disregard Factor I in considering consistent change within the factor space, for there are no significant common changes or group differences for this factor. This means, therefore, that the projection of Factor II on Factor III is of greatest interest in the analysis of change. Using this projection, we may plot the means for each group at each phase and compare their relative positions at each time period. The space defined by Factors II and III is primarily concerned with the description of social interaction in the groups, and therefore the changes represent changes in the members' descriptions of group behavior. Table 8.10

TABLE 8.10. *Mean Factor Scores for Groups by Phase*

	Factor I		Factor II		Factor III	
Phases	Bales	Dunphy	Bales	Dunphy	Bales	Dunphy
1	−0.0941	−0.2275	0.4698	0.2750	0.1718	0.8042
2	−0.1894	0.3086	1.0040	−0.2571	0.1480	0.8277
3	0.4260	−0.0040	0.6493	0.1007	−0.5250	0.1412
4	0.0615	−0.1366	−0.3388	−0.3996	−0.9995	−0.0795
5	0.1661	−0.2205	−0.3910	−0.6844	−0.9918	−0.0072
6	0.1822	−0.1975	−0.2109	−0.6988	−0.4216	−0.3695

shows the mean factor scores for groups by phase and Figure 8.2 shows the means plotted on a projection of Factor II on Factor III.

Both groups begin in the *LEADERSHIP* quadrant and end in the *WITHDRAWAL* quadrant. They are, in fact, remarkably similar in the second semester, since for both groups all three scores are in this quadrant, but the routes by which they reach this final position are

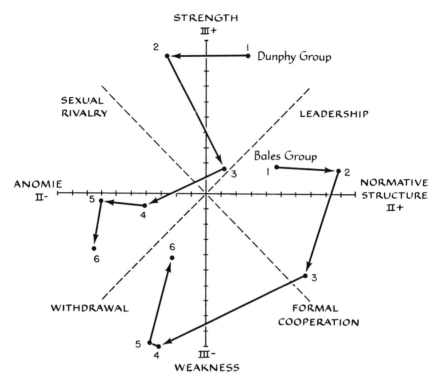

FIGURE 8.2. Group trends: Mean scores on factors 3 and 4 plotted by phase.

quite different. Dunphy's group is initially higher on *STRENGTH*, remains high in Phase 2 but moves in the opposite direction from Bales's group toward *ANOMIE,* assuming a position associated with *SEXUAL RIVALRY*. In the third phase, the reports show a neutral position as far as these issues are concerned. We may regard this as a working through of the concern with personal strength, since the score on this factor is considerably lower. Bales's group, beginning with an initially higher concern with *NORMATIVE STRUCTURE,* moves to a very high position associated with that factor in Phase 3. This po-sition indicates a high concern with the *AUTHORITY* relation-ship, which is resolved in the third phase by an interim solution to the problem, *FORMAL COOPERATION* indicating overt submis-sion to authority. One can relate these differences between the groups to the effects of the initial division of the groups and to the status char-acteristics of the instructors. Bales's group, faced with a strong authority figure, concentrated on the authority problem in the first semester. On the other hand, Dunphy's group, faced with the loss of an external authority figure, became concerned with the issue of personal strength as a way of coping with the loss of an external source of strength. This process apparently exacerbated the interpersonal rivalry in the group and aroused fears of sexual impotence.

Thus, Dunphy's group reports show initial concern with peer relationships and Bales's group with authority relationships. This has already been demonstrated, but the present description gives a much clearer picture of the dynamics of change by which these concerns developed. It also shows that these distinctive concerns lessened in significance as the groups moved into the second semester where discussion of rebellion, acting out, and loss of individual defenses make the groups appear more similar in the concerns revealed in their reports.

There is a possibility, however, that the smaller number of reports available from the second semester is responsible for the strong trends that appear in this analysis. If, for instance, the most impersonal members became disaffected and discontinued writing reports, the changing character of the reports might be due to this fact and not to changes in the attitudes of most group members. A matched-pairs analysis of variance was performed to determine the extent to which individuals changed from one semester to another and whether significant changes in one direction on the factors could be discerned for a majority of the individual members. Factor scores were therefore pooled for each semester, giving a combined semester factor score for each individual. However, for this analysis only those members were included for whom data were available from both semesters. A univariate analysis of variance was then performed on each factor for each group to determine

1. whether each individual showed a significant shift on the factor (subjects) and
2. whether a significant proportion of individuals shifted in the same direction (group).

Table 8.11 shows a large amount of individual variance on Factor I but no general group shift from the first semester to the second. It appears therefore that some individuals discuss *NEGATIVITY* a good

TABLE 8.11. Analysis-of-Variance: Changes in Factor Scores Between Semesters

Factor	Source	f Bales Group	d.f.	Sig.	f Dunphy Group	d.f.	Sig.	Direction of Group Shift Bales	Dunphy
I	Group	0.64	1,15	N.S.	0.99	1,19	N.S.		
	subjects	5.63	15,15	.01	5.20	19,19	.01		
II	Group	16.75	1,15	.01	2.86	1,19	N.S.	+ to −	
	subjects	1.18	15,15	N.S.	1.58	19,19	N.S.		
III	Group	10.91	1,15	.01	10.74	1,19	.01	− to − −	+ to −
	subjects	1.75	15,15	N.S.	1.17	19,19	N.S.		

deal in the first semester and a good deal less in the second, while the reverse is true for others. Therefore, from the point of view of the group as a whole, *NEGATIVITY* remains a consistently important topic. On Factor II, however, Bales's group as a whole moves from the positive end, *NORMATIVE STRUCTURE,* in Semester 1 to the negative end, *ANOMIE,* in the second semester. While Dunphy's group moves in the same direction, the change does not reach significant proportions. Once again it seems that the initial effect of the way in which the groups were formed precipitated the discussion of *ANOMIE* in Dunphy's group. In Bales's group, on the other hand, it becomes a much more significant problem in the second semester. There are no significant individual differences on this factor. Factor III shows a remarkably close correspondence between the two groups. Both groups show a highly significant increase in the discussion of *WEAKNESS,* and there are no significant individual differences on this factor for either group. This provides additional evidence in summary form for the major change identified earlier between the first and second semester, that is, the weakening of ego boundaries in the second semester with an accompanying consciousness of loss of identity. Thus, changes on a factor structure over time represent changes in the way in which the group situation is perceived by the group members. The factor analysis presents results that summarize and support the changes identified with the other statistical methods. In particular, it illustrates the fact that the content of reports from the two groups changed in consistent ways through the year but indicates also the way in which the different characteristics of the two instructors influenced this basic pattern in a unique way for each group.

ROLE DIFFERENTIATION AND ITS RELATIONSHIP TO THE PATTERN OF GROUP EVOLUTION

God (to Job):

Society can never think things out:
It has to see them acted out by actors,
Devoted actors at a sacrifice —
The ablest actors I can lay my hands on. . . .
        Robert Frost, "A Masque of Reason"

In the study of self-analytic groups, interest in identifying the nature and function of role types that seem to recur in different groups has been secondary only to interest in identifying an ordered sequence of phases. It has been pointed out that the emerging role types should bear some relationship to the phasal or evolutionary pattern of group development. Presumably these roles symbolize aspects of the focal conflicts facing the group at particular phases and contribute to the handling of these conflicts. Therefore, in this study I have attempted to identify the role types that developed in these two groups. Just as an attempt was made to characterize common phases for the two groups, here an attempt is made to estimate the extent to which similar roles emerged in the two groups and to identify the functions these roles performed for the participants and for the emerging social systems of the groups. It should be made clear, however, that the written reports are the primary source of information for this analysis and that therefore it is not a role in the behavioral sense that is being studied. It is more accurate to refer to it as a *role image* since it is the picture of the central person that is being transmitted to the instructor by the members of the group. On the basis of previous studies of role differentiation, the hypothesis was advanced that the images of central persons in the group would reflect a process of role differentiation within the group. In relation to the specific data being studied, it was thought that when the General Inquirer summarized descriptions of the central persons for successive phases the process of differentiation would be revealed by a stabilization over time of specific tags about each of the central persons. In addition, it was held that the pattern of differentiation would be similar in the two groups and would be indicated by similarities between the profiles of the two groups.

In order to test this, a new selection of data was made from that used for the analysis of group trends. Using the leftover lists, which include proper names, a count was made of the number of times each member was mentioned in each phase. This gave a useful index of the psychological saliency or centrality of each group member. The extent to which he occupied the group's attention was then expressed in the form of a ratio calculated as follows:

$$\frac{\text{number of times the individual is mentioned in the phase}}{\text{total number of mentions in the phase of all group members}}$$

The analysis of variance and the factor analysis both pointed to a major shift between semesters in the general character of concerns appearing in the group reports. It was decided, therefore, to choose the five most central persons in each semester in order to allow for the possible emergence of new roles to represent changing issues in the group culture.

In each group, four members maintained a central role throughout both semesters, and in each group one person who was frequently mentioned in the first semester was not among those most frequently mentioned in the second semester and vice versa. For both groups in all phases, the instructor is one of the three persons most mentioned. The instructor is also the most frequently mentioned member in the final phase of each semester. For each phase of the year, a role description was compiled for each central person by retrieving all sentences referring to him and combining these into a new unit. This yielded a composite group description of each person, a collection of subjective impressions of the person's behavior, and reactions to that behavior. Thus it is the role as seen by the group members themselves, that is, "a group portrait," rather than as seen by a relatively uninvolved and trained observer. In addition, because the descriptions are combinations of the separate member's impressions, it is those common or recurrent characteristics of their descriptions rather than those peculiar to one individual describer that give the role its characteristic profile.

The composite portrait was constructed by retrieving all sentences referring to one of the central persons and printing them out on tape. The new text was then tag tallied in the normal way so that the role descriptions were transformed into tag frequencies to allow direct comparisons to be made between the resulting profiles.

The hypothesis being tested postulated the differentiation of these role images. To test this it was necessary to construct a profile of the tags on which each of the role specialists was high. Therefore, within each group tag frequencies were used to rank central persons according to their score on each tag. This operation was performed for each phase. The individual's characteristic profile for a phase was then constructed by listing those tags for which he achieved first or second rank in that phase. It was then possible to compare the profiles for a particular individual in successive phases to determine whether tags stabilized over time. This was easiest, of course, for those persons for whom there were six profiles corresponding to six phases of centrality. Inspection of the profiles showed that the hypothesized differentiation in the descriptions did not appear, and therefore Hypothesis 4 was not supported by the available evidence.

For all individuals, the profiles did show some recurrent tags, the number in some cases representing a large proportion of the total number of tags in the profile. This seemed suggestive of continuity of image rather than differentiation, and therefore it was decided to investigate the nature of these continuities. In fact, this was supported by the review of literature where intuitive studies of self-analytic groups suggested that fully differentiated roles emerged at specific points of group evolution. This represented the other main view of the process of role differentiation, a view that was contrasted with Bales's and Slater's "evolutionary tree" hypothesis, which had been largely derived from observation of small, task-oriented groups in laboratory situations.

The stable elements of a person's image were extracted by listing the tags for which those persons with six profiles were high for at least three phases of the six. In addition, the similarity in profiles between two central members in Dunphy's group led to placing the two profiles together as "one role." External support for doing this was provided by a knowledge that these two members, in fact, seemed to play very similar roles. The profiles from one group were then compared with profiles from the other in order to determine whether similar clusters of tags were discernible in the two groups. If so, this would indicate the existence of similar role images. As there were corresponding clusters of tags between profiles, the profiles from each group were matched successively to achieve the "best fit," that is, to maximize the number of characteristic tags that one member possessed in common with a member of the other group. Thus, when taking

Bales's profile and attempting to match it successively with each of the profiles from the other group, one discovers that it matches best with Dunphy's profile. In fact, there are sixteen tags common to both profiles. Thus, these individuals are associated because they have similar profiles; the fact that they both prove to be the instructors is added evidence that the cluster of tags is not a chance assortment. Having matched these two individuals, another member was chosen from Bales's group and his profile matched against the remaining profiles in the other group. The profile showing the best fit with his was again used to indicate a person with a similar role image in Dunphy's group. The process was continued until all members who could be matched were matched.

The fact that individuals matched in this manner did play similar roles in the two groups will be demonstrated later. The common characteristics of their respective role images are presented in Table 8.12.

TABLE 8.12. Summary of the Characteristics of the Common Role Images

Instructor	Aggressor	Scapegoat	Seducer	Idol
SELVES	SELF	SELF*	OTHER	FEMALE-ROLE
NEUTER-ROLE*	OTHER	MALE-ROLE*	SENSORY-REFERENCE*	TIME-REFERENCE
JOB-ROLE*	TIME-REFERENCE	ACTION-NORM	MESSAGE-FORM	IF
IDEAL-VALUE*	SPATIAL-REFERENCE	GUIDE*	EQUAL*	CAUSE
ACTION-NORM	QUANTITY-REFERENCE*	CONTROL	APPROACH	COMMUNICATE
MESSAGE-FORM	AROUSAL	ATTACK	FOLLOW	ATTEMPT
OUGHT*	DISTRESS	GET	WORK	SEX-THEME
GUIDE	OUGHT	COMMUNITY	GET	ASCEND-THEME
CONTROL*	ATTACK*	OVERSTATE	COMMUNITY	
ACADEMIC*	MILITARY*	SIGN-WEAK	LEGAL*	
FAMILY*	RECREATIONAL	SIGN-REJECT	RECREATIONAL	
POLITICAL	OVERSTATE	AUTHORITY-THEME	SEX-THEME*	
TECHNOLOGICAL*	SIGN-REJECT*			
HIGHER-STATUS*	DANGER-THEME			
SIGN-ACCEPT				
AUTHORITY-THEME				

* Tags on which both specialists were consistently high for four or more of the six phases.
N.B. The common characteristics listed are those tags for which both incumbents ranked first or second for at least three of the six phases.

The headings of Table 8.12 are role names considered appropriate in the light of their significance for group members.

Common Role Images

The Instructor

As one would expect from the fact that this is a formal status, there is a better fit between the profiles of the two group instructors than between other corresponding role types in the two groups. In the area of PERSONS, the high tags reflect a consciousness of distance between the group and the instructor. There is a dichotomy set up between SELVES (we, us, ours) on the one hand and the instructor (HIGHER-STATUS, ACADEMIC, JOB-ROLE) on the other. This is also apparent from the high counts on NEUTER-ROLE, where the most frequently used words are member and leader.

The instructor is seen as representing the academic or "work" aspect of the course, shown by high counts on ACADEMIC and MESSAGE-FORM ("case," for example, is defined ACADEMIC, MESSAGE-FORM). Clear also is the superego representative role of the instructor as shown by high counts on IDEAL-VALUE, ACTION-NORM, OUGHT, GUIDE, CONTROL, and AUTHORITY-THEME. Considering his relative lack of participation, especially in the first semester, there is evidence here for the projection on the instructor of the superego qualities of the members.

The relative emphasis on other tags shows characteristic differences between the descriptions of the two instructors. The descriptions of Bales show higher emotional involvement (URGE: Bales high in four phases, Dunphy in two; DISTRESS 5:1; ANGER 4:2), greater emphasis on superego qualities (GOOD 4:2; BAD 2:0), higher defensiveness on all tags indicating defensiveness (NONSPECIFIC-OBJECT 3:1; UNDERSTATE 2:0), and more awareness of vulnerability (SIGN-WEAK 5:0; DANGER-THEME 4:2; DEATH-THEME 3:2). On the other hand, the description of Dunphy shows more concern with whether the group follows or ignores the instructor (SMALL GROUP 6:2; FOLLOW 5:2; AVOID 2:0).

The positions of the tags characterizing the role image of the instructor can be plotted on the various projections of the factor analysis to indicate those dimensions with which the instructor is associated. If this is done, the instructor appears to be primarily associated with *EXPRESSED* rather than *DENIED NEGATIVITY,* with *NORMATIVE STRUCTURE* rather than *ANOMIE,* and with *STRENGTH* rather than *WEAKNESS.* The role image is also very closely associated with the fusion factors *INFLUENCE, DOMINATION,* and *LEADERSHIP.*

Thus, the common image of the instructor is of a distant and judging authority figure, primarily instrumental in orientation and standing for normative control. Consistent with previous findings about the differences between the two groups in the study, the members of

Bales's group seem more emotionally involved with the instructor's authority and are therefore more defensive in writing about him and more aware of their own vulnerability in relation to him. On the other hand, attention in Dunphy's group is concentrated on following or ignoring the instructor's leadership.

The Aggressor

Both members identified as playing this role consistently seized opportunities to create rifts in group relationships, reacted strongly against the introduction of personal material, particularly when it was of a sexual nature, and seized on apparent points of weakness and vulnerability in others in order to ridicule and belittle them.

ATTACK, MILITARY, and SIGN-REJECT are the tags most strongly emphasized in the descriptions of the occupants of this role, and reading the sentences characterized by these tags indicates that the member concerned is the group specialist in aggression. In describing the actions of the aggressor, group members also recognize the danger (DANGER-THEME) to individuals and to the group in the exercise of overt aggression, and they also express guilt and anxiety (DISTRESS) about the extent to which they may be responsible for the actions of the aggressor. The association of SPATIAL-REFERENCE and QUANTITY-REFERENCE with negativity has already been fully discussed, and their occurrence as tags characteristic of the aggressor provides additional evidence for the association.

Of the tags referring to persons, SELF and OTHER are consistently high in describing the role of the aggressor. Many of the sentences tagged in this way use the words listed under these tags to emphasize the writer's lack of identification with the aggressive action. Thus, many of the sentences containing these words represent an indirect denial of responsibility for, or sympathy with, the hostility occurring in the group. It is consistent with this theme that high counts on OUGHT are also present, indicating a certain amount of moralizing about the aggressor's behavior. It is clear, however, from the inclusion of AROUSAL that the actions of the aggressor are accompanied by much emotional involvement and excitement both on the part of group members and of the aggressor himself. The OVERSTATE words which are used in connection with the role refer mainly to the extreme nature and extreme effects of the aggressor's actions. For example,

> Keith reacted to this *major* threat anxiously and irrationally, leafing through the case to find support for his crumbling mask.

The tag RECREATIONAL was generally misapplied because its occurrence here was largely associated with the word "show" (RECREATIONAL). The word is used here as a verb in the sense "he showed surprise" or "this showed us something about Keith."

It has already been shown that there was a greater concern with the problem of authority in Bales's group, and these comments make clear that this is also characteristic of role relationships. The aggressor in Bales's group directed much of his aggression toward the instructor, while this is not true to the same extent of the aggressor in Dunphy's group.

Plotting the tags that characterize the aggressor shows a close association between this role and Factor I, *EXPRESSED NEGATIVITY* versus *DENIED NEGATIVITY,* with relatively higher counts on *EXPRESSED NEGATIVITY*. This association is clearest on the projection of Factor I on Factor II where the weighting of the aggressor on the side of *ANOMIE* is also apparent. The projection of Factor I on Factor III shows that the aggressor is seen as more strong than weak, and that of Factor II on Factor III shows that his role is strongly connected with discussions of leadership.

The aggressor is seen as the "bad object" of the group, as a persecuting, rejecting, and threatening figure who arouses a high level of anxiety in the group. He is regarded as the symbol of emotional coldness and represents the maintenance of rigid individual defenses and distant relationships between members. Consonant with the concern with authority in Bales's group, the aggressor in that group is seen as directing a considerable amount of hostility toward the instructor.

The Scapegoat

The two group members identified as playing this role were each the chief object of aggressive attacks in their respective groups, and for extended periods of time they seemed to be the main focus of hostility. The descriptions of the incumbents of this role are high on two tags that are also high in descriptions of the aggressor, notably ATTACK and SIGN-REJECT. In this case, however, retrievals show a difference in that the scapegoat is generally the object of attack rather than the initiator of attack.[4] Consistent with this are the high counts on SIGN-WEAK.

High counts on SELF reveal the personal involvement of group members, expressive of their frustration and anger about the behavior

---

[4] This is clearly a case where syntax coding could have been used to advantage in distinguishing between the two roles.

of the scapegoat. In addition, there is emphasis on tags implying normative control (COMMUNITY, ACTION-NORM, GUIDE, CONTROL, AUTHORITY-THEME), and it is significant that four of these tags are also high for the instructor's role. This provides an important clue to the major reason for the scapegoating of this group member; he attempts to play an authoritative, task-oriented role (which the instructor refuses to assume) which creates the emotional involvement and anger of group members. Afraid of attacking the instructor directly, group members find a substitute who resembles him and act out the destruction of the instructor in phantasy form.

Plotting the high tags for this role against the factor structure shows that, as for the aggressor, there is a close association between this role and Factor I. The role is much more highly loaded, however, on *DENIED NEGATIVITY*. The high counts on SIGN-WEAK also link the role closely with the fusion factors *ANXIOUS-PESSIMISM, SENSITIVITY-TO-VULNERABILITY,* and *WITHDRAWAL.*

The scapegoat is an important role that emerges when groups are faced with major problems of status consensus. The description of the scapegoat that emerges from the group reports suggests important reasons for scapegoating in these particular groups. The scapegoat is seen as the weak, vulnerable object of group persecution. His rejection is seen as stemming from his overdependence on the instructor, his anxiety about the loss of individual and group controls, and his insensitivity to the responses of others. It seems likely that the members react to his anxiety because it is an exaggeration of the anxiety which they feel themselves but do not wish to recognize. Scapegoating the most anxious, most dependent member is a way the members deny and handle their own fears about dependency needs.

The Seducer

The seducer's actions are directed to weakening defenses against personal exposure and self-revelation. The name "seducer" is used because the occupants of this role tried to orient discussion about sex and intimacy, tried to seduce others into self-revelation, contributed sexual phantasies to the group, and, to some extent, acted them out, were physically attractive, and used gestures with sexual overtones. The role of seducer contrasts with that of the aggressor, who tried to inhibit the development of greater intimacy between the members of the group. In Bales's group one member (male) played the seducer role throughout the year, while in Dunphy's group the role was played by a man in the first semester and a woman in the second semester.

Tags with particularly high frequencies for this role are SEX-THEME and SENSORY-REFERENCE. The high counts on SEX-THEME derive from both direct and indirect references to sexuality and reveal that this role is oriented primarily to sexual drives and sexual phantasies. For example,

> Upon being questioned Kirk admitted that he saw reading the story as a kind of personal commitment on his part, a step in our progress towards *intimacy*.

.   .   .   .

> Kirk for example asked in his usual forthright way whether or not anybody thought the problem of *sex* was being avoided, and went on later to say that he thought the most important aspect of any adolescent relationship was the effort to reconcile tenderness and *sex*.

.   .   .   .

> In other words, Kirk was suggesting too much *intimacy*.

.   .   .   .

> However it is probable that Kirk's action was very much connected with Olga and served at the time to test the group's tolerance to emotionally charged *sexual* themes.

High counts on SENSORY-REFERENCE are particularly interesting since they indicate that members are consistently responding to the occupants of this role in a sensual manner. Even in writing these analyses while removed from the group situation, members use a large number of sensory type words in describing the actions of the seducer. A number of these references are to the characteristic silence, indicating a conflicted reaction that follows action by the seducer:

> There followed a *quieting* down of the group (which had previously been bantering among itself) which soon became dead silence.

However, there are also a large number of other sensory references:

> It was no longer a question of whether Ernest did not like Brian or Carl or Tom, it was one step removed to a plane where you said you did not have to *bare* your soul to a strange group but rather to expose your thoughts to a class.

.   .   .   .

> Ernest's story on Wednesday seemed to impress the group two ways, its sexual *tones* (which created anxiety in the group, in as much as group

members felt the group as the object of a kind of exhibitionism). . . .

.   .   .   .

For just as Joseph was chosen once, so Kirk must consider himself, because of his influential position in the group, the member to further the analogy, just as Joseph accomplished his tasks through his intelligence and *physical* charm, so Kirk hoped to do his job in the same way.

.   .   .   .

This question of whether to be *warm* and open about oneself or be *cold* and frozen-in reflects the question of intimacy in the group.

Just as the descriptions of the seducer are higher on the use of sensory words, they are also higher on the use of metaphor (EQUAL).

It would be too much *like* stabbing one's own father were we to stab the lonely hero.

.   .   .   .

Like the Pope and his church in the *Hunchback of Notre Dame* mentioned by Kirk, Dr. Bales and his course became figures of fun.

Such references make it clear that the seducer himself introduces metaphors into the group and also stimulates the use of metaphors by others in their descriptions of him. In fact, the stories and phantasies that are introduced by the seducer can be themselves regarded as extended metaphors. In the case of the seducer, the high counts on RECREATIONAL stem primarily from the word "story," and thus this tag is a more reasonable representation of the seducer's role than it is of the aggressor's. The same word, along with frequent references to cases, is also responsible for high counts on MESSAGE-FORM.

A similar theme is present in sentences tagged APPROACH, which show that the seducer "offers" and "contributes" stories and personal topics to the group, "proposes" that the group consider more personal material, becomes "involved" in the group and advocates that others become "involved" also, wants to "give" something to the group, says what "comes" to mind, and lets personal details about himself "come" out.

It appears that the seducer has a definite goal in mind for the group and works at accomplishing this goal. Thus, high counts on "work" refer not so much to instrumental or task-oriented activity as to the fact that the seducer is using his own abilities and those of others to achieve these goals. For example,

By saying that Kirk was leading the class in an improper manner, i.e., by *using* a third party as a mouthpiece, and by using the attractive technique of dropping his defenses one by one and thus exposing his inner, raw personality it appeared to me that Conrad was endeavoring to switch the class to his side.

. . . .

Kirk *uses* his ability to speak and speak well.

Thus the seducer represents movement toward greater intimacy and self-revelation and poses the problem for other group members of whether to follow his lead or not. Naturally there is ambivalence about doing this, for to expose oneself is to run the risk of making oneself vulnerable through exposing one's weaknesses. The high counts on FOLLOW reflect this ambivalence about supporting the seducer:

Several members have *followed* Kirk's lead and have begun to bring in personal aspects of themselves.

. . . .

No one has had the courage to *follow* Kirk's lead.

High counts on OTHER reflect the fact that some members did consistently support the seducer and act as a small clique referred to in the test as "they."

High counts on LEGAL derive from the use of words concerned with the maintenance of order and control in the group and the creation of a sense of responsibility, both of which are threatened by the actions of the seducer.

The counts for Kirk are enhanced by the fact that he related a story with legal implications:

On the following Wednesday, Kirk (I am sure wittingly) related to the group the story of a *murderer* who spilled his beans to a girl he was keeping hostage and was repaid ultimately with *arrest*.

The relationship of the tags characteristic of the seducer's role to the major factors drawn from the factor analysis shows the seducer's role to be primarily associated with Factor II, *NORMATIVE STRUCTURE* versus *ANOMIE* (Table 8.7). The majority of tags, however, load on the *ANOMIE* rather than the *NORMATIVE STRUCTURE* end of the factor, and the high counts on SEX-THEME link the role with *DOMINATION* and *SEXUAL RIVALRY*. Clearly separated from most of the other tags on the other end of Factor II is MESSAGE-FORM, and this gives an insight into one aspect of the ambivalence experienced by members about this role. While the seducer threatens the authoritative structure of the group, the phantasies and stories which he brings to the group and his identification with key figures in some of the cases appear to make a contribution to the task aspect of the group.

Thus the seducer is seen as the warm, sensually arousing advocate of more intimate relationships among members. He uses imaginative stories and emotive imagery to seduce members into lowering their defenses and revealing more personal details about themselves than they wish. His concern with sexuality is seen as threatening to the maintenance of both group and personal controls, since it stimulates phantasies of sexual fulfillment that members find difficult to control.

The Idol

This final role is the least distinct of the five group roles. If this role is what it seems on the limited evidence available, then this is understandable. For it is the occupant of this role, a female group member, who is the main object of the sexual phantasies of the male group members. In both groups, the "idol" was a woman who closely identified herself with the instructor, making this apparent by sitting close to him and continually supporting his authority and interpretations. The analogy between this role and that of the mother in the family is clear. Thus, while the occupant is overtly involved in supporting the instructor's authority, her close identification with him seems to involve a component sexual phantasy. In playing the role of mother, she is also by implication placing herself in the role, wife, with its implications of sexual partnership. The response to her in the group indicates that group members idealize her supportive behavior as a model of "good" group behavior, but perceiving the implications of her actions, secretly cherish phantasies of her seduction.

As for the seducer role image, SEX-THEME is high, and sentences tagged in this way reflect the fact that this is because the idol is the object of attraction in the group.

> I had just spent the previous 20 minutes dwelling upon her profile in detail and it was only upon being informed that she was *married* that I was really struck by how appealing I found that profile.

> .   .   .   .

> The boys are very much *attracted* to her and attacked her much less than they would Ernest or me under a similar situation.

> .   .   .   .

But how nervous and confused it would be were not Olga there, an *attractive,* responsive but unattainable object.

. . . .

Some of Olga's ignorance of group behavior has been in reaction to her place in the overt and tacit *sexual* phantasy of the group.

. . . .

It seems to me that Tracy would like to establish a blind *intimacy* in the group, that is, relationships in which members can *expose* themselves or say what they want with a tacit agreement among them not to analyze and interpret each other's behavior.

. . . .

Her analogy connected the *homosexual* connotation of the Valentine and incest.

High counts on attempt reflect two distinct types of action:

1. attempts by the idol to guide the group on to task achievement and to support the authority of the instructor, and
2. attempts by group members, particularly the seducer, to seduce the idol from this role.

An examination of sentences connected with the other tags that are high reveals little of importance about the role except the hesitancy of members in expressing themselves about it.

The factor analysis shows that the factor with which this role is most closely associated is the fusion factor *SEXUAL RIVALRY* versus *FORMAL COOPERATION,* and this is a clear portrayal of the significance of the role. It is exactly this problem of the choice between these two extremes that is posed by the occupant of this role. At an overt level, the idol is highly task-oriented and conforming, but both she and the group members are involved in her acting out a mother-wife role. Naturally, the extent to which this is communicated to the instructor in the weekly analyses is limited, particularly in Bales's group, where there is less expression of sexuality in the notes.

Thus, the idol is the female member who identifies herself closely with the instructor, supporting his authority, advocating conformity, and playing a motherly role. As a central figure in the group phantasy of incest, she is the object of sexual rivalry among the male group members. Because of the nature of this phantasy, the character of the role does not emerge clearly from the reports to the instructors and therefore is largely inferred from group interaction.

Role Differentiation: Conclusions

The investigation of the images of the central roles in each group showed that very similar roles emerged in the two groups and that these roles had equivalent symbolic meanings for the members of the two groups. Apart from the instructor, four informal roles were distinguished in each group and were referred to according to their characteristic function as aggressor, scapegoat, seducer, and idol. These group roles represent the externalization and dramatization of internal conflicts experienced by group members in the relative absence of external restraints and the breakdown of traditional normative expectations.

Studying the distinctive role images that emerge in the group reports does not reveal a process of *differentiation* of the kind originally hypothesized. That is, there is no clear indication that over time certain tags have progressively higher counts for one specialist and lower counts for others. Instead, it appears that most of the common role types are differentiated by the second phase and that the group's image of the role persists relatively unchanged throughout the two semesters. Given the rapidity with which the roles are differentiated, a closer study of the process of differentiation would depend on the use of interaction measures.

The five common role types that have been identified should not be thought of as a complete roster of group roles but rather as the most persistent and significant. That the roles are meaningful in terms of the way in which group members view the group is shown by their close relationship to the structure of the factor analysis of the group reports. Another way of summarizing the factor analysis is to regard Factor I as the aggressor versus the scapegoat (the direct expression of aggression versus its denial) and Factor II as the instructor and the idol ("father" and "mother"), representative of normative structure, versus the seducer, representative of incestuous wishes and fears, and hence the weakening of *NORMATIVE STRUCTURE*. Similarly the roles bear a clear relationship to the results of the analysis of variance where two dominant concerns of the first semester were shown to be aggression (ATTACK) and (SEX-THEME). It is at this time that the roles of aggressor and seducer become counterposed in the groups. The expression of aggression is played out in the relationship between the aggressor and the scapegoat, and similarly the expression of sexuality is played out between the seducer and idol. The group roles represent the externalization and dramatization of conflicts centering around the handling of primary processes in the relative absence of external restraints and the breakdown of traditional normative expectations. Thus, the role specialists become symbols of the major alternatives that the group faces in the evolution of its culture. Through the interaction of the specialists in the context of group response, patterns of action are evolved to resolve these basic dilemmas. As Frost suggests in the words at the head of this section, "Society can never think things out, it has to see them acted out by actors."

Some regularities exist in the relative significance of these roles at various phases in the group's evolution. The scapegoat, for instance, seems to assume major importance in the first semester. This role achieves most references in Dunphy's group in Phases 1 and 2 and in Bales's group in Phase 3. A major decline in the percentage of references to this role occurs after the scapegoating takes place (Dunphy's group, Phase 2; Bales's group, Phase 3). The aggressor, on the other hand, seems to remain a significant figure throughout the year. There is an interesting relationship between the seducer and the instructor roles, for references to the seducer peak in the middle phase of each semester, while references to the instructor peak in the final phase of each semester, suggesting that the problem of intimacy has two definite phases and that it may be directly relevant to the problem of identification with the instructor. It looks as if an attempt to solve this problem is made in each semester, but the solution reached in the first semester goes against greater intimacy, while in the second semester the solution is, with some reservations, for it. It is particularly at this latter stage that the role of idol is important in that, as love object, the occupant of this role stands firmly for sublimation of sexual impulses in the interests of group goal achievement.

The derivation of this constellation of roles from focal conflicts in the experience of socialization is evident. The roles include a clearly defined "father figure," a rather shadowy "mother figure," two dominant siblings who stand respectively for the free expression of libidinal drives and for their repression. In addition, there is a weaker sibling who can be victimized whenever frustration reaches too high a level. The evidence for the projection of images of significant objects internalized in the process of socialization is clear. In fact, the phantasy clearly supports Guntrip's summary of the nature of the system of internal objects that is the result of socialization in the nuclear family:

The final result, an Oedipus complex — an internally felt and phantasied situation that has become a persisting structural feature of a given individual mind — by no means corresponds exactly to the real outer parental situation. It is more akin to a final summary form in which the problem relationships of the child's infancy life come to be preserved in his mental make-up. It would be better to call it the "Family Complex," the inner representation of what the child ultimately comes to feel about his position vis-à-vis both parents and taking up into itself, as it does, his relationships with siblings as well.

(Guntrip, 1961, 310)

Another interesting relationship seems to exist between these roles and the roles of task leader and sociocenter so frequently identified in group studies. The instructor's role appears similar to that of the task leader, being perceived as high on power and closely associated with the task. The role of idol appears similar to that of the sociocenter, being supportive of the authority of the task leader and directed toward the maintenance of the normative structure and group cohesion.[5]

Where, then, do the other roles come from, since we have no evidence that they take over functions performed by these two roles? It seems likely that they represent the wishes for free expression of basic drives that were first repressed in the family and remain under control in smoothly functioning groups through the differentiation and integration of roles representative of the father and mother. This differentiation allows the projection of effective parental models on the part of most group members and thus the smooth and rapid institution in the new setting of previously internalized controls. However, the failure of the instructor to play a clearly recognizable and acceptable instrumental role threatens these controls and opens the way for the projection and acting out of the repressed phantasies. In their most clearly identifiable form, these phantasies are oedipal in nature, although they also involve elements of earlier origin. The working through of these phantasies results first in a good deal of anxiety, followed by a feeling of inner tension accompanied by immobilization on the part of most group members as they identify with the role specialists who represent alternate poles of the focal conflict. Finally,

[5] The analogy between the roles of task leader and sociocenter, on the one hand, and father and mother in the family, on the other, has already received extended treatment by Parsons and Bales (1953).

a resolution of the problem is worked out which for most members again follows the pattern established in the family: identification with the authority figure and the sublimation of impulses in the interests of achievement and rationality.

A fuller study of the significance of these roles in the development of a group mythology was made by studying the recorded interaction of the group meetings themselves. Since the General Inquirer was not used for this phase of the study, only a summary of the results of this analysis will be presented here.

Briefly, both the roles just discussed and the qualitative phasal changes identified by the General Inquirer were found to play a very significant part in the development of the group mythology. The first group myth, dominating Phase 1, centers about the role of the instructor who is seen as a weak and impotent authority figure. This period culminates in the scapegoating of a weak member of the group, who represents the instructor. In the second myth, dominating Phases 2 through 4, the instructor is seen as a secretly strong but malicious and manipulative figure. This period is characterized by a clear differentiation of the roles of aggressor and seducer and the dramatization of the tension between them. The aggressor stands for rigid concealment and control of sexual impulses, the seducer for emotional exposure and gratification of sexual impulses. Members polarize around these figures, but the aggressor eventually appears as the stronger figure. Consequently defenses against exposure and gratification of sexual impulses become more entrenched. Progress on the group task is inhibited by these developments, and fears of group disintegration emerge. Finally, new phantasies develop that express wishes for a more personal and trusting emotional climate. A third myth develops in Phases 5 and 6 of a utopian group in which members are involved in creative work, communicate honestly and act with understanding and compassion toward one another. There are accompanying phantasies of a messiah or hero who will overthrow the old patterns of behavior and introduce the new. This represents the reconstruction of the image of the instructor into an ego-ideal that can then be internalized to harness motivations of the members to this goal. Finally, the aggressor is overthrown and the group ideal is partly realized. In this process, the idol plays an important role in reintegrating the group before the course ends.

CLOSING REMARKS

This analysis must be regarded as tentative as far as establishing phase movements and role differentiation in self-analytic groups. We have no way of knowing how representative these two groups are of self-analytic groups in general. The findings are suggestive and need wider testing to establish the extent of their validity. More important, perhaps, the study indicates the usefulness of an automated system of content analysis in efficiently and reliably handling large bodies of text. This opens up a wide range of possibilities for further studies.

BIBLIOGRAPHY

Arsenian, J., E. V. Semrad, and D. Shapiro (1962), "An Analysis of Integral Functions in Small Groups." *International Journal of Group Psychotherapy,* Vol. 12, 421–434.

Bales, R. F. (1953), "The Equilibrium Problem in Small Groups." In T. Parsons, R. F. Bales, and F. A. Shils, *Working Papers in the Theory of Action.* Glencoe, Ill.: The Free Press, 111–161.

Bennis, W. G., and H. A. Shepard (1956), "A Theory of Group Development." *Human Relations,* Vol. 9, 415–437.

Bion, W. A. (1959), *Experiences in Groups.* New York: Basic Books.

Crow, E. L., F. A. Davis, and M. W. Maxfield (1960), *Statistics Manual.* New York: Dover Publications.

Dunphy, D. C. (1964), "Social Change in Self Analytic Groups." Ph.D. Dissertation, Department of Social Relations, Harvard University.

Guntrip, H. (1961), *Personality Structure and Human Interaction.* New York: International University Press.

Kassebaum, G. C., A. S. Couch, and P. Slater (1959), "The Factorial Dimensions of the M.M.P.I." *Journal of Consulting Psychology,* Vol. 23, 226–236.

Kuder, F. G. (1954), "Expected Developments in Interest and Personality Inventories." *Educational and Psychological Measurement,* Vol. 14, 265–271.

Leary, T. (1957), *Interpersonal Diagnosis of Personality.* New York: Ronald Press.

Mann, R. D. (1966), "The Development of the Member-Trainer Relationship in Self-Analytic Groups." *Human Relations,* Vol. 19, 85–115.

Mills, T. (1964), *Group Transformation: An Analysis of a Learning Group.* Englewood Cliffs, N.J.: Prentice-Hall.

Slater, P. E. (1953), "Role Differentiation in Small Groups." *American Sociological Review,* Vol. 20, 300–310.

POLITICAL SCIENCE

Political science research has provided much of the impetus behind the development of existing content analysis procedures. Analyses of propaganda materials, political speeches, diplomatic notes, and documents from political pressure groups represent the kinds of research that have made objective content analysis methods a natural area of interest for many political scientists. Following this tradition, the three papers in this section are examples of how the General Inquirer has been used to investigate problems and issues of political relevance. These papers all differ in topic, kind of materials, dictionaries used, and research design. A brief discussion of these differences will serve as an introduction to these studies.

In the first article, Holsti applies Heider's cognitive balance model to international affairs and tests predictions by analyzing diplomatic notes written by leading Chinese and Soviet decision makers during four periods of high East-West tension and three relatively relaxed periods. The dictionary used in this study is the Stanford Political Dictionary that is described in Chapter 5. The results of this analysis should give added incentive to those interested in the interdisciplinary study of political events.

Smith, Stone, and Glenn's content analysis of Presidential Nomination Acceptance Speeches is an exploratory and descriptive study of candidates and parties. This investigation makes interesting use of factor analytic techniques to plot the change of issues of the parties' candidates over a period of 36 years. Both the Harvard III Dictionary and the McPherson Lobbying Dictionary are used in this study.

Namenwirth and Brewer's work with editorials from four Western "elite" newspapers is partly on the level of testing hypotheses and partly exploratory. Similarities and differences between newspaper orientations and their changes over time are investigated with particular emphasis on the degree of interest in and the attitudes toward integration of the Atlantic Alliance versus national consciousness. For this study, Namenwirth has supplemented the Harvard III Dictionary with tag categories derived from theoretical statements of Karl Deutsch.

CHAPTER NINE

External Conflict and Internal Consensus: The Sino-Soviet Case

Ole R. Holsti
Stanford University

INTRODUCTION

To the student of international relations, one of the most fascinating developments within the international system since World War II has been the changing relations among stages within the Communist subsystem, and particularly those between China and the Soviet Union.[1] Apart from their historical and contemporary significance, these events can provide an example of more general theoretical considerations in the study of international politics. For example, to what factors should one attribute the dispute? Did the conflict be-

[1] An earlier version of this paper was read at the annual conference of the American Psychological Association, September 1964. The preparation of the data presented here was supported in part by the U.S. Naval Ordnance Test Station, China Lake, California, under Contract N123 (60530) 34292A. I am indebted to members of a graduate seminar, taught jointly by Robert C. North and myself, who coded the documents for July–August 1963; to P. Terry Hopmann for making available documents relating to the Korean and Vietnam crises; to Richard A. Brody, Richard R. Fagen, David J. Finlay, Joseph B. Kadane, and Jan F. Triska for their useful comments on an earlier draft of this paper; to Kuan Lee for his invaluable help in all aspects of analyzing the data by computer; and to the Stanford Computation Center for a generous grant of time on the IBM 7090, which made the processing of the data possible.

tween the Soviet Union and China originate in the clashing personalities of Khrushchev and Mao? Is this an illustration of the hypothesis that authoritarian states are invariably expansionist and that, owing to geographical location, these two nations were bound to clash? Or is the conflict related to a basic structural change within the international system, a transformation from a tight bipolar configuration to one with less rigid alliances? Each of these explanations of Chinese and Soviet policy has its advocates who cite supporting historical examples. The difficulty, as Rosenau (1964) has pointed out, is not the existence of multiple explanations of state behavior but rather the absence of a theory of international relations that postulates the conditions under which each of these interpretations may be relevant.

The study of Sino-Soviet relations also brings into focus certain problems of research strategy. Social scientists who seek to analyze political behavior at the international level labor under a number of handicaps, not the least of which concerns the availability of data. Recently, political scientists have become increasingly concerned with the perspective of the actor and his definition of the situation, rather than with the perspectives and situational definitions of the investigator. Without neglecting the analysis of organizations and institutions, the basic premise underlying this approach is that the behavior of nations "is determined by the way in which the situation is defined subjectively by those charged with the responsibility for making choices" (Snyder et al., 1962, 212). Although we habitually personify nation-states by referring to Soviet actions or American policies, this is in fact a convenient but sometimes misleading way of identifying decisions made by individuals in Moscow or Washington who are empowered to commit the resources of their respective states in the pursuit of international goals. However, direct access to foreign policy leaders is always severely restricted in time and space. Even the scholar fortunate enough to gain access to decision makers of his own nation cannot do so at those times when much of the most theoretically relevant research might be undertaken, as, for example, during a crisis situation. Moreover, many of the leaders deemed important, such as those of Communist China, are never available. The best one can usually do under these circumstances is an ex post facto study of one party in the crisis situation, such as the analysis of the American decision to resist aggression in Korea (Snyder and Paige, 1958).

The research problems inherent in the study of international relations are magnified for the student of Sino-Soviet relations; here the normal difficulties are compounded by cold war politics. Even the post-Stalin thaw in the Soviet Union, which has facilitated some types of research by Western scholars, has not materially eased the problems in the study of foreign policy. Clearly, many standard methods of social science research (the personal interview, the questionnaire, or the participant-observer of decision makers in action) can rarely be used. An instrument for measuring attitudes "at a distance" is needed. This is perhaps the primary rationale for using content analysis on decision-makers' documents. Thus, it is not surprising that many studies of Soviet-bloc politics have relied to some extent on one or more of the many available techniques of content analysis (Whiting, 1960; Jakobson and Lasswell, 1949; Leites and Pool, 1949; Leites, Bernaut, and Garthoff, 1951).[2]

A major drawback to the use of content analysis is found in the very nature of the technique itself; even elementary forms of the method, such as simple word counts, require extensive expenditure of scarce research resources. Moreover, most manual techniques of content analysis lack flexibility and suffer from a limited ability to deal with complex units of analysis, such as the theme, with a high level of reliability.[3]

Recent developments in programming high-speed computers for content analysis have helped to solve the dilemma. The General Inquirer system of automated content analysis has substantially reduced manual labor in data preparation while materially increasing speed, reliability, and flexibility of analysis.

The Stanford Dictionary for the General Inquirer measures *frequency* and *intensity* of attitudes, as found in written documents, along three dimensions: positive affect–negative affect; strength–weakness; activity–passivity. These dichotomized dimensions correspond to the evaluative, potency, and activity dimensions that have been found to be primary in human cognition in a variety of cultures (Osgood, Suci, and Tannenbaum, 1957; Osgood, 1962). The dictionary thus reflects the assumption that decision makers make discriminations according to how they perceive themselves, other nations,

---

[2] However, content analysis is but one of many research approaches to politics within the communist subsystem. For a recent survey of these, see Triska (1964).

[3] For further discussion of these problems, see Lasswell, Lerner, and Pool (1952), Berelson (1952), Pool (1959), and Holsti, Loomba, and North (in press).

and events — or any stimulus — along these three dimensions. This does not assume that two persons will agree whether a given attitude object is good or bad, strong or weak, active or passive but rather that these three factors account for an overwhelming proportion of the variance.

HYPOTHESIS AND DATA

The hypothesis to be examined states that intrabloc relations vary systematically according to the level of interbloc conflict. That is,

> During periods of heightened tensions between the East and the West, relations between China and the Soviet Union will be characterized by higher consensus, whereas during periods of decreasing tension, there will be a lower level of consensus.

The hypothesis can be considered as an application of a more general proposition regarding group cohesion; namely, that out-group pressure, in this case resulting from East-West conflict, tends to reduce in-group (Sino-Soviet) dissonance, whereas the absence of external pressure tends to increase those differences (Mack and Snyder, 1957, 215; Coser, 1956, 88).[4] Variations of this hypothesis may be found in many of the classical theories of the causes of war.

One test of the hypothesis might be to examine Chinese and Soviet perceptions of each other during periods of high and low interbloc conflict. The tendency of Communist leaders to use allegory, indirect attack, obscure jargon, and even omission renders direct analysis of Chinese and Soviet decision makers' attitudes toward each other extremely difficult.[5] For example, during the October 1962 missile crisis, Chinese decision makers ignored the role of the Soviet Union

---

[4] Leighton (1945) found a similar phenomenon among groups in Japanese relocation camps during World War II, as did Grinker and Spiegel (1945) in their study of cohesion among bomber crews. See also Cartwright and Zander (1956, 73–134) and Blake and Mouton (1962).

[5] "But because the realities of the dispute were carefully concealed and because in public utterances neither side attacked the other by name, it was impossible, even as late as the early autumn of 1962, to prove the extent and bitterness of the quarrel without the most elaborate documentation; and, although this had up to a point been done, very few people in the West were any the wiser because, to understand the documentation, the reader first had to master the code-language of Communist polemics" (Crankshaw, 1963, 7). For a further discussion of this point, see the introduction to Zagoria's (1962) analysis of Sino-Soviet relations.

in a seemingly calculated manner, preferring to regard the events in the Caribbean as a Cuban-American affair.[6]

An alternative approach is to adopt an indirect research strategy. There is more or less general agreement among students of Sino-Soviet relations that a major source of friction between China and the Soviet Union concerns the proper policy to be pursued toward the West in general and the United States in particular. The Soviet Union has intermittently taken a position of partial accommodation toward the West, whereas Chinese leaders have opposed any such relaxation as contradictory to the principles of Marxism–Leninism.[7] Thus it should be possible through content analysis to trace the pattern of Sino-Soviet consensus in terms of perceptions of American policy. That is, perceptions of the United States should provide a useful and valid index of the level of agreement or disagreement between Chinese and Soviet decision makers. The numerous references to American policy in most Chinese and Soviet documents are a further advantage of this approach.

The hypothesis can now be restated in more operational terms:

Chinese and Soviet attitudes toward the United States will tend to be similar in periods of high interbloc conflict, whereas during periods of decreasing tensions, attitudes toward American policy will diverge.

The data may yield four configurations of Chinese and Soviet attitudes toward the United States, shown in Figure 9.1.

The major theoretical assumption underlying this operationalization, a premise informed by a considerable literature relating to cognitive balance, is that consensus can be defined as the "existence, on the part of two or more persons, of similar orientations toward something" (Newcomb, 1959, 279). Or, stated somewhat differently, these four attitude structures are in balance only if the relationship between the

---

[6] In all the Chinese documents of October 26–31, 1962, that were analyzed in this paper, only five direct references were made to the Soviet Union.

[7] "This Chinese Communist assessment of the likelihood, desirability, and criteria of peaceful coexistence was clearly at variance with the Soviet view that there was no alternative to coexistence but war and that 'realistic' and 'sober' American circles were beginning to understand that" (Zagoria, 1962, 242).

"The Chinese rejected all three explanations of Soviet coexistence tactics: that nuclear weapons left no other choice but a more moderate approach to the West, that the Bloc could ultimately triumph with a minimum of revolutionary violence, and that it was necessary to pursue Bloc aims with a maximum of flexibility" (*Ibid.,* 304).

FIGURE 9.1. Configurations of Chinese and Soviet attitudes toward the United States.

Soviet Union and China is associative ($+$) in patterns 1 and 2, and dissociative ($-$) in patterns 3 and 4 (Heider, 1946; Newcomb, 1953; Osgood and Tannenbaum, 1955; Festinger, 1957; Rosenberg *et al.,* 1960).

Two further assumptions are incorporated into this research design. If the "strain toward balance" is to be operative, (1) the attitude object must be *salient* for the actors (Abelson, 1959) and (2) they must be *aware of each other's attitudes.* Thus the United States must be an attitude object of central concern to China and the Soviet Union, and the latter two nations must be cognizant of each other's views. Even a casual survey of Sino-Soviet–American relations for the period 1950–1965 indicates that these two conditions are fully satisfied.

The data used in this study consist of 38 Soviet and 44 Chinese documents, a total of nearly 150,000 words, written in seven periods selected from the years 1950–1963. The periods include two during which East-West relations were relatively calm, four of extremely high tension, and one in which a major crisis was in the process of resolution without recourse to violence:

1. June 28–29, 1950   The outbreak of the Korean war.
2. September 15–25, 1959   Premier Khrushchev's visit to the United States.
3. April 12–25, 1961   The American-supported invasion of Cuba.
4. October 22–25, 1962   The most intense period of the Cuban missile crisis.[8]

[8] The division of the missile crisis into two periods at October 22–31 is based on an earlier study (Holsti, Brody, and North, 1965). This division of the crisis period corresponds to the turning back of the Soviet ships which had been headed for Cuba, the first indication that violence on the high seas might be avoided. For the purposes of this paper, the first (June 1950), third (April 1961), fourth (October 22–25, 1962), and seventh (February 1965) periods are considered to be those of high interbloc conflict. The other three periods, highlighted by Soviet-American negotiations at Camp David, the settlement of the missile crisis, and the Test Ban Treaty, are those of lower international tension.

5. October 26–31, 1962   The "bargaining period" in which the missile crisis was resolved.

6. July 25–August 5, 1963   The signing of the Test Ban Treaty by the United States, Soviet Union, and Great Britain.

7. February 8, 1965   The United States decision to bomb North Vietnam.

After the periods of analysis had been selected, the entire verbatim text of publicly available documents authored by designated decision makers was content analyzed.[9]

Prior to punching the text on IBM cards, three coding operations were performed: (1) complex sentences were separated into one or more themes; (2) the syntactical position of key words in the text was identified by a system of numerical subscripts; and (3) each theme was characterized as to time and mode of expression. For example,

CV   All freedom-loving/3 peoples/3 of the world/3 must/4 oppose/4 Washington's/7 policy/7 of nuclear/7 blackmail/7.

CD   The Soviet-Union/3 recognizes/4 the industrial/7 achievements/7 of the United-States/7.

These codes identify the subject-verb-object (3-4-7) relationship, links between modifiers and referents, time (C = current), and mode of expression (V = imperative; D = indicative).[10]

The primary analysis was carried out through a direct table program written in *BALGOL* (Armour, 1964). Scores on the evaluative, potency, and activity dimensions were tallied for (1) actions in themes in which the United States was the agent and (2) qualitative characteristics ascribed to the United States. The dictionary contains approximately 3,600 words, including such terms as nuclear, blackmail, industrial, and achievement, which have been tagged and scaled for

---

[9] For example, during the Cuban missile crisis, every available document written by Premier Khrushchev, Foreign Minister Gromyko, Defense Minister Malinovsky, and Ambassador Zorin was coded and analyzed. In addition, some unsigned editorials appearing in authoritative organs of government policy, such as the Chinese newspapers *Jen-min Jih-pao* and *Red Flag*, have been included. A similar procedure of selecting documents was followed in all but the Korean and Vietnam crises, for which the initial radio commentaries were used.

[10] A small second dictionary serves to cross-reference all proper names, permitting references to "Washington" and "United States" to be retrieved together if desired.

intensity along the three dimensions.[11] This permits rapid and accurate calculations of attitudes, as revealed in the Soviet and Chinese documents, toward the United States. A General Inquirer retrieval program was used on a sample of the data to ensure the validity of the scoring in the context of the theme. In addition, the leftover lists were checked against the text, and all relevant items were scored by hand.

FINDINGS

The documents analyzed lend strong support to the hypothesis. They also corroborate the assertions by a number of scholars that some aspects of the Sino-Soviet dispute, which was clearly public by 1963, have their roots in the 1950's: Zagoria (1962) begins his analysis in 1956, whereas two other recent studies date the conflict from 1958 (Crankshaw, 1963, 8; Floyd, 1963, 67).

During periods of high East-West tension, Soviet and Chinese documents reveal consistently similar attitudes. The American decision to resist the invasion of South Korea brought forth unequivocal denunciation from both the Soviet Union and China. The period of the Bay of Pigs invasion was marked by an absence of censure by Soviet and Chinese leaders regarding the policies of each other, and during the initial days of the missile crisis in October 1962, both Chinese and Albanian criticism of Soviet policy ceased. Despite two years of increasingly vocal disagreement, the responses from Moscow and Peking to the bombing of North Vietnam revealed few differences.[12] The content analysis data disclose that during all four crisis periods, Chinese and Soviet attitudes toward American policy were quite similar: both perceived the United States predominantly on the negative, strong, and active ends of the evaluative, potency, and activity dimensions. The raw scores on the three dimensions for the seven periods are given in Table 9.1, and converted into percentages in Figure 9.2. These data indicate clearly that Soviet and Chinese perceptions of American policy converged during the periods of intense interbloc conflict over Korea, Cuba, and Vietnam.

[11] The dictionary actually consists of about 3,600 word stems; words with regular endings such as e, s, es, ed, and ing removed. Thus the working capacity of the dictionary is probably closer to 10,000 words.

[12] A more extensive study of the Korean and Vietnam crises has shown a high degree of consensus among nine members of the Communist system (Soviet Union, China, Albania, East Germany, Poland, Hungary, Rumania, Bulgaria, and Czechoslovakia) to both events (Hopmann, 1965).

TABLE 9.1. Soviet and Chinese Perceptions of United States Policy — Weighted (Frequency × Intensity) Totals

| | U.S.S.R. | | | | | | |
	June 28–29 1950	Sept. 15–25 1959	April 12–25 1961	Oct. 22–25 1962	Oct. 26–31 1962	July 25– Aug. 5 1963	Feb. 8 1965
Positive	7	754	39	23	61	10	6
Negative	49	226	211	258	80	10	104
Strong	87	746	279	359	126	35	135
Weak	3	117	27	16	25	3	3
Active	76	530	264	289	159	21	139
Passive	10	242	63	53	50	5	2
	China						
Positive	16	31	125	3	27	86	1
Negative	157	70	1196	269	1040	774	125
Strong	120	140	1055	243	816	675	116
Weak	2	11	81	17	63	20	2
Active	142	114	954	216	818	499	115
Passive	8	21	75	18	75	59	2

On the other hand, sharp differences between China and the Soviet Union appeared in periods marked by a more relaxed international atmosphere. When Premier Khrushchev visited the United States in 1959, the Chinese did not directly denounce the Soviet leader. Attacks against American policy were stepped up, however, with a warning that "the imperialists will never give up their policy of war and aggression of their own accord," intimating that accommodation with the West should be avoided (Zagoria, 1962, 242). At the same time, compared to Chinese statements, the Soviet documents revealed a vastly different attitude toward the United States, particularly along the evaluative dimension.

During October 1962, initial Chinese support for the Soviet Union in regard to the offensive missiles in Cuba did not survive the détente that brought the immediate crisis to an end. Direct analysis of the documents (geared to a mutual assessment by Chinese and Soviet leaders) reveals far less of the disagreement than the comparison of their attitudes toward the United States. After the Kennedy-Khrushchev agreement of October 28, for example, Jen-min Jih-pao editorialized that "The people of the world cannot under any circumstances lightly put their trust in the empty promises of United States

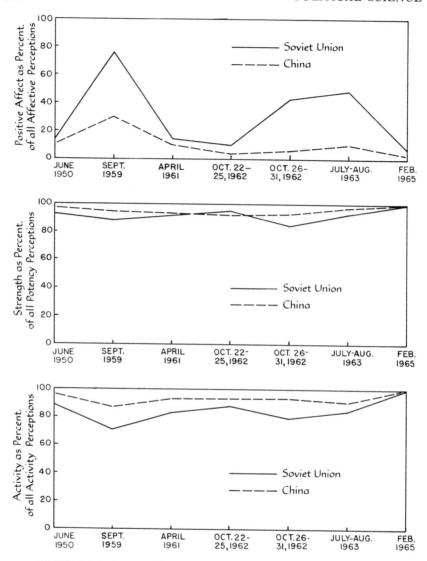

FIGURE 9.2. Soviet and Chinese perceptions of United States policy.

aggressors," implying that Premier Khrushchev had done so. The same editorial went on to praise Fidel Castro for the "justified and absolutely necessary" opposition to the on-site inspection agreed to by the United States and Soviet Union.

Subsequent developments have confirmed the thesis that the Kennedy-Khrushchev agreement was a major irritant in the relations between Moscow and Peking. Within weeks after the immediate crisis had passed, differences regarding the settlement in Cuba became more pronounced. The *Jen-min Jih-pao* editorial of November 18 stated that, "It is pure nonsense to say that 'peace has been saved by withdrawing Soviet missiles.' " *Pravda,* on the other hand, editorialized that "Neither bourgeoise propagandists nor other falsifiers can conceal the main fact that Soviet policy saved world peace and preserved the Cuban revolutionary movement." (Quoted in Floyd, 1963, 325.) In a report presented by Mikhail Suslov to the plenary meeting of the Central Committee of the Communist Party of the Soviet Union on February 14, 1964, the following charge was made against China:

> The Chinese leaders tried to paralyze the efforts that the U.S.S.R. and other socialist countries were making to turn back the menace of world war. Even at the very moment when the Cuban crisis was at its most intense point, the Chinese Government extended the armed conflict on the Sino-Indian frontier.
>
> (Quoted in Joxe, 1964, 85)

Since July 1963, the rift between the Soviet Union and China clearly has been brought out into the open. The documents of the period reveal little of the former reticence against direct attack. For example, the Chinese charged that

> The people of the world can draw only one conclusion. They (Soviet leaders) have betrayed the interests of the Soviet people and of all countries in the world, and have raised their hands and surrendered to United States imperialism.
>
> (Kuo Mo-jo, August 1, 1963)

> Incontrovertible facts show that the Soviet government has sold out the interest of the Soviet people and the interests of the people of the socialist camp, including the Chinese people, and the interests of the people living throughout the world.
>
> (*Jen-min Jih-pao,* July 27, 1963)

The Soviet replies were equally polemical. Premier Khrushchev charged Peking with "political irresponsibility" and lack of respect for "the sovereignty of the Soviet state."

To test the hypothesis regarding the effects of interbloc tension on the convergence of Sino-Soviet perceptions, the data have been aggregated into the situations of high and low East-West conflict in Table 9.2. The results indicate that during the peak periods of the two

TABLE 9.2. *Differences in Soviet and Chinese Perceptions of United States Policy During Periods of High and Low East-West Tension*

HIGH INTERBLOC CONFLICT			LOW INTERBLOC CONFLICT		
(June 1950; April 1961; Oct. 22–25, 1962; Feb. 1965)			*(Sept. 1959; Oct. 26–31, 1962; July–August 1963)*		
	U.S.S.R.	China		U.S.S.R.	China
Positive	75	145	Positive	825	144
	(10.8%)	(7.7%)		(72.3%)	(7.1%)
Negative	622	1747	Negative	316	1884
	(89.2%)	(92.3%)		(27.7%)	(92.9%)
Strong	860	1534	Strong	907	1631
	(94.6%)	(93.8%)		(86.2%)	(94.6%)
Weak	49	102	Weak	145	94
	(5.4%)	(6.2%)		(13.8%)	(5.4%)
Active	768	1427	Active	710	1431
	(85.7%)	(93.3%)		(70.5%)	(89.7%)
Passive	128	103	Passive	297	165
	(14.3%)	(6.7%)		(29.5%)	(10.3%)

Because the data in Tables 9.2 and 9.3 are based on a weighted (frequency $\times$ intensity) score, rather than frequency alone, the chi-square test of statistical significance cannot be used. It is clear from the table, however, that differences between China and the Soviet Union increase during periods of low East-West tension.

Cuban crises, differences in perception of American policy were consistently smaller than in those of the other three periods. During times of high interbloc tension, both Soviet and Chinese decision makers perceived American policy as overwhelmingly negative, strong, and active.

In the other three periods, there was a considerable divergence. Table 9.2 reveals the existence of wider differences between Chinese and Soviet perceptions of American policy during times of relatively low interbloc conflict along all three dimensions. For example, under conditions of high East-West tension, both Chinese and Soviet perceptions of American policy on the evaluative dimension were approximately 90 percent negative. With more relaxed relations between the East and the West, however, the figures for negative affect were 27.7 percent and 92.9 percent for the Soviet Union and China, respectively. The data thus support the hypothesis that decreased interbloc conflict tended to increase differences between the Soviet Union and China.

Further evidence of the growing differences between China and the

Soviet Union is indicated in their attitudes toward the Nuclear Test-Ban Treaty. Content analysis of the documents reveals the degree to which the Chinese leaders, who characterized the treaty as a "dirty fraud" (Chinese Government, July 30, 1963) and as "a United States–Soviet alliance against China, pure and simple" (*Jen-min Jih-pao*, July 27, 1963) differed with the Soviets in regard to the treaty (Table 9.3).

TABLE 9.3. *Chinese and Soviet Perceptions of the Test-Ban Treaty, July–August 1963*

	U.S.S.R.	China
Positive	256	26
	(98.5%)	(31.3%)
Negative	4	57
	(1.5%)	(68.7%)
Strong	209	77
	(80.7%)	(74.8%)
Weak	50	26
	(19.3%)	(25.2%)
Active	161	57
	(49.8%)	(64.8%)
Passive	162	31
	(50.2%)	(35.2%)

Tables 9.2 and 9.3 also indicate that differences between the Soviet Union and China under conditions of high and low tension are registered most clearly along the evaluative dimension. That is, both Chinese and Soviet leaders perceived the United States as strong and active, although in differing proportions, rather than as weak and passive under *both* conditions of intercoalition conflict. Under conditions of low tension, however, Chinese and Soviet perceptions of American policy are on the opposite ends of the evaluative dimension. The result supports other studies that have found the evaluative dimension of cognition to be the most important (Osgood, 1962; Levy and Hefner, 1964).

SUMMARY AND CONCLUSION

The purpose of this chapter has been to demonstrate the use of automated content analysis in the study of international relations "at a distance." The hypothesis that a high level of intercoalition conflict tends to increase intracoalition unity and more relaxed relations between blocs tend to magnify differences within the alliance was examined in the context of Sino-Soviet relations. Eighty-two documents written by leading Chinese and Soviet decision makers in seven periods during the years 1950–1965 were content analyzed through the Stanford version of the "General Inquirer" on the IBM 7090.

The results indicated that during the peak period of the crises over Korea, Cuba, and Vietnam, both Chinese and Soviet perceptions of American policy were overwhelmingly on the negative, strong, and active ends of the evaluative, potency, and activity dimensions. During the three periods of lower East-West tension, differences between Chinese and Soviet perceptions were greater than in the high tension periods on all three dimensions.

Although the data lend strong support to the hypothesis examined here, it seems advisable to interpret the results with great caution. It would be particularly hazardous to conclude that other factors, such as those of personality, ideology, or domestic politics, play no significant role in the relations between China and the Soviet Union. Specifically, the high degree of consensus between Moscow and Peking regarding American policy in Vietnam does not preclude the existence of other factors that might prevent a Sino-Soviet reconciliation. A more tenable conclusion might be that East-West tension may be a necessary but not sufficient condition for Sino-Soviet cohesion.

Whether even this limited interpretation of the findings is applicable to other contexts is, of course, a question for further research. A parallel study of the effects of East-West tensions on cohesion within NATO, for example, would shed further light on whether or not the findings presented here can be generalized.

BIBLIOGRAPHY

Abelson, Robert P. (1959), "Modes of Resolution of Belief Dilemmas." *The Journal of Conflict Resolution*, Vol. 3, 343–352.

Armour, Anne (1964), "A BALGOL Program for Quantitative Format in Automated Content Analysis." Stanford University, mimeographed.

Berelson, Bernard (1952), *Content Analysis in Communication Research*. Glencoe, Ill.: The Free Press.

Blake, Robert R., and Jane S. Mouton (1962), "The Intergroup Dynamics of Win-Lose Conflict and Problem-Solving Collaboration in Union-Management Relations." In Muzafer Sherif (ed.), *Intergroup Relations and Leadership*. New York: John Wiley & Sons.

Cartwright, Dorwin, and Alvin Zander (1957), *Group Dynamics*. Evanston, Ill.: Row, Peterson.

Floyd, David (1963), *Mao Against Khrushchev*. New York: Praeger.

Grinker, Roy R., and J. P. Spiegel (1945), *Men Under Stress*. Philadelphia: Blakiston.

Heider, Fritz (1946), "Attitudes and Cognitive Organization." *The Journal of Psychology*, Vol. 21, 107–112.

Holsti, Ole R. (1964), "An Adaptation of the 'General Inquirer' for the Systematic Analysis of Political Documents." *Behavioral Science*, Vol. 9, 382–388.

Holsti, Ole R., with the assistance of Richard A. Brody and Robert C. North (1965), "Measuring Affect and Action in International Reaction Models: Empirical Materials from the 1962 Cuban Crisis." *Peace Research Society, Papers II*, 170–190.

Holsti, Ole R., Joanne K. Loomba, and Robert C. North (in press), "Content Analysis." In Gardner Lindzey and Elliot Aronson (eds.), *The Handbook of Social Psychology*. 2nd ed. Reading, Mass.: Addison-Wesley.

Hopmann, R. Terry (1965), "Cohesion in the Communist System During Two Periods of International Crisis." Stanford University, mimeographed.

Jacobson, Sergius, and Harold D. Lasswell (1949), "Trend: May Day Slogans in Soviet Russia." In Harold D. Lasswell and N. Leites and associates (eds.), *Language of Politics*. New York: George E. Stewart, 1949. Cambridge, Mass.: The M.I.T. Press, 1965.

Joxe, Alain (1964), "La crise cubaine de 1962 — Entraînement contrôlé vers la dissuasion réciproque," *Stratégie*, Vol. 1, 60–87.

Lasswell, Harold D., Daniel Lerner, and Ithiel de Sola Pool (1952), *The Comparative Study of Symbols*. Stanford, Calif.: Stanford University Press.

Leighton, Alexander (1945), *The Governing of Men*. Princeton, N.J.: Princeton University Press.

Leites, Nathan C., and Ithiel de Sola Pool (1949), "Interaction: The Response of Communist Propaganda to Frustration." In Harold 'D. Lasswell and N. Leites and associates (eds.), *Language of Politics*. New York: George W. Stewart, 1949. Revised Edition. The M.I.T. Press, 1965.

Leites, Nathan C., Elsa Bernaut, and Raymond Garthoff (1951), "Politburo Images of Stalin." *World Politics*, Vol. 3, 317–339.

Levy, Sheldon G., and Robert Hefner (1964), "Multi-dimensional Scaling of International Attitudes." *Peace Research Society, Papers I*, 129–165.

Mack, Raymond W., and Richard C. Snyder (1957), "The Analysis of Social Conflict — toward an Overview and Synthesis." *The Journal of Conflict Resolution*, Vol. 1, 212–248.

Newcomb, Theodore M. (1953), "An Approach to the Study of Communicative Acts." *Psychological Review*, Vol. 60, 393–404.

——— (1959), "The Study of Consensus." In Robert K. Merton *et al.* (eds.), *Sociology Today*. New York: Basic Books.

Osgood, Charles E. (1962), "Studies on the Generality of Affective Meaning Systems." *American Psychologist*, Vol. 17, 10–28.

Osgood, Charles E., George J. Suci, and Percy H. Tannenbaum (1957), *The Measurement of Meaning*. Urbana, Ill.: University of Illinois Press.

Osgood, Charles E., and Percy H. Tannenbaum (1955), "The Principle of Congruity in the Prediction of Attitude Change." *Psychological Review*, Vol. 62 (1955), 42–55.

Pool, Ithiel de Sola (1959), *Trends in Content Analysis.* Urbana, Ill.: University of Illinois Press.

Rosenberg, Milton J., Carl I. Hovland, William J. McGuire, Robert P. Abelson, and Jack W. Brehm (1960), *Attitude Organization and Change.* New Haven, Conn.: Yale University Press.

Rosenau, James N. (1964), "Pre-Theories and Theories of Foreign Policy." Paper delivered to Conference on Comparative and International Politics, Northwestern University, April.

Snyder, Richard C., H. W. Bruck, and Burton Sapin (1962), *Foreign Policy Decision Making.* New York: The Free Press of Glencoe.

Snyder, Richard C., and Glenn Paige (1958), "The United States Decision to Resist Aggression in Korea." *Administrative Science Quarterly,* Vol. 3, 341–378.

Stone, Philip J., Robert F. Bales, J. Zvi Namenwirth, and Daniel M. Ogilvie (1962), "The General Inquirer: A Computer System for Content Analysis and Retrieval Based on the Sentence as a Unit of Information." *Behavioral Science,* Vol. 7, 484–498.

Triska, Jan F. (1964), "The Rift in the Communist World." *Background: Journal of the International Studies Association,* Vol. 8, 143–150.

Whiting, Alan (1960), *China Crosses the Yalu.* New York: Macmillan.

Zagoria, Donald S. (1962), *The Sino-Soviet Conflict,* 1956–1961. Princeton, N.J.: Princeton University Press.

CHAPTER TEN

A Content Analysis of Twenty Presidential Nomination Acceptance Speeches[1]

Marshall S. Smith
Harvard University

with Philip J. Stone
Harvard University

and Evelyn N. Glenn
Harvard University

THE PROBLEM

The study of the content of speeches by major political candidates and leaders has a long and varied history. Journalists have written many columns on the basis of qualitative content analyses of political

[1] This chapter is condensed from Smith *et al.*, "A Content Analysis of Twenty Presidential Nomination Acceptance Speeches," February 1965. The text of the speeches was drawn from three sources: the Official Proceedings of the Republican National Convention for the years 1928 through 1960; the Official Proceedings of the Democratic National Convention for the years 1928 through 1960; and *The New York Times* of July 17 and August 27, 1964. Computer time for the study was provided by the Harvard and M.I.T. computation centers. Other costs were borne directly by the authors.

speeches and documents. Particularly since 1930, political speeches and documents have been subjected to a number of objective, systematic, and quantitative studies.

The variables traditionally measured by political science content analysts are constructed of words, phrases, and themes considered as symbols of direct political significance. McDiarmid (1937) looked at words and phrases symbolic of national identity, of fundamental constitutional principles, and of national historical significance in the speeches of candidates for the American presidency from the years 1884 to 1920. James Prothro (1956) tested four hypotheses related to conservatism and the New Deal by generating content categories made up of certain words and phrases that appear to be symbolic of positions taken about various political issues and ideologies. Hayworth (1930) considered 24 categories in a study that concentrated on examination of the forms and frequency of mention of such political topics as party achievement, party loyalty, party record, social class appeals, and reference to certain campaign issues.[2]

Although the content categories used in this study may directly or indirectly indicate the same types of concern studied by political scientists, the organizing frames of reference of the category systems (the theoretical concerns that give coherence to the two sets of content categories used here) arise primarily from psychological and sociological theories. These categories measure such concepts as roles, emotions, social-emotional actions, institutional contexts, status connotations, and psychological themes rather than such primarily political concepts as party loyalty, party record, or symbols indicating national identity and constitutional principles. The imposition of such a framework on political speeches can be expected to elicit results that are both congruent and incongruent with those elicited by a more conventional political framework.

At the time of this study one of the category systems, the Psychosociological (Harvard III) Dictionary, described in Chapter 5, had been used primarily for the study of problems of a directly psychological or sociological nature. The other dictionary was developed to analyze domestic political lobbying data. The organization of this dictionary and the choice of categories within it were primarily di-

---

[2] The press coverage of political elections has also received considerable study from content analysts. See Stempel (1961), Rucker (1960), and Danielson and Adams (1961).

rected by sociological theory (McPherson, 1964). Table 10.1 shows the tag categories of the lobbying dictionary.

TABLE 10.1. McPherson Lobbying Dictionary Tag Variables*

Pattern Variables	Semantic Differential	Societal Interchange Tags	Other Dichotomous Tags
SELF-ORIENTATION	STRENGTH	MONEY	STRONG-ADVOCACY
COLLECTIVITY-ORIENTATION	WEAKNESS	POWER	MILD-ADVOCACY
		INFLUENCE	
		COMMITMENT	STRONG-OPPOSITION
ASCRIPTION	POSITIVE		MILD-OPPOSITION
ACHIEVEMENT	NEGATIVE		
			FREEDOM
AFFECTIVITY	ACTIVE		RESTRICTION
NEUTRALITY	PASSIVE		
			OVERSTATE
UNIVERSALISM			UNDERSTATE
PARTICULARISM			
			PROVISION
DIFFUSENESS			INADEQUACY
SPECIFICITY			

Selected Tags Borrowed from the Harvard III Psychosociological Dictionary (Modified by McPherson†)

GROUP	ATTACK	GOOD
NONSPECIFIC-OBJECT	AVOID	BAD
TIME-REFERENCE	ACTION-NORM	ECONOMIC
QUANTITY-REFERENCE	DEVIATION	POLITICAL
COMMUNICATE	MESSAGE-FORM	LEGAL
APPROACH	THOUGHT-FORM	RELIGIOUS

* This dictionary was developed for the study of lobbying literature and domestic political testimony in the United States Congress. The dictionary contains a number of categories suggested by the theoretical work of Talcott Parsons (McPherson, 1964).

† While McPherson uses these tag names the entry words comprising them in his dictionary are not necessarily the same as those under the same tags in the Harvard III dictionary. Therefore, in a document run on both dictionaries, the scores for the tags named GOOD may be quite different.

To some extent then, this study can be considered a test of the utility of both dictionaries in analyzing a set of data alien to the types for which the dictionaries were originally constructed. In this context one position on the issue of general- versus specific-usage content categories might be that the use of a general psychological and sociological framework is not justified with primarily political documents and that the structuring of the documents along other than political lines will only lead to unjustified conclusions. Another position might be that the use of a general psychological and sociological framework will offer new insights into the interpretation of documents because it offers the possibility of viewing the data from a perspective different than that of traditional political analysts.

It is rare that the inception of a research study can be accurately traced to one particular event or time. Without question, however, this study can be traced to the night of the 1964 Republican candidate's nomination acceptance speech. The excitement and controversy generated by this speech and the resulting political commentary seemed to center around two issues; the differences between Mr. Goldwater and the probable Democratic nominee and Mr. Goldwater's position as "in" or "out of" the political "mainstream" of the Republican party. Generalizations of these two questions result in the three major areas of research of this study.

1. The isolation of differences between the speeches of Republican and Democratic party candidates.
2. The discovery in political speeches of trends over time common to both Republican and Democratic candidates.
3. The use of content analysis category systems to isolate differences between the 1964 presidential candidates.

The study is primarily descriptive and hypotheses generating. No specific hypotheses are tested. No statistical inferences are made to larger populations of speeches. Statistics are used as heuristic devices for the discovery and ordering of differences and trends. Logical inferences are made to conscious intention, to unconscious motivations and attitudes of the candidates, and to historical antecedents.

The Data

Appropriate to the precipitating event, the data used in the analysis are the acceptance speeches of the Republican and Democratic nominees for President from the year 1928 to the year 1964.

No changes were made in the texts and each word was analyzed. The speeches were coded for two descriptive variables: party affiliation and year of delivery. Table 10.2 gives some relevant data about the speeches.

A number of problems exist in data of this sort. Since campaign speeches are not written solely by the candidate himself, inferences made about the candidates from the content of the speeches may not

TABLE 10.2. Relevant Information about the Speeches

Year	Republican	Number of Words	Number of Sentences	Democrat	Number of Words	Number of Sentences
28	Hoover	7,931	418	Smith	8,580	385
32	Hoover	7,064	345	Roosevelt	4,203	191
36	Landon	4,047	215	Roosevelt	1,987	104
40	Willkie	5,607	340	Roosevelt	3,521	127
44	Dewey	2,334	139	Roosevelt	1,742	71
48	Dewey	1,368	80	Truman	2,754	126
52	Eisenhower	1,141	51	Stevenson	1,727	77
56	Eisenhower	4,317	185	Stevenson	2,927	145
60	Nixon	5,201	198	Kennedy	2,179	108
64	Goldwater	2,878	143	Johnson	1.799	125

be valid.[3] The speeches are the product of trained speech writers, political advisors, and, to some extent, the candidate. However, as the overt behavior of the candidate in a standardized situation, the speeches are a direct stimulus to the party that he represents and to the nation's electorate. Furthermore, the candidate himself gives the speech and accepts responsibility for its content. An analysis of the speeches, however, should not be confused with an analysis of the men who gave them. The text of a single speech given in a traditional situation is not an adequate sample of a man's behavior. Thus, this is a study of twenty speeches, not thirteen men.[4]

One unique aspect of these data also deserves mention. The speeches are important documents, at least at the time of their delivery, and are entirely in the public domain, thus each has been subjected to extensive qualitative content analysis by journalists, political

[3] White (1956), in a comment on Prothro's paper, considers this problem in some detail.

[4] Even though most of the speeches were given before National Conventions by the candidates themselves, certain irregularities in situation do exist in these data. The practice of giving the speeches at the convention was started by Roosevelt in 1932. Before that time, it had been customary for the candidate to stay away from the convention. Hoover's 1928 speech was a national radio broadcast specifically directed to the committee that notified him of the nomination. Smith's 1928 acceptance of the nomination was by letter to the nominating committee of the Democratic party. Willkie, in 1940, accepted over a national radio broadcast originating from his home town; and Roosevelt in 1944 also accepted by radio. In every case, however, the talk was published nationally and represented the reply of the man chosen as his party's candidate for President. Further, in every case but Smith's, the speech was verbally spoken to a nationwide audience.

professionals, and the general public. Many of the speeches contain passages that have become political folklore. For instance, Roosevelt in 1932, "I pledge you, I pledge myself to a new deal for the American people" — Kennedy in 1960, "I am asking each of you to be pioneers toward the new frontier" — and Goldwater in 1964, "I would remind you that extremism in the defense of liberty is no vice. And let me remind you also that moderation in the pursuit of justice is no virtue." To many people these phrases symbolize the speeches in which they occur and are remembered when the speech itself has been forgotten. To consider only these phrases would be a qualitative, unstandardized procedure, and an invalid exercise within a quantitative frame of reference such as this study provides. A quantitative analysis allows for comparison (in this case, between speeches) and should provide results that can be related to the many qualitative analyses.

Choice of Content Categories

The two systems of content categories used are the Psychosociological Dictionary (Harvard III), developed at the Harvard Laboratory of Social Relations (see Chapter 5), and William McPherson's Domestic Political Dictionary, developed at Harvard for use in the study of lobbying text. Table 10.1 contains a list of the categories developed by McPherson.

Three reasons for the choice of these dictionaries should be mentioned.

1. This research offered the possibility of testing the generality of two content category systems developed with psycholgical and sociological data rather than with political data in mind.
2. Each dictionary was constructed before this research was initiated; it was felt that this situation might help reduce bias on the part of the researchers.
3. The organizing theories behind the category systems were well known to the researchers.

Research Strategy

This study follows the three-stage research strategy described in Chapter 7, and the order in which we present and discuss results is based on these three stages. Because of space limitations here, only the results of Stages I and II are described in detail.[5]

[5] For a detailed discussion of the interpretations of the factor spaces in Stage III, see Smith, Stone, and Glenn (1965, 35–47).

Stage I is an examination of the tag tally graphs and an interpretation of outlying scores of Goldwater and Johnson. Examples of graphs of tag scores that vary over time and discriminate between the two political parties are given, but the primary emphasis is on the use of the graphs and hand retrievals to point out differences between Goldwater and Johnson.

Stage II contains an analysis of the tags that appear to increase and decrease in frequency of reference over the years 1928 to 1964 and an analysis of those tags discriminating between the two political parties. A measure, which is computed exactly like the standard product-moment correlation coefficient, is employed as a descriptive measure of the linear association of the frequency of occurrence of the individual tags with time. The measure used to assess the differences between the parties might properly be called a "coefficient of variation of the differences between group averages." The formula employed in calculating this measure is identical to the formula used in the computation of the well-known Student's *t*-statistic. The differences between the measures used here and the commonly used statistics is simply in their function. In this study, no index of significance will be applied to the results; the measures are used as heuristic devices for descriptive purposes.

Another measure is used to demonstrate the differences between groups on individual tags: the number of misclassifications of speeches when the two speeches in a single year are considered a matched pair.

In Stage III of the analysis, we broaden our approach to include the interrelationships between the separate tags. Here we use principal components analysis, chosen in the multivariate stage of analysis because

1. Components analysis requires no hypothesis about the data.
2. It isolates the major orthogonal dimensions of a cluster of tags, thus reducing the number of variables to interpret and the chances of spurious association with our variables of interest. This is of particular importance since we are dealing with far fewer observations than measures.
3. Scores on these dimensions can be easily derived.

In keeping with the approach in Stages I and II, components analysis has been employed strictly for descriptive purposes. The components, as composite variables, can be interpreted by inspecting the tags that compose them. As just observed, scores on the components can easily be calculated. Scores for each speech were calculated for each component. By treating the factors (components) as single variables, we can then apply tests to measure time trends and differences between the parties as we do with single tags in Stage II of the analysis. Further, we can look at the differences between individual candidates based on their locations in the factor-score space. Thus we have a general framework, formed by the interrelationships of the content categories and the influence of all 20 speeches, within which to compare the speeches of Goldwater and Johnson.

In the following discussion of results, the scores referred to will, unless otherwise noted, always be *index scores* computed in the tag tally phase of the General Inquirer program. Although often required in General Inquirer analyses, no transformations on the index scores were considered necessary for this analysis. For ease of presentation, however, the index scores are multiplied by one thousand. Thus an index score of .027 will be presented as a score of 27.

RESULTS AND DISCUSSION

Stage I, Visual Interpretation of Graphs

The visual inspection of tags (Stage I analysis) is particularly useful for the comparison of particular speeches rather than for investigating over-all trends or group difference.

The general utility of Stage I types of analysis, however, should not be underestimated in a descriptive analysis of this sort. As a dramatic demonstration of this utility, note the graphs of five tags, shown in Figure 10.1: three from the Psychosociological Dictionary, IDEAL-VALUE, URGE, and ARTISTIC, and two from the Lobbying Dictionary, ECONOMIC and ACHIEVEMENT. Next to the graphs are samples from the list of entry words defining the tags.

The five graphed tags were chosen with our three areas of interest in mind. The graph for the tag ECONOMIC shows a clear decrease in frequency over time, and the scores for the Republican speeches are noticeably greater for the ACHIEVEMENT tag. Each of these concepts will be discussed in detail and in relation to other tags in the analysis of Stages II and III.

The graphs for the other three tags, URGE, ARTISTIC, and IDEAL-VALUE, demonstrate the power of this stage of analysis for investigating differences between pairs of subjects and deviant scores for particular subjects. The analysis of outlying scores is frequently over-looked when summary statistics are employed. In this particular analysis, we are specifically looking for outlying scores on either the Goldwater or Johnson speech. Because differences between Goldwater's and Johnson's speeches are considered later only in terms of factor scores as composite variables, a complete analysis of the deviant scores of their speeches will be made at this stage. A description of these three tags (graphed in Figure 10.1) will serve as an example of the procedure we employ when analyzing deviant tags.

As inspection of the graph reveals, Johnson's speech contains almost twice as many references to the category URGE as any of the other speeches. The entry words for this tag are largely terms relating to the processes of wanting and needing. Hand retrievals show that Johnson uses these terms while characterizing the American people, particularly in relation to domestic concerns. He used the refrain, "Most Americans want. . . . And so do I" seven times in his speech. The tag IDEAL-VALUE contains "culturally defined virtues, goals, valued conditions, and activities." It is not surprising to find that all the candidates mention terms that contribute to scores on this category. In terms of frequency of mention, Dewey's confident second acceptance speech far exceeds all others, but both Goldwater and Johnson are among those who refer most frequently to this category. Goldwater's references center on mention of the words "free," "freedom," and "liberty." These three words are mentioned a total of 40 times and constitute over one third of his total frequency of mention of this category. Only Nixon (32 mentions in a longer speech) approaches Goldwater in reference to these particular values. Goldwater's references to "free" and "freedom" are usually unspecific, with the exception of two instances: "free economy" and "free trade." Mr. Johnson mentions "freedom" or "liberty" eight times, but he usually defines it as freedom from economic want or victimization by impersonal forces. Table 10.3 contains examples of quotes containing these terms from Goldwater's and Johnson's speeches.

The last tag graphed, ARTISTIC, demonstrates that the frequency of tag occurrence does not have to be large for a tag to reveal relevant information. Goldwater's speech has almost twice the frequency of words falling in this tag as any other speech. Retrievals show that his references are primarily descriptions of American constitutional government as a "great framework," "a system of beauty," "inspiring"

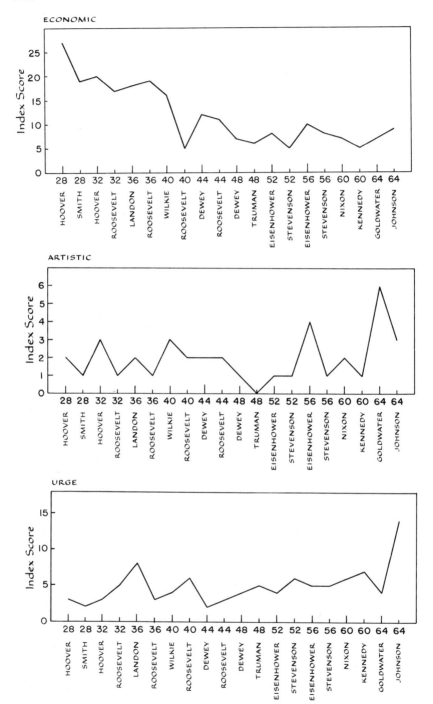

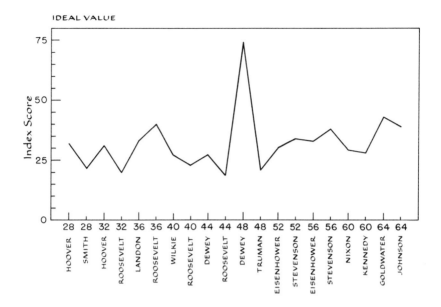

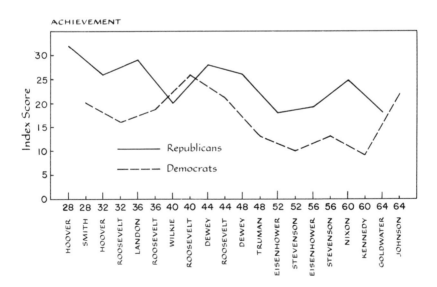

FIGURE 10.1. *Presidential Acceptance Speech tag index scores.*

TABLE 10.3. Hand Retrievals from Johnson and Goldwater Speeches for the Terms "Free," "Freer," and "Freedom"

JOHNSON: The man who is hungry, who cannot find work or educate his chil-
            dren, who is bowed by want, that man is not fully *free*. For more
            than thirty years, from social security to the war against poverty, we
            have worked to enlarge the *freedom* of man.

            As a result, Americans today are *freer* to live as they want to live,
            pursue their ambitions, meet their desires and raise their families
            than at any time in our history.

GOLDWATER: This party, with its every action, every word, every breath and every
            heartbeat has but a single resolve, *freedom*.

            We Americans understand *freedom*.

            The tide is running against *freedom*.

---

to the world, and based on the acceptance of God as the "author" of freedom.

Outlying Tags

The discussion of URGE, IDEAL-VALUE, and ARTISTIC has focused on the ways in which these tags discriminate the speeches of Goldwater and Johnson from the other speeches in the study. They are, however, only three tags of many that differentiate the speeches of the 1964 candidates from the speeches of their predecessors. Outlying tags are easily isolated by use of the graphic form of analysis employed in Stage I. However, since there are a total of 131 different tags measured in this analysis, we employed only those tags on which the speeches of Goldwater or Johnson received scores that were either the highest or lowest among all candidates. These tags are contained in Table 10.4. To demonstrate that these tags represent relevant differences and not just random high and low occurrences, we must not only show how the individual tags occur in the speeches but also that the concepts which these tags measure relate conceptually to each other and to our intuitive notions about the speeches.

The high outlying tags for the Johnson speech clearly point out the explicit emphasis on leader-follower relationships. Johnson's frequent use of the phrase, "Most Americans want. . . . And so do I," has already been mentioned. This explicit definition of goals is further emphasized by such phrases as, "These are the goals toward which I

*TABLE 10.4. Extreme Tags in the Goldwater and Johnson Speeches**

Psychosociological Dictionary			
Johnson		Goldwater	
High	Low	High	Low
MALE-ROLE	AROUSAL	CAUSE	SMALL-GROUP
NEUTER-ROLE	EXPEL	ARTISTIC	IF
TOOL	NONSPECIFIC-OBJECT	SIGN-WEAK	EQUAL
QUANTITY-REFERENCE	ECONOMIC	FEMALE-THEME	ATTACK
GUIDE			GET
FOLLOW			
URGE			
LEGAL			

Lobbying Dictionary			
Johnson		Goldwater	
High	Low	High	Low
NONSPECIFIC-OBJECT	MILD-OPPOSITION	DEVIATION	STRONG-ADVOCACY
UNIVERSALISM	ACTIVE	THOUGHT-FORM	
DIFFUSENESS	SPECIFICITY		

* High and low scores are defined as those scores that are either highest or lowest or tied for highest or lowest with only one other speech when compared to all other speeches. This convention was adopted so as not to include the very low frequency tags for which every speech has almost the same frequency.

will lead, if the American people choose to follow" and "We will try to lead you as you were led by. . . ." This unique orientation for our study is reflected in the high scores for the Johnson speech on the tags GUIDE, URGE, and LEGAL, which indicate positive goal oriented leadership and for the tag FOLLOW, which measures the reciprocal relationship to this leadership. The leader implied by these tags is unquestionably Johnson. As demonstrated by the high frequency in the Johnson speech of the tags MALE-ROLE and NEUTER-ROLE, the followers are mankind and the American people. The speech is further characterized by high reference to words such as unanimous, every, and unity (UNIVERSALISM) and words like general, total, and whole (DIFFUSENESS). Very low reference is made to words such as exclude, peculiar, and special, which denote differentiation on the basis of some characteristic (SPECIFICITY) and to words which denote rejection or exclusion (EXPEL). The picture here is of a strong leader appealing to a broad electorate. The appeal is widespread and universal in nature, and reference to particular characteristics are generally avoided. The rather low-pitched tone of the speech, demonstrated by low reference to the tags AROUSAL and MILD-OPPOSITION, complements the appeal to a widespread consensus.

The tags listed for the Goldwater speech suggest a very different picture. The high reference to categories identifying weakness and failure, SIGN-WEAK and DEVIATION, is in distinct contrast to Johnson's tactic of listing society's wants and needs. Goldwater's speech contains six consecutive sentences, each beginning with the word failures. ("Failures cement the wall of shame in Berlin.") This form of rhetoric makes a striking comparison to Johnson's repeated, "Most Americans want. . . ."

Just as the definition of problems is different in the Goldwater speech than in the Johnson speech, so is the approach to those problems that are enunciated. The speech has a very low frequency of mention of words indicating emphatic support, STRONG-ADVOCACY, and words specifying positive action orientation, GET. Instead, the approach articulates the failures and identifies them as causes to be corrected by the Republican party. Toward the middle of Goldwater's speech, the phrases, "It is the cause of Republicans . . ." and "It is our cause . . ." occur seven times. The definite commitment suggested by the high frequency of the tag CAUSE is reinforced by the very low frequency of conditional words (IF).

Using outlying scores to characterize a speech is certainly not without problems; we are dealing with only a small subset of the categories and not with the over-all profile of the speeches. It was felt that the factor analysis in Stage III of this analysis would give a broader base for the total comparison of the speeches than attempting to deal with total profiles at this stage. Further, in the initial choice of extreme tags and in the interpretation of these tags, bias on the part of the investigator can be important. For this reason, an explicit definition of extreme tags was used, and all tags meeting this definition were listed.

Stage II

The second stage concentrates on analysis of shared trends over time and on differences between the speeches of the Republican and Democratic candidates. No techniques that point out differences between, or particular characteristics of, Goldwater and Johnson were employed at this stage. As stated earlier, descriptive statistical techniques are used to identify those variables relevant to our areas of

*TABLE 10.5. Tag Variables Changing over Time**

Psychosociological Dictionary			Lobbying Dictionary		
Plus	*Minus*		*Plus*	*Minus*	
Roles			*Pattern-Variables*		
SELVES +54			SELF-	ACHIEVEMENT	−45
MALE-ROLE +54			ORIENTATION +48	PARTICULARISM	−49
Groups			*Dichotomous Tags*		
	SMALL-GROUPS	−53		PROVISION	−64
	LARGE-GROUPS	−40			
Environments			*Societal Interchanges*		
	SOCIAL-PLACE	−47	INFLUENCE +40	MONEY	−77
Cultural				POWER	−52
	ACTION-NORM	−61	*Other Tags*		
	THOUGHT-FORM	−46	GROUP	QUANTITY-	
Emotion			NONSPECIFIC-	REFERENCE	−50
URGE +51	PLEASURE	−45	OBJECT +57	ACTION-NORM	−54
Thought			COMMUNICATE +45	ECONOMIC	−81
NOT +42	IF	−51		LEGAL	−46
Social-Emotional Actions					
COMMUNICATE +54	APPROACH	−42			
ATTACK +50	CONTROL	−59			
Evaluation					
	OUGHT	−43			
Impersonal-Actions					
ATTEMPT +43					
Instituitonal-Contexts					
RECREATIONAL +45	ECONOMIC	−85			
	TECHNOLOGICAL	−75			
Psychological-Themes					
	SIGN-STRONG	−56			
	SIGN-AUTHORITY	−70			

* A rather arbitrary decision was made to fix a cutoff point for inclusion of variables. Any variable with an absolute correlation score of 40 or over was included. For convenience the decimal points were removed. Tags in the plus column increase linearly over time; those in the minus column decrease in frequency of occurrence over time. The *N* for the computation of the correlation coefficients is 20.

interest. Tables 10.5 and 10.6 show the relevant variables and the measures for the analysis of time trends and differences between Republicans and Democrats.

Trends over Time

In Table 10.5, many more tags correlate with time negatively than positively. One implication is that the dictionary is better suited to measure the concerns of the past than of the present. In some specific instances this is a real problem, but in general the same percentage of words is tagged for the later speeches as for the earlier. A second possibility, therefore, is more plausible, that the concerns of the more

TABLE 10.6. Republican–Democrat Differences*

Psychosociological Dictionary

Republicans Greater than Democrats

Tag	$\bar{X}_r$	$\bar{X}_d$	t	Misclassifications	Tie
SELVES	32.5	22.0	2.3	3	0
FEMALE-ROLE	2.1	0.9	2.4	0	5
OUGHT	11.3	8.0	2.2	1	1
WORK	20.2	15.7	2.6	2	0
ARTISTIC	2.6	1.3	2.4	0	2
LOWER-STATUS	3.1	1.6	2.3	1	3
DISTRESS	5.6	5.0	0.6	2	2
GUIDE	10.3	9.2	0.8	2	1
TECHNOLOGICAL	14.3	11.1	1.5	2	0
SIGN-ASCEND	37.5	32.0	1.2	2	0
AUTHORITY	23.3	19.2	1.5	2	0

Democrats Greater than Republicans

Tag	$\bar{X}_r$	$\bar{X}_d$	t	Misclassifications	Tie
EQUAL	3.0	4.3	-1.7	1	1
OTHER	15.5	18.6	-1.0	2	1
URGE	4.3	5.7	-1.2	2	1
BODYPART	2.9	3.7	-1.1	1	3

Lobbying Dictionary

Republicans Greater than Democrats

Tag	$\bar{X}_r$	$\bar{X}_d$	t	Misclassifications	Tie
FREEDOM	11.1	6.7	1.8	2	1
RESTRICTION	3.6	2.4	2.1	1	3
GROUP	72.2	69.4	2.2	2	0
SELF-ORIENTATION	41.3	30.7	2.4	3	0
ACHIEVEMENT	24.0	16.9	3.0	2	0
SPECIFICITY	5.9	4.3	2.2	3	0
ECONOMIC	13.2	10.4	1.0	2	0
DIFFUSENESS	20.2	18.0	1.4	3	0
ACTION-NORM	11.5	10.4	0.7	2	2

Democrats Greater than Republicans

Tag	$\bar{X}_r$	$\bar{X}_d$	t	Misclassifications	Tie
POWER	14.7	16.1	-1.0	2	1
NONSPECIFIC-OBJECT	8.5	9.1	-0.4	2	1

* Five statistics are reported in this table, the mean index score for each party, a t score computed exactly like the ordinary t-statistic for differences between the means of two groups, the number of misclassifications if we consider the candidates in a single year as a matched pair, and the number of ties between the matched pair. Two criteria were employed for inclusion of a tag in the table: (1) a t score of absolute magnitude greater than 2 or (2) the number of correct classifications greater than 5 and the number of classifications less than 4.

recent speeches are more diffuse and general than the concerns of the earlier speeches. Credence is given to this interpretation when it is noted that even as the power and scope of the presidential office has increased over the years, the length of the acceptance speeches has remained the same or slightly decreased. The nominee is forced to consider more topics because the office is of greater breadth, and thus he cannot devote much attention to any particular topic.

A striking degree of similarity appears in the results of the analyses using the two dictionaries. In both, the highest absolute correlation with time is a tag measuring ECONOMIC concerns (-85 and -81). Associated with this decrease is one of similar magnitude by the tag TECHNOLOGICAL in the Psychosociological Dictionary and the tags MONEY and PROVISION in the Lobbying Dictionary. The decrease in reference to the ECONOMIC and MONEY tags is not unexpected considering the preoccupation with business in the late 1920's and the economic problems created by the depression in the 1930's. Their association with the tags TECHNOLOGICAL and PROVISION is slightly more complex. The intercorrelation between the ECONOMIC and TECHNOLOGICAL tags in the Psychosociological Dictionary is 70. This can be partly attributed to the fact that such words as "job," "occupation," "farm," and "factory" appear on the list of entry words of TECHNOLOGICAL. Words such as "automation," "computer," and "research" do not appear on this list. The high concern over unemployment rates during the depression years and the decrease in the number of people working on farms and in the traditional factory settings appear to contribute more to the decrease in frequency of this tag than the more obvious interpretation of a decrease in concern with scientific technological advance. McPherson defines the tag PROVISION as including "the means of correcting social problems and provisions embodied in legislation." Retrievals show that the highest references to this tag were found in the depression years of the early 1930's and that these references reflect concern over the social legislation that was passed and proposed during this period. The only speech to match the depression-year speeches in high frequency of mention of the tag PROVISION is Truman's, in which he criticized the record of the Eightieth Congress by citing specific acts of legislation on which they failed to act. Although the factor analysis will automatically cluster the tags for us at the next stage of analysis, it is convenient at this stage to make intuitive clusters for the purpose of interpretation. We could consider the tags ECONOMIC, MONEY, and TECHNOLOGICAL as a cluster representing traditional business and farming concerns. PROVISION, however, is not a specific measure of these concerns and is not included in this cluster.

Continuing to look at the tags correlating negatively with time, a second cluster is suggested. In the Psychosociological Dictionary, references to normative modes of behavior (ACTION-NORM), words implying limiting action (CONTROL), moral imperatives (OUGHT), terms signifying strength (SIGN-STRONG), and authority (SIGN-AU-THORITY) suggest that the earlier speeches were written within a framework differing from that of the later speeches, a framework encouraging reference to specific authority relationships, to obligations, duties, and to accepted standards of behavior. The tags POWER, ACTION-NORM, and LEGAL in the Lobbying Dictionary support this cluster. We do not mean to imply a decrease in the strength, control, and authority of the federal government or even a decrease in a sense of moral obligation; it is simply that the society and the problems facing the candidates are now more complex and less amenable to direct specific solutions. The above-mentioned decreases in the tags PROVISION, ECONOMIC, and TECHNOLOGICAL appear to support this interpretation. Further, the tags PARTICULARISM and QUANTITY-REFERENCE both signify a decreasing use of terms dealing with specific, concrete facts and figures.

Consideration of the tags correlating positively with time reveals three tentative clusterings: terms indicating drive states (URGE) and implying goal directed activities (ATTEMPT), words connoting negation (NOT) and hostile aggressive action (ATTACK), and words indicating communication (COMMUNICATE in both dictionaries) and "means of affecting the behavior and decisions of others except through authority relations" (INFLUENCE). The wants and needs of the society are mentioned, and terms implying that they should be corrected are more highly referenced, but the specific structure within which they will be corrected is less highly referenced. There is the further implication that reliance on a structured framework has been replaced by reliance on modes of communication and influence.[6]

[6] Certain tags listed in Table 10.5 have not been discussed. Primary among these are the group tags, SELVES, SMALL-GROUP, and LARGE-GROUP, in the Psychosociological Dictionary and SELF-ORIENTATION and GROUP in the Lobbying Dictionary. It would appear that there is a contradiction in results between the dictionaries — a simple though incomplete answer is that both of the McPherson tags include the words "we" and "us," which appear under the tag SELVES and are not included in the Psychosociological Dictionary tags measuring groups.

Republican–Democrat Differences

Table 10.6 lists those tags that satisfy our criteria for distinguishing between the speeches of the Republicans and Democrats.

Again the most striking feature is an imbalance in the results. Of the 26 tags listed in Table 10.6, 20 occur with greater frequency in the speeches of the Republican candidates. A second interesting feature of these results partially explains this imbalance. If we look back to Table 10.5, we find a large correspondence between the tags seen linearly associating with time and those discriminating between the parties. Five tags from the Psychosociological Dictionary and seven tags from the Lobbying Dictionary appear in both tables. The two charts in Table 10.7 give some insight into this overlap.

TABLE 10.7. *Relationships of Tags Found Both to Vary over Time and to Differ Between Parties*

Psychosociological Dictionary			Lobbying Dictionary		
	R > D	D > R		R > D	D > R
Plus with time	SELVES	URGE	*Plus with time*	SELF-ORIENTATION GROUP	NONSPECIFIC-OBJECT
Minus with time	OUGHT TECHNOLOGICAL AUTHORITY		*Minus with time*	ACHIEVEMENT ECONOMIC ACTION-NORM	POWER

In each table, the cell defined by more frequent occurrence in Republican speeches and by negative correlation with time contains three variables. This is not to say that the frequency of occurrence of these tags in Republican speeches is decreasing less rapidly than in Democratic speeches. On the contrary, for some of these tags the decline in usage in Republican speeches is faster than it is for the Democratic speeches. This situation is demonstrated in Figure 10.1 for the tag ECONOMIC. The score for the Hoover speech in 1932 was 27, while the score for Goldwater's speech was only 7, a decrease of 20 points. The Democrats, on the other hand, started with a high score of 19 in 1928 and their lowest score was 5 in 1960, a difference of 14 points. In all but two years, however, the Republican speeches contain higher frequency of mention than their rivals. For other tags, the Republican speeches simply began at a higher level and have decreased at the same rate as the Democrats. However, for all six tags, if we interpret the negative association as a trend over time, the Republican speeches generally lag behind the Democratic speeches. Making this assumption enables us to interpret the correspondence in Republican speeches between the tags with higher frequency and negative correlations with time. Five of these six tags were instrumental in defining the two clusters in the discussion of negative trends over time: the decline in reference to ECONOMIC and TECHNOLOGICAL concerns and the decline in frequency of mention of AUTHORITY relationships, moral obligations (OUGHT), and normative patterns of behavior (ACTION-NORM). The sixth tag, ACHIEVEMENT, has many entry words in common with TECHNOLOGICAL and ECONOMIC.

These results correspond well with the notion that the Republican party is generally more conservative than the Democratic party. The Republican speeches can be characterized as more conservative than the Democratic speeches in two ways: (1) those concepts that occur more frequently in the Republican speeches also tend to correlate negatively with time, and (2) the Republican speeches give greater emphasis to clusters of concepts defining traditional concerns and highly structured techniques for dealing with issues.

The concept POWER, seen in Table 10.3 to correlate negatively with time and to occur more frequently in Democratic speeches, appears to contradict somewhat the interpretation of high frequency of mention of structured authority relationships in the Republican speeches. Although the concepts POWER and AUTHORITY-THEME do have a number of overlapping entry words, there is an important qualitative difference between the lists. The tag AUTHORITY-THEME in the Psychosociological Dictionary contains entry words "connoting the existence or exercise of power." The tag POWER is primarily composed of word connoting just the exercise of power. Words such as tradition, routine, established, conservative, and responsibility are contained in the AUTHORITY-THEME list and not in the POWER list. Thus we have a little extra handle on the interpretation of differences between the parties. The Republican speeches are seen to have higher frequency of mention of traditional, established references to authority, while the Democratic speeches place greater emphasis on particular pragmatic means of controlling the behavior of others.

Two tags appearing in the cells of Table 10.3 — URGE and NON-SPECIFIC-OBJECT — are defined by positive correlation with time and occur more frequently in the speeches of the Democratic candidates.

These two tags give some support to the notion that the Democrats lead in changing approaches to problems. In the section on time trends, we noted that the speeches given in the later years of the study were more concerned with the mention of wants and needs of the society and less concerned with specific methods of dealing with these needs. This nicely complements the Democrats' lower frequency of mention of structured, traditional modes of dealing with problems.

The upper left cells of Table 10.3 contain three tags that are mentioned more frequently by Republican candidates and that correlate positively with time: SELVES, GROUP, and SELF-ORIENTATION. All of these tags contain the entry words our, us, and we, and both SELVES and GROUP also contain ourselves. Since these four words comprise the total list of entry words for the tag SELVES and since the three tags have similarly different means in the Republican and Democratic speeches, it seems reasonable to assume that these differences are a function of these words. The predominant use of these inclusive pronouns is in reference to the candidate's party or to Americans in general. Unsubstantiated theorizing might suggest that the higher frequency of mention of these terms in Republican speeches is a product of the Republican party's status as a minority party. The theory might be that the Republican candidates perceive one of their problems to be the public's image of their party as one composed of elite groups. Perhaps they try to solve this problem by identifying themselves with all Americans and to use the inclusive plural pronouns for this purpose. At the same time, the Republicans must present a picture of a united party, and so the candidates refer to the party as we, us, and our.

Returning to Table 10.6, we see that there are a number of tags not included in Table 10.7 that lend support to the interpretation of greater Republican than Democratic emphasis on economic and technological issues and structured ways of dealing with issues. On the left side of Table 10.6, the tags WORK and GUIDE have many entry words in common with the tags ACHIEVEMENT and AUTHORITY. On the right side, the tag SPECIFICITY from the Lobbying Dictionary indicates a discrimination among objects, a specific framework through which to differentiate on the basis of some characteristic.

Another particularly interesting pattern of tags can be seen in Table 10.6. In the formulation of his dictionary for the study of lobbying groups, McPherson hypothesized that the FREEDOM and RESTRICTION tags in his dictionary would occur more frequently in text from conservative groups than in text from liberal groups. The tags are constructed to measure references to individual initiative, liberty, and freedom from centralized authority (FREEDOM) and to indicate a concern with interference and limitations imposed by outside authorities (RESTRICTION). McPherson's hypothesis relating to this rather straightforward measure of an attitude toward centralized government was substantiated by his own research, and if one accepts the notion that the Republican candidates are generally more conservative than their counterparts, it is also confirmed in this study.[7]

Stage III

As described earlier, Stage III of this analysis investigates the interrelationships of the tag categories in an attempt to delineate the principal dimensions of these relationships and to analyze the scores of the various speeches on these dimensions. The technique employed was principal components analysis. Two separate analyses were computed, one for each dictionary. No variates were excluded, and factor scores (in standard score form) were computed. Two factors were retained for each analysis. The factors in the principal position show a high degree of conceptual relevance to the questions of party difference and trends over time, thus rotational procedures were unnecessary. The amount of variance accounted for by the first two components for each analysis is shown in Table 10.8. The large amount of variance ac-

[7] A number of other conceptually exciting tags from the Psychosociological Dictionary are listed in Table 10.6 as occurring more frequently in the speeches of the GOP candidates. The tag ARTISTIC has already been discussed in the Stage I comparison of Goldwater and Johnson. The higher frequency of words indicating states of despair, shame, or failure (DISTRESS) might be a function of the fact that Republicans are more often in the challenger role in this study and are thus indentifying failure and weakness in the previous administration. The greater use of terms indicating FEMALE-ROLES and in particular the words she and her appears to be related to identification of the party and the country as having female gender, although the frequency of this tag is too low to be confidently interpreted. The problem of low frequency is also apparent in studying the tag LOWER-STATUS, which is composed of words specifically referring to roles in our society that are considered as lower status rather than peer or higher status. It might be hypothesized that the same structured framework that enables the Republican candidates to make references to moral obligations as demonstrated by the tag OUGHT enables them to reference lower status roles. Finally the tag ASCEND-THEME, composed of words associated with rising, falling, fire, and water and constructed to measure intensity of concerns related to the Icarus complex, also has higher frequency of occurrence in Republican speeches. The complexity of this tag, while rich in theoretical implications, makes it very difficult to interpret in a univariate analysis. The major dimensions of this tag, however, are very nicely defined in Stage III of this analysis.

TABLE 10.8. Percentage of Variance Accounted for by Principal Components

Psychosociological Dictionary		Lobbying Dictionary	
Factor	Percentage of Variance	Factor	Percentage of Variance
I	14.8	I	19.9
II	10.2	II	13.1
SUM	25.0	SUM	33.0

counted for by two factors, the small number of observations, and the conceptual relevance of the two sets of dimensions influenced the decision to retain only two factors.[8]

Interpretation of the Factor Spaces

Table 10.9 lists the tags with absolute loadings greater than .39 on either Factor I or Factor II for both of the analyses.[9]

The interpretation of the spaces defined by the factors is facilitated by referring to Figures 10.2 and 10.3, which show plots of these tags in the two-dimensional spaces. The terms on the plots appearing in capital letters are the labels given to the dimensions of the spaces defined by the tags. Following the procedure advocated by Kassenbaum, Couch, and Slater (1959), not only the primary dimensions are named but labels are also applied to the axes at 45-degree angles to the primary dimensions. The factor score-plots corresponding to the factor spaces are shown in Figures 10.4 and 10.5. When a candidate has given more than one acceptance speech, the appropriate year is shown next to his name. The exact scores of the speeches on the two primary axes for each analysis are listed in Table 10.10.

As seen in Figures 10.2 and 10.3, the factor spaces for the two analyses are quite similar. In each analysis the positive end of Factor I is labeled *UNIVERSALISTIC LEADERSHIP.* In the Lobbying

[8] This is a fairly large amount of variance accounted for in comparison with other studies using similar General Inquirer dictionaries. One reason is, of course, that we have only an *N* of twenty and thus only twenty positive latent roots with an average of 5 percent of the trace accounted for by each root.

[9] Five tags other than those meeting the specified criterion are also included in the description of the factor space in the Psychosociological Dictionary analyses. These tags, URGE, CAUSE, SIGN-WEAK, AVOID, and CONTROL, all had loadings of over .30 on one of the two factors and were felt to be of sufficient theoretical importance to be included in the analysis.

TABLE 10.9. Tags with Absolute Loadings Greater than .39 on Factor I or Factor II

Psychosociological Dictionary
Factor I*

Variable	I−	II	Variable	I+	II
ECONOMIC	−84	18	AFFECTION	67	30
ACTION-NORM	−74	07	ASCEND-THEME*	66	41
PLEASURE	−67	−10	HIGHER-STATUS	63	17
SOCIAL-PLACE	−66	31	SELVES*	59	45
OUGHT	−63	02	BODYPART	59	−12
TECHNOLOGICAL*	−63	45	MALE-ROLE	59	−02
THOUGHT-FORM	−58	00	RELIGIOUS*	58	41
AUTHORITY*	−57	50	SIGN-ACCEPT	54	09
NATURAL-OBJECT*	−52	42	RECREATIONAL	53	−33
FEMALE-THEME	−49	08	IDEAL-VALUE*	53	46
SMALL-GROUP	−49	−22	SENSE-REFERENCE	51	08
IF	−48	−17	ATTEMPT	51	20
SIGN-STRONG	−41	28	MILITARY	46	30
CONTROL	−38	26	FOLLOW	43	−04
CAUSE	−36	−08	NEUTER-ROLE	42	−04
SIGN-WEAK	−30	−30	THINK*	42	−49
			URGE	34	22

Factor II*

Variable	I	II−	Variable	I	II+
NOT	25	−69	SPATIAL-REFERENCE	17	58
SELF	31	−62	WORK	−01	55
COMMUNICATE	33	−60	NATURAL-WORLD	34	54
DEATH	−30	−50	LEGAL	15	54
THINK*	41	−49	AUTHORITY*	−57	50
SENSE	05	−47	APPROACH	−34	49
EQUAL	10	−47	FOOD	−17	48
UNDERSTATE	−07	−42	COMMUNITY	−03	46
SIGN-REJECT	−02	−40	IDEAL-VALUE*	53	46
DANGER-THEME	06	−40	SELVES*	59	45
AVOID	−04	−30	TECHNOLOGICAL*	63	45
			NATURAL-OBJECT*	−52	42
			RELIGIOUS*	58	41
			ASCEND-THEME*	66	41

Lobbying Dictionary
Factor I

Variable	I−	II	Variable	I+	II
ACTION-NORM	−87	20	SELF-ORIENTATION	83	36
MONEY	−86	29	OVERSTATE	70	28
PROVISION*	−66	52	GROUP	68	35
MESSAGE-FORM	−65	−27	INFLUENCE	66	21

TABLE 10.9. Cont.

Lobbying Dictionary

Factor I

Variable	I−	II	Variable	I+	II
ECONOMIC*	−56	64	UNIVERSALISM	64	32
INADEQUACY	−53	29	NONSPECIFIC-OBJECT	61	−25
POWER	−52	25	POSITIVE	60	28
LEGAL	−48	58	DIFFUSENESS*	59	50
QUANTITY-REFERENCE	−46	19	COMMITMENT*	51	48
POLITICAL	−42	−09	FREEDOM	46	36
			RELIGIOUS	42	11
			AFFECTIVITY*	41	−41

Factor II

Variable	I	II−	Variable	I	II+
COMMUNICATE	06	−54	ACHIEVEMENT	−03	71
TIME-REFERENCE	26	−50	ECONOMIC	−56	64
NEGATIVE	10	−50	RESTRICTION	03	59
AVOID	−06	−47	LEGAL	−49	58
GOOD	34	−45	COLLECTIVITY	36	53
AFFECTIVITY*	41	−41	PROVISION	−66	52
			ASCRIPTION	23	51
			COMMITMENT	48	51
			DIFFUSENESS	59	50
			PARTICULARISM	−18	43

* Tags with loadings of over 40 on both Factor I and Factor II.

Dictionary the tags INFLUENCE, UNIVERSALISM, POSITIVE, and GROUP, and in the Psychosociological Dictionary MALE-ROLE, SIGN-ACCEPT, HIGHER-STATUS, ATTEMPT, FOLLOW, and URGE represent the positive end of this dimension. At the negative end of Factor I, clusters of tags representing economic and monetary concerns appear: MONEY, ACTION-NORM, POWER, and QUANTITY-REFERENCE in the Lobbying Dictionary and in the Psychosociological Dictionary ECONOMIC, ACTION-NORM, OUGHT, THOUGHT-FORM, and PLEASURE. The positive end of Factor II in the Lobbying Dictionary analysis is labeled *INDIVIDUAL ACHIEVEMENT* and the negative end *REJECTION;* at the positive end the tags ACHIEVEMENT, PARTICULARISM, and RESTRICTION load heavily. At the negative end, the important tags are NEGATIVE, COMMUNICATE, and AVOID. In the Psychosociological Dictionary, the positive end of Factor II is represented by the tags COMMUNITY, FOOD, WORK, and LEGAL and at the negative end the tags DAN-

TABLE 10.10. Factor Scores

Psychosociological Dictionary

Republican Speeches				*Democratic Speeches*			
Year	*Candidate*	*I*	*II*	*Year*	*Candidate*	*I*	*II*
1928	Hoover	−1.15	0.97	1928	Smith	−1.57	0.89
1932	Hoover	−1.80	0.34	1932	Roosevelt	−1.01	−0.47
1936	Landon	−1.32	0.70	1936	Roosevelt	0.55	1.02
1940	Willkie	−0.30	−1.22	1940	Roosevelt	−0.29	−0.57
1944	Dewey	0.25	0.16	1944	Roosevelt	−0.57	−0.19
1948	Dewey	1.65	1.86	1948	Truman	−0.51	−1.34
1952	Eisenhower	1.34	1.84	1952	Stevenson	1.23	−2.04
1956	Eisenhower	0.29	−0.27	1956	Stevenson	0.78	−0.44
1960	Nixon	0.67	−0.49	1960	Kennedy	0.84	−1.06
1964	Goldwater	−0.15	0.03	1964	Johnson	1.07	0.27
	SUM	−.52	3.89		SUM	+.52	−3.89

Lobbying Dictionary

Republican Speeches				*Democratic Speeches*			
Year	*Candidate*	*I*	*II*	*Year*	*Candidate*	*I*	*II*
1928	Hoover	−1.05	1.43	1928	Smith	−1.72	0.59
1932	Hoover	−1.28	0.88	1932	Roosevelt	−0.83	0.08
1936	Landon	−0.78	1.19	1936	Roosevelt	−0.08	0.77
1940	Willkie	−0.49	0.00	1940	Roosevelt	0.07	−0.41
1944	Dewey	1.09	0.25	1944	Roosevelt	0.03	−0.81
1948	Dewey	1.33	0.73	1948	Truman	−1.71	−1.15
1952	Eisenhower	1.90	1.07	1952	Stevenson.	0.26	−2.33
1956	Eisenhower	−0.02	−0.22	1956	Stevenson	0.66	−1.05
1960	Nixon	0.53	−0.74	1960	Kennedy	0.20	−1.64
1964	Goldwater	0.39	0.47	1964	Johnson	1.49	0.91
	SUM	+1.63	+5.05		SUM	−1.63	−5.05

GER, SIGN-REJECT, SENSE, EQUAL, AVOID, and UNDERSTATE. The dimension is labeled *NORMATIVE COMMUNITY STRUCTURE* on the positive end and *REJECTION OF NORMATIVE STRUC-TURE* on the negative end.

In both analyses the upper-right fusion factor I+II+ is labeled *MORAL COMMITMENT*. The tags falling into this sector are similar: AFFECTION, ASCEND-THEME, SELVES, RELIGIOUS, IDEAL-VALUE, and MILITARY in the analysis using the Psychosociological Dictionary, and DIFFUSENESS, COMMITMENT, and FREEDOM in the Lobbying Dictionary analysis. At the opposite end of this dimension in the Psychosociological Dictionary analysis (the fusion factor end I−II−), the label *CRISIS* has been applied to reflect the influence of the tags

DEATH, SIGN-WEAK, and IF. In the Lobbying Dictionary analysis, the space I—II— is not well defined, but the tags POLITICAL and MESSAGE-FORM and the particular speeches that score heavily on this dimension reflect the label *DIRECT LEGISLATIVE ACTION ORIENTA-TION.* The fusion factor in the quadrant I—II+ in the Psychosocio-logical Dictionary analysis is labeled *STRUCTURED AUTHORITY.* The tag categories loading heavily on I—II+ are AUTHORITY, TECH-NOLOGICAL, NATURAL-OBJECT, CONTROL, SIGN-STRONG, APPROACH, and SOCIAL PLACE. At the opposite end, inspiring the label *INDI-VIDUAL COGNITIVE APPROACH* are three tags: THINK, COM-MUNICATE, and SELF-REFERENCE. In the Lobbying Dictionary the space I—II+ is labeled *ECONOMIC LEGISLATIVE CONCERNS* and the opposite end, I+II—, is labeled *AFFECTIVITY.* The tags LEGAL, ECONOMIC, and PROVISION load into I—II+, and the tags AFFECTIVITY, GOOD, and TIME-REFERENCE load into I+II—.

As noted earlier, more extensive arguments can be made in defense of the labeling. However, a dramatic indication of the correspondence between these factor analyses and some of the results of the Stage I and Stage II analyses can be seen by looking at the relationship of the factor scores with our first two areas of interest: trends over time and differences between parties.[10]

[10] We must remain aware of three important facts while interpreting dimensions defined by factor analytic techniques. (1) The structure of the factor space and the correlations between the various concepts are, of course, determined by the particular uses of words by the particular candidates measured here. Thus, if Kefauver had been nominated for President in 1956 instead of Stevenson, it might have affected certain correlations between the variables and thus affected the factor space. We note that this is a very good reason not to make the mistake of drawing inferences from this study to future or past candidates, since by no stretch of the imagination do these speeches represent a random sample of acceptance speeches. (2) A very im-portant reason exists for lumping all of the variables of a particular dictionary together in a factor analysis. Unlike attitude scales or questionnaires measuring par-ticular concerns with separate questions, a speech or written document consists of practically unrestrained response to a certain situation. There are no yes-no restric-tions or seven-point scales to confine the response of the subject to the stimulus. There is no way to control the candidate's interrelating of issues with means or with personal attitudes, and thus separation of levels becomes practically impossible. (3) The reader can probably think of a number of reasons for rejecting even the very weak assumptions made about the data in the application of the technique of prin-cipal components analysis: nonindependence of tags and nonadditivity of tag fre-quencies because of the constraints of the language and nonsubstitutability of entry words within certain tags are only two possible reasons for rejection. A slightly more subtle objection is produced by the construction of the two dictionaries used here, since in each dictionary the same entry words are often shared by more than one tag. Thus, there are a number of part-part correlations that affect the makeup of the factor space.

Time Trends and Party Differences

As seen in Table 10.11 the scores on Factor I for both analyses correlate quite highly and positively with time (.726 and .738). The early speeches in this study tend to have negative scores on this factor,

TABLE 10.11. Relationship of Scores on Principal Components to Time and Political Party

Psychosociological Dictionary			Lobbying Dictionary		
	Factor			Factor	
	I	II		I	II
r with time	.726	−.27	r with time	.738	−.41
t between parties	−.25	1.73	t between parties	.73	2.22
Democratic mean	+.05	−.39	Democratic mean	−.16	−.50
Republican mean	−.05	+.39	Republican mean	+.16	+.50

and the later speeches have positive scores. (See Table 10.10 and Figures 10.4 and 10.5.)

The scores of the candidates on Factor II for both analyses correlate moderately and negatively with time (−.27 and −.41). Given these two sets of figures, we could roughly plot a time dimension onto Figures 10.2 and 10.3. This time dimension would extend from the quadrant I+II− to the quadrant I−II+ in the figures and from the box in both figures labeled *TIME,* through the origin, and down into I−II+. Conceptually the correspondence between the ends of this hypothetical *TIME* dimension and the results of the Stages I and II analysis is clear. The general movement of the speeches is from *TRADITIONAL ECONOMIC ORIENTATION* and *STRUC-TURED AUTHORITY* to *INDIVIDUAL COGNITIVE AP-PROACH* and *UNIVERSALISTIC LEADERSHIP* in the Psychosociological Dictionary analyses. Many of the same variables defining these dimensions were isolated in the Stage II discussion of time trends and party differences.

Returning to Table 10.11, we note that for both analyses the *t* scores comparing the means of the Democratic and Republican speeches on Factor II are moderately large and positive. In both cases, the Republican speeches have a substantially larger mean score than the Democratic speeches. The mean scores for the Republican and Democratic speeches are plotted in Figures 10.4 and 10.5. As was

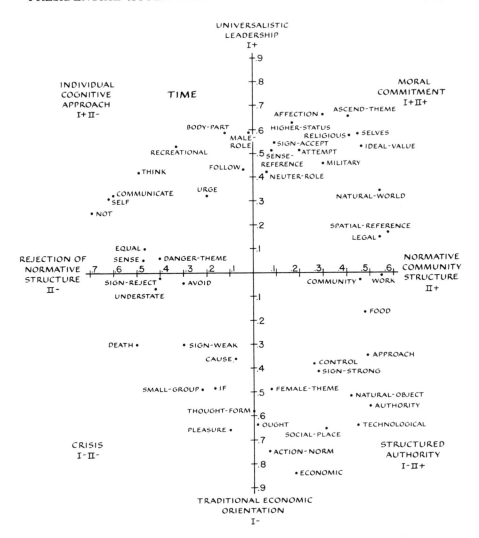

FIGURE 10.2. Factor loadings: Harvard III dictionary.

noted with the time dimension, considerable congruence can be seen
between this analysis and the analysis of differences between the two
political parties in Stage II. Those tags listed in Table 10.6 as occurring more frequently in Republican speeches tend to occur on the
positive side of Factor II, while those occurring more frequently in
Democratic speeches occur on the negative side of Factor II.

In summary, there is an over-all time trend toward the upper-left

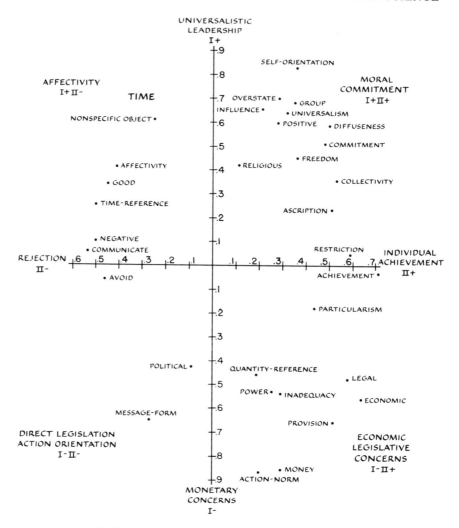

FIGURE 10.3. Factor loadings: Lobbying dictionary.

quadrant. Earlier candidates from both parties tend to be in the lower right, more recent ones toward the upper left. At any particular time, the Republican candidate should be more toward the right. With this frame of reference, we turn to the comparison of the candidates for each election.

Comparison of Pairs of Candidates' Speeches

Often an interpretation of a factor analysis makes good sense only to the interpreter. In a situation with many variables, measuring many

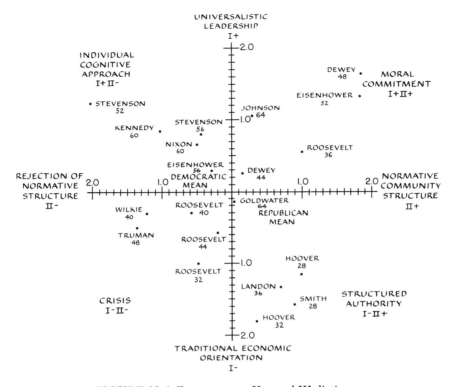

FIGURE 10.4. Factor scores: Harvard III dictionary.

different levels of conceptualization of behavior (roles, motives, social-emotional activity, institutions, psychological themes) the situation becomes very complex. We have been constantly juggling variables that relate to at least three different aspects of the speeches:

1. The issues raised by the candidates.
2. The articulated approach of the candidates to these issues.
3. The relationship of the candidate to his audience, immediate and national, as measured directly by his use of pronouns and reference to party, country, and so forth, and indirectly by his psychological attitude such as confidence, defensiveness, and so forth.

Possibly a better approach to the analysis of these data would have been to construct dictionaries to measure separately each of these aspects of variables that are consistent with a particular level of interest. A description of these 20 speeches should not, however, totally separate these aspects because they are in no sense independent. Their expression in a given speech is interactive for at least three reasons: the

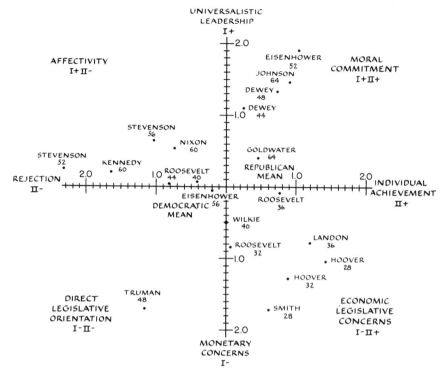

FIGURE 10.5. Factor scores: Lobbying dictionary.

party of the candidate, the year of the candidate's speech, and the personality of the candidate.

To study the effect of these aspects and to control for the year of delivery, we chose the strategy of working with pairs of candidates: Hoover and Smith in 1928, Hoover and Roosevelt in 1932, and so on through the ten presidential election years. Each pair of candidates for a given year was compared in the context of the factor spaces on the three specified levels of analysis and the common and party specific trends noted. A residual benefit of this approach is that we conclude by comparing the candidates of 1964, Goldwater and Johnson.

Within the context of our factor analyses, little difference appears to exist between the 1928 candidates. In both plots, Hoover and Smith are located in the lower-right quadrant. Their emphasis is on economic, monetary, and technological issues, and their means are within a framework of structured authority relationships and moral imperatives indicated by the tags POWER, ACTION-NORM, AUTHORITY-

THEME, OUGHT, CONTROL, SIGN-STRONG, and LEGAL. No tags measuring role references are located in this quadrant, but the concerns occurring here are negatively correlated with the tag SELF in the Psychosociological Dictionary.

Hoover's 1932 speech also appears in the lower-right quadrant (Figures 10.4 and 10.5). Since he was faced with the necessity of defending his pre- and postdepression policies, his speech can be characterized as largely concerned with MONETARY and ECONOMIC issues to be resolved within the traditional framework. Hoover did not shy from articulating a number of policies to relieve the crisis and to be carried out by the federal government, but he did continue to stress his ultimate goal, which was oriented toward the local business philosophy. Roosevelt's 1932 speech, while located in the same quadrant in the Lobbying Dictionary analysis, marked the beginning of a trend away from the negative end of Factor I. Figure 10.1 shows that Roosevelt's 1932 speech has the second highest mention of the tag URGE. His explicit recognition of the wants and needs of the society is combined with a movement, relative to Smith's speech, toward the negative end of Factor II, which for both analyses is characterized by Truman's and Willkie's issue-oriented speeches. No tags referencing specific roles or role orientations are located in this quadrant. (See Figures 10.2 and 10.3.)

Again, in 1936, the Republican nominee, Landon, is located in the lower-right quadrant of both of our analyses, indicating high frequency of mention of many of the same issues that appeared in the earlier speeches of Hoover. Roosevelt's 1936 speech dramatically continued the trend of Democratic party candidates toward the positive end of Factor I. In the terms of our analysis of scores on the Psychosociological Dictionary, his movement toward the positive end on this factor was premature, since no other candidate received as high a score until Dewey in 1944. In the context of our analysis, the speech is seen to be quite different from the other three Roosevelt speeches. It is less issue oriented and moves away from the quadrant I+II— toward the quadrant I+II+, signaling emphasis on *MORAL COMMITMENT*. By 1936, the frequency of reference to the concept SELVES was higher for the Democratic candidate for the first time, reflecting the broad electorate to whom Roosevelt was appealing.

The speeches of the 1940 and 1944 candidates can be considered together. All four speeches emphasized foreign policy to a greater extent than the other speeches up to this time and all pledged a united front in the war effort. Roosevelt's 1940 and 1944 speeches are grouped very closely together in both analyses. Although not particularly outstanding in any one of our dimensions, they are both slightly less positive than Roosevelt's ('36) speech on Factor I and slightly more negative on Factor II, a movement back toward *CRISIS* in the Psychosociological Dictionary analysis and toward *DIRECT LEGISLATIVE ACTION* in the Lobbying Dictionary analysis. Willkie's 1940 speech closely resembles the Roosevelt speeches on our dimensions. He viewed himself as "a liberal Democrat who changed his party affiliation because he found democracy in the Republican party and not in the New Deal." As can be seen in the analysis of the Psychosociological Dictionary scores, his speech resembles the very specific issue-oriented speech of Truman. Although Willkie claimed that "An acceptance speech is a candidate's keynote, a declaration of his broad principles," his long speech outlined "the problems of our great domestic economy, as well as our national defense. . . ." Dewey, on the other hand, faced with the current participation of the United States in the war, questioned the present policies only in a broad, largely nonissue-oriented manner. This approach, shown by his position in quadrant I+II+ (*MORAL COMMITMENT*) in both analyses, was later magnified in his 1948 speech and in Eisenhower's 1952 speech.

Truman's very direct "hell-raising" speech contrasts sharply with the elevated nonissue orientation of Dewey (1948). An indication of this can be seen by listing some words that occur a number of times in the Truman speech but do not occur at all in the Dewey speech. Table 10.12 contains a short list of those words. Truman spoke of his struggle with the Eightieth Congress and of the need for specific legislative action on many issues. Dewey equated his own and his party's ideals with the ideals of the American people, and in a broad statement he called for a *MORAL COMMITMENT* to these principles: "When these rights are secure in this world of ours the permanent ideals of the Republican party shall have been realized. The ideals of the American people are the ideals of the Republican party."

Neither Eisenhower (1952) nor Stevenson (1952) devoted much attention to specific issues or legislative programs.[11] Stevenson's sensi-

[11] The Eisenhower (1952) speech was so nonissue oriented that he did not even mention the conflict in Korea.

TABLE 10.12. Occurrences of Words Indicating Issue Orientation in the Speeches of the 1948 Candidates*

Word	Number of References	Word	Number of References
act(s)	5	income	10
bill	24	legislation	3
benefit(s)	10	price(s)	9
committee(s)	6	tax	4
congress	19	teachers	2
did	8	United Nations	2
dollars	6		
get	13		
housing	11		

* The words listed occur in the Truman speech and do not occur in Dewey's 1948 speech. The number of references in the Truman speech is listed next to the word.

tive, introspective examination of his own role and of the role of the Democratic party and the American people in modern society contrasts sharply with Eisenhower's interpretation of the campaign as a "battle" and the Republican party's role as leading a "crusade." To the American electorate and within the context of our analysis, these two men represent extreme positions. Eisenhower's image as a war hero returning home from Germany to unite and lead the Republican party to victory was entirely congruent with the style and emphasis of his speech. Stevenson's speech, while articulate in style, offered only complex analyses of generally misunderstood problems. No other candidate in the study is located so far out on our dimension of *MORAL COMMITMENT* as Eisenhower, and no other candidate is located so far out on the dimensions of *INDIVIDUAL COGNITIVE APPROACH* and *REJECTION* as Stevenson. In fact, the speeches of the following years may be considered as compromises of these two extreme positions. The 1956 speeches of these same two candidates can be interpreted in this manner; perhaps Stevenson's approach was tempered by his loss in 1952, and Eisenhower's by four years of presidency. Each candidate dealt more with specific issues than in his earlier speech and in the framework of our analyses, each moved toward the center of our factor score spaces, the Eisenhower speech more acutely than the Stevenson speech.

The speeches of Nixon and Kennedy are similar in many respects to the speeches of the 1956 candidates. Both speeches are moderately issue oriented; both contain references to foreign as well as to domestic issues; neither speech proposes extensive specific legislation. The means orientation of the Kennedy speech concentrates on defining the spirit of the "New Frontier," while the Nixon speech concentrates on continuing and "building on" the previous accomplishments of the Eisenhower administrations. None of the speeches of the 1956 and 1960 candidates are outstanding in emphasis of any particular pronoun or role reference. Figures 10.4 and 10.5 show the speeches of Nixon and Kennedy located quite close together. In the framework of our factor analyses, each represents a compromise of the extreme positions defined in the 1952 speeches. It is further evident from inspection of these figures and the factor-loading plots that these speeches deviate very little from their expected position on the dimension defined by the correlations of time with our factors.

If we make the assumption that the candidates from the various years spoke as representatives of their parties (as collectivities), then we see that within the factor-score spaces the paths of the parties to reach like positions in 1960 were quite different. The Republican party speeches, with one exception, are all located on the positive side of Factor II. Their early speeches (1928, 1932, 1936) all lie in the quadrant defined by monetary and economic concerns and structured authority relationships. Willkie's speech (the exception noted earlier) can be viewed in this context as the first of four major Republican changes in emphasis. His approach, however, was not followed by Dewey in 1944. Dewey's speech, the second major change, was located on the positive side of Factor II (*NORMATIVE COMMUNITY STRUCTURE* and *INDIVIDUAL ACHIEVEMENT*) though now the party, as represented by his speech, had de-emphasized the concerns of the negative end of Factor I and instead was moving out on the fusion factor dimension (I+II+) labeled *MORAL COMMITMENT*. The speeches of Dewey in 1948 and Eisenhower in 1952 have been seen to lie on the extreme of this dimension. The third major change in emphasis was noted in the discussion of Eisenhower's 1956 speech, which is located on the negative side of Factor II. This speech and Nixon's 1960 speech are seen to be little different from the corresponding speeches of their Democratic opponents. The fourth major change in Republican party emphasis occurred in 1964.

The path of the Democratic party speeches is marked by five major changes. In general, the Democratic speeches are located on the negative side of Factor II in both analyses. Smith's speech in 1928 was very similar to the early Republican speeches. The first change came with Roosevelt's 1932 speech (moving toward the positive end of Factor I and the negative end of Factor II) relative to the Smith speech. This movement away from the traditional issues and approaches preceded by eight years a similar movement by the Republican Wendell Willkie. Although Roosevelt's 1936 speech (the second major shift) can be viewed as a return to the concerns of the positive end of Factor II, the shift can also be interpreted as a function of his wide national popularity rather than as a function of a change in policy. The location of the Roosevelt 1940 and 1948 speeches close to the center of our factor-score spaces reinforces this latter interpretation. The third shift in Democratic emphasis was short-lived. Truman's policy-oriented approach was directly opposed to the appeal made by his opponent. In terms of our analysis, the 1948 speeches are further apart than any other pair of speeches in our study. The fourth major shift was also short-lived, occurring in Stevenson's 1952 speech. His dramatic movement toward the positive end of Factor I and the negative end of Factor II was modified in the fifth major change in emphasis, his 1956 speech. This speech has already been interpreted as being very similar to Kennedy's 1960 speech, and in the context of our analyses it is seen to be located between Stevenson's 1952 position and Eisenhower's 1952 position.

Johnson's speech can be viewed as a continuation of this last approach. As mentioned earlier, his emphasis on leader-follower relationships and on specification of the wants and needs of the society is unique to our sample. His over-all orientation, however, including lack of emphasis on specific legislative programs, and his broad appeal to the electorate was similar to the speeches of the 1956 and 1960 candidates. Thus, within this framework, Johnson's speech does not represent a major shift in Democratic party emphasis. His position in the factor-score spaces (Figures 10.4 and 10.5) shows some deviation from speeches of the previous eight years, but might be considered to correspond to an "expected" movement on the time dimensions with emphasis on *UNIVERSALISTIC LEADERSHIP.*

Goldwater's speech, however, can be interpreted as the fourth major shift in Republican party emphasis. Relative to the speeches of the recent candidates, Goldwater's speech represents a move toward the positive ends of Factor II (*NORMATIVE COMMUNITY STRUC-*

TURE and *INDIVIDUAL ACHIEVEMENT*) and the negative ends of Factor I (*MONETARY* and *TRADITIONAL ECONOMIC CONCERNS*). One explanation of this movement might be that Goldwater's speech is simply a partial return to high frequency of mention of the concerns that characterized the early speeches in our study. This is not, however, the situation. Goldwater's speech was characterized in the Stage I analysis as being particularly high in the identification of problems in terms of the weaknesses and failures of the previous administration. He saw the correction of these "failures" as a "cause" for the Republican party. His speech was further characterized by high frequency of mention of the words "free" and "freedom" and low frequency of occurrence of the tag GET, a variable indicating action orientation. In the earlier stage, we also note that his speech contained only a few references to tags indicating economic concern (ECONOMIC in the Psychosociological Dictionary and MONEY in the Lobbying Dictionary). At the same time, the scores for this speech on the variables POWER, AUTHORITY-THEME, and ACTION-NORM are generally higher than for any speech since 1936. Thus we can see that the Goldwater speech does not represent a general over-all return to the types of issues and positions that define the quadrant I—II+ (*MONETARY CONCERNS, ECONOMIC LEGISLATIVE CONCERNS* and *INDIVIDUAL ACHIEVEMENT* in the Lobbying Dictionary analysis, and *TRADITIONAL ECONOMIC ORIENTATION, STRUCTURED AUTHORITY,* and *NORMATIVE COMMUNITY STRUCTURE* in the Psychosociological Dictionary analysis). The very high frequency of mention of the words "free" and "freedom" lead to high scores on the tags FREEDOM, IDEAL-VALUE, and ASCEND-THEME, which characterize the upper-right quadrants (*MORAL COMMITMENT*). The speech has relatively high frequency of occurrence of tags suggesting the traditional authority structure, but low frequency of mention of tags indicating the traditional economic issue concerns. The picture is thus of a candidate combining the traditional authority orientation with an emphasis on a *MORAL COMMITMENT* to solve modern-day problems.

SUMMARY AND CONCLUSIONS

This paper reports an application of two content analysis category systems derived from psychological and sociological theory to the study of twenty well-known political speeches. All Democratic and Republican Presidential Nomination Acceptance Speeches from 1928 to 1964 were analyzed. Three methodological aspects of the study should be considered:

1. A three-stage research strategy was used to study the content of the speeches. This approach was also used in the presentation of the results. Stage I consisted of analysis of graphed results and focused on differences between the 1964 candidates. Stage II used univariate summary measures to determine which tag categories apparently varied linearly in frequency over time and which categories distinguished between the parties. Stage III consisted of a principal component analysis of the category systems and an analysis of the scores of the speeches on the resulting components. This approach was considered by the investigators to be useful for structuring and organizing the comparisons and analysis procedures employed in the study. The utility of the three-stage design for the presentation of results is less clear; the approach may help the reader understand the analysis decisions made by the investigator, but there was redundancy in presenting the information. It should be noted that while this approach may be useful for a descriptive, hypothesis-generating study, it probably should not be followed for a primarily hypothesis-testing study.

2. This was the first General Inquirer study to use two distinct sets of dictionary categories in an analysis. Insofar as the results from both analyses were congruent, the use of two systems can be considered as both complementary and redundant. Certain issues, however, were clarified by simultaneous use of the two category systems. For example, the tag POWER in the Lobbying Dictionary and the tag AUTHORITY-THEME in the Psychosociological Dictionary were both found to correlate negatively with time. POWER, however, was found to occur more frequently in speeches of the Democratic candidates and AUTHORITY-THEME was found to occur more frequently in Republican speeches. Although both tags support the finding of diminishing reliance over time on structured normative ways of expressing solutions to problems, the differences between the entry lists of the tags pointed out an important difference between the political parties that might otherwise have been overlooked. The Republican speeches had higher frequency of mention of traditional, established references to authority while the Democratic speeches had higher frequency of mention of terms implying pragmatic means of exercising control.

3. In the introduction to the paper the question of the value of imposing a psychological and/or sociological framework on political data

was raised. Neither dictionary was constructed in a framework typical of former political content analyses. The utility or value of this type of analysis should not, of course, be judged in the absence of a second comparative analysis of the same speeches, an analysis employing a traditional political-science-oriented category system. To the extent, however, that a coherent set of results did evolve from the data, we feel that the choice of dictionaries was justified.

The analysis focused on characteristics of the speeches from which inferences could be made about trends over time common to the candidate of both parties, differences between the candidate of the two parties, and ways in which the 1964 candidates differed from each other and from the other candidates represented in the study. These characteristics can roughly be grouped into three areas: issues raised by the candidate, the exercise of means of dealing with the issues, and characteristics reflecting personality aspects of particular candidates.

Over time, there is a general decrease in reference to words and phrases indicating concern with domestic economic issues. The issue orientations in later speeches tend to be more diffuse, generally covering many domestic areas as well as foreign policy issues. This decrease in emphasis on traditional economic concern is paralleled by a negative correlation with time for a cluster of tags referring to normative modes of behavior, moral imperatives, and words signifying strength and authority. This suggests that 30 or 40 years ago the structure of society was such that men attempting to exercise power and control over others could rely on specific authority relationships, on obligations and duties, and on accepted standards of behavior.

In recent speeches, less use has been made of relatively direct means of control and persuasion. Instead, there has been a steady increase over time of clusters of tags referring to need and desires, goal-directed behavior, and indirect-influence attempts. In recent years, candidates have attempted to win others to their position by appealing to the needs and desires of their audience, by indicating specific means that will be taken to achieve desired goals, and by attempting to affect the behavior and decisions of others without appeal to authority relationships.

These trends have been consistent for speeches by members of both parties, but the Republicans have been generally slower to abandon the appeals to both the domestic economic issues and to the traditional established authority structure for resolution of problems. While the Republicans have a higher frequency of mention of tags relating to established authority and moral imperatives, the Democrats place greater emphasis on particular pragmatic means of controlling the behavior of others. At the same time, the Republican speeches were seen to have a greater frequency of words referring to normative community structure, to individual initiative and liberty, and to freedom from centralized authority.

Within this general framework, combinations of political situations and personality characteristics of certain candidates apparently interacted to produce important deviations. In 1948, for example, both Truman and Dewey deviated from the preceding speeches. Truman, in an uphill battle for election, placed great emphasis on enumerating many specific issues while attacking the incumbent congress. Dewey apparently took the strategy of elevating himself above specific controversies and issued a broad moral appeal to the electorate. Similarly, Eisenhower in 1952, enjoying a widespread popularity, also spoke in general moral tones, making only a few references to specific issues. Stevenson, in the same year, spoke introspectively about his own presidential qualifications while examining in an intellectualized fashion the complexities of modern society. It is not surprising that the personality of a candidate for the office of President of the United States should produce a distinctive stamp on the candidate's, nomination acceptance speech. Each of the speeches, however, had identifiable components reflecting the changing importance of issues and methods over time and the impact of their affiliation with one of the two political parties. An analysis of these speeches then should consider both elements.

The final focus of comparison was on the speeches of the 1964 candidates. Johnson's speech, adding to the general trend, was oriented toward persuasion and appeals to needs and desires. A repeated rhetorical device was the use of the phrase, "Most Americans want. . . . And so do I." The speech was characterized by high reference to leadership and to words such as unanimous, every, unity, and general. The picture projected is that of a confident and strong leader appealing to a broad electorate. The appeal was widespread and universalistic in nature.

Goldwater's speech, in contrast, was atypical in that it scored high on variables related to direct power appeals, authority themes, and moral commitment. These were generally more pronounced than for any speech since 1936. The issues with which he dealt, however, were not the traditional economic concerns but the failures and weakness of the previous administration. Goldwater's speech therefore reflected a belief in the power of traditional authority structure and moral commitment to resolve the problems of contemporary society.

BIBLIOGRAPHY

Danielson, W. A., and J. B. Adams (1961), "Completeness of Press Coverage of the 1960 Campaign." *Journalism Quarterly,* Vol. 38, 441–452.

Hayworth, D. (1930), "An Analysis of Speeches in the Presidential Campaigns from 1884–1920." *Quarterly Journal of Speech,* Vol. 16, 35–42.

Kassenbaum, G., A. Couch, and P. Slater (1959), "The Factorial Dimensions of the MMPI." *Journal of Consulting Psychology,* Vol. 23:3, 226–236.

McDiarmid, J. (1937), "Presidential Inaugural Addresses: A study of verbal symbols." *Public Opinion Quarterly,* Vol. 1:79–82, July.

McPherson, W. (1964), "Lobbying and Communications Processes." Paper read at American Political Science Association Meeting, Chicago.

The New York Times, July 17, 1964, and August 27, 1964.

Official Proceedings of the Democratic National Convention, 1928–1960.

Official Proceedings of the Republican National Convention, 1928–1960.

Prothro, J. W. (1956), "Verbal Shifts in the American Presidency: A Content Analysis." *American Political Science Review,* Vol. 50:3 (Sept.), 726–739.

Rucker, B. W. (1960), "News' Services Crowd Reporting in the 1955 Presidential Campaign." *Journalism Quarterly,* Vol. 37, 195–198.

Smith, M. S., P. J. Stone, and E. Glenn (1965), "A Content Analysis of Twenty Presidential Nomination Acceptance Speeches." Department of Social Relations, Harvard University, February, mimeographed.

Stempel, G. H. III (1961), "The Prestige Press Covers the 1960 Presidential Campaign." *Journalism Quarterly,* Vol. 38, 157–163.

White, H. B. (1956), "Commentary on Prothro's Content Analysis." *American Political Science Review,* Vol. 50:3 (Sept.), 740–750.

CHAPTER ELEVEN

Elite Editorial Comment on the European and Atlantic Communities in Four Countries[1]

J. Zvi Namenwirth
Yale University

Thomas L. Brewer
Yale University

INTRODUCTION

This study considers the question of whether political integration has increased or declined with the European and Atlantic Com-

[1] The authors wish to acknowledge the advice and assistance of Karl W. Deutsch and Richard L. Merritt of Yale. They also wish to thank Philip J. Stone and Marshall S. Smith of Harvard for their criticisms and aid in computation, and Hayward R. Alker and Robert L. Peterson for valuable comments on an earlier draft. Erik Steiner deserves special mention for his computer programming and operation. In addition, several other people have participated at various stages of the data preparation and analysis: Michiko Leiserson, Janica Towne, Kathleen Dilzer and Fred Bamber. Mike Farrell has contributed summaries of editorials and prepared several of the tables. Research utilized in this chapter was supported in part by the United States Arms Control and Disarmament Agency. Any judgments or opinions expressed herein are those of the authors and do not necessarily reflect the views of the United States Arms Control and Disarmament Agency or any other department or agency of the United States government. This study was initiated as part of a larger project conducted at Yale University under the direction of Karl Deutsch. Additional financial aid during the final stages of preparation of the paper came from the Yale Political Data Program, which is supported by a National Science Foundation Grant and administered by Bruce M. Russett.

401

munities during the past decade. Specifically, we have attempted to assess this by measuring trends of elite orientations in four countries: Britain, France, West Germany, and the United States. These orientations are inferred from editorial comment published in four "prestige" newspapers: *The Times* (London), *Le Monde, Frankfurter Allgemeine Zeitung,* and *The New York Times.*

CONCEPTS AND THEORIES

The process of supranational integration consists of changes in four constituent elements: decision-making patterns (both official and unofficial),[2] transaction flows,[3] and mass[4] and elite perspectives. Although elite perspectives are the major concern in this paper, we do not imply that elite orientations are necessarily the most important component in the process. Neither do we imply that there are no relationships among the four components. Indeed the interplay between the objective constituents (decision-making patterns and transaction flows) and subjective ones (mass and elite perspectives) provides one of the most important but unexplored facets of the process of integration. Changes in elite orientations, however, do provide a dimension of the process; to the extent that elite orientations in the four countries included in our study have become more supranational, there has been greater integration in the Western European and Atlantic areas.

In a previous study of the North Atlantic area, the organizing concepts of this investigation have been further substantiated by Karl Deutsch:

> By *integration* we mean the attainment, within a territory, of "a sense of community" and of institutions and practices strong enough and wide-

[2] A supranational trend in regional institutions in Western Europe for the period of 1946–1961 has been documented and explicated by Namenwirth (1963). Haas (1958), in his study of the European Coal and Steel Community, and Lindberg (1963), in his study of the European Economic Community, both give theoretical and empirical treatment of the patterns of authoritative and nonauthoritative decision making in Western Europe.

[3] Transaction flows refer to the pattern of intercountry movements in trade, mail, students, immigration, etc. For indications of the relevance of such movements to supranational integration, see Deutsch (1954) and Russett (1963). Transaction flows in Western Europe and the North Atlantic area are presented by Russett (1963) and by Alker and Puchala (1965).

[4] Donald J. Puchala (1964) has conducted an analysis of responses to questions about Western European integration in USIA public opinion polls during the period of 1952–1961.

spread enough to assure, for a "long" time, dependable expectations of "peaceful change" among its population.

By *sense of community* we mean a belief on the part of individuals that they have come to agreement on at least this one point: that common social problems must and can be resolved by processes of "peaceful change."

(Deutsch, 1957, 5)[5]

Elaborating on this latter concept, he states,

The kind of sense of community that is relevant for integration . . . is a matter of mutual sympathy and loyalties; of "we feeling," trust, and mutual consideration; of partial identification in terms of self-images and interests; of mutually successful predictions of behavior, and of cooperative action in accordance with it — in short, a matter of perpetual dynamic process of mutual attention, communication, perception of needs, and responsiveness in the process of decision-making.

(Deutsch, 1957, 36)

Counterpoised to the concept of political community at the international level is the concept of nationalism, or national self-consciousness:

National consciousness . . . is the attachment of secondary symbols of nationality to primary items of information moving through channels of social communication, or through the mind of an individual. Not wit, but "French wit"; not thoroughness, but "German thoroughness" . . . .

(Deutsch, 1953, 146)

With these conceptual formulations in mind, two operational indices of changes in elite orientations were selected: (*a*) *attention to national and regional symbols and* (*b*) *the degree of similarity in the orientations in the four countries.* Attention to national and regional symbols provides an index of national and regional consciousness. Thus increasing attention to *regional* symbols and at the same time declining attention to *national* symbols indicate increasing regional integration: opposite trends conversely imply decreasing integration. Likewise, similarity of elite orientations is another indication of growing regional integration since such similarity is a prerequisite for the probability of "mutually successful predictions of behavior." Without

---

[5] Although we have referred to integration as a *process,* and the passage cited defines it as a *condition,* the citation is otherwise in accord with our own notion. See Haas (1958, 16) and Lindberg (1963, 5–6).

these shared frames of reference, any common understanding or action is quite difficult to establish and maintain.

Using these two sets of indices, we have attempted to answer the following questions: (*a*) What are the differences over time and among countries in attention to national and regional symbols? and (*b*) What are the differences over time and among countries in the similarity of orientations?

DICTIONARY CATEGORIES

The theoretical concerns thus far explored provide the rationale for the list of dictionary categories incorporated in our content analysis. The particular dictionary used in this investigation was devised by adding several tag categories to a list of 83 taken from the Harvard III Dictionary. Most of the tag categories of the dictionary are well suited to the needs of this study; among them are some traditionally important aspects of political orientations: ECONOMIC, MILITARY, and LEGAL. The tags of the Harvard III Dictionary enabled us to determine the similarity in elite orientations in terms of some fundamental sociological and psychological concepts.

The existing dictionary was expanded for the following reasons and in the following manner. To facilitate the investigation of growing similarity in orientations, we created the tag categories SOVIET, AMERICAN, BRITISH, FRENCH, GERMAN, EUROPEAN, ATLANTIC, NATIONALIST, UNIFICATION, and INTERNATIONAL-INSTITUTION. The five national categories (SOVIET through GERMAN) largely contain references to governmental and military personnel, other politicians, names of capitals, and national institutions. Similarly, the two regional categories comprised supranationally employed personnel and names and institutions identified with such international authorities. The tag NATIONALIST contains articulated references of nationalist policies and creeds, sovereignty, self-determination, autarky, and tariff. The tag UNIFICATION is a list of synonyms describing political and/or economic cooperation and unity. The tag INTERNATIONAL-INSTITUTION contains the names of all Western European and Atlantic treaties, institutions, and offices. This list of tags can be divided into two qualitatively distinct groups. Whereas NATIONALIST and UNIFICATION articulate ideological concerns, the other seven concepts contain terms describing concrete features of the national and supranational political processes. Of these descriptive categories, the four national and two regional categories were also used to test our hypotheses about changing concerns with national and regional matters in the process of integration.

To improve our understanding of editorial criticisms of existing political arrangements, we created a number of fairly general categories, such as CORRUPTION, INCOMPETENCE, COLLECTIVE-STATIC, INDIVIDUAL-STATIC, COLLECTIVE-DYNAMIC, and INDIVIDUAL-DYNAMIC. Since these categories did not differentiate among either papers or years, further discussion seems superfluous.

ELITE NEWSPAPERS

This source of elite orientations selected for analysis is the "prestige" newspaper editorial. The use of prestige papers as sources of elite attitudes was introduced in *The Hoover Institute Studies* conducted in the early 1950's. Justifying the selection of one elite newspaper per country, the authors stated,

> . . . In each major power one newspaper stands out as an organ of elite opinion. Usually semiofficial, always intimate with the government, these "prestige papers" are read by public officials, journalists, scholars, and business leaders. They seldom have large circulations, yet they have enormous influence. They are read not only in their own countries, but also abroad by those whose business it is to keep track of world affairs. They differ among themselves, but despite national and temporal differences, they are a distinct species. It is generally possible to name with fair confidence one paper in any given country which plays the role of prestige paper at any given time.
>
> (Pool, 1952, 1)

There is, therefore, an assumption that there is a rather high correlation between the content of prestige paper editorials and the orientations of national political elites.

RESEARCH DESIGN AND METHODS

The editorials analyzed in this study constitute a stratified random sample drawn from a list of all editorials dealing with European or

Atlantic topics in 1953 and 1963.[6] The sample consists of 192 editorials divided evenly between the two years and among the four papers, thereby allowing for time and country comparisons. The stratified sample contains six editorials per quarter, four quarters per year for each paper and year.

To increase confidence in our findings, a procedure was devised whereby the 24 editorials for each paper and year were numbered consecutively, and the eight strata (4 papers × 2 years) of editorials were further split in half by an odd-even number procedure. This procedure resulted in two nearly independent subsamples of 96 editorials, each of which was analyzed separately. Two nearly independent experiments were consequently performed.

To analyze differential concerns with the 99 dictionary categories, the General Inquirer program produced absolute and percentage frequencies of the words in each category for each editorial.[7] The percentage frequencies are ratios of the frequency of specific categories to the frequency of all words contained in each editorial. These percentage frequencies enabled us to control for the variable lengths of editorials, and they were the basic data of all further analysis.

All 99 categories were subjected to a two-way analysis of variance in order to ascertain differences between the units of comparison. Thus *newspaper* and *year* are the main effects of this design. The *interaction* describes particular combinations of newspaper and year effects. The analysis of variance revealed which of the 99 categories discriminated among years, newspapers, or interaction, or any combination of these three effects. Furthermore, these discriminations were established separately for the two split-half samples. If differential frequencies among the units of comparison are to be attributed to any of these three analysis-of-variance effects, then one would expect that both the magnitude and direction of such effects would occur equally in the two samples.

The following decision rule was established to determine significant discriminators. First, an effect must be significant at the 5-percent level or better in one of the two samples. Second, the same effect

[6] The year 1963 was selected because it was the latest complete year at the time the study was initiated, and 1953 was selected because it was the first year for which all issues were available for all four papers. (Issues of *Frankfurter Allgemeine Zeitung* prior to November 1952 did not exist.)
[7] To stabilize variances across units of comparison, the percentage frequencies were transformed by an arc sine square root transformation.

must be significant in the same direction at the 10-percent level or better in the other sample. The rationale for this decision rule is given by the joint probability of such an effect, considering the two samples to constitute two independent samples. Since the joint probability of an effect in the same direction at the 5-percent and 10-percent levels is about 1 percent,[8] our decision rule resulted in a rather conservative estimate as to whether the null hypothesis of no differences should be rejected. On the other hand, our decision rule has increased the probability of Type II errors in our investigation; we have assumed that certain tags do not discriminate between certain units of comparison, though in fact they did. Considering the exploratory nature of our investigation, we have been willing to make such Type II errors; although small but significant differences may not have been recognized, we are confident that such differences that have been recognized are a true characteristic of the total list of editorials from which our samples are drawn.

According to the stated decision rule, 40 categories discriminate significantly among the three effects. The discriminating categories are reviewed according to direction and significance in Tables 11.1 and 11.2. Significant interaction effects, occurring in only three cases, seem of limited importance and are therefore not reported here. (Probability levels are indicated in percentages.)[9]

At the 5-percent significance level, one may expect that by chance alone 5 of the 99 variables would be significant discriminators for each main effect. As the preceding tables show, however, our specific decision rule to establish significant effects greatly decreases such a chance finding. Furthermore, by using a particular analysis-of-variance model (Bock, 1963) that first tests the effects of a number of dependent variables at once before testing the effects for each of those variables separately, the probability that our findings would be due to chance circumstances has been practically eliminated from our design.

The significant discriminators and a number of categories of special theoretical importance were correlated across all editorials and sub-

[8] According to Stouffer's technique whereby

$$z = \frac{\text{sum of normal deviates}}{\sqrt{\text{number of observation.}}}$$

See Mosteller and Bush (1954).

[9] Probability levels of *separate* P's are equal or smaller than indicated values. Probability levels of *total* P's in descending order are indicated by rounded estimates.

TABLE 11.1. *Significant Differences Among All Newspapers in 1953 and 1963 with Respect to Differential Concern with Certain Categories*

	Total P (Percent)	Odds*					Evens*				
		NYT†	LT†	FAZ†	LM†	P (Percent)	NYT†	LT†	FAZ†	LM†	P (Percent)
SMALL-GROUP	.006	1	1	1	1	.1	1	1	1	1	.1
IDEAL-VALUE	.010	1	1	1	1	2.5	1	1	1	1	.1
SIGN-AUTHORITY	.080	1	1	1	1	2.5	1	1	1	1	1.0
SOVIET	.080	2	1	1	1	14.0	1	1	1	1	.1
LEGAL	.200	1	1	1	1	2.5	1	1	2	1	2.5
UNIFICATION	.400	1	1	1	1	1.0	1	1	1	1	12.0
POLITICAL	.900	2	1	1	1	11.0	2	1	1	1	4.0
FOOD	.030	2	2	2	2	1.0	2	2	2	2	1.0
INTERNATIONAL- INSTITUTION	.600	2	2	2	2	10.0	2	1	2	2	2.5
EXPEL	1.000	2	1	2	2	10.0	2	2	2	2	5.0

* 1 = Higher percent in 1953.
  2 = Higher percent in 1963.
† NYT = *The New York Times; LT = The Times* (London); *FAZ = Frankfurter Allgemeine Zeitung; LM = Le Monde.*

sequently factor analyzed in a number of ways. Again the analyses were conducted separately for each of the two split-half samples. A few variables were dropped from the analysis since they did not contribute to the resulting factor structure, but most of the variables were retained. A variety of both theoretical and mathematical rotations of the principal-component factor structure neither changed nor improved the comprehensibility of the underlying dimensions.

Comparing the factor structures of our two samples reveals that there is a similarity among the first four factors. This similarity is further confirmed by a mathematical comparison suggested by Ahnavaara (1954). The results of this comparison are produced in Tables 11.3 and 11.4.

Once it had been decided to limit the analysis to the first four factors, the principal component unrotated factor structure was determined for the total sample of 192 editorials. The resulting factor structure is presented in Table 11.5. The factor structure was interpreted inductively by three procedures. First, we attempted to define each end of the factors by inspection of such categories that loaded

TABLE 11.2. *Significant Differences Among Four Newspapers with Respect to Differential Concern with Certain Categories*

	Total P (Per-cent)	Odds*				P (Per-cent)	Evens*				P (Per-cent)
		NYT†	LT†	FAZ†	LM†		NYT†	LT†	FAZ†	LM†	
SELVES	.006	4	1	3	2	0.1	4	1	3	2	1.6
IDEAL-VALUE	.006	4	2	3	1	1.0	4	2	3	1	.1
POSSESS	.006	4	3	1.5	1.5	1.0	4	3	1	2	.1
MILITARY	.006	4	3	2	1	2.5	4	3	2	1	2.5
POLITICAL	.006	4	3	2	1	.1	4	3	2	1	.1
SIGN-ASCEND	.006	4	1.5	3	1.5	1.0	4	1	3	2	.1
UNIFICATION	.006	4	2.5	2.5	1	1.0	4	2	3	1	.1
SOCIAL-PLACE	.02	4	3	2	1	5.0	4	3	2	1	.1
AMERICAN	.02	4	1	2	3	1.0	4	2	1	3	1.0
ATLANTIC	.02	4	3	1	2	1.0	3	4	1	2	1.0
EUROPE	.02	3.5	2	3.5	1	5.0	3.5	2	3.5	1	.1
MALE-ROLE	.05	3	2	1	4	10.0	3	2	1	4	.1
THINK	.30	1	2	4	3	2.5	1	2.5	2.5	4	5.0
AVOID	.30	3	2	1	4	10.0	3	2	1	4	2.5
SPACE	.10	4	3	2	1	1.0	4	3	2	1	5.0
NOT	.10	1.5	1.5	4	3	5.0	1.5	1.5	4	3	1.0
DANGER-THEME	.10	4	2.5	2.5	1	1.0	4	3	1	2	5.0
BRITISH	.10	3	4	1	2	5.0	3	4	1	2	1.0
SOVIET	.10	4	2	1	3	5.0	3	2	1	4	1.0
JOB-ROLE	1.0	4	2.5	1	2.5	5.0	4	1	2	3	10.0

* 4 = Highest frequency.
  1 = Lowest frequency.
  † *NYT = The New York Times; LT = The Times* (London); *FAZ = Frankfurter Allgemeine Zeitung; LM = Le Monde.*

highly on either end of the factor. Second, the question was raised whether the resulting conception of a four-dimensional simple structure could account for the location of such categories that had loadings on more than one factor. The dimensional position of fused categories indeed confirmed the interpretation of our four factors. Finally, after determining the factor score of each of the 192 editorials, we selected the editorials with the most extreme loadings on the four factors. The question was then raised whether the factors or themes did in fact describe the major content of extreme editorials. For the extreme editorials, this was always the case, a further con-

TABLE 11.3. Matching Even and Odd Factor Loadings*

Word Categories	Evens				Odds			
	I†	II‡	III§	IV	I†	II‡	III§	IV
ATLANTIC	.63			.36	.69		−.32	.30
MILITARY	.68		.43		.62	−.34	−.30	
DANGER-THEME	.43			.43	.52			.32
REJECT	.27		.59		.39			
SOVIET	.56	.37			.65			
AMERICAN	.42			.47	.49			
WORK	−.42				−.44			
INTERNATIONAL-INSTITUTION	−.53	−.35			−.49			
EUROPEAN	−.50	−.63			−.74			
ECONOMIC	−.78			.32	−.57	.30		
POLITICAL	.38	−.76				−.68	.30	
IDEAL-VALUE		−.73				−.69		
UNIFICATION		−.72				−.56		
NATIONALIST		−.63				−.34		
ACCEPT		−.50				−.57		
ACTION-NORM		−.30	.53	−.35		−.66	−.28	
LEGAL		−.21	.33	−.46		−.56		
FOOD	−.48				−.32	.34		
AUTHORITY			.40	−.54			−.23	−.49
LARGE-GROUP	.54		.42		.47	−.38		
TOOL			.31		.40		−.45	
MALE-ROLE	.54		−.45	−.50	.57		.33	
JOB-ROLE	.51	−.32	−.37		.33	−.37	.20	
SOCIAL-PLACE			−.26	.45			.35	.37
FRENCH	.37	−.41	−.20			−.39	.38	
GERMAN	.30		−.37	−.32			.39	
ATTACK			.60	.39	.42			
AVOID				−.31				−.31
SELVES				.34				.28
NONSPECIFIC-OBJECT								
NOT								
POSSESS	.47	−.30		.45	.54			.37
SIGN-WEAK							.30	

* By comparing (1) the factor loadings of 33 selected categories of the even sample with (2) the loadings of these same categories presuming the dimension structure of the odd sample.

† Loadings below 30 have generally been omitted. (All factor analytic solutions are performed by computer programs written by K. J. Jones and W. W. Cooley of Harvard University and P. R. Lohnes of the University of Buffalo).

‡ In Factor II, the signs of the Odds and Evens are the reverse of the Totals.

§ In Factor III, the signs of the projected Odds are the reverse of the signs of the Evens.

TABLE 11.4. *The Correlations Between the Subsequent Pairs of Factors of the Two Factor Matrices for Even and Odd Samples**

	Odd Factors					
Even Factors	1	2	3	4	5	6
1	.83	.50	−.04	.18	−.12	.10
2	−.30	.63	−.15	.46	.13	.18
3	.05	−.24	−.63	−.16	.34	.24
4	.03	−.33	−.15	.70	−.03	−.25
5	.25	.13	−.21	−.20	.24	−.15
6	−.06	.06	.24	−.12	.14	.27

* It will be noted that the correlation matrix is nonsymmetrical and that the diagonal values are not unity. The closer to unity the diagonal values, the greater the similarity between subsequent pairs of factors.

firmation of our factor interpretations. (Brief descriptions of the extreme editorials for each factor are included with the factor interpretations in the following section reporting our findings.)

After the factor scores of each editorial for the four factors were determined, an analysis of variance was performed on the two split-half samples. Once it was ascertained that the significant effects were in all cases duplicated in the two samples, the analysis of variance was repeated on the total sample (in the manner just reported).

FINDINGS

To report our substantive findings, we shall first briefly indicate the results of the year comparisons of the COUNTRY, REGION, UNIFICATION, and INTERNATIONAL-INSTITUTION categories. The analysis of variance of the separate tags (as reported in Table 11.1) indicated that only three of the categories added to the General Inquirer list showed a significant difference over time. It will suffice to note here that there was significantly more concern in 1963 than in 1953 with reference to INTERNATIONAL-INSTITUTION, but less concern with UNIFICATION symbols in 1963 than a decade before. The paradoxical nature of this finding will be further discussed in the final section of the paper.

On the other hand, none of the four COUNTRY or two REGION categories showed a significant difference over time. On the basis of this finding one is tempted to conclude that there was no change in the

TABLE 11.5. *Factor Loadings of Selected Word Categories on Four Dimensions for the Total Sample*

Word Categories	Dimensions			
	I	II	III	IV
ATLANTIC	70			38—
MILITARY	69			
DANGER-THEME	57			35—
REJECT	42		—29	
SOVIET	55			
AMERICAN	46			44—
WORK	—44			
INTERNATIONAL-INSTITUTION	—51			35—
EUROPEAN	—65			
ECONOMIC	—75			35—
POLITICAL		77		
IDEAL-VALUE		75		
UNIFICATION		75		
NATIONALIST		55		
ACCEPT		61		
ACTION-NORM		58	—41	
LEGAL		44		—41
FOOD	—48	—29		
AUTHORITY			52	—54
LARGE-GROUP	43		.53	
TOOL	36		41	
MALE-ROLE	56		—33	
JOB-ROLE	54		—44	
SOCIAL-PLACE			—50	
FRENCH			—41	
GERMAN			—45	—32
ATTACK				31
AVOID				—34
SELVES				
NONSPECIFIC-OBJECT				
NOT				
POSSESS	47		32	30
SIGN-WEAK				

degree of integration between 1953 and 1963. This important point will also be dealt with in the final section of the paper.

Turning from the analysis of separate categories to the analysis of thematic positions as expressed by the factor analytic procedures, both time and country comparisons provide a picture that is clearly at variance with the previous findings. In reporting such factor analytic findings, we shall first state our interpretations of the factors. Having named the factors, we shall then proceed to document the interpretations by presenting a summary of the editorials best representing such factoral themes (this is, extreme factor-score editorials). Finally, the comparison of factor scores between papers and years will be presented and interpreted. (In all tables, numbers refer to factor loadings and average factor scores, multiplied by 100).

DIMENSION 1: NATO PERSPECTIVE VERSUS COMMON MARKET PERSPECTIVE [10]

This dimension indicates that the editorials generally consider *either* the Atlantic military alliance and the Soviet-American nuclear confrontation *or* European economic and institutional matters. Only in rare instances are these two themes treated in the same editorial. This interpretation is based on the factor loadings shown in Table 11.6.

TABLE 11.6. Factor Loadings for Dimension 1

Category	Positive Loading	Category	Negative Loading
ATLANTIC	70	ECONOMIC	−75
MILITARY	69	EUROPEAN	−65
DANGER-THEME	57	INTERNATIONAL-	
MALE-ROLE	56	INSTITUTION	−51
SOVIET	55	FOOD	−48
JOB-ROLE	54	WORK	−44
AMERICAN	46		
LARGE-GROUP	43		
REJECT	42		
TOOL	36		

The term "NATO perspective" suggests that one aspect of this factor refers to the Atlantic military alliance in the context of a bipolar world. The emphasis here is on a direct nuclear confrontation between the United States and the Soviet Union. The extreme editorial

[10] This factor explains 16 percent of the total variance. Dimensions 2, 3, and 4 explain, respectively, 11 percent, 8 percent and 7 percent of the variance.

for this end of the factor appeared in *The New York Times* under
the title, "After the Treaty." The following is a précis of the position
taken:

> The Nuclear Test-Ban Treaty is a promising beginning of a new epoch in
> East-West relations. More extensive agreements will depend on Khrush-
> chev who has indicated that, although he will not use nuclear weapons,
> he intends to continue his drive toward Communist world domination.
> As for France, Kennedy may persuade her to adhere to the treaty if
> the United States treats her like Britain and supplies her with the same
> information now given to the British. If France adheres to the treaty
> now, she may later join in building a NATO nuclear force and thereby
> restore Western solidarity.
>
> (July 28, 1963)

On the other hand, "Common Market perspective" refers to economic
and institutional issues in Western Europe. This factor interpretation
is again confirmed by the actual content of the extreme editorial for
this end of the dimension. The editorial appeared in *Frankfurter
Allgemeine Zeitung* under the title "EEC Quality," and the com-
mentator noted,

> The term "EEC — Quality," which was used frequently by entrepre-
> neurs at the Frankfurt-Fair, refers to goods which in price and quality
> can compete against Common Market goods in spite of Common Market
> tariffs. Its frequent usage implies that the Common Market is already an
> accepted concept in the minds of such entrepreneurs.
>
> (February 22, 1963.)

The time and paper comparisons for this first dimension indicate
that there is a significant difference between *The New York Times*
and the three European papers.[11] While *The New York Times* has
increased its already high concern with ATLANTIC and MILITARY solutions to world problems, the Europeans have moved away from these
concerns, toward EUROPEAN ECONOMIC and INSTITUTIONAL problems. In particular, *Frankfurter Allgemeine Zeitung* increased its
already high concern with European matters. *Le Monde* reversed its
position from a high concern with Atlantic issues to a substantial
interest in European matters. *The Times* (London) maintained a
rather low contribution to the Atlantic aspect of the dimension, with
a slight decline over the decade. These trends can be easily noted in
Table 11.7. An analysis of variance shows significant differences

[11] Significant at .001 level.

TABLE 11.7. Average Contributions to Dimension 1

	Factor Scores			Rank	
	1953	1963	Change	1953	1963
The New York Times	05	66	61	4	1
The Times (London)	12	02	−10	3	5
Le Monde	43	−19	−62	2	6
Frankfurter Allgemeine Zeitung	−30	−79	−49	7	8

Positive Scores: Atlantic Military Alliance and Soviet-American Nuclear Confrontation.
Negative Scores: European Economic and Institutional matters.

Interaction: Significant at 0.1 percent level.
Newspaper: Significant at 0.1 percent level.
Year: Not significant.

among the four papers and a significant interaction effect. The interaction effect indicates the divergence over time between *The New York Times* on the one hand and the three European papers on the other hand. The net effect over time is consequently not significant.

DIMENSION 2: IDEALIZED FUTURE VERSUS CONCRETE INTERESTS AND DIFFICULTIES

This dimension refers to another pair of opposite thematic concerns. One involves the future and the desirability of a supranational legal framework for European unification, including a concern with NATIONALISM as well.[12] The other aspect of the dimension refers to daily and divisive issues hampering unification; there is an emphasis on agriculture in this regard. Table 11.8 presents the factor-loading

TABLE 11.8. Factor Loadings for Dimension 2

Category	Positive Loading	Category	Negative Loading
POLITICAL	77	FOOD	−29
UNIFICATION	75		
IDEAL-VALUE	75		
SIGN-ACCEPT	61		
ACTION-NORM	58		
NATIONALIST	55		
LEGAL	44		

[12] The interpretation of the negative end of this dimension is rather speculative since only one category loaded on the negative end of the factor. The content of the category FOOD includes references not only to agricultural topics, which of course have been quite problematic for the European communities, but also references to the "chicken war," which was a problematic issue in the Atlantic community.

data on which these interpretations were based. For this factor, the definition of "the idealized future" end of the dimension is validated by the extreme editorial appearing in an edition of *The New York Times*:

> The Consultive — Assembly of the Council-of-Europe endorsed the tentative plans to unite six nations in a Federated Community, which would exist under a constitution providing for the supranational political, military, and economic authorities. The constitutional Assembly, representing the six nations, conflicted with the Consultive Assembly on the issue of national sovereignty. Nevertheless, unification is on the march and statesmen should be able to reconcile differences.
>
> (January 20, 1953)

The extreme example of the other end of this dimension is found in *Frankfurter Allgemeine Zeitung,* which commented on European and trans-Atlantic agricultural controversies. Even though our original interpretation was based on a minimal factor loading, this interpretation is surprisingly confirmed by the content of the editorial that follows and several other editorials with extreme factor scores on this end of the dimension.

> The Federal Government has agreed to suspend the EEC levy on pork imports; but since pork is scarce outside the EEC, Germany may have to turn to the abundant supply of poultry from America and Denmark. Germany could allow an inflow of this foreign poultry, as it did in 1959, in order to give the consumer a cheap means to remedy the meat shortage. Thus Germany should stop the chicken war with the United States.
>
> (November 30, 1963)

TABLE 11.9. Average Contributions to Dimension 2

	Factor Scores			Rank	
	1953	*1963*	*Change*	*1953*	*1963*
The New York Times	83	56	−27	1	2
The Times (London)	22	−43	−65	4	6
Le Monde	−39	−60	−21	5	8
Frankfurter Allgemeine Zeitung	27	−46	−73	3	7

Positive Scores: Idealized Future.
Negative Scores: Concrete Interests and Difficulties.

Interaction: Not significant.
Newspaper: Significant at 0.1 percent level.
Year: Significant at 0.1 percent level.

As Table 11.9 suggests, *The New York Times* has retained much of its idealism and supranationalism over the ten-year period. The European papers, by contrast, have tended to be rather skeptical — or realistic according to their own perceptions — at least in 1963. *The Times* (London) and *Frankfurter Allgemeine Zeitung* shifted away from the idealistic position in 1953 to the skeptical one in 1963. *Le Monde* increased its already substantial contribution to the skeptical end of the dimension. In other words, the European papers have become more alike over the decade while *The New York Times* has become unique in its emphasis on idealistic supranationalism.

DIMENSION 3: COSTS OF SUPRANATIONAL ALLIANCES VERSUS FRANCO-GERMAN POLITICAL CONTROVERSIES

The underlying theme of this dimension is a concern with national obstacles to supranational arrangements. This concern is expressed in either of two ways: the dangers and costs of military involvements and changes therein for each member country, or Franco-German controversies related to the European community. Evidences of these themes may be seen in the loadings in Table 11.10. The predominance

TABLE 11.10. Factor Loadings for Dimension 3

Category	Loading	Category	Loading
LARGE-GROUP	53	SOCIAL-PLACE	−50
AUTHORITY	52	GERMAN	−45
TOOL	41	JOB-ROLE	−44
MILITARY	37	FRENCH	−41
		SIGN-ACCEPT	−41
		MALE-ROLE	−33
		DANGER-THEME	−29

of concern with the cost of regional military arrangements in the extreme editorial from *The Times* (London) once again verifies the interpretation of the factor:

> The cost of the multilateral Polaris fleet could be too great for Britain which has the final word in deciding whether to accept the American proposal. The heaviest burden of cost would come when Britain reached the most expensive stage of her own Polaris program; then economies would have to be made in conventional forces.
>
> (May 16, 1963)

The predominance of Franco-German controversies in the *Frankfurter Allgemeine Zeitung* editorial, which was extreme on the other end of the dimension, similarly corroborates our understanding:

> Adenauer seems to be having difficulty establishing as warm a relationship with the present French Foreign-Minister, Bidault, as he had with the former one, Schuman. A recent lengthy discussion between Adenauer and Bidault may help the relationship; but in the long run French foreign policy depends on the solutions to many internal fights which at present are unpredictable. West Germany simply must wait until French policy is made clear.
>
> (August 11, 1953)

According to the editorial comments, only Franco-German politics are related to restraining concerns toward European and/or Atlantic integration; and by implication, neither American nor British symbols are unequivocally related to such restraints. As a matter of fact, American symbols are related to either the "NATO perspective" (discussed earlier) or to pressures for increasing integration in the Atlantic area (as will be discussed in connection with Dimension 4).

An analysis of variance reveals that there are no significant differences either over time or among the four papers in this dimension. The similarity of the papers in this regard implies two quite different conclusions that can be related to integration. On one hand, as we have asserted above, the similarity of outlook suggests a greater degree of integration. On the other hand, however, the continuing concern with the psychic and material costs of supranational arrangements and the domestic contribution demanded by them indicate a lack of enthusiasm for the arrangements.

DIMENSION 4: AMERICAN PRESSURES FOR INTEGRATION VERSUS LEGAL TEMPORIZING AND RESTRAINT

The factor loadings given in Table 11.11 indicate that the underlying theme of this dimension is a concern with the status quo of European and Atlantic politics. First there is an American pressure for fusion and extension of existing institutional arrangements at the international level, both Atlantic and European. As the summary of the extreme editorial indicates, these American pressures are perceived as including economic issues:

TABLE 11.11. Factor Loadings for Dimension 4

Category	Loading	Category	Loading
AMERICAN	44	AUTHORITY	− 54
ATLANTIC	38	LEGAL	− 41
DANGER-THEME	35	AVOID	− 34
INTERNATIONAL-INSTITUTION	35	GERMAN	− 32
ECONOMIC	35		
ATTACK	31		

Under the impact of Kennedy's European trip, President De Gaulle has relented on his adamant stand against the "Anglo-Saxons," has agreed to discussions between the EEC and Britain on all political and economic problems, and has agreed to further preparation for the "Kennedy-Round" of tariff-cut talks.

(The New York Times, July 13, 1963)

On the other hand, the opposite end of the dimension describes an orientation toward conserving the existing order in the European and Atlantic world by the introduction of legal consideration and other restraining and conservative measures. The editorials attribute the latter orientations especially to the Germans, although German editorials do not necessarily see matters in the same light. A comment by *The Times* (London) on the "Painful Inches" toward ratification of the European Defense Community authenticates the reference to one end of the dimension as including legal restraints:

France, Belgium, Germany, and other individual states are having political and legal difficulties in ratifying the EDC. In Germany although the Bundestag passed the bills to ratify the treaties, the Bundesrat, acting within its ill-defined sphere in the legislative process established by the 1949 constitution, is holding up ratification because of internal political difficulties.

(April 28, 1953)

Table 11.12 indicates the year and paper differences for this dimension. The figures indicate that by 1963 supranational integration had become more closely identified with American pressures and initiatives than in 1953. This trend is especially marked in *The New York Times,* for its score increased by a factor of six over the decade. Lesser shifts in the same direction occurred in all three European papers as well. *The Times* (London) and *Frankfurter Allgemeine Zeitung* reversed their positions; in 1953 they were oriented toward

TABLE 11.12. Average Contributions to Dimension 4

	Factor Scores			Rank	
	1953	1963	Change	1953	1963
The New York Times	22	135	113	2	1
The Times (London)	−37	15	52	5	3
Le Monde	−74	−37	37	6	5
Frankfurter Allgemeine Zeitung	−37	12	49	5	4

Positive Scores: American Pressure for Integration.
Negative Scores: Legal Temporizing and Restraint.

Interaction: Not significant.
Newspaper: Significant at 0.1 percent level.
Year: Significant at 0.1 percent level.

the legal and conservative end of the dimension but became oriented toward American pressures by 1963. Meanwhile, *Le Monde* maintained its position of concern with the conservative and legal aspect of the dimension, although to a lesser extent in 1963 than in 1953.

Nevertheless, one can conclude that this dimension indicates that *The New York Times* seems to perceive a different world from that of its European counterparts. It continues to be intent on American activism, focusing on efforts to merge military and economic supranational instrumentalities. These efforts, however, find little support in the European press. As a matter of fact, the findings suggest that the linkage between military and economic policies — either by extension of the Atlantic community or by a transformation of the European institutions — is a theme created by *The New York Times* commentators.

GRAPHIC SUMMARY

The findings of the factor analysis can be further explicated by a graphic representation of combinations of factors. Figures 11.1, 11.2, and 11.3 can be read in the following manner. Changing positions are indicated for each paper by an arrow. The *origin* of the arrow signifies its position in 1953, and the *head* of the arrow signifies its position in 1963. The *length* of the arrow indicates the magnitude of the change. The *direction* of the arrow indicates the direction of the change. Measurements along the axes are based on the factor loadings reported in the preceding tables.

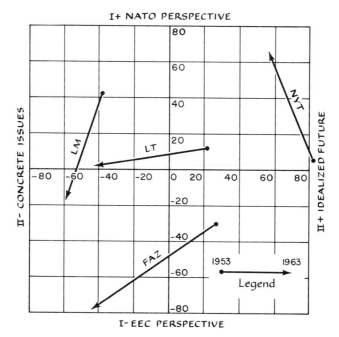

FIGURE 11.1. *Changing positions of four prestige papers from 1953–1963: Factor dimensions I × II.*

Inspection of the three figures shows that the magnitude of change is often the largest for *The New York Times*. Furthermore, the change usually shows *The New York Times* moving in a different direction from the three European papers, while the three European papers either converge or move in a similar direction. Thus, *The New York Times* over time is increasingly different from the European papers, while the European papers move in the same direction and/or become more alike.

CONCLUSIONS AND DISCUSSION

What, then, may we conclude about integration in Western Europe and the Atlantic alliance? Was there a greater or lesser degree of integration in 1963 than in 1953? We have three sets of indicators, not all of which point to the same conclusion.

One set of indicators includes the country and region symbols, which frequencies would presumably suggest unambiguous conclusions about the degree of integration; but we have found that there

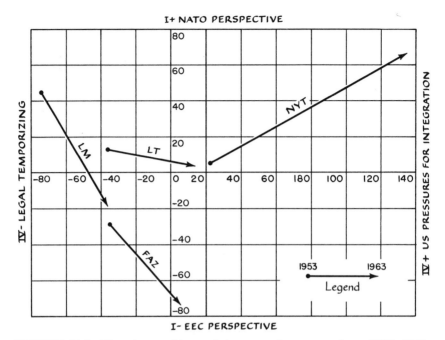

FIGURE 11.2. Changing positions of four prestige papers from 1953–1963:
Factor dimensions I × IV.

were no significant differences in the frequency of references to these
symbols between the two years. Hence, on this basis alone, one would
conclude that the degree of integration in both Western Europe and
in the Atlantic alliance was essentially the same in 1953 and 1963.

In any case, the other two sets of indicators suggest quite different
conclusions. First, there are the three categories NATIONALISTIC, UNI-
FICATION, and INTERNATIONAL-INSTITUTION. As previously noted,
there was no significant difference over time in the frequency of occurrence of words labeled NATIONALISTIC. References to UNIFICATION
and INTERNATIONAL-INSTITUTION, however, did vary significantly
over time: UNIFICATION symbols decreased and references to INTER-
NATIONAL-INSTITUTION increased. At first thought, one might regard
these two trends as paradoxical. Further reflection, however, suggests that there is a plausible explanation for these trends. At a minimum, one can state that these trends indicate a change in the nature
of the concern with integration. In 1953, integration was viewed in
more idealistic and abstract terms and less in terms of institutional
arrangements and policies, but by 1963 the idealism and abstract

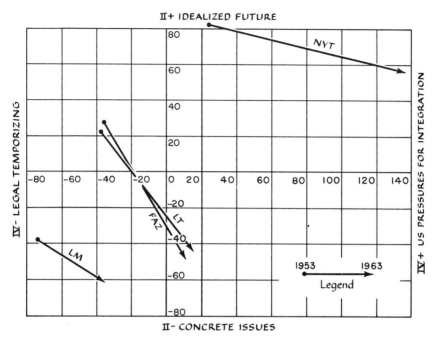

FIGURE 11.3. *Changing positions of four prestige papers from 1953–1963: Factor dimensions II × IV.*

concerns became less prominent than the institutional and policy concerns. A recollection of Dimension 2 corroborates these conclusions. Dimension 2 suggests that the European papers shifted to a more intense concern with "concrete interests and difficulties" by 1963, as opposed to concern with the "idealized future." On the other hand, *The New York Times* maintained its attention to the "idealized future." Thus, we can conclude that this changing nature of the concern was in evidence for the European papers but not for the American.

One may with some confidence suggest that these trends not only represent a change in the *nature of the concern* with integration but also imply a *greater degree* of integration. The increased European interest in the European institutions and their policies reflects the growing penetration of supranational activities into the domestic scene. Hence the editorial commentators have been forced to discuss European unification more and more in terms of practical, day-to-day politics, rather than in terms of utopian expectations. Meanwhile, *The New York Times* has continued to discuss Atlantic unification in utopian terms. Consequently, we suggest that there has not only been a change in the *nature* of the European concern with integration but that this change implies in turn a greater *extent* of European integration. However, these trends describe neither changing orientations of American commentators nor orientations pertaining to Atlantic integration.

The analysis of all four dimensions, as indicators of generalized orientations or outlooks, reinforces the same conclusion, that there is increased integration in Western Europe and decreased integration in the Atlantic area. These conclusions are, in this case, based on the finding of increased similarity among the European papers and an increased difference between them and the American paper. To underscore the point, it seems appropriate to reiterate quickly the interpretations of the dimensions. Dimension 1 reveals that *The New York Times* is more attentive to Atlantic military alliance and the Soviet-American confrontation, while the Europeans are more concerned with European economic and institutional matters. *The New York Times* has continued to view unification in idealistic terms, while the Europeans concentrate on current policies and difficulties. And, finally, *The New York Times* expresses much greater interest in American pressures for Atlantic and European cooperation than the European papers.

In addition to our conclusions, there remain several issues prompted by the study. One such issue is the value of using national and regional symbols as indexes of integration. It will be recalled that Dimension 1 reveals that, except for American references, country symbols are *independent* of regional symbols. Whereas Atlantic symbols loaded highly on one end and European references on the other end of that dimension, only the American references of the four country categories were also associated with either of the region categories. In other words, the level of concern with regional symbols in no way enables one to predict the level of concern with national symbols, and vice versa. This evidence thus places in doubt the proposition that during the process of integration attention to regional symbols increases at the expense of attention to national symbols.

A second issue refers to an important assumption mentioned in the introduction to the paper, namely, that one can infer elite orientations from editorials in "prestige" newspapers. It has been frequently stated elsewhere that the elite press provides a stable index of the attitudes of the national political elite (Pool, 1952, and Schramm, 1959), and biographical data for the editors of the prestige papers incorporated in the *Hoover Institute Studies* support this contention. The authors of those studies discovered that the editors of "prestige" papers tend to come "from the same social circles as members of the elite," share their "education and other attitude-forming experiences," and "maintain close contact with members of the government" (Pool, 1952, 120–140). But the evidence thus remains circumstantial and inconclusive. To increase confidence in this assumption, we are preparing comparative analyses of elite and mass papers in Britain and the United States. For purposes of the study reported in this paper, however, we have adopted the traditional assumption that prestige editorials do in fact reflect elite orientations.

Finally, it will also be recalled that Dimension 1 indicates that economic and military matters are rarely discussed together. Rather they are considered exclusive of each other: the commentators speak *either* about economic issues *or* about military issues. Furthermore, military matters are nearly always associated with the East-West nuclear confrontation and its dangers: negative affect is an inherent element of the military perspective. This unexpected finding warrants further discussion.

The conceptual distinction between matters military and economic appears to be a mapping device whereby new and unfamiliar events are cognitively organized within a familiar framework. As such, the mapping device serves two circular though distinct functions. First, by placing novel phenomena in a known conceptual environment, it suggests that the novel events can be understood, controlled, and predicted within the context of a familiar order. Second, insofar as the established intellectual procedures and orientations master subsequent events, they conserve the various established ways of looking at the world. Thus, once the observer has decided whether an event is either economic or military, it becomes part of previously established orientations. This ordering procedure therefore fulfills functions usually attributed to ideology.[13] The thematic positions discovered by factor analysis therefore may well describe differential ideological positions concerning the European and Atlantic communities.

In European and Atlantic politics, the mapping of events as either military or economic is likely to have had important consequences

[13] For example, see Geertz (1964) and Lane (1962, 13–16).

for regional integration. This conceptual distinction and the fears associated with military matters explain European rejections of suggestions for increased Atlantic integration, economic and military. Atlantic cooperation is perceived as a military arrangement and is therefore considered in a basically negative context.

On the other hand, this conceptual distinction may help to explain the success of European integration, since it has been perceived almost exclusively in economic terms. The abortive attempt to establish the European Defense Community in the early 1950's is one of the more obvious exceptions to the preponderance of economic considerations. And, as is well known, the French have recently interjected military considerations into the politics of European cooperation.

If this insertion of military concerns continues, it seems likely that it will have serious debilitating effects on European integration. This speculation is based on the assumption that the tendency to view events as either military or economic is pervasive. If it is, then European cooperation will be thought of more and more as a military question, not an economic one. And it will suffer from the negative attitudes inevitably associated with military phenomena in a nuclear age.

BIBLIOGRAPHY

Ahnavaara, Y. (1954), "Transformation Analysis of Factorial Data," *Annales Academiae Scientarium Fennicae,* Series B.

Alker, Hayward R., and Donald Puchala (1965), "Trends in Economic Partnership in the North Atlantic Area," mimeographed.

Bock, Darrell R. (1963), "Programming Univariate and Multivariate Analysis of Variance," *Technometrics,* V, 1.

Deutsch, Karl W. (1953), *Nationalism and Social Communication.* New York: The Technology Press of the Massachusetts Institute of Technology and John Wiley & Sons.

——— (1954), *Political Community at the International Level.* New York: Doubleday.

——— (1955), "Symbols of Political Community." In Lyman Bryson, *et al.* (eds.), *Symbols* and *Society,* 14th Symposium of the Conference on Science, Philosophy and Religion, New York: Harper and Brothers.

Deutsch, Karl W., *et al.* (1957), *Political Community and the North Atlantic Area.* Princeton, N.J.: Princeton University Press, 1957.

Geertz, Clifford (1964), "Ideology as a Cultural System." In Apter, David (ed.), *Ideology and Discontent.* New York: The Free Press of Glencoe.

Haas, Ernst (1958), *The Uniting of Europe.* Stanford, Calif.: Stanford University Press.

Lane, Robert E. (1962), *Political Ideology*. New York: The Free Press of Glencoe.

Lindberg, Leon (1963), *The Political Dynamics of European Economic Integration*. Stanford, Calif.: Stanford University Press.

McPherson, W. R., D. C. Dunphy, R. F. Bales, P. J. Stone, and D. M. Ogilvie (1963), "A Revised Psychological and Sociological Dictionary for the General Inquirer," mimeographed.

Merritt, Richard L. (1953), "Nation-Building in America: The Colonial Years." In Karl W. Deutsch, and William Foltz (eds.), *Nation-Building*. New York: Atherton Press.

Mosteller, F., and R. R. Bush (1954), "Selected Quantitative Techniques." In G. Lindzey (ed.), *Handbook of Social Psychology*, Reading, Mass.: Addison-Wesley.

Namenwirth, J. Zvi (1963), *Bureaucratic Power and European Unification*, Ph.D. dissertation, Harvard University.

—— (forthcoming), "Confirming British Attitudes toward Atlantic and European Integration" and "American Editorial Comment on the Korean War."

Pool, Ithiel de Sola (1951), *Symbols of Internationalism*. Stanford, Calif.: Stanford University Press.

——— et al. (1952), *The "Prestige Papers": A Survey of Their Editorials*. Stanford, Calif.: Stanford University Press.

Puchala, Donald J. (1964), *Western European Attitudes on International Problems*, Research Memorandum No. 1, Yale Research Memoranda in Political Science.

Russett, Bruce M. (1963), *Community and Contention*. Cambridge, Mass.: The M.I.T. Press.

Schramm, Wilbur (ed.) (1959), *One Day in the World's Press*. Stanford, Calif.: Stanford University Press.

PERSONALITY

Both papers in this section utilize the General Inquirer for individual case analysis. The first paper (Paige) demonstrates a method of "trait" analysis, and the second (Ogilvie) points out the danger of interpreting the meaning of tag scores without retrievals.

The major contribution of Paige's analysis lies in his attempt to answer G. W. Allport's call for a method to conceptualize materials from one individual without having to compare that individual with the universe. Paige takes a well-known series of letters written by a single individual (Jenny) over eleven years and uses the General Inquirer to identify Jenny's unique traits or personal dispositions. He is then able to put this trait analysis together with important events in her life and sensitively trace Jenny's reactions to changing circumstances. An interesting aspect of this study is that these letters have been analyzed before and Paige compares his results with the results obtained by others.

In the other paper of this section, Ogilvie discusses tree-building and retrieval procedures that assist investigators in ordering data once they have been tagged by the computer. By means of a case study, some of the faults of making interpretations on the basis of tag scores alone are demonstrated, and strategies of systematically reworking the data are introduced.

CHAPTER TWELVE

Letters from Jenny: An Approach to the Clinical Analysis of Personality Structure by Computer

Jeffery M. Paige
University of Michigan

INTRODUCTION

Revealing personal documents, such as letters, diaries, or autobiographies, carry great human as well as psychological fascination. Such self-description can provide an endless source of hypotheses about the dynamics of an individual or of people in general. Collections of letters, published diaries, and autobiographies are, however, difficult subjects for psychological study. Too often that which is noted and remembered is a theme important to the reader or researcher and not to the author. Gordon Allport (1942) has suggested that personal documents are not accepted as respectable scientific data because of the vague and introspective nature of many studies based on them.

One way of interjecting objectivity into the study of personal documents and of extracting general notions from the complexity of an individual life is through content analysis. Although quantifying themes of documents does not ensure that the numerical results will be useful or even interesting, it does at least guarantee that when another observer follows a similar set of rules he will arrive at similar results. Content analysis currently lacks the sophistication and sensitivity to thematic innuendo of the trained clinical observer, but if used properly it can detect themes that the clinician's more global reading may miss. Content analysis reorganizes the material of documents in ways that make new insights possible, and it provides a means of checking the insights against reliable, quantitative data.

The present study uses the General Inquirer system to explore the structure of a single personality in the manner of a clinical psychologist. In order to have a standard by which to judge the results of this content analysis, we chose data that had been subjected to exhaustive clinical analyses. These data are a series of 167 letters written by an elderly woman, Jenny Masterson (a pseudonym), to her son's college roommate, Glenn, and his wife, Isabel. The letters were originally published by Allport (1946) as a valuable source of data about personality, and he has used them extensively in his teaching to illustrate personality theories. Recently he republished most of the letters, along with a collection of analyses of them, written from a variety of psychological traditions. Allport has also listed trait names (Allport, 1964, 198) that have been used by students and clinicians in describing Jenny. Thus a considerable backlog of descriptions of Jenny exist, ranging from the notes of undergraduates to sophisticated psychoanalytic interpretations. The literature on Jenny includes a hand content analysis of the letters carried out by Baldwin (1942) in which a set of *ad hoc* categories was used. The analysis presented here differs from Baldwin's because the General Inquirer allows for a more exhaustive content analysis with a much larger set of general categories (The Harvard III Dictionary) rather than *ad hoc* categories; and it differs, too, in the extensive use made of the numbers generated by the analysis.

The worth of the study presented here, or of any other content analysis of personal documents, depends on whether it tells us something about the structure of personality and whether the results are comparable in general content and in psychological depth with those of clinical observers. Within this chapter we shall try to provide tentative answers to both of these questions.

Jenny's History

Jenny was born in Ireland in 1868 of Protestant parents, but the family moved to Canada when she was five. She grew up strong-willed and independent, with a dislike of the puritan conventionalism of her family. When she married, she chose a divorced American railway inspector. The marriage created a permanent rift between Jenny and her family, for the family considered the divorce a disgrace. Jenny had worked from the time of her father's death, when she was eighteen, to support her family, and in marriage she felt uncomfortable being supported by a man, "like a kept woman," as she put it. Her husband died while she was pregnant with her only child, Ross, and she never remarried.

Jenny's letters contain frequent, nostalgic descriptions of Ross's childhood years. She was apparently happy, although she worked long hours at menial jobs in order to spend extravagantly on Ross. She sent him to private schools; and when he was at Princeton, she saw to it that he had enough spending money not to be embarrassed by his wealthier schoolmates. After Princeton, Ross served briefly in the ambulance corps in France and then returned to the United States to a life without immediate job prospects or long-range goals.

Jenny had always resented Ross's attachments to women, starting with the wife of one of his professors, who seemed to Jenny to be overly attentive to her handsome son. When Ross finally married, Jenny was outraged and never forgave him his betrayal. She left New York, where Ross lived, and went to Chicago. It is from Chicago that the first letter of this series was written. Perhaps she wrote to Ross's college roommate in hopes of reliving the happy experiences of Ross's college days. The eleven-year correspondence continued until Jenny's death in 1937.

During this period, she lived in Chicago, Montreal, Manhattan, and the Bronx, in apartments, and finally in an institution for the elderly. She worked in an art store, as a children's nurse, and as a scrub-woman. Her contacts with Ross were tempestuous and short-lived. After his death of a mastoid infection contracted while vacationing with a woman, Jenny's rage knew no bounds. To the end of her life, she accused the woman of murdering her son and engaged in a petu-lant legal battle for Ross's meager estate.

A short time after Ross's death, Jenny committed herself to an institution for the elderly; and in the months before her own death she became unbearably difficult. She refused to face the other inmates when she encountered them in the halls and attacked one of them by hitting her over the head with a pail. At the time of her sudden death, the superintendent of the institution had been considering sending her to an institution for the insane. Jenny's letters are concise and direct. She practiced no conscious deception and wrote in a natural, brilliant style. The subjects of her letters, herself, the events around her, the people she knew, may have been quite different from her descriptions, but Jenny's letters do not present a factual account of her last eleven years. They are, rather, a verbal picture of her subjective world. Her son's college roommate and his wife were a sympathetic audience to whom Jenny could express her need for affection, her violent hatreds, her prejudices, values, sorrows, isolation, and her persistent struggle with an intractable environment. Glenn and Isabel saw Jenny only twice during the period of their correspondence. The letters are a monologue and do not reflect the development of a dyadic relationship.

The intensely personal quality of the letters and the fact that Jenny dwelled on herself, rather than on the events around her, make the letters a promising source of verbal data for a General Inquirer analysis.

General Procedure

Two main approaches were used to develop a description of the structure of Jenny's personality. Both are essentially idiographic, that is without reference to norms scaled in the general population or to comparisons with other people. Both approaches compare Jenny with herself over time and are concerned with two general kinds of temporal change: first, day to day shifts of mood and immediate environment that lead to changing topics in individual letters; second, gradual structural changes in personality that lead to the emotional disorganization evident toward the end of Jenny's life. The apparent variation of individual letters does not indicate a lack of internal consistency in Jenny's personality. Her personality, "the dynamic organization within the individual of those psychophysical systems that determine his characteristic behavior and thought" (Allport, 1961, 28), remains relatively constant. Each letter shows us the pattern of Jenny's personality from a different perspective.

Factor analysis was used to extract the underlying dimensions of Jenny's personality from the variance in the letters as a whole. Long-term personality changes were studied by examining changes in single tags over the eleven-year span of the letters.

Factors and Traits

Our content analysis of the letters follows the "descriptive factor analysis" strategies outlined in Chapter 7. The single letter is the basic temporal unit upon which the factor analysis was based. Tag tallies were obtained for each letter, and the results were used to generate a table of correlations and a factor structure.

All 83 tags of the Harvard III Dictionary, plus tags for the following references were correlated with one another: ROSS, GLENN, ISABEL, FAMILY (in Canada), ROSS and JENNY (combined), NEW YORK, CHICAGO, and MONTREAL. Positive correlation indicates that co-occurrence of tags within the same letter are more frequent than would be predicted by chance alone. Thus the table of correlations reveal which psychological concepts on the tag list are associated in Jenny's written train of thought and presumably in her mind.

A number of schemes were tried in an attempt to interpret the clusters of tags making up each factor. The factors might have referred simply to the different locales from which the letters were written, the people with whom Jenny happened to be dealing at the time, or the situational pressures to which she was exposed. They might have represented a clinical typology, such as the psychoanalytic (oral, anal, phallic) or the Jungian (extrovert, introvert). However, none of these interpretations proved satisfactory. The most useful scheme was to consider each factor as a personal trait expressed in a number of different situations.

The notion of trait has been developed by a number of personality theorists, notably Allport (1937), Eysenck (1953), and Cattell (1946). Allport defines a trait as a neuropsychic structure rendering stimuli and responses "functionally equivalent." Eysenck defines trait simply as an "observed constellation of individual action tendencies." For Cattell a trait is a "mental structure," an inference made from observed behavior to account for its regularity and consistency. The common element of these definitions seems to be that a trait is a grouping of behaviors that can be considered equivalent from the point of view of the personality being studied. Thus a trait is a class or grouping of equivalent behaviors. Although there is some dispute over the exact basis for traits, the theorists seem to agree that this is a useful way of specifying dimensions in personality.

The theorists agree, too, that there are two general kinds of traits. Allport distinguishes between personal dispositions, descriptive of a single individual, and those that are distillations of elements common to a large number of personalities. Cattell makes a similar distinction between unique and common traits. Most factor analytic studies of personality, notably those of Cattell (1946) and Eysenck (1953), have attempted to isolate traits that can be found in almost everyone. In a search for general norms, these studies have lumped together measurements on a great number of people and have submerged individual personality structure. Allport (1937) has argued that more consideration should be given to idiographic studies of traits, studies that deal with the structure of a particular personality, rather than sacrificing the pattern of a single life to statistically convenient norms. The factors derived from the General Inquirer analysis represent the fine structure of a single personality as opposed to the general norms produced by most factor analytic studies of personality. In the discussion that follows, we shall use the general term, trait, but with the understanding that these are *unique* personal dispositions.

The factor structure summarizes the principal intercorrelations within letters among the tags of the General Inquirer system. It constructs groupings of Jenny's verbal behavior that are to some extent equivalent, that is, tending to correlate with one another. Thus it is not surprising that the notion of trait, which we have argued is basically a grouping of equivalent behaviors, should be useful in understanding the factor structure. The factor structure operationalizes Jenny's personality traits in terms of her own verbal behavior. This is not to imply that any factor analysis of a series of letters will produce a list of traits. If Jenny had been sending postcards back to Glenn and Isabel from a European trip, a factor analysis might produce one factor from each country visited. It is the primarily personal nature of Jenny's concerns that make the letters so psychologically revealing.

Each factor was defined by examining clusters of high-loading tags and by careful reading of the five letters with the highest factor scores, that is, those letters whose content best represents the factor. The

TABLE 12.1. Tags Loading on Factors I–III

Loading	Factor I	Factor II	Factor III
.7	MALE-ROLE	MESSAGE-FORM	
.6	ROSS BAD, COMMUNICATE, SIGN-REJECT	ECONOMIC	PLEASURE
.5	ANGER FEMALE-ROLE	POSSESS ATTEMPT ROSS	ISABEL
.4	HIGHER-STATUS		THINK, ACADEMIC, PEER-STATUS
.3	NOT ATTACK	CAUSE, APPROACH, WORK OUGHT, GLENN	SELVES, OTHER, GLENN URGE GOOD MALE-THEME, RJ SIGN-ACCEPT COMMUNICATE
.2			
.1			
.0			
−.1			
−.2			
−.3	WORK, MOVE MONTREAL	SIGN-AUTHORITY, OVERSTATE TIME-REFERENCE	FEMALE-ROLE TIME-REFERENCE THOUGHT-FORM, SIGN-STRONG, HIGHER-STATUS AVOID
−.4	GLENN, POSSESS SENSORY-REFERENCE	SELVES, PLEASURE AVOID DISTRESS MOVE BODY-PART	QUANTITY-REFERENCE SIGN-AUTHORITY JOB-ROLE WORK SIGN-WEAK
−.5	ATTEMPT CLOTHING, SPACE REFERENCE, TECHNOLOGICAL	NATURAL-WORLD NEUTER-ROLE LOWER-STATUS SIGN-WEAK	MEDICAL
−.6		SENSE	
−.7	SELF		

text and tag listing was examined at some length to determine the cause of a high score on a given tag in a given letter. The first eight factors, accounting for almost half (44.6 percent) of the variance, were examined. Table 12.1 gives a breakdown of the tags appearing in the first three factors.

Factor I: Aggression Management

The positive pole of this factor is concerned with people rather than things, strong feelings rather than emotional neutrality. MALE-ROLE and ROSS both refer to the frequency with which Jenny mentions her son. MALE-ROLE is primarily triggered by the word "he." The other personal tags involve women. FEMALE-ROLE is triggered by feminine pronouns and by all references to occupations normally associated with women. HIGHER-STATUS is associated with the text word "lady," which Jenny often uses sarcastically to describe Ross's friends, while LOWER-STATUS is associated with the word "prostitute," an equally frequent epithet for Ross's women. Several tags of interpersonal relationships, ANGER, ATTACK, SIGN-REJECT, and BAD, refer to negative feelings of aggression. The letters with the highest factor scores describe bitter arguments (one aspect of the high loadings on COMMUNI-CATE) between mother and son in which Jenny usually attacks Ross's present mistress. In these letters, comments appear about the low morals and evil intentions of modern women and about Ross's ingratitude. Letters with slightly lower factor scores still contain unfavorable mention of Ross and women but also refer to financial problems. One letter discusses Ross's failure to support his mother in her old age and his inability to hold a job.

The negative pole includes references to SELF, to travel (SPACE-REFERENCE, MOVE, MONTREAL, ATTEMPT), physical and economic objects (CLOTHING, TECHNOLOGICAL), and to economic activities (WORK, POSSESS). GLENN is the only personal tag to appear. The letters grouping themselves about this pole generally deal with Jenny's frequent trips, especially to Montreal. (She was usually on the move when the frustrations of the existing situation became unbearable.) The two letters with the highest scores are both addressed to Glenn and deal with Jenny's preparations to go to Canada. She feared she might die in an accident while en route and in these letters she discusses the settlement of her estate (LEGAL) with Glenn. She was afraid of losing her money and sewed it into the hems of her garments before each trip. The letter refers to her few possessions and contains plans for Glenn to claim her suitcases on her return. In other letters, she speaks of her attempts to find work; this involves much running about but no long journeys. All the letters indicate that Jenny was in continual movement from place to place, worrying about money, revealing no strong emotions, and dealing with objects rather than people.

If there is a single underlying trait in the two poles of this factor, it would seem to be in the management of aggressive tendencies, so apparent in Jenny's interpersonal relations. Her relationship with Ross was certainly the most important, if not the only, close personal relationship she maintained after the death of her husband, and Ross brought other people into her life. In this relationship, Jenny's aggression was manifested in her continual arguments with Ross, her name calling, her rages at other women. When she disliked people or was annoyed by a situation, she would take flight in a physical journey, into her work, or in frenetic job hunting. Jenny's frequent moves were usually a result of a desire to get away from someone, usually Ross, in order to take revenge by rejecting him. Significantly, the three letters with the highest positive scores were all written shortly after Jenny had broken with Ross, just after she had begun her correspondence.

Perhaps the best example of Jenny's alternative methods of handling aggression appears starkly in her final years in the institution. Then she would turn her face to the wall or withdraw into her room to avoid other patients, or else she would respond with violent, upprovoked, physical and verbal attacks. The common element of these opposite responses was her frequent expressions of hatred for the institution and its inmates. Thus, Jenny's response to the hostility she frequently felt was to fight or to flee. Direct attack and avoidance, overt aggression and rejection, are two forms of a single, underlying trait.

Factor II: Possessiveness

The most cursory reading of Jenny's letters indicates that much of her life revolved around Ross. Thus it is not surprising to find his presence or absence affecting a second dimension of her personality. The positive pole of Factor II includes ROSS, as well as references to money and written financial agreements (MESSAGE-FORM) and finances in general (ECONOMIC). Although APPROACH is an interpersonal tag, it includes many words of impersonal exchange: give, bring, offer. These words cause the high score. In this case, POSSESS indicates the possession of money; EXPEL is triggered by the single word "send"; and SIGN-ACCEPT is triggered by words suggestive of impersonal exchange of objects. These tags create the impression of getting and sending that seems to characterize this pole. OUGHT and ATTEMPT (in this case represented by the word "claim") indicate a concern for financial obligation. CAUSE is used infrequently to speculate about Ross's motives. The high loading on WORK is a result of two words, "pay" (again economic interchange) and "sew." "Sew" is associated with the frequent references to clothing in letters with high factor scores. Jenny held onto her money by sewing it into the lining of her coats, and she kept people close to her by carrying their names in her purse.

The general impression of a retentive, interpersonal relationship involving money and financial obligation, getting and sending, is confirmed by letters with high factor scores. These letters describe Jenny's cautious financial dealings with Ross and with a Mr. Pratt, with Ross's agreement not to marry for a year after he had signed a year's lease on an apartment for Jenny and himself, and with his marriage to a woman whom, Jenny claimed, he thought would support him. In these letters, Ross almost appears as a business associate, bound by contracts and monetary exchanges.

The negative pole of Factor II describes Jenny's relationships with children. The two lowest-scoring letters were written when Jenny worked in the nursery; the next three contain references to Ross as a child, or to Donald (Glenn and Isabel's first child). NEUTER-ROLE, LOWER-STATUS, and SIGN-WEAK, used variously in the definitions of boy, girl, child, and baby, have very negative scores and are evenly distributed through the five sample letters. Some tags involve only the situation in the nursery. HIGHER-STATUS and SIGN-AUTHORITY refer to Jenny's supervisors in the home, DISTRESS to her shame at yielding to the "barbaric" disciplinary methods of the home and to her poor physical condition. Jenny's descriptions of the corporal punishment administered by the other matrons makes BODY-PART a significant tag. AVOID refers to her extended efforts to quit the nursery entirely.

The experience in the nursery was generally unpleasant, but Jenny took joy in her charges. In the letters from the nursery period, the few sentences mentioning PLEASURE most often refer to Jenny's affection for the children. Similar references to PLEASURE occur in letters about Ross as a child and about Glenn's son Donald. SELVES, the collective "we," includes Jenny's references to herself and the other matrons but also the mutuality she felt with the children. Jenny apparently perceived her relations with children with particular vividness (SENSE), "Oh, you should 'see' little Eddie, the darling, lovely boy of three." Jenny frequently compared children metaphorically to natural beauty (NATURAL-OBJECT): "My little 'sunbeam' boy. . . ." References to past time trigger TIME-REFERENCE. Many of Jenny's pleasurable references are in nostalgic letters, memories of a hansom cab ride through Chicago with Ross, Ross standing nervously with Glenn at their first Princeton exam.

In both of these situations, the common element might be called possessiveness. Its alternative expression appears in Jenny's maternal needs, and in her retentive characteristics. In both situations, Jenny was concerned with controlling people: little children in the nursery, Ross through financial arrangements. Much of her anger at her supervisors in the home and her intense desire to avoid them may have been a result of her frustrated attempts to care for the children in her own way. Jenny's need to control other people could hardly be satisfied in a situation in which she herself was controlled. At the retentive pole, the letters deal with periods in her life in which Jenny had recently broken with Ross or was about to break with him. The economic retentiveness, the care for Ross's financial obligations to Jenny, the emphasis on money that had passed between them were all attempts to hold Ross, the adult, with the same force with which she had held him as a child. When Ross was not in her life (and in all the letters at the negative pole he is not), Jenny satisfied her need for maternal possession by caring for other children or by reminiscing about Ross as a child. In Jenny, a mother's joy in caring for children merged with a desire to possess and control the destiny of her offspring.

Factor III: Need for Affiliation

The positive pole of Factor III deals with Jenny's relationship with Glenn and Isabel, referred to by the tags GLENN, ISABEL, SELVES, and PEER-STATUS (you). ACADEMIC refers to Jenny's tendency to associate Glenn with the pleasant days when he and Ross were at Princeton together and to Jenny's love of books. One letter deals with a book, *Marco Polo,* which Glenn and Isabel had sent to Jenny on the eve of one of her many journeys. THINK is triggered by the word "know," used in sentences such as, "I have known Glenn and . . . I want to 'know' you [Isabel]." GOOD is high because of Jenny's many favorable evaluations of Glenn and Isabel. In this case, SIGN-ACCEPT and COMMUNICATE both suggest interpersonal communication. PLEASURE, the highest positive tag, indicates that Jenny's friendship with Glenn and Isabel is one of the pleasantest parts of her generally unhappy life. URGE, which includes words like "need" and "help," is an expression of Jenny's dependence on Glenn and Isabel and her need for their personal support: "I hope and pray most earnestly that we may be friends. I need you." RJ (references to Ross and Jenny collectively) is high because Jenny tends to associate Glenn's family with the happy days when she and Ross were together. The negative pole portrays most of the misfortunes in Jenny's life. HIGHER-STATUS, SIGN-STRONG, SIGN-AUTHORITY, and FEMALE-ROLE all refer to the women Jenny met in her many jobs. The women were frequently in positions of authority.

JOB-ROLE and WORK refer to the jobs themselves; DEATH, MEDICAL, and SIGN-WEAK refer to Jenny's difficulties in finding jobs, the stresses of hard work, and her poor health. AVOID occurs in sentences in which Jenny speaks of "losing her grip" or committing suicide. THOUGHT-FORM is triggered by the word "plan" and indicates Jenny's concern for her economic future. At this pole, the letters discuss Jenny's misfortunes, physical misery, her lack of work, and the hardships of the jobs she does hold. She threatens suicide. She uses the word "merely" (QUANTITY-REFERENCE) to suggest that she is unfortunate: "I merely became ill . . ."

The common dimension of these two poles seems to be Jenny's affiliative needs for Glenn and Isabel. In the letters with high positive scores, these needs are directly expressed by telling Glenn and Isabel how much she needs and depends on them, by praising them and their home, by talking of the joy she takes in their friendship. The letters describing her misery are a more subtle request for the same personal relationship. The letters at the negative pole tend to exaggerate Jenny's condition. They stress her hardships, her struggles, and the infrequency of her rewards. In these letters, Jenny also appeals to Glenn and Isabel for affection and attempts to arouse their sympathy by vivid descriptions of her misery.

A Comparison of Factors and Common Sense Traits

We have described the first three factors in some detail in order to demonstrate the method used to interpret them and to demonstrate how intimately each factor is connected with the fabric of Jenny's life. It should be noted that in this limited space it is impossible to discuss every tag in detail. We have merely presented summaries, with much specific evidence omitted.

Table 12.2 briefly describes the first eight factors and gives an account of Jenny's life situation when they appeared. The factors are listed in descending order of variance. It should be noted that these variance scores only tell us the frequency of the appearance of a trait in Jenny's written reflections during a single decade of her life. As such, the list does present a picture of the relative prominence of each of these traits in Jenny's personality.

The list of traits is an abstraction from the actual structure of personal dispositions in Jenny's personality. The complete definition of any factor and its corresponding trait can be obtained only by careful examination of the relevant letters and tag clusters. As Table 12.3 indicates, each factor is intimately connected with Jenny's actual behavior as expressed in the letters. The factors are not the result of an *a priori* theoretic scheme or an intuitive notion of what Jenny must have been like.

The factor descriptions correspond roughly to a list of "common sense" traits described by Allport (1964). Allport asked 36 undergraduates to characterize Jenny in terms of her traits. The students extracted 198 trait names. Many of these, of course, were synonymous or closely related, and Allport grouped them into clusters which represent characteristics recognized by a number of different judges. While the correspondence between the two lists is certainly not one to one, there is considerable overlap. In general both the human judges and the content analysis picked up the same major themes, but the cataloging systems used are somewhat different.[1]

Jenny's cynicism, her sarcasm, and her frequent quarrels are all forms of aggressive behavior and as such are organized in a single factor by the General Inquirer analysis. Much of Jenny's hypochondria and her morbid fixation on death seemed to be a means of evok-

[1] G. W. Allport (1964, 201) presents a pairing slightly different from that in Table 12.3.

TABLE 12.2. *Jenny's Most Prominent Traits and the Situations in Which They Appear*

Trait	Mode of Expression
Aggression	Deprecatory invective, especially directed at Ross and women; anger, arguments with Ross. Indirectly expressed in travel and job hunting.
Possessiveness	A combination of nurturant and retentive needs. Expressed in Jenny's joy in caring for children, including Ross when he was younger, and in her later attempts to bind her son to her by legal and financial means.
Need for Affiliation	Expressed directly by telling Glenn and Isabel how much they are depended upon, by praising them and their home, by writing of the joy she takes in their friendship. Indirectly expressed by exaggerated descriptions of distress intended (probably unconsciously) to invoke sympathy.
Need for Autonomy	Optimism and happiness in being able to support herself despite poverty and lack of skills. Pride in ability to find work and perform hard jobs. Frustrated by supervision, especially during the period of the nursery.
Need for Familial Acceptance	Frequent attempts to return to Canada and be reconciled with her sisters, to visit and live with them. Indirectly expressed by associating family values (that is, aesthetic values) with her own family situation — she and Ross.
Sexuality	Jenny's romantic descriptions of her relationship with her son — hansom cab rides by moonlight, trips to the country. Indirectly expressed by her vicarious sharing (by identification with Isabel) in the affection evident to her in Glenn's family.
Sentience	Jenny's sentience, her love of art, literature, and natural beauty. Also expressed by her need to be dependent on Glenn and Isabel, to assume a subordinate position, to be helped and supported.
Martyrdom	Description of the nobility of Jenny's sacrifices for others, particularly for Ross. Also expressed by complaints that her sacrifices are unappreciated and bring her only grief, and descriptions of the burdens she must bear.

ing Glenn's and Isabel's sympathy, and in the factor structure, letters dealing with death and ill health fell on the same factor as those dealing with direct attempts to ingratiate herself with Glenn and Isabel. The trait names that Allport characterized as sentimental are words such as retrospective, maternal, dweller in the past, all of which refer

TABLE 12.3. Factorial and Common Sense Traits

Factorial Traits	Allport's Common Sense Traits
aggression	quarrelsome, suspicious aggressive
possessiveness	self-centered
need for affiliation	cynical, morbid
sexuality	sentimental
need for familial acceptance	
need for autonomy	independent, autonomous
sentience	aesthetic-artistic
martyrdom	self-centered
(no parallel)	dramatic, intense

to Jenny's reminiscence about her half-romantic relationship with her son or to her attempts to reconcile herself, at least in memory, with her family. There seems to be no parallel in the General Inquirer analysis to many trait names that deal with the dramatic style of Jenny's life. Apparently the intuitive reader readily perceives stylistic and expressive qualities of the letters, while the factor analysis is bound more closely to actual situations. The comparison between Allport's common sense traits and the factor structure suggests that automated content analysis is sensitive to the same kinds of themes as a human observer.[2]

LONG-TERM CHANGES OF PERSONALITY

In this section, we turn to longer trends stretching over much of the last decade of Jenny's life, changes in the structure of personality itself. Although Jenny never found life comfortable, she became increasingly disturbed in her last eleven years. Why did Jenny's adequate, if not happy, adjustment deteriorate into maladjustment? The answer is to be found in long-term changes in her physical and interpersonal environment and in her personality itself.

In order to examine some of these long-term changes, the text was divided into fifteen "natural sections," each section ending at a change in Jenny's physical or interpersonal environment. The first period in-

[2] A similar comparison might be made between these factors and the constellations found by Baldwin (1942). Basic differences in the selection of categories makes such comparisons difficult. Baldwin begins with themes quite specific to Jenny and plots the frequency of coexistence in the same context of thought.

cludes her Chicago letters, the second, her trip home to Montreal, the third, her stay alone in New York before her reconciliation with Ross. The remaining twelve sections reflect her frequent trips and many jobs. It was necessary to divide the long, relatively uniform years of institutional life into somewhat more arbitrary periods involving changes in attitudes toward her deceased son. Tag totals were obtained from each of the fifteen periods and a subsystem of the General Inquirer automatically generated graphs of tag scores as a function of time for each of the tags. The graphs were inspected for long-term trends, and inferences were checked by retrieving sentences from relevant sections.

Three tags, SELF, ROSS, and MALE-ROLE (the last two are for the most part identical), are highly variable but are related in an interesting way. When Jenny was alone, she naturally wrote much of herself. The earliest letters, written just after her break with Ross, mark such a period of isolation: SELF-references are high. As her contacts with the world gradually increased, as she searched for a job, for a place to live, she referred less often to herself, and when she saw Ross again, SELF references and, presumably, self-centeredness are at a minimum. Isolation and crisis were always associated in Jenny's life. When she broke with Ross, when he died, when she was in the institution for the elderly, Jenny was alone. In times of crisis she did not seek other people, but instead concentrated more intensely on herself and thereby increased the apparent severity of her problems.

When Jenny did not write of herself, she wrote of her son. The curves of SELF and ROSS are mirror images of one another (Figure 12.1), at least up to the time of Ross's death. When SELF is high, ROSS is low, and vice versa. When Jenny was with her son, she was less concerned about herself, and thus Ross might have served as a stabilizing influence, helping her to bear her many problems. At the end of her life, Jenny mainly writes of herself and scarcely mentions Ross. Although her relationship with her son was tumultuous, it drew her out of herself and provided human contact. When her son was gone and her memory of him waned, Jenny turned inward. The superintendent of the institution remarked that before her death, Jenny had begun to turn her face to the wall when she met other women in the corridors, a psychic turning away that had begun shortly after her son's death.

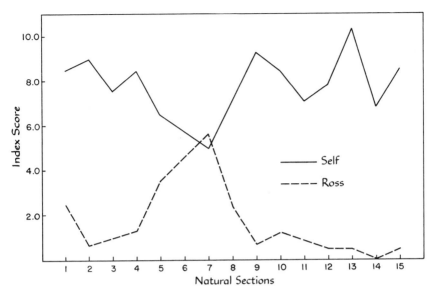

FIGURE 12.1. Graphs of tags ROSS *and* SELF *across natural section time periods.*

Few tags show a constant trend over the entire fifteen sections, but a number of them change near the end of Jenny's life, particularly in the final two sections, Jenny's last two years and her most psychically troubled time. Each of these tags was translated into a retrieval question, and the retrieved sentences were examined in detail. We can now summarize the results.

Attack

Jenny refers to overt aggression during her period of work in the nursery, immediately after Ross's death, and in her last years in the institution. In the nursery, Jenny describes the aggression that the matrons directed primarily at the children: "We had not a thing to beat the babies with." During the legal dispute, Jenny reiterates the crimes of the "chip" — "She killed Ross all right." "She killed Ross, morally and physically." It is interesting that during the final year of her life, she again spoke freely of aggression. She again describes the evils of Ross's "chip," "and that is why the chip killed him," but adds a new element, a lengthy description of her battle with a nurse, "I . . . pounded her breasts, her head and face. . . ." A retrieval of all of Jenny's aggressive statements reveals that such an admission is extremely rare. This trend toward greater overt aggressiveness is indicative of Jenny's losing battle to control her aggressive impulses, which earlier had been expended in name calling or travel.

Academic

At the end of her life, Jenny became increasingly concerned with things of the mind. Cut off from any possibility of human companionship by the death of her son, her dislike of women, and the senility of many of the residents in the institution, she turned to reading newspapers and great books and to a lecture series. "So I have started my study of Grecian history all over again." "There are eight volumes, Shakespeare in calf best paper and print, student's edition, good glossary and notes. . . ." "They have lectures and 'gallery talks' almost every day." Jenny's academic-aesthetic interests persisted and became more intense at the end of her life. She used art and literature as a substitute for the human warmth she was unable to find.

Overstate

This tag includes words such as always, never, really, impossible, and a high score indicates a tendency toward exaggeration and rigidity. Excessive use of words in this category indicates a tendency to see the world in a black-white, oversimplified form, to be dogmatic and extreme in judgments. UNDERSTATE, the complementary category, indicates judicious reserve and a cautious attitude toward the future. OVERSTATE increases over Jenny's entire letter writing period but is particularly high in the period of institutional life. The subjects of overstatement remain relatively constant throughout her life. Other people, Jenny's physical and mental condition, and life in general are notably bad. Glenn, nature, and culture are exceptionally good. In the final years, this bifurcation between people with whom she had immediate contact and her values became more and more extreme. In the last year of her life, Jenny found the other women in the home intolerable: "I looked at this extremely plain, unattractive old creature and felt pity." She lost all patience with the officials of the home: "This will be the first of a series of tales of my experience with those infernal hypocrites and liars, and double dealers, the damn Catholics, and the equally damn Y.W.C.A." Her health and talk about it were worse than ever: ". . . seems every nerve, muscle and cord in my body was dragged and strained. . . ." Her avoidance of other people was total: "But I never see anyone. . . ." "I do not answer at all, there is nothing to answer. . . ." Art and nature became even more highly valued — "My love has always been the red rose . . ." and art is ". . . the only thing in the world that has lasting qualities. 'All things pass, art alone remains with us, the bust outlives the throne, the coin, Tiberius!' " Finally she still felt close to Glenn and Isabel: "Thank you so much for that perfectly lovely card. . . ." At the end of her life Jenny's world was divided into two extremes, bad people, who surrounded her in the home and were to be avoided, and the beauties of art and nature, which were to be admired.

Death

Jenny's thoughts turned to death more and more in her last years in the home. She had spoken frequently of death at another period in her life, just before her reconciliation with Ross. In her last two years, she contemplated suicide: "that I am damned to remain here, barring accident, until I take the law into my own hands." About the death that surrounded her in the home: "The old women here are just sitting around waiting to die." She spoke of her own poor physical condition: "Life is as usual with me sort of a living death." There are also indirect, almost poetic, references to death pervading the things she loved: "[the roses] are still here on my shelf near the window. They remained fresh for a long time, and I left them in the vase. . . . Now and then a leaf falls off, but on the whole they are still themselves, and you." The atmosphere of the home and Jenny's advancing years were reasons enough for thoughts of death.

Jenny's life, as she expressed it in her letters, changed notably in the two years before death. She was more isolated than she had been at any time in her life and concentrated more on herself. Her memories of Ross became fainter. For support, she increasingly turned to her aesthetic values, her love of literature, and her appreciation of natural beauty. Her dislike of authority figures became more intense. She used animal names to express her disgust, assuming what she perceived as a male role. Her aggressive drives began to be overt. She battled physically with nurses and other patients. She avoided the other members of the home as much as possible. The bifurcation between her values and her interpersonal needs became more and more extreme. People were hated and avoided. Jenny withdrew into herself with her beloved literature and art.

The following etiology of Jenny's mental deterioration is based on the evidence from the time-trend analysis just summarized and on the constellation of the traits isolated in the factor analysis. Her sharp trend toward withdrawal, punctuated with occasional aggressive outbursts, was a result of the interaction of her personality structure with three major events: Ross's death, her entrance into the institution, and her final rejection by her family. Ross fulfilled many of Jenny's deepest needs, her desire to possess and control, her sexuality, and, to a certain extent, her affiliativeness. With Ross gone, Jenny lost all hope of controlling his life and all possibility of intimacy with him. Instead of seeking other friends, Jenny behaved as she had in the past by isolating herself and thus frustrating her affiliative needs. There were no opportunities for Jenny to nurture anyone in the institution. On the contrary, her life was prescribed by the authorities. Jenny's entrance into the institution frustrated her need for autonomy. She became angry and disturbed at the feminine directors, just as earlier she had hated her supervisors in the nursery. Not only was her need for autonomy frustrated by the institution, but she lost one of the principal outlets for her aggressions: avoidance. Jenny could not remove herself physically from the institution as she had from the nursery. Instead she rejected others by drawing into herself. The avoidance of others by hiding in herself was not as satisfactory an outlet for aggression as avoidance by travel and an active life.

The home situation and the death of Ross frustrated most of Jenny's basic traits: aggression, possessiveness, need for autonomy, affiliativeness, and sexuality toward Ross. Her final unsuccessful trip to Canada frustrated still another: her desire to be accepted by her family. When her sister failed to sign over $1,000 worth of property to Jenny so that she could enter Canada, Jenny was unequivocably rejected. She returned to the institution where the single trait she could express, her love of art and literature, assumed central importance in her life.

When her indirect modes of expressing aggression were impossible, she turned to direct modes. When all of her interpersonal needs were frustrated by her environment and her own aggressiveness, she turned inward to herself and her sentient needs.

SUMMARY

The General Inquirer has enabled us to find out much about Jenny Masterson, but what has the study of her letters told us about automated content analysis? Content analysis, in conjunction with factor analysis, makes possible a description of the unique traits that make up the structure of individual personality. Unlike the usual factor analysis study of personality, the traits are unique to the personality studied. The fine structure of personality is not sacrificed for global personality dimensions. The factor structure provides an operational definition of the notion of trait by tying it closely to Jenny's own verbal behavior. The traits thus derived correspond to the major common sense traits listed by human readers, but the results of the content analysis are repeatable and are not subject to the distortions of subjective readings. The analysis of changes in tags over the entire period of the letters allows us to describe more accurately changes in Jenny's personality than could the clinical observer. Although the General Inquirer analysis does not solve the riddle of Jenny's personality, it does provide a stable, quantified picture of her personality in terms of her own verbal behavior.

BIBLIOGRAPHY

Allport, G. W. (1937), *Personality: Psychological Interpretation.* New York: Henry Holt.

——— (1942), *The Use of Personal Documents in Psychological Science.* New York: Social Science Research Council Bulletin, 49.

——— (1961), *Pattern and Growth in Personality.* New York: Holt, Rinehart and Winston.

——— (ed.) (1964), *Letters from Jenny.* New York: Harcourt, Brace & World.

"Anonymous Letters from Jenny." (1946), *Journal of Abnormal and Social Psychology.* Vol. 41, 315–350, 449–480.

Baldwin, A. L. (1942), "Personal Structure Analysis: A Statistical Method for Investigating the Single Personality." *Journal of Abnormal and Social Psychology.* Vol. 37, 163–183.

Cattell, R. B. (1946), *Description and Measurement of Personality.* New York: World Book Co.

Eysenck, N. J. (1953), *The Structure of Human Personality.* New York: John Wiley & Sons.

CHAPTER THIRTEEN

Procedures for Improving
the Interpretation of Tag Scores:
The Case of Windle

Daniel M. Ogilvie
Harvard University

INTRODUCTION

One of the obvious advantages of using computers as research tools in the social sciences is that they speed up statistical analyses and assist the investigator in conceptualizing large amounts of data that he otherwise would not be able to handle in a convenient time period. In extending this advantage, we now find ourselves in the fortunate position of having computer systems capable of rapid manipulation of verbal data. The operations have become particularly useful to psychologists working in the area of content analysis and have led to at least one computer system that rapidly categorizes words under predesignated lists. The appearance of this system has been met with enthusiasm by a number of investigators. However, beneath this enthusiasm (often completely covered by it) lies the difficult and neglected problem of validating the interpretations.

This issue of interpretive validity should be salient to all users of the General Inquirer. We shall briefly define part of this problem by tracing the steps of the researcher who has some documents he wants content analyzed. He hears that the General Inquirer might well be the system he is looking for. He reads the literature available on the system, understands what it does with the data, finds that several of the tags could be relevant to some of the variables that interest him, and subsequently makes arrangements to have his materials processed. The data are punched, run on the General Inquirer, 4,100 words are defined, and the results are returned to him. In looking over his printout, he finds that eight or nine tags are high for one document and low for another. After thinking about these findings for a while, a theory begins to emerge that is slightly different from the theory he had previously had in mind, but it is a theory that seems to hang together. If he has the time, he may retrieve some sentences from the two sets of data; he will find sentences that support his now well-internalized theory, and finally he will write up his findings. It may never occur to him that the results could be entirely spurious. After all, he has analyzed his data on a computer, the latest and most sophisticated research tool. If it occurs to him to ask the developers of the system if his results are valid, they are hard put for an answer. They know that tags have not been applied to his data in a random fashion; they know that a great deal of time was spent in making up and revising the dictionary; yet a real "feel" of what is going on and a real "faith" in interpretation is lacking. The point is admittedly overdrawn, but the basic issue of "how confident can we be about our interpretations" remains, and this is the problem discussed in this paper.

We shall approach this problem of validity by making what is essentially an idiographic case study. The focus of this analysis is on one individual, Windle, who was one of ten members of an all male undergraduate course organized along the lines of a training group. Over the period of two semesters this group met for one hour three times a week, for a total of 76 sessions. During this time, they were observed through a one-way mirror. One of the observers categorized their interaction by using a revised form of the Bales Interaction Process Analysis system (IPA). (Some of the information extracted from these recordings will become useful in the analysis to follow.) For 15 or 20 minutes after each session the members wrote about what had occurred. They were given freedom to discuss a wide range of topics: their feelings about the group or an individual member, the relevance of one of their assigned cases to the happenings in the group, their thoughts about the comments or lack of comments of the instructor, and so on. The average length of these Post-Meeting Reaction Questionnaires (PMRQ) was between 200 and 250 words. In this attempt to evaluate the General Inquirer, we shall be dealing primarily with an analysis of Windle's PMRQ's from Session 8 through Session 25.

We will ask ourselves the following questions: Are the differences on tag scores between Windle and the other group members meaningful? Do they fit with an intuitive understanding of him? Do these differences point to any new insights that are still consistent with Windle's general behavior patterns? Are the General Inquirer results at all congruent with Windle's group interaction as measured by IPA? In other words, we will look at the problem from an intuitive viewpoint with the help of an outside criterion.

PROCEDURE

First let us look at Windle's Interaction scores as compared to the scores of the entire group. Figure 13.1 has been constructed in the following manner: to obtain the group percentage scores, the group totals for Sessions 8 through 25 were summed separately for each of the 12 categories, and these 12 summations were in turn divided by

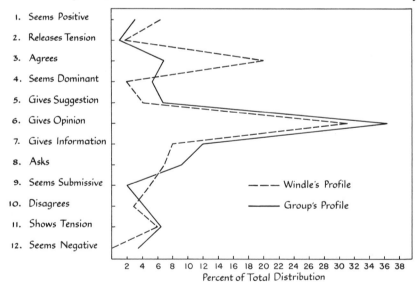

FIGURE 13.1. Windle's IPA distribution compared to group's distribution.

the grand total of all scores. Windle's percentage scores were obtained by the same procedure after his totals were extracted from the group's total.

In the Socioemotional areas, we can clearly see that on the average Windle (1) shows more positivity than the other group members, (2) agrees a much greater number of times than the others, (3) is not dominant, (4) submits frequently, and (5) expresses little negativity. To establish the statistical significance of such differences has always been a tricky problem for IPA users. However, a satisfactory description of the data can be made by first calculating the percentage scores each individual obtained in each category for every session. For example, we start with Person number 1, calculate his percentage distribution over the 12 categories for Session 8, do the same for Session 9, and so on: then continue with the same procedure for Person number 2, and so on. We may then select a category that interests us and rank order each person on that category for each session. In other words, for the data presented here, we have 18 sessions and therefore each person is ranked 18 different times for one category. To these ranks we can apply the Kolmogorov-Smirnov one-sample test, which tells us whether our obtained ranks for any one person can be expected by chance. When using this procedure, one must be careful to specify where the obtained distribution differs from the expected distribution because this test has the peculiar characteristic of pointing up significance when the individual's ranks are consistently on the mean. That is, if one subject out of a group of 9 members is always ranked number 5, his obtained distribution will still differ significantly from the expected distribution. Using this test, Windle's ranks came out on the high side of the distribution for categories 1, 3, and 8; low on categories 4 and 12. See Table 13.1 for the significance levels.

TABLE 13.1. *IPA Categories That Discriminate Windle from This Group*

Category	Direction	D	Significance Level
Positive	High	.65	.01
Agrees	High	.59	.01
Dominant	Low	.39	.10
Submissive	High	.33	.10
Negative	Low	.27	n.s.

What has all this told us about our subject? He looks like an agreeable, pleasant person, someone who is easy to get along with. He appears to be submissive and nonobtrusive. It is probably easy to get him to go along with just about anything. In fact, he has a self-admitted need to be liked, to be one of the boys. His attempt to be liked comes out in the form of a general orientation to please the other person.

With these impressions of Windle in mind, let us go directly into an analysis of his PMRQ's. As with the IPA analysis, we have the advantage of comparing Windle's tag frequencies with the tag frequencies of the other group members. In preparing these data for processing, the PMRQ's for six members[1] were divided into four sections of comparable length. That is, the data for each person was divided in such a way that after every four or five PMRQ's a tag tally could be taken. If the data are of sufficient length, this division seems to be helpful in establishing a criterion of consistency. In comparing Windle's score on a given tag with the scores of the other group members, we are again faced with the problem of how large the difference has to be before we find it "interesting." Again one possible solution is to rank the individuals on the basis of their scores for a certain tag. This is obviously not possible when we have only one score per person, and it is hardly worthwhile with anything less than four scores per person. In our case, we have 6 subjects and 4 tag counts for each person, giving every member 4 ranks out of a possible 24 positions for each tag. The Kruskal-Wallis one-way analysis of variance by ranks will tell us how often a cluster of ranks for any one person could have happened by chance. Using this statistic, we find that Windle's high ranks on two tags (AVOID and AROUSAL) had the probability of occurring by chance one time in a hundred. Further, his high rankings on the over-all distribution for the tag SIGN-REJECT was significant at the .05 level. Although these low probabilities of occurrence give us a sense of confidence, we are not convinced that we need to concern ourselves solely with just those tags which, by these measures, turn out to be significant. For example, valuable information may possibly be obtained by splitting the tag scores at the median so that half of the scores lie on one side and half on the other. In our case, if all of

---

[1] Four members have been excluded from this analysis because they were rather unfaithful in their attendance and consequently left us with a sparse amount of PMRQ data.

Windle's scores for a particular tag cluster are on one side of the median, we know that at least he is consistent in using (or not using) words that have been classified under that tag word. Using this procedure, we find that, compared to the rest of the group, Windle was high in his use of 11 tags and low on 4. These tags are placed under their respective subdivisions in Table 13.2.

TABLE 13.2. Tags That Distinguish Windle from the Other Group Members

HIGH		LOW
SELF	*Persons*	
MESSAGE-FORM	*Culture*	SELVES
AROUSAL DISTRESS	*Emotion*	
	Thought	THINK
COMMUNICATE ATTACK AVOID	*Socioemotional Actions*	
	Impersonal Actions	ATTEMPT
ACADEMIC	*Institutional Contexts*	
SIGN-STRONG SIGN-WEAK SIGN-REJECT	*Psychological Themes*	

And suddenly we appear to be in trouble. Here we are confronted with a list of tags that could not possibly have been applied to words from the pen of Windle. What has happened to IDEAL-VALUE, AFFECTION, PLEASURE, GOOD, APPROACH, and FOLLOW? Certainly they would be more congruent with our record of his pleasant, agreeing, and submissive external behavior. Instead, we get AROUSAL, DISTRESS, ATTACK, AVOID, SIGN-STRONG, SIGN-WEAK, and SIGN-REJECT. Suddenly the solution to this incongruity leaps out at us. Windle is compensating for his submissiveness, for being pushed around, by attacking the other group members. Secretly he despises them. Underneath his pleasant mask he is seething with anger. He is expressing his revenge through print. This mode of theorizing is dangerously convincing, and it is exactly the kind made possible by the General Inquirer. We rapidly scan the data and immediately find sentences such as,

"Steve had no business bringing that guest today," or "Larry made me angry in today's meeting." Out of 3,339 words, or 265 sentences, we will find many examples to support our new-found theory, and it will not take too many examples to sell the theory. Despite the fact that the results are not quite what we had expected to find, this does not bother us; we have a much better theory than we had hoped for.

Our point is obvious. We begin the analysis of our data by looking over the tag frequencies, but it must not end there. Our initial impression of the meaning of the tag tallies may be correct, but we must do more than select a few exemplifying sentences to validate our conceptualization. The addition of the 1401 tag tally and retrieval systems and the tree-building procedures to the General Inquirer package have greatly facilitated our efforts to understand the data at hand. So, for the time being, let us forget about this interpretation of Windle's tag tallies. Let us try to minimize our biases and allow the two sets of data to speak for themselves.

Our procedure will be to compare Windle's documents with those of another group member whom we shall call Gale. In processing the data with the 1401 programs, we attempted to find those tags that best differentiated between the two sets of documents by building a tree to account for a large percentage of Windle's sentences and a smaller percentage of Gale's. At each node, the sentences on the "yes" side of the node were retrieved, and the tags on the "no" side were totaled. By taking a tag tally at each node, the data were progressively reduced by using the better tag discriminators at each node. Studying the retrievals at these nodes increases our chances of better understanding what is happening as the tree structure grows. We must keep in mind that this procedure is just a strategy of organizing sentences in a systematic, comparative way, a heuristic that we hope will lead to improved interpretation. The tree that was developed is shown in Figure 13.2.

At each nonterminal node appears the name of the tag used to discriminate between the documents. The numbers on the left branches indicate the number of sentences containing the tags specified by the retrieval questions. The figures in parentheses refer to the percentages of sentences retrieved. The first number of each pair pertains to Windle's sentences, the second to Gale's. On the right branches, the figures indicate the number and percentage of sentences not yet discriminated.

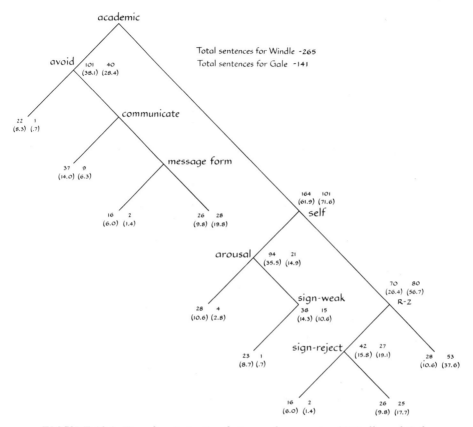

FIGURE 13.2. Tree discrimination between documents of Windle and Gale.

The tag ACADEMIC was one of the obvious choices for the first node because (1) the tag tally showed that Windle had higher counts on it than the other members, and (2) despite this difference, it still retrieved a large proportion of Gale's sentences. (It retrieved 38.1 percent of Windle's sentences and 28.4 percent of Gale's sentences.) A tag tally of these sentences revealed a large difference between Windle and Gale on the following categories: AVOID, COMMUNICATE, and MESSAGE-FORM. These three tags were used for the next three nodes. Combined, these three nodes accounted for 28.3 percent of Windle's sentences and only 8.4 percent of Gale's. A sample of these sentences is given in Table 13.3.

From Windle's retrievals, we detect a rather compulsive concern about the cases used as teaching devices in this course. This concern was relatively absent in Gale's PMRQ's. Note that the "seething anger"

TABLE 13.3. Sample Sentence Retrievals for Windle and Gale

Retrievals on ACADEMIC, AVOID
Windle

The group succeeded in avoiding the case for 40 minutes.

The presence of a girl partially explains the avoidance of the last meeting's "homosexual" discussion.

The absence of 5 members of the group produced the topic of discussion of today's meeting.

In my opinion we were actually avoiding the cases, the reading, etc.

Some members of the group desire to escape from the tasks of the course and to avoid being confronted with the great amount of knowledge. . . .

Their discussion was avoiding the type of conversation and analysis I am interested in in relation to this course.

Today, however, I did feel that more people . . . agreed with me and shared my frustration and my annoyance toward Steve for his continual avoidance of case analysis.

Gale (Only one sentence retrieved.)

Perhaps we can learn to hate without fear.

Retrievals on ACADEMIC, COMMUNICATE
Windle

If the level of discussion had continued it would have been dangerous to my own and, in my opinion, the group's ability to rationally discuss a case.

We have to discuss the case again.

Our discussion resulted in some renewed introspection on my part.

. . . because I could participate more in the discussion.

Frank nodded when I suggested this reason.

Steve led the discussion away from such analyses.

Gale has led the discussion during the past week or two.

Throughout most of today's session I felt the same frustration that I have mentioned previously about irrelevant discussions.

Gale

The slight hesitancy to initiate a discussion of sexual factors was easily overcome.

The case discussion partially accounts for today's virtual lack of rough interpersonal contact.

Absenteeism may portend a drastic identification crisis with reference to this group for that individual.

TABLE 13.3. Cont.

Retrievals on ACADEMIC, MESSAGE-FORM

Windle

It seemed obvious that the group seemed threatened by the case from the start.

We must get down to the case at all costs.

We should discuss the case no matter what.

Like Allen Jennings (case son), I felt a conscious desire for independence.

Upon return to case studies people still tended to fight for their own ideas.

Gale

The case material was characterized by a marked adaptiveness for purposes of abstraction and projection at the hand of the group.

This also accounted for the divergence of approaches to an analysis.

---

hypothesis finds little to support it here. Any anger that is expressed is in the form of criticism of those who block case discussion, of those who lead the group away from case analysis.

Windle forces us to consider the role of case materials in the course these students were taking. This course is structured primarily around three tasks: the members have (1) assigned readings to consider, (2) cases to discuss, and (3) their own group to analyze. Generally each group goes through an extended period of self-analysis during which there is little discussion of the readings or cases. Windle's group was going through such a stage. But this obviously bothered him. Time after time he writes, "We must get back to the cases." Why should this be? One reason could be that the analysis of the group was threatening to him and the cases offered an escape. Another possibility concerns his guilt about the group not living up to the instructor's expectations by avoiding part of the assigned course work. A third possibility (associated with the second) is that he is writing to be accepted by the instructor. That is, he could be saying in effect, "Look, I want to discuss the cases, but these fellows are holding me back. Don't blame me for their lack of cooperation." To decide the fruitfulness of these interpretations, let us return to the data to see if the remainder of the tree sheds more light on any or all of them.

Since we have removed all sentences containing words defined by ACADEMIC, the data have been reduced to 164 sentences for Windle and 101 sentences for Gale. A tag tally of these remaining sentences reveals a substantial difference between Windle and Gale in writing in the first person (SELF). In turn, a tag tally of these sentences showed different counts on AROUSAL and SIGN-WEAK: Windle scores high on both. The combination of SELF and AROUSAL leads us to believe that we are coming close to verification of the hypothesis that Windle expresses emotional excitement in his PMRQ's normally withheld in live interaction. Some of the power-packed words that could be raising his total in this category are arouse, awake, emotion, instinct, energy, excite, impulse, restless, and so forth. The actual retrievals, however, again betray this hypothesis. Twenty-four of the 28 retrievals were caused by the words "felt" and "feeling." Some examples are

> And it is the same feeling (or worry) about exclusion that makes me fear my own absenteeism.
>
> I may have felt I had let him down.
>
> I felt a sudden pang of guilt at what I had done.
>
> I felt a tremendous degree of relief.
>
> My feeling today was again one of frustration.
>
> I felt disgust at myself and the rest of the group.

Here, then, is an instance of being misled by the General Inquirer's dictionary. We had expected to find sentences containing expressions of emotional excitement, but at first glance these retrievals seem to have little relevance to our preconceptions. On the other hand, we should not be too hasty in our dismissal of these sentences from the AROUSAL category. Let us look at them for a moment. Out of the array of topics Windle could have chosen to write about, he consistently chose to tell us how he felt. He is obviously very sensitive to the effects of external situations and stimuli on his internal state. His emotions appear to fluctuate with the situation. This in itself is not alarming, nor is it at all unusual. The unusual aspect of it is Windle's strong awareness and concern with such fluctuations.

It could still be debated whether or not the word "felt" belonged on the AROUSAL list. Possibly SENSE would be a better category for it. Consider the following sentence: "I felt that the ship was not making much forward progress in the rough seas." "Felt" in this sentence could just as well be replaced by "sensed." On the other hand, when Windle says, "I felt frustrated," he is not just saying, "I sensed frustration." He is describing an internal state. A solution to this problem would be to place the attributive "felt" on the SENSE list and the verbal "felt" on the AROUSAL list. But beneath the issue of the placement of one word lies a much greater problem. We have seen how the consistent use of one word can affect the tag totals. That is, just one word repeated often enough may be responsible for a high count on a certain tag. Therefore, when we rely on the tag tally as our sole source of information, we risk the possibility of entirely missing the meaning of the tag distributions. Just because the count is high on a particular tag does not mean that we understand what it means. Perhaps the only solution to this problem is to do just what we have done here, make retrievals on the basis of that tag word and study the sentences extracted from the documents.

Having removed the sentences containing reference to SELF and AROUSAL in Windle's case, we come to the next node, which is SELF, SIGN-WEAK. (The reader may want to refer to Figure 13.2 to pick up our location.) At this node, we begin to pick up some "old stuff." The sentences retrieved by SELF and SIGN-WEAK look familiar to us. The picture is becoming consistent. Consider the following sentences:

> This discussion of homosexuality frightened me to an almost unbearable level.

> I, for one, was becoming worried and too a little guilty.

> I did worry though about somehow antagonizing the absent members.

> I think that I did feel a little hesitant about voicing some of my more "far out" speculations.

> I fear that Gale will "argue me down."

> And it seemed to me that there was a more general discomfort in the group than ever before.

Here we find Windle expressing his need to be accepted by the members of the group. He does not even want to offend absent members, not because such attacks might be inherently unfair but because of the fear of reciprocation. Such reciprocation would be damaging to his self-esteem and would produce evidence of nonacceptance. He even hesitates to express his own ideas because of the fear of being "argued down." In other words, he appears to need constant surface reinforcement that he is an accepted member. In the preceding sentences, we again find Windle to be intimately aware of the external environment and of his emotional reactions to it.

Let us look now at the final node of our tree. After removing the sentences referring to SELF, a tag tally of the remaining sentences in both documents pointed out that the tag R-Z was very high for both sets. First R-Z must be explained. As the PMRQ's were being coded, references to other group members were specified by the use of a special code for each member. Each time the General Inquirer tagging program encountered one of these special codes, it defined it by R-Z. In this case, then, the counts on R-Z refer to the number of times the two writers mentioned other group members in the sentences that remained to be discriminated. It was decided to extract those sentences containing references to other members and run a tag tally on them. The tag concept that differentiated best between these two sets of sentences was SIGN-REJECT. The sorts of sentences retrieved from Windle's PMRQ's by the specifications R-Z, SIGN-REJECT are exemplified by the following:

> The group had been rebelling against Steve.
>
> Then Burgess finally suggested that we "kick him out" of next week's meeting.
>
> We effectively crucified Gale.
>
> As if, as Dr. . . . put it, we were considering the remains of a deposed God.
>
> The analytical forces criticized him last week.
>
> Steve's actions have prevented the rest of the group from establishing the "give and take. . . ."

These examples help to clarify the context in which Windle uses words which are generally associated with negative actions. Rather than appearing in the context of slashing attacks on others, it comes out in rather mild reporting of the day's events: "the group rebels . . . ," "Analytical forces criticize . . . ," and "other members prevent. . . ."

DISCUSSION AND CONCLUSIONS

We now come to the question, "Have we learned anything about Windle by using the General Inquirer procedures?" Consider the following paragraph that Windle wrote in one of his early PMRQ's:

. . . I felt that the Seiton family situation was, in one or two respects, quite similar to that in my own family but . . . I was reluctant to reveal this 'intimate' detail directly to the other members of group. (Although I was not at all hesitant in drawing from my experience in formulating opinions about the Seitons.) I suppose, then, that I am still somewhat afraid of not being received as a 'regular guy' by the other members of the group.

Here Windle reveals a little bit about his own family life. The Seiton family is a short case study assigned in the course. The case describes a group situation in which all the members of the family try to please one another. On the surface, this sounds as if it should lead to a fulfilling and rewarding family experience. However, when each member of the family is trying to do what the other wishes to have done, nobody is quite sure what the other person really wants. For example, the case describes several instances in which one member of the family gets involved in a project solely because he senses that another member wants him to do it. Ironically, that "other" family member had no interest in the project whatsoever.

Windle recognizes this situation, but he is "reluctant to reveal this intimate detail to the other members of the group." The Seitons avoided intimacy too. But Windle was "not at all hesitant in drawing from [his] experience in formulating opinions about the Seitons." This is a rather blatant attempt to please the reader of his PMRQ, whom Windle no doubt suspects is judging the quality of his work. His statement could have been taken almost straight from the catalogue description of the course. Along this line, recall that a substantial proportion of his PMRQ was devoted to a discussion of the avoidance of the cases. This, too, could have been motivated by a need to please (and be accepted by) his reader.

Finally, Windle wants to be accepted as a "regular guy." He has revealed his technique of trying to accomplish this task. He first senses the situation (a necessity for a Seiton family member), and then makes certain that his internal mood is fluctuating properly with this situation. This ensures him against making inappropriate responses. His constant agreement, positivity, and submissiveness also assure him of at least surface acceptance.

All in all, we have a picture of a person who is almost neurotically "other-directed." The breeze blows and Windle is carried with it. As far as we have gone in this analysis, the General Inquirer has helped to piece together a consistent life style. It has given us added insight into the methods by which one person deals with his environment. In a very real sense, we have permitted the two sets of data to speak for themselves and have not attempted to squeeze them into a preformed cast. Our earlier "seething anger" hypothesis can now be viewed as the result of faulty inference. We had inferred that Windle's documents contained the results of frustrating submission, false positivity, and superficial pleasantness. But in retrospect we wonder why we expected his interpersonal tactics to be different in the two situations. He wanted to be liked by his fellow group members. He also wanted to be viewed as a good, cooperative, likable student by the researchers. A more thorough consideration of the situation might have made us more aware of the level on which Windle would approach his writing task. As we gain experience with different source materials and as we take advantage of the flexibility of the General Inquirer, we will gradually increase our understanding of the kinds of information we may expect to extract from different types of documents.

CLINICAL PSYCHOLOGY

The two papers in this section attend to important but difficult issues. In the first paper, Maher, McKean, and McLaughlin report on three studies of language pathology. The difficulties of obtaining samples of thought-disordered language are discussed in the introduction to these studies, and the circularity that often plagues such research is described. Their carefully worked out designs enable the investigators not only to specify rules by which judges separate samples of thought-disordered language from normal language but also allow them to draw at least tentative conclusions about the sources of the documents. Besides presenting a lesson in research design and replication, this paper demonstrates how the General Inquirer can assist in summarizing information on more than one level. For example, since past research in language pathology has covered syntactic and semantic characteristics of disordered language, the authors' use of syntax marking enables them to attempt to replicate both sorts of findings at once. This is an excellent documentation of the time-saving features of computer methods.

The next article, written by Psathas and Arp, is a convenient reminder that the above-mentioned "time-saving features of computer methods" should not be confused with "quick and easy research." In this paper, the complex problem of analyzing therapist-patient interaction is taken up, and several months' work with a single corpus of data is discussed. Their efforts have centered primarily around developing a dictionary that adequately differentiates between the statements of interviewers whose interviewing styles were experimentally

467

manipulated. Striking a balance between empirical discrimination and theoretical usefulness, the authors describe the evolution of this dictionary that eventually will be used to investigate therapist-patient interaction in a variety of circumstances.

CHAPTER FOURTEEN

Studies in Psychotic Language[1]

Brendan A. Maher[2]
University of Wisconsin

Kathryn O. McKean[3]
Boulder, Colorado

Barry McLaughlin[4]
Harvard University

For many years, psychopathologists have been concerned with the problems posed by the language disturbances found in severe behavior disorders, and most particularly in the language of schizophrenia. Generally speaking, it is possible to identify two classes of

[1] The studies reported here were made possible by the cooperation of a large number of psychologists at hospitals throughout the United States. We would like to take this opportunity of expressing our gratitude to the following people, who sent documents to us, provided background history, and helped in a variety of other ways. Our thanks are due to Dr. Douglas A. R. Peyman, Alabama State Hospital; Mr. Robert de von Flindt, Arizona State Hospital; Dr. Irvin Hart, Atascadero State Hospital; Dr. Trent E. Bessent, Metropolitan State Hospital; Dr. Herman O. Schmidt, Norwich State Hospital; Dr. Martin Cohen and Dr. Sophie Leschen, Jacksonville State Hospital; Mr. Joseph Gruber, Manteno State Hospital; Mr. Jack G. McCombs and Dr. Ernst S. Klein, Peoria State Hospital; Dr. Werner Franz Kuhn and Mr. Earl W. Furlan, Central State Hospital; Dr. Loren Fitzhugh, New Castle State Hospital; Dr. Robert Schaef, St. Louis State Hospital; Dr. Jane Kraus and Dr. Grace Surber, New Hampshire State Hospital; Dr. Bernard S. Aaronson, New Jersey Neuro-Psychiatric Institute; Dr. David Cavanaugh, Buffalo State Hospital; Mrs. Elizabeth Kerchner, Edward J. Meyer Memorial Hospital; Dr. Thomas F. Graham, Massillon State Hospital; Mr. Donald J. Whalen, Clarks Summit State Hospital; Dr. Vincent J. Freschi, Embreeville State Hospital; Dr. Joseph A. Cammarata and Dr. Herbert I. Levit, Dixmont State Hospital; Dr. Richard Sanders and Dr. George Hunter,

problems to which answers have been sought. The first is the problem of identifying characteristics of psychotic language in order that it may be distinguished reliably from other kinds of language pathology (for example, those found in simple illiteracy, organic disorders, mental deficiency, and so on). The second is that of relating these characteristics to some more comprehensive understanding of the psychotic disorder itself.

Space does not permit a thorough survey of the hypotheses that have been advanced in response to these questions. Nor is it possible to cover the empirical research that they have generated. Certain previous lines of investigation are, however, germane to the data that are to be reported here, and we shall include a brief account of these. A fuller discussion of this general topic area is to be found elsewhere. (Maher, 1966).

THE RELIABILITY OF JUDGMENT OF SCHIZOPHRENIC LANGUAGE

Before we can discuss sensibly the problems of discovering the characteristics of schizophrenic language, it is necessary to be sure

Philadelphia State Hospital; Mr. Stephen Treat, Fairview State Hospital; Dr. Harold Smolinsky, Wernersville State Hospital; Dr. Paul C. Young and Mr. Harry G. Davis, Big Spring State Hospital; Mr. Daniel V. Taub, Arkansas State Hospital; Dr. James P. Judge, Fairview State Hospital; Dr. Charles R. Shearn, Colorado State Hospital; Mr. Adam Fikso, Chicago State Hospital; Dr. Philip Bower, Elgin State Hospital; Mr. William R. Brader, Logansport State Hospital; Dr. Winifred S. Graves, Madison State Hospital; Dr. William Zimmerman, Osawatomie State Hospital; Dr. W. T. Miller, Kansas Treatment Center, Topeka State Hospital; Dr. Robert F. Long, St. Peter State Hospital; Dr. William J. Reizicka, Nevada State Hospital; Dr. Francis M. Canter, Hastings State Hospital; Mr. O. Lee Duff, Gowanda State Hospital; Dr. Soon Duk Koh and Mr. Fred Humphrey, State Hospital Jamestown; Dr. James G. Bond, Toledo State Hospital; Mr. Joseph Bansavage, Woodville State Hospital; Dr. Elmore Martin, South Carolina State Hospital; Dr. Eugene Engen, Yankton State Hospital; Dr. Bertha Duncan, Big Springs State Hospital; and Mr. Donald Eldred, Vermont State Hospital.

Our thanks are also due to Dr. Philip Stone, to whom we owe a debt of gratitude of great proportions, and to Dr. Chad Gordon, Carl Anderson, Dr. Hugh Cline, and Marshall S. Smith, all of the Department of Social Relations, Harvard University, Miss Jean Melchowitz of Radcliffe College, and Dr. Louis Sherman of the Veterans Administration.

[2] Professor of Psychology. Acknowledgment is given for support provided by Grant No. MH 5505 from the National Institute of Mental Health, which assisted in the conduct of some of this work.

[3] Study I was conducted largely by Mrs. McKean (McKean, 1963) with assistance from Grant No. NSF-G22841 from the National Science Foundation.

[4] Mr. McLaughlin conducted Study III while supported by a United States Public Health Service Fellowship (1-F1-MH-22, 445).

that observers can agree that certain samples of the language are diagnostic of schizophrenia and that others are not. In a word, the matter of interjudge reliability must be established with confidence before we may turn to the fine-grained analysis of the language. There is already a substantial body of literature on this issue, the major source being the work of Hunt and his students at Northwestern University (for instance, Hunt and Jones, 1958a, 1958b). From the work of this group, it appears that experienced clinicians agree very closely with each other when asked to rate brief language samples for degree of "schizophrenicity," and that these judgments overlap closely with those made by naive undergraduates when faced with the same task. In other words, the professional and the layman generally agree about what is and what is not schizophrenic language. However, attempts to define the cues in the language that generate these judgments were less revealing. One study (Hunt and Jones, 1958a) indicates that clinicians and undergraduates correlated schizophrenicity highly with lack of "communicability." In this context, communicability was defined as the provision of a "public, understandable meaning" in the sample versus a "purely personal, private meaning whose significance is apparent only to the patient himself." In this study rank-order correlations between schizophrenicity and communicability are −.90 and −.84 for the clinicians and the undergraduates, respectively. Unfortunately, many systematic patterns of distortion may be laid upon the language to produce lack of communicability. As samples of language pathology from other kinds of patients were not included, it is unknown whether other kinds of incommunicability exist that might be judged to reflect disorders other than schizophrenicity.

One of the first aims of the studies described here was to identify the systematic differences between language judged to be thought disordered and language judged to be free from thought disorder. A certain element of circularity tends to plague research into this problem; if we use judges to sort samples into thought disorder versus normality, then we may simply be studying the judging habits of the sorters rather than any independently consistent attribute of psychotic pathology. Where the judges are mental health professionals, the high degree of mutual agreement might conceivably reflect their common training in descriptive diagnosis. We would succeed in learning something about judges and little about patients. On the other hand, the judges may well be responding to verbal symptoms that are critically related to other aspects of the psychosis, and when we discover the cues to which the judges react we find some important features of the psychopathology of the writers.

There is no obvious escape from this dilemma. However, we may study the judging principles of both professionals and laymen by analyzing the content of documents that are judged to be in the two categories without regard to the presence or absence of actual pathology in the authors. The first two studies described in this report deal with the problem of the principles of judgment, but use documents produced by patients under conditions of spontaneity. This, of course, offers the possibility of discovering explicitly the rules that judges use implicitly when diagnosing thought disorder from language samples; it also offers the possibility of relating characteristics of the samples to other facts that may be known about the writers.

The nature of these implicit cues has been the source of many hypotheses. Two general kinds of hypothesis have been advanced: those relating to the formal attributes of language and those relating to the thematic aspects.

Formal Characteristics of the Language

Some investigators have turned their attention to the syntactical and grammatical aspects of the language of psychotics, ignoring the question of content or theme. Among the simplest versions of this approach is the use of the *type-token ratio* (TTR), a ratio obtained by dividing the number of different words (types) by the total number of words (tokens) occurring in the sample under analysis. Fairbanks (1944) and Mann (1944) have both reported that the TTR's of hospitalized schizophrenics were lower than those of normal college student controls. Congruent findings have been reported by Whitehorn and Zipf (1943) and by Lorenz and Cobb (1954) who found that paranoid schizophrenic patients tend to repeat words more than normal adults. The General Inquirer makes possible an analogous comparison; in this case the ratio to be computed is that of the total number of different tags to total words tagged in the sample. As each tag subsumes a number of different words, the ratio is not numerically identical with the TTR. However, if we accept the assumption that (for unspecified reasons) the schizophrenic patient uses an impoverished range of vocabulary (hence the lower TTR), then he should also generate a smaller number of tags than his normal control comparison.

We note in passing that in the studies just now cited, the educational level of the pathological and control populations was not equated, making it difficult to conclude that the differences obtained necessarily reflect pathology.

A second popular comparison has been the *adjective-verb quotient* (*AVQ*). This measure was first developed by Busemann (1926), who reported that an increase in the denominator (verbs) was found in school children rated as unstable by their teachers. The studies of Mann (1944) and Fairbanks (1944) already cited found higher AVQ's in their normal samples than in their schizophrenic patients. The differences did not, however, attain statistical significance.

Contradictory findings have been reported with regard to a number of other formal aspects. Arguing that the schizophrenic patient is characterized by unusual egocentricity, Shneidman (1948) felt that the use of self-referring pronouns would be particularly high in their language. Fairbanks (1944) and Ellsworth (1951) found that the use of first-person singular pronouns was greater in schizophrenic subjects than in normals. However, Lorenz and Cobb (1954), Mann (1944), and White (1949) failed to find this. In fact, White reported a tendency of her schizophrenics to avoid the use of personal pronouns or topics of self-reference.

Fairbanks (1944), studying parts of speech, reported that significantly fewer nouns, conjunctions, prepositions, adjectives, and articles were used by schizophrenic patients compared to the freshman control group. Ellsworth (1951), on the other hand, found that fewer pronouns and adjectives were used, but more verbs and nouns. To complete the confusion, Mabry (1955) found no differences between patients and controls with regard to parts of speech.

Thematic Aspects of the Language

One of the most articulated hypotheses about the content of thought-disordered language has been advanced by Mednick (1958). He proposes that the major mechanism at work in the genesis of disordered thought and language is the avoidance of thinking about threatening subjects. Thus, irrelevant associations serve the hedonistic purpose of keeping the patient safely on the periphery of concern about his more profound psychological difficulties. Mednick considers this state of affairs to be the end product of a process in which the patient begins in an acute psychotic state marked by considerable overt anxiety, expressions of fear, and panic. Thence by degrees he moves to a calmer state of chronicity in which anxiety is effectively avoided by the irrelevance of thought content. While it is clear that an adequate test of this hypothesis requires a comprehensive study of the longitudinal changes occurring from the acute state onward, certain deductions of a grosser sort may be made. Specifically, we should expect to find that the language of the thought-disordered patient contains fewer direct references to anxiety, fear, or apprehension than would that of a patient who is still in the acute state.

A more complex approach to the same rather crude comparison may be made by calculating not simply the differences in overt references to anxiety but by weighing these against overt reference to anxiety reduction or relief. Such a measure was developed by Dollard and Mowrer (1947) in the *distress-relief quotient (DRQ)*. This method classifies words, clauses, and sentences as to whether they communicate distress, relief from distress, or neither. From Mednick's hypothesis we should expect that thought-disordered language would produce lower DRQ's than the language of patients whose thought does not appear to be disrupted. Within the analytic framework provided by the Harvard III Dictionary, a similar measure may be obtained by computing the ratio of distress tags to relief tags, working with the dictionary definition of the tags as described in Part I of this book.

Further thematic differences have been described by Gottschalk and Gleser (1964). They compared the speech of chronic and acute schizophrenics, brain-damaged patients, nonschizophrenic psychiatric patients, general medical patients, and normal adult controls. Characteristic of schizophrenia were themes in the following categories: others avoiding self, self unfriendly to others, others unfriendly to self, disorientation, physical illness, psychological malfunctioning, malfunctioning of indeterminate origin, unsureness of own performance, need of control, denial of affect, these supplemented by signs of a more general character, such as erroneous or bizarre statements, repetition of phrases or clauses, and questions to the interviewer. While these distinguished schizophrenic subjects from most other groups, they did not clearly differentiate between schizophrenic and brain-damaged patients. There was some tendency for the latter to produce more statements of disorientation, while the former produced more statements of interpersonal relationships.

Clearly not all of these thematic categories have homologs in the General Inquirer Dictionary. However, some tag comparisons may be made fruitfully, and will be reported later in this present paper.

Against the background of the hypotheses and findings that have been reviewed here, the present writers conducted a series of investigations with the aid of the General Inquirer procedure. We shall now describe these in detail.

STUDIES WITH THE GENERAL INQUIRER

This series of studies was performed with concern for some basic problems of methodology. A prime consideration was the fact that it is difficult to elicit gross symptomatology from psychotic patients under the circumstances of a typical psychological experiment. Past experience suggested that specimens of schizophrenic thought disorder would be obtained better under conditions of spontaneity than by requiring the patient to verbalize on a selected topic under laboratory conditions. Diurnal fluctuations in the clinical status of a patient, the difficulty in selecting a stimulus topic that is sure to produce pathological reactions, and the well-known difficulty in getting patients to attend to the requirements of a formal experimental procedure led us to seek our data in a different way. Instead, we decided to contact a large number of mental hospitals throughout the United States and ask the cooperation of the staff in providing us with letters, documents, diaries, or other written material that they knew had been written spontaneously (that is, not at staff request). This procedure was adopted with full cognizance that we thereby forfeited certain kinds of control that are highly desirable for this kind of research.

Specifically, we did not know whether all cooperating hospitals used the same criteria to send us documents, and we did not know exactly in what circumstances each document was written. In the case of letters, it was safe to assume that those sent to us were biased in the direction of pathology as presumably the more normal letters written by patients were forwarded to the addressee rather than to us.

From this preliminary inquiry a very large number of documents were received ranging from long-term sets of diaries to curt obscenities scrawled on matchbook covers. As the documents were received, they were coded as to the hospital of origin, but no other information was available at that time about the writer. Subsequently, a questionnaire was sent back to the cooperating hospital asking for data on the patient's age, sex, date of admission, date of first admission to any mental hospital, most recent diagnosis, and the hospital's classification on an acute versus chronic and on thought-disordered versus non-thought-disordered categories. These questionnaires were not sent out until after the relevant documents had been sent for computer analysis so that the selection of documents was made "blind" as to these background data.

Study I. Correlates of Judged Pathology

In the first study, 53 documents were selected that met the following criteria. All sentences of opening greeting and of closing salutation were excluded from the documents. Using a table of random numbers, we selected a line of the text and the sample began with the first sentence on that line or on the lines immediately following. Fifty words were counted from that point, and there the sample was terminated, provided it concluded a sentence or a clause. If it did not, the sample was extended to include all of the clause in which the 50th word occurred. Only documents long enough to meet this selection standard were used. These samples were then coded as to syntax for General Inquirer use. The system of syntax coding was based upon the division of the text into simple thought sequences, or single units of thought. Each unit included a subject, verb, objects, and modifiers plus the source of the thought, the attributive subject, and the verb. The text was divided into these units, and each word was assigned to one of the following categories by its function in the text:

Code	*Function*
/1	Subject and incorporated modifiers — all words that together form the concept which acts with respect to the verb.
/2	Nonincorporated subject modifiers — words that identify the subject in relation to something else that is not the subject.
/3	Predicate verbs, excluding all auxiliaries and future infinitives.
/4	Verb modifiers including all time references as to when thought is operative — including conventional adverbs and time, place, and space referents of action indicated by the verb.

/5   (Direct) object and incorporated modifiers — all words that together form the concept of what is acted upon by the subject.

/6   Nonincorporated object modifiers — words that identify the direct object in relation to something else which is not part of the direct object.

/7   Indirect objects and all modifiers.

/8   Attributive nouns: Example:
       I think that . . .

/9   Attributive verbs: Examples:
       I hope that . . .
       He says that . . .
       The fact is that . . .

An example of the syntax coding of a text sample is given as follows:

THEN/4 I/1 BEGAN/3 TO SYMPATHIZE/3 WITH THE GERMANS/5 AND THE NAZIS/5 + AND (I/1) TAKE/3 A BELLIGERENT/5 ATTITUDE/5 TOWARD MINORITY/6 GROUPS/6, JEWS/6, NEGROES/6, ITALIANS/6. I/1 ALSO LOOKED/3 UP PEOPLE/5 S NAMES/5 IN THE GERMAN/4 ENGLISH/4 DICTIONARY/4, + PEOPLE/1 WHO HAD LIVED/3 IN THE SAME/4 ROOMING/4 HOUSES/4 WITH ME/4. A WOMAN/5 S NAME/5 LIKE KAMJANTER/5 I/1 DECODED/3 TO MEAN/3, + IT/8 IS A PITY/9 TO FIGHT/3 HIS FUTURE/5.

Once coded in this way, the documents were submitted for analysis by the General Inquirer.

The group of 53 documents comprised a subsample drawn from the initial supply in the following way. From the first group of documents, a total of approximately 100 documents were sorted by one of the present writers (then an undergraduate) into three categories; thought disorder, normal, and unusable (unreadable, too short for use, or too illiterate for adequate handling by the General Inquirer). Documents that fell into the first two categories were then examined to eliminate any duplication of the same author-patient. Fifty-three texts then remained that were to be used in the analysis. A second judge, also an undergraduate, repeated the sorting independently. Interjudge agreement on this sorting was 69.3 percent over-all, with agreements of 63.3 percent on the thought-disorder group and 77.3 percent on the normal group.

Using the first judge's sorting as the basic division of the groups, the subgroups totaled 30 thought disordered and 23 normal documents. Additional judging was done by three experienced clinical psychologists from the Veterans Administration hospitals of the Boston area. These three judges agreed with this division 80.8 percent, 80.0 percent, and 76.9 percent, respectively. Finally, when the questionnaire data were received from the cooperating hospitals, the overall basic sorting was found to agree with the attending clinician's judgments in 74 percent of the cases. Accepting the hospital clinician's diagnosis as the validity criterion, this agreement broke down into 96.6 percent overlap in the judgment of cases as thought disordered, but only 42.9 percent agreement in the judgment that thought disorder was absent. This difference in distribution across the two categories was not statistically significant (chi-square = 0.440 with 1 df). It seems likely that the ward clinician will attach a diagnosis of thought disorder whenever the verbal behavior of the patient has exhibited this, even though much of the verbal behavior may be quite normal. Thus the diagnosis of the patient's status by reading a randomly selected letter is much more likely to produce a false negative diagnosis than a false positive one. This accounts for the very high degree of agreement in the case of the thought-disordered group versus the lower agreement about the authors of normal documents.

This close agreement by the experimental judge and the ward clinician was paralleled by a similarly close overlap between the judgment that a document was thought disordered and the hospital diagnosis of schizophrenia. Ninety-three percent of those documents judged thought disordered came from patients with a diagnosis of schizophrenia, but only 47.9 percent of those judged normal came from patients with diagnosis of some other kind. This is to be expected, as a diagnosis of schizophrenia may be made on many other grounds, in the absence of overt thought disorder.

Purpose of the Study

It must be made clear that the major purpose of this study was to discover those language attributes that influence judges to regard a sample as pathological. It was not intended to investigate the clinical correlates in the patients who had written the samples. Strictly speaking, it would have been possible to do this study by generating artificial documents, reflecting the investigators' preconceptions about the cues judges use, and then testing to see if these cues were in fact influential in the judgments. As the current state of the literature provides no convincing basis for any preconceptions, it was decided to use real documents and to let "nature" put the important dimensions in.

However, because of the manner in which the study was conducted it proved possible to get ancillary data of a rather crude kind about the writers. We have already discussed the relationship of the judgment of the document to the hospital diagnosis of the patient. Additional personal data are given in Table 14.1.

TABLE 14.1. *Mean Age and Chronicity Differences for Authors of Normal and Thought-Disordered Documents*

	Mean		SD				
Measure	D	N	D	N	t	df	P
Age (in years)*	45.5	36.3	12.4	11.9	2.40	51	.01 < p < .05
Number of Years Ill**	12.8	4.9	8.4	4.7	4.01	49	p < .01
Age Became Ill***	32.6	31.4	8.8	11.3	1.36	49	N.S.
Percent of Life Ill****	26.6	13.1	13.1	12.4	3.86	49	p < .01

* Age = 1963 − year of birth.
** Number of years ill = 1963 − date of first admission (in years).
*** Age became ill = Age − number of years ill.
**** Percent of life ill = Number of years ill/age × 100.

Here we see that in this study the author of a document judged to be thought disordered was older than the author of one judged normal. Both groups had been first recognized as mentally ill at approximately the same age, but the older group had — necessarily — now reached greater chronicity and had spent a greater percentage of their life in the hospital. This age difference may well be a sampling artifact, for in the subsequent cross-validation (Study II) this age difference was not found. No particular significance can be attributed to it at this point, although it did reach statistical significance in this case.

The absence of relationships between the subtle judgments of thought disorder in written language and gross variables such as age should not surprise us. Theoretically we should expect relationships with other complex forms of behavior, especially cognitive behavior, attentional phenomena, and the like. However, we must reiterate that such was not the purpose of this study. Rather our main aim was to identify the cues used in judging the language rather than the author characteristics that might be related to language usage.

Results

Syntax Differences

The frequency of use of each General Inquirer syntax category was computed by hand. In addition a count was made of the number of words marked for syntax in each sample. A correction in these scores was necessary because of the different number of total words in each sample. The disorganized group averaged 67.1 words per sample, while the normal group had a mean of 61.3 words per sample. To correct for the unequal sizes of the samples, the raw frequency obtained for each category in a sample was divided by the total words in that sample. The resulting index scores were used in all statistical tests. Table 14.2 reports the percentage means of the index frequencies for the two groups.

TABLE 14.2. Percentage Means of Index Frequencies for Each Syntax Mark and Total Marked Words per Sample

Group	Condition									Total
	Subject	Subject Modifier	Verb	Verb Modifier	Object	Object Modifier	Indirect Object and Modifier	Attributive Noun	Attributive Verb	Marked per Sample
D	17.6	2.3	10.3	11.0	17.7	1.2	1.1	1.1	1.1	63.5
N	16.5	1.3	11.2	15.1	12.3	0.9	1.3	1.8	2.1	62.6

The difference between the two groups on the index frequencies of marked words per sample was not significant ($t = 0.6712$, 51 *df*, $p > .20$).

A comparison was made between the frequency of subjects and the frequency of objects per sample. From the index scores, a simple measure of qualitative difference was determined. If the frequency of subjects used exceeded the frequency of objects used in a given sample, that sample received a plus; if the reverse was true, the sample received a minus; and if the index frequencies were equal, the sample received a zero. Table 14.3 shows the results obtained by this method. A chi-square test for differences between the frequencies of plus and minus samples was significant. (The zero scores were omitted from the chi-square test because of the zero frequency in one cell and a correspondingly low frequency in the other cell.)

A comparison of the difference in magnitude of the index ratios (obtained by dividing the object index score into the subject index

TABLE 14.3. Comparison of Frequency of Use of Subject and Object

| | Groups | | |
Conditions	D	N	Sum
+ (Subject > object)	13	17	30
0 (Subject = object)	2	0	2
− (Subject < object)	15	6	21
Total Ss	30	23	53

Chi-square $= 4.010$, 1 df, $.05 > p > .02$.

score) was almost significant ($t = 1.76$; 50 df, $.10 > p > .05$). A comparison was made of all other syntax categories coded in the texts. No significant differences were found between the two groups in their usage of each syntax category.

The number of different words (DW) per sample was counted by hand. Raw frequencies were corrected for different sample size by dividing the total words in a given sample into the raw frequency of different words for that sample (the TTR). The disorganized group averaged 70.8 percent different words, and the normal group averaged 74.3 percent different words. A test for difference between means was not significant ($t = 1.630$, 51 df, $.20 > p > .10$).

Thematic Differences (Tag Tallies)

The tag tally differences between the two groups are summarized in Table 14.4. The table includes only those tags in which the index

TABLE 14.4. All Tags with Index Ratio of 2.0 or Above

| Disorganized Group High | | Normal Group High | |
Tag	Index Ratio	Tag	Index Ratio
JOB-ROLE	2.3	SMALL-GROUP	2.0
NATURAL-OBJECT	2.0	BAD	2.0
SENSORY-REFERENCE	2.0	GUIDE	2.2
NATURAL-WORLD	2.5	FOLLOW	2.0
PLEASURE	3.0	WORK	2.2
EQUAL	2.0	MOVE	3.0
APPROACH	3.0	GET	3.3
ATTACK	5.0	EXPEL	4.0
LEGAL	5.5	ARTISTIC	2.0
MILITARY	3.0	RECREATIONAL	4.0
POLITICAL	3.3	MALE THEME	5.0

ratio between the two groups equaled or exceeded 2.0. Because of the lack of independence between one occurrence of a tag in an author's text and another occurrence in the same text, it is not possible to meet the assumptions required for normal statistical comparison of these differences. Hence the index ratios are simply descriptive of the differences between the two groups and cannot be taken as statistically reliable.

Two additional criteria of difference were applied to the data. The first of these is the presence of an index ratio that is equal to or greater than 2.0, where at least one of the two groups produced this tag a minimum of ten times. This eliminates all index ratios that are high but dependent upon very low absolute raw frequencies. Results from the application of this criterion are given in Table 14.5.

TABLE 14.5. *Tags with Minimum Absolute Frequency of 10 and Index Ratios of 2.0 or More*

Tag D	Tag N	Index Ratio	High Group
NATURAL-WORLD	*	2.5	D
*	GUIDE	2.2	N
*	WORK	2.2	N
*	MOVE	3.0	N
*	GET	3.3	N
LEGAL	*	5.5	D
POLITICAL	*	3.3	D

* Frequency below 10.

Seven tags met both of these criteria. Three were high for the thought-disordered group: NATURAL-WORLD (environments), LEGAL, and POLITICAL (institutional contexts). The other four were high for the normal documents: GUIDE (social emotional action), WORK, MOVE, and GET (impersonal actions).

These two criteria are admittedly rather severe for a study the purpose of which was the discovery of differences rather than the demonstration of them from some existing theoretical base. Thus an index ratio of as low as 1.5 might be impressive where the absolute values of the numbers going into the ratio are relatively large. Where this more lenient criterion is used, certain additional tags appear to be of interest.

Retrieval Differences

When retrievals were made of the sentences in which these seven tags occurred, more specific information was obtained. The high count of NATURAL-WORLD tags for the thought disordered group was found to be due mainly to the high frequency of scientific words by that group. Retrievals of LEGAL and POLITICAL tags showed that the thought disordered frequently used words like "criminal," "judge," "murdered," "politician" while normals did not use them at all.

In studying the other four high tags (GUIDE, WORK, MOVE, GET) as verbs, the sentences retrieved fell into two general patterns. One pattern — SELF acts — was used much more frequently by normals than by disorganized writers [index ratio 4.3 (N)]. Examples of this type of sentence are

> *I taught* part of a year
> In the ninth grade, *I played football*
> *I moved* to El Paso with my parents

The other pattern — a subject acts on SELF — was used with almost equal frequency by both groups [index ratio 1.2 (N)]. Examples of this type of sentence are

> I want you to help me
> I was committed here three years ago
> It is putting a damper on my spirit

When combined with retrievals, the tag tally data uncovered other differences between the two groups.

1. Normals made more references to themselves (higher use of "I") than did the disorganized group.

2. The tag NOT was used more frequently by normals than by the disorganized group. Inspection of retrieved sentences showed that this difference was due entirely to the high frequency of use of the word "not" in 76 percent of their negative sentences.

3. Normals used the tag THINK more frequently than did the other group. This difference was observed to be due to the fact that normals used the attributive phrase "I feel/9 that . . ." in 24 percent of their responses while the disorganized group did not employ this phrase in any of their sentences. Omitting this phrase from the frequency count,

the two groups used THINK words almost equally [corrected index ratio 1.2 (N)].

4. Normals used words dealing with communication more often than did the disorganized group. A large proportion of the words used by the normal group (82 percent) were verbs dealing with the act of communication (said, write, tell, ask, talk). For the disorganized group, only half (50 percent) of the words used were verbs dealing with the act of communication. The index ratios obtained by separating these two uses were 2.3 (N) for verbs dealing with the action of communication, and 2.0 (D) for all other communication words (examples — mostly nouns — are an answer, a request, a deal, television, voice, telephone).

5. An interesting reversal was noted in the use of the female pronoun (she or her) by the two groups. As a subject, "she" was used more frequently by normals than by the disorganized group [index ratio 3.0 (N)]. As an object, "her" was used more frequently by the disorganized group [index ratio 3.0 (D)]. Although there were more males in both groups, there was no difference in the ratio of males to females between the two groups, so this observation is probably not due to bias from sex differences between the two groups.

DRQ Differences

Two measures were made of the DRQ using the emotion tags. One consisted of the index frequency of the DISTRESS tag divided by the DISTRESS tag frequency plus the PLEASURE tag frequency. The second measure consisted of the sum of all the arousal tags (AROUSAL + URGE + DISTRESS + ANGER divided by the sum of the arousal tags plus the sum of the relief tags (PLEASURE + AFFECTION). The re-

TABLE 14.6. Measures of DRQ

Tag(s)	D		N	
	f^*	Index	f	Index
Distress	18	8	9	6
Distress + Pleasure	26	12	10	6
(1) DRQ	.69	.68	.90	1.0
Arousal	37	17	24	16
Arousal + Relief	51	23	28	18
(2) DRQ	.73	.74	.86	.89

* f = Raw frequency.

sults of both these measures are reported in Table 14.6. In both cases, the disorganized group had the lower DRQ indicative of lower tension.

Summary of Conclusions

From this study certain differences seemed to emerge between the documents in the two groups. These differences could not be analyzed by conventional statistical techniques and hence are reported here as descriptive observations subject to the fate that might befall them in later cross-validation. No interpretations are offered at this point but will be made later on.

1. Documents judged to be free from thought disorder used fewer objects per subject than did those judged pathological. This may be related to the more frequent appearance of the use of "self (as subject) acts" as a sentence form, rather than the sequence, "A subject acts on an object." Alternatively, it may be a consequence of the diminished focusing of attention as a sentence progresses toward its end. This latter possibility will be discussed later.

2. Documents judged normal contained more qualifiers per verb than those judged pathological. These results were not statistically significant, but they are in line with the observations of Ellsworth (1951).

3. The disorganized group was found to be significantly older than the normals. Since both groups had approximately the same age of onset, the disorganized group has been hospitalized longer and their condition can be considered to be chronic with respect to the normals.

4. The disorganized group showed a tendency to use fewer qualifiers per verb than did the normals, although the difference was not statistically significant. The results are in line with Ellsworth's observations (1951).

5. The difference between the two groups on mean percent of different words used per sample was not statistically significant, but the normals tended to use more different words per sample than the disorganized group. These results agree with those obtained by Lorenz and Cobb (1954) and Mann (1944). They indicate, according to Lorenz and Cobb (1954) and Whitehorn and Zipf (1943), a tendency for the disorganized patients' writing to be less diverse and flexible and more repetitious and rigid than the writing of normals.

6. The tag tally data point to two different content areas of interest

for the two groups. The normal group made many more references to personal experiences and actions than did the disorganized group. They wrote about themselves with reference to their life experiences: their schooling, their travels, their families, their communities, and their personal activities and feelings. The disorganized group, on the other hand, dealt more with thematic material such as religion, science, life, death, sex, law, politics, and war. These findings corroborate White's data (1949). White found that schizophrenics avoided personal themes or references and preferred to substitute "universal themes, of a complex nature, . . . for the simpler personal themes."

7. Normals made more references to self than did the disorganized group. Lorenz and Cobb (1954), in their analysis of spoken language, found that schizophrenics used "I" slightly less frequently than did normals, while all other patient groups used "I" more frequently than normals. The normals' more frequent references to themselves seem to be due to a greater interest in themselves and their own life. It may also be due to the autobiographical nature of many of the "normal" documents. A similar observation was made by Mann (1944). She noted that the normals in her study (college freshmen) used more first person references than did her schizophrenic subjects. She concluded that the task of writing a "life story" usually tended to increase the number of references to self.

> This may actually have operated to increase the frequency of self-reference for the freshmen, but for the schizophrenic patients, this effect may have been counteracted to a large extent by their tendency to enumerate, and to get off the track in recounting their life histories by describing certain places, events, or things with little or no reference to their own relation to such places, events, or things.
>
> (Mann, 1944, 73)

8. The normals' highly exclusive use of the word "not" as opposed to a more varied choice of negative words by the disorganized group agrees with data obtained by Fairbanks (1944). However, Fairbanks found that schizophrenics used considerably more negative words than normals, a finding that does not agree with the results of this study.

9. The disorganized group had a lower DRQ, indicating that they are under less tension than the "normal" group. These data are in agreement with conclusions reached by Mednick (1958).

Study II. Replication Investigation of Correlates of Judgment

With the foregoing conclusions in hand, the present writers proceeded to a second investigation that was essentially a replication of
the first. On this occasion four judges were used. Each judge read 60
of 80 documents that were selected as before. However, sample length
was increased from 50 to 100 words. Thus each document was read
by three judges. These judges were graduate students in English at
Harvard University, and they were asked to sort the documents that
displayed pathologically deviant language usage from those that appeared normal in language usage. Interjudge agreements ranged over-
all from 86.0 percent to 69.4 percent between the various pairs of
judges. Complete agreement was reached on 41 documents, and the
remaining 39 were assigned according to the majority judgment.
From this judgment, 53 documents were judged pathologically disordered and 27 as not thought disordered. Questionnaire data were
not subsequently available on three of the latter group, one of the
patients having died and the other two having been transferred. The
judging procedure was repeated once again with clinicians from the
Veterans Administration Hospitals of the Boston area. The pooled
judgments of the clinicians (three per document) agreed 85 percent
with the selection already made.

There were no statistically significant differences in background
data on the group of 77 authors. We may note here that the age at
which both groups became ill is about the same as that found in Study
I. The differences between the four groups (Study I plus Study II) are
not significant. In the light of this the greater age of the authors of
disordered documents found in Study I may be regarded as sampling
deviation. The age itself, 45.5 years, is very close to the age of the
authors of normal documents in this study, 46.2.

Of this total sample, 68 patients were judged to be thought disordered by the ward clinician at the cooperating hospital. This included 92 percent agreement on the positive identification of thought
disorder from the documents, but only 24 percent agreement on the
absence of it. Thus the majority of documents in both groups were
produced by people judged to be thought disordered by these attending clinicians.

The method of analysis of these documents by the General Inquirer
differed in one respect from the first study. A revised system of syntax

identification was used (McKean, McLaughlin, and Maher, 1963).
The main purpose of the revision was to include identifying categories
for qualifiers and modifiers.

Noun subject(s) and predicate noun(s)	/1
All modifiers of subject(s)	/2
All verbs except auxiliaries	/3
All verb modifiers including all reference to when, where, how, and why action occurs	/4
Noun object(s)	/5
All modifiers of object(s)	/6
Indirect object(s) and all modifiers	/7
Attributive noun(s)	/8
Attributive verb(s)	/9

Results

For the purpose of brevity, this section of results will be confined
to these differences that appeared both here and in the first study.
Index scores and ratios were computed as before. The data here are
based on the complete 80 documents.

Subject/Object Relationships

In Table 14.3, we saw that the thought-disordered group included
significantly more documents in which the number of objects used
exceeded the number of subjects, and that this distinguished them
significantly from the nondisordered group. A similar comparison in
this study was made, and it showed the same results: the disordered
group revealed a significantly higher number of documents that had
an object total exceeding the subject total. Additionally, the magnitude of the index ratios of subject/object that failed to reach significance in Study I, did so in Study II. Here the *t* value for the difference
was significant at the .05 level. The respective index ratios were
THOUGHT-DISORDERED, 1.4; NORMAL, 0.78.

As this difference had been sustained in both studies, a closer look
was taken at both the numerical and the semantic aspects of it. For
each a plot was made of the distribution of subject/object ratios obtained by each document, to attempt to ascertain a cutoff ratio that
would optimally distinguish between documents likely to be judged
disordered and those not. This analysis established that ratios of 3.0
or higher (3 objects per subject) were found only in documents

judged thought disordered, the total number of cases concerned being 8, while ratios of between 2.00 and 2.99 included a further five cases of thought disorder, but only one case judged to be normal.

Retrieval of texts that included the high ratios was then carried out to permit examination of their semantic features. A distinctive aspect of many of them was the tendency to produce chains of noun associations at the end of sentences (that is, where the noun occupies an object role). One example may be cited:

I/1 LIKE/3 COFFEE/5 CREAM/5 COWS/5 ELIZABETH TAYLOR/5

The sequence of object nouns that appears in this sentence appears to be a simple chain of associations, each noun providing an association stimulus for the one that follows immediately, and so on down the line. Two interesting issues arise here, that may have some relevance to theory. In the first place, this effect is most striking at the end of a sentence and not elsewhere in the sentence form. This provokes the speculation that the attentional mechanisms that are necessary to the maintenance of coherent language are weaker at the end of a sentence than elsewhere. Possibly the "period" point is one at which the disruptive influences of strong but irrelevant associations are most likely to override the inhibitory mechanisms that preserve the integrity of the sentence while it is still uncompleted. Bleuler (1911, 26) cites a patient who in describing a walk with her family listed them as "father, son" and then added "and the Holy Ghost." An important test of this proposition might be made by comparing this kind of pattern in the English language with the loci of disruptions to be found in languages that have a high frequency of sentence structure involving a verb ending (for instance, some Germanic constructions).

A second observation relates to the relatively normal nature of the interfering associations. *Coffee* to *cream* to *cows,* and so on, and *father* to *son* to *and Holy Ghost* appear to be chains of fairly common associations. They do not appear to be bizarre or idiosyncratic in themselves. Rather they seem to occur in the manner suggested elsewhere by the work of Chapman (1958), who found that normal associates intrude irrelevantly into the conceptual performance of schizophrenic subjects. Within the context of this chapter, there is no ready way to quantify this possibility, but the basic technique of the General Inquirer lends itself to modification in the form of dictionaries of associates to words as well as the present dictionary of rationally meaningful tag categories.

Adjective/Verb Qualifier Ratios

The effect described in Study I was found here only in very attenuated form. The ratio for thought-disordered documents was 0.89, while for the normal documents it was 1.10. The difference between these ratios was not statistically significant. The statistical insignificance of this conclusion, plus the similar insignificance of the similar finding in Study I, suggests that this is at best a trivial trend and not likely to act as a cue to judges.

Self-References

The index ratio of self-reference words was again high in favor of the normal documents. In this case, the ratio was 2.0 (the normals making twice as many references as did the disordered documents).

Different Words

Once again the range of vocabulary usage was calculated by tabulating the percentage of different words used in the two samples and weighing for differences in sample lengths. The figures obtained were comparable with those found earlier (72 percent for the thought-disordered documents and 73.7 percent for the normal documents), but they were not significantly different from each other. This measure may be abandoned as unfruitful in future research.

Thematic Aspects

Once again the disordered group included a higher number of references to political themes. At first sight this difference did not appear to be as great as had been the case in Study I. However, a comparison of the retrievals showed that the documents in Study II had, coincidentally, several references to "state hospital" and the occurrence of the word "state" had led to a political tagging of the entry. Removing these entries, the difference between the groups remained large (4.0), with the retrieved material reflecting largely a concern with world politics, domestic subversion, and the like. Concern with *religion* was also evident, as well as science and themes of life and death. No differences were found in the number of sex themes appearing in the two groups.

On the other hand, the difference between the groups on GUIDE, WORK and MOVE tags shrank considerably, and it seems unlikely that the earlier results could be acceptable as evidence of the rules judges use in making their diagnoses from the language samples.

Distress-Relief Quotient

The DRQ was calculated as before. For the two groups, the quotients produced were 0.815 for those who were thought disordered and 0.750 for the normals. The difference between these two values is low (much smaller than in Study I), while both of the values lie at the low end of the range implied by the results of Study I. Here again, it seems clear that a high DRQ is not a necessary cue to the judgment of thought disorder.

General Conclusions

At the outset, we pointed out that the purpose of the first two studies was to discover the cues that reliably distinguish those documents judged to be thought disordered from those judged to be normal. While it is to be expected that this division would have some parallel in the diagnosis of the patients who wrote them, this was not inevitable. A patient who writes letters 10 percent of which are thought disordered will be diagnosed as thought disordered. However, a judge trying to estimate the diagnosis from a random sample of the patient's writings would be likely to draw a normal rather than a disordered document.

Bearing this in mind, we can suggest that some cues that operate to influence the judgment of documents are

1. Disruptive chains of association: These occur chiefly at the end of sentences, consist usually of chains of common association and are reflected by a proportion of objects to subjects in the text.

2. Self-references: A greater number of references to the self is related to judgment of normality. This is accompanied by a greater number of sentences in which the subject (the writer) acts upon some object. It may be regarded as related to the greater frequency of active verbs (guide, control, work) appearing in normal documents, but the evidence for this is somewhat tenuous.

3. Thematic: Concern with universal themes of a political, religious, or scientific nature is very characteristic of the disordered

document, being much rarer in the normal. Per contra, the normal document is more likely to include references to the personal life and concerns of the writer as they arise in his immediate community.

Anxiety themes, as measured by the variant of the DRQ used here, do not appear substantially different in the two groups.

Clearly, many of the factors that must influence judgment were not revealed by this procedure; those that were should be tested by the systematic generation of documents (or selection of them from real patients) that meet and do not meet these criteria in order to provide cross-validation data. However, they provide a point of departure and have perhaps moved us a little further along the road from the initial hypothesis that lack of communicability is a central variable in such judgments.

Study III: Patient Differences: The Process-Reactive Dimension

While the foregoing studies may have given us some crude insights into the variables that influence judges, they do not tell us anything about the patients. This is the state of affairs envisaged in our opening discussion. Consequently, in the third study, we turned our attention to discovering differences between groups of documents selected because the clinical status of the writers was known and could be used to group the documents in some significant fashion.

The Process-Reactive Dimension in Schizophrenia

Psychopathologists have begun to turn from the study of gross diagnostic categories of schizophrenia (paranoid, simple, hebephrenic, and catatonic) to the examination of categories based upon more comprehensive measurement of the patient's behavior, both present and past. One of the most promising dimensions of this kind is the PROCESS-REACTIVE classification of schizophrenia. While the distinction between process and reactive schizophrenia dates to Bleuler's (1911) use of the terms to distinguish patients with poor from those with good prognosis, the classification, which is dimensional rather than dichotomous, rests upon two polar definitions of the ends of the continuum. A reactive patient typically has a good psychological history, good physical health, normal siblings, a normally protective and accepting mother, an accepting father, is well adjusted in school, experiences domestic troubles without behavioral pathology, is extraverted in behavior and interests, is heterosexual, experiences sudden onset of psychosis with pertinent stress present, shows verbal aggression, responds well to treatment, has minor paranoid trends, shows no sensations of self-change, no somatic delusions, and retains personal decency. On the other hand, the process schizophrenic patient has a history of early psychological trauma, poor physical health, psychopathological siblings, an overprotective or rejecting mother, a rejecting father, has school difficulties, shows great behavioral changes when there are family troubles, is introverted in behavior and interests, lacks heterosexuality, experiences an insidious and gradual onset of psychosis without external stress, displays physical aggression, does not respond well to treatment, has massive paranoid trends, little capacity for alcohol, is aware of changes in the self, has somatic delusions, and loses decency. Prognosis for the reactive patient is relatively good, while for the process patient it is poor.

Inspection of the previous paragraphs will indicate that language behavior per se plays only a small part in the definition of process or reactive schizophrenia. The dimension rests heavily upon measures of general social adjustment, occupational adequacy, speed of onset, and so forth. The kinds of verbal symptom that play a part in the judgment of thought disorder play very little part in the assignment of a patient to either the reactive or process end of this continuum. There are, however, reasons to suppose that the basic differences between process and reactive patients might be accompanied by differences in their language usage.

A number of important differences have been discovered between patients at the ends of the process-reactive dimension. Fuller descriptions are available elsewhere (Crider, Maher, and Grinspoon, 1965). From analysis of them it seems quite possible that the reactive subject is in a heightened state of arousal (or anxiety) with concomitant narrowing of attention, while the process schizophrenic patient is in a state of pathologically low arousal with broad attention span and consequent difficulty in the effective inhibition of distracting input. Venables (1964) has presented this thesis as a basis for interpretation of the behavioral differences that have been reported.

Insofar as thought disorder may be regarded as occasioned by difficulty in the exclusion of irrelevant associations into consciousness, then we should expect to find differences between process and reactive groups in their language productions and in ways that are related to the judgmental criteria of thought disorder already described in the previous two studies. It was with this in mind that the third study was done.

The data of this study came from documents collected some years previously at Boston State Hospital.[5] These were letters or other material written in the patients' spare time.

Many of the documents collected were unsigned, and others were illegible or too short for purposes of the study. Examination of the useful material yielded a list of 117 names. The records of Boston State Hospital were then examined to ascertain the diagnostic category and other information about these patients. It became apparent that some patients had written under several names, and records for a few patients were not available. Sixty of the remaining patients were found to be diagnosed schizophrenic, and 32 belonged to other diagnostic categories: traumatic psychosis, epilepsy, chronic brain syndrome, syphilitic meningo-encephalitis. Two of the nonschizophrenic patients were dropped because of schizophrenic symptoms, leaving a total of 60 schizophrenic and 30 nonschizophrenic patients.

Experimental psychopathologists have generally turned to the Phillips Scale (Zigler and Phillips, 1961) to measure the process-reactive aspects of a patient's clinical status. This scale is applied to the patient's case history. It provides a method of scoring the case history for such items as frequency of heterosexual activity, length of time a job has been held, competence levels implied by the job, educational level reached, etc. High scores are in the direction of greater adequacy and normality of the patient's premorbid history. High scores are at the reactive end and low scores at the process end of the continuum.

The records of the schizophrenic patients were then examined to rate the patients on the six variables of the Phillips scale. Following Phillips' procedure, the Dictionary of Occupational Titles was employed for scoring the occupational level variable, and the individual's score was his average on those variables where information was available (thus if information was available for only four of the six variables, the individual's score was the total divided by four). If the patient scored over 1.00 on the Phillips scale and if he was not in the hospital

[5] The data employed in this study were originally collected by Dr. R. S. Johnson of the Boston State Hospital for research purposes. Following Dr. Johnson's untimely death, the research was not carried out and the data remained unanalyzed. Dr. John Arsenian of the same hospital and Mrs. Johnson kindly made the data available to us.

two years after the material used in this study was written, he was classified as acute-reactive schizophrenic. If his score on the Phillips scale was under .70 and if he was still in the hospital two years after this material was written, he was classified chronic-process schizophrenic. The remaining patients were placed in a mixed group of reactive-process (or acute-chronic) schizophrenics. These particular cutoff points on the Phillips scale were chosen arbitrarily so that each group had twenty patients.

It will be noted that, besides scores on the Phillips scale, information was available as to chronicity. Because the written material had been gathered about ten years prior to the study, it was possible to determine whether the patient was in the hospital two years later by comparing the dates on the letters with the patient's records. This was done. It might be noted, parenthetically, that a correlation between the Phillips scale and length of stay in the hospital, with age partialed out, was $-.328$ ($p < .05$). This provides some evidence for the validity of this instrument as a prognostic indicator.

Samples of approximately 100 words were taken from the written documents of the 90 patients. The opening sentence of each document was omitted, and the sample began with the sentence closest to a word randomly selected as before. One hundred words were counted from the beginning of the chosen sentence, and the sample ended with the completion of a sentence as close as possible to the 100th word. Thus at times the sample was slightly under and at times slightly over one hundred words. Because of this variability, ratio scores are used in the analysis of the results. The system for coding syntax was that employed in Study II. In addition, a system of coding grammatical categories was used in this study (McLaughlin and Maher, 1963). The grammatical categories were as follows:

N — noun
V — verb, including gerunds and participles
J — adjective
D — adverb
P — first person pronoun (singular)
R — repetition of a noun, adverb, adjective, or verb (except verb "to be")
G — negative construction
A — allness words, which allow of no exception: all, always, fully, nothing, every, and so on.

Q — verb modifiers that modify or qualify the main verb (excluding auxiliaries "to be" and "have"): should, can, could, tried to, did, and so on.

B — ambivalent constructions, those words which may express ambivalence or hesitancy on the part of the speaker: but, if, however, probably, and so on.

An example of a document completed for grammar and syntax is now given:

I/1P AM/3V OF I-BUILDING/5N BOSTON-STATE-HOSPITAL/5N. WITH MY/4P NOSTRILS/4N CLOGGED/4V AND WINTER/4N HERE/4D I/1P CHANCED/3V TO BE READING/3V THE MAGAZINE/5N + THAT/5 MENTHOLATUM/1N ADVERTIZED/3V FROM. KINDLY/4D SEND/3V IT/4 TO ME/7P AT THE BOSTON-STATE-HOSPITAL/4NR AT 591-MORTON-STREET/4N DORCHESTER-24-MASSACHUSETTS/4N, UNITED-STATES/4N OF AMERICA/4N. SEND/3VR IT/5 TO LOUIS-MEEHLMAN/7N IN CARE/4N OF LOUIS-MEEHLMAN/4NR + AND ME/1P WHO/1 ANSWERS/3V BY NAME/4N OF LOUIS-MEEHLMAN/4NR WILL CARE/5VR FOR IT/5 MYSELF/7P. THANKS/3V EVERLASTINGLY/4DA. MERRY/6J NEW-YEAR/5N. THANKS/3VR MENTHOLATUM/4NR COMPANY/4N. FOR MY/4P NOSE/4N FOR MY/4P NOSE/4NR FOR MY/4P NOSE/4NR FOR MY/4P NOSE/4NR FOR MY/4P NOSE/4NR FOR MY/4P NOSE/4NR.

In analyzing the data, three comparisons were made: (1) differences between three schizophrenic groups, reactive, reactive-process, and process ($n = 20$, $N = 60$); (2) differences between two schizophrenic groups, reactive and process (above or below a Phillips scale score of .80, respectively; $n = 30$, $N = 60$); and (3) differences between schizophrenic and nonschizophrenic patients ($n = 60$ and 30, respectively; $n = 90$). Since ratio scores were employed, nonparametric tests were used: the Mann-Whitney test for two samples and the Kruskal-Wallis for three samples (Siegel, 1956).

Results

Grammatical characteristic. The tendency to *repeat words* in written language samples was slightly more pronounced in process than acute schizophrenics. However, the effect was not statistically significant. This is in line with our previous findings that chronic patients are thought disordered, and acute patients more similar to normals in their thought processes. No difference was found between schizophrenics and nonschizophrenic patients in the same hospital. The uselessness of this measure seems to be quite clear.

The use of pronouns of *personal reference* was not more marked in schizophrenic than in other patients. This is in line with the findings of Lorenz and Cobb (1954) and Mann (1944), and argues against Shneidman's contention (1948) that schizophrenic patients manifest an extraordinary interest in themselves. Thus while our previous data suggest that self-reference may be used by judges as a cue, it does not seem to correlate with either schizophrenic nonschizophrenia, nor with the process-reactive dimension.

Subject/object ratios. The schizophrenic patients used slightly more objects per subject than did the nonschizophrenics, but the difference is extremely slight and clearly nonsignificant. An examination of the documents themselves shows few if any cases where chains of interfering associations entered into the text, and hence the absence of the differences found in the two previous studies is not surprising. At the present moment, it appears that where high ratios exist they are likely to be judged thought disordered, but the absolute probability that they will be found in a randomly selected document from a schizophrenic patient is not high.

No difference was found in the use of *negative words* by the schizophrenic and nonschizophrenic patients. The process schizophrenics gave more negatives than reactive schizophrenics, but this difference was not statistically significant.

Schizophrenic patients gave about the same number of *nouns* and *verbs* per sample as did nonschizophrenic patients. The reactive schizophrenics used more nouns and less verbs than the process schizophrenics (the difference between verbs was statistically significant). In addition, the ratio of *adjectives* to *verbs,* while not differing between schizophrenic and nonschizophrenic patients, was statistically significant between process and reactive schizophrenics. The process schizophrenics tended to have a lower adjective-verb quotient than reactive schizophrenics. Another measure, that of the ratio of *nouns* and *verbs* to *adjectives* and *adverbs,* showed a slightly greater use of nouns and verbs relative to adjectives and adverbs on the part of reactive as compared to process schizophrenics. The difference on this ratio was significant when schizophrenic and nonschizophrenic patients were compared; the schizophrenics had the larger noun-verb/adjective-adverb ratio.

Verb qualifiers tended to be greater for process than reactive schizo-phrenics. This effect approached but did not attain statistical signifi-cance. The results are somewhat in disagreement with those of Ellsworth (1951) and our own Study I where we found that chronic patients tended to use fewer qualifiers per verb than other patients. However, the measures employed in those studies are not identical with those used here.

Bleuler (1911) and Meehl (1962) observed that *ambivalence* is one of the core characteristics of the behavior of schizophrenic pa-tients. It is thought that such behavior is symptomatic of a person functioning under competing motives. Consequently, it was felt that schizophrenic language samples would show more ambivalent con-structions as measured by the use of words such as but, if, probably, seems, and so on, than the language samples of nonschizophrenic patients. While differences in the use of such ambivalent constructions were minimal between schizophrenic groups, the difference between schizophrenic and nonschizophrenic patients was significant, but in the direction opposite to what was expected. The nonschizophrenic group used significantly more ambivalent constructions than schizo-phrenic subjects did.

If chronic (process) schizophrenics are more disorganized in their thought processes, it would seem likely that the average length of a *thought unit* would be smaller for them than for the reactive patients. Dividing each language sample into the number of segments that could stand by themselves as sentences, it was found that process schizophrenics did tend to break their messages into shorter units than reactive patients did, but the difference was not significant.

All of the grammatical comparisons, including those discussed in the previous paragraphs, are given in Table 14.7.

Thematic characteristics. The seven tags that had been of some interest in previous studies were examined in this one also: NATURAL-WORLD, LEGAL, POLITICAL, GUIDE, WORK, MOVE, and GET. Summing the NATURAL-WORLD, LEGAL, and POLITICAL tags for messages used in the present study showed a significantly greater use of these tags by reactive patients when compared with process patients. The same was true for the GUIDE, WORK, MOVE, and GET tags. The differences on these tags for schizophrenic and nonschizophrenic patients were not significant.

A similar analysis was made for the sum for each individual of the

TABLE 14.7. Mean Scores for Grammatical Characteristics (Representing occurrence per 100 words)

Category	Reactive	Process	R-P	Reactive	Process	Schizo-phrenic	Nonschizo-phrenic
Repetitions	4.16	7.66	6.55	5.49	6.74	6.14	6.53
Personal "I"	8.22	9.36	6.39	7.36	8.60	8.01	7.94
Self (subject)	3.84	5.01	3.18	2.56	4.46	4.01	4.05
Self (object)	1.01	.93	.98	1.02	.92	.97	1.08
Negatives	1.24	1.74	1.64	1.36	1.71	1.54	1.62
Subjects	6.38	7.86	6.97	6.81	7.33	7.07	7.53
Objects	6.27	6.54	6.58	6.57	6.37	6.47	6.74
Nouns	15.76	15.10	17.41	17.58	14.60	16.09	15.79
Verbs	19.48	21.04	18.28	18.19	21.01*	19.60	19.22
Noun-verb/ adjective-adverb	3.83	3.33	3.21	3.61	3.30	3.46	2.81*
Adjective/verb	.37	.29	.41*	.39	.31*	.35	.36
Qualifiers	2.42	3.24	2.44	2.20	3.19	2.70	2.53
Ambivalent constructions	1.80	1.67	1.53	1.68	1.64	1.66	2.06*
Average length of thought unit	10.45	9.23	9.26	10.09	9.18	9.64	8.89

* $p < .05$.

tags, COMMUNITY, FAMILY, ACADEMIC, RECREATIONAL and of the tags MILITARY, SCIENCE, SEX, and DEATH. In both cases, the difference was in favor of the reactive schizophrenics, but not statistically so. Again the differences between schizophrenic and nonschizophrenic patients were not significant. On both the COMMUNICATION and the THINK tags, the process schizophrenics were higher than reactives; and in the second case, the difference was statistically significant. No other significant differences were found between tags. A summary presentation of the major comparisons is given in Table 14.8.

DRQ. The same measure of DRQ that was applied in Studies I and II revealed that chronic process schizophrenics had a slightly, but not significantly lower DRQ than did the reactive group. Control nonschizophrenic patients had higher DRQ than the schizophrenic group, but again the difference was not statistically significant.

DISCUSSION

Direct comparison of the results of this study with those of previous studies is difficult because of differences in control groups. Our first two studies, for example, used control groups of documents judged

TABLE 14.8. Mean Scores for Thematic Characteristics (Representing occurrence per 100 words)

Category	Reactive	Process	R-P	Reactive	Process	Schizo-phrenic	Nonschizo-phrenic
Distress-Relief Quotient	.75	.65	.68	.72	.67	.69	.79
Sum Tags NATURAL-WORLD, LEGAL, POLITICAL	12.50	5.60	21.05	19.70	6.40*	13.05	9.67
Sum Tags GUIDE, WORK, MOVE, GET	48.90	33.50	38.65	46.80	33.90*	40.35	41.23
Sum Tags COMMUNITY, FAMILY, ACADEMIC, RECREATIONAL	33.05	25.45	21.60	28.47	24.93	26.70	22.37
Sum Tags SEX, DEATH, MILITARY, SCIENCE	20.04	18.85	19.05	20.37	18.50	18.43	21.17
COMMUNICATE	16.20	20.85	16.90	15.90	20.07	17.98	17.57
THINK	9.20	12.40	6.60	6.43	12.36*	9.40	11.60*

$* p < .05.$

not to be disorganized, and as we have seen this group consisted of schizophrenic and nonschizophrenic patients. Most other studies have used normals as controls. In contrast, the control group here consisted of nonschizophrenic patients in the same hospital. For the most part, differences in grammatical and thematic characteristics of written samples between this control group and the schizophrenic patients were small and statistically insignificant.

There are, however, several exceptions to this rule. In two cases the difference between schizophrenic and nonschizophrenic patients reached statistical significance, and two other cases approached significance. The noun-verb/adjective-adverb ratio was higher for schizophrenic patients than for nonschizophrenic patients. If we assume that under high-drive states there should be less tendency toward modification of noun and verb forms because increases in drive weaken the capacity for discriminative qualification, then this would suggest more intense motivations in the schizophrenic patients. On the other hand, the use of ambivalent constructions was significantly more marked in nonschizophrenic patients, suggesting a greater level of anxiety on the part of these patients than on the part of schizophrenic patients. This is supported by a higher DRQ and shorter average thought-unit length in messages of nonschizophrenic patients.

However, the difficulty with such comparisons (a difficulty which besets all previous studies in this area) is that it assumes schizophrenia to be a unitary process. Most likely, the differences between schizophrenic and nonschizophrenic patients or normal individuals will depend on the type of schizophrenic patients used in the comparison. Lumping together different types of schizophrenic patients merely serves to obfuscate these differences. For this reason, the focal point of interest in this study has been the comparison between types of schizophrenic patients, where the typology employed is based on the reactive-process distinction as a function of life history and chronicity of illness.

The present findings give support to Mednick's (1958) hypothesis to the extent that the reactive-process classification parallels his acute-chronic classification. The DRQ was slightly higher for the reactive group; concern with the immediate personal concerns of the family, community, and schooling was more marked. Personal activity — as reflected in the themes relating to work, achievement, movement, and resolve — was also higher. However, remote themes (those that should be found in chronic patients because of their anxiety-reducing potential) were also higher in the reactive patients. Topics such as science, politics, the law, and the natural world were very significantly higher; and on the face of it, this does not support Mednick's position.

In general, however, our findings could be summarized as follows: Acute reactive schizophrenic patients' writings show more anxiety than those of chronic process patients. They are more concerned with external matters, ranging from the community to the world at large, and their concern is in personal, concrete, and abstract universal themes. On the other hand, the process chronic patient shows significantly more emphasis upon "inner" mental activity with a concomitant low concern for external matters and with a greater emphasis upon passivity rather than activity.

The findings of this study, and indeed of all three studies, should be regarded as the outcome of tentative forays into a wilderness of problems that besets the analysis of psychotic language. Dictionaries are needed that will reflect more closely important clinical and theoretical variables in the study of psychopathology. However, the beginnings made here with the avowedly broad-ranging dictionary of the General Inquirer provide reasonable ground for hope that comprehensive studies can be made in the near future. Certainly, the application of high-speed computer technology has brought the study of patients' documents into the realm of feasibility in a way that has not been possible with the manual procedures of the past.

BIBLIOGRAPHY

Bleuler, E. (1911), *Dementia Praecox, or the Group of Schizophrenias.* New York: International University Press.

Busemann, A. (1926), "Die Erregungsphasen der Jugend." *Zsch. f. Kinderforsch,* Vol. 33, 115–137.

Chapman, L. J. (1958), "Intrusion of Associative Responses into Schizophrenic Conceptual Performance." *Journal of Abnormal and Social Psychology,* Vol. 56, 374–379.

Crider, A., B. A. Maher, and L. Grinspoon (1965), "The Effect of Sensory Input on the Reaction Time of Schizophrenic Patients of Good and Poor Premorbid History." *Psychonomic Science,* Vol. 2, 47–48.

Dollard, John, and O. H. Mowrer (1947), "A Method of Measuring Tension in Written Documents." *Journal of Abnormal and Social Psychology,* Vol. 42, 3–32.

Ellsworth, Robert B. (1951), "The Regression of Schizophrenic Language." *Journal of Consulting Psychology,* Vol. 15, 387–391.

Fairbanks, Helen (1944), "The Quantitative Differentiation of Samples of Spoken Language." *Psychological Monographs,* Vol. 56, No. 255, 19–28.

Gottschalk, Louis, and Goldine Gleser (1964), "Distinguishing Characteristics of the Verbal Communications of Schizophrenic Patients." *Disorders of Communication,* Vol. 42, 400–413.

Hunt, William, and Nelson F. Jones (1957), "The Reliability of Clinical Judgment as a Function of Clinical Experience." *Journal of Clinical Psychology,* Vol. 13, 377–378.

——— (1958*a*), "The Reliability of Clinical Judgments of Asocial Tendency." *Journal of Clinical Psychology,* Vol. 14, 233–235.

——— (1958*b*), "Clinical Judgment of Some Aspects of Schizophrenic Thinking." *Journal of Clinical Psychology,* Vol. 14, 235–239.

Lorenz, Maria, and Stanley Cobb (1954), "Language Patterns in Psychotic and Psychoneurotic Subjects." *Archives of Neurological Psychiatry,* Vol. 72, 665–673.

Mabry, Mary (1955), "A Study Comparing the Language Characteristics of Scattered and Non-Scattered Schizophrenics with Normals." *Dissertation Abstracts,* Vol. 15, 457–458.

McKean, Kathryn O. (1963), "An Analysis of Selected Samples of Normal and Disorganized Language Productions of Mental Patients." Senior honors thesis, Radcliffe College.

McKean, Kathryn O., B. McLaughlin, and B. A. Maher (1963), "A Revised System of Syntax Identification in the General Inquirer Computer System." Dittoed memorandum. Center for Research in Personality, Harvard University.

McLaughlin, B., and B. A. Maher (1963), "Syntactical and Grammatical Identification in the General Inquirer Computer System: A Further Revision." Dittoed memorandum. Center for Research in Personality, Harvard University.

Maher, Brendan A. (1966), *Principles of Psychopathology*. New York: McGraw-Hill.

Mann, Mary B. (1944), "The Quantitative Differentiation of Samples of Written Language." *Psychological Monographs*, Vol. 56, No. 255, 41–74.

Mednick, Sarnoff A. (1958), "A Learning Theory Approach to Schizophrenia." *Psychological Bulletin*, Vol. 55, 316–325.

Meehl, P. E. (1962), "Schizotaxia, Schizotypy, Schizophrenia." *American Psychologist*, Vol. 17, 827–838.

Shneidman, Edwin (1948), "Schizophrenia and the MAPS Test." *Genetic Psychology Monographs*, Vol. 38, 145–223.

White, Mary A. (1949), "A Study of Schizophrenic Language." *Journal of Abnormal and Social Psychology*, Vol. 44, 61–74.

Whitehorn, John, and George Zipf (1943), "Schizophrenic Language." *Archives of Neurological Psychiatry*, Vol. 49, 831–851.

Venables, P. E. (1964), "Input Dysfunction in Schizophrenia." In B. A. Maher (ed.), *Progress in Experimental Personality Research*. Vol. I. New York: Academic Press.

Zigler, E., and L. Phillips (1961), "Social Competence and Outcome in Psychiatric Disorder." *Journal of Abnormal and Social Psychology*, Vol. 63, 264–271.

CHAPTER FIFTEEN

A Thematic Analysis of Interviewer's Statements in Therapy-Analogue Interviews[1]

George Psathas
Washington University

Dennis J. Arp
Washington University

INTRODUCTION

This study reports the development, testing, and application of a thematic analysis for the classification of therapist interventions in psychotherapeutic interviews. The data, comprising therapy-analogue interviews, constitute a more limited range of materials than actual psychotherapeutic sessions, but our aim is eventually to extend this system to such materials as well.

Some of the better-known attempts to deal with the lexical content of individual therapy protocols include those of Dollard and Auld (1959), Lennard and Bernstein (1960), Murray (1956), Gottschalk

[1] This research was supported by a grant from the U.S. Public Health Service, National Institute of Mental Health, MH 08664–01. Computations were done with support provided by the Washington University Computer Center under National Science Foundation Grant G–22296.

and Gleser (1963), Strupp (1960), and the recent computer analysis proposed by Harway and Iker (1964). Despite some interesting similarities and differences between our approach and the approaches of these researchers, we have not attempted systematic comparisons nor have we developed a dictionary or retrieval system to replicate any of these systems. Instead we have attempted to develop an empirically based set of content themes through the intensive analysis of both patient and therapist statements in therapeutic interviews. A set of therapy-analogue interviews collected by Heller (1963) were analyzed in order to test the validity and applicability of certain features of the General Inquirer system with data of this type. Only two of the several problems investigated will be described here.

The first problem concerns the differentiation of interviewer conditions in the interviews collected by Heller. He had given the interviewers special instructions in role playing. That their actual conduct varied according to the instructions was shown in the analysis of the subjects' (interviewees') behavior (Heller, 1963) and by the judgment of skilled observers who listened to recordings of the interviewers' verbal interaction. Heller's study did not subject the interviewers' behavior to detailed content analysis. Since the styles of interviewer conduct varied along theoretically important dimensions (activity-passivity and friendliness-hostility), a study of the specific manner in which interviewers differed could conceivably reveal important content dimensions that could be applied later to the analysis of statements generated by therapists in therapeutic interviews.

Our second concern is intimately related to the first in that it involved the delineation of distinctive content themes that not only might distinguish friendly and hostile interviewers, for example, but would also provide meaningful classifications of interviewers' or therapists' statements.

THE DATA AND PROCEDURE

Heller (1963) presented subjects, undergraduate psychology students, with a standard case study narrated on tape by an actor portraying a college student seeking guidance for personal problems. Immediately after listening to the stimulus material, subjects were asked to participate in a 15-minute interview, with one of four different types of interviewers. Subjects were given the following instructions:

1. As a starter for the *first five minutes* you should remember and report as much about the tape as you can (Description condition).
2. For the *next five minutes* you should discuss how you would solve the situation on the tape (Solution-Proposal condition).
3. For the *last five minutes* you should talk about yourself — about how you seem different or like the person on the tape (Identification condition).

Attempting to vary interpersonal behavior along the dimensions of activity (Active versus Passive) and affect (Friendly versus Hostile), Heller devised interviewer roles and trained speech and theater graduate students as interviewers. A description of the four roles devised is as follows:

1. *Active-Friendly* interviewer (AF). This interviewer leads the interview by encouraging verbalization but not directing the content of the discussion. He is sympathetic, friendly, and considerate of the interviewee. He is supportive and helpful. He speaks often, tends to be verbose, and uses nonverbal signs of approval.

2. *Passive-Friendly* interviewer (PF). This interviewer allows the interviewee to lead the interview. He is agreeable, friendly, and interested. He is laconic but agrees readily when he does speak. He uses nonverbal signs of approval.

3. *Active-Hostile* interviewer (AH). This interviewer leads the interview by requesting verbalization, but he does not direct the content of the discussion. Although not in extreme form, he shows disdain, disapproval, and lack of appreciation for the interviewee's approach to the task. He speaks often, tends to be verbose, and uses nonverbal signs of disapproval.

4. *Passive-Hostile* interviewer (PH). This interviewer allows the interviewee to lead the interview. He is aloof and shows lack of interest. He is laconic but voices skepticism or disapproval when he does speak. He uses nonverbal signs of disapproval.

Twelve interviewers, three per condition, were trained to perform one interviewer role. Each interviewer saw eight subjects. Three interviews in each condition were selected for the present analysis, one from each interviewer. The data consist of twelve interviews drawn from four different conditions, one interview from each of the three interviewers in each condition.

Since interviewers' statements were relatively infrequent as compared with subjects' statements, the three five-minute phases of the interview (Description, Solution-Proposal, and Identification) were combined in order to increase the number of statements to be analyzed. Since each interviewer was instructed to maintain his particular orientation throughout the entire interview (active-friendly interviewers were expected to be active-friendly in each phase of the interview and to convey this to the subject), no major differences were expected between the phases of the interview. One initial indication that no differences existed is that there were no statistically significant changes in the number of words or sentences found when the phases were compared.

Our analysis was based on the Harvard III Dictionary. In the tag tally phase of our investigation we discarded 41 Harvard III tags that had zero frequency in over half of the cell entries, across as well as within treatment conditions. This eliminated spurious significance.[2] Three other tags from the Harvard III Dictionary were eliminated because they were duplicates of the special codes. These special code tags, added in the initial coding and data preparation procedures, refer primarily to the tense of verbs, or to the sex, kinship, and social status of persons mentioned in the interview. Thus, the total number of tags used was 53.

DESCRIPTION OF DIFFERENCES

The analysis of interview conditions for each tag revealed several tags that discriminated between interviewers. Those that had the lowest rates of error (in the sense of inappropriate tagging as judged from an examination of the meaning of the sentence) and reflected statistically significant differences between interview conditions are given in Table 15.1.

Sentences that contained words classified by the tags just listed were retrieved. After a detailed analysis of these sentences, we came to two conclusions.

First, even though statistically significant differences between interviewer conditions were discovered, reliance on tag tally results was not sufficient to permit a reliable interpretation of the meaning of the differences. This was especially true because of the high rates of error discovered when sentences retrieved by a single tag specification

---

[2] These tags tended to occur with extremely low frequencies if they occurred at all.

TABLE 15.1. Tags Showing Statistically Significant Differences Between Interviewers by Condition

Categories and Tags	Active vs. Passive	Friendly vs. Hostile
Persons		
OTHER	A > P†	
NEUTER-ROLE	A > P††	
Physical Qualifiers		
SPACE-REFERENCE		H > F**
Environments		
SOCIAL-PLACE		H > F*
Culture		
MESSAGE-FORM	P > A**	F > H††
THOUGHT-FORM		H > F*
Emotion		
AFFECTION	P > A*	F > H*
Thought		
THINK	P > A*	
Evaluation		
OUGHT	A > P*	
Social-Emotional Actions		
FOLLOW		F > H††
AVOID		H > F†
Impersonal Actions		
WORK		H > F*
Institutional Contexts		
ECONOMIC		H > F*
Psychological Themes		
ASCEND-THEME	A > P*	
AUTHORITY-THEME	A > P††	F > H††
OVERSTATE		F > H††
SIGN-ACCEPT		F > H††
FEMALE-THEME		H > F*
Special Codes		
EQUAL-STATUS	A > P†	
FEMALES	A > P*	
HIGHER-STATUS	A > P*	
MALES	A > P**	
NON-FAMILY	A > P††	
PRESENT TENSE		H > F††

* $p < .10$.
** $p < .05$.
† $p < .025$.
†† $p < .01$.

were examined. The type of error that was of greatest concern was the inappropriate or inaccurate classification of a word under one tag heading when its meaning in context was something different. The special usages and meanings in verbal interaction and in interviews of the kind being studied could not have been anticipated in the construction of the Harvard III Dictionary. We began to realize that a dictionary constructed especially for therapeutic interviews would be desirable in the long run, but at this point we were not ready to build one ourselves. Instead, we proceeded with the same dictionary to test whether other approaches, such as combinations of tags, would provide additional insights into the differences between the experimental conditions and whether we could devise new methods for analyzing this same set of data.

Our second conclusion involved the realization that combinations of tags or of tags and words must be used as the basis of subsequent retrievals in order to describe better the content of themes that were becoming apparent after the inspection of retrievals.

Our first strategy to detect themes involved clustering tags that had shown statistically significant differences.[3] Statistical discrimination within this cluster produced a series of smaller clusters. A major problem with this method was that a cluster arrived at by this empirical procedure did not necessarily contain a set of statements that could readily be interpreted. In other words, we found that at times this strategy forced us to sacrifice theoretical relevance for statistical significance. The dependence of any interpretation on a dictionary that produces low rates of error in retrievals and includes tags that are theoretically relevant for the content being analyzed became more and more apparent. Building on this fact, we came closer to the construction of a new dictionary.

THEME ANALYSIS

Our next step was based on the results of the previous stages. However, in contrast to the cluster analysis which started with tags that already showed discriminatory power, we did not try to select any particular combination that had differentiated between conditions. Instead we asked whether what we already knew about the content could help us to construct themes based either on tags, combinations of tags and words, or words alone. If a meaningful theme could first be constructed, we would next determine whether it discriminated between conditions. Even if it failed to discriminate, we would still have developed a theme that could be applied to other interview material of the same type.

One of the first themes noted in the interviewers' statements was

---

[3] Tags with high rates of error were omitted from the development of the cluster.

based on the tags OUGHT, SIGN-ASCEND, and SIGN-AUTHORITY. The words "would" and "should" were used in declarative and interrogative forms of sentences to give some kind of suggestion or to prod the interviewee to begin or continue. Calling this theme *PRODDING-SUGGESTION,* we then examined other sentence retrievals to determine whether other words, presently located in other tag lists, were actually being used in the same way. This search revealed that the following words were likewise indicative of this theme: give, make, must, begin, tell, talk, and report. In addition, in these sentences the frequent reference to the interviewee as subject led us to conclude that this information should also be included in the theme. Examples are

Tell me how *you would* solve the situation.

How *would you* apply this (problem) to yourself?

(*You*) *make* it (comparison) a little clearer.

So then *you would* just *tell* him to speak right up to the fellows in the fraternity (club).

Would you talk about those problems?

By using actual words rather than tags in new retrieval specifications, we created in effect a new dictionary tag consisting of all words on this list plus interviewee as subject. Sentences were retrieved within each condition and tested for the presence of significant differences. However, no statistically significant differences in the frequency of *PRODDING-SUGGESTION* were found for Active versus Passive or Friendly versus Hostile interviewers, although there was a tendency for passive interviewers to be lower on this theme ($X^2 = 2.27$, $df = 1$, $p < .20$).

We were also interested in whether different phases of the interview might be differentiated by the frequency of this theme, a problem that had not yet been examined in any systematic fashion. This question is especially relevant in assessing the validity of the dictionary since the experimental conditions require the interviewer to be certain that the subject moves from describing the problems in the tape-recorded case to proposing solutions and then to comparing himself with the case. However, the exact manner in which interviewers might vary their behavior within each phase could not be completely specified. Furthermore, the themes that we might discover in the examination of the data were not to be selected in terms of their ability to differentiate between phases of the interview. If they did reveal differences, it would be an indication that variations in interviewer behavior from one phase to another could be detected through the dictionary or through the new themes being constructed.

Combining all interviewers and comparing phases of the interview revealed that the Solution-Proposal phase had the highest proportion of *PRODDING-SUGGESTION*[4] ($X^2 = 13.57$, $df = 2$, $p < .01$). The interviewers urge the subject to provide adequate solutions for the problem and use *PRODDING-SUGGESTION* more frequently in this phase.

A second theme generated by interviewers seemed appropriately described as *PROBING-REFLECTION*. Words such as feel, think, want, see, said, say, find, mean, speak, or suggest together with interviewee as subject (you think . . . , you say . . . , you mean . . .) constitute the elements of this theme. There is a certain amount of interpretation in the declarative form of statements that include this theme, but the interpretation is not deep.

In contrast to *PRODDING-SUGGESTION,* the frequency of this theme does differentiate interviewers by condition. The passive interviewers are higher than the active ($X^2 = 3.81$, $df = 1$, $p < .10$), and the hostile interviewers are higher than the friendly ($X^2 = 16.50$, $df = 1$, $p < .001$). The passive-hostile interviewers generate the highest frequencies for this theme, and the active-friendly interviewers generate the lowest. We are able to show this in analyzing interaction effects by examining the contribution to chi-square of each condition treated separately. (The contribution to chi-square for each condition is PH $= 20.22$, PF $= 1.00$, AH $= 1.14$, and AF $= 4.94$.) The PF and AH interviewers' frequencies are within the range of chance expectation. It appears that PH interviewers try to shift the burden of participation to the subject, stressing that it is he who has taken a particular position and not agreeing or identifying themselves with him if possible. If this is, in fact, perceived by the subject as passive hostility, the implications of too great a concentration on *PROBING-REFLECTION* statements by an interviewer-therapist deserve further study. Examples of the types of statements included here are the following:

---

[4] Where two words are used in describing a theme, such as *PRODDING-SUGGESTION,* the first refers to interrogative and the second to declarative forms.

Well that is one solution *you* have *mentioned.*

Then *you* still *think you* can identify with him.

You said you remembered that he wanted to kill himself.

Are *you saying* that *you see* a lot of differences or do *you see* some similarities?

When used in an interrogative form, this theme seems to be more probing than reflecting. For example,

Any other kinds of solution that *you* can *think* of?

Do you see any other solutions to some of the things *you mentioned?*

Can *you think* of anything more about his folks (parents)?

Unlike the *PRODDING-SUGGESTION* theme which showed differences by interview phase, this theme remains relatively constant throughout each phase.

Continuing this same procedure, we identified eight themes and developed lists of words, combinations of words, and words with their grammatical context (for instance, interviewee as subject of the sentence), which in essence produced a new dictionary specifically designed to classify all statements generated by the interviewers. The results of this analysis and a brief description of each theme are presented in summary form in Tables 15.2, 15.3, and 15.4.

Table 15.3 shows that of all statements generated by interviewers over all conditions, at least one of the eight themes is contained in an average of 82 percent of the statements. We had attained at least one goal, that of inclusiveness.

For each theme, comparisons of interviewers by each condition were made. From the results summarized in Table 15.4, it is possible to characterize the different interviewer styles. To be an active interviewer means that one tends to be higher than expected on expressions of *AGREEMENT*. To be passive is to be higher than expected on *PROBING-REFLECTION,* to stress the subject's *ABILITY-POTENTIAL,* to give more *DIRECT-URGING* statements, and use more *OPEN-ENDED PROBES*. These themes, considered together, seem to indicate that the low activity rate of passive interviewers is associated with statements that may serve to keep the subject talking on specific topics. In contrast to simple agreement, which may operate as a general reinforcer for the continuation of any topic, the other types

TABLE 15.2. Analysis of Themes: Interviewer Statements

PRODDING-SUGGESTION

Urges the other to do something, to take a course of action, asks other to continue.

PROBING-REFLECTION

Asks for more information or opinion, reflects subject's previous statements, makes
mild interpretation.

ABILITY-POTENTIAL

Asks other if he can do something, suggests that other use his ability or potential,
refers to what other can do.

DIRECT-PRAISE

Praises, compliments, or thanks the other.

AGREEMENT

Expresses passive acceptance, agreement, or understanding (one subdimension is
the utterance "mm hmm" spoken by itself called "mild agreement").
   a. mild agreement
   b. other agreement

NEGATION

Direct use of negative qualifiers (this theme overlaps with and generally negates
another theme).

DIRECT-URGING

Asks, urges, or directs the other to go on, continue, or return to another topic.

OPEN-ENDED PROBE

General probe asking for more information, an opinion, or ideas, usually without
reference to any specific topic.

---

*TABLE 15.3. Number and Percent of Total Sentences Accounted For
by Eight Themes by Condition*

		Sentences Accounted For	
Condition	*Total*	*N*	*Percent*
ACTIVE	513	414	81
PASSIVE	176	142	81
FRIENDLY	441	370	84
HOSTILE	248	186	75
PASSIVE-HOSTILE	71	58	82
PASSIVE-FRIENDLY	105	84	80
ACTIVE-FRIENDLY	336	286	85
ACTIVE-HOSTILE	177	128	72

TABLE 15.4. *Summary of Chi-Square Analysis of Each Theme by Condition*

Active-High Passive-Low	Passive-High Active-Low	Friendly-High Hostile-Low	Hostile-High Friendly-Low
AGREEMENT**	PROBING-REFLECTION*	DIRECT-PRAISE††	PROBING-REFLECTION††
	ABILITY-POTENTIAL†	AGREEMENT††	ABILITY-POTENTIAL*
	DIRECT-URGING**		DIRECT-URGING**
	OPEN-ENDED PROBE†		OPEN-ENDED PROBE*
			NEGATION**

* $p < .10$.
** $p < .05$.
† $p < .01$.
†† $p < .001$.

of statements can lead the subject to focus on specific topics. An examination of subjects' behavior is necessary in order to determine what the content of their interaction is in response to interviewer comments of each type. The analysis of interaction sequences is necessary to determine the effect of particular interviewer comments, but at this point we have not begun to analyze the subjects' responses.

Turning to the friendly-hostility dimension, we find that Hostile interviewers are high on four of the same themes that distinguish the Passive interviewers: *PROBING-REFLECTION, ABILITY-POTENTIAL, DIRECT-URGING,* and *OPEN-ENDED PROBES* (see Table 15.4). *NEGATION* is the only theme on which Hostile interviewers are higher than expected and the Passive interviewers are not. Both conditions have less than the expected amount of *AGREEMENT* references, but the Hostile interviewers are also low on *DIRECT-PRAISE* statements. While one may differentiate hostility from passivity on two themes, *NEGATION* and *DIRECT-PRAISE,* the evidence leads to the conclusion that passivity and hostility seem to be intercorrelated, or at least the combination of the two has a cumulative effect.

This cumulative effect can also be seen in the Active and Friendly interviewers. Both are high in their use of *AGREEMENT* and have less than the expected amount of *PROBING-REFLECTION, ABILITY-POTENTIAL, DIRECT-URGING,* and *OPEN-ENDED PROBES.* The distinguishing themes for Friendly interviewers are their greater use of *DIRECT-PRAISE* and the nonutilization of *NEGATION.*

When the magnitude and direction of the contribution to the chi-square is examined for the four interaction conditions, the two conditions that show the greatest contrast, as might be expected from our earlier analysis of the independent dimensions, are the PH and the AF. They are polar opposites on four themes in that the PH group is highest for *PROBING-REFLECTION, ABILITY-POTENTIAL, DIRECT-URGING,* and *OPEN-ENDED PROBES,* while the AF group is the lowest. On *AGREEMENT,* the AF group is highest and the PH group is one of the two lowest. For the *DIRECT-PRAISE* theme, the AF group is second highest and the PH group second lowest.

When we contrast the PH group with the AH group, no such polar oppositions can be found, and the contrast between the AF group and the PF group reveals that the AF group is lowest on *ABILITY-PO-TENTIAL* references while the PF group is second highest. Examining the PH and PF conditions, the only major oppositions found are that the PH group is highest on *PROBING-REFLECTION* while the PF group is second lowest, and the PF group is highest in *DI-RECT-PRAISE* whereas the PH group is second lowest. The addition of hostility to the passivity dimension is thus responsible for an increase in *PROBING-REFLECTION* and a decrease in *DIRECT-PRAISE.* The addition of friendliness produces converse effects on this dimension in that *DIRECT-PRAISE* increases while *PROBING-REFLECTION* diminishes.

Similarly, when we compare the differences for the AF and AH groups, we find that the addition of friendliness to the activity dimension results in a decrease of *PROBING-REFLECTION* and an increase in *DIRECT-PRAISE* and *AGREEMENT.* The AH group is correspondingly opposite on these dimensions in that they are lowest in *AGREEMENT* and *DIRECT-PRAISE* and second highest in *PROBING-REFLECTION.* These kinds of contrasts between conditions enable us to specify in more detail how interviewers behave as they attempt to "create" a particular experimental condition.[5]

Overlap Among Themes

In conducting our analysis of themes and in examining sentences retrieved, it became apparent that particular kinds of overlaps (the

---

[5] Because of the small number of cases in each condition, we chose not to use the analysis of variance in the statistical analyses. However, it should be apparent that a replication study with a large number of observations would make this possible.

joint occurrence of two or more themes per sentence) were more likely to occur than others. Furthermore, the frequency with which a given theme overlapped with another differed according to the nature of the theme rather than with the frequency of its occurrence in the total document. Table 15.5 presents the frequencies and percentages for each theme. As can be seen by inspection of this table, the most frequent theme, *AGREEMENT,* is least likely to overlap with other themes when one considers only the percentage of times this theme is found alone. This theme, because it includes expressions such as

TABLE 15.5. *Frequency and Percent of Overlap and Nonoverlap for Eight Themes*

		Overlap	No Overlap	Total	Percent of Total
PRODDING-SUGGESTION	N	84	29	113	
	Percent	(74)	(27)		13.8
PROBING-REFLECTION	N	106	59	165	
	Percent	(64)	(36)		20.1
ABILITY-POTENTIAL	N	94	16	110	
	Percent	(85)	(15)		13.4
DIRECT-PRAISE	N	13	25	38	
	Percent	(34)	(66)		4.6
AGREEMENT	N	36	154	190	
	Percent	(19)	(81)		23.2
NEGATION	N	49	25	74	
	Percent	(66)	(34)		9.0
DIRECT-URGING	N	7	10	17	
	Percent	(41)	(59)		2.1
OPEN-ENDED PROBES	N	99	14	113	
	Percent	(88)	(12)		13.8
ALL THEMES	N	332	488	820	
	Percent	(40)	(60)		

"Mmm hmm" and "I see," which are often independent interventions, is most likely to occur alone. However, because it is a frequent theme, the total number of overlaps expected is greater than for *DIRECT-URGING* and *DIRECT-PRAISE,* which have low frequencies in the overlap column of 7 and 13 in Table 15.5. Of the other themes, *OPEN-ENDED PROBES* is the least likely to occur by itself (12 percent) and *ABILITY-POTENTIAL* (15 percent) next in order. When examined in sentences, these themes are seen as requiring the presence of other words for meaning. They also tend to co-occur with certain other themes, although Table 15.5 does not show the other themes with which they are most frequently associated. The results suggest that an examination of the combined occurrences of particular themes can help us to determine whether new meanings evolve when specific themes occur together. Further, the examination of patterns of overlap can reveal which themes are more likely to co-occur or be dependent on one another. Distinctive patterns of co-occurrence may also be associated with interviewer styles. This would indicate how interviewers use different patterns of themes to create their distinctive styles of behavior.

In making this comparison, we looked at all sentences in which two or more themes occurred. We determined the theoretical probability of the co-occurrence of any pair of themes first, and then compared this with the actual frequency. For example, the pair *PRODDING-SUGGESTION* and *PROBING-REFLECTION* occurs with an actual frequency of 34, but the theoretical frequency expected is 6.6.[6] This

[6] The calculation of the expected frequencies is accomplished by using a random sampling model for an infinite population. The probability values are computed to control for the base rate of overlap for a given theme (for instance, the proportion of *PRODDING-SUGGESTION* references is given by $113/820 = .1378048$, but the proportion of overlap is given by $84/820 = .1024390$ and that for nonoverlap $29/820 = .0353658$); control for the base rate or frequency for each condition (for instance, the PH interviewers have a total of 38 sentences that overlap with another theme as opposed to the AF interviewers who have a total of 96 sentences that overlap with another theme); and to also control for the probability of obtaining a particular kind of overlap in sentences containing two, three, four, or five overlapping themes (for instance, here we determine what on the basis of chance alone would be the probability of getting two particular themes to overlap when eight themes are available and there are only two themes in a sentence, or the probability when there are three, four, or five themes in the sentence, and so on). As an example, consider the following: the probability of obtaining an overlap of *PRODDING-SUGGESTION* (A) and *PROBING-REFLECTION* (B) in a sentence with only two themes is given by the product of their separate proportions for overlap (or $84/240 \times 106/820$). But since this event can occur in two ways (either an AB may occur or a BA may occur) the product is doubled. The result is .0296370. Our empirical data show

TABLE 15.6. Comparison of the Actual and Expected Overlap for Three Types of Co-occurrences*

	AB		AC		BC	
	PRODDING-SUGGESTION and PROBING-REFLECTION		*PRODDING-SUGGESTION and ABILITY-POTENTIAL*		*PROBING-REFLECTION and ABILITY-POTENTIAL*	
Condition	*Observed*	*Expected*	*Observed*	*Expected*	*Observed*	*Expected*
PASSIVE-HOSTILE	5	1.14	2	1.02	13	1.27
PASSIVE-FRIENDLY	5	1.07	7	.97	11	1.19
ACTIVE-FRIENDLY	17	2.86	11	2.56	14	3.19
ACTIVE-HOSTILE	7	1.56	6	1.38	7	1.73
TOTAL	*34*	*6.63*	*26*	*5.93*	*45*	*7.38*
FRIENDLY	22	3.93	18	3.51	25	4.38
HOSTILE	12	2.70	8	2.40	20	3.00
ACTIVE	24	4.37	17	3.94	21	4.91
PASSIVE	10	2.25	9	1.99	24	2.46

* The observed frequencies do not include the overlap in 2 sentences that contained 5 themes as the expected frequencies were not calculated for sentences with greater than 4 themes.

comparison, only a part of which is tabulated in Table 15.6, shows that some pairs of themes tend to co-occur with a frequency greater than that based on a chance model. Of these pairs, three will be

---

that there are 26, 22, 65, and 43 sentences with only two themes in a sentence for the PH, PF, AF, and AH interviewers, respectively. To obtain the expected frequencies for each condition, the probability of an AB overlap is multiplied by the number of sentences with only two themes per sentence, and the result is .69, .58, 1.72, and 1.14, respectively. The procedure is similar for sentences containing three themes and for which *only* the probability of obtaining a two-theme overlap, such as AB, is desired. However, one must consider that these two elements may overlap in a sentence with three elements in at least three different fashions. One may have an A and a B and any one of the remaining themes (N). There are six different ways in which this may be arranged so the probability is equal to $6 \times 84/820 \times 106/820 \times 298/820$. The probability for AAB and BBA is similarly computed but there are only three ways in which each can occur and each is thus tripled. The probability of an AB overlap in a sentence with only three themes is now the sum of the three kinds of occurrences (that is .0380791). This value is then multiplied by the number of sentences which contain three themes for each of the experimental conditions. The process is continued for sentences with four themes. The expected frequencies for each interviewer condition and for each kind of sentence (those with only two themes, those with only three themes, and those with only four themes) are totaled and yield 6.63 expected AB overlaps for all interviewer conditions. This is much less than the actual frequency of AB overlap, which is 34. (See Table 15.6.)

mentioned for illustrative purposes. The procedure followed here is sufficiently general so that any analysis of themes in a specified unit can be examined in the same way. The discovery of significantly associated themes is of interest, but of even greater interest is the combination of pairs of themes that have some theoretical relevance for the understanding of the interviewer's interaction. Some examples of frequent overlapping pairs are *PRODDING-SUGGESTION* (A) and *PROBING-REFLECTION* (B); *PRODDING-SUGGESTION* (A) and *ABILITY-POTENTIAL* (C); and *PROBING-REFLECTION* (B) and *ABILITY-POTENTIAL* (C). These three pairs occur with greater than chance expectancy, and when such statements occur they represent a different emphasis from those in which one theme or the other occurs.

B&A *You think* then setting up the schedule *would* solve one of his
      B   A
problems.

B&A In terms of the social situation *you find* that the social conflicts
                                B
are not the kind that *you would* have.
           A

A&C But now (*tell*) just straight facts that *you can* remember.
         A   C

A&C (*Tell*) just anything that *you can* possibly remember from the
     A   C
tape (record).

B&C And ah what solutions do *you think* he *might* have?
                      B   C

B&C *You think* he *can* look at the problems differently.
      B   C

B&C Then *you* still *think you can* identify with him.
          B   C

The co-occurrences of themes A&B, A&C, and B&C represent the varied emphasis that the interviewers may place on the subject's statements by juxtaposing these common themes. As might be expected, a theme occurring alone tends to be found in a shorter sentence, but the length of the sentence with two or more themes is not its major distinguishing characteristic. In sentences with two or more themes, qualifications are introduced, emphasis and clarification are made concerning what the subject has said or is being requested to say, more specificity is apparent, and general interest in whatever the subject will say is being communicated. Again, we need to extend our analysis to the subject's responses to these multitheme statements in order to learn how such sentences are interpreted and how they function.

How meanings can change because of their sequential appearance is worth exploring. Some sentences are fairly complex. For example, the sequence of themes for one (declarative sentence) is *REFLEC-TION, SUGGESTION, POTENTIAL, REFLECTION, REFLECTION, REFLECTION* (B, A, C, B, B, B). From a knowledge of these themes, we would guess without looking at the exact sentence itself that it conveys to the subject the following: the interviewer first reflects what the subject has said, or he refers to his feelings, thoughts, or ideas; then he suggests a course of action dependent on how much the subject is able to do, and finally he makes three more references to the subject's feelings, thoughts, or ideas by employing reflective themes. When we examine the actual sentence it reads, "Let *us see, you would* ah, ah, *try* to explain that his parents *wanted* to do this for the best, I *think you said.*" The general meaning of the sentence is fairly successfully captured by the shorthand description of the themes though there are some errors. For example, "parents wanted" is classified as a reflection that is equivalent to "you feel" or "you think," and it is retrieved because the interviewee is the subject of the whole sentence. Our interpretation, without looking at the actual usage, was that the interviewer is referring to something the interviewee "wanted." However, at one level of interpretation it is possible to note that by referring to what the "parents wanted" the interviewer *is* actually referring to what the interviewee thinks the parents wanted, and in this sense it is a projection of the interviewee's feeling state. Without considering sequence or multiple occurrences, this sentence would be classified as *SUGGESTION, REFLECTION, POTENTIAL.*

The possibility of making "blind" reconstructions of sentences becomes very real the more we learn about how themes co-occur, which themes most frequently co-occur, and what new meanings emerge when certain patterns of co-occurrence are found. By calculating the appropriate probabilities that themes will co-occur, the data from any interview can be examined to determine whether particular patterns are more or less frequent than chance models would predict. The distinctiveness of interviewer styles would be more immediately apparent if observed frequencies could be automatically compared with theoretically expected ones by means of a program that could compute the discrepancy on a first run after the data were tagged. The consideration of a program that incorporates this feature of simultaneous classification and analysis represents an additional challenge in the extension of the General Inquirer system.

EPICRISIS

The series of exploratory operations by which the themes were developed (proceeding from the analysis of individual tags to clusters of tags) was a necessary step, but one that does not need to be repeated. Even though significant differences were revealed in these steps, we chose to develop a new set of categories, more promising both descriptively and theoretically. The results of this alteration to the Harvard III Dictionary were quite fruitful. The significant differences between interviewer styles are encouraging even though they could not be anticipated. That Passive-Hostility and Active-Friendliness were the most contrasting conditions was not demonstrated by the earlier analyses. Only after themes were developed was this contrast apparent. Heller (1963) came to the same conclusion, but he chose to investigate the interviewees' reactions rather than the thematic patterning in the interviewers' verbalizations. He found that the AF interviewers were best liked and that the PH interviewers were least liked ($p < .01$). Our independent analysis of these two conditions discovered this polar opposition from a different vantage point, and perhaps future studies will permit us to list more of those characteristics contributing to the interviewees' likes and dislikes.

The development of a set of themes that can be built into the dictionary tags now allows us to probe further into these interviewer styles. For instance, we would like to know how subjects respond to interviewer statements of one type in contrast to another. Does hostility, when total activity rate is suppressed, create greater problems of communication than active hostility, and if so, how are these communication problems manifested? Active-Friendly interviewers tend to be high on simple acts of *AGREEMENT*. But if statements that include only this theme are removed, how else do they differ, that is, is it possible that there are other distinctive features of their statements and that their rates on other themes are no different from other interviewer styles? If so, the creation of an Active-Friendly style may be due to the addition of one theme rather than the reduction of others.

The results obtained in our analysis of overlapping themes has provided a method for developing computer programs that will automatically produce a contingency analysis and yield more information as to which particular types of co-occurrences are an integral part of a given interviewer style. It will also enable us to discern whether these particular types of co-occurrences are the result of linguistic rules in the English language, the result of the interviewers' task, or due to the limited vocabulary that emerges in therapeutic interactions. Further explorations with these themes will reveal how particular patterns of overlap alter the meanings of interventions and how crucial the sequence or repetitiveness of themes may be in conveying the desired message to the interviewee. It may well be that the crucial determinants that other content analysis systems have not yet discovered were due to the absence of high-speed automated processing methods that could handle such complex contingencies.

Some of the next steps in this research are by now obvious. The development of a new dictionary for interviewers' statements needs to be tested against another set of similar materials in an effort to replicate the results of the present study. Since additional interviews obtained by Heller (that were not analyzed here) are available, this step is possible. After replication, analysis-of-variance procedures can be used because a larger number of cases will be available.

Most important, however, will be the extension of the present set of themes to the analysis of real therapeutic interviews. At the same time, we are continuing the analysis of the subject's interaction in order to develop a set of discriminating themes that can later be applied to the analysis of patient interaction. Our selection of a set of data with a more limited range of variation, that is, interviewers' statements, was a deliberate strategy in developing our procedures. The more difficult task of extending the same methods to subjects, patients, and to real therapeutic interviews lies ahead.

BIBLIOGRAPHY

Auld, F., Jr., and E. J. Murray (1955), "Content Analysis Studies of Psychotherapy," *Psychological Bulletin,* Vol. 52, 377–395.

Dollard, J., and F. Auld, Jr. (1959), *Scoring Human Motives: A Manual*. New Haven, Conn.: Yale University Press.

Gottschalk, L. A., and G. C. Gleser (1963), *Manual of Instructions for the Verbal Behavior Method of Measuring Certain Psychological Variables including Some of the Theoretical Bases*. Department of Psychiatry, University of Cincinnati.

Harway, H. I., and H. P. Iker (July 14, 1964), "Objective Content Analysis of Psychotherapy by Computer." Paper presented at the 1964 Rochester Conference on Data Acquisition and Processing in Biology and Medicine. Rochester, New York.

Heller, K. (1963), "Interpersonal Style in an Interview Analogue." Paper presented at the symposium, "Social Influence, Counseling and Psychotherapy," American Psychological Association meetings, Philadelphia.

Lennard, H. L., and A. Bernstein (1960), *The Anatomy of Psychotherapy*. New York: Columbia University Press.

Murray, E. J. (1956), "A Content-Analysis Method for Studying Psychotherapy." *Psychological Monographs*, Vol. 70, No. 13 (Whole No. 420).

Strupp, H. (1960), *Psychotherapists in Action*. New York: Grune & Stratton.

SOCIAL PSYCHOLOGY

The first paper in this section (Ogilvie, Stone, and Shneid-man) discusses one of the earliest studies with the General Inquirer. It was the first piece of research to take full advantage of all features of the system that existed at that time (1962). The data were syntax marked; retrievals were made on the basis of the syntax positions of tagged words; leftover lists were systematically explored. In a limited sense, then, this is a landmark document. It will be noted that from our present position of computer technology, this study was far from elegant. For example, although the rudiments of contingency analysis were recognized, the half-computer, half-manual procedures of sort-ing and categorizing sentences would now be handled by a more sophisticated use of retrieval questions. But despite those features that in retrospect appear to have a "hit or miss" quality, the results of the analysis were unusually clear. Distinct and understandable differences between genuine and simulated suicide notes were uncovered, a fact that was particularly gratifying at a time when encouragement was welcome.

The second article is Ramallo's study of documents produced by successful and unsuccessful volunteers for Operation Crossroads Africa. Curiously, in his earlier work with related material, Ramallo found that reports written by unsuccessful volunteers resembled simu-lated suicide notes and the reports of successful volunteers resembled genuine suicide notes in respect to positions on a "thought-involve-ment" dimension. The former pairs used more "thought-related" words, and the latter pair made more use of "concrete-action" types of words.

These initial results were later modified, and it was found that successful volunteers wrote concurrently about both *subjective (thought) and objective (concrete) elements of experience to a greater degree than did their unsuccessful counterparts. In addition to describing his work with these dimensions, Ramallo also discusses several unexpected problems in method that he encountered in the course of his research.*

These problems (such as variable sentence length and use of percentage scores) required special statistical treatment, and his presentation should be helpful to those who encounter similar difficulties in the future.

These two studies use versions of the Harvard III Dictionary, a dictionary that is placed in the category of "general dictionary" in Chapter 4. By contrast, the last paper in this section focuses on a "specific dictionary." Specific dictionaries were previously described as containing a limited number of tag categories that are used to measure variables considered crucial to the researcher's theoretical orientation. Our example is McLaughlin's construction of a dictionary that categorizes responses to the open-ended "Who Am I?" questionnaire in a manner that enables him to examine self-perceived identity of certain groups of college students. Using this measure, McLaughlin investigates response differences between students from public and private school backgrounds and also traces changes in self-perceived identity within each group over a four-year period. The success of this research has encouraged our efforts to take advantage of the richness of open-ended materials without having to sacrifice needed objectivity.

CHAPTER SIXTEEN

Some Characteristics of Genuine Versus Simulated Suicide Notes

Daniel M. Ogilvie
Harvard University

Philip J. Stone
Harvard University

Edwin S. Shneidman
Suicide Prevention Center
Los Angeles, California

THE NOTES AND THE PROBLEM [1]

Thirty-three genuine suicide and 33 simulated suicide notes were made available to members of the research team by Edwin S. Shneidman. The genuine notes were selected from 721 suicide notes collected from folders of suicide cases in Los Angeles county for the ten-year period of 1945 to 1954. This sample included only those notes written by suicide victims who were male, Caucasian, Protestant, native born, and between the ages of 25 and 59. For comparative purposes, simulated suicide notes were obtained fron nonsuicidal individuals who

---

[1] For more complete information about these notes and the research related to them, the reader is referred to *Clues to Suicide* edited by E. S. Shneidman and Norman L. Farberow (New York: McGraw-Hill, 1957).

were all also male, Caucasian, Protestant, and native born, and who were matched with genuine note writers with respect to age and occupational level. The simulated note writers were instructed to make their notes sound as real as possible, to write as if they were actually planning to take their own life. Through the use of the General Inquirer, we were able to distinguish between genuine and simulated suicide notes.

The Dictionary[2]

The dictionary used in this study was the Harvard II Psycho-sociological Dictionary (forerunner of our current dictionary.) That category system, like the Harvard III Dictionary, was divided into first-order tags (discrete, independent categories) and second-order tags (nonindependent categories). The first-order tags were sub-divided into *ROLES, OBJECTS, EMOTIONAL STATES,* and *ACTIONS.* All **Things** were either *ROLES* or *OBJECTS,* and all **Processes** were either *EMOTIONAL STATES* or *ACTIONS.* The second-order tags were classified as referring to either *INSTITUTIONS, STATUSES, QUALITIES,* or *SYMBOLIC REFERENTS.*

First Inspection of Tag Score Differences

The genuine and simulated notes were processed separately. The tags that appeared to differentiate between the sets (total difference of .03 percent or greater) are presented in Table 16.1.
Roughly summarizing the differences revealed in Table 16.1, we found that the genuine suicide notes are slightly more diversified in their use of the eight general categories in our theoretical scheme. With the exception of *EMOTIONAL STATES* and *INSTITUTIONS,* the genuine notes have relatively higher counts on some tags under all categories. On the other hand, the simulated notes do not have any higher scores in the following categories: *OBJECTS, STATUSES,* and *QUALITIES.* Moreover, the simulated notes make relatively little use of the *ROLES* category.

More specifically, the greatest difference seems to be that the genuine note writers concentrate more heavily on tags referring to **Things** (*ROLES* and *OBJECTS*) and *qualities,* whereas the simulated note

---

[2] Since an understanding of the results of this study is not contingent upon a full understanding of the dictionary that was used, a complete presentation of the tag categories will not be undertaken here.

TABLE 16.1. Tags That Discriminate Between Genuine and Simulated Notes

---

FIRST-ORDER TAGS

Things

ROLES		*OBJECTS*	
(Genuine)	(Simulated)	(Genuine)	(Simulated)
SELF*	SELVES	ARTIFACT	
OTHER		PLACE	
MALE-ROLE			
FEMALE-ROLE			

Processes

EMOTIONAL STATES		*ACTIONS*	
(Genuine)	(Simulated)	(Genuine)	(Simulated)
	ANXIETY-FAIL	COMMUNICATE	THINK
	ANXIETY-UNABLE	POSSESS	SENSE
	DISTRESS	GET	IF
		ATTACK	NOT
			MOVE
			AVOID
			DIRECT
			GOALS

SECOND-ORDER TAGS

INSTITUTIONS		*STATUSES*	
(Genuine)	(Simulated)	(Genuine)	(Simulated)
	ACADEMIC	HIGHER-STATUS	

QUALITIES		*SYMBOLIC REFERENTS*	
(Genuine)	(Simulated)	(Genuine)	(Simulated)
QUANTITY-REFERENCE		SEX-THEME	DEATH-THEME
BAD		MALE-THEME	UNDERSTATE

---

* Tags that appear in this table are those which had comparatively "high" counts for the set (genuine or simulated) under which they are listed.

writers have their heaviest concentration on tags referring to **Processes.** The use of tags under **Things** and *qualities* by genuine note writers appears to represent a greater emphasis on specifics. On the other hand, the high counts on tags under **Processes** might well reflect a more general use of words indicating the operation of cognitive processes for the simulated note writers (words such as think, sense, if, goals). Another difference between the two types of notes is the tendency for the genuine notes to use sentences with words referring to themselves in the first person and to others (male and females), whereas the simulated note writers tend to refer more to themselves and others simultaneously by using the word "we." Equally interesting is the complete absence of tags under *EMOTIONAL STATES* for the genuine notes. This reflects a relative lack of direct references to emotion. Also we find that the genuine notes are high on the symbolic tags SEX-THEME and MALE-THEME, possibly indicating an underlying concern with sex which is not recognized on the conscious level.

Leftover Revelations

The words that were not found in the dictionary and thereby were printed out as leftovers were reviewed. First it was found that the dictionary defined a higher percentage of words in the simulated notes (92 percent) than were defined for the genuine notes (86 percent). In other words, 8 percent of the words in the simulated notes were not defined, whereas 14 percent of the words from the genuine notes went without definition. In addition to this finding, the words in the two lists differed in content. Specifically, 64 percent of the leftover words from the genuine notes could be classified in one of the following five categories: proper names, places, objects, numbers, and time. By contrast, only 32 percent of the leftover words from the simulated notes could be classified under these categories. This finding supports one of our initial interpretations of the differences on tag counts between the two sets of notes. That is, the genuine note writers used very specific, concrete references in their messages.

Retrieving and Judging Sentences

Previous to processing the genuine and simulated notes, they had been coded and syntax marked. For our purposes, this was important in two respects. First, pronouns could be identified. If the writer referred to his sister by using the pronoun "you," the information that "you" meant sister and sister meant female was not lost. Second, since sentence "parts" (subject, verb, object, and so on) had been specified, initial tag-score differences between the sets of notes were further divided into differences with respect to parts of speech. For example, the summary score for the tag FEMALE-ROLE revealed that genuine note writers referred to females more frequently than did simulated note writers. Further inspection of the printout revealed that the greatest difference lay in the genuine notes' references to females in the *subject* position of the sentence (154 occurrences of female as subject for the genuine notes compared to 64 occurrences for the simulated notes). Making use of this rather substantial difference, we retrieved all sentences from both sets of notes that matched our Female-as-Subject specification.

Working from the printout of the retrieval of these sentences, we found that all sentences from both genuine and simulated notes could be classified under one of the following three categories:

1. Writer is making a request or is giving an instruction or command to a woman.

Examples: You (female) get in touch with Mary Jones (female) at once.
You (female) please get a lawyer.
You (female) be happy.
You (female) teach him (son) to grow into a fine man.

2. Writer is giving information or expressing opinions (given as information) about a woman.

Examples: She lives close by.
Soon she (daughter) will dominate you.
She packed her bag.
Mother meant good.

3. A woman has acted upon the writer, over and above straight information.

Examples: She kept after me.
Helen (female) gave it (pen) to me.
And (wife) left me.
But she (mother) drove me to my grave.

Table 16.2 gives the percentage distribution of sentences retrieved and classified from both genuine and simulated notes with respect to these categories.

We see that genuine note writers gave a smaller percentage of instructions to females, but they had a higher percentage of sentences giving information about women and sentences implying that a woman had directed action toward the writer. The latter two findings seemed reasonable, but the first finding created difficulties insofar as it was incongruent with our evolving notion of a suicide victim's terse concreteness. An investigation of those sentences in which the writer was giving commands or instructions indicated that they could

TABLE 16.2. *Classifications of "Female-as Subject" Retrievals*

	Genuine	Simulated
Instruction	29%	45%
Information	55%	50%
Female acting upon writer	15%	06%
	$n = 152$	$n = 64$

Independently rated by three judges not familiar with the materials with 95 percent agreement.

be further classified into two relatively clear categories. These categories were

1. Instructions are of a specific nature.
Examples: You (female) tell my folks.
          You (female) please take care of my bills.
2. Instructions are of an unreasonable or vague nature.
Examples: You (female) do not be mean with me, please.
          You (female) find a new life for yourself.

Three judges who were not familiar with the materials independently judged these "instruction" sentences as belonging either in the *specific* or *vague* categories. There was complete agreement among raters. The results showed that when genuine writers gave instructions, 55 percent of these instructions were specific and direct. Only 25 percent of the instructions given by the simulated note writers had this quality; the other 75 percent were of a vague, noninstrumental nature.

Moving away from the women in the lives of genuine and simulated suicide note writers, we recall that another difference between the two sets of notes appeared when we considered tags under the **Processes** division of first-order tags. The simulated notes were overrepresented by tags falling under this division. Quite generally, we remarked that this might reflect a greater use of decision-making words on the part of the pretenders. To investigate this possibility further, we chose to concentrate on sentences that were retrieved on the basis of containing words that had been defined by the tag THINK. Fifty-nine sentences were recovered from the genuine set compared to 54 sentences from the simulated set.[3] It was noted from these retrievals

[3] For the most part, genuine notes were longer than simulated notes. Thus, even though more THINK sentences were retrieved from the genuine set, the percentage difference of such sentences remains in the simulated note writers' favor.

that two types of words were responsible for raising the tag count for THINK. The first type included words such as think, recall, reason, remember, explain, consider, decide, and so forth. The second type included the words know, knew, known. Normally when words in the first list are used in a sentence they serve to indicate that the writer is attempting to solve a problem or is using his reasoning processes in some way, for instance, "I am thinking of all the problems we have shared." On the other hand, when "know" is used in a sentence, it indicates that a problem has been solved, knowledge has been gained, a decision has been made; for example, "I knew that if I went to the doctor, I would. . . ."

This distinction within the category THINK differentiated between the genuine and simulated notes in the following manner. Fifty-eight percent of the genuine notes originally retrieved as matching the specification THINK contained a form of the word "know." When the distribution is viewed in a slightly different manner, 19 of the 33 genuine notes contained sentences using a form of the word "know." By contrast, only 8 of the 33 simulated suicide notes contained "know" sentences.

We may conclude that the simulated note writers tended to use words indicating the operation of problem-solving modes, whereas the genuine note writers' use of the word "know" reflects the fact that a final decision has been made. Partial substantiation of this view is gained when we recall that, along with the tag THINK, other tags referring to intellectual processes (SENSE, IF, ACADEMIC) were more frequently used by the simulated note writers than by the genuine note writers.

DISCUSSION AND SUMMARY

Before summarizing the results of our analysis, it is instructive to review briefly the results of these same paired notes in an analysis conducted by Gottschalk and Gleser (1960). By using a hand method of classifying words into objects, processes, spatial relations, and so forth (a method similar to our computer method), they summarized that the categories of words that typify genuine suicide notes include a relatively high percentage of references to people and things, places or spatial relations, and a relatively low percentage of references to cognitive processes. We too found that genuine notes had a relatively high percentage of references to people, places, and things when we (1) compared the frequencies of tags under *ROLES* and *OBJECTS* and (2) compared the two lists of leftover words. The results of our analysis of *specific* versus *vague* requests made by the note writers using "Female-as-Subject" warrant us to note the possibility that the genuine note writers not only made more specific mention of names, places, and objects but they were much more specific in their entire final communicative attempt than were the simulated note writers. Again, in line with Gottschalk and Gleser's findings, we pointed out that the simulated note writers used a large number of words that were defined by the tags indicating the use of cognitive processes. The results of the analysis of the tag THINK and the high counts on tags SENSE, IF, and ACADEMIC for the simulated note writers added support to this finding. Contrasting these results for simulated note writers we found that the genuine suicide note writers tended to use the word "know" more often. This finding can also be viewed as another example of the genuine note writers' specificity as opposed to the generality of the simulated notes.

As a demonstration of the usefulness of these findings in discriminating between the genuine and simulated notes, Stone carried out the following procedure. First he developed a discriminant function for distinguishing between the first 15 pairs of notes. The three factors that, when combined, best discriminated between these pairs were

1. References to concrete things, persons, and places (higher for genuine notes).
2. Use of the word "love" in the text (higher for genuine notes).
3. Total number of references to processes of thought and decision (higher for simulated notes).

The first and third criteria were taken from the findings just discussed. The addition of the second factor (use of the word "love") was the result of further exploration of the text word differences between these 15 documents.

The discriminant function developed from these factors was simple and straightforward: the score on the third measure was subtracted from the sum of the scores of the first two measures. This index correctly discriminated 13 of the 15 pairs of notes.

Stone, who was not familiar with the remaining 18 pairs of notes, then applied the discriminant function to them. After making his predictions on the basis of the index scores, we found that he had correctly separated 17 of the 18 paired notes.

More elaborate functions for discriminating between real and simulated suicide notes could be obtained by combining stepwise multiple regression techniques with the tree-building procedures described in Chapter 3. Our further explorations have shown that the task becomes much more difficult, however, if the notes are not available in matched pairs, as they were for Stone. Assuming that age and socioeconomic information is available, a more realistic procedure would be to collect more notes and develop separate discrimination formulas and norms as needed for each major age and socioeconomic group.

In summary, the question asked at the outset of this study was "Can we find differences between genuine suicide notes and simulated suicide notes by using the General Inquirer procedures?" We found that we could find differences and that those differences were substantial. More often than was true of the simulated notes, genuine notes contained specific information, used names of people, places, and things, made frequent mention of women, and gave instructions to others that were concrete enough to be actually carried out. By contrast, the simulated suicide notes contained a greater percentage of "thinking" words, suggesting that the issue of suicide was being pondered, reasoned with, and probably rationalized.

BIBLIOGRAPHY

Gottschalk, L. A., and Goldine Gleser (1960), "An Analysis of the Verbal Content of Suicide Notes." *British Journal of Medical Psychology*, Vol. 33, 195–204.

Shneidman, E. E., and N. L. Farberow (1957), *Clues to Suicide*. New York: McGraw-Hill.

CHAPTER SEVENTEEN

The Integration of Subject and Object in the Context of Action: A Study of Reports Written by Successful and Unsuccessful Volunteers for Field Work in Africa

Luis I. Ramallo

Universidad N.S. de la Asunción (*Paraguay*)

EDITORIAL NOTE

   The "thought-action" dimension that was found to be crucial in making understandable differentiations between genuine and simulated suicide notes has also been usefully employed in other analyses. For example, in the next study to be reported, Ramallo discusses a "think-involvement" dimension that he found helpful in his study of successful and unsuccessful volunteers for a program called Operation Crossroads Africa (an organization whose goals and activities are roughly comparable to those of the Peace Corps). Ramallo's report consists of sections from a longer paper in which he discusses efforts of modern Existential Phenomenologists to show a continuity between consciousness and action and to demonstrate how this continuity depends on the integration in consciousness of the subjective and objective elements of human experience. Ramallo restates this Existential position in the form of the following hypothesis: "The products of consciousness of people engaged in successful and meaningful action will show a better integration of subjective and objective elements than the products of unsuccessful agents."

By letting one cluster of tags define "subjective elements" and another cluster define "objective elements," Ramallo tests his hypothesis by tabulating sentences in which tags from these two lists co-occur.

Much of the philosophical orientation that guided Ramallo's study has been sacrificed here to make space for a more thorough discussion of his research design and descriptions of some of the difficulties he encountered in his analysis and how these problems were solved.

THE DATA, CRITERION, MEASURES, AND RESEARCH DESIGN

The data for this study were obtained through the cooperation of an organization called *Operation Crossroads Africa,* whose purpose is to give carefully selected young adults a novel exposure to field experiences in a foreign country.[1] This private organization provides work sites in many different African countries where groups of 10 to 12 Americans engage in an eight-week period of work and interaction with African young people. Isaacs (1961) has published his own participant observer study of Crossroads. His account leaves one with the impression that the experience provided by Crossroads is carefully balanced between an intellectual approach to the understanding of a novel world and the type of service orientation (getting a job well done) that is the main emphasis of the *Peace Corps* and other similar field-action programs.

One hundred-fifty Crossroads Volunteers (VV) formed the initial population of this study. The volunteers were informed that we wished to collect from them written reports of an open-ended nature, describing their summer experience in Africa with the ultimate purpose of learning something about this particular kind of experience. The tasks presented to them were as follows:

1. During the orientation session, four days previous to departure time, the VV completed two tasks:
   a. A modified group version of Murray's TAT, from which some motivational measures could be taken.

[1] I cannot overstress the magnificent quality of the cooperation given by Rev. Dr. James Robinson, the founder and director of Crossroads, and by the staff, leaders, and volunteers of the 1963 Crossroads.

Computing time for this study was supported by the National Science Foundation, Grant No. GP–2723.

   b. A fictional report, under the following set of instructions:

> We are interested in devising methods of assessing the effective-
> ness of field service projects such as OCA. We believe that one
> of the best methods for doing this is to receive from the par-
> ticipants themselves reports of their personal participation in the
> project. As part of our research, we are interested in finding out
> what your expectations are for your summer in Africa. One way
> of discovering this is to have you write reports now as if you
> had been in the field for half the summer.
>
>   Please bear in mind the following attitude as you write this
> simulated report: please write a report trying to cover the fol-
> lowing areas: your job, living conditions your work and contact
> with host-countrymen, leisure time, yourself, etc. Write as fully
> and frankly as possible. Imagine that you are writing this report
> to individuals who are honestly concerned with evaluating a
> program such as this.
>
>   You may spend as much time as you feel appropriate for this
> type of report, up to about an hour. Thank you for your time
> and cooperation.

2. During the eight weeks of their African experience, they were asked
to complete two field reports, one two weeks after their arrival and one
about a week prior to their return to the United States, both under instructions similar to the ones for the simulated report and under the
same open-ended conditions as to length and style.

Ratings and the Selection of Subjects

   All of the volunteers were rated by field supervisors on the following
variables:

   Maturity and judgment
   Concern for others
   Relating to Africans
   Intellectual curiosity
   Creativity
   Leadership
   Willingness to follow rules
   Contribution to work
   Ability to express self
   Group responsibility
   Tactfulness

   The initial plan was to use Crossroads' own evaluation of the VV
as the criterion variable for selecting the high-, medium-, and low-

success groups. However, the criterion ratings did not allow finely graded differentiations, mostly because all but a few VV performed in an excellent manner. Since ratings showed a clearly bimodal distribution (with most of the VV tightly clustered at the upper end) an alternate plan was adopted. This strategy involved the formation of just two criterion groups, one formed by those VV who were rated as clear failures and the other by an equal number of VV taken from the very top of the distribution.

Of the two VV groups obtained from the ratings, the high-success group is made up of six males and ten females. All of them completed at least one of the tasks. The low-success group consists of seven males and nine females. Four of them (two males and two females) did not write any of the reports and are excluded from this study.

The total available data for the final samples are summarized in Table 17.1. The lower rate of returns for the TAT and fictional re-

TABLE 17.1. *Data Available (Number of Protocols) for the High- and Low-Success Groups of VV**

	TAT	*Fictional*	*Field 1*	*Field 2*
High VV	8	9	16	14
Low VV	11	9	12	10

* Maximum possible N for each cell: high $= 16$, low $= 12$.

port resulted from the fact that some of the groups were absent from the original testing session. The returns for the Field 2 reports were affected by the traveling schedules of two of the groups. We are left, then, with 79 percent of the total possible number of protocols for the VV who completed at least one of the tasks.

Method of Analysis

The testing of this kind of open-ended written material for the degree of "existential concreteness" had to involve some kind of content analysis. For the field reports, a measurement strategy was decided upon that involved the General Inquirer and made use of selected first-order tags from the Harvard III Dictionary. The reasons for this choice were both methodological and empirical. The flexibility and reliability of this instrument, together with its ability to handle large numbers of documents of different length and to match any number of co-occurrence specifications that would be involved in a test of two-theme integration provided methodological advantages. Previous studies by Ogilvie, Stone, and Shneidman (1962) and Ramallo (1962) showed that a particular division of tags (from the Harvard II Dictionary) would discriminate between different kinds of documents. The two clusters of tags could easily be identified as *THOUGHT* (or internal and intransitive action) and *INVOLVE-MENT* (or external and transitive action). Ogilvie found that fictional suicide notes were high on *THOUGHT* and low on *INVOLVE-MENT*, while real notes presented an opposite relationship. In Rama-llo's study, it was found that successful field workers received high counts of *INVOLVEMENT* while unsuccessful workers used more *THOUGHT* words in their reports. Although these differences did not reach a level of significance, they were consistent. They tend to give the impression that protocols from people who were more in-volved (real suicides, successful workers) could be differentiated from the protocols of uninvolved people (fictional suicides, unsuccessful workers) by the use of these particular clusters of tags.

Further analysis of these preliminary data, under the guidance of existential theory, indicated that a more significant way to deal with these differences might be to measure the extent to which words from the two kinds tended to co-occur in a single sentence than to record straight counts on the two clusters. Thus our strategy involves focusing on a functional aspect of speech rather than on a formal one. Sapir has expressed the relationship between these two kinds of elements.

> Radical (or grammatical) element and sentence — these are the primary *functional* units of speech, the former as an abstracted minimum, the latter as the esthetically satisfying embodiment of the unified thought. The actual *formal* units of speech, the words, may on occasion identify themselves with either of the two functional units; more often they medi-ate between the two extremes, embodying one or more radical notions and also one or more subsidiary ones. We may put the whole matter in a nutshell by saying that the radical and grammatical elements of lan-guage, abstracted as they are from the realities of speech, respond to the conceptual world of science, abstracted as it is from the realities of ex-perience, and that the word, the existent unit of living speech, responds to the unit of actually apprehended experience, of history, of art. The sentence is the logical counterpart of the complete thought only if it be felt as made up of the radical and grammatical elements that lurk in the recesses of its words. It is the psychological counterpart of experiences,

of art, when it is felt as indeed it normally is, as the finished play of word
with word. (Sapir, 1921, 33)

Linguistic research on sentences has been extremely rare, never
going beyond some developmental studies and the question of principal and subordinate clauses. We have to rely on the common-sense
concepts expressed by Sapir and say that when a person places a
period between two sentences in written speech he is somehow giving
us a "piece" of his experience that has a unity of its own. In this sense,
the sentence as a unit of reported experiences is the unit of information in this study.

Table 17.2 presents the list of General Inquirer tags that make up

TABLE 17.2. Tags from the Harvard III Dictionary (General Inquirer)
That Make Up the Think and Involvement Indexes

THINK	INVOLVEMENT
sense	communicate
think	approach
if	guide
cause	control
ought	attack
ideal value	avoid
	follow
	attempt
	work
	move
	get
	possess
	expel

the two clusters of words we define as *THOUGHT* and *INVOLVE-
MENT*. These tags are all regular first-order tags from the Harvard
III Dictionary.

The research design called for the processing of each individual
protocol for the three conditions and for the two groups (high- and
low-success VV) and then having the General Inquirer calculate the
percentage of sentences in each case that meet the general specification
of containing at least one word from each of the two clusters of tags.
The hypothesis being tested can be operationally described as follows:

1. The high-success group will show a higher percentage of *THINK-
   INVOLVEMENT* (*T-I*) sentences than the low-success group for
   all conditions.

2. There will be a trend toward higher percentages of *T-I* sentences in the high-success group and little or no change for the low-success group across conditions, especially from the fictional to the field conditions.

RESULTS

The results for the two groups and three conditions are presented in Table 17.3.

TABLE 17.3. *Number of "T-I" Sentences for the Two Criterion Groups and Three Conditions (In percentages of total number of sentences in each cell)*

	High-Rated VV*	Low-Rated VV	U-Test
Fictional Report	44.5%	45.4%	n.s.
Field 1 Report	50.9%	38.5%	$p. \leq .025$ (one-tailed)
Field 2 Report	60.0%	42.2%	$p. \leq .025$ (one-tailed)

* Mann-Whitney U-test for differences in change from Fictional to Field 1 ($N_1 = 9$ and $N_2 = 9$ matched pairs).

The main hypothesis is well supported. The only discrepancy appears to be in the fictional reports, where no differences are found between the two criterion groups. This is not very upsetting, since, as far as actual experience is concerned, the fictional situation is obviously of a neutral character. This seems to be one of those cases in which you realize how you should have predicted after you see the results. The crucial result, moreover, concerns the variability found for the high-success group in the predicted direction, and the lack of variability for the low group. This means that the high-success group did react to their field experience in a concrete way. As far as this existential dimension goes, the transition from fictional to field condition seems irrelevant for the low-success group, but highly relevant for the successful VV.

An inspection of *T-I* and non-*T-I* sentences revealed that non-*T-I* sentences were clearly of two kinds: either strictly instrumental ("The site for our building had not been cleared") or merely speculative ("There is so much to do and to see"). The *T-I* sentences, on the other hand, have an integrated flavor that fits closely the dimension that concerns us ("It seems to be necessary to let many of the things we see, i.e. disease, poor sanitation, etc., bounce off to a certain degree").

The correct interpretation of the results demands that we ascertain that it is indeed the relatively larger amount of two-theme co-occurrence that is responsible for the observed differences. This can be tested by conducting several analyses of variance involving the individual tags that make up the two clusters. An analysis of the tag scores for high versus low VV on the 19 tags involved in the T-I measure showed that for the fictional report two tags are significantly different by themselves: OUGHT (mean higher for Low VV, $p. \leq .01$) and MOVE (mean higher for High VV, $p. \leq .01$). For the Field 1 report, only one tag has independent significance: APPROACH, its mean being higher for the Low VV ($p. \leq .05$). For the Field 2 reports, none of the 19 tags reaches independent significance between the two criterion groups. When we compare these findings with the trends across conditions, it is quite apparent that our T-I results can hardly be attributed to what any of the tag counts by themselves can achieve. An analysis of variance for each of the two clusters of tags shows that the *INVOLVEMENT* words by themselves differentiate the high and low fictional reports, while the *THOUGHT* words differentiate the Field 1 reports, and neither cluster differentiates between the Field 2 reports. Again, this is of no help in explaining the T-I differences, since it is not consistently related to the high-low trend in T-I sentences.

Another possible source of difficulty could be the widely different length of the protocols; they range from 100 to 1,000 words. Stone (1965) has indicated that a rough minimum for a reliable frequency count is about a thousand words of text. Since many of the protocols did not fit this criterion, it had to be shown that the lack of reliability would not apply when the supertags *THINK* and *INVOLVEMENT* are used. Obviously, when a larger number of words are involved in a count, we expect a higher correlation with the total number of words in the text. It was found that for the protocols in the present study, the product-moment correlations between total number of words in the protocol and the raw number of *THOUGHT* words on the one hand and the raw number of *INVOLVEMENT* words on the other are substantial enough to indicate high reliability. Table 17.4 presents the correlations for the different kinds of protocols.

TABLE 17.4. *Product-Moment Correlations Between Length of Protocol and Word Counts Related to the T-I Measure for All Reports* (Raw numbers)

Variables	Fictional	Field 1	Field 2
Total *N* words and *THINK* words	.836	.888	.918
Total *N* words and *INVOLVEMENT* words	.923	.915	.919
Total *N* words and *T-I* sentences	.929	.869	.860

The use made of percentages in the *T-I* measure could also be affected by the variable length of the protocols. In this case, contrary to the previous one, we would hope for a low correlation between total number of words and the percentage of *T-I* sentences. Table 17.5

TABLE 17.5. *Product-Moment Correlations Between Length Factors of Protocols and Percentage Number of T-I Sentences for All Reports*

Variables	Fictional	Field 1	Field 2
Total *N* words and Percent of "*T-I*" sentences	.45	.19	.23
Total *N* sentences and Percent of "*T-I*" sentences	.24	$-.05$	.05

presents the pertinent product-moment correlations, for both total number of words and total number of sentences. The size of the correlations is low except in the case of the fictional reports. This finding seems to give even more support to the conclusion just reached concerning the neutral character of the fictional condition, since under conditions irrelevant to the *T-I* dimension one would expect that length of document would affect the *T-I* percentages.

Another more troublesome problem arose from an unexpected characteristic of the protocols. Under all three conditions the average number of words per sentence was consistently higher for the High VV. Since theoretically a longer sentence has a higher probability of containing co-occurrence words, there was a question of whether this stylistic fact alone could perhaps account for the findings. Even before conducting any tests, there were several reasons for not accepting this interpretation. First, differences in sentence length apply to all the conditions, while the *T-I* findings clearly vary across conditions. Second, if we were faced with the dilemma of attributing *T-I* findings to the length of the sentences or to say that *T-I* sentences are longer because they have to be more complex, it seems that we would have more reason to accept the second alternative: there is no obvious reason why sentence length per se should be the discriminating factor.

It turns out that the correlations between sentence length and number of *T-I* sentences are low for the field reports and fairly high for the fictional report: .47 for the fictional, 17 for Field 1, and .16 for Field 2. Sentence length, incidentially, is by itself a better predictor for separating the two criterion groups than *T-I*. In the Field 2 reports, for example, all of the VV in the high group have word/sentence averages of over 20, while not a single V in the low group reaches an average of 20. Thus, any partial correlation scheme that would control for sentence length simply controls away the variance between the two groups. The size of the correlation between sentence length and number of *T-I* sentences indicates that we are faced here with a case of two fairly independent variables that nevertheless both correlate with a single criterion. This is further supported by a reassess-

TABLE 17.6. Number of T-I Sentences for Three Sentence-Length Intervals for the Two Criterion Groups and for Three Conditions (In percentages of total number of sentences in each cell)

Sentence Length	Fictional	Field 1	Field 2
Short*			
High-Rated VV	11.5	12.3	13.6
Low-Rated VV	14.4	14.8	13.6
Medium**			
High-Rated VV	26.8	40.4	50.4
Low-Rated VV	41.2	34.9	37.7
Long†			
High-Rated VV	72.2	73.1	78.8
Low-Rated VV	71.6	70.3	68.6

* Less than 10 words.
** Between 10 and 20 words.
† More than 20 words.

ment of the data separately for three sentence-length intervals. Table 17.6 shows the results of this analysis.

It seems clear from this second analysis that the medium-length sentences are responsible for the differences in the T-I findings, even though a test of discrepancy scores between fictional and field conditions is significant for both medium and long sentences, indicating that both types of sentences reflect the main over-all finding of change in T-I for the high VV and no change for the low VV.

SUMMARY

The existential position that there is a continuity between consciousness and action and that this continuity depends on an integration of subjective and objective elements of human experience was restated in the form of the following hypothesis: the products of consciousness of people engaged in successful and meaningful action will show a better integration of subjective and objective elements than the products from unsuccessful agents.

This hypothesis was tested by means of a content analysis of reports written by Volunteers for Operation Crossroads Africa. It was inferred that integration between objective and subjective elements would be reflected in the co-occurrence of objective and subjective words in the same sentence. The measure of objective and subjective elements consisted of several tags from the Harvard III Dictionary of the General Inquirer.

Two criterion groups, separated by means of supervisor ratings, wrote reports that differed in the amount of integrated sentences. No differences appeared under the neutral condition of fictional reports written before departure to Africa. In the two field reports, the predicted differences between high- and low-success VV's were statistically significant. These differences did not reflect the influence of any one tag alone, nor were they affected by the relative length of the reports, the use of percentages, or the fact that one of the groups consistently wrote longer sentences.

BIBLIOGRAPHY

Isaacs, H. R. (1961), *Emergent Americans: A Report on Crossroads Africa.* New York: The John Day Co.

Ogilvie, D. M., P. J. Stone, and E. Shneidman (1962), "Some Characteristics of Genuine vs. Simulated Suicide Notes: A General Inquirer Study." Dittoed. Harvard University: Laboratory of Social Relations.

Ramallo, L. I. (1962), "Working Paper on the Application of the General Inquirer (a Computer System) to the Analysis and Evaluation of Reports from Field Service Volunteers." dittoed. Harvard University, Social Relations 272, 1962.

Sapir, E. (1921), *Language: An Introduction to the Study of Speech*. New York: Harcourt, Brace & Company.

Stone, P. J. (1965), "An Introduction to the General Inquirer: A Computer System for the Study of Spoken or Written Material." dittoed. New York: Simulmatics Corporation.

CHAPTER EIGHTEEN

The WAI Dictionary and Self-Perceived Identity in College Students

Barry McLaughlin
Harvard University

INTRODUCTION

Colby (1960) tells the fable of an object from outer space that suddenly arrived on earth and resisted all efforts by the physicists and astronomers to determine its composition, structure, or function. Finally a psychologist asked, "Who are you?" and the object replied, "Ralph." The psychologist's question seemed innocent enough, but its informational yield was enormous. It bears upon what some psychologists (Holt, 1964) regard as the most important issue in personality research — that of identity.

Few concepts in the history of psychology have articulated the *Zeitgeist* of an era more accurately than the concept of identity has ours. Existential meditation and autobiographic self-examination are the orthodox genres of contemporary paperback culture. Identity, with its implication of uniqueness, self-determination, and personal dignity, is a red, white, and blue term. The Judeo-Christian tradition and the American heritage stress the immeasurable worth of individual identity. What is more, every person is conscious that he stands at the center of a unique network of relationships, experiences, and influences. He is different and he knows it.

Contemporary identity concern has come repeatedly to the attention of psychiatrists and clinical psychologists. Interest in identity is particularly prominent in this literature. There are, however, converging lines of thought from other areas of psychological science. Social psychologists have recently stressed the function of personal and social identity within the larger social matrix. Theorists in personality research have come to concern themselves with the self and the self-concept as dimensions of special relevance to behavior. In this chapter, an attempt will be made to work out a theoretical concept of identity consistent with previous formulations that will bear the strain of operational tests. A method will be described for measuring dimensions of identity, and the method will be employed to investigate specific aspects of identity concern among college students.

Self-Perceived Identity: Theoretical Perspective

Identity is a dynamic and complex concept. A person does not have an identity once and for all. Certain aspects of identity are relatively fixed, but others fluctuate considerably. The phenomenon described by Erikson as an "identity crisis" (1959) is viewed as a time in which identity elements are reintegrated and reassimilated within the context of social and maturational pressures. These pressures are especially prominent during adolescence and youth when identity problems become salient. Theoretically, three conceptualizations of identity have contributed to the present formulation: the work of Erik Erikson in clinical psychology, symbolic interaction theory in social psychology, and the study of the self-concept in personality theory.

The theoretical formulations of Erikson are of central importance in understanding the present concept of identity. In particular, his stress upon psychosocial development and upon the crises precipitated by changes in the individual's surroundings are of considerable relevance for understanding the population from which the sample used in this research was drawn. However, this research is restricted to identity as it is known in conscious awareness, leaving out of account what Erikson described as an "unconscious striving for continuity of personality" (1959, 102). This dimension of identity is of extreme importance in clinical work, but it must be analyzed and treated by clinical methods.

Erikson noted the complexity of meaning of the identity concept. He felt that identity could be adequately understood in all of its richness only if it were studied from a variety of angles — biographic, pathographic, and theoretical — and if the term were allowed to retain all of its connotations. The resulting ambiguity was felt to be necessary and helpful for delineating significant problems. Some theorists (Lynd, 1958) agree with Erikson in his insistence on openness of meaning; other theorists (Lichtenstein, 1963) disagree and feel that attempts should be made to attain greater clarification.

One such attempt was Goffman's introduction of a threefold typology of identity. This formulation (Goffman, 1963) contains a basic subjective-objective dimension of identity, of which ego identity (in the sense sometimes used by Erikson) is at the subjective pole. In this sense, identity is private and even unconscious. A private-public dimension spans the objective side of the subjective-objective dimension, giving three types or descriptions of identity (Figure 18.1).

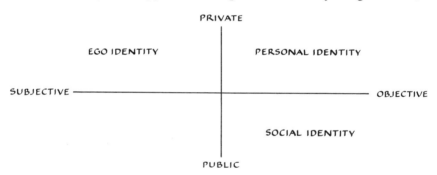

FIGURE 18.1. *A typology of identity concepts (adapted from Goffman, 1963).*

The identity concept employed here appears on the right side of the diagram. Ego identity as a private and subjective feeling or as a sense of self-sameness does not fall within the compass of the present research. On the other hand, the concept of identity used here is not equivalent to Goffman's personal and social identity. Goffman apparently regards identity as an epiphenomenon of social interaction. For him, identity is "part of other persons' concerns and definitions regarding the individual whose identity is in question" (1963, 105–106). While this issue may be more epistemological than psychological, the position taken here is that identity is not merely social roles and personal qualities as others define them for a person. Rather identity — in line with Mead's thinking in symbolic interaction theory and Erikson's in clinical psychology — is, at least in part, self-defined.

The importance of self-definition has been stressed in particular by Rogers and his followers in their discussions of the self-concept. As experiences occur, they are related to the self-concept. Depending on the self-concept, the experience will be symbolized accurately, perceived consciously, and organized into the self-structure; or it might be ignored because it is not important to the self-structure, or even denied and distorted because it is threatening to the self. Consequently, Rogers insists that a person's notion of himself is a complex and significant factor in his behavior. The complexity of the self-concept involves at least four dimensions: (*a*) the individual's abilities and characteristics as he perceives them, (*b*) his perception of himself in relation to other people, (*c*) his values, and (*d*) the goals and ideals to which he aspires.

Drawing from all of these formulations, a construct called "self-perceived identity" is used in this research. Stated simply, this construct includes elements of self-perceived identity, each reflecting the theoretical emphasis of a different area of psychological science:

   a. A personally defined set of relationships (clinical psychology).
   b. Derived from and maintained in a social context (social psychology).
   c. Consisting of a more or less organized synthesis of personality dimensions (personality theory).

To understand the construct adequately, its empirical referents should be described.

Empirical Methods

Many of the instruments used to assess perceptions of self and identity (rating scales, adjective check lists, Q sorts, and so forth) suffer from a major defect. In each case, the universe of responses is predefined for the subject. An adequate instrument should be such as to allow the person to define his own universe of responses. That is, the instrument should be open ended. Such methods, however, are difficult to quantify, and for this reason researchers have preferred simpler methods. On the other hand, assessing self-perceptions by the simpler but more constricting approaches such as Q sorts, adjective

check lists, and rating scales has been sharply criticized (Wylie, 1961).
Consequently, it is desirable to devise a method of handling open-
ended responses in an objective and quantifiable manner. The General
Inquirer system for content analysis offers a means of solving some of
these problems.

The open-ended questionnaire used in this research was entitled
"Who Am I?" (WAI). Subjects were given a sheet of paper with
20 lines on it and the following instructions:

There are 20 numbered blanks on the page below. Please write 20
answers to the simple question "Who Am I?" in the blanks. Just give

TABLE 18.1. Examples of Responses to the WAI Questionnaire

Student A
A student at Harvard
An unimportant being in this vast world and universe
I try to obtain recognition and differentiate myself from others
Have above average looks, intelligence, and ability
One constantly preoccupied with death
I cannot accept organized religion
Resent those who classify me without letting me show them what I am and
  what I can do
I enjoy parties and getting drunk
I have an interest in grades not so much for myself but for what others will think
I do not know what I want out of life other than to receive pleasure from what
  I am doing
I need to be with other people
Feel uneasy when alone
Not introverted yet long to be so
I want and need the material love of a girl — this is something I have never had.

Student B
A very intelligent United States Negro at Harvard
The first son of my father
The grandson of my maternal grandmother
The half-brother of my half-brother
An alumnus of (a certain) high school
A permanent resident of (home town)
Former (home town) grand spelling champion
A member of the National Honor Society
One of the recipients of 1960 (certain) scholarship
Summer employee of (a certain) park in (home town)
The only undergraduate from (home town)
First graduate of (a certain) high school to enter Harvard
First member of both parents' lineage to leave (home state) to attend college
Future leader in Africa or some underdeveloped area

20 different answers to this question. Answer as if you were giving the answers to yourself, not to somebody else. Write the answers in the order that they occur to you. Don't worry about logic or "importance." Go along fairly fast, for time is limited.

(Kuhn and McPartland, 1954, 69)

Samples of the responses of two college freshmen are given in Table 18.1.

A dictionary for the General Inquirer system (WAI Dictionary) was developed for measuring self-perceived identity, and the categories of the dictionary were both theoretically and empirically derived. Previous research and theory, especially Rogers' formulations concerning the dimensions of the self-concepts, as well as the constraints of the data used to construct the dictionary (a sample of 200 WAI questionnaires) led to a system of 30 categories comprising eight dimensions of self-perceived identity (see Table 18.2). The dictionary has been revised three times and at present consists of about 3,000 words and 50 idiom routines. Further information about category

TABLE 18.2. Tags for the Who Am I (WAI) Dictionary

a. Roles	*d. Cognitive and Behavior Orientations*
1. MALE-ROLE	16. ACCEPTANCE-ORIENTATION
2. STUDENT-ROLE	17. REJECTION-ORIENTATION
3. INTELLECTUAL-ROLE	18. ACTION-ORIENTATION
4. FAMILY-ROLE	19. COGNITIVE-ORIENTATION
5. INTERPERSONAL-ROLE	20. ACHIEVEMENT-ORIENTATION
6. SOCIAL-GROUP-ROLE	*e. Self-Evaluations*
b. Values and Interests	21. POSITIVE-SELF-EVALUATION
7. RELIGIOUS-REFERENCE	22. NEGATIVE-SELF-EVALUATION
8. POLITICAL-REFERENCE	23. NEUTRAL-SELF-EVALUATION
9. ECONOMIC-AND-STATUS-REFERENCE	*f. Psychological States*
10. AESTHETIC-REFERENCE	
11. PHYSICAL-REFERENCE	24. SIGN-CONTENT
12. RECREATION-AND-SPORTS-REFERENCE	25. SIGN-DISCONTENT
c. Temporal and Spatial Orientations	26. SIGN-NEED
13. PAST-ORIENTATION	*g. Expressive Modes*
14. FUTURE-ORIENTATION	27. OVERSTATE
15. PLACE-ORIENTATION	28. UNDERSTATE
	29. NEGATIVE
	h. Consensual Human Identity
	30. CONSENSUAL

selection, dictionary entries, and validation procedures is available in the author's doctoral dissertation (McLaughlin, 1965).

Subjects in this research are members of a large sample of Harvard undergraduates of the class of 1964 investigated in the Harvard Student Study, a longitudinal survey of college life (King, 1963). Data from these students were utilized without reference to names or other personal identifying information. WAI questionnaires for four years for all subjects (about 250) in the sample and other data from the Harvard Student Study constituted a wealth of longitudinal information about personality and were thought to be of particular interest for theoretical reasons because of the importance of identity concerns during this phase of the life cycle (Erikson, 1959).[1]

SELF-PERCEIVED IDENTITY AND THE COLLEGE STUDENT

In Erikson's terms, identity formation involves a crisis. Basically, such a crisis requires that a person pass through a situation of emotional and mental stress demanding significant changes in self-perception within a short period of time. The severity of this crisis varies greatly in different individuals. For each it involves a "task," a personal synthesis of the models, values, and ideals offered by society (Erikson, 1959). The more differentiated and heterogeneous the elements from which this identity must be built, the more difficult the task. In the liberal arts college, the young person is deliberately and in principle confronted with a plurality of divergent and incompatible interpretations, values, and ideals. He is exposed to a multiplicity of ideas and, especially in the urban liberal arts college community, comes in contact with a diversity of individuals. The person must somehow establish his own identity within this complex world. This is not to say that all individuals pass through an identity crisis during the college years, but merely that certain forces are present during this period of a person's life that make such a crisis more probable.

In this study, an attempt was made to examine some of the changes Harvard undergraduates undergo in the course of their four years of college. This particular population was felt to be of interest because it represents a high caliber of college student at a liberal arts college.

[1] The author is indebted to Dr. Stanley King of Harvard, who graciously permitted the use of these data.

The official culture is tolerant and open. Freshman courses encourage the student to adopt a critical view of his prior values, judgments, and ways of assessing experience. The atmosphere of the college is one of critical examination and openness to change.

The impact of Harvard, however, is dependent on the prior characteristics of the student. Some academically inclined students come to college interested in the faculty and intellectual environment, while others come to college uncertain of their goals. Some students expect to change and comply readily with the norms and customs of the college culture. Others drop old customs and habits reluctantly. Such differences were the variables of concern in a larger study (McLaughlin, 1965). One major difference between Harvard students relates to their previous background. In this paper, the difference between private and public school graduates will be discussed.

Private and Public School Graduates

It is not unreasonable to expect differences between private and public school graduates at Harvard. A common stereotype regards the private school graduate as typically "Harvard." He wears Ivy League clothes on arrival and is thought to be quite sophisticated about Harvard's demands. Private school graduates are likely to come to college with a number of their fellows from the same school. They are the "in-group" from the beginning, and the public school graduate, who knows no one else, must strive to gain admission to this group by accommodating himself to its values and tastes. Harvard, after all, is a private school and not a state university.

In a study of public and private school graduates at Harvard, McCarley (1959) found that interview material from a sample of 24 freshmen, 12 from private and 12 from public schools, confirmed the stereotypes. The private school graduates saw Harvard to be much like the schools they had left. There was a greater freedom but basically little had changed. They mentioned the social restraint, the Ivy League clothes, the uniformly high intelligence of their classmates. All of this was quite new to the public school graduate, and the intellectual competition in particular caused a great deal of anxiety and concern.

However, the freshmen from public schools, in spite of their concern about the competition and the work load, reacted with more or less immediate intellectual engagement. They soon became immersed in their work. The private school graduate, on the other hand, was typically more casual. The general reaction of this group was a denial of concern about academic competition and the work load.

Moreover, the private school graduates denied nonacademic stresses as well. These students reported little difficulty in adjustment. In fact, the very uniformity in tone and wording of their statements suggested that they were merely repeating what they were taught to believe and wanted to believe. At any rate, the interviews confirmed the stereotypes and indicated that public school graduates reported considerable stress and subsequent change in themselves and their outlook, while the private school graduates reported little stress and little change.

McCarley, however, was not satisfied. He wanted to know if there were different levels of change. Possibly the interviews merely tapped an outer surface and had little to do with the core of identity. The students were therefore given a self-report questionnaire (a Q-sort) and asked to sort conceptions of self as real at the present time and as ideal upon graduation from college. These measures flatly contradicted the interview data. A quite different picture of change appeared in the two groups. All of the students seemed to share a general consensus about the type of person they would like to be at graduation, but public school graduates saw themselves as already close to what they wanted to be in the future, anticipating little change over the four years. Private school graduates, in contrast, thought of themselves as presently far from the ideal.

The ideal of both groups was an individual with high intellectual standards, creative, productive, sure of himself and his values, and independent. For the public school graduate at Harvard, intellectual commitment of this nature was assumed. For the private school graduate, it had to be generated. Private school graduates had to reorient themselves. To survive the work load, they were forced to abandon some of their role as warm, spontaneous, and outgoing "playboys." Instead, like the public school graduates, they had to assume the role of dedicated and hard-working "grinds." Therefore, change at this level was more pronounced among private school graduates.

McCarley's (1959) study highlighted the complexity involved in assessing the effect of the Harvard culture on individual identity. What is expressed outwardly may be misleading, and less straightforward methods are likely to be more successful. McCarley, however, did not systematically follow up his study through the four years of college.

This will be attempted here with a much larger sample of students. Hopefully, the WAI data will confirm McCarley's findings and yield additional information about the effect of the urban, liberal arts college culture upon self-perception.

Measurement Procedures

The quantitative data were from two principal sources. The first of these are the tags of the General Inquirer process. Verbal material from WAI protocols were coded according to the categories stipulated in the WAI dictionary. The second source of data is the Harvard Student Study material as it bears on the issues of interest in this research.

The unit of analysis upon which the tag tallies were based was the entire response rather than individual words. The reason for this was to prevent erroneous inferences based on the accumulation of tags in one or a few responses. For example, the response, "a pre-med student in biology at Harvard college," would be coded Student Role four times (the words pre-med, student, biology, and college) if individual words were the unit of measurement but only once when the total response was the unit. It seemed preferable to avoid such redundant coding. Since occasional subjects failed to give twenty responses, it was also necessary to employ percentage data.

A hand check was necessary to ensure that the computer did not mis-tag the data. Where mis-tagging occurred, the results were corrected by hand. The main sources of mis-tagging were defects in preliminary computer procedures. For example, a special subroutine was required to handle negative constructions involving self-evaluations and psychological states. For the initial analyses this subroutine did not function adequately and hand tagging was necessary. Occasional mistakes and the incidence of rare words that did not occur frequently enough to warrant inclusion in the dictionary necessitated other corrections.

To assess the amount of change in self-perceived identity that occurred over a two-year period, the difference between scores on each tag for those two years was computed, and all of the differences were summed to give a total change score. Since raw measures of change so computed do not take into account differential extremities of change (thus 15 units of change plus 15 units would be equal to 25 units of change plus 5 units), the amount of change for each tag over the two-year period was squared so that larger changes might be weighted more. Thus:

$$\Sigma (A - B) = [A(1) - B(1)]^2 + [A(2) - B(2)]^2 + \cdots [A(30) - B(30)]^2$$

where $\Sigma(A - B)$ is the total amount of change on all tags between first (A) and second (B) years, $A(1)$ is the score for a given subject on the first tag in first year, $B(1)$ for the first tag in second year, $A(2)$ for the second tag in first year, and so forth to $B(30)$, which is the score for a given subject on the 30th tag in the second year.

The same procedure was followed to assess the amount of change occurring between second and third, and third and fourth years. One difficulty with the data was subject loss either because students dropped out of college or failed to continue in the Harvard Student Study. Thus WAI protocols were available for 243 subjects in first year, 207 subjects in second year, 173 subjects in third, and 152 subjects in fourth year. Consequently, data for all four years were not available for all subjects. In some cases, change could be assessed across three years only, in other cases two years, and in some cases no measure of change was possible.

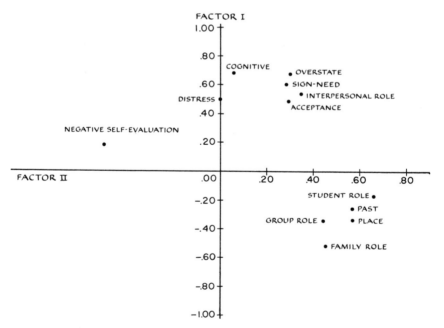

FIGURE 18.2. The plot of factor I against factor II for 243 freshmen WAI protocols.

Another measure is of interest here. A factor analysis of the tag tally scores was employed. In analyzing first year WAI protocols, two pronounced factors were obtained. The first of these was a cluster of tags relating to concern in the area of interpersonal relations. The factor scores of freshmen subjects on Factor I were employed as indices of social anxiety and concern over interpersonal relations. Subject A in Table 18.1 had a moderately high score on Factor I. The second factor involved a cluster of tags relating to the past and one's background and accomplishments. The factor scores on Factor II were taken as a measure of the tendency on the part of the subject to describe himself in terms of his past identity and past accomplishments. Subject B in Table 18.1 had a high score on Factor II. The plot of Factor I against Factor II is given in Figure 18.2. The loadings are given in Table 18.3. It should be noted that the factors are not rotated; it is the clustering that is of central interest.

TABLE 18.3. Factor Loadings for Factors I and II for Freshman Year

Factor I		Factor II	
Amount of variance accounted for:	15.14		9.83
Factor loadings:			
OVERSTATE	.74	STUDENT-ROLE	.66
COGNITIVE-ORIENTATION	.73	PAST-ORIENTATION	.61
UNDERSTATE	.63	PLACE-ORIENTATION	.61
SIGN-NEED	.59	SOCIAL-GROUP-ROLE	.53
INTERPERSONAL-ROLE	.54	NEGATIVE SELF-EVALUATION	−.49
NEGATIVE	.54	FAMILY-ROLE	.45
SIGN-DISCONTENT	.48		

The other measures used in this research were from the Harvard Student Study. One of these, the discrepancy between real and ideal self, is based on the sum discrepancy between factor loadings on four factors from Semantic Differential measure of the concepts Self-As-I-Am and Self-As-I-Would-Like-to-Be. The measures of academic achievement were percentile ratings with 99 representing the highest percentile.

Private School Graduates and the Valedictorian Type

In the present sample, 94 students were graduates of private high schools and 148 were graduates of public high schools. There were the expected differences between the two groups: private school graduates were predominately from the Northeastern part of the country and from higher socioeconomic levels than were public school graduates. In line with McCarley's (1959) findings, the graduates of public schools did better academically in the first year, were more concerned with their role as students, and showed less discrepancy between real and ideal self than private school graduates. All of these differences were statistically significant (Table 18.4). Other differ-

TABLE 18.4. *Mean Scores for Public and Private School Graduates in Freshman Year*

	Public	N	Private	N	t
Percentile	56.91	(147)	46.06	(93)	2.78†
Discrepancy	19.65	(144)	23.59	(91)	2.13‡
STUDENT-ROLE*	15.04	(137)	12.10	(88)	2.11‡
POSITIVE SELF-EVALUATION	9.56	(137)	10.83	(88)	<1
NEGATIVE SELF-EVALUATION	7.78	(137)	8.78	(88)	<1
SIGN-CONTENT	2.00	(137)	2.62	(88)	<1
SIGN-DISCONTENT	5.39	(137)	6.20	(88)	<1
Factor I	.01	(137)	.07	(88)	<1
Factor II	.10	(137)	−.09	(88)	1.43
Change (between 1st and 2nd years)	409.96	(106)	471.85	(64)	<1

* General Inquirer tags represent percent occurrence per 20 responses.
† $p < .01$.
‡ $p < .05$.

ences were not significant, although the consistently higher scores on SELF-EVALUATIONS and PSYCHOLOGICAL-STATE tags may point to a greater tendency on the part of private school graduates toward introspection. These subjects also were slightly higher than public school graduates on social anxiety as measured by Factor I. As might be expected, loadings on Factor II were higher among public school graduates, suggesting that members of this group had a more pronounced tendency to identify themselves in terms of the past and their past accomplishments. Finally, the data suggested that the private students changed more in self-perceived identity during the first two years of college than public school graduates.

These findings are generally consonant with McCarley's (1959) and indicate that the so-called "identity crisis" with the changes it induces is a more marked phenomenon among private school graduates than among public school graduates. Apparently the concern of private school students over their academic inferiority and the anxiety they experience resulting from the discrepancy between their real and ideal selves led to changes in their perceptions of self-identity. However, a further breakdown of the data warned against accepting this conclusion without qualifications.

It was felt that there might be differences among public school graduates. In particular, students who did exceptionally well in high school might differ from other public school graduates. Forty-four percent of the public school graduates in the sample were either first or second in their graduating class. For operational purposes, this group of 64 students will be referred to as the "valedictorian type."

When the valedictorian types were compared with other graduates of public high schools, they were found to perform better academically and to be slightly more concerned with their role as students (Table 18.5). On the other hand, the discrepancy between real and ideal self

TABLE 18.5. *Mean Scores for Public and Private School Graduates with the Further Distinction of Valedictorian and Non-valedictorian Types*

	Nonvaledictorians	N	t*	Valedictorians	N	t†	Private School	N
Percentile	44.77	(83)	4.64‡	65.22	(64)	4.42‡	46.06	(93)
Discrepancy	18.76	(80)	2.41§	23.17	(64)	<1	23.59	(91)
STUDENT-ROLE	14.34	(76)	<1	16.21	(61)	2.23§	12.10	(88)
POSITIVE SELF-EVALUATION	9.37	(76)	<1	9.84	(61)	<1	10.83	(88)
NEGATIVE SELF-EVALUATION	7.82	(76)	<1	7.71	(61)	<1	8.78	(88)
SIGN-CONTENT	1.94	(76)	<1	2.10	(61)	<1	2.62	(88)
SIGN-DISCONTENT	4.28	(76)	1.96	6.65	(61)	<1	6.20	(88)
SIGN-NEED	4.26	(76)	1.19	5.95	(61)	<1	5.14	(88)
Factor I	−.13	(76)	1.67	.15	(61)	<1	.07	(88)
Factor II	.05	(76)	<1	.15	(61)	1.43	−.09	(88)
Change (between 1st and 2nd years)	436.48	(62)	1.41	372.55	(44)	1.81	471.85	(64)

* The *t*-test is between nonvaledictorians and valedictorians.
† The *t*-test is between valedictorians and private school graduates.
‡ $p < .01$.
§ $p < .05$.

was significantly higher among valedictorian types than among other graduates of public high schools. There was also more SIGN-DISCONTENT and SIGN-NEED. This dissatisfaction was apparently the result of nonacademic concerns. The evidence for this comes from the higher scores on Factor I, which represent more social anxiety and interpersonal concern among valedictorian types.

In spite of this, the valedictorian types were more stable in their self-perceived identity. They were more inclined to view themselves in terms of past achievements, and this may have helped them stabilize their identity. At any rate, there was a pronounced stability, although the discrepancy between real and ideal self was almost as large for the valedictorian types as it was for the private school graduates (Table 18.5).

When valedictorian types and private school graduates were compared, there were significant differences in academic achievement and concern with STUDENT-ROLE in favor of the valedictorian types. Private school graduates were higher on self-evaluation tags, but valedictorian types showed more SIGN-DISCONTENT and SIGN-NEED. None of these differences, however, was statistically significant. There were only slight differences in social anxiety, but valedictorian types identified themselves in terms of the past to a much greater extent than did private school graduates. Finally, the valedictorian types showed more stability in self-perceived identity, although the difference did not reach statistical significance.

These findings seem to indicate that the discrepancy between real and ideal self is not in itself a force making for identity crises and subsequent change. Valedictorian types were just as dissatisfied with themselves as were the private school graduates, but the areas of dissatisfaction were quite different. Presumably the high-discrepancy and the NEGATIVE SELF-EVALUATION scores of private school graduates were the result of their academic inferiority and concern in this area. The priority put upon academic competence and intellectual values by the Harvard culture led them to change their self-perceptions. On the other hand, the area of dissatisfaction for valedictorian types was the social and interpersonal area. The strong dedication of these students to their academic careers prevented any shifting of interest, although they were acutely aware of their limitations in nonacademic areas. The core of their identity, rooted in the commitment and successes of the past, remained relatively unchanged.

A question that emerges from this research is whether these findings persist over time. McCarley (1959) hypothesized that they would and that the private school graduate would necessarily change to accommodate himself to the work ethic of the Harvard culture. The attempt was made to test this hypothesis here since it was possible to follow the subjects through their four years of college. Because the central concern of this research is self-perceived identity, the main source of data was the WAI questionnaire.

Two tags in particular were found to be relevant to the hypothesis. These were INTELLECTUAL-ROLE and ACHIEVEMENT-ORIENTATION (Table 18.6).

TABLE 18.6. Mean Scores on Relevant Tags Across the Four Years of College

	1st Year	2nd Year	3rd Year	4th Year	N
INTELLECTUAL-ROLE					
Valedictorian	10.03	8.16	8.86	8.39	36
Nonvaledictorian	7.10	6.58	6.58	6.53	37
Private School	7.91	6.77	6.60	8.93	47
ACHIEVEMENT-ORIENTATION					
Valedictorian	4.14	4.25	6.56	4.42	36
Nonvaledictorian	4.38	3.52	3.67	4.22	37
Private School	4.07	3.87	3.57	5.43	47

Since there is a possible artifact resulting from subject-loss in the course of four years, only the subjects for whom data were available for all four years are included in this analysis. Analyses of variance for these data revealed a significant main effect for the different groups

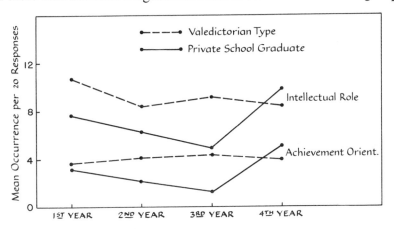

FIGURE 18.3. Mean scores of private school graduates and valedictorians on intellectual role and achievement orientation tags over four years of college.

on the INTELLECTUAL-ROLE tag. It can be seen from the data that the nonvaledictorian public school graduates score lower, for the most part, on both INTELLECTUAL-ROLE and ACHIEVEMENT-ORIENTATION, and that the valedictorian public school graduates are initially higher but eventually lower on both tags than the private school graduates (Figure 18.3). A 4 × 2 analysis of variance between these two groups, however, did not reveal a significant interaction effect.

These findings lend general support to McCarley's (1959) hypothesis. The need he observed among private school graduates in freshman year to reorient themselves to intellectual values and achievement does seem to affect self-perceived identity over time. In the course of four years, the private school graduate accommodates himself to the orientation of the public school valedictorian type. Intellectual pursuits take on a greater importance in his life, and he becomes more concerned with intellectual values. He becomes more of a "grind" and less of a "playboy."

DISCUSSION

The research reported here is a part of a study of crisis and change among college students (McLaughlin, 1965). "Crisis" may be too dramatic a term for the present purposes, but it conveys the meaning necessary to describe a situation of emotional and mental stress that requires a significant alteration of outlook within a short period of time. The alterations of outlook of interest are those changes that occur in the specific area of self-perception and identity.

Some further examples are illustrative of the type of research possible with a construct such as "self-perceived identity" as measured by General Inquirer procedures. For instance, when subjects were divided on the basis of the discrepancy between expected and actual academic achievement, those who did poorer than they had predicted changed most in self-perceived identity during the first two years of college, expressed more anxiety and self-deprecation, and tended to define their identity more in terms of nonacademic roles than other subjects.

Data were also obtained indicating that students with a basically functional or professional orientation to college were more stable in self-perceived identity than students who were less certain of how college fit into their life plan. Furthermore, those students without definite goals were found to use group memberships and social activities as means of stabilizing their self-perceptions. That is, by identifying with a group, these students apparently were able to resolve some of the uncertainties and ambiguities of their own identity.

Upon further investigation, students who dropped out of college were found to be more anxious, covertly although not overtly, than nondropouts. Dropouts were also lower in measures of competitive achievement and, while not actually inferior, tended to be pessimistic about their abilities. Thus, this low self-esteem was in effect a self-fulfilling prophecy.

Hopefully, this research demonstrates the value of the WAI questionnaire as an open-ended measure capable of tapping nuances of self-perceived identity. The great advantage of such a measure is that the subject defines his own universe of responses. The disadvantage (and the reason previous investigators have preferred Q-sorts, rating scales, and adjective check lists) is that open-ended responses are difficult to code. However, General Inquirer procedures are ideally suited to such data: responses are typically short and directed toward a domain somewhat circumscribed by the orienting instructions of the questionnaire.

BIBLIOGRAPHY

Colby, K. M. (1960), *An Introduction to Psychoanalytic Research.* New York: Basic Books.

Erikson, E. H. (1959), "Identity and the Life Cycle." *Psychological Issues,* Vol. 1, 1–171.

Goffman, E. (1963), *Stigma: Notes on the Management of Spoiled Identity.* Englewood Cliffs, N.J.: Prentice-Hall.

Holt, R. R. (1964), "Forcible Indoctrination and Personality Change." In P. Worchel and D. Byrne (eds.), *Personality and Change.* New York: John Wiley & Sons, pp. 289–318.

King, S. H. (1963), "Harvard Student Study: Progress Report." Harvard University, mimeographed.

Kuhn, M. H., and T. S. McPartland (1954), "An Empirical Investigation of Self Attitudes." *American Sociological Review,* Vol. 19, 68–76.

Lichtenstein, H. (1963), "The Dilemma of Human Identity." *Journal of American Psychoanalytic Association,* Vol. 11, 173–223.

Lynd, Helen M. (1958), *On Shame and the Search for Identity.* New York: Harcourt, Brace & World.

McCarley, R. (1959), "A Walk around Harvard Yard." Unpublished honors thesis, Harvard University.

McLaughlin, B. (1965), "Identity and Personality: a Study of Self-Perceived Identity in College Students." Unpublished doctoral dissertation, Harvard University.

Rogers, C. (1959), "A Theory of Therapy, Personality, and Interpersonal Rela-
    tionships as Developed in the Client-Centered Framework." In S. Koch
    (ed.), *Psychology: A Study of a Science*. Vol. 3, New York: McGraw-Hill,
    pp. 184–256.
Wylie, Ruth (1961), *The Self Concept*. Lincoln, Neb.: University of Nebraska
    Press.

CROSS-CULTURAL STUDIES

*Over the past few years, data processed by the General In-
quirer have been mounting so that now we stare in amazement at the
hundreds of boxes of punched cards that have been collected. Although some of these boxes contain materials that will never be processed again, other boxes contain valuable collections of materials that
can be used for a variety of research purposes. One such collection
comes from the combined resources and efforts of Davis and Colby
who, between them, have recently assembled folktales from 55 primitive societies. The method by which folktales from 46 of these societies
were collected is described in the paper by Kalin, Davis, and McClelland. However, the purpose of this paper is not to demonstrate how
one goes about collecting folktales but to investigate the relationship
between the use of alcohol and the expression of themes in folktales.
For this investigation Kalin, Davis, and McClelland have constructed
a dictionary that is intended to explicate variables that have been considered important by other researchers and/or by themselves in discovering and understanding the psychological correlates of alcoholism.*

*The second paper is a report of a study comparing projected (from
now to the year 2000) autobiographies written by Radcliffe and Egyptian students. In this paper, Dahlberg and Stone assume that these
two groups of students draw on their past experiences, societal norms,
and cultural expectations when faced with the task of structuring and
discussing their projected futures. Given this assumption, the authors
proceed to itemize modal differences between the structure of American and Egyptian families and on this basis predict tags that should*

discriminate between autobiographies. This study, then, is not as much a test of a theory as it is a test of validity of specified tag categories. Simply stated, the question asked in the paper is, "Do certain tags measure what we expect them to measure?"

In the final paper, Colby discusses the development of an anthropological dictionary that he is designing to discriminate between cultures. Colby takes the position that many cross-cultural studies have suffered by an attempt to apply traditional psychological concepts to the problem of uncovering cultural differences. In most cases, these studies have demonstrated large within-culture variation that tends to minimize (or cover up) between-culture differences. In this paper, it is argued that we need cultural categories if cultural differences are to emerge. The process of constructing a dictionary of this kind is described, and work that has been done on validating the categories is discussed.

CHAPTER NINETEEN

The Relationship Between Use of Alcohol and Thematic Content of Folktales in Primitive Societies[1]

Rudolf Kalin
University of California, Davis

William N. Davis
Harvard University

David C. McClelland
Harvard University

INTRODUCTION

The present study is part of a larger project undertaken to shed light on the question: "Why do people drink alcoholic beverages

[1] This research was supported by a grant to D. C. McClelland by the National Institute of Mental Health, United States Public Health Service. The authors are greatly indebted to the following people for their generous assistance during various stages of the research: To Philip J. Stone, Marshall S. Smith, and Miss Janica Towne for providing invaluable help in the conceptual and technical aspects of the General Inquirer; to Benjamin N. Colby for letting us use some of his folktale collections; to Irvin L. Child for making available drinking ratings before they were published; to H. Eric Wanner and Jon Rolf for assistance in the final stages of the data analysis; to Mrs. Ellen Davis for keypunching the folktales.

in moderate and excessive amounts?" Specifically, the purpose of this investigation is to find psychological correlates of heavy drinking in primitive societies by relating the thematic content of folktales to drinking behavior. In order to present a rationale for our approach, it seems appropriate to state some general assumptions underlying it. One is that the consumption of alcoholic beverages is meaningfully related to the cultural, social, and psychological characteristics of the consumers. Although this position is almost too obvious to be made explicit, it is not shared by some students of alcohol, who see, for example, the reason for excessive drinking to be exclusively biological or social.

A second major assumption concerns the usefulness of the cross-cultural method. This method permits us to test a hypothesis generally. A conclusion about drinking behavior based on observations of a limited group of Americans or Europeans can hardly generate a general theory of the use of alcohol. Such a theory requires a general test, which the cross-cultural method can provide. Previous studies using this method (Horton, 1943; Field, 1962; Davis, 1964; Bacon, Barry, and Child, 1965) have related various economic, social, and child-training variables to the use of alcohol. The earlier investigators have typically explained their findings by postulating various "states of mind." For example, in Horton's study "anxiety" was *inferred* from high subsistence insecurity. Bacon, Barry, and Child inferred "dependency conflict," again a psychological concept implying a certain state of mind, from observations about child training, that is, from observations of external events. It is clear that these psychological concepts, which have the status of hypothetical constructs, are several steps removed from the observations on which they are based. The present study works with data that deal more directly with states of mind, namely folktales.

Our third assumption is that folktales reflect the modal or typical mental content of the people in a society. From this assumption it follows that a comparison of the thematic content of folktales of societies varying in their drinking behavior reveals the state of mind associated with various drinking patterns. If, for example, Horton's hypothesis is correct that fear or anxiety is a relevant variable for understanding the function of alcohol, we should expect themes of fear to occur at different rates in folktales of societies with different drinking patterns. It should also be clear that we take thematic fear to be a more direct index of "general level of anxiety" (if such a concept is useful at all) than the number of subsistence hazards.

But what justification do we have to assume that folktales represent the modal thoughts, or mental content, of the members in a society? By phrasing this question differently: "Do folktales reflect something meaningful and stable about societies?" we are really asking the methodological questions of validity and reliability. Previous research has related the content of folktales to other aspects of culture and has indicated that folktales are indeed psychologically meaningful aspects of a society. For example, Wright (1954) found that folktales in which aggression is displaced tend to appear in tribes in which the socialization of aggression in children is severe. McClelland (1961) has reported a positive relationship between achievement themes in folktales and the percentage of males engaged in full time entrepreneurial activity, an activity characteristic of people with frequent thoughts of achievement.

The reliability of folktales is treated in greater detail later.

METHOD

The general strategy employed in the present research was to select a representative sample of primitive societies for which adequate folktale collections and information concerning drinking behavior were available. The following rules guided this selection procedure.

Selection of Folktales

The sample consists of 46 folktale collections, with each collection representing the folk literature of one primitive culture. In order to be included in the sample, each collection had to contain at least 4,000 words and about 10 separate tales. (Only 9 tales were available for 8 collections, and 1 collection has only 8 tales.) However, on the average, each collection consists of about 8,000 words and 14 tales. Whenever an exceedingly large corpus of tales was discovered, 10 to 14 tales were randomly selected for analysis. Another rule for selection concerns the reputability of the source. Clearly, it was necessary to select collections that had not been substantially changed during translation. Therefore the introduction to each collection was carefully scrutinized. If the author made any mention of editing the text or of changing it in any way, the collection was considered unacceptable. About two thirds of the collections used in this study were gathered by profes-sional scholars, such as folklorists and anthropologists. The remaining tales were collected by amateurs (missionaries or government officials) who made no mention of having altered the original versions and, in most cases, clearly stated that no such alteration had occurred. A further rule for inclusion in the sample concerns the content of the folktales. It was decided to discard any tales that are either origin myths or historical legends from the recent past. Also excluded were folktales that primarily consist of religious ritual or ceremonial in-structions. These types of tales were omitted because it was felt that their content is probably not determined by the commonplace thoughts and problems of the average members of a given culture.

Selection of Societies

In addition to the restraints imposed upon the sample by the rules governing the selection of folktales, the following rules guided the selection of societies.

Only cultures were selected whose location, relative to one another, would tend to discourage transferal of folktale themes. Within the limits of the availability of folktale sources, each collection was drawn from a different subcultural area (Murdock, 1962–1965). Where this was not possible, that is, where it was necessary to use two or more sources within the same subcultural area, an attempt was made to select collections from cultures having different linguistic affiliations (Murdock, 1962–1965). Thirty-four of the 46 cultures in the sample were selected using these two criteria. For the six pairs of exceptions (Thonga–Basuto; Ganda–Kikuyu; Ifaluk–Ulithi; Carib–Taulipang; Chiricahua–Jicarilla; Palaung–Khasis), where geographical subcul-tural area and linguistic affiliation was the same, it was determined that the members of each pair be separated from each other by a number of other cultures. Because of this geographical distance and because each member of each pair constituted a distinct culture by itself, it was felt that these collections could be legitimately included in a sample designed to maximize independence of cases.

To ensure that societies in the sample would not only be independ-ent but also representative of all the major cultural areas of the world, an effort was made to select the same number of cultures from each major geographical area. In addition, attention was paid to the geo-graphical distribution of the cultures chosen within each major area.

To a certain extent, the hope of equalizing representation has been realized. Although exact equality is impossible, it is possible to include a substantial number of cultures from each area. The distribution is as follows: Africa, 9; Insular-Pacific, 7; Eurasia, 9; North America, 14; South America, 7.

A final criterion for inclusion was the availability of adequate measures of alcohol consumption for the culture. The drinking ratings compiled by Child, Bacon, and Barry (1965) were used for this study. Two ratings in particular were chosen: "general consumption" and "frequency of drunkenness." General consumption is a rating of the amount of alcohol consumed in a given society relative to other societies. It is essentially a quantity variable. Frequency of drunkenness is a rating of the relative frequency of drunkenness of the members of one society relative to others.

Dictionary Construction

The dictionary used in the present study is designed to explore a number of different possibilities with regard to the psychological correlates of drinking. When first completed, the dictionary contained 95 tags and about 4,000 entry words. The Thorndike-Barnhart Comprehensive Desk Dictionary was used in the construction of the tags.

In its initial form, the Alcohol Dictionary was divided into several different groups of tags. Each group was designed to test one particular idea about the psychological correlates of drinking. For example, seven different tags were constructed to test the general validity of Horton's work on correlates of primitive drinking. This aspect of the study provides a good example of the advantages indicated in the introduction of the use of folktales over an approach like Horton's in testing general hypotheses. Let us take four of Horton's major variables: general level of anxiety, insecure food supply, type of economy, and insobriety. Horton *hypothesized* that anxiety is positively related to insobriety. He *assumed* that insecure food supply was an index of anxiety. He *found* that insecure food supply was directly related to insobriety. But even though the results bore out the hypothesis, the assumed relationship between insecure food supply and anxiety remains questionable, as Lemert (1954) has pointed out. The results obtained by Horton may very well have nothing to do with the anxiety reduction hypothesis, a point that has also been made by Field (1962), who explains the relationship between insecure food supply and insobriety by the high association between insecure food supply and type of economy (hunting and gathering societies versus those with higher agriculture). Field also maintains that it is not anxiety that drives hunters to drink but the fact that their social organization is looser than that of societies with highly developed agriculture. Whoever is right, it is clear that Horton's approach leaves much to be desired. He uses four major variables. The relationship among the variables is theoretically as well as empirically far from clear. What has been shown empirically is that insecure food supply relates to type of economy and that both relate to insobriety. What has not been shown is that insecure food supply relates to anxiety and that anxiety, measured more directly, relates to drinking.

In the present approach, relevant variables representing action, as perceived by ethnographers, and thought, as reflected in folktales, can be interrelated. The most direct test of Horton's hypothesis can be made with the tag FEAR. Other tags, closer to Horton's observations, were entitled RICH (full, plenty, sated), POOR (hunger, meager, needy), FOOD (meal, milk, food), FARM-HERD (farmer, grain, pasture), HUNT-GATHER (hunt, hunter, trap).

The other groups of tags included in the Alcohol Dictionary were designed to test the following theories and hypotheses: (1) need for sentience (Kalin, 1964; Kalin, McClelland, and Kahn, 1965); (2) the psychoanalytic view of the importance of oral concerns; (3) Bacon, Barry, and Child's (1965) theory of dependency conflict; (4) Field's (1962) ideas emphasizing social disorganization; (5) impulsivity, and (6) sex identity.

When the Alcohol Dictionary was first completed, many of the tags contained an overabundance of entry words. That is, tags were frequently "overloaded" by including as many words as possible that might be related to the concept in question. The procedure was deliberate. It was felt that by exhausting the number of entry words for a given tag, we would greatly reduce the possibility of missing crucial words, and as a result, a lengthy analysis of the usually ambiguous leftover list probably would not be necessary. In order to arrive at a more concise definition of "overloaded" tags, extensive retrievals were made to determine the relative contribution of individual words to tag index scores and to ascertain the frequency with which certain words were being mistagged. Thus, by overloading and retrieving most of the tags in the Alcohol Dictionary, it was possible to compose a tag wherein all the entry words were not only theoretically relevant but also frequent enough to contribute to the final index score.

The retrieval strategy was used for yet another purpose. Many of the theoretically important concepts in the study of drinking are not very well defined insofar as their referents in folktales are concerned. How, for example, do we define "conflict over dependency"? The retrieval strategy enabled us to reduce the original text to those passages that might conceivably have something to do with dependency. With this greatly reduced text, it then became possible to find quickly a tentative definition of the concept and then to work empirically toward a final definition.

Analysis and Present State of Research

At the time of this writing, the project is far from completed. The analyses carried out to date have involved dividing the folktale collection of each society in half, in order to obtain two samples of approximately equal length and with an equal number of different tales. On the average, each half contains about 4,000 words and approximately 7 tales.

The Alcohol Dictionary was then used to tag one half of the text from each of 46 societies. Changes were made in the dictionary on the basis of the resulting tag tallies and extensive retrievals. While some tags were left essentially unchanged, others were considerably altered. The other half of the text was then tagged with the revised version of the dictionary. Correlation coefficients were then computed between all the tag tallies (index scores) and the drinking ratings in both halves of the text separately. Each tag tally from the first half of the text was also correlated with the corresponding tally of the second half.

We have obtained some clear results, but we do not have complete confidence in some promising tags nor do we understand them fully. For one thing, the effect of the difference in the dictionaries used on the two halves is as yet unclear. Also, there is still inadequate knowledge of the entry words responsible for many tags. And finally, there still is too much mistagging in several tags. Below we present the results on which extensive work has already been done. Later on, some of the more tentative but suggestive results are also mentioned.

We are presently engaged in "purifying" about 40 of the original list of tags. We plan to write yet another dictionary on which both halves of the text will be run again.

RESULTS AND DISCUSSION

Reliability of Folktales

In psychological measurement the concept of reliability is very important. Several kinds of reliability are distinguished, but generally reliability deals with the question of the stability of measurements. It is desirable to obtain stability across different observers (the computer, of course, is a perfectly reliable "observer" of content) and across different observations. To deal with this latter problem, one needs to measure the same variable by different observations (for instance, test-retest, split-half, odd-even). A reliable instrument, or a reliable variable, obtains when these different observations yield similar results. Although this is not a formal reliability study since our dictionary was in continual flux, the same observation was made on two different occasions (that is, two samples of folktales from each of 46 societies were tagged and tallied). The size of the correlation of the same tag applied to the first and second halves of the text across the 46 societies gives an indication of the reliability of that tag.

This procedure differs from the situation in psychological measurement in some important respects. When the reliability of a psychological test consisting of several items is determined, there is always a known source of variance, that is, an invariant characteristic, associated with each of the two sets of measures. For example, if we have two forms of a test designed to measure the same variable, and we administer the two forms to a number of people and correlate the two sets of measures, we know that at least part of the difference between the measures can be attributed to the difference between the two forms. We also know one aspect of the forms that is invariant, namely, the items they contain. When we correlate two sets of tag tallies based on two samples of text, there is nothing invariant in each sample that is similar to an identical set of items across people. The attribution of one half of a body of text to one of the two sets of measurements is arbitrary. Because in our situation there is more unexplained variance, we should expect the reliability coefficients of our tags to be generally lower than those obtained with reliable psychological tests.

With these general comments in mind, we can now apply the concept of reliability to our folktales. How do we interpret a high reliability coefficient? Literally, it simply means that a given group of words occurs with similar frequencies in two sets of texts from the same society. Expressed differently, it means that the frequency of a given group of words is more similar in different samples of text from within societies than in samples of text from different societies. However, the meaning of reliable tags is subject to various interpretations. One possible reason for consistency in folktales within a society is that all the tales from that society come from the same source. Source, in this context, can mean that the same anthropologist gathered the tales, that the same informant told the tales, or that the same translator rendered them into English. The effect of an identical source is probably a relatively consistent style. For example, if the tales in some societies are told in the first-person singular, whereas in others they are told in the third person, we obtain high consistency in the use of pronouns.

Besides reflecting a consistent source, reliable tags can also reflect consistency within a society. That is, a tag may tap a cultural or psychological characteristic that is reflected consistently in folktales within a society and varies across different societies.

In some instances, it may be difficult to decide whether a reliable tag reflects stylistic or psychologically meaningful consistency. However, we have attempted to make this decision with some of our tags. The results are shown in Table 19.1.

Table 19.1 presents the reliability coefficients of a selected list of tags. Included were only those tags that did not differ extensively in the two dictionaries used. It should be noted, however, that in most of these tags a few minor differences exist in the entry words of the two dictionaries. Table 19.1 also presents the means and standard deviations of the frequencies of the tags (occurrence per 1,000 words).

It is evident from Table 19.1 that several of our tags are quite stable across the two halves of the text. Although the interpretation is not totally unequivocal, we can make some reasonable guesses as to the meaning of this stability. The tags called psychological and sociocultural are likely to reflect meaningful societal concerns. The tags SELF, SELVES, and OTHER, however, are more likely to mirror stylistic or formal aspects of the folktales, possibly more characteristic of the storyteller or translator than of the society itself. It is possible, of course, that these tags have psychological meaning in addition to the

TABLE 19.1. *Means, Standard Deviations, and Reliability Coefficients for a Selected List of Tags*

Tag Names	First Half of Text		Second Half of Text		Correlation Coefficient (N = 46)
	Mean*	S.D.	Mean	S.D.	
Psychological					
FEAR‡	1.50	1.17	1.52	1.14	.20†
TIME CONCERN‡	41.35	9.68	38.85	8.43	.62
MISER‡	1.74	.99	1.74	1.11	.31
ACQUIRE	7.76	3.09	8.67	3.58	.44
RATIONAL THINK‡	1.83	1.19	1.98	1.21	.50
CHANGE‡	1.43	1.01	1.52	1.47	.61
NOT	9.09	3.11	8.67	2.90	.65
WANT‡	2.00	.98	2.04	1.44	.45
Sociocultural					
FORMAL ORGANIZATION‡	3.76	2.33	4.28	3.13	.57
HIGH STATUS‡	2.63	2.93	3.06	3.50	.52
CLOTHING‡	1.96	2.07	1.79	1.37	.37
DOMESTIC‡	1.87	1.69	2.20	1.86	.42
Stylistic					
SELF	18.61	13.37	18.30	11.62	.73
SELVES	4.07	2.60	4.41	2.51	.36
OTHER	34.93	11.86	34.20	8.53	.59

* Average frequency of index scores (occurrence per 1,000 words).
† With $N = 46$, if $r = .24$ $p < .05$; if $r = .34$ $p < .01$ (one-tailed tests).
‡ Minor differences in entry words of tag in dictionaries used on first and second halves of text.

formal characteristics. For example, the frequent and consistent use of words relating to the self may reflect egocentrism. At this point, interpretations of this sort are mere speculations.

Some of the psychological and sociocultural tags listed in Table 19.1 clearly represent consistent concerns rather than consistent style. For example, CHANGE (change, turn into, become, transform) refers to statements of a change of state. Examples are "He turns into an animal," "He is transformed into a spirit," and so forth. Further results on this tag and an additional discussion are presented later. MISER is defined by words referring to hoarding, concealing, retaining. ACQUIRE is composed of words like acquire, grab, take, and so forth. RATIONAL THINK consists of thought, think, plan, and so forth. In WANT, we find hope, want, need, wish and so forth. Since all these tags quite clearly refer to *content,* rather than *formal* characteristics, we have good reason to believe that they reflect consistent concerns.

The inclusion of TIME CONCERN and NOT among the psychological tags is somewhat questionable. Tabulation of entry words for TIME CONCERN indicated that most of the tag was carried by such words as after, when, and so forth. Since these words are simply grammatical markers and do not refer to content, we do not know how much the content related words in TIME CONCERN contributed to the correlation. The case of NOT (not, never) is similarly doubtful. It is possible, however, that we are dealing with a formal characteristic that has psychological significance, namely denial, restraint, or inhibition.

FEAR is one tag included in this list with a rather low reliability. The correlation does not even reach acceptable statistical significance. It is an interesting tag, however, in that it has quite substantial relational fertility (to be discussed). This suggests that a theme need not be consistently present in a body of text in order to be meaningful and important. More generally, it is apparent that a tag need not be reliable yet can still be valid insofar as it relates meaningfully and consistently to other variables.

The meaning of the sociocultural tags should be fairly clear from the names. FORMAL ORGANIZATION includes words that denote legal, political, and formalized social organization (conference, governor, manager). HIGH-STATUS denotes positions or occupations with high social status (general, chief, judge). CLOTHING includes articles of clothing, and DOMESTIC is made up of words denoting domestic utensils and activities.

The interpretation of substantial reliability coefficients of content-related story characteristics reflecting societal consistency has been made in another context. McClelland (1961) scored the content of childrens' readers from various modern nations for the Need for Achievement and correlated the scores based on two subsets of stories from the same societies. In an evaluation of this work, Brown came to the conclusion that "if the amount of achievement imagery in a story were purely a function of the personality of its author and in no sense a reflection of the national atmosphere one would expect the two sets of scores for a single nation to be unrelated. In fact these correlations were impressively large; for the stories collected in the 1920's the correlation was .671 and for the later set it was .594. This fact argues strongly that the amount of achievement content in these stories at a given time is a national characteristic." (Brown, 1965, 455).

The fact that the General Inquirer approach to content analysis can establish societal consistency has implications beyond the major purpose of the present study. High reliability of a tag does not merely indicate stability of the concerns of a society. A high reliability co-efficient also means that the variable on which two sets of measures are taken forms a stable dimension along which the cases (societies) can be placed. For example, the fact that CHANGE correlated .61 in the two halves of the text does not simply mean that a society mentioning change of state in some folktales is also likely to mention it in others. It also means that change forms a dimension on which a given society can be placed. Whether or not the dimension is meaningful is another question to be established by finding correlates of this dimension with other variables in the societies. Still, the present approach is useful in pointing out new dimensions or variables that can be studied nomothetically across cultures.

Folktale Content and Drinking

The drinking rating used in the statistical analyses is a combination score (sum) of the "general-consumption" and "frequency-of-drunkenness" ratings developed by Bacon, Barry, and Child (1965). The reason for this procedure was our interest in "heavy drinking," defined as combination of high consumption and frequent drunkenness. The two measures also correlate very highly ($r = .77$).

The thematic correlates of heavy drinking that have been established thus far are presented in Table 19.2.

The tag FEAR as it originally appeared in the dictionary showed a consistently negative (though not significant) relationship with drinking. Retrievals and tabulation of entry words, however, showed that only some aspects of FEAR are consistently related to drinking. Originally, the tag contained words relating to flight and to possible behavioral consequences of fear (scream, tremble, and so forth). Retrievals showed that these more indirect references to fear resulted in frequent mistags ("the trembling trees"). When the FEAR tag was purified (by hand) to include only very direct references to fear (fear, scared, terrified, and so forth), the correlations with drinking were

TABLE 19.2. Relationship Between Thematic Tags and Drinking Ratings

	Correlations with Combined Drinking Score		
Tag Names	Whole Text	First Half of Text	Second Half of Text
FEAR (original)	−.24*†	−.13	−.23
FEAR (purified)	−.42§	−.34‡	−.30‡
HUNT-GATHER (original)	.47§	.44§	.32‡
HUNT (purified)			.44§
AGGRESSIVE IMPLEMENT (original)	.30†	.26†	.19
FEMININE-MAN (original)	.23	.15	.24†
DOMESTIC-MAN (purified)			.33‡
CHANGE (original)	.27†	.20	.27†

* All significance tests are two tailed.
† .10 > p > .05.
‡ p < .05.
§ p < .01.

greatly improved and became statistically significant. This finding, therefore, shows that the more direct references to fear appear in the folktales of a society, the less likely its members are to engage in heavy drinking. This result is significant in view of the prominent role of fear or anxiety in many theories of drinking. Note that Horton (1943) predicted just the opposite, that is, that fear or anxiety would show a positive relationship with insobriety.

The present inverse relationship is not the only evidence that questions Horton's hypothesis. Field (1962) presented the results of several other measures of fear (fear of spirits) and found them to be unrelated to drinking. Field also reported a negative correlation between aggression socialization anxiety and insobriety. In addition, Bacon, Barry, and Child (1965) reported a negative correlation between anal socialization anxiety and their rating of frequency of drunkenness. It is unclear whether these various measures of fear or anxiety are equivalent, or even have anything in common. It is even doubtful that a concept like general level of anxiety in a society is meaningful at all.

It is probably possible to interpret the present inverse relationship between fear and drinking as still supporting the anxiety reduction hypothesis. One could say that the reason little fear is expressed in the folktales of heavy drinking societies is that fear has been reduced through heavy drinking. This kind of interpretation would then have to explain the motivation for continued excessive use of alcohol in these societies.

One can also argue that actual fear (fear as experienced by the members of a society) and thematic fear are inversely related. It is then possible to interpret the inverse relationship between thematic fear and drinking to mean that heavy drinkers are more scared than light drinkers, that they are so afraid, in fact, that they avoid mention, maybe even thought about, fear. Further results in Table 19.2, however, indicate that it is not timidity, but a lack of it, that is associated with heavy drinking.

The strongest relationship obtained so far is between the tag HUNT-GATHER and drinking. Retrievals were made and it was discovered that despite the strong association with drinking, several problems remain. Semantically ambiguous words are included under this tag, and therefore frequent mistagging results. Examples are "game" (hunt or play) and "gather" (one can gather anything). Another problem is created by the word "meat." Although meat can be used in a hunting context, it is more frequently used in other ways. Consequently, the retrieved HUNT-GATHER tag (for the second half of the text only) was hand coded and only direct references to hunting and trapping were counted. References to gathering are too infrequent to be of any use. The purified HUNT tag somewhat improved the correlation with drinking. The result indicates that in societies with heavy drinking, themes of hunting are prominent in folktales. A concern with hunting also seems incompatible with fear. That is, a brave hunter should not be afraid. The fact that heavy drinkers are concerned with hunting supports the foregoing contention that it is not timidity, but a lack of it, that goes with heavy drinking.

The relationship between AGGRESSIVE IMPLEMENT and drinking may be related to the previous result. AGGRESSIVE IMPLEMENT consists of entry words such as spear, arrow, and so forth. These words can be used either in an aggressive or hunting context.

The tag FEMININE-MAN is a combination tag, defined by the co-occurrence in the same sentence of a male character (father, man, he) and CLOTHING, DOMESTIC, and a tag called FEMININITY. The purpose of this tag was to provide information on the possible relationship between sex identity and drinking. Since the tag is a complex one and theoretically very important, much work was done on the retrievals of tagged sentences. These analyses show that the FEMININITY component resulted mostly in mis-tagging. Femininity was defined by words like round, little, light, and so forth. As these words are quite ambiguous, such references as "he went round the house," "after a little while he . . ." got coded. The retrievals of the tag FEMININE-MAN in the second half of the text were therefore hand scored. References were counted in which men were clearly in a feminine context. Examples are, "he took his teeth to make a necklace," "She dressed him in a skirt," "he cooked meat," "he set aside cooked rice for his wife." This purified tag was then called DOMESTIC MAN, and it can be seen from Table 19.2 that the relationship of this theme with drinking is quite significant.

Taken by itself, the suggestion that in heavy drinking societies males in folktales are frequently seen in domestic contexts is rather curious. However, other evidence points to the theory that heavy drinking males have a basic feminine identity. Davis (1964) found that societies with couvade (those in which men display pregnancy symptoms, that is act out a distinctly feminine role) tend to be higher in frequency of drunkenness than societies where the custom of couvade is absent. A similar finding was obtained by Munroe (1964) who discovered that among the Black Caribs, those men who show strong couvade were rated to be heavier drinkers than men showing weak couvade.

In this context, MacAndrew's (1965) study differentiating male alcoholic outpatients from nonalcoholic psychiatric outpatients on the basis of being alcoholic or nonalcoholic by means of the MMPI is quite relevant. He found that alcoholics tend to endorse items like "I like to cook," "I would like to wear expensive clothes," "The one to whom I was most attached and whom I most admired as a child was a woman (mother, sister, aunt or other woman)" much more frequently than the control subjects. The correspondence between these items and the tag DOMESTIC MAN is certainly striking.

The suggestion that heavy drinkers have a basic feminine identity should not be taken to mean that this is their consistent and all pervasive identity or, that they are latent homosexuals. Munroe (1964) found that couvade males tended to curse more (a masculine trait), and in our folktales heavy drinking societies are concerned with hunting and aggressive or hunting implements. At this time, it is possible only to speculate why men with basic feminine characteristics coupled with certain masculine concerns should take to heavy drinking. Perhaps a drinking bout simultaneously fulfills these two seemingly contradictory needs. Horton (1943) reports that a typical drinking bout in primitive societies generally involves sexual and especially aggressive acting out which is then followed by extreme passivity (passing out). It is quite clear, then, that during drinking both the role of the brave hunter (aggressive behavior) and of a woman (complete passivity) can be acted out.

Although the tag CHANGE did not quite reach an acceptable significance level, it does provide another interesting lead into the dynamics of drinking. Investigation of retrievals indicate that the removal of the entry word "become" would improve the relationship with drinking. Although "become" can reflect a change of state, it is more equivocal than such phrases and words as turn into, change into, transform. At least two interpretations of the relationship between this tag and drinking are possible. One is that the tag may reflect the frequent transformations undergone by people who are frequently drunk. It may also be related to the dual sexual identity of heavy drinkers, that is, a man becomes a woman and then a man again.

Thematic Content of Folktales and Ethnographic Ratings

Since most of the societies in our sample are among those for which various ethnographic ratings are available (Murdock, 1962–1965), it was possible to relate the thematic content of folktales (thought system of a society) with ethnographic ratings (description of the action or reality system). A very general and important question concerns the relationship between these two systems. The results presented in Table 19.3 are relevant to this point.

How do the thought and action systems in similar realms relate to another behavior? Specifically, how do hunting themes in folktales and the extent to which the economy of a society depends on hunting relate to drinking behavior? Table 19.3 shows that both the thematic and the behavior variable are positively associated with the combination drinking score. While the correlation between hunting economy and this drinking rating does not quite reach an acceptable significance level, we can have confidence in the relationship because both Field (1962), and Barry, Buchwald, Child, and Bacon (1965) have reported a significant positive correlation between hunting economy and frequency of drunkenness (which constitutes one of the two com-

TABLE 19.3. *Intercorrelations Among Some Thematic Variables and Ethnographic Ratings*

Variables	Variables		
	2. r (N)	3. r (N)	4. r (N)
1. Combined Drinking Rating	.44§ (46)	.20 (43)	−.42§ (46)
2. Thematic Hunt†		.22* (43)	−.44§ (46)
3. Hunt Economy‡			−.08 (43)
4. Thematic Fear			

* .10 > p < .05.
† Purified HUNT tag, based on second half of text only.
‡ Ratings from Murdock, *Ethnographic Atlas* (1962–1965). Information available on only 43 societies.
§ p < .01.

ponents of our combined drinking score). Also, in our sample, hunting economy correlates .32 ($N = 43$, $p < .05$) with frequency of drunkenness. It appears, therefore, that hunting, as represented in both the thought and action system, is similarly related to heavy drinking.

A second question concerns a direct comparison of the thought and action systems. Specifically, what is the correlation between hunting economy and themes of hunting in folktales? Table 19.3 shows this correlation to be .22 ($.10 < p > .05$). While we cannot be very certain that the correlation is real, that is not due to chance, its small size points to an interesting situation. The small covariance of hunting in behavior and thought (that is, the relatively great independence of the two) suggests that the thoughts of a heavy drinking society can be concerned with hunting without necessarily being engaged in such hunting activity. In other words, the hunting theme has functional significance (that is, it is related to drinking) beyond being simply a reflection of reality.

Table 19.3 also contains information relevant to Horton's major assumptions. One of these is that subsistence insecurity is an index of the general level of anxiety within a culture. The ratings of subsistence insecurity were not immediately available to us, but since subsistence insecurity is highly correlated with type of economy (Field, 1962), the relationship between dependence on hunting economy and our tag FEAR represents a reasonable test of Horton's assumption. Table 19.3 shows that the two variables are not related. It is of further interest to note the correlation between the tags FEAR and HUNT. The significant negative correlation indicates that the two themes are mutually exclusive (within the limits of the correlation). These results, in conjunction with the relationship of fear and drinking presented earlier, fail to support Horton on two counts. One is that fear is not positively but negatively related to drinking, and the other, that a concern with fear is not positively but, if anything, negatively associated with a hunting economy.

To conclude the present section, we can say that although thought and reality as represented in thematic content and ratings of behavior have aspects in common, there are enough differences between the two to warrant their separate investigation. This section has also demonstrated that by analyzing the content of folktales one can directly test psychological assumptions that would otherwise remain only as assumptions.

Other Promising Findings

In addition to the results presented earlier, a number of other interesting relationships between thematic variables and the drinking ratings were discovered. However, either because of insufficient work on them (lack of knowledge concerning the significant entry words and of the extent of mis-tagging), or because of inconsistencies between the two halves of text (probably due to changes in the dictionary), they are not reported here in detail. Some general impressions are presented in order to indicate the direction in which we are headed.

The results on the occurrence of kinship terms in folktales definitely suggests that societies varying in their drinking behavior mention different combinations of kin terms. For example, the terms uncle, aunt, niece (collateral kin, Romney and D'Andrade, 1964) occur much more frequently in heavy drinking societies. Thus an obvious next step is to relate the use of kin terms to social structure variables (for example, marital residence, descent) since these variables have been found to relate to drinking (Field, 1962). Another reason for relating them is that the saliency of various kinship terms in folktales can be expected to covary with the saliency of a particular kinship structure.

Based on incomplete results, it is also our impression that the following theories and hypotheses on drinking deserve further attention: Among the components of sentience proposed by Kalin, McClelland, and Kahn (1965) and Kalin (1964), aggression looks especially promising. The validity of the concept of inhibition proposed by the same investigators is suggested by negative relations between drinking and TIME CONCERN, RATIONAL THINK, and NOT. The psychoanalytic notion that drinking is associated with orality also deserves further work, because positive relationships between drinking and the tags FOOD and INGEST were found.

GENERAL DISCUSSION AND FUTURE PLANS
Some Methodological Points

It is quite clear that the present study can be criticized on various counts. One can argue that statistics are used inappropriately because percentage scores do not lend themselves properly to parametric statistics. The fact that the study is as much an exploration as hypothesis testing can lead to the criticism that it is merely a "fishing" expedition," and as such simply capitalizes on results obtained by chance. Subject to the same criticism is the fact that the dictionary has been, and still is being, revised. There is one answer to all these criticisms. In order to have faith in any conclusion (hypothesis or theory), the results on which the conclusion is based need to be cross-validated in several contexts. Unfortunately, there are not many more primitive societies available that meet the criteria for selection described earlier. However, cross-validation can be achieved in other ways. We are presently collecting TAT stories from alcoholics. A finding that alcoholics differ from nonalcoholics in the content of their TAT's in the same way that folktales of heavy and light drinking societies are different would represent a confirmation of the present results.

Another way in which the context of the cross-validation can be varied is by using different instruments to tap the same variables. An example of this is the MMPI study (MacAndrew, 1965).

And finally, faith in a theory comes when we understand it sufficiently to test it experimentally. In the case of a theory of drinking, this can be achieved when the experimental arousal of whatever theoretically makes people drink results in increased alcohol consumption.

Folktales and Reality

Going beyond the special topic of alcohol consumption, we plan to shed more light on the general problem of the relationship between the thematic content of folktales and other aspects of primitive cultures. It is our plan to relate variables describing the social structure of societies and childhood socialization techniques to folktale content as well as to drinking ratings. Thereby we can obtain information on the etiology of heavy drinking as well as provide knowledge on the more general question of how social structure and child training are reflected in the projective system.

BIBLIOGRAPHY

Bacon, M. K., H. Barry, and I. L. Child (1965), "A Crosscultural Study of Drinking: II. Relations to other Features of Culture. *Quarterly Journal of Studies on Alcohol,* Supplement No. 3, 29–48.

Barry, H., III, C. Buchwald, I. L. Child, M. K. Bacon (1965), "A Crosscultural Study of Drinking: IV. Comparison with Horton Ratings." *Quarterly Journal of Studies on Alcohol,* Vol. 3 (1965), 62–78.

Brown, R. (1965), *Social Psychology.* New York: The Free Press of Glencoe.

Child, I. L., M. K. Bacon, and H. Barry, III (1965), "A Crosscultural Study of Drinking: I. Descriptive Measurements of Drinking Customs. *Quarterly Journal of Studies on Alcohol,* Supplement No. 3, 1–28.

Davis, W. N. (1964), "A Crosscultural Study of Drunkenness." Unpublished Honors Thesis. Harvard College.

Field, P. B. (1962), "A New Crosscultural Study of Drunkenness." In Pittman, D. J., and Snyder, C. R. (eds.), *Society, Culture and Drinking Patterns.* New York: John Wiley & Sons, 48–74.

Horton, D. (1943), "The Functions of Alcohol in Primitive Societies: A Crosscultural Study." *Quarterly Journal of Studies on Alcohol,* Vol. 4, 199–320.

Kalin, R. (1964), "Alcohol, Sentience, and Inhibition: An Experimental Study." Unpublished doctoral dissertation, Harvard University.

Kalin, R., D. C. McClelland, and M. Kahn (1965), "The Effects of Male Social Drinking on Fantasy." *Journal of Personality and Social Psychology,* Vol. 1, 441–452.

Lemert, E. M. (1954), "Alcohol and the North West Coast Indians." *University of California Publications in Culture and Society,* Vol. 2, 303–406.

MacAndrew, C. (1965), "The Differentiation of Male Alcoholic Outpatients from Nonalcoholic Psychiatric Outpatients by Means of the MMPI." *Quarterly Journal of Studies on Alcohol,* Vol. 26, 238–246.

McClelland, D. C. (1961), *The Achieving Society.* Princeton, N.J.: Van Nostrand.

McCord, W., and J. McCord (1960), *Origins of Alcoholism.* Stanford, Calif.: Stanford University Press.

Munroe, R. L. (1964), "Couvade Practices of the Black Carib: A Psychological Study." Unpublished doctoral dissertation, Harvard University.

Murdock, G. (ed.), "Ethnographic Atlas." (Series) *Ethnology,* Vols. I–IV (1962–1965).

Romney, A. K., and R. G. D'Andrade (1964), "Cognitive Aspects of English Kin Terms." *American Anthropologist,* Vol. 66, No. 3, Part 2 (Special Publication), 146–170.

Wright, G. (1954), "Projection and Displacement: A Crosscultural Study of Folktale Aggression." *Journal of Abnormal and Social Psychology,* Vol. 49, 523–528.

CHAPTER TWENTY

Cross-Cultural Contrasts
in Interpersonal Structuring

Frances M. Dahlberg
Cornell University

Philip J. Stone
Harvard University

INTRODUCTION

Often two essays will tell the same story but will differ dramatically in the extent of placing characters into specified roles, in making dominance and submissive relationships explicit, in specifying symbols of social status, in putting behavior into what we call in Chapter 5 an "institutional" setting, and in utilizing social values to indicate a moral imperative. In constructing the Harvard III Dictionary, considerable care was given to including categories for each of these different aspects of structuring the social world.

A story may be given any of several forms of structuring. Some essays may make time and space relationships explicit, taking care to specify when and where each event occurred. Others may emphasize task structure, identifying events in terms of their relationship to overall goal attainment. The different aspects of "interpersonal structuring," in contrast, emphasize normative patterns of social control.

Occasionally, the tendency to specify different aspects of "interpersonal structuring" is a manifestation of what Adorno *et al.* (1950)

describe as the authoritarian personality. Yet its inherent relationships with other apparent components of authoritarianism, such as (Bass, 1955) dogmatism, misanthropy, xenophobia, suggestibility, and acquiescence, is far from demonstrated. Until then, it makes sense to study these other components separately.

This chapter considers the effectiveness of the Harvard III Dictionary categories in identifying different aspects of interpersonal structuring. While the dictionary may successfully measure these aspects, the *inference* drawn from these measurements will still depend on the situation. A high frequency may reflect a cultural norm or situational pressure and be quite functional within such circumstances. A low frequency may reflect situational pressures that keep a basic tendency of the "source" from being expressed.

Our test case in this instance is a cross-cultural comparison of essays written by students of college age. Differences in interpersonal structuring are occasionally considered to be a cultural characteristic, reflecting cultural patterns of family hierarchy and early socialization. If we are to demonstrate interpersonal structuring as a cultural pattern, then we must demonstrate that the pattern is characteristic of productions from members of one culture and not characteristic of productions from members of another.

Our task is twofold. First we would like to demonstrate one instance in which the different aspects of interpersonal structuring co-occur as a pattern. Second, we wish to show that this pattern can function as a cultural characteristic.

THE CATEGORIES

In delineating dictionary categories, two parallel strategies were employed. One was to create an extensive, second-order tag, containing a large number of denotative and connotative entries referring to the stratified structuring of interpersonal relationships. This category was labeled SIGN-AUTHORITY. Such a category places all of one's measurement resources into a combined index. Success in applying such a category is gratifying, but one may be hard pressed to determine what aspects of the category are causing it.

The second approach is to create a number of more specific tag categories representing different aspects of the concept. Interpersonal structuring was expected to be reflected in the higher use of the action categories CONTROL, GUIDE, and FOLLOW in the role designations MALE-ROLE, FEMALE-ROLE, JOB-ROLE, plus the second-order role tags HIGHER-STATUS and LOWER-STATUS in the specificity of institutional settings — especially in ACADEMIC, LEGAL, POLITICAL, and ECONOMIC, in the interpersonal moral imperative use of OUGHT, and the social legitimizations of IDEAL-VALUE. A measurement of interpersonal structuring is not thought to be represented in any one of these tags alone, but in the high scores of a group of tags.

THE TEST

The tendency to express interpersonal structuring should vary greatly according to the test situation. For example, given a particular TAT picture, a respondent may tell a story that does not involve extensive interpersonal structuring, even though this characteristic figures strongly in his own personality. As the personality has many facets, usually only a limited number of aspects can be elicited within any single test.

In this research, a test was used that requires at least some structuring of a future closely relevant to the ego. The question is what kinds of structuring take place. This future autobiography procedure, as first suggested by A. Szalai of Hungary and implemented by Gillespie and Allport (1955), has instructions essentially as follows:

> Beginning at the present (your past life history, up to now, need not be told), write a few pages concerning your expectations, plans and aspirations for the future. There is no required length for these essays: anything from 4 to 8 pages (or about 1000 or 2000 words) would be quite acceptable. . . . Although you need not follow a strict chronological method, year by year or decade by decade, it would be well to write first of the near future as you see it, and then of the expectations appropriate to successive periods of middle age and later life. . . .
>
> (Gillespie and Allport, 1955, 41)

In 1948, Gillespie and Allport (1955) undertook a cross-national survey of ten countries to explore differences in attitudes of youth. They used this future autobiography assignment in conjunction with a questionnaire and collected their data in the United States, New Zealand, South Africa (including Afrikaners, English, Bantus, and Indians), Egypt, Mexico, France, Italy, Germany, Japan, and Israel.

SELECTION OF CONTRASTING CULTURES

The Egyptian culture stands out within this collection as giving considerable emphasis to specified interpersonal relationships. As described by Marjarian (1959) and others, Egyptian culture strongly stresses patriarchal and hierarchical authority. Within the family, roles of dominance and submission are clearly defined, and sex roles are acutely differentiated. Parents are seen as distant, forbidding, and stern. The father, even in liberal Egyptian families, is the decision maker and final authority; much formal deference is given to him. The child is taught to conform to the wishes of the elders and to avoid being a discredit to the family.

The teachings of the Islam religion reinforce this early family training. Emphasis is on submission to the ruling hand of God and acceptance of fate. Man is considered inherently good but weak and subject to temptation. Society exists to protect its members and to discipline them to subject themselves to God. This pattern extends to other sections of Egyptian life. As might be expected, positions in government carry high prestige. Within both the society and the family, authority is autocratic and arbitrary (Harris, 1957, 338–343).

In his comparison of 473 Egyptian Students with 822 United States students, Melikian (1959) found that the Egyptians had significantly higher scores on the Adorno et al. F scale. The questionnaire Gillespie and Allport used as part of their 1948 cross-cultural survey shows, for example, that 46 percent of the Egyptian students of the sample believed that their destinies are controlled by external circumstances, as compared to 15 percent of the United States student sample.

A United States sample, such as the Radcliffe students, should tend to provide in contrast a less interpersonally structured outlook. Jacob reports (1957, 12–37) that American students when ranking issues as to their importance place self-interest, social acceptance, and friendship high, and they show relative apathy in political and community activities. Similarly, Barton (1959) finds that self-development, promoting pleasure for others, and establishing fine relationships with other persons receive highest scorings on a check-list procedure.

The Egyptian sample in this study offered the advantage of being written in English. Thus we were able to circumvent the problem of translation and the possibility of building in relationships in the translation process. Our comparison thus consists of two sets of essays written in English.

From the essays collected by Gillespie and Allport,[1] two samples of 20 were randomly picked, one from the 32 essays available from the Women's Teaching Institute in Alexandria, and another from 97 essays available from Radcliffe.[2] In both groups, the essays were each several pages long. A check was made of the Radcliffe sample to see that it represented different parts of the country.

This sample of Egyptian females had been educated in a Western tradition. They form an elite group in a land of then only 25 percent literacy and cannot be used as an example of the model Egyptian personality. Yet as Dujiker and Frijda (1960, 167) point out, the study of national elites representing ideals of value systems among different social classes is needed as well as sample representations of a country as a whole. It is doubtful that the young girls, despite their education, would not reflect the overriding tone of their culture.

INITIAL IMPRESSIONS

Before enlisting the computer, it makes sense to read carefully the essays. Perhaps some unanticipated artifact will make them actually quite different from what might be expected. Perhaps important differences will appear that are beyond the capacity of our dictionary.

A casual reading of a sample of essays from the two cultures gives the strong impression that the "future autobiography" technique has been successful in eliciting major cultural differences in attitudes. These differences do not seem to be an artifact of language ability; the Egyptian girls appear to have mastered the vocabulary and sentence-structure complexity of English enough that they could have written a Radcliffe essay had it been in their nature.

As one extends his impressionistic reading to more than a few essays from each culture, it becomes difficult to keep a balanced perspective on the many contrasts that occur. The way a particular essay is written will tend to highlight certain characteristics and lead the reader to ignore others. Across essays, one tends to be so struck, for example,

[1] We appreciate Gillespie's and Allport's generosity in making their data available to us.
[2] The selection of females rather than both males and females stems from the hypotheses of a larger study by Dahlberg (1963) not discussed here.

by the nationalism of the Egyptians that other differences become subsumed. The number of comparisons in this task of context analysis makes us quite ready to enlist the computer for further assistance.

The casual reading of the essays showed no major reason to add entries or change categories within the Harvard III Dictionary. The essays of both cultures were written in everyday language. The nationalism of the Egyptian essays included reference to some political figures and conditions, but these would all appear on the leftover list and could be handled separately.

ANALYSIS PROCEDURES

In comparing the Egyptian and Radcliffe writings, our unit of reference is the essay. For each tag, the 40 essays (20 from each group) are rank ordered together from high to low according to their word tag tally index scores. If the rank ordering of the Radcliffe and Egyptian essay scores on a tag are randomly intermixed, the expected sum of the rank assignments for each group is 410. The Mann-Whitney test determines the significance of the difference between the actual sum of ranks for each group and this expected value.

Table 20.1 shows the tags on which the Egyptian essays significantly tended to have higher scores. Table 20.2 shows tags on which the

TABLE 20.1. Tags Tending to Have Higher Scores on Egyptian Essays (Harvard III Dictionary)

Tag	Sum of Ranks	Significance Level
SIGN-AUTHORITY	289	.01
JOB-ROLE	293	.01
FEMALE-ROLE	304	.01
HIGHER-STATUS	346.5	.05
LOWER-STATUS	300.5	.01
IDEAL VALUE	289	.01
OUGHT	286	.01
LEGAL	340.5	.05
MEDICAL	348	.05
POLITICAL	309.5	.01
RELIGIOUS	284.5	.01
GUIDE	246	.01
FOLLOW	286	.01
URGE	346.5	.05
GOOD	256	.01

TABLE 20.2. *Tags Tending to Have Higher Scores on Radcliffe Essays* (*Harvard III Dictionary*)

Tag	Sum of Ranks	Significance Level
SELVES	308	.01
SMALL-GROUP	279	.01
OVERSTATE	314.5	.01
UNDERSTATE	270	.01
RECREATIONAL	300.5	.01
TIME	285	.01
SPACE	289	.01
QUANTITY	328	.05

Radcliffe essays significantly tended to be higher. Altogether, 18 of the 83 tags in the Harvard III Dictionary show differences significant at least at the .01 level, many of these being considerably more significant than that. The question, however, is not whether more tags showed significant differences than would be expected to occur by chance (we did not expect many tags to differ) but whether the pattern of tag differences is as expected.

EGYPTIAN RESULTS

Turning first to our broad category SIGN-AUTHORITY, we find that the Egyptian essays tend to have much higher scores, the difference being significant considerably beyond the .01 level. The 40 tag index scores show a wide range of distribution, from a low of 0.8 percent to a high of 3.9 percent. While one Radcliffe essay tends to score very high, none of the Egyptian essays score in the lower quartile. Thus, a high SIGN-AUTHORITY score is a reliable characteristic of our Egyptian sample.

For the more specific categories, we first expected that the action tags CONTROL, GUIDE, and FOLLOW would be higher for the Egyptian essays. As Table 20.1 indicates, the scores for GUIDE and FOLLOW are each significantly higher for the Egyptian essays at the .01 level. A check of the tag CONTROL shows that it occurs too infrequently for between-group differences to be feasible. While the two highest scores (0.7 and 0.6 percent) are both Egyptian, the rest of the scores all intermix at 0.4 percent or less, and for many essays in both groups the tag did not appear at all.

A check of the contexts in which GUIDE occurred indicated that an artifact might be causing the differences: The Egyptian girls were at a teaching institute. Most all of them mentioned "teaching" and "education" as being a part of their lives, both these words being entries in the GUIDE category. To check for these effects, a retrieval (described in Chapter 3) was made on the category GUIDE with references to (TEACH(and (EDUCAT(removed; thus, sentences containing such words as teach, teacher, educate, education were no longer counted in either the Egyptian or Radcliffe essays. While this adjustment reduced the amount of difference between the two groups on the tag GUIDE, enough difference remained to be statistically significant.

Apart from the context of teaching, the GUIDE and FOLLOW categories are thus more characteristic of the Egyptian essays. The following examples suggest this emphasis:

Women *imitate* men. . . .

Society *helps* and *protects* widows.

I shall *respect* his opinions.

She will *serve* her country. . . .

Next, we expected the Egyptian essays to be more role conscious, with more references to MALE-ROLE, FEMALE-ROLE, and JOB-ROLE as well as to the second-order categories of HIGHER-STATUS and LOWER-STATUS. As can be seen in Table 20.1, all of these except MALE-ROLE show significant differences in the expected direction.

As discussed in Chapter 4, the categories MALE-ROLE and FEMALE-ROLE in the Harvard III Dictionary both have the unfortunate characteristic of including both familiar pronouns (he, him, his, she, hers) and role names (woman, mistress, father, and so forth). Since there is the tendency for these categories to occur in the same sentence, the separating pronouns and role names by retrieval procedures is laborious.

Within the Egyptian group, a retrieval shows that references to FEMALE-ROLE were often descriptions of women's place in society, be it the writer, her daughter, sister, or women in general:

I shall become a school *mistress*. It is a great thing for a *girl* to be a teacher who can prepare for the country a strong generation by teaching *her* pupils good manners and habits, and the love of God and work and faithfulness to their country.

My *daughter* may be a lawyer who defends the cause of the right and fights against injustice and oppression.

Egyptian society treats *women* too severely. We should sacrifice ourselves in defense of our cause. We should endeavor hard to actualize our principles even if we are banished and persecuted. Why should Egyptians insist upon keeping *women* within high walls as if *she* were a beast — an unpardonable blunder?

Within such assertions, however, the subjugated female outlook also, appears:

Her (wife's) first duty is to entertain her husband and see that he is not bored. He should forget all his troubles and sufferings in *her* presence.

MALE-ROLE is a highly frequent tag in both the Egyptian and Radcliffe essays. While over-all frequencies are about the same, we can investigate further using co-occurrence retrieval procedures to see if there are differences in how the tag is used. This exploration is described as an example in Chapter 3, pages 114 to 116. A retrieval is first made of all sentences in both the Egyptian and Radcliffe essays which contain one or more references to MALE-ROLE. A tag tally is then made of these retrieved sentences. As described in Chapter 3, the Egyptian use of MALE-ROLE was found to co-occur more with JOB-ROLE, SIGN-STRONG, SIGN-ACCEPT, HIGHER-STATUS, and RELIGION than in the Radcliffe essays. Each of these tags shows a larger between-group difference ratio as a co-occurrence with MALE-ROLE than they do in the data as a whole.

When the same procedure is used with the Radcliffe essays, they show high MALE-ROLE co-occurrences only with SIGN-WEAK, WORK, and PEER-STATUS. Most of the co-occurrences of PEER-STATUS and MALE-ROLE represent the double tagging of the word "husband." The future husband figures quite strongly in the Radcliffe essays as a close companion in common activities.

Thus the Egyptian essays generally show more concern with the specification of roles and hierarchial status. MALE-ROLE appears equally frequent in both groups, but in terms of co-occurrences it is treated quite differently by each group; These co-occurrence differences are again in accord with our general expectations.

As expected, institutional specificity appears more often in the Egyptian essays. Four institutions, LEGAL, MEDICAL, POLITICAL, and RELIGIOUS, are significantly higher in Table 20.1. For the Radcliffe essays, only one institutional category, RECREATIONAL, appears significantly higher in Table 20.2. While we did not specifically predict Egyptians would be higher on RELIGION, and we note that Egyptian essays are not higher on ACADEMIC or ECONOMIC, the over-all trend is very much as expected. In fact, the high counts on RELIGION may primarily be due to the tendency of the Egyptian essays to have a religious ending:

> May *God* protect us all

> May *God* will my hopes and aspirations to come true

> May *God* realize all my wishes

> I shall be grateful to *God* in his *heavens.*

Obligations and duties are frequently mentioned in the Egyptian essays. The significantly high scores on OUGHT (Table 20.1) reflect a high sense of interpersonal responsibility.

Finally, the Egyptian essays are much higher in references to IDEAL-VALUE. (Table 17.1). Many of these refer to interpersonal relationships:

> I shall teach her *faithfulness, courage* and sacrifice.

> I will marry my sons to good, *virtuous,* and well educated girls.

> Our home shall be a *paradise* whose inhabitants enjoy happiness, love, *faithfulness* and *harmony.*

> *Honesty* exists no more and vice has gained mastery over *virtue.*

> I shall engrave upon their souls the best rules of conduct and the most *valuable* manners.

Socially approved competence is also important:

> I am promoted through *efficiency* and long *experience.*

> I admire *culture, skill* and *competence.*

> I hope for continuous *success* in my examinations, to do my work properly and *faithfully,* to have a distinguished and praiseworthy personality.

The repeated reference to social ideal values stands out in the casual reading of the essays. While a number of improvements might be made in this dictionary category, this is one difference between cultures that is so apparent as to be unquestionable.

EGYPTIAN RESULTS, NONPREDICTED

One cannot help but be impressed with the amount of nationalism and ambition expressed in the Egyptian essays. Their wants and upward expectations are made clear:

> Anyone who has no hopes is similar to a fruitless tree. Every wise person looks ahead into the future and prepares himself for the coming days.

> Egypt will advance through reformation and improvement.

> Since the beginning of creation, man has been a creature of different hopes and great aspirations.

> I expect Egypt will occupy an eminent position among nations.

> I will participate in the reform of the youth and raising the standard of living in Egypt.

> And so I will not retire until I have done my complete duty to my country and my God.

Many of these references are responsible for the significantly high scores (Table 20.1) on the tag URGE:

> I *want* to play my part in the feminine movement of *reform*.

The remaining tag appearing in Table 20.1 is GOOD. This unexpected difference between the two groups stems mainly from an esthetic emphasis appearing in the Egyptian essays:

> Our house has a *beautiful* garden.

> The children are dressed in *beautiful* clothes.

> Our marriage ceremony will be *splendid* and *beautiful*.

Interpersonal structuring as a concept does appear to be useful in describing the Egyptian essays, at least insofar as it provides contrast between Egyptian and Radcliffe essays. Of the 15 significant differences found and listed in Table 20.1, 13 fit into the predicted pattern. Only a few of the predicted differences did not occur. One of these, CONTROL, was simply due to low frequency counts. The others were less central to the concept.

But suppose we reverse our focus and examine those tags that are high for the Radcliffe essays. Do any of these hint of a concern for interpersonal structuring? If not, how then have the Radcliffe students handled the structuring demands of the autobiography assignment?

RADCLIFFE RESULTS

Generally the Radcliffe essay patterns support the previous college student studies of Jacob (1957), Barton (1959), and others. A great amount of attention is given to the family and the companionship it offers. The emphasis on the family unit is reflected in the frequencies of the tag SMALL GROUP (Table 20.2).[3] The high degree of identity in the family is reflected in the extensive use of "we" and "our" (SELVES) in describing family activity. Structure and differentiation within the family is decidedly de-emphasized. Indeed as one Radcliffe student explicitly stresses:

> I would like to be the sweet, loveable, knitting person who always has cooky jars full and enough time to listen to her grandchildren's troubles. Yet I would like to be a young looking and acting grandma whom her children call by her first name.

The Radcliffe essays tend to emphasize the structure of time and place sequences. Often a dramatic scenario is used, giving names to yet unmet husbands and unborn children, and giving specific details of yet unbegun events:

> Right after my second child, Diane, was born, my husband's back was injured on his way to an emergency call one night. He was hit by a hit and run driver and was in the hospital for four months. During this time, I was forced to go to work in order to keep our children fed and clothed.

> We bought a 3000 acre ranch located about 140 miles north of Los Angeles near the Nevada border, but on the western slopes of the Sierras. The nearest town was fifteen miles away. David continued his work on wheat diseases and every once in the while found time to write a report for the people at Davis.

> My husband and I shall settle down in a home of our own and indulge in our hobbies. I can raise tropical goldfish and carve bad pieces of sculpture and discuss nothing in particular with my friends.

---

[3] The tag SMALL GROUP focuses in these documents on references to the family per se. The second-order tag FAMILY is not useful here because it also includes extensive lists of household materials, and so on.

Such time and place structuring becomes reflected in significant differences (Table 20.2) for the tags TIME, SPACE, and QUANTITY. The frequent mention of travel in Europe and intimate family vacations causes high counts for the tag RECREATIONAL. The dramatic quality of the writing leads to higher scores on both OVERSTATE and UNDER-STATE, emphasizing contrast.

Taken together, the focus on a personal life within the companion-ship of the family, the dramatic specificity, and the emphasis on per-sonal and family pleasures, has led Gillespie and Allport to use G. Almond's (1950) term "privatism" in characterizing the Radcliffe essays. While a number of Radcliffe essays mention social work and community activities, these mentions are more in terms of a temporary personal outlet rather than an intensive concern for changes in society. The primary referent is the personal world of the family.

SUMMARY AND CONCLUSIONS

This chapter has outlined a concept of interpersonal structuring, specifying how it should be manifest in both a broad, second-order Harvard III category loosely titled SIGN-AUTHORITY and in a pattern of tags including GUIDE, CONTROL, FOLLOW, MALE-ROLE, FEMALE-ROLE, JOB-ROLE, HIGHER-STATUS, LOWER-STATUS, OUGHT, IDEAL-VALUE, plus a number of the tags considering institutional specificity. As a study in one aspect of dictionary validity, a set of Egyptian and Radcliffe "future autobiographies" were examined for differences in interpersonal structuring. The SIGN-AUTHORITY tag and the pattern of more specific tags were much as expected, showing statistically significant differences. The validation of interpersonal structuring thus appears to warrant further development and substantiation. Its mani-festation as a cultural pattern is clearly evident.

BIBLIOGRAPHY

Adorno, T. W., Else Frenkel-Brunswik, Daniel J. Levinson, and R. Nevitt Sanford (1950), *The Authoritarian Personality,* New York: Harper & Bros.

Almond, G. A. (1950), *The American People and Foreign Policy.* New York: Harcourt Brace.

Barton, Allen H. (1959), *Studying the Effects of College Education.* New Haven, Conn.: Edward W. Hazen Foundation.

Bass, Bernard M. (1955), "Authoritarianism or Acquiescence?" *Journal of Abnormal and Social Psychology,* Vol. 51, 616–623. Reprinted in Mednick, M., and S. Mednick, *Research in Personalities.* New York: Holt, Rinehart and Winston.

Dahlberg, F. M. (1963), "From Now to the Year 2,000." A.B. thesis, Radcliffe College.

Duijker, H. C. J., and N. H. Frijda (1960), *National Character and National Stereotypes.* Amsterdam: North Holland Publishing Company.

Gillespie, James M., and Gordon W. Allport (1955), *Youth's Outlook on the Future: A Cross-National Study,* New York: Doubleday.

Harris, George L. (1957), *Egypt.* New Haven, Conn.: Yale University Human Relations Area Files.

Jacob, Philip E. (1957), *Changing Values in College.* New York: Harper & Bros.

Melikian, Levon (1959), "Authoritarianism and Its Correlates in the Egyptian Culture and in the United States," *Journal of Social Issues,* Vol. 15, No. 3, 58–70.

Marjarian, Pergrouhi (1959), "Adjustment in the Family and Patterns of Family Living." *Journal of Social Issues.* Vol. 15: 3, 28–44.

CHAPTER TWENTY-ONE

Development and Applications of an Anthropological Dictionary[1]

Benjamin N. Colby
Museum of New Mexico

INTRODUCTION

Scholars have long been interested in folktale themes, motifs, and plots as indicators of culturally important characteristics (Boas, 1935; Lévi-Strauss, 1955; Thompson, 1955; Propp, 1958; Jacobs, 1959; and Opler, 1959). Psychologically oriented anthropologists have extended this interest to the study of Thematic Apperception Test stories to explore the relationships between culture and personality. However, these investigators have found it difficult to locate themes from projective test compositions that show low variation among individuals of the same culture and high variation between members of different cultures (DuBois, 1944; Vogt, 1951; Wallace, 1952; Kaplan, 1954; and Lindzey, 1961). For Thematic Apperception Tests, the difficulty is that the protocols are usually analyzed with categories designed for studying personality — which is everywhere heterogeneous — rather than for studying cultural character-

[1] The research reported on in this chapter was supported by NIH grants M-4711, M-4975, MH-08301, and MH-08854.
I wish to acknowledge my indebtedness to Professor Bert Kaplan for making available several unpublished Navajo and Zuni TAT stories.

istics that (by definition) are constant over a variety of personality types within the same culture. Here we describe our attempts to formulate categories for analyzing folktales, TAT's, and other projective materials on a *cultural* level.

Our strategy for constructing such categories has included a search for categories in culturally distinctive folktales. We felt that folktales are more culturally representative than other kinds of texts and would therefore be the best point of departure for developing cultural tags. A folktale is a collective product of many minds in a cultural group. Even if a people borrow from another society, they usually provide their own special stamp in the retelling.

After presenting our dictionary and discussing its evolution, we shall report on some preliminary work on validating the categories. For this aspect of our work we will draw on the analysis of Navajo and Zuni TAT compositions. We concentrate on the Navajo and Zuni comparisons because the tribes are already well described in the literature, and thus we can draw parallels between what is known (culturally) about the tribes and modal differences revealed in TAT responses.

THE EARLY DICTIONARIES

The first Anthropological Dictionary was a combination of tags from the Kluckhohn binary value categories (1956) and tags derived from folktale studies. The Kluckhohn value tags formed the nucleus, to which were added tags derived from an earlier Harvard Psychosociological Dictionary (many were subdivided or modified in the process) and tags from the folktale studies which were made up of words used in characterizing or synopsizing the folktales of a number of cultures we had studied previously. Other tags were brought in to test anthropologically interesting hypotheses. Preliminary tests of this dictionary were made to see whether the tag categories would in fact prove useful in differentiating between cultures. As a result, some basic revisions were attempted, resulting in what we shall refer to as the second dictionary.

In revising the tag definitions for the second dictionary we attempted to deal with the high variation in frequency between specific entry words of each tag. High-frequency words would often "mask" important low-frequency words, and without retrievals a simple tag tally did not provide the more detailed information needed for interpretation. Further, we found that many of the low-frequency tags had to be lumped together into larger tags if statistically significant results were to be obtained.

In addition to these changes, we also changed tag titles. The most frequent entry words were sometimes chosen as names to represent the tag previously misrepresented by a low-frequency entry word title; shifts in large numbers of entry words or additions of many new entry words called for a different tag title that would be more appropriate to the changed tag; and in some cases, tag titles that were self-explanatory were chosen.

Upon the completion of the second dictionary, we made a pilot study of ten cultures. This resulted in a number of interesting findings. For example, tags measuring what we thought to be a latent sex imagery were complementary to the tags of manifest sex imagery. The latent sex category included tags containing references to possible symbols for both genitalia and sexual actions. The overt sex category concerned direct references to affection and sexual acts. From this finding, one might infer that inhibition in matters of sex may result in indirect outlets in the symbolic content of folktales. (The rank-order correlation for this was $-.55$, prob. $< .06$).

On the other hand, a coincident rather than complementary relationship was found for what were first called latent and overt orality tags, but which may more cautiously be called a possible measure of latent "gastrointestinal" concern ($r = +.66$, prob. $< .05$). The gastrointestinal measure consisted of the tags FULL, RELEASE, and EMPTY. The overt orality measure consisted of the tags ORAL and FOOD. These tags showed significant covariation and so may be presumed to be tapping a common variable.

Among other coincident distributions of this kind was one for what are now the RATIONAL and TRUTH tags. The first dictionary had three tags concerned with rationality: FOOLISH, WISE, and PLAN. Together, these three tags were in coincident distribution with the TRUTH tag when compared along a continuum of rank order of frequency. Two exceptions arose which are out of coincident distribution by not more than two cultures. These findings suggested that a single underlying characteristic existed which was tapped by these three tags and by the TRUTH tag. Consequently, the entries for FOOLISH, WISE, and PLAN were lumped together to make a new tag called RATIONAL.

Further changes of this kind were made in the dictionary, and a new sample of seven cultures was run to test the validity of the results of the previous study. Findings concerning latent and overt sex and orality were not repeated in this study but the RATIONAL-TRUTH correlation was.

Perhaps the most exciting finding that emerged from the studies using the second dictionary revolves around a combination of the HEALTH and SICKNESS tags (which separately are of very low frequency). In both samples, we noticed that cultures emphasizing health and sickness de-emphasized various types of kinesthetic activity requiring use of the muscles in athletic and other strenuous activities (as measured by the KINESTHETIC tag). We also observed that a SHAME tag was inversely related to the KINESTHETIC tag and positively correlated (at the .05 level) with the combined scorings of HEALTH and SICKNESS. A hand retrieval of sentences containing words of the SHAME tag suggested that the correlating variable had to do with the feelings of the people involved rather than with acts of shaming per se. Considering these tags to be some measure of an emotional state, we checked other emotional categories. In the seven culture run we found a correlation of HEALTH and SICKNESS with the ANGER tag at the .01 level of significance. Thus it appeared that those cultures emphasizing kinesthetic activity were less likely to be preoccupied with emotional states and frustrations relating to persons and were more concerned with satisfaction or disappointment in mastering the physical, nonsocial environment. This was supported when a study of relationship between KINESTHETIC and other categories revealed a correlation with the EFFICACY tag (which may possibly measure a concern with achievement, success, and efficacy primarily in nonsocial matters) at the .01 level of significance. If true, KINESTHETIC cultures are less concerned with personal emotions and social relationships in their activities and more concerned with efficacy and achievement in themselves. HEALTH-SICKNESS cultures are more caught up with personal emotions in their activities and are more likely to be preoccupied with the social consequences of their activities. We will explore these interrelationships further in future work.

Drawing upon the results of these validation studies with the second dictionary, we consolidated what we had learned in a third revision. This revision included only tags which had been shown to have sufficiently high frequency counts to be useful and which distinguished between cultures in our samples. It was thus a significant step toward the creation of a dictionary consisting of tags measuring cultural rather then personality differences and representing variables of theoretical significance to anthropologists. In addition, we had come to be increasingly interested in measuring the different kinds of plots developed by different cultures, so that the categories were arranged to relate to this interest.

TAG ORGANIZATION OF THE THIRD ANTHROPOLOGICAL DICTIONARY

The tags of the third anthropological dictionary are grouped into five main sections: (1) Plot Structure, (2) Behavioral Systems, (3) Mental Processes, (4) Analytic-Experimental, and (5) Second-Order Tags. The second-order tags could be redistributed among the first three sections, but because they are not independent they have been kept separate to avoid confusion in correlation studies.

Plot Structure

This section is subdivided according to the *characters* in the plot structure and *action* or *plot movement*. For instance, the first group of the *characters* subsection consists of family roles, an area of major concern to anthropologists. The KIN-AFFINAL tag lists terms for husband, wife, and in-laws. The husband and wife subdivisions can be used conjunctively with the SEX-MALE and SEX-FEMALE tags to study the ratio of references to men and women in stories, which may well be a significant factor in distinguishing between cultures. The KIN-CONSANGUINEAL tag lists lineal, collateral, and nonnuclear family kin terms, a subdivision based on components traditionally used in studies of kinship semantics. The degree to which the extended family participates in myths and folktales may prove to be a revealing characteristic easily tallied with this subdivision.

The CHILDREN tag focuses on children and the way children are conceptualized. For example, Americans tend to glorify childhood and give much more attention to children than the French, who ignore their children and look upon childhood as a state to be grown out of as soon as possible. The Germans are child centered in still another way. This tag should illuminate these differences in a study of short stories from these three countries which is planned shortly.

The second group of the *characters* subsection consists of pronoun tags. The three-person tags can yield a variety of measures. One is the degree of conversation reported in the text as indicated by the frequency of first- and second-person pronouns. With the degree of conversation as a controlled variable, it may then be possible to derive measures of detachment versus identification from ratios among first-, second-, and third-person frequencies. Though the PERSON-OTHER tag counts only the plural of the third person (along with the second person), the singulars for the third person are in the SEX-MALE and SEX-FEMALE tags so that an over-all count of third-person references can be made by a combination of the two tags with the third-person plural subdivision of the PERSON-OTHER tag. This measure may be very useful in studying personal relationships in folktales and TAT's. We have given a detailed description of this section of the dictionary in order to illustrate the distinctive kinds of emphases represented in it. However, we shall limit our description of the rest of the dictionary in order to conserve space.

The first group of tags in the *plot movement* subsection is designed to indicate basic orientation and movement in space and time. The second group of tags consists of tags referring to actions, such as COMMUNICATION and WORK, and problem situations, such as DIFFICULTY and TRIED. Tags in this area should reflect cultural differences in the kinds of pursuits actually carried on in a society, such as hunting and agriculture, and also basic differences in orientations to action in general. Many of the focal points in plot structure center around problem situations, and tags under this heading will aid the study of the various ways cultures cope with a wide range of difficulties.

Behavioral Systems

The second part of the dictionary treats the three behavioral systems: *personality, social,* and *cultural.* The *personality* subsection has been divided into body, emotions, and abilities. The *body* subdivision contains tags relating to the body and the living process which are important constituents of the self-image.

As far as the body is concerned, for example, recent developments in theories of psychosomatic processes have made us curious about whether some cultures emphasize certain parts of the body more than others and whether any other characteristics correlate with such emphasis. It may be possible to relate our results to various theories about body boundary image. Hopefully, differences in this area will also relate to emotional differences that can be measured by the tags designed to tap emotional dispositions. These are among the most conceptually clear and important tags of the dictionary.

The *social system* tags all deal with various aspects of social relations. They are divided into tags representing different kinds and levels of cooperation and control. The *cultural system* tags are, of course, particularly important and will be used for studying cultural values and norms. Of particular interest also are object tags, which are new to the dictionary. In the past, we omitted object words because they were often so specific to a particular culture that cross-cultural comparisons were difficult. The word elephant, for example, might be frequent in stories from India but would never appear in Eskimo tales. If some of these object words were to be included in other tags, their sporadic high frequency would mask the effect of the tags' other entry words. Now, however, we have included many object words, although unanticipated objects peculiar to a particular culture will still end up on leftover lists. We have, for instance, divided the NATURAL OBJECT tag into ANIMAL, PLANT, and INANIMATE, a division made with the Rorschach categories in mind. We believe that significant differences between these generalized kinds of natural objects may well relate to other cross-cultural variables. Similarly, we have constructed another tag called, for want of a better name, GREEK ELEMENTS, consisting of words for earth, air, fire, and water. The tag may be useful in cross-cultural studies of metaphors and symbolism. Thus some tags from the first dictionary that were excluded from the second dictionary because they were considered culture-specific were reincorporated into the third dictionary.

Mental Processes

These are divided into three main classes: *explanation, description,* and *perception.* Explanation tags will be used to study logical processes and to inventory the types of questions asked. The description categories deal with size, form, and quantity and already have shown interesting cultural emphases, as have the categories of *perception.*

Analytic-Experimental

The analytic-experimental tags measure such things as connective words related to the logical structure of folktales. Other tags are intended for studies of idioms and special word relations.

Second-Order Tags

Most entry words of the second-order tags correspond exactly to those of the Harvard III Dictionary. Those that do not are similar enough to permit direct comparison and were included especially for this reason.

EXAMPLE FINDINGS OF A PILOT STUDY

Throughout the discussion of our dictionary, we have tried to convey our method of constructing categories. It has involved several stages of interaction between data and dictionary with modifications of the dictionary at each stage. We will now discuss some of the results of a pilot study intended to shed further light on the usefulness of certain categories. For this pilot study, the TAT protocols of 15 Navajo and 12 Zuni veterans (of similar age) were used (Kaplan, 1957).

The first finding demonstrates a link between the frequency of a particular class of preoccupations in TAT texts and the main economic orientation in Zuni culture.

In the TAT stories of the Zuni, there is more concern with forms of moisture than in the Navajo stories (Table 21.1).

TABLE 21.1. Moisture Concern*

Entry Words	Frequency per Hundred Words	
	Navajo	*Zuni*
snow	.018	.071
snowing	.007	.000
rain	.007	.029
raining	.000	.004
rainy	.000	.004
clouds	.007	.025
TOTAL	.039	.133

* Totals are significant at the .05 level with the *t* Test.

The Zuni are crop growers. During the summer they need rain to mature their corn, and during the winter they need snow to supply the early spring moisture to germinate their corn. The meteorological concern of the Zuni contrasts with the sheep-herding, nonagricultural Navajo who are their neighbors and directly relates to the traditional

Zuni means of livelihood. Thus, by a purely statistical count of the frequency with which meteorological terms appear in TAT's we have an idea of their relative importance.

The General Inquirer was also used to investigate subjective statements about dominant themes. A number of anthropologists who have studied Navajo life have commented upon the Navajo theme of travel and movement (Astrov, 1950; Hoijer, 1951; Kluckhohn, 1949; Landar, 1959; and Spencer, 1957). There seems to be a mental set that predisposes the Navajo to think in terms of travel. In their conversations, myths, and rituals, Navajos describe the circumstances of travel at great length. We decided to test this with a TRAVEL tag, composed of the following entry words: bridge, crawl, creep, crossroad, departure, embark, expedition, highway, horseback, journey, road, roadside, sail, street, stroll, lane, march, path, travel, traveler, vagabond, voyage, walk, wander, wayside.

The mean index scores of Navajos and Zunis for the TRAVEL tag were .273 and .175, respectively, which is a statistically significant (.05 level, *t* test) difference. We then examined the retrievals and found that the entry words walk, wander, travel, sail, horseback, and creep were, with one exception, used to indicate actual travel. They appeared more frequently in the Navajo (.170) than in the Zuni (.065) protocols. But entry words such as street, road, and bridge appeared more often in the Zuni stories. Further study indicated that the Navajo used words in the TRAVEL tag to represent the idea of travel and the Zuni used words in the TRAVEL tag for orientation and setting.

There are other differences in over-all tag frequency which appeared to be important and will warrant further study. The Navajo stories tell of individuals who are more expressive in their sadness and are more intimately concerned with their close relatives than the Zuni characters, who are sad for direct, personal reasons (because they lack friendship or have been rejected by others or because of their own misbehavior or misfortune).

A look at the AFFECTION retrievals showed not only a higher frequency of AFFECTION tags for the Navajo (which had been predicted on the basis of personal contact with Navajo and Zuni Indians) but also more intimate demonstrations of affection by Navajos between men and women, especially husband and wife, as reflected in their sentences. The Zuni sentences were usually more formal and perfunctory. The general impression from comparing the two groups of sentences is that the Zuni stories are emotionally more "shallow" in interpersonal affection than the Navajo stories.

Though the Zuni are more interested in social power and dominance as measured by the DOMINANCE tag, the Navajo are concerned with physical power, use of the muscles, and bodily contact. The KINESTHETIC, POWER, and TIRED tags show an emphasis on the use of muscles. The WANT tag also shows a focus on the development of physical strength in Navajo stories. An unexpectedly high count for the KEEP tag was due to the high number of times the entry word "hold" appeared in Navajo stories. In most cases, this seemed to indicate bodily contact (to hold on to someone).

Of great importance (particularly for cognition studies) is the question of picture structuring and tag pervasiveness. Some culture themes may appear almost randomly in specific pictures but persistently and pervasively show up in the tag counts no matter what pictures are used. On the other hand, a picture can be so structured that similar stories are told by members of both cultures, revealing little cultural or personality information. And finally, a picture can evoke entirely different responses from each cultural group.

A tag tally by story number rather than by individuals was made to study those tags showing the greatest cultural variability by picture.[2] For example, TRAVEL A words are frequent in the Navajo stories for TAT picture 9. On the other hand, Zunis use more TRAVEL A words in their responses to picture 20. Considering all the pictures, however, the Navajo interest in travel was much stronger than that of the Zuni. Twenty-two tags showing the greatest cultural difference by picture were selected for retrieval. Of these, 13 (ranging in average frequency from .015 to .108 with a mean of .042) failed to reveal sufficiently consistent differences by picture. The nine remaining tags ranged in average frequency from .040 to .290 with a mean of .102. But even with these latter tags, the differences were not large. Higher

[2] Here as elsewhere in this paper I treat consistent differences between the two groups as cultural. Perhaps "nonpersonality nonchance characteristics" would be more accurate though confusing. Clearly some of the differences between the Zuni and Navajo stories reflect differences in education and acquaintance with the dominant Anglo culture of the area, both being higher for the Zuni. These may not be considered cultural factors in the idiom of some, but I prefer to so include them. Other consistent differences arise as a result of the test situation, different attitude of the test administrator, and so forth.

frequency tags and a much larger sample are necessary. Two of these nine cases will be described.

Picture 18 shows a man standing awkwardly with shoulders back and eyes closed. The hands of another person are on him but the darkness of the picture obscures all but the hands of the second person. Eight of the 15 Navajos said the man was drunk, had difficulty walking or traveling home, and was being helped by someone. In another case, the man was said to have difficulty walking because he was sleepy. There were only two case in the Navajo stories where the hands belonged to someone intent on doing evil. In the Zuni stories, only 2 of the 12 stories involved the idea of drunkenness, while 5 out of the 12 dealt with robbery or murder.

Another difference was noted for picture 1 of a boy with a violin. The Navajos spoke of "wondering" or "thinking" about how to play or fix the violin. In contrast, the Zunis tell stories emphasizing the actual playing of the violin and spoke more often about career and ambition. In the only Zuni story that emphasized the learning process itself, the boy "followed the directions." This tendency fits in very well with our ethnographic experience. The Navajo mode of learning is one of observing and then doing rather than one of formal instruction in which a person describes step-by-step just what to do, which seems to be the Zuni method.

The notion of contrastive opposition developed by. F. de Saussure (1959) in linguistics can also be applied to thematic emphasis such as the Navajo concern for travel. Twelve out of 15 Navajos responded to one of the Murray TAT pictures that shows a group of men resting or sleeping by stating that the men were resting in the middle of a journey. The Zuni, on the other hand, thought of the men in the picture either as resting from work or as lazy or out of work. Only 1 of the 12 Zunis mentioned travel.

While the Navajo idea of rest is a conceptual opposite of travel in one direction, "home" is its opposite in another. The Navajo think of home more as an end state or goal after a period of travel. This conception appeared in Navajo stories more than twice as often as in Zuni stories. Further, "home" appears more frequently at the conclusion of Navajo stories than in Zuni stories. This is shown in the tables that follow. Table 21.2 shows the gradual increase in frequency for the word "home" in Navajo TAT stories from the begin-

TABLE 21.2. Plot Structure of Home in Navajo TAT's

1.	.	.	.	.	.	17	
2.	.	.	.	.	.	.	20
3.	.	.	.	.	.	.	24
4.	.	.	.	.	.	.	24
5.	.	.	.	.	.	.	. 28

ning (first part) to the end (fifth part) of the stories. The Kendall's rank correlation coefficient *tau* between this sample and a linear increasing model is .95. Table 21.3 shows the pattern of frequency for

TABLE 21.3. Plot Structure of Home in Zuni TAT's

1.	.	.	.	.	.	11
2.	.	.	.	.	.	10
3.	.	.	.	.	.	. 16
4.	.	.	.	.	.	. 15
5.	.	.	.	.	.	12

the word "home" in Zuni TAT stories from the beginning (first part) to the end (fifth part) of the stories. The Kendall's rank correlation coefficient between this sample and a linear increasing model is .20.

When a Navajo arrives home, it is usually at the end of the story; there is nothing more to tell. For the Zunis, though, something may be going on in the home that is important in the respondent's story.

This particular type of analysis involving the shape or structure of narrative concern may eventually lead to the mapping of one or more "cognitive templates" (Colby, 1966a and b) for the construction of stories, either in TAT's or folktales, which are used by natives when producing stories. In the most recent studies of Eskimo and Japanese folktales, 23 percent of the independent tags showed significant patterns at better than the .01 level of significance (using the chi-square flatness test).

This concludes the discussion of our work with and on the Anthropological Dictionary. In addition to using it to describe cultural differences expressed in TAT's and folktales, we hope to test various theories concerning the functions of folktales and myths and provide some evidence on the relationships between themes expressed in projective materials and overt behavior. We also have plans to develop a dictionary in Ixil (a Mayan language of Guatemala) for a more microscopic analysis of variations on a theme in a single culture.

BIBLIOGRAPHY

Astrov, M. (1950), "The Concept of Motion as the Psychological Leitmotif of Navaho Life and Literature." *Journal of American Folklore,* Vol. 63, 46–47.

Boas, F. (1935), *Kwakiutl Culture as Reflected in Mythology.* Memoirs of the American Folklore Society.

Colby, B. N. (1966*a*), "The Analysis of Culture Content and the Patterning of Narrative Concern in Texts." *American Anthropologist,* Vol. 68, No. 2, Part 1, 374–388.

———— (1966*b*), "Culture Patterns in Narrative." *Science,* Vol. 151, No. 3712, 793–798.

DuBois, C. (1944), *The People of the Alor.* Minneapolis, Minn.: University of Minnesota Press.

Kaplan, B. (ed.) (1957), *Primary Records in Culture and Personality.* Vol. I. Madison, Wis.: The Microcard Foundation.

Hoijer, H. (1951), "Cultural Implications of Some Navaho Linguistic Categories." *Language,* Vol. 27, 117.

Jacobs, M. (1959), *The Content and Style of an Oral Literature.* New York: Viking Press, Viking Publications in Anthropology, Vol. 26.

Kaplan, B. (1954), *A Study of Rorschach Responses in Four Cultures.* Papers of the Peabody Museum of Archeology and Ethnology, Harvard University, Vol. 42, No. 2.

de Saussure, F. (1959), *Course in General Linguistics.* New York: The Philosophical Library, Inc.

Kluckhohn, C. (1949), "The Philosophy of the Navaho Indians." In F. C. S. Northrup (ed.), *Ideological Differences and World Order.* New Haven, Conn.: Yale University Press, 1949.

———— (1956), "Toward a Comparison of Value-Emphasis in Different Cultures." In L. D. White (ed.), *The State of Social Sciences.* Chicago: University of Chicago Press.

Landar, H. J. (1959), "Four Navaho Summer Tales: Part Three." *Journal of American Folklore,* Vol. 72, 298–309.

Lévi-Strauss, C. (1955), "The Structural Study of Myth. *Journal of American Folklore,* Vol. 68, 428.

Lindzey, G. (1961), *Projective Techniques and Cross-Cultural Research.* New York: Appleton-Century-Crofts.

Opler, M. E. (1959), "Component Assemblage and Theme in Cultural Integration and Differentiation." *American Anthropologist,* Vol. 61, 955–964.

Propp, V. (1958), *Morphology of the Folktale.* Indiana University Monograph of the International Journal of American Linguistics, Publication 10.

Spencer, K. (1957), *Mythology and Value: An Analysis of Navaho Chantway Myths.* Philadelphia: American Folklore Society.

Thompson, S. (1955), *Motif-Index of Literature.* Bloomington: Indiana University Press.

Vogt, Evon Z. (1951), *Navaho Veterans: A Study of Changing Values.* Papers of the Peabody Museum of Archeology and Ethnology. Harvard University, Vol. 41, No. 1.

Wallace, A. F. C. (1952), *The Modal Personality Structure of the Tuscarora Indians as Revealed by the Rorschach Test.* Washington, D.C.: Smithsonian Institute, Bureau of American Ethnology, Bulletin 150.

OTHER APPLICATIONS

Two Special Directions

Finally, we come to two studies that fall outside the six major areas of research. The first article (Stone, Dunphy, and Bernstein) discusses problems of understanding purchasing behavior in terms of the psychological image formed of the product and the sociological network of formal and informal human communications. In the second article (Ellis and Favat), we turn to a discussion of the application of the General Inquirer to literary analysis, with illustrations from a study of Mark Twain's Huckleberry Finn.

The "product image" article summarizes several "open-ended" survey strategies in relation to building models in business. This is the only paper in Part II that considers the important topic of content analysis applications to survey research. Other General Inquirer analyses under way in survey research are adding to our knowledge and capabilities in this area. For example, Frisbie and Sudman (1966) have shown that the General Inquirer approach can handle many of the routine categorization tasks currently made manually by coders at survey research centers. The "product image" chapter outlines several research strategies that would not be feasible without computer content analysis assistance.

The paper on literary analysis utilizes the Harvard III Dictionary to study recurrent themes in Huckleberry Finn. *While only a few trends are illustrated in the article, it is evident that the basic categories provided by the general dictionary provide a useful reference for studying themes that have interested those who have studied* Huckleberry

Finn *in the past. The chapter also points up the usefulness of the retrieval listings in bringing together sentences from different parts of a text. As cited in I. A. Richard's quote at the head of Chapter 2, the overlap between the social sciences and literary analysis is more than has been commonly realized. Perhaps past theoretical terminology and measurement procedures have contributed to the maintenance of this overdrawn separation.*

CHAPTER TWENTY-TWO

The Analysis of Product Image

Philip J. Stone
Harvard University

Dexter C. Dunphy
Harvard University

Alex Bernstein
Simulmatics Corporation

INTRODUCTION

Ours is a society of packaged commodities. Detergents, political candidates, legislative bills, community action programs, minority group causes, and new model automobiles are all products competing for the awareness, attention, acceptance, and supportive action (purchase, vote, and so on) of the public. Far from being a simple entity, a product is a complex stimulus, communicated both formally and informally, and perceived in complex ways. This chapter considers the application of various open-ended techniques for studying the images of products and the organizations that produced them. We outline strategies for comparing product-image similarity, both as presented and perceived, as well as methods for assessing and predicting the over-all impact of these images as formally and informally communicated to the consumer. Much of our experience is drawn from applied content analysis research conducted for clients by the Simulmatics Corporation in New York City.

An investigator cannot necessarily assume that a simple equation exists between the image presented in the mass media and the image retained by the consumer. The mass media present but one source of image. People are also influenced by what others are saying about the product and doing with it. Product representatives with direct contact include retail sales and service personnel. "Unofficial" representatives include the new owner, the person who has casually heard about the product, and the person who very much wants the product but cannot afford it. All these people are likely to have attitudes about the product, and, inasmuch as these attitudes have conversational value within a social interaction, they may be discussed at length. In some cases, the content of a discussion may be restricted by norms about what an "official" representative may properly say, yet the representative's attitude toward the product may be effectively communicated nonetheless. Some persons may win respect as being informed about a product, and so may have a particular effect on the opinions of others.

Traditional research into product image has concentrated mainly on the image of the product as conveyed through mass media. Relatively little attention has been given to changes in that image as it is received and discussed by the audience.

COMPONENTS OF AN IMAGE

We find it important to distinguish between three main aspects of a product image. The first is what is referred to in Chapter 2 of this book as a "theme"; this may take the form of a simple story of what happened with a product when certain specified conditions prevailed. "My neighbor's 1961 X brand car simply fell apart when it was left outside in the winter" would be an example of such a theme. The second aspect is the image proper, such as "X brand cars are inexpensive but have a poor finish." The third aspect is the net evaluation, such as "X brand cars may have a poor finish, but in California weather they are a good buy." It should be noted that the same or similar image information may result in a different evaluation, depending on its relative importance to the individual. In the same way, a number of factors may affect whether a set of themes results in a particular image.

In this chapter, we consider how themes, images, and evaluations are affected both by psychological predispositions of the audience and by patterns of communication within the audience. The application of a model for each process is proposed, and the role of content analysis is described.

A PSYCHOLOGICAL MODEL

Following the thesis put forth by Stefflre (1965, and in press), we hypothesize that the way a person responds to a new product will depend on the relation of the new stimulus to the context provided by his past experience. To quote Stefflre,

> "Each group behaves toward the new things in a manner that is similar to the manner in which they behave toward items they see the new items similar to. Groups or individuals may vary in terms of (1) their notions of what is similar to what, and (2) what items elicit what behaviors."

In order to utilize this notion for content analysis of product image, we need to know three things about the respondents:

1) their behavior toward past items they perceive as similar to the new item

2) their perception of past items they perceive as similar to the new item

3) their perception of the new item

(Stefflre, 1965, 12)

Several procedures may be used to ascertain the similarity between the perception of the new item and of the past items. Stefflre proposes the use of rating scales, free associations, and distributional similarity in spoken language. It is to the last of these alternatives that content analysis may make a useful and highly sensitive contribution.

In the context of studying synonymy, Rubenstein and Goodenough (1965) instructed subjects to write two sentences each at least ten words in length using a particular word as a noun. Each subject made up sentences for 50 words, the sentences in fact averaging 13.5 words each. The similarities and differences between sentences for two particular words could then be compared (Goodenough, 1965) by making a General Inquirer sentence tag tally for each set. For example, the two words "car" and "automobile" were compared [1] using a special

---

[1] The research design was constructed such that people who wrote sentences for "car" were different from those who wrote sentences for "automobile," thus avoiding the subjects having a conscious contrast.

dictionary consisting of the tags SPEED, ACCIDENTS, MOVEMENT, NEG-
ATIVE, MAINTENANCE, UP-TO-DATE, MACHINERY, USEFUL, POSITIVE,
PERSON-REFERENCES, PLACE-REFERENCES, ACQUISITION, LOOKS. As
an exercise, the reader might wish to guess which tags are most associated with which "car" and which were most associated with "automobile." In fact, the tag tally profiles were quite similar for most tags,
including SPEED, LOOKS, MACHINERY, UP-TO-DATE, and MOVEMENT.
The word "automobile" was slightly more associated with ACCIDENTS
and NEGATIVE references. The "car" was much more associated with
POSITIVE and USEFUL, but also ACQUISITION and MAINTENANCE. Using
a different dictionary, Goodenough also compared the sentences for
the words "journey" and "voyage." The word "journey" was found to
connote more discomfort and hardship, while the term "voyage" con-
noted more physical danger. It would seem travel agents do well to
use other terms.

Several advantages of using an open-ended procedure for assessing
perceived similarity are evident. Rating scales have the limitations of
confining the respondent to the alternatives provided by the experimenter. By encouraging the construction of sentences concerning the
product and other related products, multifaceted imagery including
significant themes may be elicited. A dictionary can be constructed and
adjusted, using mis-tagging and leftover lists and cues for adjustment,
until the data have been adequately described.

An interesting alternative open-ended format for assessing perceived
similarity is to have the words "I think of X as . . ." on a sheet of
paper followed by 15 or 20 empty lines to be filled in by the respondent. This format provides not only a number of themes, images, and
evaluations concerning each product but also records the sequence in
which the responses are brought forth. In Chapter 17 of this book,
McLaughlin describes one application of this format to the somewhat
different problem of studying self-identity, the instructions in this case
reading "I think of myself as. . . ."

Open-ended information can also be important in the Stefflre model
in ascertaining the events that led up to a past purchasing behavior.
For example Zola (1963) asked 66 Italian, 87 Irish, and 43 Anglo-
Saxon patients in an "open-ended focussed interview" about the factors
that led up to their consulting a doctor. In brief, Italians tended to go
to the doctor when the symptoms interfered with social or personal
relations (such as making them irritable). Another Italian pattern was
to seek treatment when they experienced a situational or interpersonal

crisis; when everything else goes wrong, they are likely to decide to take care of a continuing medical symptom by going to the doctor. The Irish tended to go only after they received the sanction of others, when the responsibility for making the visit could be imputed to someone else. The Anglo-Saxons tend to go primarily when the symptoms interfered with their work or physical activity.

When viewed in this way, the seeking of medical aid is a decision contingent on a sequence of prior events, the sequence differing for various ethnic groups. Open-ended techniques become important in studying these history patterns, whether it is seeking medical aid, buying a car, or deciding to write a congressman. While hand analysis is quite satisfactory for small samples, larger national samples become much more feasible with an assist from the computer.

Within a psychological model such as Stefflre's, content analysis can play a significant role in the analysis of open-ended material, both in ascertaining the perception of items and in obtaining the sequence of past decision behaviors.

A COMMUNICATIONS MODEL

The interplay of mass media and interpersonal communication has been studied with a "community controversy" model developed by Abelson and Bernstein (1963). The model has been applied to a variety of situations, including fluoridation issues and school board elections revolving around *de facto* desegregation. Surveys are used to assess how the issues are perceived, to test exposure to particular media of communications, and to identify the characteristics of other persons in the community with whom the issue is likely to be discussed. As Abelson and Bernstein describe,

> The model specifies processes by which each individual may change as the campaign progresses. Changes can be effected in two ways: 1) by exposure to public "assertions" from "sources," these appearing in communication "channels" (broadly defined), 2) via conversations with others who have a stand on the issue and who may also make assertions.

Part of the input to the model then is content of local communication channels:

> The standard local communication channels are represented in the computer, and can be loaded each simulated week with appropriate assertions from sources. (For research purposes, the distribution of asser-

tions would be pre-determined and used as an independent variable. For field purposes, the assertions would instead be determined by the content analysis of actual channels.)

(Abelson and Bernstein, 1963)

Given the appearance of certain assertions in certain channels, the model can predict how these will be perceived and the extent to which they become part of informal communication patterns and so result in a modification of the existing product image. Some issues may spread rapidly and forcefully through informal communication channels to affect attitudes and subsequent voting or consumption patterns. Others may be salient in the media but "sleepers" in informal communications and so ultimately may fail to influence action.

Much of our work at Simulmatics has been concerned with content analysis of text in mass media. Using a dictionary described later, we are concerned not only with the isolation of particular themes or assertions but also with assessing over-all change in attitude toward a topic, a change that is often noted by a conspicuous absence in further mention, or an over-all change in tone in repeating old themes.

A fully fledged monitoring system designed to maintain contact with fluctuations in product image would have two aspects: first, a consistent monitoring of mass media, including those media directed at particular groups of specialists and representatives (for instance, trade journals); and second, a set of open-ended survey research techniques to monitor "gossip," not only as stemming from the mass media but also as completely arising and circulating in informal channels. The approach has to be open-ended because of the difficulty in anticipating what issues may arise in informal communication. Giving careful attention to rapport, the research might include probes as to what the respondent has heard about the product in recent conversations, what he thinks his retailer thinks about it, what his neighbor thinks about it, and so on. In order to be sensitive to continuous changes in image, the investigator must pick up information as it is reported and the sources to which it is accredited by the respondent.

In a large-scale survey, different aspects of an image can be picked up and monitored, both geographically and within various strata of consumers. The relative salience of certain aspects of the image in the mass media can be compared with the relative salience of the same aspects in the minds of the respondents. The analysis must also be able to pick up new attitudes and themes as they are engendered and spread within informal communication. Those products that represent complex stimuli (for instance, an election issue or a new model automobile) pose major problems when it comes to analyzing the themes, images, and evaluations brought forth in open-ended survey material. It is at this point that the capacity of the computer to content analyze such information becomes a key resource.

GENERAL INQUIRER DICTIONARIES FOR MEASURING PRODUCT AND COMPANY IMAGES

We have been developing product-image dictionaries and scoring routines designed to measure the three aspects of product image discussed earlier. We have used different dictionaries to assess images of competing products and political candidates and to monitor changes in these images over time within trade journals, promotional literature, and survey responses. Table 22.1 illustrates some of the dictionary categories used for assessing more general patterns of commercial product image. In the example given, "product properties" are divided into lists of assets and liabilities, the assets including STRENGTH, VERSATILITY, ECONOMY, RELIABILITY, and APPEARANCE, the liabilities including WEAKNESS and EXPENSE. By checking for the qualifiers, an assessment is made of the evaluative content of the image. Thus the tag MANY plus the tag ASSETS combine to give an evaluation *HIGH-RATE,* as does the combination of FEW and LIABILITIES. Similarly an INCREASE in STRENGTH is scored as being *SUM-IMPROVEMENT,* while an INCREASE in MAINTENANCE would be a *SUM-DECLINE.*

In addition to such general categories, particular dictionaries adapted to the study of particular kinds of products have categories relevant to those kinds of products. For example, if the product is a piece of machinery, words and phrases have to be included in special categories for specifying major parts and functions of the machine. Retrieval procedures can then be used to separate out and analyze sentences referring to these aspects.

A number of categories within a product-image dictionary may be devoted to the image of the producing company rather than to the particular product. Very often the product image is strongly influenced by the company image, and so categories relating to the relative stability of the company, its policies, delivery, and servicing are highly relevant. Considerable attention is often warranted also for categories

TABLE 22.1. Tag Categories of a Product Image Dictionary

PRODUCT PROPERTIES	INSTITUTIONAL-REFERENCES
STRENGTH	ROLES
VERSATILITY	ORGANIZATION
ECONOMY	MANAGEMENT
RELIABILITY	FINANCE
APPEARANCE	MARKETING
TOTAL ASSETS	CONSUMPTION
WEAKNESS	SCIENTIFIC
EXPENSE	TECHNOLOGICAL
TOTAL LIABILITIES	
	PRODUCT-AREAS
QUANTITY	TRANSPORTATION
MANY — LARGE	DOMESTIC
FEW — SMALL	EDUCATION
METRICS	DEFENSE
RELATIONAL	ENGINEERING
TOTAL QUANTITY	
	MATERIALS
HIGH-RATE	COMPONENTS
LOW-RATE	ACTIONS
CHANGE	NEED
INCREASE	USE
DECREASE	FACILITATE
STASIS	COMMUNICATE
TRANSFORM	PROCESS
TOTAL CHANGE	STRESS
SUM-DECLINE	LOGIC
SUM-IMPROVEMENT	CAUSE
TIME	NOT
PAST	
PRESENT	STYLE
FUTURE	EMPHASIS
UNIT	UNDEREMPHASIS
TOTAL TIME	EMOTIONAL
	EVALUATION
	GOOD
	BAD

emphasizing different orientations to action on the part of the company: Is the company perceived as focused on research and development? On efficient marketing? Is it past, present, or future oriented?

Some special content analysis categories are needed for each product-image research problem, but the kinds of categories employed are fairly standard and the basic strategy is transferable from one application to another. As we develop more experience in a broader range of contexts, we believe we can evolve a highly efficient and sensitive general-purpose instrument for image analysis.

SUMMARY

We have outlined over-all strategies that we believe hold considerable promise for the study of product image. These strategies are new in that computer-aided content analysis of open-ended material can be used to map the presentation and perception of a product. By utilizing research designs that go beyond the simple tabulation of characteristics of the overt image in the mass media, a comprehensive analysis can be undertaken to determine the attitudes and predict the actions of consumers.

BIBLIOGRAPHY

Abelson, R., and A. Bernstein (1963), "A Computer Simulation Model of Community Referendum Controversies." *Public Opinion Quarterly,* Vol. 27, 93–122.

Goodenough, J., personal communication, 1965.

Rubenstein, H., and J. B. Goodenough (1965), "Contextual Correlates of Synonymy." *Communications of the Association for Computing Machinery,* Vol. 8, 627–633.

Stefflre, V. (1965), "Simulation of People's Behavior toward New Objects and Events." *American Behavioral Scientist,* Vol. 8, 12–15.

——— (in press), *Language and Behavior.* Reading, Mass.: Addison-Wesley.

Zola, I. (1963), "Sociocultural Factors in the Seeking of Medical Aid — A Progress Report." *Transcultural Psychiatric Research,* Vol. 14, 62–65.

CHAPTER TWENTY-THREE

From Computer to Criticism: An Application of Automatic Content Analysis to the Study of Literature

Allan B. Ellis
Harvard University

F. André Favat
Harvard University

> For the use of a telescope, especially after its great development in the seventeenth century, so enlarged the whole range of what its possessors could see and do that, in the end, it was a factor in changing their whole picture of the world. . . . The potential capacity of the digital computer to process non-numerical data in novel ways . . . is so great as to make of it the telescope of the mind.
> Margaret Masterman, "The Intellect's New Eye," 1962

   Language specialists—among them linguists, literary historians, scholars, and critics—are finding the computer increasingly applicable to the activities that lie within their provinces. Instances in which computer technology has directly enhanced the efforts of the literary scholar, for example, are abundant.[1] Attribution and influence studies, comparisons of variant texts, thematic analyses, and the like—studies employing such techniques as automatic word counts, machine-constructed concordances, and parsing of sentences—represent only a sample of the activity in the field and indicate only a few of the possible applications of computers to the study of literature.

One relevant technique that is not widely used by the literary scholar and critic, however, is automatic content analysis. As recently as 1962, Hays observed: "Other subfields of automatic language-data processing intersect more crucially with psychology: automatic content analysis of novels and editorials, of discussion group transcripts, of field and clinical interviews lies just ahead. . . ." (Hayes, 1962, 396). Since that time the development of the General Inquirer has made possible the application of automatic content analysis to each of these areas. Especially promising to the literary scholar is the General Inquirer's application to the novel and, more generally, to criticism.

Whether a piece of literary criticism is considered to be an aberration or a revelation depends not only upon what the critic asserts about a literary work but also upon what he proposes as evidence to support his assertion. When F. R. Leavis (1950, 167) states that the imagery in *The Golden Bowl* "is not immediate and inevitable, but synthetic," he supports his assertion by presenting his readers with evidence in the form of excerpts from the text. The literary critic, consciously or not, usually gathers such evidence by analyzing the content of the text, seeking out patterns, categorizing them, finding their conjunctions, and the like. Content analysis, then, seems to be one part of the process of literary criticism, a process that moves from reading to analysis to evaluation.

Our discussion here is of an application of General Inquirer procedures to Mark Twain's *The Adventures of Huckleberry Finn*—an investigation designed to determine more exactly the role automatic content analysis can play in the study of a novel and in the process of literary criticism.

Huckleberry Finn, or any similarly complex novel, when viewed through the General Inquirer, permits, and indeed stimulates, a num-

---

[1] Evidence of this is found, for example, in the *Newsletter* of the American Council of Learned Societies (May 1965), which reports nearly 70 cases of research in progress in languages and literature, and in the *Literary Data Processing Conference Proceedings* (Bessinger and Parrish, 1964), which contains descriptions of the use of automated data-processing techniques by literary scholars.

ber of approaches: we might examine Huck in his relationship to society, to nature—with particular reference to the land or river scenes —to other characters such as Tom and Jim, or to some specific part of the story such as the concluding chapters. We have chosen to examine Huck in his relation to death, for although few readers would call *Huckleberry Finn* a novel of death, few others could read the book and not be aware of Huck's repeated references to and associations with this theme.

Because our interest centered on Huck, the text which we submitted to the tagging routine of the Psychosociological Dictionary consisted of those sentences in the book "spoken" by him. These sentences were grouped by chapter and included his part of the dialogue with other characters as well as his first-person narrative, thus excluding only those statements made by other characters.

Retrieving on the DEATH tag, which includes such words as autumn, cry, dark, end, mourn, rest, separation, and still, we found that every chapter in the book was represented by such sentences as

. . . so then I didn't care no more about him, because I don't take no stock in dead people. (Chapter 1)

The stars were shining, and the leaves rustled in the woods ever so mournful; and I heard an owl, away off, who-whooing about somebody that was dead, and a whippowill and a dog crying about somebody that was going to die. . . . (Chapter 1)

I fetched the pig in, and took him back nearly to the table and hacked into his throat with the ax, and laid him down on the ground to bleed. . . . (Chapter 7)

They won't ever hunt the river for anything but my dead carcass. (Chapter 7)

And he said if a man owned a beehive and that man died, the bees must be told about it before sun-up next morning, or else the bees would all weaken down and quit work and die. (Chapter 8)

I got to feeling so mean and so miserable I most wished I was dead. (Chapter 16)

Every time a man died, or a woman died, or a child died, she would be on hand with her "tribute" before he was cold. (Chapter 17)

But he said it warn't no use, nothing but to be dead and done with it all could do him any good; though he said it often made him feel easier and better for a while if people treated him according to his rights. . . . (Chapter 19)

He was often moaning and mourning that way nights, when he judged I was asleep. . . . (Chapter 23)

Well, then . . . how'll it do to saw him out, the way I done before I was murdered that time? (Chapter 34)

We obtained tag tally graphs on this corpus to learn more about the many different contexts in which the DEATH retrievals occurred, and found that among the categories in these sentences, those of NATURAL-WORLD, SELF, OTHER, MALE-ROLE, FEMALE-ROLE, and FAMILY seemed to predominate.

Because of such sentences as

I set down again, a-shaking all over, and got out my pipe for a smoke; for the house was all as still as death now. . . . (Chapter 1)

Some thought it would be good to kill the families of boys that told the secrets. (Chapter 2)

I liked all that family, dead ones and all, and warn't going to let anything come between us. (Chapter 17)

The girls said they hadn't ever dreamed of seeing the family separated or sold away from town. (Chapter 27)

we felt it would be of particular interest to examine further the co-occurrences of the DEATH and FAMILY tags and, in that way, determine more exactly Huck's relationship to these two themes.

On a number of occasions after his escape, Huck is presented with situations in which he finds it necessary to fabricate a story that will explain his presence to people who confront him. His method is to assume a fictitious identity and to create a fictitious background. We found that the death and the family themes appear throughout these passages and, in fact, form the substance of the lies. For example:

Then I told her my father and mother was dead, and the law had bound me out to a mean old farmer in the country thirty mile back from the river. . . . (Chapter 11)

They all asked me questions, and I told them how pap and me and all the family was living on a little farm down at the bottom of Arkansaw, and my sister Mary Ann run off and got married and never was heard of no more, and Bill went to hunt them and he warn't heard of no more, and Tom and Mort died, and then there warn't nobody but just me and pap left, and he was just trimmed down to nothing, on account of his troubles; so when he died, I took what there was left. . . . (Chapter 17)

My folks was living in Pike County, in Missouri, where I was born, and they all died off but me and pa and my brother Ike. (Chapter 20)

On the basis of such sentences, we examined occurrences of Huck's impersonations that had not been retrieved, and found, for instance, that he suggests imminent family death in order to get the owner of the ferryboat to go out to the wrecked *Walter Scott,* and implies it in his attempts to ward off the men in the skiff by hinting that his family, aboard the raft, has smallpox.[2]

The association of death and family is not only present in Huck's fabrications but attends other family situations as well. Two of these were the Boggs-Sherburn and the Grangerford episodes. Having retrieved death-family sentences on each of these, we returned to the text to further examine them.

In the Boggs-Sherburn story, the killing of Boggs received the major emphasis, and the last-minute entrance of his daughter imposes the family component upon the incident. Huck relates:

That young girl screamed out and comes rushing, and down she throws herself on her father, crying. . . . (Chapter 21)

Then they pulled his daughter away from him, screaming and crying and took her off. (Chapter 21)

Death and family are more organically related, however, in the Grangerford story, for indeed the family lives with death. One of the very first things we learn of them is:

This was all there was of the family now, but there used to be more — three sons; they got killed and Emmeline that died. (Chapter 18)

Emmeline, the painter and poetress of death, produced in pictures and

---

[2] That "smallpox" is a death-associated word in *Huckleberry Finn* is evident in the famous "Raftsmen passage." One of the men rants,

I'm the . . . copper-bellied corpse-maker. . . . I'm the man they call Sudden Death and General Desolation! Sired by a hurricane, dam'd by an earthquake, half-brother to the cholera, nearly related to the smallpox on the mother's side.

Interestingly, those of Huck's lies regarding his background but not concerning death and family are those not of his own making. For instance, the Duke and the King cast Huck into the role of their "valley," and it is Aunt Sally who hastily concludes that Huck is Tom Sawyer come to visit.

words a kind of death that Huck struggles to understand,[3] and eventually even this family is further disrupted by the deaths of Buck, his father, and his two brothers.

It may be possible to say that the association of family and death found in these initially retrieved sentences was a result of Huck's experience and intuition, a combination that tells him that posing as a parentless waif will get him the most sympathy from the people who question his presence and therefore assure his being able to maneuver out of the situation. But it is more likely that no such simple impetus gives rise to the association of family and death. We assume that the things Huck says, whether they be true or not, are indications of the things that concern him. The association, then, of death and family can be seen as a manifestation of one of his deepest preoccupations.

We can say that Huck has no family. The young band of robbers almost exclude him because he has no parents, and even Huck himself does not propose that having pap as a father constitutes having a family. And when we turn to the text to locate the context in which the retrieved sentences occur, we find that all of Huck's lies about his dead mothers and fathers do, in fact, take place after Jim discovers pap's body in the floating house. And so, Huck, more than even he himself realizes, throughout the rest of the book has no family.

Moreover, it is clear that Huck is deeply aware that the family is subject to external forces that disrupt it. The law may separate a child from its father, or may bind a child to a farmer, and the institution of slavery can separate a mother from her children. And thus it is not surprising that in his fabrications Huck presents himself as the product of a family disrupted by that ultimate destroyer, death.[4]

A number of words are used throughout the novel to denote the parent members of the family unit, including ma, pa, old man, pap, and, infrequently, mother and father. Drawing any conclusions about Huck's pattern of usage of these terms would necessitate the constructing of a new dictionary category, PARENT, or, as an expedient, the devising of a complete retrieval question set that included all those

---

[3] Throughout the book Huck has difficulty in coping with death. He "don't take no stock in dead people," cannot write a death-tribute for Emmeline, cannot relate the Grangerford deaths, and finds the mourning for the dead Peter Wilks "disgusting."

[4] While we do not here concern ourselves with other dimensions of death in relation to Huck, it is apparent that it is not a unidimensional theme. Thus, just as death is the disrupter that separates Huck from his family, real or imagined, so is death the liberator that separates him, however imperfectly, from society.

words used by Huck to denote the parent members of the family. To get a preliminary notion of Huck's parent referents, however, we chose to retrieve on the words "pap" and "father," which he uses most and least frequently, respectively, to refer to his father.

We found that in only one instance does Huck use the word "father" to denote pap, and that this one sentence is notably impersonal and legalistic.

> . . . so he said courts mustn't interfere and separate families if they could help it; said he'd druther not take a child away from its father. (Chapter 5)

The retrievals on "pap," were another matter. They presented to us, in convenient juxtaposition, those sentences that involved Huck's description of his father. We found in nearly all of them that Huck saw his father as animal-like.

> So I went to him that night and told him that pap was here again, for I found his tracks in the snow. (Chapter 4)

> I slipped the ramrod down it to make sure it was loaded, and then I laid it across the turnip-barrel, pointing towards pap, and set down behind it to wait for him to stir. (Chapter 6)

> . . . and pap he always said it, too, though he warn't no more quality than a mudcat himself. (Chapter 18)

We returned to the text to examine these sentences more closely in their contexts. We found, as in Chapter 6, where Huck and pap are in the cabin, that there were whole passages in which the pap-animal connection existed.

> . . . so now he raised a howl that fairly made a body's hair raise, and down he went in the dirt, and rolled there. . . . Pretty soon he was all fagged out, and fell down panting. . . . By and by he raised up part way and listened, with his head to one side. . . . Then he went down on all fours, and crawled off . . . and wallowed in under the old pine table. . . . By and by he rolled out and jumped up to his feet looking wild, and he see me and went for me. (Chapter 6)

And with such sentences in mind as

> His hair was long and tangled and greasy, and hung down, and you could see his eyes shining through like he was behind vines. (Chapter 5)

> There warn't no color in his face, where his face showed; it was white; not like another man's white, but a white to make a body sick, a white to make a body's flesh crawl — a tree-toad white, a fish-belly white. (Chapter 5)

that sentence prefiguring pap's death:

> They judged it was him, anyway; said this drownded man was just his size, and was ragged, and had uncommon long hair, which was all like pap; but they couldn't make nothing of the face, because it had been in the water so long it warn't much like a face at all. (Chapter 3)

returns to us with greater force indeed.

The procedures followed in obtaining and analyzing these retrievals do not, of course, exhaust the possibilities of the General Inquirer system. In fact, the value of the General Inquirer obtains because it encourages further analysis.

We will be able, for example, to conduct an automatic theme analysis, where we will, in effect, construct two texts, one composed of all those sentences with DEATH occurrences, and the other composed of the remaining and therefore NON-DEATH sentences. By comparing the two we will be able to determine which categories are common to both and any categories particularly characteristic of each.

We will be able to examine the words forming the subcategories of the DEATH tag in the Psychosociological Dictionary. We noticed in our DEATH retrievals, for example, that the word "still" caused a number of sentences to be presented for our inspection. We found that on some occasions the association of "still" and death was direct:

> . . . for the house was all still as death now. . . . (Chapter 1)

On certain occasions, stillness pervaded the natural world into which Huck escapes:

> . . . and the stars over us was sparkling ever so fine; and down by the village was the river, a whole mile broad, and awful still and grand. (Chapter 2)

and on other occasions the stillness of the passively floating drift-logs, which have a certain death quality to them, seemed analogous to Huck, who is also "dead" throughout most of the novel, as he floats on the river raft.

The moon was so bright I could 'a' counted the drift-logs that went a-slipping along, black and still. . . . (Chapter 7)

Another alternative available to us is the construction of a new dictionary. In using the present General Inquirer dictionary for our work with *Huckleberry Finn,* we risk overlooking one of the cautions referred to earlier (Chapter 6); namely, that although a general dictionary may be used for a variety of texts, the contents of each text may possess a number of distinctive aspects that make the application of a general dictionary to them inappropriate. Such a new dictionary would categorize words with particular reference to the text, and in this way be conscious, for example, of words whose meanings may have been different at the time the novel was written, or which are peculiar to the text. By constructing a new dictionary we could include in the DEATH tag words such as ghost, coffin, ashes, hacked, hung, which do not now appear in categories useful for our purposes. In addition, certain categories are presently missing from the Psychosociological Dictionary that are especially relevant to an analysis of Huckleberry Finn. For instance, in our study of death it would seem reasonable for us to also examine the notion of birth, especially in view of the interplay of death and rebirth that abounds in the story (Lynn, 1958) and because of such incidents as Huck's and Jim's discussion of the way the stars came into being and Huck's comment, in the concluding chapters, about "being born again." In a new dictionary, a BIRTH tag would permit us to retrieve the appropriate sentences.

We may also regroup the text. For example, knowing that the book divides into alternating scenes of land and river, it is possible to group Huck's sentences into these units and thus explore such things as the occurrence of certain themes as they appear in two or more of the large segments. The hypothesis, for instance, that the kinds of death references in the land chapters differ from those in the river chapters can be easily tested.

Another possible regrouping is by separate texts, composed of appropriate sentences, for each of the voices Huck uses to speak, narrate, paraphrase, and so on. These groupings will permit us to examine what sorts of concerns Huck manifests in each of these voices and therefore enable us to determine which concerns link the voices together and which ones make them different.

Furthermore, instead of excluding Jim, Tom, pap, or the King and the Duke, we may include their statements, but as separate texts. This will permit us not only to examine other characters in the ways we have examined Huck but also to make comparisons between two or more of them. In addition, with such a grouping, we will be able to explore aspects of the book such as repetition and variation (Baldanza, 1955) that are present in such occurrences as

Huck:

> Then away out in the woods I heard that kind of a sound that a ghost makes when it wants to tell about something that's on its mind and can't make itself understood and so can't rest easy in its grave, and has to go about that way every night grieving. (Chapter 1)

Jim (to Huck):

> Doan' hurt me — don't! I hain't ever done no harm to a ghos'. (Chapter 8)

Tom (to Huck):

> Don't you play nothing on me, because I wouldn't on you. Honest injun, you ain't a ghost? (Chapter 33)

We have described here not an instrument nor a computer program but rather a process in which the principles of content analysis provide a set of systematic procedures for obtaining data that can be transformed by the literary critic into evidence. The computer provides the opportunity for the different examination and reordering of data, and the literary critic, thus aided, directs his attention to that part of the process to which he is essential—reasoning, evaluating, and judging. Such a process requires that the computer and the critic be allies and that each provide those capabilities that can, in concert, substantially enrich the whole critical procedure.

The fact that the computer has aided the scholar does not mean that this critical procedure has been violated. There is the same reading of the text and the same grouping of it in ways appropriate to the hypothesis. The difference lies in the fact that the critic now does not need to count, search, and sort the material himself in order to find evidence for his hypothesis. The computer performs this function for him and presents the resulting data for his evaluation. The computer does not usurp the critic's essential functions but, in fact, enhances them. The critic is able to operate unhampered by the clerical obstacles involved in the search for evidence; and assured of the practicality of searching for and working with his data, he can now, in fact, ask questions that previously he could have only wished to ask.

The suggestion is here that distinctions drawn about the relationship between quantitative and qualitative activities have been misleading. Parrish (1964) reports that some feel these activities rest along a continuum and that others feel they are mutually exclusive. But we should not conclude from these discussions — especially in light of the success with which the General Inquirer has been applied to the general problem of textual analysis — that the central issue is whether or not the quantitative and qualitative worlds are different from each other. We stipulate their difference and concern ourselves instead with the ways in which the characteristic functions of each can contribute to the critical act. We do not require that the telescope be of the same substance as the astronomer.

BIBLIOGRAPHY

Baldanza, F. (November 1965) "The Structure of *Huckleberry Finn,*" *American Literature,* Vol. 27, 347–355.

Bessinger, J., and S. Parrish (eds.) (1964), *Literary Data Processing Conference Proceedings,* New York: IBM.

"Computerized Research in the Humanities: A Survey." (May 1965) *ACLS Newsletter,* Vol. 16, 13–24.

Hays, D. (1962), "Automatic Language Data Processing." In H. Borko (ed.), *Computer Applications in the Behavioral Sciences.* Englewood Cliffs, N.J.: Prentice-Hall, 395–421.

Leavis, F. R. (1950), *The Great Tradition,* London: Chatto and Windus.

Lynn, K. (Spring 1958), "Huck and Jim," *Yale Review,* Vol. 47, 421–431.

Masterman, M. (April 27, 1962), "The Intellect's New Eye," *The Times* (London) *Literary Supplement.*

Parrish, S. (1964), "Summary of Proceedings." In J. Bessinger and S. Parrish, *Literary Data Processing Conference Proceedings,* New York: IBM, 3–10.

TOPIC INDEX

NAME INDEX

645

TAG INDEX, HARVARD THIRD PSYCHOSOCIOLOGICAL DICTIONARY TAGS

ACADEMIC	126, 144, 175, 184, 292, 295, 301, 302, 306, 311, 312, 313, 315, 326, 327, 437, 441, 457, 461, 499, 500, 529, 533, 591, 598
ACTION-NORM	126, 174, 179, 292, 296, 299, 302, 313, 315, 326, 327, 330, 361, 373, 377, 382, 383, 410, 415
AFFECTION	175, 180, 292, 295, 298, 382, 384, 457, 484, 508
ANGER	175, 180, 310, 311, 327, 437, 484
APPROACH	126, 175, 292, 297, 326, 332, 361, 373, 382, 437, 439, 457, 481, 541, 543
AROUSAL	175, 180, 292, 298, 315, 326, 328, 370, 373, 457, 462, 484
ARTISTIC	144, 175, 184, 310, 366, 367, 370, 371, 374, 481
ASCEND-THEME	176, 185, 292, 295, 306, 307, 326, 382, 384, 508
ATTACK	175, 292, 297, 298, 310, 311, 315, 316, 326, 328, 329, 336, 361, 371, 373, 376, 410, 437, 438, 457, 481, 529, 541
ATTEMPT	175, 182, 326, 376, 382, 383, 437, 438, 440, 457, 541
AUTHORITY-THEME	176, 186, 292, 295, 311, 315, 326, 327, 330, 374, 377, 378, 382, 397, 410, 417, 508
AVOID	175, 251, 292, 295, 298, 311, 312, 313, 315, 327, 361, 382, 384, 410, 437, 440, 442, 457, 508, 529, 541
BAD	114, 173, 175, 181, 327, 361, 437, 481, 529
BODY-PART	174, 374, 382, 437, 440
CAUSE	173, 175, 180, 326, 371, 373, 382, 437, 440, 541
CLOTHING	174, 178, 437, 438
COMMUNICATE	126, 156, 175, 182, 310, 313, 315, 326, 361, 373, 376, 382, 437, 438, 442, 457, 499, 500, 529, 541
COMMUNITY	136, 144, 175, 184, 292, 296, 301, 302, 310, 315, 326, 330, 382, 499, 500
CONTROL	175, 326, 330, 373, 376, 382, 541, 591, 595, 601
DANGER-THEME	176, 186, 292, 295, 303, 307, 310, 311, 313, 315, 326, 327, 328, 382, 383, 410, 413, 417
DEATH-THEME	176, 186, 292, 295, 303, 311, 312, 313, 315, 382, 442, 499, 500, 529, 630, 631, 635, 636
DEVIATION	174, 179, 181, 292, 295, 306, 307, 310, 311, 312, 315, 361, 371, 373
DISTRESS	126, 136, 175, 180, 292, 295, 310, 311, 312, 315, 326, 327, 328, 374, 437, 457, 484, 529
ECONOMIC	144, 176, 184, 238, 361, 366, 371, 373, 375, 382, 383, 396, 410, 413, 437, 439, 508, 591, 598
EQUAL	126, 173, 175, 180, 292, 295, 298, 299, 301, 311, 312, 326, 332, 371, 374, 382 384, 481
EXPEL	175, 182, 371, 408, 440, 481, 541
FAMILY	126, 144, 176, 184, 292, 295, 313, 315, 326, 499, 500, 631
FEMALE-ROLE	104, 106, 114, 115, 121, 124, 127, 144, 174, 177, 292, 295, 296, 311, 312, 313, 315, 316, 326, 374, 437, 438, 442, 529, 530, 591, 594, 596, 601, 631
FEMALE-THEME	176, 185, 292, 295, 307, 371, 382, 508
FOLLOW	175, 182, 311, 312, 315, 326, 327, 333, 371, 382, 383, 457, 481, 508, 541, 591, 594, 596, 601
FOOD	148, 174, 178, 382, 408, 410, 413
GET	126, 136, 175, 182, 292, 299, 326, 371, 372, 481, 482, 498, 500, 529, 541
GOOD	114, 126, 173, 175, 181, 315, 327, 361, 437, 457, 594, 599
GUIDE	114, 125, 126, 175, 292, 295, 306, 310, 311, 312, 315, 326, 327, 330, 371, 374, 481, 482, 498, 500, 541, 591, 595, 596, 601
HIGHER-STATUS	115, 144, 147, 176, 292, 295, 306, 315, 326, 327, 382, 383, 437, 438, 440, 442, 591, 594, 596, 597, 601

649

Lacking an adequate theory of the relationship between social scientific variables and how they are expressed in language, the social scientist falls back on his intuitive understanding, which is naturally subject to error. As the material in this book will reveal, much of our current success in content analysis derives from the lessons of past research. These lessons lead to further refinements and practical means of compensating for the inadequacies of the theory. Chapters 4 and 5 consider these lessons in further detail.

"Systematic and Objective"

These are the aspects of content analysis most stressed by previous writers. Berelson, in probably the most widely referenced definition of content analysis, defines it as "a research technique for the objective, systematic and quantitative description of the manifest content of communication." (Berelson, 1954, 489). Berelson uses the term "objective" to indicate that the procedure should be explicit, one that can be replicated exactly by other analysts. "Systematic" for Berelson means that "*all* the relevant content is to be analysed in terms of *all* the relevant categories" (Berelson, 1954, 489) in order to secure unbiased information for the hypotheses being tested. Similarly, Cartwright proposes to "use the terms 'content analysis' and 'coding' interchangeably to refer to the objective, systematic, and quantitative description of any symbolic behavior" (Cartwright, 1953, 424). Objectivity and systemization are requirements not specific to content analysis, but they are necessary for any procedure to be appropriate for scientific inquiry.

Contrary to its apparent implication, to be "systematic" does not always require that all the sampled text be inspected. Often the question is whether or not a characteristic appears in a text, not how often it appears. In such cases, the text need be inspected only until an occurrence is found.

Similarly, a scientific inquiry need not have the additional characteristic of being quantitative in the sense of counting frequencies. The qualitative-quantitative dimension, which will be discussed in Chapter 2, has been a source of considerable confusion and argument. The procedure of content analysis refers only to the systematic and objective identification of specified characteristics. Whether these occurrences are counted after they are identified depends on the hypotheses being investigated.

The implementation of procedures on a computer insures that they are both systematic and objective. The nature of a computer program requires that both the categories and the rules for identifying and recording characteristics occurring in the data be explicitly stated. The computer then systematically applies the categories and rules to the data in a completely objective manner. Whether the measurement procedure was reasonable or best suited to the inferences being made may be debated, but the procedures themselves are explicit and clear. The fluctuations resulting from the biases and fatigue of the coder do not enter into the analysis process itself when a computer is used, nor is there any problem of securing intercoder reliability.

"Within Text"

Our definition is not concerned with problems of record*ing* information but of analyzing the patterns of information as contained in a record*ed* text. Within this book, all texts analyzed are in English. There is no reason why the text need be limited to English; indeed, General Inquirer procedures are currently used to study text in Tzotil, the language of the Zinacanten Indians in the Chiapas Highlands of Mexico. Another project is currently under way that will require the analysis of text in German. The General Inquirer procedures described in this book might also be used to study a phonetic transcription or the notation text of an observer's recording of playground interaction.

Working with text materials often provides information not otherwise available. Many important changes of society and of the people who live in it are richly documented by text information. Text often becomes the most important resource for testing hypotheses about changes over the years. The investigator need not be present with his measuring instruments either before or after or during the event. Text is also often naturally produced and available in situations in which the investigator could not or cannot intrude.

Past definitions of content analysis have not limited it to text material but have included all aspects of communication or symbolic behavior. In verbal behavior, the text may be only part of the communication. Indeed, as Bernstein (1964*a*) has pointed out, the language used in many social situations is a "restricted code in which the text content is actually of secondary importance in the communication process." A number of writers, including Allport and Vernon

(1933), Ruesch and Kees (1956), and contributors to the Sebeok, Hayes, and Bateson volume (1964), have stressed the importance of various paralinguistic cues. In limiting our definition to text, we are not denigrating the importance of these phenomena. Rather we are stressing they will be adequately handled by content analysis only when they can be notated in textual form.

"Research Technique"

The final component of our definition emphasizes that content analysis is carried out in the context of a research design. Research findings are always relative, based on the characteristics of one text as compared with another. The texts to be compared depend on the hypotheses being tested. For example, if we compare one man's public speeches with another man's family dinner conversation, we will probably learn more about the differences between public speeches and family dinner conversations than we will learn about the differences between the two men. Some studies will attempt to hold the situation constant while studying different respondents. Other studies will purposely vary the situation to study its effect.

If the hypotheses concern differences in the treatment of a topic, the first task is to select documents relevant to that topic. For example, a study of newspaper editorial changes in attitudes toward the common market (Chapter 11) first must select editorials that consider the topic. Procedures for choosing text to be included in a study should be explicit.

For some research problems, the investigator may sample a large amount of data and "wash out" unrepresentative situational or topic effects as much as possible. For example, in the study of long-term, self-analytic groups (Chapter 8), it is difficult to control for occasional member absences or particular variations in topics discussed. By sampling an adequate amount of material over a number of occasions, the sample comes to represent the over-all attendance configurations and topic concerns of the group.

Research design, then, is an important part of the context in which content analysis takes place. We have considerably more to say about it in Chapters 6 and 7.

OVERVIEW: A MODEL OF CONTENT ANALYSIS

Our definition presents content analysis as a research tool to be used by the social scientist in making inferences; what is measured in content analysis depends on the theory being investigated. This context is needed not only to gain a proper perspective on content analysis but to differentiate it from other activities that may appear to be similar but are for other purposes. In this section, we shall present a content analysis model, and we shall then use this model to specify what content analysis is not.

Past discussions of content analysis have often given little consideration to its larger context. While Berelson's definition specifies that content analysis is "a research technique," little further emphasis is made of its research purpose. In fact, Berelson argues that many valid content analysis studies are undertaken solely or primarily to describe characteristics of content:

> In a great many studies there is no real problem of inference at all. This is true for all those content analyses in which the description of content itself is the primary objective. Such studies can be said to contain implicit inferences about the causes or the consequences of the content — and some contain them explicitly — but such inferences are in the nature of addenda to or reformulations of the basic data. Thus a trend study of newspaper content can be considered material for inferences about the changing character of press controls and/or about the changing character of public attention. But such "inferences" are usually nothing but reformulations in other terms of the content analysis itself.
>
> (Berelson, 1954, 516–517)

We feel that the researcher has an obligation both to himself and to his public to explicate clearly the inferences he is making. As we describe in Chapter 2, many content analysts, often preoccupied with measurement, have felt that they should stay at the level of fact and let the reader draw the conclusions. Actually content analysts invariably use at least a rudimentary theoretical framework in the very design of categories and rules for their application. Its rationale, purpose, and implications when applied to the data should be made explicit.

Our content analysis model is represented in Figure 1.1. Primary importance is given to the theory being investigated. The theory determines the texts to be compared (that is, the research design), the